D0519922

Readings in
Global Health

A research anthology collected from the

American Journal of Public Health

Editor
Omar A. Khan, MD, MHS, FAAFP

Associate Editors
Sir Michael Marmot, MBBS, MPH, PhD, FRCP, FFPHM
Carlos Castillo-Salgado, MD, JD, MPH, Dr. PH
Neal Nathanson, MD
John Seffrin, PhD
Stanley A. Plotkin, MD
Garth Graham, MD, MPH
A. Mushtaque R. Chowdhury, PhD
Allan Rosenfield, MD
Beth Kirkpatrick, MD

APHA
PRESS

American Public Health Association
Washington, DC
2008

American Public Health Association
800 I Street, NW
Washington, DC 20001–3710
www.apha.org

All chapters except for the overview chapters of each section were originally published in the American Journal of Public Health. Specific journal volume and issue details appear at the bottom of each page.

Georges C. Benjamin, MD, FACP
Executive Director

Printed and bound in the United States of America
Set in: Cremona and Franklin Gothic
Interior Design and Typesetting: Terence Mulligan
Cover Design: Jennifer Strass
Printing and Binding by Port City Press, Baltimore, Maryland

ISBN: 978-0-87553-187-8

800 08/08

Table of Contents

Section Two: HIV/AIDS

Section Three: Tobacco

Section Four: Vaccines

Section Seven: Infectious Diseases

Acknowledgements and Dedications

To my wife, friend and partner (all the same person), Salwa. To my son, Zareef, who in spite of my railing against population growth, provides a strong emotional reason for perpetuating the species.

For my colleagues at APHA notably Ellen Meyer, Director of Publications and Terence Mulligan—both of them untiring, patient and wise—for shepherding this collection to completion. To Dr. Georges Benjamin, for his leadership and providing an environment at APHA which encourages responsibility and innovation.

For my able Associate Editor colleagues: people of great distinction in the various fields of global health, who gave generously of their valuable time to contribute to this project.

I am grateful for the many institutions and projects which have allowed me to develop my thinking and practice in global health. Wilmington Friends School, for a strong Quaker philosophy encouraging service to others. The University of Pennsylvania, for providing the desire to outperform people's expectations. The University of Vermont, for being my spiritual home in so many ways; providing me medical training as well as a setting of breathtaking natural beauty, to teach, learn, and listen in the company of wise and informed colleagues and students. The Johns Hopkins University, for providing an outstanding public health education; work experience in international development; and enduring friendships. Writers Without Borders, and my co-principal, Tim Brookes, for providing a new way of looking at global health, through the lens of the written word.

For the many friends and extended family I am grateful to have, who suffer erratic communications and unexpected drop-ins, and provide me continuous intellectual stimulation. For my parents, siblings, and grandparents who encouraged me, and my uncle, Javed Gilani, who was and is the main medical influence in my life: thank you.

To my colleagues who work with the primary care project Shushasthya in Dhaka, Bangladesh; the name in Bengali translates to a most fitting closing statement: Good health!

Omar Khan
Havre de Grace, MD & Burlington, VT
2008

Special Dedication

The Editor and Publications Board of the American Public Health Association dedicate this to their colleague and friend, the late Ellen Meyer, APHA Director of Publications.

Introduction

| Omar A. Khan, MD MHS, FAAFP, Clinical Assistant Professor and Attending Physician, Dept. of Family Medicine, University of Vermont College of Medicine; Attending Physician, Dept. of Family Medicine, Christiana Care Health System and Dept. of Pediatrics, A.I. duPont Hospital for Children

Global health is part of the fabric of public health. Whether in academics or practice, the health sciences—including public health and medicine—as well as the related social sciences, have contributed and benefited from the study of this field. Yet it is still regarded as a new or emerging area, and there are several reasons for this.

The study of the health of people around the globe is not new, but it is constantly reinventing itself. In part, this is because the discipline of global health is fundamentally an amalgam of several overlapping areas. Within public health alone, one brings to bear on global health several aspects of environmental health, epidemiology, biostatistics, infectious diseases, chronic diseases, nutrition, health systems, anthropology—and that's just the start. The aforementioned are what we can consider overarching subjects which underpin the more specific, thematic areas of interest to specific populations: geriatric health, maternal and child health, reproductive health, mental health, and so forth. As innovations occur in each discipline, whether broad or narrow, overarching or thematic, thus too does the discipline itself change—slowly but inexorably, and occasionally requiring a new name to describe the new techniques, modes of study, and approaches which happen to prevail at the time.

Medicine is, for better or for worse, separate from public health in most fields of study in the U.S. It too has made its own contributions to global health; indeed, many practitioners of the field have been trained physicians seeking to cure ailments of "the third world." The field of tropical medicine developed out of these efforts, evolving towards having a variety of ways for modern-day physicians to do global health. This area requires special mention. From the point of view of sustainable health improvements in less-developed settings, there is, in general, little to recommend individual physicians going abroad for short-term work without the underpinnings of a broader health system. While there certainly are medical interventions—cataract surgeries, fistula repairs—which are amenable to an approach of brief exposure, the public health perspective would always seek to integrate a broader, longer-term approach which would include elements of technology transfer, cultural respect, and non-interference in the host situation.

Unfortunately, these elements are too often disregarded in pursuit of a different agenda of "missionary medicine": short-term (and shortsighted) projects; religious proselytizing; and inadequate emphasis on sustainability. Public health has its own version of ethical lapses in the global arena, notably inadequate protection for research participants in developing settings; contributing to the brain drain abroad; and generally, a double standard applying to Western and non-Western participants.

This selection of readings is meant to introduce the reader to some particular issues we feel are relevant to global health today. In doing so, we hope it whets the reader's appetite for more. It is neither exhaustive nor encyclopedic; it is our sincere hope the reader will seek out more extensive material and experiences in their areas of interest.

This selection is indebted to material originally published by APHA in the *American Journal of Public Health*. The papers herein are largely as they originally appeared; however, they have been restructured by our Associate Editors into areas matching the focus of this book. The material has been given additional context by their original Editorials which appear here for the first time.

The Section on "Social Context of Global Health" is introduced by Prof. Sir Michael Marmot, Chairman of the Commission on Social Determinants of Health, with a Foreword by Dr. Carlos Castillo-Salgado of the Pan American Health Organization (PAHO). "HIV/AIDS: Prevention, Control, Treatment" is introduced by Prof. Neal Nathanson, Associate Dean for Global Health at the University of Pennsylvania. The section on Tobacco is introduced by Dr. John Seffrin, CEO of the American Cancer Society. The "Vaccines" section is introduced by Prof. Stanley Plotkin of Aventis. Dr. Garth Graham, Director of the Office of Minority Health, and Deputy Assistant Secretary of Health, provides the Foreword for the section on "Health Disparities". The section on "Children, Adolescents & Family Health" is fortunate to have two editors: Prof. Mushtaque Chowdhury, Dean of the James P. Grant School of Public Health of BRAC University, and Prof. Allan Rosenfield, Dean of the Mailman School of Public Health of Columbia University. Dr. Beth Kirkpatrick, Associate Professor of Infectious Diseases at the University of Vermont introduces the section on "non-HIV Infectious Diseases." I round off the collection with a discussion of other sources of global health information with an "Annotated Bibilography of Global Health."

Each section presents some of the finest thinking on that particular topic, with added context from a luminary in that field. The information will necessarily give way to better and more current thoughts, and we anticipate this collection to be updated through the years as new information becomes available.

In this writer's view, a major challenge for those of us involved in the field(s) of global health is to make connections between disparate disciplines, and to reach across the subject-specific boundaries and borders which separate health and medical professionals as surely as geographic boundaries do. This selection is a start towards this first aim.

The second—and most important—challenge is to make sure that amid the busy travel schedules, the life-saving vaccine work, the immediate medical relief surgery, the groundbreaking research- we never forget those whose lives we seek to improve. Easier said than done, for it also means regarding each other on a personal level, whether "over there" or "at home," as human beings worthy of compassion and respect.

We wish you happy and healthy reading. Drop us a line with any additional thoughts!

Foreword: The Social Determinants of Health Global Health and Resolving Tensions

| *Professor Sir Michael Marmot MBBS, MPH, PhD, FRCP, FFPHM; Chairman, Commission on Social Determinants of Health; Director, UCL International Institute for Society and Health; Professor of Epidemiology and Public Health, University College London*

Dramatic inequalities in health exist among countries. A girl born in Zambia can expect to live 43 years, at today's age-specific mortality rates; a girl in Japan, 86 years. Within countries, too, there are dramatic inequalities in health. When, a few years ago, it was pointed out that African-American men in New York City had lower life expectancy than men in Bangladesh[1] people were skeptical. In fact the finding that the least well-off in rich countries have worse life expectancy than the average in some poorer countries is all too pervasive.[2]

The importance of this latter finding suggests that we should not think of health in low and middle income countries as "their" problem, or "ours" only in so far as we have a touch of altruism. But the problem of global inequalities in health is "our" problem. We are all involved in that we have large health inequalities within all our countries, rich and poor, and there are large inequalities between countries.

There is a second reason why we should see global health inequalities as "our" problem, wherever "we" happen to be. We are all getting the same health problems. While it is true that there are some health problems that are unique to low income countries, there are more that are common to low, middle, and high income countries. Of about 57 million deaths a year, world wide, 18 million are from communicable disease, including HIV/AIDS, 33 million from non communicable disease, and five million from injuries and violence. People in low income countries are suffering from tropical diseases at the same time as they have a large burden of non-communicable disease and injury. In middle income countries, overwhelmingly, the health burden is non-communicable disease and injury. If the problems are common, so should be the solutions.

A third reason for a global approach to health problems is the issue of globalization itself. Brown et al, in this collection, quote Yach and Bettcher's definition of globalization as "the process of increasing economic, political, and social interdependence and integration as capital, goods, persons, concepts, images, ideas and values cross state boundaries." Those of us concerned with alcohol and health have learned that though alcohol may be a good friend—why else would people indulge—it is bad enemy. So it is with globalization: a good friend and a bad enemy.

The set of global arrangements that we have and their effect on disempowering the poorest of the world, both people, communities and, indeed, whole countries are not epiphenomena. Our global arrangements are central to the issue of global health.

What then should an approach to global health look like? The papers in this collection illustrate a number of important tensions—which at times may be quite destructive of efforts to improve global health—but may also be, if resolved appropriately, quite creative. Economic orthodoxy or social programs? Where should health be on the development agenda? Economic development leads to better health or health leads to economic development? Disease control or development of health systems? The health care system or wider determinants? Theory and practice?

There is a continuing tension between disease control and development of health systems. Vast amounts of money are earmarked for control of specific diseases such as malaria, HIV/AIDS, and TB. These have been labeled vertical programs—a minor triumph for trigonometry. We have before us the shining example of smallpox eradication that shows what can be done. Against this is the argument for development of health systems, particularly comprehensive primary care—horizontal programs. Here, the rationale is that we want not just less of one disease but less of all of them and better health. Inevitably, someone would resolve the tension by saying not vertical or horizontal but diagonal.[3]

The discussion of vertical or horizontal implies that health problems should be tackled within the health sector. There is the tacit assumption that inequities in health equate with inequities in health care—an assumption that is not consistent with the evidence. Brown, Cuetho and Fee point out that within WHO there have always been tensions between social and economic approaches to population health and technology or disease-focused approaches. They write: " These approaches are not necessarily incompatible, although they have often been at odds. The emphasis on one or the other waxes and wanes over time, depending on the larger balance of power, the changing interests of international players, the intellectual and ideological commitments of key individuals…"

3

As a key exponent of the importance of wider issues, Ilona Kickbush describes the development of health promotion. It aimed to move health policy from a risk factor approach to strategies that address the determinants of health and empower people to participate in improving the settings in which they live and work.

Currently, I chair the Commission on Social Determinants of Health, set up by the Director-General of WHO, that is in the tradition of acting on the wider determinants of health.[2] An important part of our approach is not to ignore health systems but to argue that they could do their jobs better if there were appropriate attention to the social determinants of health.

If, however, one accepts that health and, more particularly, health equity result from our set of social, economic, and political arrangements, whose responsibility is it? Within a country it may be that the actions of the minister of finance have more impact on health equity than the actions of the minister of health. Yet the minister of health, and those who advise her, are likely to have more knowledge and involvement in improving health than the minister of finance and his advisors. Clearly, the minister of health has an important stewardship and advocacy function, and should have at her disposal the data and evidence that make the case for actions to improve health and health equity.

We have seen this play out globally with WHO and the World Bank. In 1990 the World Bank's loans for health were greater than WHO's budget. And by 1996 the Bank's loans for health, nutrition, and population were $13.5 billion—dwarfing WHO's budget. The Bank, and its sister institution the International Monetary Fund, while not quite the global ministers of finance, have a big influence on ministers of finance. WHO, as with ministers of health, needs not only to play the expert role within the health sector but be the advocate, the steward for the wider influences on health and the measurer of health, health equity, and their determinants.

As with ministers of finance so with the Bank: its record in the determinants of health is a checkered one. Jennifer Prah Ruger charts the history of the Bank from its origins as an institution that equated development with the growth of Gross Domestic Product. There was a clear, if somewhat simple, theory: economic growth equals development. Power plants and transport infrastructure were more likely to attract loans than 'social overheads' such as eliminating malaria, reducing illiteracy, building vocational schools. That changed when Robert McNamara moved poverty reduction to center stage and the Bank started with social sector loans. As is now well documented, the Bank's operations in the 1990s were dominated by a new theory: the Washington Consensus. This takes a variety of forms but essentially believes in small government, reduction of deficits, and the market to solve problems of poor countries.

We have heard a great deal of well justified criticism of structural adjustment and neo-liberalism, not least from Joseph Stiglitz, former chief economist at the World Bank.[4] The discussion must not stop there. To quote the title of Stiglitz's later book, the issue is "Making Globalisation Work." There are signs that the Bank has recognized the health effects of its wider sets of policies. In the health sector, its advocacy of privatization and user fees will continue to attract vigorous criticism as evidence accumulates on the adverse impacts on people of low income.

Theory of a different sort played a major role in the development of Latin American Social Medicine. Deborah Tajer emphasises the intersection of science and politics. This is not only the stuff of academic tea room discussions. Chillingly, members of the social medicine movement were imprisoned or died. Two main fields of endeavor for these committed people were workers' health and the relation of societal policies to health. They provide good examples of how a well-worked out theory can guide explicit action.

One part of their theory appears to be rejection of the mind-body relation. I presume that there is concern that this is somehow an effete worry of people free from the pressures of poverty and that it detracts attention from the real social, economic, and political causes of ill-health. I have heard these criticisms elsewhere.[5] The fact that objective social conditions impact on the operations of the brain and hence affect physical as well as mental health makes a focus on social conditions even more important.[6] Wilkinson's work would, indeed, add force to Tajer's observation that poverty in Latin America is largely due to income inequality, not overall lack of wealth.

The papers in this volume give a fine background to new developments in global health. A rediscovery of the importance of primary health care is now on the agenda of the WHO as are the social determinants of health. There is growing recognition that economic growth is important for the bottom billion of the world's population[7] but that much more than economic growth is needed for development to improve the quality of lives of the global population. Improvements in health will be the measure and the result of such a comprehensive approach to development.

References

1. McCord C. Excess mortality in Harlem. *N Engl J Med* 1990;322:173-7.
2. Marmot M. Achieving health equity: from root causes to fair outcomes. *Lancet* 2007;370(9593):1153-63.
3. Frenk J, Gonzalez-Pier E, Gomez-Dantes O, Lezana MA, Knaul FM. Comprehensive reform to improve health system performance in Mexico. *Lancet* 2006 October 28;368 (9546):1524-34.
4. Stiglitz JE. Globalization and its Discontents. London: Allen Lane; 2002.
5. Lynch JW, Davey-Smith G, Kaplan GA, House JS. Income inequality and mortality: importance to health of individual income, psychosocial environment, or material conditions. *Br Med J* 2000;320:1200-4.
6. Marmot M, Wilkinson RG. Psychosocial and material pathways in the relation between income and health: a response to Lynch et al. *Br Med J* 2001;322(7296):1233-6.
7. Collier P. T*he Bottom Billion: Why the Poorest Countries Are Failing and What Can Be Done About it.* New York: Oxford University Press; 2007.

Overview of Social Determinants of Health Section

| *Carlos Castillo-Salgado, MD, JD, MPH, Dr. PH; Special Advisor, Forum for Public Health in the Americas, Pan-American Health Organization (PAHO); Associate Professor, Department of Epidemiology, Bloomberg School of Public Health, Johns Hopkins University*

During the last part of the twentieth century, the paradigm of public health has been profoundly influenced by a medical-centered culture and the premise that individual behavioral modification and "individual health responsibility" were the main thrusts for the success of health promotion and protection of the population. This vision of public health was effective in diverting the attention from fully addressing the "causes of the causes" of the public's health. Under this prevalent paradigm, the key for successful public health programs was the promotion of accepting individual health responsibilities and behavioral changes with minimum or reduced activities targeted to modifying the prime environmental, social, nutritional, and economic forces operating in the society as the main determinants of health. These determinants were presented as equal components of the health process, as were individual choices for obtaining health and welfare. As a consequence of this vision, individual will power was seen as the force needed to overcome the environmental and societal pressures of the determinants of health.

The twelve articles presented in this section reflect the active debate rethinking of the role of social determinants of public health at national and global levels.

As illustrated in the selected articles, during the past 20 years there have been important changes in the global public health landscape. Public health in many parts of the world is still in "disarray," an expression used by the United States Institute of Medicine in its 1988 report on the "Future of Public Health"[1]. Many new public health initiatives and partnerships have been developed in response to contending global and national threats of emerging or re-emerging infectious diseases and their response challenges. The health care sector reform, the inconclusive policy agenda of smoking and health, the acceleration and expansion of the cancer epidemic, and the unprecedented levels of the obesity epidemic are coupled with the new dimensions of bioterrorism and bio-security that in a synergistic way affect both developed and less developed countries of the world and have had an enormous impact on the health conditions of billions of people.

The articles of this section blend the debates of the economic globalization and global trade with the emergence of "global health" as a new concept needed to respond to the same forces shaping international trade agreements and sector health reforms all over the world. The emergence of new strategic partners and new public-private partnerships occurred as the World Bank increased its involvement in shaping the priorities of the public health agenda. Additionally, the Bill and Melinda Gates Foundation and other private organizations became significant players, providing strategic funds, while the World Health Organization (WHO) began losing its role as the main driver of international health priorities and programs.

As mentioned before, the concept of global health emerged during the last decades of the twentieth century to accommodate the new dynamics and actors of public health at the international level. As presented by T.M. Brown, M, Cueto and E. Fee[2], the term is the product of a separation of "international health" and a model where the key actors of public health were governments and international agencies such as WHO and UNICEF. These authors link the historical appearance of the term "global health" with the power struggle between those traditional drivers of international health with the new drivers/partners from powerful international financial institutions such the World Bank (WB) and International Monetary Fund (IMF) as well as private sector organizations such as the Global Funds for AIDS, Tuberculosis and Malaria.

J. Prah Ruger[3] documents the historical transformation of the World Bank (WB) from being a multilateral international financial institution with limited presence in international health projects to becoming in more recent years a major financial contributor to global health. This reading offers a historical account of the Bank's priorities and development philosophy over its six decades of existence. Also, it analyses the increase in the Bank's lending programs for international health projects as malnutrition and ill health were identified as the two main symptoms of poverty in the *World Development Report, 1980.* The *World Development Report, 1993: Investing in Health* was the first report devoted entirely to health, opening the doors for the Bank to become a major driver of health sector reforms and global health. The article includes a description of the criticisms about the Bank's practices of market-oriented health sector reforms and the introduction of the DALYs to global health burden assessments.

From a different angle, D. Tarantola[4] discusses the concept of global health and its implications for National Governance. As presented in this brief commentary, the concept of global health became more prevalent as health is seen "beyond geopolitical boundaries and including not only governments but nongovernmental stakeholders and actors." The role of the private sector and the new health venture models known as public-private partnerships are linked to this new global health concept. The resulting global health ventures such as the Global Fund on HIV/AIDS, Tuberculosis and Malaria also bring potential risks for poor countries to accept "choices made by donors on their behalf," raising important issues of how to develop investment priorities and governance in global public health.

R Klein[5] discusses the lessons learned from the international experience for health care reform in the United States and other developed countries such as Britain, Canada, France and Germany. As presented in this essay, a key aspect of the politics of health systems reform has been the growing dissatisfaction with the existing systems to offer adequate cost-containment mechanisms ("too much money is spent protecting few people") and to guarantee schemes offering comprehensive health care. A critique of the role played by economic theory i n shaping social policy is presented, including the benefits of competition and the importance of incentives in health care systems. Also, it is postulated that traditional criteria for evaluating health care systems of "comprehensiveness, value for money, and equity," should add "the ability of health care systems to adapt and change," citing the examples of the current information technology and evidence-based medicine. Differences in political culture, history, institutions, and local circumstances are important parts of the political landscape of health care reform.

Globalization of public health information may facilitate the removal of barriers to the accessibility and utilization of such information and knowledge in an immediate and direct way. Access to key information about medical developments and new public health choices may benefit billions of people. However, this could also bring risks if that knowledge is misused or directed to the unhealthy patterns of consumption and unsafe products and services. Globalization is transforming the way governments are addressing public health in such areas as global trade of food products, water, medications, tobacco, and alcohol distribution services, as well as regulation of occupational and environmental health and health care services.

E.R. Shaffer et al[6] present a critical assessment of the linkages between international trade agreements and public health. They describe the history and forces shaping the main international trade agreements and review their implications and adverse effects for public health. An important issue discussed in this essay is how trade enforcement is superseding World Trade Organization (WTO) member countries' internal laws, including public health regulations. A listserve on globalization and health is presented. This website posts information on key organizations studying the public health effects of global trade. A challenge of public health is to critically review its linkages with global trade and to reduce its negative health effects on populations.

D. Barr[7] reviews the effectiveness of the new public-private partnerships in addressing the problems of health and welfare systems worldwide. This type of partnership has been proposed as a new model to improve the delivery of health and welfare services in developing countries. The author provides an overview of the history of public-private partnerships in the health sector and describes the main components of a research protocol commissioned to evaluate the effectiveness of this type of partnership for addressing unmet health needs. The globalization of the national economies and its "marketization efforts" in their health care systems provided the opportunity to explore these new models as a better approach for the improvement of health and welfare systems. The discussion includes a summary of the three main forces contributing to the development of this model, the types and nature of the partnerships and the main elements and key questions of a protocol for evaluating the effectiveness and assessing equity issues of public-private partnerships.

I. Kickbush[8] addresses the new public health and health promotion movement of the last part of the twentieth century and reviews the contribution of the World Health Organization (WHO) in this process. The movement is presented as a reorientation of health policy priorities using strategies addressing the determinants of health and empowering people to participate in improving the health of their communities. The author notes that the focus of health policy remains on expenditure rather than in investment, particularly when public health is integrated with the general welfare policy. The discussion is centered in describing the key action areas of two major international health initiatives: the strategy of "Health for All" (where WHO positioned health at the center of the human development policy), and the Ottawa Charter for Health Promotion with its five key action areas. Also, this analysis documents the two approaches used by WHO (WHO "Health for All" targets and the Setting approach) to disseminate and apply the health promotion approach.

As described by N. Krieger[9] and D. Tajer[10], as part of a growing awareness of the public health impact of diverse international trade agreements and social policies, some regions of the world have been affected in an increasing level of social inequities in the health of their populations. Latin America has been classified by most economic and social agencies as the most inequitable region of the globe. This situation has stimulated the growth of movements in Latin America from the civil society and academic institutions aimed at the development of new theoretical frameworks that explicitly identify the social determinants of health inequalities which can be used to guide their elimination through collective action for collective health. The roots, trajectory and contributions of the Latin American Social and Collective Medicine movement are presented.

T. Pang[11] documents in this section how the ongoing genomics revolution may change how diseases are diagnosed, prevented, and treated. Equitable international mechanisms and global collaboration will be needed to ensure that the advances of applied genomics are shared for the health improvement of the people living in developing countries, avoiding the potential "genomics divide" between the rich and poor nations. The impact of genomics on global health spans not only microbial pathogens and infectious diseases, but also the prevention, diagnosis, and management of chronic diseases including cancer, diabetes, mental disorders and cardiovascular diseases. The author postulates that "genomic epidemiology" could be a new approach for studying the molecular, metabolic, and disease profiles of thousands of subjects. However, it is also noted that genomics bring many challenging issues such as ethical, moral, legal, and economic implications and concerns about stigmatization and misuse of genetic information. Development of effective research partnerships and accountability measures are needed to use genomics with equity in global health.

Karpati at al[12] examine a novel method using the variability in disease rates to understand the real distribution of health patterns and to gain understanding of the complex interactions between contextual socioeconomic determinants and health. The understanding of the relationship between the social context and health is postulated as being reflected in the health variability at the ecological level. The observed differences in health variability might reflect the impact level of the social determinants on vulnerable populations.

Contrasting the conventional schemes of classification of diseases,

P.W. Setel al al[12] propose the development of a new working framework for the classification of the disease burden in low-income countries that could better assist policymakers and planners in the selection of their populations' health needs and priorities. Distinctions of "causes" and "effects" of diseases provide a direction of the new disease classification criteria, "broad care needs." Likelihood of mortality (low and high) and chronicity (acute and chronic) are contrasted in a two-by-two contingency table yielding a four-way effect-oriented broad care needs classification scheme. This classification scheme is seen as a useful tool serving policymakers. Additional modeling of potential costs and health benefits could be also used with this classification framework.

These articles provide excellent presentations and discussions of several key interconnected public health issues that illustrate part of the debate of the social determinants on global health.

As described in the readings of this section, the increasing complexity of the public health arena at the global and national levels has resulted in a new paradigm of global health and the participation of new stakeholders. These new stakeholders may bring new agendas and propose health priority changes. It is important to avoid the superposition of opposing health agendas that frequently result in "unhealthy" redundancy of competing policies and projects that leave health organizations and agencies working in parallel while missing opportunities for synergies and reducing the impact for better health of large populations.

Recently, the interests of multiple groups, from civil society, governments, academia, the scientific community, and international agencies, have opened new avenues toward improving the health of the most vulnerable populations. The goal is to reduce the health inequalities by tackling the interventions of the key social determinants of health. Part of this global movement has been the creation of the International Society for Equity in Health (ISEqH)[14], the formation of Departments of Global Health in differ-

ent universities and research institutions, and the proliferation of different political and grassroots movements all over the world to work for equity in health. Of special importance is the recent work of The Commission on Social Determinants of Health (CSDH)[15]. This commission was created in 2005 by WHO to mobilize civil society, governments, international organizations, and the scientific community to address the social determinants of health and to propose modifications in the way public health interventions are implemented. M. Marmot[16], chairman of the Commission, has indicated that in addressing the social gradients in health, we need to "focus not only on the extremes of income poverty but on the opportunity, empowerment, security, and dignity that disadvantaged people want in rich and poor countries alike."

References

1. Institute of Medicine. *The Future of Public Health*. National Academies Press, 1988. p.19
2. Brown TM, Cueto M, Fee E. The World Health Organization and the Transition From "International" to "Global" Public Health. *Am J Public Health*. 2006; 96:62-72
3. Prah RJ. The Changing Role of the WORLD BANK in Global Health. *Am J Public Health*. 2005; 95:60-70
4. Tarantola D. Global Health and National Governance. *Am J Public Health*. 2005; 95:8
5. Klein R. Lessons for (and From) America. *Am J Public Health*. 2003; 93:61-63
6. Shaffer ER, Waitzkin H, Brenner J, Jasso-Aguilar R. Global Trade and Public Health. *Am J Public Health*. 2005; 95: 23-34
7. Barr DA. Ethics in Public Health Research: A Research Protocol to Evaluate the Effectiveness of Public-Private Partnerships as a Means to Improve Health and Welfare Systems Worldwide. *Am J Public Health*. 2007; 97:19-25
8. Kickbusch I. The Contribution of the World Health Organization to a New Public Health and Health Promotion. *Am J Public Health*. 2003; 93:383-388
9. Krieger N. Latin American Social Medicine: The Quest for Social Justice

and Public Health. *Am J Public Health*. 2003; 93:1989-1991

10. Tajer D. Latin American Social Medicine: Roots, Development During the 1990s, and Current Challenges. *Am J Public Health*. 2003; 93:2023-2027

11. Pang T. The Impact of Genomics on Global Health. A*m J Public Health*. 2002; 92:1077-1079

12. Karpati A, Galea S, Awerbuch T, Levins R. Variability and Vulnerability at the Ecological Level: Implications for Understanding the Social Determinants of Health. *Am J Public Health*. 2002; 92:1768-1772

13. Setel PW, Saker L, Unwin NC, Hemed Y, Whiting DR, Kitange H. Is It Time to Reassess the Categorization of Disease Burdens in Low-Income Countries?. *Am J Public Health*. 2004; 94:384-388

14. International Society for Equity in Health. www.iseqh.org

15. WHO. Commission on Social Determinants of Health. Geneva: World Health Organization, 2006

16. Marmot M. Health in an unequal world. *Lancet* 2006 Sep 12; 368 (9552): 2081-94

The Standard of Care Debate: Can Research in Developing Countries Be Both Ethical and Responsive to Those Countries' Health Needs?

| David Wendler, PhD, Ezekiel J. Emanuel, MD, PhD and Reidar K. Lie, MD, PhD

ABSTRACT

To avoid exploitation of host communities, many commentators argue that subjects must receive the best methods available worldwide. Others worry that this requirement may block important research intended to improve health care, especially in developing countries.

To resolve this dilemma, we propose a framework for the conditions under which it is acceptable to provide subjects with less than the best methods. Specifically, institutional review boards should assume a default of requiring the "worldwide best" methods, meaning the best methods available anywhere in the world, in all cases.

However, institutional review boards should be willing to grant exceptions to this default for research studies that satisfy the following 4 conditions: (1) scientific necessity, (2) relevance for the host community, (3) sufficient host community benefit, and (4) subject and host community nonmaleficence.

INTRODUCTION

The distribution of health care around the world is marked by dramatic inequalities. Individuals in developed countries typically have access to safe water, new vaccines, and effective medications; individuals in developing countries often have access to little or no health care at all. These inequalities in health care have contributed to significant inequalities in health, with individuals who happen to live in the developing world experiencing far greater disease burdens and far shorter lives than individuals in the developed world. These inequalities have also led to a debate over what clinical investigators can do to improve health care in developing countries and thereby reduce health disparities between rich and poor.[1-6]

To protect host communities from exploitation, most commentators argue that efforts to improve health care in the developing world should never involve research that uses less than the "worldwide best"[7] methods, meaning the best methods available anywhere in the world.[8-15] Most notably, paragraph 29 of the Declaration of Helsinki states: "The benefits, risks, burdens, and effectiveness of a new method should be tested against those of the best current prophylactic, diagnostic, and therapeutic methods."[7] Similarly, Shapiro and Meslin, chairman and executive director of the US National Bioethics Advisory Commission write: "In our view, an experimental intervention should normally be compared with an established, effective treatment . . . whether or not that treatment is available in the host [developing] country."[16(p140)]

A ban on research using less than the worldwide best methods would definitively address the potential for such research to exploit host communities. Yet, such a ban may also block important research designed to improve health care for the world's poor. Is it possible to address the potential for exploitation while allowing research that has the potential to benefit the host communities?

The debate over what standard of care should be required for individuals participating in research trials typically focuses on research conducted in developing countries by investigators from developed countries. This focus makes sense. Most clinical research is conducted by investigators from developed countries, and most communities lacking access to good health care are located in developing countries. Nonetheless, researchers from developing countries may also exploit host communities. And communities in developed countries sometimes lack access to the best methods available worldwide, increasing the potential that they may be exploited. A complete analysis, then, should address the potential for exploitation independent of the nationality of the investigators, or the geographic location of the study.

SCIENTIFIC NECESSITY

Some critics argue that research using less than the best methods available worldwide—medications, procedures, interventions, vaccines—is never scientifically necessary.[9,10,15] They conclude that requiring the best methods in all cases would allow investigators to obtain the same scientific information while providing greater benefits to subjects. This argument has focused on the controversial HIV vertical transmission trials.

So-called long-course treatment, also known as the 076 regimen, was—and remains—the best method for preventing transmission of HIV infection from mother to child. Unfortunately, the "early prenatal visits, intravenous

TABLE 1— Outcomes of Short-Course AZT Vertical Transmission Trials: 1999–2000

Trial, Country, Year	Placebo Transmission Rate, %	Short-Course Transmission Rate, %	Long-Course Transmission Rate, %
076 Regimen, United States, 1999	25.5	NA	8.3
Placebo trial, Thailand, 1999	18.9	9.9	NA
Ivory Coast, 1999	24.	15.7	NA
Ivory Coast, Burkina Faso, 1999	27.5	18.0	NA
Equivalence, Thailand, 2000	NA	10.5	6.5
Nevirapine, Uganda, 1999	25.1	13.1	NA

Note. AZT = zidovudine; NA = not available.

infusion during labor, and cost" associated with long-course treatment make it neither affordable nor feasible in developing countries, where the burden of HIV disease is greatest.[17(p786)] To identify a method to help individuals in developing countries, investigators compared a less expensive, more easily administered "short course" of zidovudine (AZT) to what these individuals typically receive to prevent vertical transmission—namely, no treatment at all. Criticism of these trials was widespread, with commentators arguing that the control arms could have used long-course AZT rather than no treatment, thus reducing the number of HIV-infected babies in the trials without undermining the scientific importance of the resulting data.[8–10,13]

Before the start of the short-course trials, data from South Africa showed wide variation in the HIV vertical transmission rate in untreated individuals over time, even at the same location.[18] These data provided compelling evidence, *ex ante*, that any assessment of short-course AZT needed an untreated control arm to determine whether the intervention was better than no treatment at all. This need for a no-treatment control arm

was confirmed by the results of the trials themselves.

The transmission rates found in the trials—18.9% to 27.5% in the placebo arm[19–23] and 9.9% to 18% in the short-course arm—confirm that an equivalence trial could well have shown a long-course transmission rate of 8%, and a short-course transmission rate of 17% (Table 1). Comparing this short-course transmission rate to the 076 placebo transmission rate of 25% would suggest that short-course treatment is better than placebo and possibly worth pursuing. Yet, the variability in the placebo transmission rate reveals that the placebo rate in an equivalence trial might have been 19%, suggesting that short-course treatment was not worth pursuing. The important point is that this result was a realistic possibility *at the outset,* implying that the trials needed a no-treatment arm to determine whether the short course was better than no treatment at all.

The literature, perhaps shaped by the debate over the HIV vertical transmission trials, has focused on what investigators may use as *controls* in clinical trials. Yet, a total ban on research using less than the best methods would also prevent investigators

from assessing active agents that are expected to be less effective than the worldwide best methods. This frequently overlooked implication of a total ban on less than the best methods is illustrated by the landmark nevirapine trials.

Approximately 75% of HIV vertical transmission occurs during or after delivery.[24] Thus, a treatment administered during delivery might offer a feasible, economical way to reduce HIV vertical transmission in developing countries, despite the fact that it would not affect the 25% of transmission that occurs during gestation.[25] This line of reasoning led investigators to nevirapine, a well-tolerated, low-cost, potent antiviral. A single 200-mg oral dose of nevirapine given during labor passes quickly through the placenta and has a long serum half-life.[26] Hence, a single dose of nevirapine given to the mother during labor, and to the infant within 72 hours of birth, might offer a feasible and affordable treatment for vertical HIV transmission in developing countries.

Because nevirapine does not offer protection against the approximately 25% of vertical transmission that occurs in utero, it was recognized at the time that it would be less effective

American Journal of Public Health | June 2004, Vol 94, No. 6

than long-course AZT therapy. Hence, the requirement that trial participants receive the worldwide best methods implies that participants may not receive nevirapine alone, precluding assessment of nevirapine as a single agent. The human costs of this requirement are highlighted by the fact that trials conducted on nevirapine as a single agent have revolutionized perinatal HIV treatment in developing countries, potentially saving millions of lives.[27]

Determining whether a trial using less than the best methods is scientifically necessary requires clinical judgment based on the relevant probabilities: What are the chances the trial will answer an important question? What are the chances the same question can be answered by a trial using only the best methods? Because there is no infallible algorithm to answer these questions, institutional review boards will have to decide whether to allow less than the best methods on a case-by-case basis. To maximize subject benefit, institutional review boards should assume a default of requiring the best methods in all cases. From there, institutional review boards should allow research using less than the best methods only when scientifically necessary to answer an important question.

HOST COMMUNITY RELEVANCE

Provision of the best methods to everyone in the world would render incremental improvements in health care for developing countries otiose. To take just 1 example, approximately 10 million children die each year from diseases that could be prevented by aid amounting to less than 1% of the gross national product of developed countries.[28,29] Provision of such aid would save millions of lives and render unnecessary any research to assess whether less than the best methods may be partially effective in combating these diseases. Tragically, this aid has not been provided. In this context, research using less than the best methods sometimes represents the best hope for communities in developing countries to address their most significant health needs. When it does, when these trials address an important health need of communities in developing countries, the moral importance of helping the poor provides a strong argument in their favor.

SUFFICIENT HOST COMMUNITY BENEFIT

Even when scientifically necessary, and relevant to an important health concern of the host community, research using less than the best methods retains the potential to exploit host communities by failing to provide them with a fair level of benefits. The fairness of the benefits to the host community depends on the burdens and risks it bears and the extent to which others benefit from its participation in the trial.[30] In particular, as the host community assumes greater burdens, or others enjoy greater benefits from its participation, the institutional review board should insist that the host community receive correspondingly greater benefits to ensure a fair trial.

Beforehand, it may be unclear whether the tested method, even if proved effective, will be implemented in the host community. In such cases, the fact that the trial addresses an important health concern may not in itself offer a fair level of benefits. Similarly, trials may produce so much benefit for others that the information provided to the host community does not represent a fair proportion of the overall benefits.[11] In these cases, the host community should receive additional benefits, such as development of clinics or training of nurses, to ensure that the overall benefits it receives are fair given the burdens it experiences and the benefits others receive from its participation.[30]

The need for a fair level of benefits highlights the fact that a ban on research using less than the worldwide best methods, although intended to *minimize* the potential for exploitation, may *increase* it in practice. To ensure that the host community receives sufficient benefits, investigators might focus their research on methods that the host communities can implement, if proved successful. Insisting that investigators use the worldwide best methods may force them to abandon these attempts to assess methods that can be implemented in the host communities, thereby increasing the chances for exploitation.

SUBJECT AND HOST COMMUNITY NONMALEFICENCE

The principle of nonmaleficence implies that research using less than the best methods should be allowed only when it will not make research subjects or the host community prospectively worse off.[31] To satisfy this requirement, such research should not harm the existing health care system. For instance, research should not rely on nurses or laboratories that are needed to care for patients in the host community. Second, it is important to ensure that research using less than the worldwide best methods does not make subjects prospectively worse off than they would be in the absence of the trial. Provided there is clinical equipoise between the proposed new treatment and the local methods of care, individuals who enroll will receive either the methods they would have received otherwise, if any, or a method not known to be inferior to it.[32] When this condition is met, research participation can offer subjects an important benefit by providing access to medical interventions not otherwise available to them.

Satisfaction of these 4 conditions—scientific necessity, host country relevance, sufficient benefit, nonmaleficence—ensures that research using less than the worldwide best methods addresses an important health concern of the host community and offers the host community sufficient benefit without making subjects worse off. This potential to help the world's poor provides an important ethical argument in favor of allowing such research.

POSSIBLE OBJECTIONS

These trials violate investigators' clinical obligations.

The US National Bioethics Advisory Commission and others

argue that researchers gain moral obligations to provide the best care possible when they enter into clinical relationships with research subjects.[31,33–35] This view implies that investigators should not conduct research using less than the best methods even when it satisfies the 4 conditions outlined: a potential for future benefit, no matter how great, cannot justify the violation of researchers' obligations to provide present subjects with the best methods. Although this argument seems compelling, it is not clear that it accurately reflects clinicians' obligations.

Clearly, investigators have clinical obligations that go beyond the scientific needs of particular research trials. Investigators cannot justify trials using less than the best methods simply by arguing that in the absence of the trial, subjects would receive nothing. For instance, an investigator working in the developing world cannot decide against providing her subjects with cardiopulmonary resuscitation at little or no cost simply on the grounds that, in her absence, they would not receive it. At the same time, investigators' clinical obligations do not seem to imply they must provide the worldwide best methods in all cases. It is widely agreed that investigators assessing whether aspirin reduces mortality from heart attacks in a developing country would not be required to provide subjects with coronary artery bypass surgery,[36] much less coronary intensive care in case of a myocardial infarction.[37] What implications does the fact that clinicians need not provide these worldwide best methods have for the standard of care debate?

One's moral obligations depend in part on the costs associated with the available alternatives.[38–40] Whether I have a moral obligation to save a drowning child depends upon what is required, and what I must forgo. If I can save the child at little or no cost to myself or others, then I am obligated to do so. If saving the child would put me at great risk of death, or prevent me from saving several other children, I am not obligated to do so.

Physicians' obligations to their patients are similarly shaped by the relevant costs. This is obvious, although often implicit, in the context of standard medical care. To take an example relevant to developing countries, the Elizabeth Glaser Pediatric AIDS Foundation devoted a $100 million grant from the US Agency for International Development to blocking vertical transmission of HIV from mother to child in the developing world.[41] Long-course AZT therapy (the 076 regimen) is the worldwide best method for blocking vertical transmission of HIV from mother to child. Hence, the claim that clinicians are obligated to provide those for whom they care with the best methods implies that the clinicians working on this project are obligated to provide long-course AZT to block vertical transmission of HIV.

Assuming a cost of $250 per mother–child pair treated, provision of long-course AZT would translate into approximately 65 000 fewer HIV-infected children compared with the background infection rate without treatment. Conversely, devoting the same money to single-dose nevirapine, at $4 per mother–child pair, translates into approximately 270 000 fewer HIV-infected children compared with the background infection rate without treatment. That is, providing nevirapine rather than long-course AZT has the potential to save an additional 200 000 lives.

This difference supports the claim that the foundation made the ethically appropriate choice—supply nevirapine—even though its decision entails that the foundation's clinicians will fail to provide the worldwide best methods to block vertical transmission when they could have done so. This conclusion suggests that the provision of less than the best methods can be consistent with physicians' clinical obligations when providing the best methods would entail unacceptably high costs. Determining exactly how high the associated costs must be to justify providing less than the best methods will be difficult, and institutional review boards will have to use their judgment. Under the proposed 4 conditions, researchers may use less than the best methods only when their use is scientifically necessary to address an important health concern of the host community. Insisting that researchers provide all subjects with the best methods in such cases would entail a high cost, represented by the importance of the health concern that thereby goes unaddressed.

These trials rely on a double standard.

Some commentators argue that it is unethical to conduct research in the *developed* world using less than the best methods. Hence, allowing such trials in the *developing* world relies on a double standard: "Acceptance of a standard of care that does not conform to the standard in the sponsoring country results in a double standard in research. Such a double standard . . . permits research designs that are unacceptable in the sponsoring country."[8(p854)]

The fact that a particular trial design is allowed in one place but not another does not in itself constitute a double standard.[42] For there may be relevant differences—environmental, genetic, social, cultural differences—that render the same design acceptable in one place, but not the other. To take a straightforward example, no one would argue that approving research using bovine-derived drugs in the United States but not in India constitutes an ethical double standard.

Because patients in developed countries typically have access to the worldwide best methods, research using less than the best methods typically does not have sufficient social value to justify its risks. In contrast, such research may have sufficient social value in developing countries, where the existing standard of care is something less than the worldwide best. This suggests that research using less than the worldwide best methods can be ethically acceptable in developing countries, even though the very same research would be unethical in a developed country.

Furthermore, when a developed country makes a reasonable decision not to provide a worldwide best treatment on grounds of cost-effectiveness, it may be acceptable to conduct research in that country on less effective methods.[43] For instance, a new type of erythropoietin has been developed that is expected to be as effective as existing versions for postchemotherapy supportive care, and more easily administered. During the time this newer drug is on patent, it is likely to be very expensive, and a developed country may decide on cost-effectiveness grounds to provide its citizens with the older, less-convenient version. Assuming this decision is a reasonable one, it seems ethically acceptable to conduct trials in that country that compare proposed new treatments to the older version, rather than the worldwide best version.

These trials are counterproductive.

Some critics argue that research using less than the best methods may be counterproductive, reducing pressure on host governments to reform, or pharmaceutical companies to provide treatments at an affordable price. "The issue of the affordability of drugs should be tackled by getting governments, pharmaceutical companies, donors, and other international agencies to cooperate in making drugs cheaper rather than by looking for other, probably inferior, regimens for people in less-developed countries."[44(p842)]

This possibility highlights the importance of assessing the ethical acceptability of research using less than the best methods in light of *all* feasible alternatives. If an individual study, or even series of studies using less than the worldwide best methods would impair a realistic chance that the host country will receive state-of-the-art health care for the condition under study, such studies should be prohibited. However, when there are no realistic alternatives for the foreseeable future to address the health concern in question, use of less than the worldwide best methods may represent the best hope for the host communities. Here too, institutional review boards must use their judgment. What are the chances that the research use of less than the best methods will lead

to the development of a feasible and economical treatment? What are the chances, in the absence of these trials, that the best methods will be provided for the condition in question?

SUMMARY

Critics rightly point out that research using less than the worldwide best methods has the potential to be scientifically unnecessary, counterproductive, exploitive, inconsistent with investigators' clinical obligations, and based on an ethical double standard. Fortunately, these possibilities, although important, are not inevitable. Investigators should be allowed to use less than the worldwide best methods only when doing so is ethically appropriate and has the potential to provide sufficient benefit for the host communities. Specifically, institutional review boards should assume a default of requiring the best methods in all cases and approve research using less than the worldwide best methods only when it satisfies the following 4 conditions: (1) scientific necessity: investigators must use less than the worldwide best methods to answer the scientific question posed by the trial; (2) relevance for the host community: answering the scientific question posed by the trial will help address an important health need of the host community; (3) sufficient host community benefit: the trial will produce a fair level of benefit for the host community; and (4) subject and host community nonmaleficence: subjects and the host community will not be made prospectively worse off than they would be in the absence of the trial.

About the Authors

The authors are with the Department of Clinical Bioethics at the National Institutes of Health, Bethesda, Md. Reidar K. Lie is also with the Department of Public Health and Primary Health Care, University of Bergen, Norway.

Correspondence: Requests for reprints should be sent to David Wendler, PhD, Department of Clinical Bioethics, National Institutes of Health, Building 10, Room 1C118, Bethesda, MD 20892 (e-mail: dwendler@nih.gov).

Acknowledgments

The work for this project was completed as part of the authors' responsibilities as employees of the National Institutes of Health.

Notes

The opinions expressed are the authors' own and do not reflect any position or policy of the National Institutes of Health, Public Health Service, or Department of Health and Human Services.

Contributors

D. Wendler conceived the project and wrote the first draft of the article. All the authors helped revise the article.

References

1. Macklin R. After Helsinki: unresolved issues in international research. *Kennedy Inst Ethics J.* 2001;11:17–36.
2. Levine RJ. The "best proven therapeutic method" Standard in clinical trials in technologically developing countries. *IRB: Rev Human Subjects Res.*1998;20:5–9.
3. Lie RK. Ethics of placebo-controlled trials in developing countries. *Bioethics.*1998;12:307–311.
4. Varmus H, Satcher D. Ethical complexities of conducting research in developing countries. *N Engl J Med.*1997;337:1003–1005.
5. Resnik DB. The ethics of HIV research in developing nations. *Bioethics.*1998;12:286–306.
6. Killen J, Grady C, Folkers GK, Fauci AS. Ethics of clinical research in the developing world. *Nature Rev.*2002;2:210–215.
7. Declaration of Helsinki, paragraph 29, revised October 2000. Available at: http://www.wma.net/e/home/html. Accessed January 10, 2004.
8. Lurie P, Wolf SM. Unethical trials of methods to reduce perinatal transmission of the human immunodeficiency virus in developing countries. *N Engl J Med.*1997;337:853–856.
9. Angell M. The ethics of clinical research in the third world. *N Engl J Med.*1997;337:847–849.
10. Angell M. Ethical imperialism? Ethics in international collaborative clinical research. *N Engl J*

*Med.*1988;319:1081−1083.

11. Angell M. Investigators' responsibilities for human subjects in developing countries. *N Engl J Med.*2000;342:967−969.

12. Rothman KJ, Michels KB. The continuing unethical use of placebos. *N Engl J Med.*1994;331:394.

13. Rothman D. The shame of medical research. *The New York Review of Books.* Available at: http://www.nybooks.com/articles/13907. Accessed January 10, 2004.

14. Annas G. Prominent opinion: the ethics of international research trials in the developing world. *J Med Ethics.*2001;2:7010.

15. Brennan TA. Proposed revisions to the Declaration of Helsinki—will they weaken the ethical principles underlying human research? *N Engl J Med.*1999;341:527−531.

16. Shapiro HT, Meslin EM. Ethical issues in the design and conduct of clinical trials in developing countries. *N Engl J Med.*2001;345:139−142.

17. Dabis F, Msellati P, Meda N, et al. 6-month efficacy, tolerance, and acceptability of a short regimen of oral zidovudine to reduce vertical transmission of HIV in breastfed children in Cote d'Ivoire and Burkina Faso: a double-blind placebo-controlled multicentre trial. *Lancet.*1999;353:786−792.

18. Karim SSA. Placebo controls in HIV perinatal transmission trials: a South African's viewpoint. *Am J Public Health.*1998;88:564−566.

19. Conner EM, Sperling RJ, Gelber R, et al. Reduction of maternal–infant transmission of human immunodeficiency virus type 1 with zidovudine treatment. *N Engl J Med.*1994;331:1173−1180.

20. Shaffer N, Chuachoowong R, Mock PA, et al. Short-course zidovudine for perinatal HIV-1 transmission in Bangkok, Thailand: a randomized controlled trial. *Lancet.*1999;353:773−780.

21. Wiktor SZ, Ekpini E, Karon JM, et al. Short-course oral zidovudine for prevention of mother-to-child transmission of HIV-1 in Abidjan, Cote d'Ivoire: a randomized trial. *Lancet.*1999; 353:781−785.

22. Lallemont M, Jourdain G, Le Coeur S, et al. A trial of shortened zidovudine regimens to prevent mother-to-child transmission of human immunodeficiency virus type 1. *N Engl J Med.*2000;343:982−991.

23. Guay LA, Musoke P, Fleming T, et al. Intrapartum and neonatal single-dose nevirapine compared to zidovudine for prevention of mother-to-child transmission of HIV-1 in Kampala, Uganda: HIVNET 012 randomised trial. *Lancet.*1999;354:795−802.

24. Rouzioux C, Costagliola D, Burgard M, et al. Estimated timing of mother-to-child human immunodeficiency virus type 1 transmission by use of a Markov model: the HIV infection in newborns French collaborative study group. *Am J Epidemiol.*1995;142:1330−1337.

25. Consensus statement. Science, ethics, and the future of research into maternal infant transmission of HIV-1. *Lancet.*1999;353:832−835.

26. Mirochnick M, Fenton T, Gagnier P, et al. Pharmacokinetics of nevirapine in human immunodeficiency virus type 1–infected pregnant women and their neonates. *J Infect Dis.*1998;178:368−374.

27. Marseille E, Kahn JG, Mmiro F, et al. Cost effectiveness of a single-dose nevirapine regimen for mothers and babies to decrease vertical HIV-1 transmission in sub-Saharan Africa. *Lancet.*1999;354:803−809.

28. Jha P, Mills A, Hanson K, et al. Improving the health of the global poor. *Science.*2002;295:2036−2039.

29. Attaran A, Sachs J. Defining and refining international donor support for combating the AIDS pandemic. *Lancet.*2002;357:57−61.

30. Participants in the 2001 Conference on Ethical Aspects of Research in Developing Countries. Fair benefits for research in developing countries. *Science.*2002;298:2133−2134.

31. National Bioethics Advisory Commission. Ethical and policy issues in international research: clinical trials in developing countries. Available at: http://www.georgetown.edu/research/nrcbl/nbac/pubs.html. Accessed January 10, 2004.

32. Freedman B. Equipoise and the ethics of clinical research. *N Engl J Med.*1987;317:141−145.

33. Lurie P, Wolfe SM. HIVNET nevirapine trials [letter]. *Lancet.*1999;354:1816.

34. Lurie P, Wolfe SM. Science, ethics, and the future of research into maternal infant transmission of HIV-1 [letter]. *Lancet.*1999;353:1878−1879.

35. Omene JA. Science, ethics, and the future of research into maternal infant transmission of HIV-1 [letter]. *Lancet.*1999;353:1878.

36. Bloom BR. The highest attainable Standard: ethical issues in AIDS vaccines. *Science.*1998;279:186−188.

37. Kass N, Faden R. HIV research, ethics, and the developing world. *Am J Public Health.*1998;88:548−550.

38. Kagan S. *The Limits of Morality.* Oxford, England: Oxford University Press; 1989:64−70.

39. Raz J. *Practical Reason and Norms.* Oxford, England: Oxford University Press; 1975:15−32.

40. Beauchamp T, Childress J. *The Principle of Biomedical Ethics.* 5th ed. Oxford, England: Oxford University Press; 2001:14−21.

41. Brown D, Faler B. US to give AIDS foundation $100 Million Grant. *Washington Post.* August 1, 2002:A8.

42. Orentlicher D. Universality and its limits: when research ethics can reflect local circumstances. *J Law Med Ethics.*2002;30:403−410.

43. Freedman B. Placebo-controlled trials and the logic of clinical purpose. *IRB.*1990;12:1−6.

44. Msamanga G. Letter to the editor. *N Engl J Med.*1998;338:842.

Lessons for (and From) America

| *Rudolf Klein, MA*

ABSTRACT

Drawing lessons from international experience for health care reform in the United States requires striking a difficult balance between historical determinism and free will, between cynical pessimism and naïve optimism. The key to this puzzle may lie in a paradox: the United States is the most successful exporter of public health policy ideas and instruments yet has failed to build an effective health care system.

General ideas (like notions about the role of competition) and microinstruments (like diagnosis-related groups) travel better than do health care systems. Ideas can be adapted to local circumstances, and instruments may easily fit into preexisting systems.

Importing systems from countries with different histories and institutions would require a tectonic shift in the American political landscape.

INTRODUCTION

International Comparisons hold out one clear lesson for the United States: the Declaration of Independence was a blunder. If only the colonists had been patient, if only they had tolerated British rule for a few more decades, they would in due course have received the blessings of a Westminster-type constitution. Just like Britain herself, and ex-colonies like Canada and New Zealand, they would have had a system of majoritarian government that enables the executive to enact its legislative program. And given such a system of majoritarian government, it is almost certain that the United States would long since have enacted some form or other of comprehensive health care insurance. As it is, American exceptionalism is reflected both in its constitutional arrangements—and the generous opportunities these offer to special interests to obstruct, delay, or sabotage legislation even if it has the support of a majority of the population—and the lack of anything resembling a scheme of comprehensive health care.

To draw such a lesson may seem absurd. History is not a film that can be rerun or remade. In any case, the central contention is highly questionable. Constitutional arrangements are surely only part of the explanation for America's unique failure among rich countries to adopt national health insurance, since these did not prevent the introduction of Medicare and Medicaid despite the opposition of the medical profession and other interests.[1]

The point of going back to the Declaration of Independence is to remind ourselves about a central dilemma in any lessondrawing exercise. This is how best to strike a balance between assuming that history is all—that the past of individual countries determines the future—and assuming, contrariwise, that policymakers have a free hand in adopting whatever foreign exemplars take their fancy. This article elaborates on this theme: historical determinism versus free will in lesson drawing—and how best to steer a course between cynical fatalism and naïve optimism.

PRISONERS OF THE PAST?

A strong interpretation of historical determinism would suggest that policymakers are prisoners of the past. From this perspective, the notion of path dependency not only explains past history but also predicts the future. The ideas, institutions, and interests inherited from the past shape, and constrain, what can be done in the present. In the case of the United States, past policies have created powerful interest groups (notably for-profit insurers and providers) with the financial and political resources to resist attempts to reform the system to their disadvantage.[2] And they operate within a political system that provides ample scope for wrecking tactics; witness the opposition to the Clinton plan.

What, then, is the point of seeking to draw lessons—about, say, the best way of funding a comprehensive health care system—from countries whose history has not created similarly powerful interest groups and whose political systems do not afford similar opportunities for wrecking strategies? Skepticism is compounded when we consider other factors, such as differences in political culture: can policies reflecting a commitment to the concept of social solidarity be exported to a country conspicuously lacking any such tradition?

The more optimistic free-will approach would argue that systems do change, and not always in ways that can be predicted: social scientists are skilled in rationalizing ex post facto what has happened in terms of the specific institutional and cultural inheritance of individual countries, but accurate ex ante facto predictions based on these same factors are conspicuously rare. Windows of opportunity, as we know, do open, often unexpectedly.[3] However, we badly lack convincing window-opening theories; we are better at explaining continuities than discontinuities, paths rather than turnings. And when windows do open, it will be those policy advocates with well-grounded proposals and persuasive arguments (for example, evidence that a particular policy works well elsewhere) who will be best placed to exploit the opportunity.

So even if foreign exemplars offer options that may seem totally unrealistic in today's circumstances, there is no way of telling when they might become relevant and appealing. Indeed, optimists might even argue that acting on the assumption of policy free will could actually bring it about by stretching the imaginations and challenging the assumptions of decisionmakers and the wider public, while historical determinism can all too easily become self-fulfilling by creating a corrosive pessimism about the possibilities of change. In which case, distilling lessons for America from the experience of other countries becomes a useful, if contingent, exercise.

The best way of addressing these contrasting views is perhaps by disaggregating the notion of lesson drawing by distinguishing between different kinds of policies and arenas. The politics of systems reform will be different from the politics of introducing change within the framework of an existing system. And, in turn, the politics of within-system change may vary from issue to issue, bringing different actors and different interests into play. Some may rouse ideological passions: the introduction in the 1990s of mimic markets in Britain's National Health Service (NHS) is a case in point.[4] These changes did not affect the principles or funding mechanisms of the NHS, but they caused much outrage— all the more so because they were seen as an example of lesson drawing from the United States, of all countries (a warning that the perceived prove-

nance of lessons may be an important factor in determining their reception). Other changes may be more technical in character and therefore involve much smaller but concentrated constituencies, such as the medical profession, with a passionate self-interest in the issues at stake.

THE POLITICS OF SYSTEMS REFORM

Starting with systems reform, there is indeed one overriding lesson that emerges from the contributions in this issue: there is no one lesson or formula for creating, and funding, the kind of comprehensive, universal health care system that other advanced countries take for granted but that the United States has found so elusive. Germany and France have insurance-based systems; Britain has a tax-based system. Both models offer a complex mixture of strengths and weaknesses. The insurance-based systems appear to be more successful in creating high-standard services, offering choice to the consumer. But the method of finance inflates labor costs, has higher administrative costs than a tax-based system, and is also less progressive. Conversely, Britain's tax-based, progressively financed system has been conspicuously successful in containing costs but much less so in terms of standards of service, let alone consumer choice.

The case of Britain is worth pondering on further as a warning of the pitfalls of lesson drawing. Lessons drawn tend to vary over time as perceptions shift. So, for many decades, Britain was held out as the supreme exemplar of successful cost containment—as indeed it was. However, at the turn of the millennium, the Labour Government decided that the political costs of successful cost containment were too great. The medical profession and others who had argued that the NHS had been seriously underfunded appeared to be vindicated as the government announced extra billions for the NHS to cut waiting lists, improve services, and introduce (eventually) patient choice.

So what conclusion is to be drawn from this turnabout, from virtue suddenly turning into vice? If tax funding meant that the NHS was indeed underfunded for the first 50 years of its existence—a dubious, if widely held, assumption—does this mean that the model is fundamentally flawed? Or is the appropriate lesson to draw that the model, despite its flaws, can still be salvaged? Different answers are likely to be given to these questions, depending on the relative weight put on cost containment versus service standards.

If the first lesson to be drawn from the country contributions is that there are different paths toward achieving much the same objectives, the second lesson is therefore that all paths pose problems for the traveler. Dissatisfaction with existing systems appears to be the rule. All the countries covered in this survey are tinkering, to varying degrees, with their systems. As the country reports show, policymakers are continuously striving to repair, improve, and experiment, even in countries that appear to be doing rather well—particularly when compared with the United States.

If Britain is embarking on radical reform yet again—with the Labour Government reinventing the mimic market (market-like mechanisms designed to increase competition among public-sector providers), so loudly denounced when originally introduced by Mrs Thatcher's administration—this is perhaps no surprise, given a national consensus that the system has failed to deliver. But France has been reengineering aspects of its system, despite placing first in the World Health Organization's notorious ranking exercise. In Germany there is a vigorous political debate about how to reform the system, while Canada is awash with commissions and committees investigating options for the future. If countries are not worrying about spending too little (like Britain), they are worrying about spending too much (like France).

There are, of course, good reasons for this. On the one hand, there are exogenous pressures on health care systems. Some, like the changing demographic structure of the population, are general. Others are specific to Europe: the European Union's common currency rules about budget deficits constrain governments already fiscally stressed as a result of dipping rates of economic growth. Hence the preoccupation—Britain always excepted—with cost containment, an issue that inevitably creeps up the political agenda when economic indicators slide down. Other pressures are endogenous to health care systems. Crossnationally, the configuration of services is changing and new patterns of practice are developing. Thus a common theme across European systems is how to strike a new balance between curative and preventive interventions, between hospital and primary care.

In short, to add to the traditional criteria for evaluating health care systems such as comprehensiveness, value for money, and equity, a new one is now emerging: the ability of health care systems to adapt and change—by exploiting, for example, the opportunities offered by the combination of information technology and evidence-based medicine. Moving from systems or macropolicymaking to the next level of technical or micropolicymaking, where should we be looking for lessons about how to promote flexibility, innovation, and experimentation?

EXPORTING AMERICAN IDEAS

Ironically, the answer to that question appears to be the United States. In this respect, if in no other, it is the rest of the world that looks for lessons to the United States, not the other way around. The United States is, without doubt, a net exporter of ideas and exemplars. It is worth pondering this curious phenomenon for what it tells us about the flow of lessons from country to country. The US health care system (if indeed it can be called that) is, by common consent, a conspicuous failure: too much money is spent protecting too few people. The point does not need belaboring: critical self-examination and continuous debate about reform is part of the American health care scene. And yet American ideas—notably notions of competition—have been influential in a range of European countries. And American policy tools—for example, diagnosisrelated groups—based systems of remuneration—have been widely adopted.

Why? Consider, first, the diffusion of American notions about systems design. One plausible explanation for this is that, since the 1970s, economic theory has played an increasingly important part in shaping social policy while economic reality has been increasingly important in forcing countries to reassess their policy trajectory. Health care is no exception.[5] And it so happens that American economists—by sheer weight of numbers, quite apart from any intellectual distinction—tend to dominate the international debate, as a count of journal articles would no doubt confirm. To varying degrees, American ideas and rhetoric about the benefits of competition and the importance of incentives have therefore become naturalized in other countries—a sort of intellectual convergence based on the role of economic ideas in the policy process. Exogenous ideas have been absorbed to the extent that they speak to endogenous concerns: most specifically, how best to adapt paternalistic, solidaristic health care systems to a consumer society where individual choice is sovereign (as is the case in Britain and, to a lesser extent, Sweden and the Netherlands).

The widespread adoption of American policy tools is perhaps less surprising. One way of characterizing health care in the United States is that it represents a heroic but doomed endeavor to bring order to chaos, a never-ending battle to overcome the perversities of a system that might have been designed to fail.

It is this that spurs the participants in the system to ever-greater feats of ingenuity and inventiveness. It is this that promotes managerial, as well as technological, innovation on a scale that no other country can even begin to match. For the outside world, the US health care scene is therefore a kind of supermarket where they can shop selectively. But having shopped, they also adapt; once again, the crucial element is the local environment and context—and the extent to which imports fit, or can be made to fit, local needs.

So here the argument comes full circle. The United States will draw lessons from other countries to the extent that these are most consistent with local circumstances. In health care, there is no such thing as "the best buy" system. And lessons are learned not because of the intrinsic merits of some foreign system but because of the compatibility of its features with the institutions and ideology of the importing country. For the United States, the lessons learned are therefore likely to depend on whether increasing inequality, linked to increasing economic turbulence, produces a tectonic shift in the country's political scenery.[6]

About the Authors

Rudolf Klein is with the University of Bath, the London School of Economics, and the London School of Hygiene and Tropical Medicine.

Correspondence: Requests for reprints should be sent to Rudolf Klein, L 12A Laurier Road, London NW5 1SG, England.

References
1. Marmor T. *The Politics of Medicare.* 2nd ed. New York, NY: Aldine de Gruyter; 2000.
2. Tuohy CH. *Accidental Logics: The Dynamics of Change in the Health Care Arena in the United States, Britain and Canada.* New York, NY: Oxford University Press; 1999.
3. Kingdon J. *Agendas, Alternatives and Public Policies.* 2nd ed. New York, NY: Harper Collins; 1995.
4. Klein R. *The New Politics of the NHS.* 4th ed. Harlow, Essex, England: Prentice Hall; 2001.
5. Fox D. *Economists and Health Care.* New York, NY: Prodist; 1979.
6. Phillips K. *Wealth and Democracy.* New York, NY: Broadway Books; 2002. Cited by: Madrick J. The power of the super-rich. *New York Review of Books.* July 18, 2002:25–27.

Variability and Vulnerability at the Ecological Level: Implications for Understanding the Social Determinants of Health

| Adam Karpati, MD, MPH, Sandro Galea, MD, MPH, Tamara Awerbuch, PhD and Richard Levins, PhD

ABSTRACT

Objectives. We examined variability in disease rates to gain understanding of the complex interactions between contextual socioeconomic factors and health.

Methods. We compared mortality rates between New York and California counties in the lowest and highest quartiles of socioeconomic status (SES), assessed rate variability between counties for various outcomes, and examined correlations between outcomes' sensitivity to SES and their variability.

Results. Outcomes with mortality rates that differed most by county SES were among those whose variability across counties was high (e.g., AIDS, homicide, cirrhosis). Lower-SES counties manifested greater variability among outcome measures.

Conclusions. Differences in health outcome variability reflect differences in SES impact on health. Health variability at the ecological level might reflect the impact of stressors on vulnerable populations. (Am J Public Health. 2002;92:1768–1772)

INTRODUCTION

Recent research into the role of the social environment as a determinant of individual health has reinvigorated inquiry into the relation between context and health.[1–3] Questions regarding mechanism follow naturally from this work. A key aspect of many contextual variables is that they cannot be measured at the individual level; they are essentially group, or ecological, characteristics. Contextual factors likely interact with the large number of individual characteristics that determine health and illness, such as genetics, behavioral choices, and access to medical care.

Analyses of community factors attempt to elucidate how context affects the health of individuals.[4] Although multilevel analysis allows statistical determination of the relative effect of individual and community factors,[5] the manner in which these measures exert their effects on public health is likely to be more complex than is suggested by generalized multilevel linear models.[6,7] A more accurate understanding of the interplay between individuals and their environments requires construction of models that take into account our knowledge of interactions on various levels, contextual and otherwise, and the fact that system components are interconnected and likely display feedback loops.[8–10]

One approach to understanding complex systems is to examine variability among their components. Variability refers to the extent to which a characteristic of a complex system (e.g., heart rate or stock prices) changes over time or space. Variability in a complex system might reflect the effect of external influences ("stressors") through their interaction with the system's homeostatic mechanisms.[11]

Most evaluations of variability in complex physiological systems have been done in the context of individual clinical characteristics. For example, a decrease in heart rate variability has been shown to predict mortality after myocardial infarction.[12] For public health surveillance or for epidemiological analysis, variability in population health or its determinants may be a more informative characteristic than the absolute level of particular components. Similarly, for policy or program evaluation, variability might be a useful measure of the relative effects of different interventions.

We studied the relation between contextual effects and population health outcomes by examining mortality rates associated with several conditions in counties in New York and California. We hypothesized that, first, certain diseases or health outcomes (e.g., traumatic events or communicable diseases) are more sensitive to population socioeconomic factors than are others, reflecting the degree to which those outcomes are avoidable or preventable. Second, the rates of the outcomes that are most sensitive to socioeconomic factors also vary the most among counties, reflecting the wide distribution of responses to the stressors to which populations are exposed.

METHODS

The unit of analysis for this study was the county. We selected New York and California because they are among the most populous states in the United States and their county mortality rates are based on relatively large denominators. We excluded from the analysis any county in either state with a population of less than 15 000 persons.

TABLE 1 —Mortality Rates from Various Causes in New York and California, 1997.[a]

Outcome	New York			California		
	Mean	Range	Range/Mean	Mean	Range	Range/Mean
All-cause mortality (all ages)	829	274	0.3	453.8	228.5	0.5
All-cause mortality (≥75 y)	21655	9070	0.4	19 284.2	8714	0.5
All-cause mortality (10-24 y)[b]	120	310	2.6	75.0	155.1	2.1
Infant mortality	6.7	12.5	1.9	7.0	12.3	1.8
AIDS	4.9	53.7	10.9	3.4	24.6	7.3
Pneumonia[c]	34.4	65.1	1.9	15.8	22.3	1.4
COPD	42.7	58.3	1.4	23.5	29.6	1.3
Cardiovascular disease	286	234	0.8	89.5	75.0	0.8
Stroke	47.9	64.0	1.6	26.4	22.6	0.9
All neoplastic disease	204	107	0.5	118.8	56.1	0.5
Lung cancer	n/a	n/a	n/a	34.9	32.3	0.9
Female breast cancer	n/a	n/a	n/a	19.1	19.1	1.0
Cirrhosis	8.0	15.6	2.0	10.1	24.7	2.4
Accidents[d]	29.2	33.8	1.2	18.5	29.5	1.6
Homicide	2.6	16.7	6.3	6.7	17.7	2.6
Suicide	n/a	n/a	n/a	12.1	18.3	1.5

Note. COPD = chronic obstructive pulmonary disease; n/a = not available.

[a]New York data from 1997. California data from 1997 or aggregated from 1995-1997. New York rates are age-adjusted to New York State census population 1990. California rates are standardized to US standard population 1940. (As such, these rates are not directly comparable.) All rates are per 100 000 population.

[b]California-ages 15-24 years.

[c]California-includes influenza.

[d]California-motor vehicle accidents only.

Data

We used New York State Department of Health and California Department of Health Services data to obtain age-adjusted mortality rates in each county for the various outcomes.[13,14] Table 1 presents the mortality rates for the outcomes studied. We selected outcomes on the basis of data availability, range of clinical conditions, and consistency with previously published studies. Rates for New York were from 1997; rates for California were either from 1997 alone or were an average of rates from 1995 to 1997.

We obtained the following measures of county socioeconomic status (SES) from the US Census Bureau: unemployment rate (1997), percentage living in poverty (1995), percentage of children aged less than 18 years living in poverty (1995), median household income (1995), and high school graduation rate (1990).[15] Percentage living in poverty is defined as the percentage of households under the federal poverty threshold, adjusted for family size and composition.[16] These socioeconomic factors were chosen on the basis of data availability and consistency with previously published studies.[11,17]

Analysis

We analyzed counties in California and New York separately. We stratified counties into quartiles by each of the SES measures, calculated the average rate of each health outcome for the bottom and top quartiles, and obtained the rate ratio for a given health outcome by comparing counties in the lowest and highest socioeconomic quartiles.

We also calculated the variability of each health outcome across all counties in each state. Following Levins and Lopez, we used the range of values divided by the mean value as the measure of variability; this measure provides a useful estimate for qualitative analyses.[11] The larger the range divided by the mean value, the higher the variability of a particular health outcome across counties. No statistical inferences were based on this measure of variability. We calculated Pearson correlation coefficients between rate ratios and variability measures and examined variability in outcomes across counties, stratified by SES.

We also calculated smoothed countyspecific rates, in which the observed rate in a county was "stabilized" by replacing it with the weighted average of the county rate and all adjacent county rates; weights were proportionate to population size.[18] We repeated all of the analyses described here on the smoothed rate estimates. Finally, we compared outcome rankings and correlations derived using the range-divided-by-mean measure with rankings obtained using 2 other variability measures: interquartile range divided by mean, and the coefficient of variation (SD / mean x 100%).

RESULTS

We included 61 (98%) of 62 counties in New York and 53 (91%) of 58 counties in California in the analysis. For each outcome, Table 1 shows the mean, range, and range divided by mean across counties in both states.

In New York, the largest variability in outcomes was in AIDS mortality (range / mean = 10.9), followed by

homicide (6.3), all-cause mortality among persons aged 10–24 years (2.6), and mortality from cirrhosis (2.0). The smallest variability was observed in all-cause mortality across all ages (0.3) and among persons aged more than 75 years (0.4), as well as in mortality from neoplastic disease (0.5) and mortality from cardiovascular disease (0.8).

In California, variability was highest for AIDS (range / mean = 7.3), followed by homicide (2.6), mortality from cirrhosis (2.4), and mortality among persons aged 15–24 years (2.1). The lowest variability was in rates for all-cause mortality across all ages and for persons aged more than 75 years as well as mortality from neoplastic disease (0.5 for each) and mortality from cardiovascular (0.8) or cerebrovascular (0.9) disease. The ordering of diseases by their intercounty variability was similar between the 2 states.

Rate ratios comparing mean disease-specific mortality rates between counties in the lower and upper quar-

tiles of various socioeconomic markers are shown in Table 2. Rate ratios greater than 1.0 imply that counties with lower SES have higher disease-specific mortality than do those with higher SES.

The range of all rate ratios in New York was 0.85–4.00. The mean ratios across economic marker categories ranged from 0.98 for neoplastic disease to 2.96 for AIDS. Mean homicide and cirrhosis mortality ratios were 1.58 and 1.28, respectively. For all economic markers, all-cause mortality, all-cause mortality for persons aged more than 75 years, and mortality from neoplasms had ratios less than 1.10. Mortality from all causes in persons aged 10–24 years had a mean rate ratio of 1.26. The mean ratios for all outcomes across economic measures ranged from 1.13 (median household income) to 1.39 (percentage of persons aged < 18 years in poverty).

In California, ratios ranged from 0.40 to 2.61. The mean ratio across economic indicators for neoplastic disease rates was 1.05 (0.90 for female breast cancer and 1.12 for lung cancer). The highest mean ratios were for mortality rates from motor vehicle accidents (2.03) and for homicide rates (1.85). The mean ratio for cirrhosis was 1.27. All-cause mortality for persons aged more than 75 years, suicide, pneumonia and influenza mortality, and female breast cancer mortality each had rate ratios of less than 1.10 for all economic markers. In addition, ratios for AIDS mortality ranged from 0.40 to 0.88. Mortality from all causes in persons aged 10–24 years had a mean rate ratio of 1.31, whereas for persons aged more than 75 years the mean ratio was 0.93. The mean ratios for all outcomes across economic measures ranged from 1.13 (high school graduation rate) to 1.27 (percentage of persons aged < 18 years in poverty).

In both states, the variability (range / mean) of health outcomes across counties was strongly correlated with the mean ratio of rates between counties in the lowest and highest quartiles of economic status (measured by percentage of children < 18 years

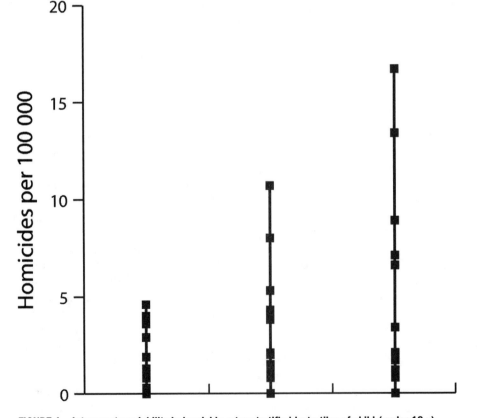

FIGURE 1 —Intercounty variability in homicide rates stratified by tertiles of child (under 18 y) poverty, New York State, 1997.

TABLE 2 -Relative Mortality Rates Comparing Counties in the Lowest to Highest Quartiles of Economic Indicators, New York and California, 1997.

Outcome	New York						California					
	Employment	Poverty	Under-18 poverty	Income	% high school grad	Row mean	Employment	Poverty	Under-18 poverty	Income	% high school grad	Row mean
All-cause mortality (all ages)	1.05	1.07	1.05	1.05	1.03	1.05	1.16	1.19	1.22	1.21	1.13	1.18
All-cause mortality (≥75 y)	0.97	0.97	0.96	1.01	0.95	0.97	0.95	0.94	0.94	0.91	0.92	0.93
All-cause mortality (10-24 y)	1.00	1.41	1.22	1.21	1.47	1.26	1.32	1.16	1.27	1.32	1.46	1.31
Infant mortality	1.04	1.14	1.04	0.96	1.17	1.07	1.24	1.35	1.41	1.29	1.17	1.29
AIDS	3.47	3.13	4.00	1.64	2.59	2.96	0.40	0.68	0.88	0.57	0.68	0.64
Pneumonia	0.92	1.11	1.09	1.10	1.01	1.04	0.93	1.07	1.09	0.88	0.99	0.99
COPD	1.01	1.22	1.10	1.16	1.12	1.12	1.35	1.32	1.34	1.47	1.19	1.33
Cardiovascular disease	1.12	1.06	1.07	1.05	1.04	1.07	1.18	1.28	1.33	1.18	1.23	1.24
Stroke	0.85	1.16	1.13	1.02	0.96	1.02	1.11	1.11	1.17	1.09	1.15	1.12
All neoplastic disease	1.01	0.97	0.97	1.00	0.94	0.98	1.07	1.02	1.05	1.12	1.01	1.05
Lung cancer	n/a	n/a	n/a	n/a	n/a	n/a	1.15	1.11	1.12	1.23	0.99	1.12
Female breast cancer	n/a	n/a	n/a	n/a	n/a	n/a	1.00	0.86	0.85	0.94	0.88	0.90
Cirrhosis	1.42	1.40	1.37	1.20	1.00	1.28	1.13	1.44	1.38	1.43	0.98	1.27
Accidents	0.91	1.25	1.13	1.17	1.23	1.14	2.56	1.71	1.75	2.38	1.76	2.03
Homicide	1.40	1.94	2.23	1.13	1.20	1.58	1.40	2.02	2.61	1.39	1.86	1.85
Suicide	n/a	n/a	n/a	n/a	n/a	n/a	0.93	1.00	0.98	1.06	0.73	0.94
Column mean	1.23	1.36	1.39	1.13	1.20		1.18	1.20	1.27	1.22	1.13	

Note. COPD = chronic obstructive pulmonary disease; n/a = not available.

living in poverty). In New York, the Pearson correlation coefficient was 0.97; in California, it was 0.70 (0.01 when AIDS was included in the calculation).

Figure 1 shows the relation between the homicide rates in New York counties and their socioeconomic status. Homicide rates for each county were plotted against tertiles of poverty (percentage of persons aged < 18 years living in poverty). Counties of lower economic status displayed greater variability in their rates of homicide than do counties with high economic status. The general trend of the relation was linear, with a positive slope; however, among counties with the lowest economic status, there were both low and high rates.

Smoothed rates showed less variability than did observed rates (range / mean for all outcomes varied from 0.2 to 6.4, compared with 0.3 to 11.0 in the original analysis); nonetheless, the trends and correlations present in the original analysis were preserved. In both New York and California, AIDS rates and homicide rates continued to display the most variability (New York AIDS range / mean = 6.4, homicide range / mean = 3.4; California AIDS range / mean = 2.0, homicide range / mean = 1.4), and mortality among persons aged more than 75 years and neoplastic disease mortality continued to display the least (range / mean = 0.2–0.3). Similarly, as expected, the magnitudes of variability for each outcome were attenuated when the coeffecient of variation or the interquartile range divided by mean were used (ranges 12%.–104% and 0.1–0.9, respectively, in New York, and 7%–200% and 0.2–0.7 in California); the ordering of outcomes by variability, however, remained largely unchanged in comparison with the ordering obtained with the range-divided-by-mean statistic (e.g., AIDS and homicide rates remained most variable and all-cause mortality and mortality from neoplasms remained least variable), as did the strong association between variability and SES sensitivity.

DISCUSSION

This analysis investigated the effects of counties' SES on their mortality rates and the variability of those rates across counties. We hypothesized that the outcomes most sensitive to SES would also exhibit the most variability. Outcomes in both New York and California that displayed high sensitivities to SES were AIDS, homicide, cirrhosis, and accidents. Outcomes in both states were most sensitive to the percentage of children living in poverty as a single indicator of SES.

All-cause mortality and certain neoplastic disease mortality rates did not differ greatly between poorer and wealthier counties. The underlying mechanisms for these health outcomes might account for the findings. Diseases with an incidence or course that is influenced by behavioral or environmental factors would be expected to exhibit sensitivity to SES, whereas diseases with genetic or other nonmodifiable causes would not. Our analysis is consistent with earlier findings and builds on previous small-area analyses in Kansas, Saskatchewan, and Cuba.[11]

A general process underlying these observations has been articulated by Link and Phelan, who postulated that access to protections and avoidance of harms underlie health outcomes that are sensitive to SES.[19] For example, in California, lung cancer mortality (largely a consequence of smoking) had a higher mean ratio than did female breast cancer mortality. In New York, cirrhosis mortality (largely a consequence of alcohol misuse) had a higher rate ratio than did neoplasms. A comparison of age-specific mortality further supports this hypothesis. In New York and California, county rates between economic strata exhibit low ratios for mortality among older persons and high ratios for youth mortality. Youth mortality has more potentially modifiable behavioral and social causes at its root than does mortality among older persons.

The economic sensitivity of AIDS was reversed in New York and California. In New York State, counties

in the lowest economic quartiles had an average of 2.96 times the AIDS rates of counties in the highest quartiles, and AIDS is particularly prevalent in poor communities of New York City. By contrast, in California, the populations with the lowest SES are both urban and rural, and AIDS incidence is more widely distributed in populations of varying SES.

Our principal measures of interest were variabilities in outcomes rather than absolute rates. Variability in mortality rates across counties was highest for the outcomes with larger SES rate ratios. AIDS mortality and homicide were the outcomes with the largest variability in the 2 states. Rates for all-cause mortality across ages and for mortality in older persons, as well as rates for neoplastic disease mortality, exhibited small variability and were generally not sensitive to socioeconomic conditions.

Although we hypothesized that variability reflects system-specific conditions (i.e., the balance among vulnerability, stressors, and protectors), variability may also be the product of random events, especially when the outcome of interest is rare or the population within which it occurs is small. Moreover, there may be confounding of the SES–sensitivity/variability relationship if rare events are also more sensitive to SES. To address these possibilities, we repeated all analyses using smoothed county-specific rates, which reduce intercounty population variability, as well as robust measures of variability, which have low sensitivity to outliers. The observed rate variability was attenuated under these circumstances, but trends in health outcome variability and associations with county-level SES were preserved.

In their examination of ecological factors contributing to adverse health effects, Levins and Lopez suggested that the relation between economic deprivation and variability in health status might be mediated by the vulnerability of populations.[11] They cited an observation by a geneticist, I. I. Schmalhausen, that "a system at the boundary of its tolerance along any dimension of its existence is more vulnerable to small differences in circumstance along any dimension."[20] Populations enduring social or economic deprivation will be more vulnerable to potential stressors than will populations of higher status. Thus, acute outbreaks of infectious diseases, environmental risks, or transient gaps in public health services will likely affect an economically deprived population to a greater degree than they would a less marginalized population.

We note, however, that these external stressors are not uniformly distributed across all disadvantaged communities, and therein might lie the source of the observed variability. Although vulnerability might result from chronic economic deprivation, the range of adverse health outcomes will depend on the degree to which each community experiences stressors and the distribution within communities of counteracting protective factors.

Variability in biological systems is increasingly seen as a marker for stresses to systems in homeostasis. Applying this insight to communities and health, we postulate that economic deprivation produces vulnerability to stressors whose nonuniform distribution across populations manifests as variability in health outcomes. One possible implication of this model is that interventions to improve public health might exert the greatest effect not by targeting particular stressors, but rather by focusing on improving general social and economic well-being, thus reducing populations' overall vulnerability.

About the Authors

At the time of the study, Adam Karpati and Sandro Galea were with the Department of Population and International Health, Harvard School of Public Health, Boston, Mass. Adam Karpati is also with the Epidemiology Program Office, Centers for Disease Control and Prevention, Atlanta, Ga. Sandro Galea is also with the Center for Urban Epidemiologic Studies, New York Academy of Medicine, New York. Tamara Awerbuch and Richard Levins are with the Department of Population and International Health, Harvard School of Public Health.

Correspondence: Requests for reprints should be sent to Adam Karpati, MD, MPH, Bureau of Community HealthWorks, New York City Department of Health, 40 Worth St, Room 1607, New York, NY 10013 (e-mail: aek3@cdc.gov).

Acknowledgments

Some of the ideas in this article were developed with the support of the Robert Wood Johnson Foundation Investigator Award and the Kansas Health Foundation.

Footnotes

A. Karpati and S. Galea collected the data, performed the analysis, and wrote the article. T. Awerbuch contributed to the study design, oversaw the analysis, and contributed to the editing of the article. R. Levins contributed to the study formulation and design, oversaw the analysis, and contributed to the editing of the article.

References

1. Kawachi I, Kennedy BP, Lochner K, Prothrow-Stith D. Social capital, income inequality, and mortality. *Am J Public Health.* 1997;87:1491–1498.
2. O'Campo P, Xue X, Wang MC, Caughy M. Neighborhood risk factors for low birthweight in Baltimore: a multilevel analysis. *Am J Public Health.* 1997;87:1113–1118.
3. Yen IH, Kaplan GA. Neighborhood social environment and risk of death: multilevel evidence from the Alameda County Study. *Am J Epidemiol.* 1999;149:898–907.
4. Susser M. The logic in ecological, I: the logic of analysis. *Am J Public Health.* 1994;84:825–829.
5. Diez-Roux AV. Bringing context back into epidemiology: variables and fallacies in multilevel analysis. *Am J Public Health.* 1998;88: 216–222.
6. Philippe P, Mansi O. Nonlinearity in the epidemiology of complex health and disease processes. *Theor Med Bioeth.* 1998;19:591–607.
7. Goldenfeld N, Kadanoff LP. Simple lessons from complexity. *Science.* 1999;284:87–89.
8. Sandberg S, Awerbuch TE, Gonin R. Simplicity vs complexity in deterministic models: an application to AIDS data. *J Biol Systems.* 1994;4:61–81.
9. Koopman JS, Longini IM Jr. The eco-logical effects of individual exposures and nonlinear disease dynamics in populations. *Am J Public Health.* 1994;84:836–842.
10. Seely AJ, Christou NV. Multiple organ dysfunction syndrome: exploring the paradigm of complex nonlinear systems. *Crit Care Med.* 2000;28:2193–2200.
11. Levins R, Lopez C. Toward an ecosocial view of health. *Int J Health Serv.* 1999;29:261–293.
12. Kleiger RE, Miller JP, Bigger JT Jr, Moss AJ. Decreased heart rate variability and its association with increased mortality after acute myocardial infarction. *Am J Cardiol.* 1987;59:256–262.
13. New York State Department of Health. Available at: http://www.health.state.ny.us/nysdoh/research/research.htm. Accessed April 2, 2002.
14. California Department of Health Services. Available at: http://www.dhs.ca.gov/hisp. Accessed April 2, 2002.
15. U.S. Bureau of the Census. Available at http://www.census.gov/hhes/www/saipe/estimatetoc.html. Accessed April 2, 2002.
16. Dalaker J. *Poverty in the United States: 1998.* Washington, DC: US Census Bureau, Current Population Reports; 1999. Series P60-207.
17. Cubbin C, Pickle LW, Fingerhut L. Social context and geographic patterns of homicide among US black and white males. *Am J Public Health.* 2000;90:579–587.
18. Devine O, Parrish RG. Monitoring the health of a population. In: Stroup DF, Teutsch SM, eds. *Statistics in Public Health: Quantitative Approaches to Public Health Problems.* New York, NY: Oxford University Press; 1998:58–91.
19. Link BG, Phelan JC. Evaluating the fundamental cause explanation for social disparities in health. In: Bird CE, Conrad P, Fremont AM, eds. *Handbook of Medical Sociology.* 5th ed. Upper Saddle River, NJ: Prentice Hall; 2000:33–46.
20. Schmalhausen II. *Factors of Evolution.* Philadelphia, Pa: Blakiston Company; 1949.

The World Health Organization and the Transition From "International" to "Global" Public Health

| Theodore M. Brown, PhD, Marcos Cueto, PhD and Elizabeth Fee, PhD

ABSTRACT

The term "global health" is rapidly replacing the older terminology of "international health." We describe the role of the World Health Organization (WHO) in both international and global health and in the transition from one to the other. We suggest that the term "global health" emerged as part of larger political and historical processes, in which WHO found its dominant role challenged and began to reposition itself within a shifting set of power alliances.

Between 1948 and 1998, WHO moved from being the unquestioned leader of international health to being an organization in crisis, facing budget shortfalls and diminished status, especially given the growing influence of new and powerful players. We argue that WHO began to refashion itself as the coordinator, strategic planner, and leader of global health initiatives as a strategy of survival in response to this transformed international political context.

INTRODUCTION

Even a quick glance at the titles of books and articles in recent medical and public health literature suggests that an important transition is under way. The terms "global," "globalization," and their variants are everywhere, and in the specific context of international public health, "global" seems to be emerging as the preferred authoritative term.[1] As one indicator, the number of entries in PubMed under the rubrics "global health" and "international health" shows that "global health" is rapidly on the rise, seemingly on track to overtake "international health" in the near future (Table 1). Although universities, government agencies, and private philanthropies are all using the term in highly visible ways,[2] the origin and meaning of the term "global health" are still unclear.

We provide historical insight into the emergence of the terminology of global health. We believe that an examination of this linguistic shift will yield important fruit, and not just information about fashions and fads in language use. Our task here is to provide a critical analysis of the meaning, emergence, and significance of the term "global health" and to place its growing popularity in a broader historical context. In particular, we focus on the role of the World Health Organization (WHO) in both international and global health and as an agent in the transition from one concept to the other.

Let us first define and differentiate some essential terms. "International health" was already a term of considerable currency in the late 19th and early 20th century, when it referred primarily to a focus on the control of epidemics across the boundaries between nations (i.e., "international"). "Intergovernmental" refers to the relationships between the governments of sovereign nations—in this case, with regard to the policies and practices of public health. "Global health," in general, implies consideration of the health needs of the people of the whole planet above the concerns of particular nations. The term "global" is also associated with the growing importance of actors beyond governmental or intergovernmental organizations and agencies—for example, the media, internationally influential foundations, nongovernmental organizations, and transnational corporations. Logically, the terms "international," "intergovernmental," and "global" need

TABLE 1— Number of Articles Retrieved by PubMed, Using "International Health" and "Global Health" as Search Terms, by Decade: 1950 Through July 2005

Decade	International Health[a]	Global Health[a]
1950s	1 007	54
1960s	3 303	155
1970s	8 369	1 137
1980s	16 924	7 176
1990s	49 158	27 794
2000–July 2005	52 169[b]	39 759[b]

[a]Picks up variant term endings (e.g. "international" also picks up "internationalize" and "internationalization"; "global" also picks up "globalize" and "globalization").

[b]Number for 55 months only.

not be mutually exclusive and in fact can be understood as complementary. Thus, we could say that WHO is an intergovernmental agency that exercises international functions with the goal of improving global health.

Given these definitions, it should come as no surprise that global health is not entirely an invention of the past few years. The term "global" was sometimes used well before the 1990s, as in the "global malaria eradication program" launched by WHO in the mid-1950s; a WHO Public Affairs Committee pamphlet of 1958, *The World Health Organization: Its Global Battle Against Disease*[3]; a 1971 report for the US House of Representatives entitled *The Politics of Global Health*[4]; and many studies of the "global population problem" in the 1970s.[5] But the term was generally limited and its use in official statements and documents sporadic at best. Now there is an increasing frequency of references to global health.[6] Yet the questions remain: How many have participated in this shift in terminology? Do they consider it trendy, trivial, or trenchant?

Supinda Bunyavanich and Ruth B. Walkup tried to answer these questions and published, under the provocative title "US Public Health Leaders Shift Toward a New Paradigm of Global Health," their report of conversations conducted in 1999 with 29 "international health leaders."[7] Their respondents fell into 2 groups. About half felt that there was no need for a new terminology and that the label "global health" was meaningless jargon. The other half thought that there were profound differences between international health and global health and that "global" clearly meant something transnational. Although these respondents believed that a major shift had occurred within the previous few years, they seemed unable clearly to articulate or define it.

In 1998, Derek Yach and Douglas Bettcher came closer to capturing both the essence and the origin of the new global health in a 2-part article on "The Globalization of Public Health" in the *American Journal of Public Health*.[8] They defined the "new paradigm" of globalization as "the process of increasing economic, political, and social interdependence and integration as capital, goods, persons, concepts, images, ideas and values cross state boundaries." The roots of globalization were long, they said, going back at least to the 19th century, but the process was assuming a new magnitude in the late 20th century. The globalization of public health, they argued, had a dual aspect, one both promising and threatening.

In one respect, there was easier diffusion of useful technologies and of ideas and values such as human rights. In another, there were such risks as diminished social safety nets; the facilitated marketing of tobacco, alcohol, and psychoactive drugs; the easier worldwide spread of infectious diseases; and the rapid degradation of the environment, with dangerous public health consequences. But Yach and Bettcher were convinced that WHO could turn these risks into opportunities. WHO, they argued, could help create more efficient information and surveillance systems by strengthening its global monitoring and alert systems, thus creating "global early warning systems." They believed that even the most powerful nations would buy into this new globally interdependent world system once these nations realized that such involvement was in their best interest.

Despite the long list of problems and threats, Yach and Bettcher were largely uncritical as they promoted the virtues of global public health and the leadership role of WHO. In an editorial in the same issue of the Journal, George Silver noted that Yach and Bettcher worked for WHO and that their position was similar to other optimistic stances taken by WHO officials and advocates. But WHO, Silver pointed out, was actually in a bad way: "The WHO's leadership role has passed to the far wealthier and more influential World Bank, and the WHO's mission has been dispersed among other UN agencies." Wealthy donor countries were billions of dollars in arrears, and this left the United Nations and its agencies in "disarray, hamstrung by financial constraints and internal incompetencies, frustrated by turf wars and cross-national policies."[9] Given these -realities, Yach and Bettcher's promotion of "global public health" while they were affiliated with WHO was, to say the least, intriguing. Why were these spokesmen for the much-criticized and apparently hobbled WHO so upbeat about "global" public health?

THE WORLD HEALTH ORGANIZATION

The Early Years

To better understand Yach and Bettcher's role, and that of WHO more generally, it will be helpful to review the history of the organization from 1948 to 1998, as it moved from being the unquestioned leader of international health to searching for its place in the contested world of global health.

WHO formally began in 1948, when the first World Health Assembly in Geneva, Switzerland, ratified its constitution. The idea of a permanent institution for international health can be traced to the organization in 1902 of the International Sanitary Office of the American Republics, which, some decades later, became the Pan American Sanitary Bureau and eventually the Pan American Health Organization.[10] The Rockefeller Foundation, especially its International Health Division, was also a very significant player in international health in the early 20th century.[11]

Two European-based international health agencies were also important. One was the Office Internationale d'Hygiène Publique, which began functioning in Paris in 1907; it concentrated on several basic activities related to the administration of international sanitary agreements and the rapid exchange of epidemiological information.[12] The second agency, the League of Nations Health Organization, began its work in 1920.[13] This organization established its headquarters in Geneva, sponsored a series of international commissions on diseases, and published epidemiological intelligence and technical

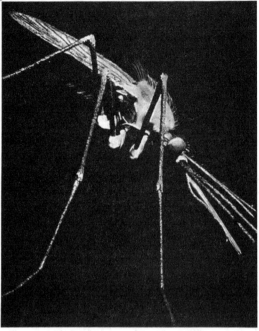

WAR ON THE MALARIA MOSQUITO!

Malaria is still the world's greatest public health problem. With modern methods it can be wiped out. This is the goal of an international eradication campaign directed by WHO.

"War on the Malaria Mosquito!" Poster produced by the Division of Public Information, World Health Organization, Geneva, 1958. Courtesy of the World Health Organization. Source: Prints and Photographs Collection of the National Library of Medicine.

reports. The League of Nations Health Organization was poorly budgeted and faced covert opposition from other national and international organizations, including the US Public Health Service. Despite these complications, which limited the Health Organization's effectiveness, both the Office Internationale d'Hygiène Publique and the Health Organization survived through World War II and were present at the critical postwar moment when the future of international health would be defined.

An international conference in 1945 approved the creation of the United Nations and also voted for the creation of a new specialized health agency. Participants at the meeting ini-

tially formed a commission of prominent individuals, among whom were René Sand from Belgium, Andrija Stampar from Yugoslavia, and Thomas Parran from the United States. Sand and Stampar were widely recognized as champions of social medicine. The commission held meetings between 1946 and early 1948 to plan the new international health organization. Representatives of the Pan American Sanitary Bureau, whose leaders resisted being absorbed by the new agency, were also involved, as were leaders of new institutions such as the United Nations Relief and Rehabilitation Administration (UNRRA).

Against this background, the first World Health Assembly met in

Geneva in June 1948 and formally created the World Health Organization. The Office Internationale d'Hygiène Publique, the League of Nations Health Organization, and UNRRA merged into the new agency. The Pan American Sanitary Bureau—then headed by Fred L. Soper, a former Rockefeller Foundation official—was allowed to retain autonomous status as part of a regionalization scheme.[14] WHO formally divided the world into a series of regions—the Americas, Southeast Asia, Europe, Eastern Mediterranean, Western Pacific, and Africa—but it did not fully implement this regionalization until the 1950s. Although an "international" and "intergovernmental" mindset prevailed in the 1940s and 1950s, naming the new organization the *World* Health Organization also raised sights to a worldwide, "global" perspective.

The first director general of WHO, Brock Chisholm, was a Canadian psychiatrist loosely identified with the British social medicine tradition. The United States, a main contributor to the WHO budget, played a contradictory role: on the one hand, it supported the UN system with its broad worldwide goals, but on the other, it was jealous of its sovereignty and maintained the right to intervene unilaterally in the Americas in the name of national security. Another problem for WHO was that its constitution had to be ratified by nation states, a slow process: by 1949, only 14 countries had signed on.[15]

As an intergovernmental agency, WHO had to be responsive to the larger political environment. The politics of the Cold War had a particular salience, with an unmistakable impact on WHO policies and personnel. Thus, when the Soviet Union and other communist countries walked out of the UN system and therefore out of WHO in 1949, the United States and its allies were easily able to exert a dominating influence. In 1953, Chisholm completed his term as director general and was replaced by the Brazilian Marcolino Candau. Candau, who had worked under Soper on malaria control in Brazil, was associated first with the "vertical" disease control programs of the Rockefeller Foundation and then with their adoption by the Pan American Sanitary Bureau when Soper moved to that agency as director.[16] Candau would be director general of WHO for over 20 years. From 1949 until 1956, when the Soviet Union returned to the UN and WHO, WHO was closely allied with US interests.

In 1955, Candau was charged with overseeing WHO's campaign of malaria eradication, approved that year by the World Health Assembly. The ambitious goal of malaria eradication had been conceived and promoted in the context of great enthusiasm and optimism about the ability of widespread DDT spraying to kill mosquitoes. As Randall Packard has argued, the United States and its allies believed that global malaria eradication would usher in economic growth and create overseas markets for US technology and manufactured goods.[17] It would build support for local governments and their US supporters and help win "hearts and minds" in the battle against Communism. Mirroring then-current development theories, the campaign promoted technologies brought in from outside and made no attempt to enlist the participation of local populations in planning or implementation. This model of development assistance fit neatly into US Cold War efforts to promote modernization with limited social reform.[18]

With the return of the Soviet Union and other communist countries in 1956, the political balance in the World Health Assembly shifted and Candau accommodated the changed balance of power. During the 1960s, malaria eradication was facing serious difficulties in the field; ultimately, it would suffer colossal and embarrassing failures. In 1969, the World Health Assembly, declaring that it was not feasible to eradicate malaria in many parts of the world, began a slow process of reversal, returning once again to an older malaria control agenda. This time, however, there was a new twist; the 1969 assembly emphasized the need to develop rural health

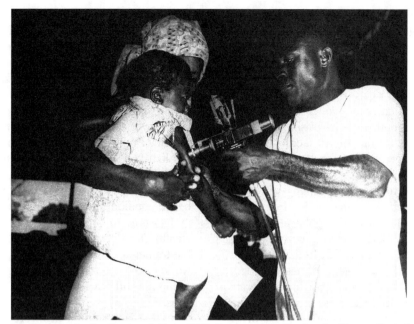

Smallpox Vaccination Program in Togo, 1967. Courtesy of the Centers for Disease Control and Prevention. Source: Public Health Image Library, CDC.

systems and to integrate malaria control into general health services.

When the Soviet Union returned to WHO, its representative at the assembly was the national deputy minister of health. He argued that it was now scientifically feasible, socially desirable, and economically worthwhile to attempt to eradicate smallpox worldwide.[19] The Soviet Union wanted to make its mark on global health, and Candau, recognizing the shifting balance of power, was willing to cooperate. The Soviet Union and Cuba agreed to provide 25 million and 2 million doses of freeze-dried vaccine, respectively; in 1959, the World Health Assembly committed itself to a global smallpox eradication program.

In the 1960s, technical improvements—jet injectors and bifurcated needles—made the process of vaccination much cheaper, easier, and more effective. The United States' interest in smallpox eradication sharply increased; in 1965, Lyndon Johnson instructed the US delegation to the World Health Assembly to pledge American support for an international program to eradicate smallpox from the earth.[20] At that time, despite a decade of marked progress, the disease was still endemic in more than 30 countries. In 1967, now with the support of the world's

most powerful players, WHO launched the Intensified Smallpox Eradication Program. This program, an international effort led by the American Donald A. Henderson, would ultimately be stunningly successful.[21]

The Promise and Perils of Primary Health Care, 1973–1993

Within WHO, there have always been tensions between social and economic approaches to population health and technology-or disease-focused approaches. These approaches are not necessarily incompatible, although they have often been at odds. The emphasis on one or the other waxes and wanes over time, depending on the larger balance of power, the changing interests of international players, the intellectual and ideological commitments of key individuals, and the way that all of these factors interact with the health policymaking process.

During the 1960s and 1970s, changes in WHO were significantly influenced by a political context marked by the emergence of decolonized African nations, the spread of nationalist and socialist movements, and new theories of development that emphasized long-term socioeconomic growth rather than short-term technological intervention. Rallying within organizations such as the Non-Aligned Movement, developing countries created the UN Conference on Trade and Development (UNCTAD), where they argued vigorously for fairer terms of trade and more generous financing of development.[22] In Washington, DC, more liberal politics succeeded the conservatism of the 1950s, with the civil rights movement and other social movements forcing changes in national priorities.

This changing political environment was reflected in corresponding shifts within WHO. In the 1960s, WHO acknowledged that a strengthened health infrastructure was prerequisite to the success of malaria control programs, especially in Africa. In 1968, Candau called for a comprehensive and integrated plan for curative and preventive care services. A Soviet representative called for an organizational study of methods for promoting the development of basic health services.[23] In January 1971, the Executive Board of the World Health Assembly agreed to undertake this study, and its results were presented to the assembly in 1973.[24] Socrates Litsios has discussed many of the steps in the transformation of WHO's approach from an older model of health services to what would become the "Primary Health Care" approach.[25] This new model drew upon the thinking and experiences of nongovernmental organizations and medical missionaries working in Africa, Asia, and Latin America at the grass-roots level. It also gained saliency from China's reentry into the UN in 1973 and the widespread interest in Chinese "barefoot doctors," who were reported to be transforming rural health conditions. These experiences underscored the urgency of a "Primary Health Care" perspective that included the training of community health workers and the resolution of basic economic and environmental problems.[26]

These new approaches were spearheaded by Halfdan T. Mahler, a Dane, who served as director general of WHO from 1973 to 1988. Under pressure from the Soviet delegate to the executive board, Mahler agreed to hold a major conference on the organization of health services in Alma-Ata, in the Soviet Union. Mahler was initially reluctant because he disagreed with the Soviet Union's highly centralized and medicalized approach to the provision of health services.[27] The Soviet Union succeeded in hosting the September 1978 conference, but the conference itself reflected Mahler's views much more closely than it did those of the Soviets. The Declaration of Primary Health Care and the goal of "Health for All in the Year 2000" advocated an "intersectoral" and multidimensional approach to health and socioeconomic development, emphasized the use of "appropriate technology," and urged active community participation in health care and health education at every level.[28]

David Tejada de Rivero has argued that "It is regrettable that afterward the impatience of some international agencies, both UN and private, and their emphasis on achieving tangible results instead of promoting change . . . led to major distortions of the original concept of primary health care."[29] A number of governments, agencies, and individuals saw WHO's idealistic view of Primary Health Care as "unrealistic" and unattainable. The process of reducing Alma-Ata's idealism to a practical set of technical interventions that could be implemented and measured more easily began in 1979 at a small conference—heavily influenced by US attendees and policies—held in Bellagio, Italy, and sponsored by the Rockefeller Foundation, with assistance from the World Bank. Those in attendance included the president of the World Bank, the vice president of the Ford Foundation, the administrator of USAID, and the executive secretary of UNICEF.[30]

The Bellagio meeting focused on an alternative concept to that articulated at Alma-Ata—"Selective Primary Health Care"—which was built on the notion of pragmatic, low-cost interventions that were limited in scope and easy to monitor and evaluate. Thanks primarily to UNICEF, Selective Primary Health Care was soon operationalized under the acronym "GOBI" (Growth monitoring to fight malnutrition in children, Oral rehydration techniques to defeat diarrheal diseases, Breastfeeding to protect children, and Immunizations).[31]

In the 1980s, WHO had to reckon with the growing influence of the World Bank. The bank had initially

Alma Ata Conference, 1978. Courtesy of the Pan American Health Organization. Source: Office of Public Information, PAHO.

been formed in 1946 to assist in the reconstruction of Europe and later expanded its mandate to provide loans, grants, and technical assistance to developing countries. At first, it funded large investments in physical capital and infrastructure; in the 1970s, however, it began to invest in population control, health, and education, with an emphasis on population control.[32] The World Bank approved its first loan for family planning in 1970. In 1979, the World Bank created a Population, Health, and Nutrition Department and adopted a policy of funding both stand-alone health programs and health components of other projects.

In its 1980 *World Development Report*, the Bank argued that both malnutrition and ill health could be countered by direct government action—with World Bank assistance.[33] It also suggested that improving health and nutrition could accelerate economic growth, thus providing a good argument for social sector spending. As the Bank began to make direct loans for health services, it called for more efficient use of available resources and discussed the roles of the private and public sectors in financing health care. The Bank favored free markets and a diminished role for national governments.[34] In the context of widespread indebtedness by developing countries and increasingly scarce resources for health expenditures, the World Bank's promotion of "structural adjustment" measures at the very time that the HIV/AIDS epidemic erupted drew angry criticism but also underscored the Bank's new influence.

In contrast to the World Bank's increasing authority, in the 1980s the prestige of WHO was beginning to diminish. One sign of trouble was the 1982 vote by the World Health Assembly to freeze WHO's budget.[35] This was followed by the 1985 decision by the United States to pay only 20% of its assessed contribution to all UN agencies and to withhold its contribution to WHO's regular budget, in part as a protest against WHO's "Essential Drug Program," which was opposed by leading US-based pharma-

ceutical companies.[36] These events occurred amidst growing tensions between WHO and UNICEF and other agencies and the controversy over Selective versus Comprehensive Primary Health Care. As part of a rancorous public debate conducted in the pages of *Social Science and Medicine* in 1988, Kenneth Newell, a highly placed WHO official and an architect of Comprehensive Primary Health Care, called Selective Primary Health Care a "threat . . . [that] can be thought of as a counter-revolution."[37]

In 1988, Mahler's 15-year tenure as director general of WHO came to an end. Unexpectedly, Hiroshi Nakajima, a Japanese researcher who had been director of the WHO Western Pacific Regional Office in Manila, was elected new director general.[38]

Crisis at WHO, 1988–1998

The first citizen of Japan ever elected to head a UN agency, Nakajima rapidly became the most controversial director general in WHO's history. His nomination had not been supported by the United States or by a number of European and Latin American countries, and his performance in office did little to assuage their doubts. Nakajima did try to launch several important initiatives—on tobacco, global disease surveillance, and public–private partnerships—but fierce criticism persisted that raised questions about his autocratic style and poor management, his inability to communicate effectively, and, worst of all, cronyism and corruption.

Another symptom of WHO's problems in the late 1980s was the growth of "extrabudgetary" funding. As Gill Walt of the London School of Hygiene and Tropical Medicine noted, there was a crucial shift from predominant reliance on WHO's "regular budget"—drawn from member states' contributions on the basis of population size and gross national product—to greatly increased dependence on extrabudgetary funding coming from donations by multilateral agencies or "donor" nations.[39] By the period 1986–1987, extrabudgetary funds of

$437 million had almost caught up with the regular budget of $543 million. By the beginning of the 1990s, extra-budgetary funding had overtaken the regular budget by $21 million, contributing 54% of WHO's overall budget.

Enormous problems for the organization followed from this budgetary shift. Priorities and policies were still ostensibly set by the World Health Assembly, which was made up of all member nations. The assembly, however, now dominated numerically by poor and developing countries, had authority only over the regular budget, frozen since the early 1980s. Wealthy donor nations and multilateral agencies like the World Bank could largely call the shots on the use of the extra-budgetary funds they contributed. Thus, they created, in effect, a series of "vertical" programs more or less independent of the rest of WHO's programs and decisionmaking structure. The dilemma for the organization was that although the extrabudgetary funds added to the overall budget, "they [increased] difficulties of coordination and continuity, [caused] unpredictability in finance, and a great deal of dependence on the satisfaction of particular donors,"[40] as Gill Walt explained.

Fiona Godlee published a series of articles in 1994 and 1995 that built on Walt's critique.[41] She concluded with this dire assessment: "WHO is caught in a cycle of decline, with donors expressing their lack of faith in its central management by placing funds outside the management's control. This has prevented WHO from [developing] . . . integrated responses to countries' long term needs."[41]

In the late 1980s and early 1990s, the World Bank moved confidently into the vacuum created by an increasingly ineffective WHO. WHO officials were unable or unwilling to respond to the new international political economy structured around neoliberal approaches to economics, trade, and politics.[42] The Bank maintained that existing health systems were often wasteful, inefficient, and ineffective, and it argued in favor of greater reliance on private-sector health care provision and the reduction of public involvement in health services delivery.[43]

Controversies surrounded the World Bank's policies and practices, but there was no doubt that, by the early 1990s, it had become a dominant force in international health. The Bank's greatest "comparative advantage" lay in its ability to mobilize large financial resources. By 1990, the Bank's loans for health surpassed WHO's total budget, and by the end of 1996, the Bank's cumulative lending portfolio in health, nutrition, and population had reached $13.5 billion. Yet the Bank recognized that, whereas it had great economic strengths and influence, WHO still had considerable technical expertise in matters of health and medicine. This was clearly reflected in the Bank's widely influential *World Development Report, 1993: Investing in Health*, in which credit is given to WHO, "a full partner with the World Bank at every step of the preparation of the Report."[44] Circumstances suggested that it was to the advantage of both parties for the World Bank and WHO to work together.

WHO EMBRACES "GLOBAL HEALTH"

This is the context in which WHO began to refashion itself as a coordinator, strategic planner, and leader of "global health" initiatives. In January 1992, the 31-member Executive Board of the World Health Assembly decided to appoint a "working group" to recommend how WHO could be most effective in international health work in light of the "global change" rapidly overtaking the world. The executive board may have been responding, in part, to the Children's Vaccine Initiative, perceived within WHO as an attempted "coup" by UNICEF, the World Bank, the UN Development Program, the Rockefeller Foundation, and several other players seeking to wrest control of vaccine development.[45] The working group's final report of May 1993 recommend-

ed that WHO—if it was to maintain leadership of the health sector—must overhaul its fragmented management of global, regional, and country programs, diminish the competition between regular and extrabudgetary programs, and, above all, increase the emphasis within WHO on global health issues and WHO's coordinating role in that domain.[46]

Until that time, the term "global health" had been used sporadically and, outside WHO, usually by people on the political left with various "world" agendas. In 1990, G. A. Gellert of International Physicians for the Prevention of Nuclear War had called for analyses of "global health interdependence."[47] In the same year, Milton and Ruth Roemer argued that further improvements in "global health" would be dependent on the expansion of public rather than private health services.[48] Another strong source for the term "global health" was the environmental movement, especially debates over world environmental degradation, global warming, and their potentially devastating effects on human health.[49]

In the mid-1990s, a considerable body of literature was produced on global health threats. In the United States, a new Centers for Disease Control and Prevention (CDC) journal, *Emerging Infectious Diseases*, began publication, and former CDC director William Foege started using the phrase "global infectious disease threats."[50] In 1997, the Institute of Medicine's Board of International Health released a report, *America's Vital Interest in Global Health: Protecting Our People, Enhancing Our Economy, and Advancing Our International Interests*.[51] In 1998, the CDC's *Preventing Emerging Infectious Diseases: A Strategy for the 21st Century* appeared, followed in 2001 by the Institute of Medicine's *Perspectives on the Department of Defense Global Emerging Infections Surveillance and Response System*.[52] Best-selling books and news magazines were full of stories about Ebola and West Nile virus, resurgent tuberculosis, and the threat of bioterrorism.[53] The message was clear: there was a palpa-

ble global disease threat.

In 1998, the World Health Assembly reached outside the ranks of WHO for a new leader who could restore credibility to the organization and provide it with a new vision: Gro Harlem Brundtland, former prime minister of Norway and a physician and public health professional. Brundtland brought formidable expertise to the task. In the 1980s, she had been chair of the UN World Commission on Environment and Development and produced the "Brundtland Report," which led to the Earth Summit of 1992. She was familiar with the global thinking of the environmental movement and had a broad and clear understanding of the links between health, environment, and development.[54]

Brundtland was determined to position WHO as an important player on the global stage, move beyond ministries of health, and gain a seat at the table where decisions were being made.[55] She wanted to refashion WHO as a "department of consequence"[55] able to monitor and influence other actors on the global scene. She established a Commission on Macroeconomics and Health, chaired by economist Jeffrey Sachs of Harvard University and including former ministers of finance and officers from the World Bank, the International Monetary Fund, the World Trade Organization, and the UN Development Program, as well as public health leaders. The commission issued a report in December 2001, which argued that improving health in developing countries was essential to their economic development.[56] The report identified a set of disease priorities that would require focused intervention.

Brundtland also began to strengthen WHO's financial position, largely by organizing "global partnerships" and "global funds" to bring together "stakeholders"—private donors, governments, and bilateral and multilateral agencies—to concentrate on specific targets (for example, Roll Back Malaria in 1998, the Global Alliance for Vaccines and Immunization in 1999, and Stop TB in 2001). These were semiautonomous programs bringing in substantial outside funding, often in the form of "public–private partnerships."[57] A very significant player in these partnerships was the Bill & Melinda Gates Foundation, which committed more than $1.7 billion between 1998 and 2000 to an international program to prevent or eliminate diseases in the world's poorest nations, mainly through vaccines and immunization programs.[58] Within a few years, some 70 "global health partnerships" had been created.

Brundtland's tenure as director general was not without blemish nor free from criticism. Some of the initiatives credited to her administration had actually been started under Nakajima (for example, the WHO Framework Convention on Tobacco Control), others may be looked upon today with some skepticism (the Commission on Macroeconomics and Health, Roll Back Malaria), and still others arguably did not receive enough attention from her administration (Primary Health Care, HIV/AIDS, Health and Human Rights, and Child Health). Nonetheless, few would dispute the assertion that Brundtland succeeded in achieving her principal objective, which was to reposition WHO as a credible and highly visible contributor to the rapidly changing field of global health.

CONCLUSION

We can now return briefly to the questions implied at the beginning of this article: how does a historical perspective help us understand the emergence of the terminology of "global health" and what role did WHO play as an agent in its development? The basic answers derive from the fact that WHO at various times in its history alternatively led, reflected, and tried to accommodate broader changes and challenges in the ever-shifting world of international health. In the 1950s and 1960s, when changes in biology, economics, and great power politics transformed foreign relations and public health, WHO moved from a narrow

Current Director General Jongwook Lee with three former Directors-General at the celebration to mark the 25th Anniversary of the Alma Ata Declaration. From left: G. H. Brundtland, H. Mahler, H. Nakajima, Lee JW. Courtesy of the World Health Organization. Source: Media Center, WHO.

emphasis on malaria eradication to a broader interest in the development of health services and the emerging concentration on smallpox eradication. In the 1970s and 1980s, WHO developed the concept of Primary Health Care but then turned from zealous advocacy to the pragmatic promotion of Selective Primary Health Care as complex changes overtook intra-and interorganizational dynamics and altered the international economic and political order. In the 1990s, WHO attempted to use leadership of an emerging concern with "global health" as an organizational strategy that promised survival and, indeed, renewal.

But just as it did not invent the eradicationist or primary care agendas, WHO did not invent "global health"; other, larger forces were responsible. WHO certainly did help promote interest in global health and contributed significantly to the dissemination of new concepts and a new vocabulary. In that process, it was hoping to acquire, as Yach and Bettcher suggested in 1998, a restored coordinating and leadership role. Whether WHO's organizational repositioning will serve to reestablish it as the unquestioned steward of the health of the world's population, and how this

mission will be effected in practice, remains an open question at this time.

About the Authors

Theodore M. Brown is with the Department of History and the Department of Community and Preventive Medicine, University of Rochester, Rochester, NY. Marcos Cueto is with the Facultad de Salud Pública, Universidad Peruana Cayetano Heredia, Lima, Peru. Elizabeth Fee is with the History of Medicine Division, National Library of Medicine, National Institutes of Health, Bethesda, Md.

Correspondence: Requests for reprints should be sent to Elizabeth Fee, PhD, History of Medicine Division, National Library of Medicine, 8600 Rockville Pike, Bethesda, MD 20974 (e-mail: elizabeth_fee@nlm.nih.gov).

Acknowledgments

The authors are grateful to the Joint Learning Initiative of the Rockefeller Foundation, which initially commissioned this article, and to the Global Health Histories Initiative of the World Health Organization, which has provided a supportive environment for continuing our research.

References

1. A small sampling of recent titles: David L. Heymann and G. R. Rodier, "Global Surveillance of Communicable Diseases," *Emerging Infectious Diseases* 4 (1998): 362–365; David Woodward, Nick Drager, Robert Beaglehole, and Debra Lipson, "Globalization and Health: A Framework for Analysis and Action," *Bulletin of the World Health Organization* 79 (2001): 875–881; Gill Walt, "Globalisation of International Health," *The Lancet* 351 (February 7, 1998): 434–437; Stephen J. Kunitz, "Globalization, States, and the Health of Indigenous Peoples," *American Journal of Public Health* 90 (2000): 1531–1539; *Health Policy in a Globalising World*, ed. Kelley Lee, Kent Buse, and Suzanne Fustukian (Cambridge, England: Cambridge University Press, 2002).

2. For example, Yale has a Division of Global Health in its School of Public Health, Harvard has a Center for Health and the Global Environment, and the London School of Hygiene and Tropical Medicine has a Center on Global Change and Health; the National Institutes of Health has a strategic plan on Emerging Infectious Diseases and Global Health; Gro Harlem Brundtland addressed the 35th Anniversary Symposium of the John E. Fogarty International Center on "Global Health: A Challenge to Scientists" in May 2003; the Centers of Disease Control and Prevention has established an Office of Global Health and has partnered with the World Health Organization (WHO), the World Bank, UNICEF, the US Agency for International Development, and others in creating Global Health Partnerships.

3. Albert Deutsch, *The World Health Organization: Its Global Battle Against Disease* (New York: Public Affairs Committee, 1958).

4. Randall M Packard, " 'No Other Logical Choice': Global Malaria Eradication and the Politics of International Health in the Post-War Era," *Parassitologia* 40 (1998): 217–229, and *The Politics of Global Health, Prepared for the Subcommittee on National Security Policy and Scientific Developments of the Committee on Foreign Affairs, US House of Representatives* (Washington, DC: US Government Printing Office, 1971).

5. For example, T W. Wilson, *World Population and a Global Emergency* (Washington, DC: Aspen Institute for Humanistic Studies, Program in Environment and Quality of Life, 1974).

6. James E. Banta, "From International to Global Health," *Journal of Community Health* 26 (2001): 73–76.

7. Supinda Bunyavanich and Ruth B. Walkup, "US Public Health Leaders Shift Toward a New Paradigm of Global Health," *American Journal of Public Health* 91 (2001): 1556–1558.

8. Derek Yach and Douglas Bettcher, "The Globalization of Public Health, I: Threats and Opportunities," *American Journal of Public Health* 88 (1998): 735–738, and "The Globalization of Public Health, II: The Convergence of Self-Interest and Altruism," *American Journal of Public Health* 88 (1998): 738–741.

9. George Silver, "International Health Services Need an Interorganizational Policy," *American Journal of Public Health* 88 (1998): 727–729 (quote on p. 728).

10. *Pro Salute, Novi Mundi: Historia de la Organización Panamericana de la Salud* (Washington, DC: Organización Panamericana de la Salud, 1992).

11. See John Farley, *To Cast Out Disease: A History of the International Health Division of the Rockefeller Foundation (1913–1951)* (Oxford: Oxford University Press, 2003); Anne-Emmanuelle Birn, "Eradication, Control or Neither? Hookworm Versus Malaria Strategies and Rockefeller Public Health in Mexico," *Parassitologia* 40 (1996):137–147; *Missionaries of Science: Latin America and the Rockefeller Foundation*, ed. Marcos Cueto (Bloomington: Indiana University Press, 1994).

12. *Vingt-Cinq Ans d'Activité de l'Office Internationale d'Hygiène Publique, 1909–1933* (Paris: Office Internationale d'Hygiène Publique, 1933); Paul F. Basch, "A Historical Perspective on International Health," *Infectious Disease Clinics of North America* 5 (1991):183–196; W.R. Aykroyd, "International Health—A Retrospective Memoir," *Perspectives in Biology and Medicine* 11 (1968): 273–285.

13. Frank G. Bourdreau, "International Health," *American Journal of Public Health and the Nation's Health* 19 (1929): 863–878; Bourdreau, "International Health Work," in *Pioneers in World Order: An American Appraisal of the League of Nations*, ed. Harriet Eager Favis (New York: Columbia University Press, 1944), 193–207; Norman Howard-Jones, *International Public Health Between the Two World Wars: The Organizational Problems* (Geneva: WHO, 1978); Martin David Dubin, "The League of Nations Health Organisation," in *International Health Organisations and Movements, 1918–1939*, ed. Paul Weindling (Cambridge, England: Cambridge University Press, 1995), 56–80.

14. Thomas Parran, "The First 12 Years of WHO," *Public Health Reports* 73 (1958): 879–883; Fred L. Soper, *Ventures in World Health: The Memoirs of Fred Lowe Soper*, ed. John Duffy (Washington, DC: Pan American Health Organization, 1977); Javed Siddiqi, *World Health and World Politics: The World Health Organization and the UN System* (London: Hurst and Co, 1995).

15. "Seventh Meeting of the Executive Committee of the Pan American Sanitary Organization," Washington, DC, May 23–30, 1949, Folder "Pan American Sanitary Bureau," RG 90–41, Box 9, Series Graduate School of Public Health, University of Pittsburgh Archives.

16. WHO, "Information. Former Directors-General of the World Health Organization. Dr Marcolino Gomes Candau," available at http://www.who.int/archives/wh050/en/directors.htm, accessed July 24, 2004; "In memory of Dr M. G. Candau," *WHO Chronicle* 37 (1983): 144–147.

17. Randall M. Packard, "Malaria Dreams: Postwar Visions of Health and Development in the Third World," *Medical Anthropology* 17 (1997): 279–296; Packard, "No Other Logical Choice" *Parassitologia* 40 (1998): 217–229.

18. Randall M. Packard and Peter J. Brown, "Rethinking Health, Development and Malaria: Historicizing a Cultural Model in International Health," *Medical Anthropology* 17 (1997): 181–194.

19. Ian and Jennifer Glynn, *The Life and Death of Smallpox* (New York: Cambridge University Press, 2004), 194–196.

20. Ibid, 198.

21. William H. Foege, "Commentary: Smallpox Eradication in West and

Central Africa Revisited," *Bulletin of the World Health Organization* 76 (1998): 233–235; Donald A. Henderson, "Eradication: Lessons From the Past," *Bulletin of the World Health Organization* 76 (Supplement 2) (1998): 17–21; Frank Fenner, Donald A. Henderson, Issao Arita, Zdenek Jevek, and Ivan Dalinovich Ladnyi, *Smallpox and its Eradication* (Geneva: WHO, 1988).

22. *The New International Economic Order: The North South Debate*, ed. Jagdish N. Bhagwati (Cambridge, Mass: MIT Press, 1977); Robert L. Rothstein, *Global Bargaining: UNCTAD and the Quest for a New International Economic Order* (Princeton, NJ: Princeton University Press, 1979).

23. Socrates Litsios, "The Long and Difficult Road to Alma-Ata: A Personal Reflection," *International Journal of Health Services* 32 (2002): 709–732.

24. Executive Board 49th Session, WHO document EB49/SR/14 Rev (Geneva: WHO, 1973), 218; *Organizational Study of the Executive Board on Methods of Promoting the Development of Basic Health Services*, WHO document EB49/WP/6 (Geneva: WHO, 1972), 19–20.

25. Socrates Litsios, "The Christian Medical Commission and the Development of WHO's Primary Health Care Approach," *American Journal of Public Health* 94 (2004): 1884–1893; Litsios, "The Long and Difficult Road to Alma-Ata."

26. John H. Bryant, *Health and the Developing World* (Ithaca, NY: Cornell University Press, 1969); *Doctors for the Villages: Study of Rural Internships in Seven Indian Medical Colleges*, ed. Carl E. Taylor (New York: Asia Publishing House, 1976); Kenneth W. Newell, *Health by the People* (Geneva: WHO, 1975). See also Marcos Cueto, "The Origins of Primary Health Care and Selective Primary Health Care," *American Journal of Public Health* 94 (2004): 1864–1874; Litsios, "The Christian Medical Commission."

27. See Litsios, "The Long and Difficult Road to Alma-Ata," 716–719.

28. "Declaration of Alma-Ata, International Conference on Primary Health Care, Alma-Ata, USSR, 6–12 September, 1978," available at http://www.who.int/hpr/NPH/docs/declaration_almaata.pdf, accessed April 10, 2004.

29. David A Tejada de Rivero, "Alma-Ata Revisited," *Perspectives in Health Magazine: The Magazine of the Pan American Health Organization* 8 (2003): 1–6 (quote on p. 4).

30. Maggie Black, *Children First: The Story of UNICEF, Past and Present* (Oxford: Oxford University Press; 1996), and *The Children and the Nations: The Story of UNICEF* (New York: UNICEF, 1986), 114–140. UNICEF was created in 1946 to assist needy children in Europe's war ravaged areas. After the emergency ended, it broadened its mission and concentrated resources on the needs of children in developing countries.

31. UNICEF, *The State of the World's Children: 1982/1983* (New York: Oxford University Press, 1983). See also Cueto, "Origins of Primary Health Care."

32. Jennifer Prah Ruger, "The Changing Role of the World Bank in Global Health in Historical Perspective," *American Journal of Public Health* 95 (2005): 60–70.

33. *World Development Report 1980* (Washington, DC: World Bank, 1980).

34. *Financing Health Services in Developing Countries: An Agenda for Reform* (Washington, DC: World Bank, 1987).

35. Fiona Godlee, "WHO in Retreat; Is It Losing Its Influence?" *British Medical Journal* 309 (1994): 1491–1495.

36. Ibid, 1492.

37. Kenneth Newell, "Selective Primary Health Care: The Counter Revolution," *Social Science and Medicine* 26 (1988): 903–906 (quote on p. 906).

38. Paul Lewis, "Divided World Health Organization Braces for Leadership Change," *New York Times*, May 1, 1988, p. 20.

39. Gill Walt, "WHO Under Stress: Implications for Health Policy," *Health Policy* 24 (1993): 125–144.

40. Ibid, 129.

41. Fiona Godlee, "WHO in Crisis," *British Medical Journal* 309 (1994):1424–1428; Godlee, "WHO in Retreat"; Fiona Godlee, "WHO's Special Programmes: Undermining From Above," *British Medical Journal* 310 (1995):178–182 (quote on p. 182).

42. P. Brown, "The WHO Strikes Mid-Life Crisis," *New Scientist* 153 (1997): 12; "World Bank's Cure for Donor Fatigue [editorial]," *The Lancet* 342 (July 10, 1993): 63–64; Anthony Zwi, "Introduction to Policy Forum: The World Bank and International Health," *Social Science and Medicine* 50(2000): 167.

43. World Bank, *Financing Health Services in Developing Countries.*

44. *World Development Report, 1993: Investing in Health* (Washington, DC: World Bank, 1993), iii–iv (quote on pp. iii–iv).

45. For a full account, see William Muraskin, *The Politics of International Health: The Children's Vaccine Initiative and the Struggle to Develop Vaccines for the Third World* (Albany: State University of New York Press, 1998).

46. Bo Stenson and Göran Sterky, "What Future WHO?" *Health Policy* 28 (1994): 235–256 (quote on p. 242).

47. G.A. Gellert, "Global Health Interdependence and the International Physicians' Movement," *Journal of the American Medical Association* 264 (1990): 610–613 (quote on p. 610).

48. Milton Roemer and Ruth Roemer, "Global Health, National Development, and the Role of Government," *American Journal of Public Health* 80 (1990): 1188–1192.

49. See, for example, Andrew J. Haines, "Global Warming and Health," *British Medical Journal* 302 (1991): 669–670; Andrew J. Haines, Paul R. Epstein, and Anthony J. McMichael, "Global Health Watch: Monitoring Impacts of Environmental Change," *The Lancet* 342 (December 11, 1993): 1464–1469; Anthony J. McMichael, "Global Environmental Change and Human Population Health: A Conceptual and Scientific Challenge for Epidemiology," *International Journal of Epidemiology* 22 (1993): 1–8; John M. Last, "Global Change: Ozone Depletion, Greenhouse Warming, and Public Health," *Annual Review of Public Health* 14 (1993): 115–136; A. J. McMichael, *Planetary Overload, Global Environmental Change and the Health of the Human Species* (Cambridge, England: Cambridge University Press, 1993); Anthony J. McMichael, Andrew J. Haines, R. Sloof, and S. Kovats, *Climate Change and Human Health* (Geneva: WHO, 1996); Anthony J. McMichael and Andrew Haines, "Global Climate Change: The Potential Effects on Health," *British Medical Journal* 315 (1997): 805–809.

50. Stephen S Morse, "Factors in the Emergence of Infectious Diseases," *Emerging Infectious Diseases* 1 (1995): 7–15 (quote on p. 7).

51. Institute of Medicine, *America's Vital*

Interest in Global Health: Protecting Our People, Enhancing Our Economy, and Advancing Our International Interests (Washington, DC: National Academy Press, 1997).

52. *Emerging Infections: Biomedical Research Reports*, ed. Richard M. Krause (San Diego: Academic Press, 1998); *Preventing Emerging Infectious Diseases: A Strategy for the 21st Century* (Atlanta: Centers for Disease Control and Prevention, 1998); *Perspectives on the Department of Defense Global Emerging Infections Surveillance and Response System*, ed. Philip S. Brachman, Heather C. O'-Maonaigh, and Richard N. Miller (Washington, DC: National Academy Press, 2001).

53. For example, Laurie Garrett, *The Coming Plague: Newly Emerging Diseases in a World Out of Balance* (New York: Farrar, Straus and Giroux, 1994).

54. Lawrence K. Altman, "US Moves to Replace Japanese Head of WHO," *New York Times*, December 20, 1992, p. 1.

55. Ilona Kickbusch, "The Development of International Health Priorities—Accountability Intact?" *Social Science & Medicine* 51 (2000): 979–989 (quote on p. 985).

56. Commission on Macroeconomics and Health, *Macroeconomics and Health: Investing in Health for Economic Development* (Geneva: WHO, 2001); see also Howard Waitzkin, "Report of the WHO Commission on Macroeconomics and Health: A Summary and Critique," *The Lancet* 361 (February 8, 2003): 523–526.

57. Michael A. Reid and E. Jim Pearce, "Whither the World Health Organization?" *The Medical Journal of Australia* 178 (2003): 9–12.

58. Michael McCarthy, "A Conversation With the Leaders of the Gates Foundation's Global Health Program: Gordon Perkin and William Foege," *The Lancet* 356 (July 8, 2000): 153–155.

The Contribution of the World Health Organization to a New Public Health and Health Promotion

| Ilona Kickbusch, PhD

ABSTRACT

The author traces the development of the concept of health promotion from 1980s policies of the World Health Organization. Two approaches that signify the modernization of public health are outlined in detail: the European Health for All targets and the settings approach. Both aim to reorient health policy priorities from a risk factor approach to strategies that address the determinants of health and empower people to participate in improving the health of their communities.

These approaches combine classic public health dictums with "new" strategies, some setting explicit goals to integrate public health with general welfare policy. Health for All, health promotion, and population health have contributed to this reorientation in thinking and strategy, but the focus of health policy remains expenditure rather than investment.

INTRODUCTION

In 1986, at an international conference held in Ottawa, Ontario, Canada, under the leadership of the World Health Organization (WHO) (and with a strong personal commitment from then Director General Halfdan Mahler), a broad new understanding of health promotion was adopted. The Ottawa Charter for Health Promotion has since exerted significant influence—both directly and indirectly—on the public health debate, on health policy formulation, and on health promotion practices in many countries.[1,2] The work on this document was spearheaded by the WHO European Regional Office and was developed over a period of 5 years of intensive research and debate. It was based on the "Health for All" philosophy,[3] the Alma Ata Declaration,[4] and the Lalonde health field concept.[5]

The Ottawa charter initiated a redefinition and repositioning of institutions, epistemic communities, and actors at the "health" end of the disease–health continuum, a perspective that had been labeled the "salutogenic approach" by Aaron Antonovsky.[6] In overcoming an individualistic understanding of lifestyles and in highlighting social environments and policy, the orientation of health promotion began to shift from focusing on the modification of individual risk factors or risk behaviors to addressing the "context and meaning" of health actions and the determinants that keep people healthy. The Canadian Lalonde report is often cited as having been the starting point of this new development. Recently the director of the Pan American Health Organization, Sir George Alleyne, reflected on this issue, stating that "it is perhaps not accidental that the impetus for the focus on health promotion for the many should have risen in Canada which is often credited with maintaining a more egalitarian approach in all health matters."[7]

In its Health for All strategy, WHO positioned health at the center of development policy and defined the goal of health policy as "providing all people with the opportunity to lead a socially and economically productive life."[3] It proposed a revolutionary shift in perspective from input to outcomes: governments were to be held accountable for the *health* of their populations, not just for the health services they provided. Lester Breslow, the father of the Alameda County study and one of the world's leading epidemiologists, had argued in 1985 that "the stage is set for a new public health revolution."[8] The Ottawa charter echoed this challenge as well as the link to public health history in its subtitle, "The Move Towards a New Public Health."

Fourteen years later, in a commentary published in the *Journal of the American Medical Association*, Breslow deemed the Ottawa charter the document that has best captured the essence of the third public health revolution by conceptualizing health as a "resource for living" and shifting the focus from disease prevention to "capacity building for health."[9] In many parts of the world, influenced in particular by WHO and the Pan American Health Organization, health promotion has come to be understood not only as an approach that moves "beyond health care" but also as a commitment to social reform and equity. The Pan American Health Organization included the categories of the Ottawa charter in its 2001 annual report, and the director's message stated: "For an organization devoted to health, such as ours, the main strategies of health promotion can find application in almost all aspects of our work."[7]

The Ottawa charter frames health as a resource that is created in the context of everyday life and defines health promotion as "the process of enabling people to increase control over, and to improve their health." It defines health as "a resource for everyday life, not the objective of living." It adds that "health is a positive concept emphasizing social and personal resources, as well as physical capabilities." Following in the footsteps of the best traditions of public health and social medicine and making full use of the research on the impact of social factors on health, it links the production of health explicitly to "prerequisites for health" such as peace, income, and housing and—most important—defines health promotion as a process of empowerment and capacity building.

The charter outlines 5 key action areas that reinforce one another with the goal of improving the health of populations: (1) the development of healthy public policies (policies supportive of health in sectors other than health), (2) the need to ensure environments supportive of health, (3) the importance of personal skills, (4) community action, and (5) the challenge of reorienting health services. A new mind-set and professional ethos are proposed for health professionals; their new role is to "enable, advocate, and mediate." This approach to health promotion found its dissemination and application through a number of channels. Here I focus on 2 of these channels: the European health targets and the settings approach.

THE WHO "HEALTH FOR ALL" TARGETS

The most important avenue for the spread and recognition of a broad understanding of health promotion was the adoption of 38 Health for All targets by the member states of the European region of WHO in 1984.[3] In essence, these targets followed the Lalonde health field concept[5] with one important distinction: the section on "lifestyles and health" did not focus on lifestyles as individual behavior changes but opted to integrate several components of the Lalonde concept in a composite approach. A paper pre-

sented at the 1983 meeting of the WHO Regional Committee of the European Region had already made the point that lifestyles needed to be understood as collective behaviors deeply rooted in context.[10] This thinking was very different from the second major influence on the work of the WHO Regional Office, the "management by objective" approach applied in the *Healthy People 2000* goals and objectives in the United States,[11] which involved commitment to a focus on individual behavior modification.

Finally, 2 sets of "lifestyles" targets were developed, one following the US "reduction of disease" model and the other following a "social model of health" approach. An advisory group of WHO European member states decided to move ahead with the latter, and the compromise was a package of 5 lifestyles and health targets that addressed healthy public policy, social support systems, knowledge and motivation, positive health behavior, and health-damaging behavior. While still addressing individual behaviors, the advisory group zeroed in on the interactions between individuals and their environments and on the political instruments needed to address health determinants. The group aimed to expand the territory of health into other policy arenas and highlighted the complex political and social processes necessary to achieve changes in health. This approach was strengthened in subsequent revisions of the targets in 1991 and 1998.[12,13]

As a matter of policy and principle, the 5 lifestyle targets were always grouped as a "package," and a new division was created within the organization to support their implementation. The working group preparing the lifestyles targets also exerted considerable influence on the nature of the European target document by proposing—as early as 1982—targets for social determinants of health. These targets were not included in the final document, but the group did succeed in gaining support for an equity in health target.

The decision to move in a direction that was quite different from the

approach chosen in the United States can be understood only by keeping in mind the strong link between public health and social reform in European public health history—the work of Villermé, Virchow, Chadwick, and Engels, to name but a few—and the role of the state in the provision of health and social services in the European region. This decision built as well on intellectual traditions in the social sciences, particularly Max Weber's understanding of lifestyles as a collective social category and Emile Durkheim's understanding of the social determinants of health as developed in his classic 1970 study, *Suicide*. Recently this understanding of lifestyles as residing at the intersection between personal and social factors[10] has been further expanded and developed as "collective lifestyles" by Frohlich and Potvin.[14] They too argue that collective lifestyles should be conceptualized as a group attribute resulting from the interaction between social conditions and behavior.

The European Health for All targets provided the new resource-based health promotion approaches a visibility far beyond the individual program and projects. Through these targets, health promotion gained legitimacy and influence and created the positive political environment for the adoption of the Ottawa charter in 1986. To date, 27 European countries have formulated health targets using the WHO policy as a starting point, as have regions, provinces, and cities.[15,16]

The most recent such attempt at the national level upholds the original orientation developed in the Ottawa charter and the WHO policy. A report published in 2001 by the Swedish National Committee for Public Health[17] (a parliamentary committee established in 1997) identified 6 main areas of strategic intent that, in effect, set both a health promotion and a health determinants agenda: (1) strengthening social capital, (2) ensuring that children grow up in a satisfactory environment, (3) improving workplace conditions, (4) creating a satisfactory physical environment, (5) stimulating health-promoting life habits, and

(6) developing a satisfactory infrastructure for health issues. Gunnar Ågren, director-general of the Swedish National Institute of Public Health, described the essence of the Swedish targets as being oriented toward health determinants rather than health behaviors.[18] This "new order" was, to a certain degree, a response to Leonard Syme's[19] repeated challenges for a new categorization of health action not based on disease categories.

It must be kept in mind, though, that while the charter and its "ecological" orientation were widely adopted, the practice of health promotion frequently continued to focus on individual behavior change, in part because its institutional base tended to be in health education. Many proponents of health promotion as a "new public health" based more on social determinants were therefore encouraged when the population health movement emerged in Canada at the beginning of the 1990s, because it provided strong arguments for a focus on social and economic determinants and for investments in the sectors that "produce health," such as education, income, and housing.[20] But population health, as the "next new thing," included very little mention of health promotion, and the chance to forge a strong alliance was lost.

In 1998, WHO's Regional Office for Europe published a detailed report exploring the intersection between population health and the Health for All strategy.[21] It underlined that the common ground between population health, Health for All, and health promotion resides in the recognition that the majority of health determinants reside outside the health sector and drew attention to the strategic competence and experience that health promotion is able to bring to the table. The more recent target documents of WHO have reinforced the commitment to address health determinants and to seek strategic entry points outside of the health sector. For example, according to WHO's recent *Health 21* document[13]:

[W]hether one is a government minister, city mayor, company director, community leader, a parent or individual, Health 21 can help develop action strategies that will result in more democratic, socially responsible and sustainable development. Health is a powerful political platform.

At the same time, the European document has strengthened the commitment to values such as equity, participation, solidarity, sustainability, and accountability, a point often considered a weakness of the population health debate, which focuses on an economic rather than a humanistic rationale. A subtle change can also be seen in the new *Healthy People 2010* goals and objectives of the United States, which now include goals related to supportive environments.

THE SETTINGS APPROACH

Developing health targets (or health goals and objectives, in the preferred US terminology)—at whatever level of governance, from organizational to international—is one mechanism of agreeing on common goals and direction, providing a "common context of interpretation" and broadening the legitimacy base for critical choices in health. The target development process in itself, if broadly conceived and implemented in partnerships beyond the health sector, produces "bridging capital."[22] Commitment to collaboration becomes a "categorical imperative," and, as a consequence, new strategic roles emerge for public health departments, health agencies, and health professionals. This is a point repeatedly underlined in comparative analyses of health targets.[12] One such challenge, for example, is how to transfer knowledge regarding what creates health and how to organize collective learning regarding how to produce health as an overall systems goal, not just a responsibility of the health sector. Governance theories stress the importance of "meso" institutions and mediating structures, which allow the dialogue between all parties to evolve and serve as a center of social learning.[23]

This shift in orientation and purpose found its strategic expression in the settings approach, the second major innovation introduced by the WHO European Regional Office in the field of health promotion.[24,25] This approach spearheaded a number of initiatives that sought to engage other actors in health, and it did so by creating a new dissemination strategy through networks. In the early 1980s, the WHO European Regional Office began to work with cities and local authorities, universities, and professional organizations, along with regions, companies, schools, prisons, and hospitals, to create networks of commitment and diffusion. These networks carried the new health policy message to a range of collaborators in other sectors, organizations, and all levels of governance. Through a myriad of meetings, consultations, publications, and other formal and informal mechanisms, an international learning process was set up for the new concept of health promotion.[26–30]

The key strategic point of the settings approach was to move health promotion away from focusing on individual behaviors and communities at risk to developing a strategy that encompasses a total population within a given setting. This followed the thinking of Geoffrey Rose[31] that an effective and sustainable public health strategy must lower the risk of the majority of individuals, not only those at the tail end of the distribution. The target of the intervention therefore moves from individuals or groups of individuals to their environments, the "settings of everyday life." The strategic objective becomes the strengthening of resources for health. The innovation of health promotion has been to include the participatory process and empowerment as part of the strategic objectives. Indeed, Rootman et al.[32] claimed that "unless empowerment is part of the strategy it cannot be called health promotion."

In 1987, the WHO Healthy Cities project was launched with the explicit aim of localizing the Health for All strategy by involving political decision makers in cities throughout Europe and by building a strong lobby for public health at the local level. What began with 11 designated WHO cities soon became a widespread "new public health movement" in which several hundred cities around the world engaged in new types of public health approaches.[33] The leaders of the project ventured that health was not something separate to be implemented by public health departments, and they challenged each social actor in the community, the private sector, the nongovernmental sector, the faith community, and the various sectors of city government to contribute to health and work with others in an "organized community effort," as expressed in the definition of public health of C. E. A. Winslow.[34]

Anthony Giddens, the British sociologist and recent director of the London School of Economics, coined the phrase "life politics" to refer to this kind of integrative approach. He postulated that we cannot continue to divide the way we do politics into vertical streams of action: separating, for example, social policy, health policy, and economic policy.[35] According to Giddens, the question faced in 21st-century politics is "How do we want to live our lives?" Accordingly—and following the WHO definition of health—the 11 qualities of a healthy city developed by the project are related to well-being and quality of life.[36]

To be recognized, cities had to fulfill a number of conditions set by WHO[37]; for example, they had to commit to a health plan, create an intersectoral committee for health, establish a Healthy Cities office and appoint a coordinator, develop a city health profile, and involve citizens and community groups. The project advocated partnership and network-based approaches of change management to allow creation of political commitment, generate visibility for health issues, embark on institutional change, and create space for innovative health action. Diffusion of knowledge and exchange of information were ensured through regular meetings of all European cities involved in the project, as well as through national and regional networks. Cities were supported in developing indicators and policies, and

a mechanism called the "multi-city action plan" was introduced that focused on priority health issues such as equity, traffic, tobacco, the elderly, mental health, and AIDS care.

The project continues to this day. There is now a strong focus on cities in Central and Eastern Europe, and the practical experience accumulated in the cities has become a source of inspiration for local health action around the world. WHO has engaged in regular project evaluations and reviews.[33] The approach has been particularly successful in the Americas, where, with the encouragement of the Pan American Health Organization, a strong "healthy municipalities network" has evolved that includes hundreds of cities.[38] In the United States, the Coalition for Healthy Cities and Communities (http://www.healthy-communities.org) has based its work on the WHO approach.

Following the Healthy Cities project, other settings approaches were developed by the WHO Regional Office for Europe: health-promoting schools, healthpromoting workplaces, health in prisons, healthy universities, and health-promoting hospitals. In all of these projects, the key intention has been to gain a "political" commitment to improving the health of the entire organization (a systems approach) and developing strategies that allow all parts of the organization to work together to improve the health of the setting. The settings projects have caught the imagination of many actors in many countries, with and without WHO support. What they achieve does not fit easily into an epidemiological framework of "evidence" but needs to be analyzed in terms of social and political processes.

Ways in which to approach the evaluation of settings programs have been outlined in a number of recent publications.[25,32,39] Such projects fulfill many of the criteria for "promising interventions" developed in the recent Institute of Medicine report focusing on health promotion.[40] Strategically, their achievement has been to move health out of the professional action frame into organizations and the com-

munity ("the context of everyday life" in the language of the Ottawa charter) and to frame health in terms of relevance to people and communities.

This active role of citizens and the community is central to the settings approach. The Ottawa charter definition of health promotion—"the process of enabling people to increase control over their health"—partly took its lead from the health definitions of the major social movements of the 1970s and 1980s (e.g., the women's health movement, the self-help movement, and the gay rights movement). Some authors, for example Petersen,[41] contend that this is not a move toward empowerment but an increased privatization of risk. However, Paquet[23] argues that the new health governance is only possible as a new type of social contract between the "strategic state" and "active citizens," which in turn reflects an understanding of health as a co-produced good within the structure of everyday life.

For example, a recent English health target document[42] (although its targets are structured around disease categories) presents itself as an intersectoral challenge for the whole of government, not just the health sector. It regards health as a "national contract" and a 3-way partnership between individuals, communities, and the government. The document then clearly lays out the responsibilities of each partner under each respective target. The health promotion approach advocated by the Ottawa charter implies that health is produced in the dynamic exchange between people and their environments. Social determinants are considered central to health creation, but at the same time people are recognized as social actors who can effect change. Indeed, the very process of involvement is considered health promoting in that it creates (for example) self-esteem, a sense of worth, and social capital.

THE THIRD PUBLIC HEALTH REVOLUTION

The first public health revolution addressed sanitary conditions and fought infectious diseases; the second public health revolution focused on the contribution of individual behaviors to noncommunicable diseases and premature death. The third public health revolution recognizes health as a key dimension of quality of life. Health policies in the 21st century will need to be constructed from the key question posed by both the health promotion and population health movements: "What makes people healthy?" Health policies will need to address both the collective lifestyles of modern societies and the social environments of modern life as they affect the health and quality of life of populations.

The 6 key areas of the new Swedish policy outlined earlier show the commitment to base a modern health policy on health determinants and indicate at the same time that we need both the analytical dimensions of population health research and the cumulative experience of health promotion practice to move ahead. Priority should be given to building healthy communities and healthy workplaces, strengthening the wide range of social networks for health, and increasing people's capabilities to lead healthy lives. The development of tools such as environmental, social, economic, and, most recently, health "impact assessments"[43,44] (or the "Verona benchmark," which relates to best practices in partnership building[45]) underlines the fact that assessments of accountability need to involve both cross-sector effects and externalities.

Population health research such as the work of Keating and Hertzman[46] helps situate policy reorientation in a wider societal context. In late modern societies, health will again—as in the first public health revolution—play a central role in wealth creation, and nation-states will need to invest in human and social capital if they are to remain competitive on a global scale. According to Keating and Hertzman, "The wealth of nations in the Information Age may depend heavily, perhaps primarily, upon their ability to promote the developmental health of their populations." From a health promotion perspective, this argument is important but not sufficient; its goal resides in well-being and quality of life.

It is this orientation that has led Swedish health policymakers to set the explicit goal of integrating public health with general welfare policy. Health for All, health promotion, and population health have all contributed to a reorientation in thinking and strategy, yet the focus of health policy remains medical care expenditures rather than investment in health determinants.[47] It is in the realm of politics, however, that the key question must be resolved: What amount of resources does a society want to invest in health and quality of life, and who should pay?

About the Authors

The author is with the Division of Global Health, Department of Epidemiology and Public Health, Yale University School of Medicine, New Haven, Conn.

Correspondence: Requests for reprints should be sent to Ilona Kickbusch, PhD, Division of Global Health, Yale University School of Medicine, Department of Epidemiology and Public Health, 60 College St, PO Box 208034, New Haven, CT 06520-8034 (e-mail: ilona.kickbusch@yale.edu).

References

1. Ottawa Charter for Health Promotion. In: *Health Promotion.* Vol. 1. Geneva, Switzerland: World Health Organization; 1986:iii–v.
2. Kickbusch I. Perspectives on health governance in the 21st century: revisiting health goals and targets. In: Marinker M, ed. *Health Targets in Europe: Polity, Progress and Promise.* London: BMJ Books; 2002:206–229.
3. *Health for All Targets.* Copenhagen, Denmark: World Health Organization; 1984.
4. *The Alma Ata Declaration.* Geneva, Switzerland: World Health Organization; 1978.
5. Lalonde M. *A New Perspective on the Health of Canadians.* Ottawa, Ontario, Canada: Information Canada; 1974.
6. Antonovsky A. *Unraveling the Mystery of Health: How People Manage Stress and Stay Well.* San Francisco, Calif: Jossey-Bass; 1987.
7. Alleyne G. The director's message. In: *Pan American Health Organization Annual Report 2001.* Washington, DC: Pan American Health Organization; 2001.
8. Breslow L. A prevention strategy: toward health in the year 2000. *Health Med.* 1985;3:43–44.
9. Breslow L. From disease prevention to health promotion. *JAMA.* 1999;281:1030–1033.
10. Kickbusch I. Lifestyles and health. *Soc Sci Med.* 1986;2:117–124.
11. *Healthy People: The Surgeon General's Report on Health Promotion and Disease Prevention.* Washington, DC: US Dept of Health, Education, and Welfare; 1979.
12. Van de Water HPA, van Herten LM. *Health Policies on Target? Review of Health Target and Priority Setting in 18 European Countries.* Leiden, the Netherlands: Netherlands Organization for Applied Scientific Research; 1998.
13. *Health 21—Health for All in the 21st Century.* Copenhagen, Denmark: World Health Organization; 1999.
14. Frohlich KL, Corin E, Potvin L. A theoretical proposal for the relationship between context and disease. *Sociol Health Illness.* 2001;23:776–797.
15. *Proceedings of the International Workshop on Target Setting, Brussels, 8–9 March 1966.* Brussels, Belgium: European Public Health Center; 1966.
16. Goumans M, Springett J. From project to policy—"healthy cities" as a mechanism for policy change for health? *Health Promotion Int.* 1997;12:311–377.
17. Swedish National Committee for Public Health. *Health on Equal Terms—National Goals for Public Health.* Stockholm, Sweden: Ministry of Health and Social Affairs; 2000.
18. Ågren G. The new Swedish public health policy. Available at: http://www.fhi.se/In. Accessed January 6, 2003.
19. Syme SL. To prevent disease: the need for a new approach. In: Blane E, Brunner E, Wilkinson R, eds. *Health and Social Organisation: Towards Health Policy for the 21st Century.* London, England: Routledge; 1996:22–31.
20. Evans RG, Barer ML, Marmor TR, eds. *Why Are Some People Healthy and Others Not?* New York, NY: Aldine de Gruyter; 1994.

21. Zoellner H, Lessof S. *Population Health—Putting Concepts Into Action.* Copenhagen, Denmark: World Health Organization Regional Office for Europe; 1998.

22. Putnam R. *Bowling Alone: The Collapse and Revival of American Community.* New York, NY: Simon & Schuster; 2000.

23. Paquet G. The new governance, subsidiarity and the strategic state. In: *Governance in the 21st Century.* Paris, France: Organisation for Economic Cooperation and Development; 2001:183–208.

24. Kickbusch I. Health promoting environments: the next steps. *Aust N Z J Public Health.* 1997;21:431–434.

25. Poland BD, Green L, Rootman I. *Settings for Health Promotion: Linking Theory and Practice.* London, England: Sage Publications; 2000:1–43.

26. Burgher M, Rasmussen VB, Rivett D, eds. *The European Network of Health Promoting Schools: The Alliance of Health and Education.* Copenhagen, Denmark: World Health Organization Regional Office for Europe; 1999.

27. Demmer H. *Worksite Health Promotion: How to Go About It.* Copenhagen, Denmark: World Health Organization Regional Office for Europe; 1995. European Health Promotion Series 4.

28. Pelikan JM, Garcia Barbero M, Lobnig H, Krajic K, eds. *Pathways to a Health Promoting Hospital.* Gamburg, Germany: Conrad Verlag; 1998.

29 Tsouros A, Dowding G, Thompson J, Dooris M. *Health Promoting Universities: Concept, Experiences and Framework for Action.* Copenhagen, Denmark: World Health Organization; 1998.

30. Whitelaw S, Baxendale A, Bryce C, MacHardy L, Young I, Witney E. "Settings" based health promotion: a review. *Health Promotion Int.* 2001;16:339–354.

31. Rose G. *The Strategy of Preventive Medicine.* Oxford, England: Oxford University Press Inc; 1992.

32. Rootman I, Goodstadt M, Hyndman B, et al., eds. *Evaluation in Health Promotion: Principles and Perspectives.* Copenhagen, Denmark: World Health Organization; 2001.

33. De Leeuw E. Healthy cities: urban social entrepreneurship for health. *Health Promotion Int.* 1999;14:261–269.

34. Winslow CEA. Winslow's definition of public health. In: *Encyclopedia Britannica.* Vol. 15. London, England: Encyclopedia Britannica Inc; 2001:740.

35. Giddens A. *Modernity and Self Identity: Self and Society in the Late Modern Age.* Cambridge, England: Polity Press; 1991.

36. Hancock T, Duhl L. *Promoting Health in the Urban Context.* Copenhagen, Denmark: World Health Organization; 1988.

37. *Healthy Cities Project: Five Year Planning Framework.* Copenhagen, Denmark: World Health Organization; 1988.

38. *Healthy Municipalities.* Washington, DC: Pan American Health Organization; 2000.

39. Nutbeam D. Evaluating health promotion. *Health Promotion Int.* 1998;13:27–44.

40. *Promoting Health: Intervention Strategies From Social and Behavioral Research.* Washington, DC: Institute of Medicine; 2000.

41. Petersen AR. Risk and the regulated self: the discourse of health promotion as politics of uncertainty. *Aust N Z J Sociol.* 1996;32:44–57.

42. Hunter DJ, Fulop N, Warner M. *From "Health of the Nation" to "Our Healthier Nation": A Case Study From England.* Brussels, Belgium: World Health Organization European Center for Health Policy; 2000.

43. *Health Impact Assessment: Main Concepts and Suggested Approach.* Brussels, Belgium: World Health Organization European Center for Health Policy; 1999.

44. Health impact assessment. *Promotion Educ.* 2001;7(theme issue).

45. McMahon L, Harvey S, Zigio E, Arnell G. Using the investment triangle—towards process guidelines. Available at: http://www.who.dk/Verona/main.htm. Accessed November 11, 2000.

46. Keating DP, Hertzman C. *Developmental Health and the Wealth of Nations.* New York, NY: Guilford Press; 1999.

47. Levin SL, Ziglio E. Health promotion as an investment strategy: considerations and theory and practice. *Health Promotion Int.* 1996;11:33–40.

Is It Time to Reassess the Categorization of Disease Burdens in Low-Income Countries?

| Philip W. Setel, PhD, Lance Saker, MD, Nigel C. Unwin, MD, Yusuf Hemed, MMed, David R. Whiting, BA and Henry Kitange, MD

ABSTRACT

The classification of disease burdens is an important topic that receives little attention or debate. One common classification scheme, the *broad cause* grouping, is based on etiology and health transition theory and is mainly concerned with distinguishing communicable from noncommunicable diseases. This may be of limited utility to policymakers and planners. We propose a *broad care needs* framework to complement the broad cause grouping. This alternative scheme may be of equal or greater value to planners. We apply these schemes to disability-adjusted life year estimates for 2000 and to mortality data from Tanzania. The results suggest that a broad care needs approach could shift the priorities of health planners and policymakers and deserves further evaluation.

INTRODUCTION

How disease burdens are characterized and categorized in terms of broad groupings is an important issue that receives little attention or debate. The application of conventional *broad cause* groups (i.e., *communicable, noncommunicable,* and *injuries*) to the disease burden determines much of the field on which important debates in international health are conducted. The broad cause view of disease burdens in developing countries has informed both influential policy recommendations that poor countries invest solely in communicable disease reduction to achieve the greatest future health returns,[1] and potent warnings that noncommunicable diseases loom as "tomorrow's pandemics" in the developing world.[2]

The time is ripe for challenging the conventional categories underlying these discussions. A move away from groupings based on *causes* to ones that stress the *effects* and *care needs* of disease burdens would be instructive. Perhaps more importantly, they may be of greater intrinsic use for high-level public health policy and services planning. Our concerns echo recent calls for a reassessment of models of health care delivery that move away from a narrow focus on acute, episodic treatment to ones that more closely reflect the increasing burden of conditions requiring long-term care and management regardless of etiology.[3]

To illustrate our point, we present a simple broad care needs scheme for categorizing the burden of disease. We then apply both the conventional broad cause scheme used in the 1990 Global Burden of Disease (GBD) study[4,5] and the proposed needs-oriented scheme to 2 sets of data: GBD *disability-adjusted life year* (DALY) estimates for sub-Saharan Africa for 2000, and community-based data on cause-specific mortality from a rural district in the United Republic of Tanzania for 2000.

CONCERNS ABOUT THE BROAD CAUSE SCHEME

Chief among the aims of the GBD 1990 study was to inform health policy and decisionmaking. Its authors used a broad classification of diseases based on etiology, epidemiological risks, and epidemiological transition theory[6] to provide a simplified bird's eye view of the many conditions constituting the total disease burden. The 3 GBD groups are:

- Group I: Communicable, maternal, perinatal, and nutritional conditions
- Group II: Noncommunicable diseases
- Group III: Injuries

Broad cause groups formulated in this way have been used to provide overarching descriptions of the type of health care and preventive measures required for the conditions within those groups.[1] The typical group I condition, for example, is a classic infectious illness requiring acute, episodic, and (depending on severity) short-term hospital care.

Of particular concern is the distinction between broad cause groups I and II. The distinction between these groups, based as it is on the *causes* rather than the *effects* of disease, provides a weak compass for setting high-level planning and priority directions and may lead decisionmakers astray in predicting the types of health intervention and care that will be needed by the populations they serve.[3] Although HIV/AIDS and tuberculosis may be infectious in nature (i.e., group I conditions), their management has much more in common with that of severe stroke (group II) than measles (group I). Conversely, treatment of appendicitis (group II) is more similar to that of bacterial meningitis (group I) than to that of lung cancer (group II).

TABLE 1– Criteria for Broad Care Needs Classification of Disease Groups

	Chronicity	
Likelihood of Mortality	**Acute**	**Chronic**
Low	Potentially curable with > 1 mo of current appropriate treatment and < 20% chance of mortality within 1 mo if untreated	Either incurable or requires > 1 mo of appropriate treatment and < 5%/y chance of developing an intercurrent episode or acute illness associated with the chronic condition, with > 20% chance of mortality within 1 mo if untreated
High	Potentially curable with > 1 mo of current appropriate treatment and > 20% chance of mortality within 1 month if untreated	Either incurable or requires > 1 mo of appropriate treatment and < 5%/y chance of developing an intercurrent episode or acute illness associated with the chronic condition, with > 20% chance of mortality within 1 mo if untreated

The use of the broad cause scheme without a broad care needs perspective to complement it could perpetuate a misapprehension about where today's care needs actually lie in many developing countries.

A BROAD CARE NEEDS CLASSIFICATION FOR HEALTH PLANNERS

We propose a simple alternative classification based on a 2-axis *health effects* or *care needs* orientation. Two of the most fundamental criteria for discriminating between the effects of different illnesses on individuals and the resulting demands on health services are (1) the length of time they produce ill health in an individual (*chronicity*) and (2) their relative likelihood of causing death (*mortality*).

Other aspects of particular illnesses, such as the availability of cost-effective preventive interventions or likelihood of disablement and the typical age at which patients are afflicted by the illness will also affect the implied need for health services. However, for the purposes of simplicity, we have limited our care needs classification criteria to the 2 parameters of *chronicity* and *mortality*. We divided these parameters into 2 groups. All major disease conditions were rated as either *acute* or *chronic* along 1 axis, and as having a *low* or

high mortality along the other. The combination of these categories yields a 4-way effect-oriented broad care needs classification scheme: (1) acute care needs, with low- and high-mortality subgroups, and (2) long-term care and management needs, with low- and high-mortality subgroups (see Table 1 for definitions).

OUR APPROACH

Comparison Using GBD 2000 DALY Estimates for Sub-Saharan Africa

Two physicians reclassified selected causes of public health importance in Africa from the 1990 GBD study into the care needs scheme. The reclassification was based on their knowledge of the typical clinical course of each disease group. It is acknowledged that the chronicity and mortality risks of some diseases differ in different settings. We have not attempted to take this into account in this illustrative exercise. Conditions placed under the 4 different categories shown in Table 1 are available from the authors. When assigning disease groups that include several subgroups of conditions, we attempted to achieve a best fit for the disease group in question. Some specific disease groups included conditions that fell into different categories within the effect-oriented scheme (e.g., digestive diseases included appendicitis [acute care need,

high mortality] and cirrhosis [long-term care need, high mortality]). In these situations we classified groups according to the most common disease in that group in the GBD study estimates. *Years of life lost* (YLLs) due to injuries were assigned to the acute care need, high-mortality category. *Years lived with disability* (YLDs) due to injuries were classified as chronic care need, low mortality. We then abstracted the predicted number of DALYs for each category from the GBD estimates and tabulated them. The results are compared with the 2000 broad cause estimates for the same list of causes, as published in the original study.[4]

It should be noted that we did not include in our analysis diseases or disease groups classified as acute care need, low mortality. Although such diseases are responsible for a significant proportion of a health service's workload, they do not represent a high number of lost DALYs. Also, for the sake of brevity, results are presented for 2 age groups only: (1) children younger than 5 years and (2) the remainder of the population.

Comparison Using Data From Tanzania

The comparison was repeated using data from the Tanzanian Ministry of Health's National Sentinel System of linked demographic surveillance sites. Since 1992, the Adult Morbidity and Mortality Project has been facilitating the establishment of this system and has engaged in demographic and cause-specific mortality surveillance among rural and urban populations amounting to approximately 1% of the total national population.[7] These data are regarded as one of the only reliable sources of longitudinal population-based mortality data in Africa.[8] Methods of data collection and surveillance areas have previously been described.[9] Briefly, they include the annual re-enumeration of the population under surveillance in the rural areas, semiannual re-enumeration in the urban area, and networks of village and neighborhood reporters who record incident deaths on a continuous basis. Trained health care workers follow up each death in the surveillance areas and administer a *verbal autopsy* interview with the kin and carers of the deceased person. When they are available from the household, data from medical records are abstracted. Probable cause of death is attributed using a list of causes derived from the *International Statistical Classification of Diseases, 10th Revision*.[10] A panel of 3 physicians assigns the cause. Coders are blind to each other's diagnosis, and cause of death is assigned when 2 coders agree. A cause is assigned in more than 90% of cases.

Only mortality data (deaths and YLLs) are available. Data from Morogoro District for 2000 were selected for presentation. Of the 3 current sentinel sites in Tanzania, Morogoro has the highest proportion of deaths with group I causes and therefore represents a good test case for the comparison of disease burden categorization schemes. YLLs were calculated with the formula published in the 1990 GBD study. We categorized causes of death available from the project into 1990 GBD broad cause categories following that source, and into the broad care needs classification scheme using the criteria previously described.

OUR RESULTS

Figure 1 compares the percentage of estimated DALYs for 2000 attributable to the broad cause and broad care needs classification schemes. Group I causes predominated among children younger than 5 years (86% of DALYs). According to the broad care needs scheme, a similar but smaller proportion of DALYs were lost to conditions requiring acute or episodic care. Only 7% of lost DALYs in children were due to noncommunicable (group II) diseases. However, taking a broad care needs perspective

suggests that over one fifth (23%) of lost DALYs expected among children in 2000 were from conditions needing long-term care and management.

In the rest of the population, 35% of lost DALYs were from group I causes. An equal proportion of lost DALYs among the population older than 5 years were from the group II set of conditions, whereas injuries and accidents accounted for 30%. From a care needs perspective, just 14% of DALYs lost were expected to be due to conditions needing acute care services, as opposed to 86% of DALYS attributable to conditions requiring long-term care and management. Note that HIV and tuberculosis are classified as group I conditions in the GBD study but are classified as high mortality and requiring long-term care and management in the effectorientated classification.

Figure 2 applies the classification schemes to mortality data from Tanzania. Among children, very similar proportions were observed in the group I and acute care needs groups (90% and 89%, respectively). The percentage (9%) of group II conditions matched the 10% of the disease burden among children needing long-term care; less than 2% of the mortality burden in children was due to group III conditions.

In the remainder of the population, group I causes of death predominated (72% of YLLs), with most of the remainder (22%) attributed to noninfectious group II conditions. This contrasts with a care needs perspective in which 44% of YLLs were due to conditions needing acute and episodic health care, whereas just under half of all mortality (49%) was caused by diseases needing long-term care and management.

DISCUSSION

In writing this article, we have sought to stimulate debate about the broad categorization of disease burdens in developing countries by proposing a simple alternative to the conventional cause-based scheme. We have also tried to point out how different categorization schemes might lead

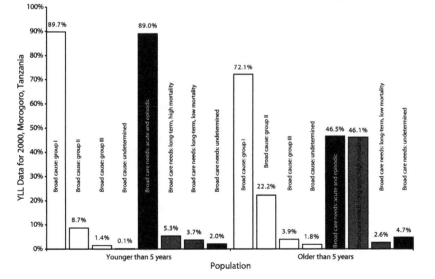

FIGURE 1— Percentage of disability-adjusted life years (DALYs) owing to broad cause and broad care needs conditions (estimates for 2000).

Note. White bars = broad cause groups; black bars = broad care needs (acute care and undetermined); gray bars = broad care needs (long-term care and management).

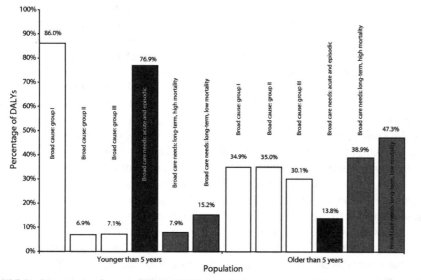

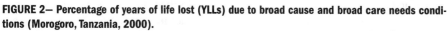

FIGURE 2— Percentage of years of life lost (YLLs) due to broad cause and broad care needs conditions (Morogoro, Tanzania, 2000).

Note. White bars = broad cause groups; black bars = broad care needs (acute care and undetermined); gray bars = broad care needs (long-term care and management).

planners to divergent conclusions about where high-level service priorities may lie. In doing so, we hope to stimulate further development of useful approaches to the categorization of disease burdens for different audiences, including policymakers and planners. In particular, there is a growing need for understanding and debating how priorities are set at the local or district level. This level is increasingly where initial planning and decisionmaking take place in the era of decentralization and health reform. At all levels, there is a need for more and better sources of data, however one may group and categorize them. New information techniques such as sentinel demographic surveillance may contribute to filling these gaps.

Two main points are suggested by this exercise. First, the effect-oriented broad care needs scheme applied to both DALY estimates and YLL data suggests that radically different approaches to health care are needed for the populations younger than and older than 5 years in Africa. As some recent high-profile publications suggest,[11] the conventional policy interpretation of a high burden in the GBD broad cause group I is that health care priorities be placed on services for communicable diseases requiring acute and episodic care. Our analysis has

shown that this interpretation may hold for the disease burden in children younger than 5 years, but for the majority of the population it may well lead in some wrong directions. When the disease burden is regrouped in such a way as to specifically reflect the care needs implied by acute versus chronic conditions, this conventional interpretation is materially changed.

Infants and younger children are burdened by conditions needing acute and episodic care, whereas the majority of the population (who are older than age 5 years) clearly need a health system that can provide long-term care and management. Among women, diseases categorized as chronic account for 75% of deaths and 83% of DALYs. Among men they account for 64% of deaths and 96% of DALYs. These differences largely reflect the fact that men are more likely to suffer serious injuries. Therefore, deaths from external causes and years lived with the disabling effects of injury are both more common in men. In addition, maternal mortality and illness substantially influence total female DALYs lost. This suggests even more strongly the need to provide services for the management of chronic conditions in health systems in Africa.

The health policy and health care requirements for chronic conditions

are substantially different from those for acute conditions, whatever their etiology. Chronic conditions require the ability of a health system to deliver treatment over a prolonged period of time. Patient education with the aim of promoting long-term behavioral change is usually a feature of care, and for most chronic conditions the aim is management rather than cure.

Second, the effect-oriented classification provides a relatively easy method for assessing the need for broad types of care. Because it does not require an in-depth understanding of the underlying abnormality and detailed management of particular diseases, it could easily be used by health policymakers and planners from nonclinical backgrounds. A greater burden of disease caused by chronic illnesses implies a greater need for the type of innovative care called for by the World Health Organization and also implies the need for a greater emphasis on preventive programs and services.

The 2 classification schemes compared in this paper are not mutually exclusive. The broad cause classification remains an informative way of summarizing the impact of major types of causes on differences in disease patterns over time and between populations. A classification based on acuteness-chronicity should better serve the needs of health care policymakers and planners. It is a matter of choosing the most appropriate classification for a given use.

We have illustrated how a classification based on chronicity and mortality could be useful to health care policymakers and planners, particularly for patients older than 5 years. Clearly, further work on this approach would be required before it could be adopted. This would include detailed modeling of the potential costs and health benefits of using such a framework for policy decisions. We hope that others will be encouraged to contribute to this work.

Acknowledgments

This article is, in part, an output of the Adult Morbidity and Mortality

Project (AMMP). AMMP is a project of the Tanzanian Ministry of Health and local councils, funded by the UK Department for International Development (DFID) and implemented in partnership with the University of Newcastle upon Tyne. The views expressed are not necessarily those of DFID. The authors also thank the District Councils and residents of Hai, Igunga, and Morogoro Districts, and Ilala, Kigoma, and Temeke Municipalities.

The following individuals are members of the AMMP Team, without whose work this publication would not have been possible: KGMM Alberti, Richard Amaro, Gregory Kabadi, Berlina Job, Judith Kahama, Joel Kalula, Ayoub Kibao, John Kissima, Regina Kutaga, Mary Lewanga, Frederic Macha, Haroun Machibya, Mkamba Mashombo, Godwill Massawe, Gabriel Masuki, Louisa Masayanyika, Ali Mhina, Veronica Mkusa, Ades Moshy, Hamisi Mponezya, Robert Mswia, Deo Mtasiwa, Ferdinand Mugusi, Samuel Ngatunga, Mkay Nguluma, Peter Nkulila, Seif Rashid, JJ Rubona, Asha Sankole, Daudi Simba. The authors also thank the District Councils and residents of of Hai, Igunga, and Morogoro Districts, and Ilala, Kigoma, and Temeke Municipalities.

Human Participant Protection

Mortality data were obtained from a Tanzanian Ministry of Health development project. Ethical clearance was not required or sought for the mortality surveillance component. All project activities were overseen by the Tanzanian Ministry of Health and representatives of local government.

About the Authors

At the time of writing, Philip W. Setel, Lance Saker, Nigel C. Unwin, and David R. Whiting were with the University of Newcastle upon Tyne Medical School, Department of Medicine, Newcastle upon Tyne, England. Philip W. Setel and David R. Whiting are also with the Adult Morbidity and Mortality Project, Ministry of Health, Dar es Salaam, Tanzania, as is Yusuf Hemed. Henry Kitange is with the Morogoro Regional Hospital, Morogoro, Tanzania.

Correspondence: Requests for reprints should be sent to Philip W. Setel, MEASURE Evaluation, Carolina Population Center, University of North Carolina at Chapel Hill, CB-1820, Chapel Hill, NC 27516.

Contributors

P. Setel and N. Unwin conceived the article. N. Unwin, L. Saker, and P. Setel designed the analysis. L. Saker, D. Whiting, N. Unwin, P. Setel, Y. Hemed, and H. Kitange participated in data preparation and carried out the analysis. P. Setel, L. Saker, and N. Unwin wrote the article, and Y. Hemed, D. Whiting, and H. Kitange assisted in editing and revision.

References

1. Gwatkin DR, Guillot M. *The Burden of Disease Among the Global Poor. Current Situation, Future Trends, and Implications for Strategy.* Washington DC: The World Bank; 2000.
2. Alberti KGMM. Noncommunicable diseases: tomorrow's pandemics. *Bull World Health Organ.* 2001;79:907.
3. *Innovative Care for Chronic Conditions: Building Blocks for Action.* Geneva, Switzerland: World Health Organization; 2002.
4. Murray CJL, Lopez AD, eds. *The Global Burden of Disease.* Boston, Mass: The Harvard School of Public Health on behalf of the World Health Organization and the World Bank; 1996.
5. Murray CJL, Lopez AD. *Global Health Statistics.* Boston, Mass: The Harvard School of Public Health on behalf of the World Health Organization and the World Bank; 1996.
6. Murray CJL, Lopez AD. Estimating causes of death: new methods and global and regional applications for 1990. In: Murray CJL, Lopez AD, eds. *The Global Burden of Disease.* Boston, Mass: The Harvard School of Public Health on behalf of the World Health Organization and the World Bank; 1996:117–200.
7. *The Policy Implications of Adult Morbidity and Mortality. End of Phase 1 Report.* Dar es Salaam, United Republic of Tanzania: Ministry of Health and AMMP Team; 1997.
8. Lopez AD, Salomon J, Ahmad O, Murray CJL, Mafat D. *Life Tables for 191 Countries: Data, Methods and Results.* Geneva, Switzerland: World Health Organization; 1999. GPE Discussion Paper Series, No. 9.
9. Setel P, Hemed Y, Unwin N, Alberti K, for the AMMP Team. Six-year cause-specific adult mortality in Tanzania: evidence from community-based surveillance in three districts 1992–1998. *MMWR Morb Mortal Wkly Rep.* 2000;49:416–419.
10. *International Statistical Classification of Diseases and Related Health Problems.* 10th rev. Vol 2. Geneva, Switzerland: World Health Organization; 1993.
11. Gwatkin DR, Guillot M, Heuveline P. The burden of disease among the global poor. *Lancet.* 1999;354:586–589.

The Impact of Genomics on Global Health

| Tikki Pang, PhD, FRCPath

ABSTRACT

Ensuring that advances in genomics are applied to the health improvement of people living in developing countries is an important contemporary challenge. In the near term, such advances are likely to alleviate infectious diseases, with longer-term benefits envisaged for chronic disorders.

To ensure that benefits are shared by developing countries, attention must be paid to complex ethical, legal, social, and economic issues, as well as to public education and engagement. Creative and equitable international mechanisms and goodwill are needed to turn high hopes into reality and allow the use of genomics to reduce health inequities between rich and poor nations. (*Am J Public Health.* 2002;92:1077–1079).

INTRODUCTION

The ongoing genomics revolution, highlighted by the sequencing of the human genome, promises to change how diseases are diagnosed, prevented, and treated. It has tremendous potential to improve health globally. Despite the flush of excitement about its potential, drugs and interventions derived from genomics are likely to be expensive, and of particular interest is how these advances will affect the health of people living in the developing countries. The reality is that many of the advances in genomics were made, and in part are owned, by the developed world, and this has given rise to the concern that a "genomics divide"[1] will be created that will further widen the equity gap in health between rich and poor nations.

Instead, genomics and related technologies should be used to narrow the existing unethical inequities in global health. A report recently released by the World Health Organization focuses on this inequity. It points out, for example, that approximately 80% of investments in genomics in 2000 were made in the United States, and 80% of the DNA patents in genomics in the period 1980 through 1993 were held by US companies.[2] Of the 1233 new drugs marketed between 1975 and 1999, only 13 were approved specifically for tropical diseases.[2]

POTENTIAL FOR HEALTH IMPROVEMENT

In recent years the genomes of nearly 50 microbial pathogens have been sequenced, and ongoing efforts to sequence the genomes of mosquito vectors (e.g., *Anopheles gambiae,* the malaria vector, and *Aedes aegypti,* the main vector for dengue fever) promise benefits in the shorter term for the control of communicable diseases.[3] Fosmidomycin, originally developed for treatment of recurrent urinary infections, showed effective anti-malarial activity when genome sequence information from *Plasmodium falciparum* revealed a common biochemical target, present in the parasite and not in the human host[4]; the drug has gone into clinical trials in less than 2 years. Clinical trials have also begun in Africa of a preerythrocytic DNA-based vaccine that gave significant protection against natural *P falciparum* infection.[5]

Although the benefits of alleviation of infectious diseases are obvious, it is now believed that the information generated by genomics will, in the long term, also play a major role in the prevention, diagnosis, and management of many diseases which hitherto have been difficult or impossible to control, including cardiovascular disease, cancer, diabetes, the major psychoses, dementia, rheumatic disease, and asthma.[6] From a public health perspective, the genomics revolution may present new opportunities for the prevention of these diseases, but before these opportunities can be realized we will need to know more about what combination of genetic and environmental factors predispose people to such diseases.[7]

New approaches to population-based epidemiological studies, such as "genomic epidemiology" to chart the molecular, metabolic, and disease profiles of thousands of subjects, may be the path to the future. A new consortium has been formed to pursue this approach, which aims to scale the relevant technologies to sample sizes appropriate for epidemiological studies.[8] The initial focus will be on diabetes and cardiovascular disease, but the goal is to develop generic tools and protocols that can ultimately be applied to other diseases.

The recent announcement of the genome sequences of 2 varieties of rice, *indica* and *japonica*,[9,10] marks another milestone in the genomics revolution with tremendous potential implications for health. Three billion people, mainly in the developing world, depend on rice as their staple diet. The sequencing of the rice genome may pave the way for better strains of rice with enhanced yields, nutritional value, and disease resistance.

IMPLICATIONS AND CONCERNS

Aside from the complex scientific and technical problems of bringing genomics to the clinic, ensuring that its benefits will be reaped by developing countries will require attention to many equally challenging issues. Genomics brings with it complex new ethical, legal, social, and economic implications, as well as concerns about risks and hazards.[11] Issues of confidentiality, stigmatization, and misuse of genetic information are high on the list of concerns, particularly the potential for creating a genetic underclass that may be denied medical insurance as a result of genetic testing and screening. Genomics has also been associated with the prospect of "designer babies," and there is a concomitant concern about creating a genetically engineered overclass and a disease-prone underclass; the higher likelihood of the former being associated with richer people in the developed world is obvious.

Issues of intellectual property rights associated with DNA sequences[12] and the potential exploitation of developing-country populations by creating genetic databases, often at the behest of companies based in the developed world,[13] are other areas of concern. While industry believes that without strong and effective global intellectual property rules, the gap between developed and developing countries will only grow in the future, there are plenty of concerns about the patentability of DNA sequences and the applications derived from them, and what implications this will have for the developing countries.

Most important, the relatively rich product pipeline of genomics-based drugs will mean a tremendous increase in the demand for clinical trial sites, many of which will be in the developing countries; this area represents an ethical minefield relating to issues such as informed consent, standard of care,

and continuing availability of the drug being tested, the price of which is often beyond the reach of poor people.[14] Finally, in the aftermath of the tragedy that took place in the United States on September 11, 2001, the utilization of advances in genomics for acts of bioterrorism and biological warfare similarly occupy the minds of many.

INTEGRATION WITH RESEARCH AND PRACTICE

Despite the tremendous potential and promise of genomics, it is very difficult to predict when its benefits for health will be realized; there are so many critical things we do not yet know about how gene products interact. Many people were surprised to learn that we have only twice as many genes as a fly or a worm.[15] Hence it is vitally important for the developing countries to maintain focus on the basics of what can be done now, particularly in the fields of public health and the development of more functional health care systems.

The main message of the World Health Organization report[2] is that medical practice will not change overnight as a result of new technologies spawned by genomics, but the long-term possibilities are such that both developing and developed countries must prepare themselves for this new technology and carefully explore its possibilities, always looking at its cost-effectiveness compared with more standard approaches to medical care. It is also vital that genomics research not be pursued to the detriment of the well-established methods of clinical practice and clinical and epidemiological research. Indeed, for its full exploitation it will need to be integrated into clinical research involving patients and into epidemiological studies in the community. It is crucially important to maintain a balance in medical practice and research between genomics and these more conventional and well-tried approaches.

In addition, it is crucial to increase the quality of education in genetics and genomics at all levels of society. If this is not achieved it will be impossi-

ble to develop an informed debate about the various issues involved, and there is a danger that those who administer health services will be unable to distinguish between hyperbole and reality in a new, uncertain, and rapidly expanding research field.

STRATEGIES FOR EQUITABLE SHARING

What strategies and actions are needed in the future to ensure that the benefits of the genomics revolution are shared by the developing countries? Strong international leadership by the scientific community, international organizations, governments, and industry is required through promotion of innovative partnerships and cooperation strategies. A key issue in the postgenomics era will be who will pay to test, develop, and deliver important vaccines, drugs, and diagnostic procedures for diseases of the developing world, and who will ensure equitable access to those who need it most.

The "Millennium Challenge Account" to improve health in the developing world, discussed at the recent Monterrey summit on financing for development,[16] could be partly used for this purpose. Given the ethical concerns associated with many of the key issues and the significant commercial interest, a proposal has also been made for a Commission on Global Genomics Governance to make recommendations for genome-related issues and activities.[17] At a higher political level, the potential of genomics to generate economic and health benefits for developing countries should be highlighted to the world's leaders. Attention to these problems at the June 2002 meeting of the G8 (the world's wealthiest nations—Canada, France, Germany, Italy, Japan, the United Kingdom, and the United States—and Russia), which is to focus on Africa, would be a visionary move on the part of these countries.

Such a call for action acknowledges that while most of the incentives to develop new drugs and vaccines are primarily of interest to markets in the industrialized world, there are enormous opportunities to apply knowledge of the genome to diseases of the poorest people as well, and that we all have a responsibility to help make these opportunities into realities.

In particular, the medical profession in the developed countries has a vital role to play. Many of the important infectious killers are being encountered with increasing frequency in richer countries and, as the provision of basic health care improves, many poorer countries are making the epidemiological transition toward a pattern of disease similar to those of the developed countries. Globally, heart disease is now the most common cause of death. The globalization of disease is a message that must be clearly understood by medical schools, research funding bodies, industry, and governments of rich countries.

The development of effective and equitable research partnerships between developed and developing countries will not only help to combat the global inequity of health care, but will also be of enormous mutual benefit to both parties. As Donald Kennedy, editor-in-chief of *Science*, aptly and succinctly put it, "What can First World science do, not for the West, but for the Rest."[18]

About the Authors

Correspondence: Requests for reprints should be sent to Tikki Pang, Research Policy and Cooperation (RPC/EIP), World Health Organization, Ave Appia, CH-1211 Geneva 27, Switzerland (e-mail: pangt@who.int).

References

1. Singer P, Daar A. Harnessing genomics and biotechnology to improve global health equity. *Science.* 2001; 294:87–89.
2. *Genomics and World Health.* Report of the Advisory Committee on Health Research. Geneva, Switzerland: World Health Organization; 2002.
3. Hoffman SL, Subramanian GM, Collins FH, Venter JC. *Plasmodium,* human and *Anopheles* genomics and malaria. *Nature.* 2002; 415:702–709.
4. Jomaa H, Wiesner J, Sanderbrand S, et al. Inhibitors of the nonmevalonate pathway of isoprenoid biosynthesis as antimalarial drugs. *Science.* 1999; 285:1573–1576.
5. Bojang KA, Milligan PJ, Pinder M, et al. Efficacy of RTS, S/ASO2 malaria vaccine against *Plasmodium falciparum* infection in semi-immune adult men in The Gambia: a randomised trial. *Lancet.* 2001; 358:1927–1934.
6. Wright AF, van Heyningen V. Shortcut to disease genes. *Nature.* 2001; 414:705–706.
7. Steinberg K, Gwinn M, Khoury MJ. The role of genomics in public health and disease prevention. *JAMA.* 2001; 286:1635.
8. Butler D. Epidemiology set to get fast-track treatment. *Nature.* 2001; 414:139.
9. Yu J, Hu S, Wang J, et al. A draft sequence of the rice genome (*Oryza sativa* L. ssp. *indica*). *Science.* 2002; 296:79–92 .
10. Goff SA, Ricke D, Lan TH, et al. A draft sequence of the rice genome (*Oryza sativa* L. ssp. *japonica*). *Science.* 2002; 296:92–100.
11. Fukuyama F. *Our Posthuman Future: Consequences of the Biotechnology Revolution.* New York, NY: Farrar Strauss & Giroux; 2002.
12. Cook-Deegan RM, McCormack SJ. Intellectual property. Patents, secrecy and DNA. *Science.* 2001; 293:217.
13. Burton B. Proposed genetic database on Tongans opposed. *BMJ.* 2002; 324:443.
14. Killen J, Grady C, Folkers GK, Fauci AS. Ethics of clinical research in the developing world. *Nature Rev Immunol.* 2002; 2:210–215.
15. Lewis F. Science's latest discovery: how much we don't know. *International Herald Tribune.* April 3, 2002:6.
16. A feast of giving. *Economist.* March 23, 2002:73.
17. Loff B. Africans discuss ethics of biomedical research. *Lancet.* 2002; 359:956.
18. Kennedy D. Science and development. *Science.* 2001; 294:2053.

Latin American Social Medicine: The Quest for Social Justice and Public Health

| Nancy Krieger, PhD

INTRODUCTION

Social justice is the foundation of public health. This controversial assertion has been the guiding principle to some, and anathema to others, ever since the rise of the modern public health movement in the mid-19th century in Europe and the Americas.[1]

Translated to the realms of theory and action, the premise that societal arrangements of power and property powerfully shape the public's health has animated diverse efforts to develop cogent frameworks that explicitly identify determinants of—and can usefully guide efforts to rectify—social inequalities in health. Examples of such frameworks in the English-language literature appearing since the mid-20th century include "social medicine," "social production of disease," "political economy of health," and, most recently, "health and human rights," "population health," and "ecosocial theory."[2] A similar discourse generated by the social, academic, and political movement collectively known as Latin American social medicine[3,4] can be found in the Spanish- and Portuguese-language literature.

CONNECTING PROGRESSIVE PUBLIC HEALTH WITHIN THE AMERICAS

Until recently, these different strands of progressive public health thinking and practice in the Americas were barely intertwined. New connections, however, are starting to be made, spurred by growing awareness of the public health impacts of diverse regional economic and social policies.[1–5] Of particular concern are neoliberal economic policies, such as the North American Free Trade Agreement (NAFTA), which result in economic austerity plans, environmental degradation, and growing intra- and interregional social disparities in health.[5]

To encourage North–South dialogue within the Americas, for example, one recent initiative, based at the University of New Mexico and involving institutional partners in Argentina, Chile, Ecuador, and Brazil, is focused on increasing access to the Latin American social medicine literature via the Internet (see http://hsc.unm.edu/lasm). Its promise is to increase the flow of ideas not only from South to North but also across the South, by providing readily accessible structured abstracts for key works translated into English, Spanish, and Portuguese. Another example, reflected in the pages of this issue of the Journal, is the special session "Latin American Social Medicine: The Quest for Social Justice and Public Health—Linking History, Data, and Pedagogy" organized at the 2002 Annual Meeting of the American Public Health Association (APHA).

The idea for this session, organized by APHA's Spirit of 1848 Caucus, arose at the caucus's 2001 business meeting. The caucus, dedicated to addressing social inequalities in health, focuses on 3 issues: the politics of public health data, the social history of public health, and progressive pedagogy (see http://www.progressivehn.org). At this meeting, Tony Casas, from the Pan American Health Organization (PAHO), asked about the similarities and differences between US and Latin American progressive public health thinking and practice. In response, we organized a session for the following year to tackle this question, consonant with our goal of building ties between people—within and across countries—who are vitally concerned about issues of social justice and public health. We decided that the appropriate venue would be our first "integrative" session, a session deliberately designed to address one topic in relation to the 3 foci of our caucus. This important collaborative effort was made possible by 2 key organizations: PAHO and the Latin American Social Medicine Association (ALAMES). ALAMES helped us decide on and secure the participation of our Latin American speakers, and PAHO covered their travel costs.

LATIN AMERICAN SCHOLARS ON "COLLECTIVE HEALTH"

The issues raised in that session, and elaborated in the articles appearing in this issue of the Journal,[6–9] underscore the importance of making explicit connections between social justice and public health—historically, empirically, and pedagogically—and acting to strengthen those connections. Reviewing the origins of Latin American social medicine as a social, academic, and political movement, Débora Tajer, professor and research director of gender studies, Faculty of Psychology, University of Buenos Aires, and past president of ALAMES, describes the founding of ALAMES in 1984, premised on the defense of health as a public good and civil right.[6] To counter conventional, reductionist, and positivist public health frameworks and programs, ALAMES has developed an alternative focus on what the association terms "the social production of the health–illness–care process."

HISTORY

Beginning with an emphasis on the role of social class and the production/reproduction of class relations and inequality in relation to state policies, the ALAMES framework has expanded to include incorporating gender analysis and engaging with human rights movements. In practical terms, this has translated to an emphasis on building ties between academics and activists, with knowledge generation and transfer used as a tool for social change. Importantly, these ties are rooted in the recognition that collective action for collective health requires not only critical scientific expertise but also frank engagement with the politics of public health. This principled stance can entail considerable risk in times of repressive governments more committed to the defense of propertied interests than to public health.

DATA

Translating theory into a guide for research and intervention, Saul Franco Agudelo, a professor and researcher with the Department of Collective Health, National University of Colombia, presents a social-medical analysis of the violence in Colombia.[7] Defining violence as "a specific form of human interaction in which force produces harm or injury to others in order to achieve a given purpose," he emphasizes that violence is a process, has a historical nature, and must be analyzed in relation to "the specific combination of cultural, economic, social-political and legal conditions that make a phenomenon historically possible and rationally understandable." Analyzing the extraordinarily high rates of homicide in Colombia, he attributes these rates to "three structural conditions—inequality, impunity, and intolerance—and three transitional processes—illegal drug traffic, the internal armed conflict, and the introduction and development of a neoliberal model."

PEDAGOGY

Finally, underscoring that pedagogy for public health does not occur only in classrooms, Asa Cristina Laurell, secretary of health, Mexico City, and a professor at the Metropolitan University of Mexico City, describes the new Broadened Health Care Model now operative in Mexico City.[8] Drawing on the legacy of progressive Brazilian health reforms in the 1980s, which asserted health as a universal social right to be guaranteed by the state, this model serves not only as an important public health initiative but also as a critical civic lesson. The key values of the Broadened Health Care Model, which aims to decrease inequality between social groups and geographic areas, are the intrinsic and equal value of all persons; the obligation of government to honor and protect the life of all human beings; and the right to health as a social right and a responsibility of government as the guardian of collective interests.

At a time when the Mexican federal government was imposing an "austerity budget" that followed the neoliberal formula of slashing services to the most vulnerable sectors of the population, the enactment of this model resulted in an alternative "austerity program" that reduced the salaries of high officials and attacked corruption. These measures enabled the initiative to secure funds to provide free health services, prescription drugs, and a monthly pension to virtually all persons aged 70 years and older (there had previously been no social security program). In addition, more than 300 000 families (out of approximately 1 million) were enrolled into a new program offering free universal health services. Other accomplishments have included increasing public participation in health programs and improving transparency of government action in all 1352 administrative sectors of Mexico City, thereby challenging conventional notions of public institutions as incapable of offering appropriate services.

Seiji Yamada, clinical associate professor of family practice, University of Hawai'i, concludes this forum by reflecting on the relevance of Latin American social medicine to other regions of the world.[9] He focuses on the public health impact of early- to mid-20th-century Japanese imperialism and mid- to late-20th- and 21st-century US imperialism on the populations of diverse Asian countries.

INTEGRATION

As demonstrated by these contributions, the work of Latin American scholars on what they term "collective health" is highly relevant to public health researchers, teachers, practitioners, and advocates in the United States and elsewhere. For fruitful engagement to occur, especially within the Americas, it will be necessary to address more than simply language barriers. For example, important Canadian work advancing progressive thinking and practice about population health, readily available in English as well as French,[10] remains unfamiliar to many public health professionals in the United States. To counter the fragmentation that many of us face—within and between disciplines, within and between work on particular diseases or health problems, and within and between different organizations geared to specific issues or social groups—a different mindset is necessary. We need not start from scratch. As demonstrated by Latin American social medicine, we can build on the core social-justice principle of solidarity to make vital connections with others to develop our thoughts, strategize, and enhance joint efforts to eliminate social inequalities in health.

About the Authors.
Correspondence: Requests for reprints should be sent to Nancy Krieger, PhD, Department of Society, Human Development, and Health,

Harvard School of Public Health, 677 Huntington Ave, Boston, MA 02115 (e-mail: nkrieger@hsph.harvard.edu).

Acknowledgments

Thanks to Luis Avilés (representing the Spirit of 1848 history subcommittee) and Babette Nueberger (representing the Spirit of 1848 progressive pedagogy subcommittee), who, along with Nancy Krieger (representing the Spirit of 1848 politics of public health data subcommittee), organized the Spirit of 1848 session "Latin American Social Medicine: The Question for Social Justice and Public Health—Linking History, Data, and Pedagogy" at the 130th Annual Meeting of the American Public Health Association, Philadelphia, Pa, November 9–13, 2002. Thanks also to PAHO and ALAMES for their generous support of the session, to the rest of the Spirit of 1848 Coordinating Committee (especially Anne-Emanuelle Birn) for their helpful comments, and to the following APHA groups for their cosponsorship of the session: the International Health, Medical Care, Public Health Education and Health Promotion, and School Health Education and Services sections; the Alternative and Complementary Health Practices special interest group; and the Asian Pacific Islander Caucus, the Health Equity and Public Hospitals Caucus, the Latino Caucus, the Socialist Caucus, the Women's Caucus, and the Vietnam Caucus.

References

1. Krieger N, Birn AE. A vision of social justice as the foundation of public health: commemorating 150 years of the spirit of 1848. *Am J Public Health.* 1998; 88:1603–1606.
2. Krieger N. Theories for social epidemiology in the 21st century: an ecosocial perspective. *Int J Epidemiol.* 2001; 30:668–677.
3. Franco S, Nunes E, Breilh J, Laurell A. *Debates en Medicina Social* [Debates in Social Medicine]. Quito, Ecuador: Pan American Health Organization and Latin American Association of Social Medicine; 1991.
4. Waitzkin H, Iriart C, Estrada A, Lamadrid S. Social medicine then and now: lessons from Latin America. *Am J Public Health.* 2001; 91:1592–1601.
5. Número especial sobre factores determinantes de la iniquidad en salud [Special issue on determinants of inequity in health]. *Rev Panam Salud Publica.* 2002; 11 (special issue): 291–490.
6. Tajer D. Latin American Social Medicine: Roots, Development During the 1990s, and Current Challenges. *Am J Public Health.* 2003; 93:2016–2020.
7. Franco S. A social-medical approach to Colombian violence. *Am J Public Health.* 2003; 93:2025–2029.
8. Laurell AC. What does Latin American Social Medicine do when it governs? *Am J Public Health.* 2003; 93:2021–2024.
9. Yamada S. Remarks on Latin American Social Medicine. *Am J Public Health.* 2003; 93:1994–1996.
10. Health Canada [Santé Canada]. Population health approach. Available at: http://www.hc-sc.gc.ca/hppb/phdd. Accessed February 2, 2003.

Latin American Social Medicine: Roots, Development During the 1990s, and Current Challenges

| Débora Tajer, PhD

ABSTRACT

Latin American social medicine arose during the 1950s and 1960s, drawing its inspiration from the social movements that emerged in France, Germany, and England in the mid-19th century.

The Latin American movement of social medicine has clear ideological goals. It is organized around the Latin American Association of Social Medicine, which was founded in 1984 and is regarded as a social, political, and academic movement. This article takes a historical perspective and presents the reasons for the emergence and identity of the association, focusing on the main developments and contributions of this movement from the 1990s until the present time.

INTRODUCTION

The source of inspiration for Latin American social medicine (LASM) is the social movements that occurred in France, Germany, and England during the mid-19th century[1] and the development of European social medicine, together with political processes whose main representative was Rudolf Virchow. LASM originated in the reformulation of medical training that took place in Latin America during the 1950s[2] and differs from traditional disciplines of hygiene, public health, and preventive medicine.[3,4] The turning point took place in the late 1960s, when the ideology underlying the preventive model then in vogue in Latin America became explicit and the possibility of constructing a social theory

in medicine arose.[1] Thus began a new and distinctive methodological tradition in the field: the critical and ideological analysis of what is usually presented as purely technical knowledge.[5]

This perspective, which appeared in the context of formalizing the contents of social sciences in health courses as part of undergraduate medical training, later advanced toward specific graduate programs in social medicine in different countries. The forerunners were the masters program in social medicine of the Autonomous Metropolitan University of Mexico in 1975 and the social medicine program of the State University of Rio de Janeiro in 1976, both supported by the Pan-American Health Organization.[3]

Although LASM is basically considered as a stream of thought and knowledge, it has strong roots in a political practice, carried out by a social actor of heterogeneous characteristics, known as the LASM movement. The link between theory and practice makes LASM an approach with explicit ideological objectives[6] that has undergone important changes throughout its nearly 40 years.

The complexity of the LASM movement may be defined when we identify its roots. They include:

- A conceptual framework within the field of public health called *social medicine* or, in Brazil, *collective health* that highlights the economic, political, subjective, and social determinants of the health-disease-care process of human collectivities.

- A political dimension represented by the attempts at political change and social transformation in Latin America, started in the 1950s, that valued the improvement of health status and equitable access to health services as essential pillars of the liberation of the people.

- An organizational modality originating in the social medicine seminars organized by the Argentine public health practitioner Juan Cesar García from the Pan-American Health Organization at the end of the 1970s and beginning of the 1980s. During the third seminar in 1984, the Latin American Social Medicine Association (ALAMES) was created.

- A view of the concept of subjectivity that is theoretically and practically based on the Marxist tradition that considers the subject as historically conditioned and at the same time a maker of history, and that values political practice as a promoter of solidary subjectivities.

ALAMES AS AN ORGANIZATION

ALAMES began in 1984 with a group of pioneers from Mexico, Ecuador, and Brazil and editorial committees of specialized journals.[7] ALAMES does not encompass the total diversity of the movement, but since its origin it has remained a leader in the region because of its role in generating, harmonizing, and promoting the production of national groups and processes.

After 19 years of work, ALAMES has become a powerful collectivity, defining itself as a social, political, and academic movement aimed at guiding public health and social medicine toward resolution of the historical and social determinants of the health-disease-care process. ALAMES is present in all countries of the American continent.

The Latin American region is very diverse, and so are the different national groups and dynamics. National ALAMES groups may be formed around graduate institutions of collective health (Brazil), medical unions (Chile-Uruguay), pro-health peasant movements (Paraguay), public health schools or masters programs in social medicine (Costa Rica, Mexico, Peru), national health movements (Colombia), self-organized groups (Argentina), groups of research-action (Ecuador), or others.

In spite of the diversity of both the region and the movement, the idea of the movement is preserved by a regional vision highlighting the coexistence of a practice that articulates social, academic, and political aspects. Such coexistence has provided a huge potential but at the same time implies countless contradictions and challenges.

ORIGINS AND MAIN CURRENT ISSUES

It is important to understand that many of the members of the LASM movement come from and belong to an academic environment[9] and consider that the generation and transmission of knowledge is a tool for change. Basic investigations—as well as the promotion of evidence-based advocacy—are promoted and undertaken according to this same theoretical framework, with the goal of contributing to the design and implementation of evidence-based counter-hegemonic public policies.[10–16]

To understand the specificity of this movement, one must understand that in Latin America the difference between the classic approach to public health and the social medicine paradigm is evidenced by:

1 LASM's definition of populations as objects of study, not conceived as a sum of individuals but rather as collectivities.[15–17]
2 Studies of health institutions aimed at understanding their logic and their capacity to reproduce relations of dominance, and at developing alternative proposals.[18,19]
3 The consideration of the dialectic relation between being healthy, being sick, and health care practices, not as unrelated situations but as a historical process described as the health-disease-care process.[20,21]
4 The introduction of sociohistorical structures as determinants of the process of the health-disease-care process of individuals and collectivites.[22,23]
5 The articulation between theory and political practice known as *praxis*[24] that defines theory as both describing reality and inspiring social change.
6 The methodological development of "differing historical, quantitative, and qualitative approaches aimed at avoiding the perceived limitations of positivism and reductionism in traditional public health and clinical methods."[8,25–27]

The clear link between politics and science, which defines the LASM movement, finds its roots in the social origin of university students, which was affected by the proliferation of free public universities in the region, and the marked political involvement of students that began during the 1960s. After graduation, this led many health care professionals to choose a professional practice that was related to the processes of political change in Latin America. Such radicalization has promoted theoretical and technical developments that resulted in the scientific sector's contributions to social changes as a daily expression of the relation between science and power.[28] The consequences included important advances and achievements but also led to the death, disappearance, and exile of many key representatives of the LASM movement.

The conceptual matrix of LASM may be found in the incorporation of social sciences into the fields of collective health, in the beginnings of dialectic materialism, and, in the 1980s and later, to several developments of the European social sciences such as those by Althusser, Bourdieu, Foucault, Giddens, Gramsci, Habermas, Heller, Laclau, and Rorty.

A field in which LASM has been a pioneer is workers' health, with major methodological contributions to incorporating the concept of social class and the process of production and social reproduction in health research.[20,29,30] The second major field includes the effect of social policies on health and health care, a redefinition of the state as a heterogeneous arena,[18] public policies in health,[31] and the effects of international relations, mainly between central and peripheral countries, as determinants of the health conditions in the latter.[22,32] In the 1980s, the main issue was the impact of economic crisis, unemployment, and inflation on the increase in poverty and worsening of health conditions in the region, as well as the process of transition toward democracy.[33] Related issues included the impact of the violence and trauma that prior authoritarian dictatorships[34] and democracies[35] inflicted on the population's health.

In addition to issues raised by specific historical events, this movement has made specific and original contributions to international collective health[6]: developments in the area of social epidemiology,[29,30] policies and practices in health,[31,36] strategic planning in health,[18,37] epistemology and methodology,[17,25–27] and the incorporation of the subjective dimension into the field of collective health.[38,39] The incorporation of the subjective dimension addressed the effects of political violence at a psychological level, and incorporated Bourdieu's[40] concept of *habitus* to understand the social and historical determinants of subjective action. The subjective dimension also addressed the contributions of psychoanalysis with its critique of the health-disease model, the body-mind relation conceived by positivism, and the inclusion of the impact of the unconscious dimension in the health-disease-care process.

LASM IN THE 1990s

During the 1990s, scientific theory and research in the LASM movement grew, and in several countries, graduate programs in social medicine and collective health were consolidated. The graduate programs contributed many systematic studies of several population health issues approached from the perspective of social medicine. One should understand that the development of graduate programs has been very uneven in the region, and the creation of new programs remains one of the current priorities for several countries.[41] Brazil is the most advanced country in terms of graduate programs, and Brazil and Mexico have the greatest state support for these activities. Other countries that have a long history in this field but lack higher academic training in the field include Argentina, Chile, Ecuador, and Uruguay. The recent creation of doctoral programs in Mexico and Colombia must be celebrated.

Understandably, the lack of higher-level graduate programs in some countries of the Southern Cone (Argentina, Chile, and Uruguay), which at the same time have greatly developed social medicine, can be partly attributed to the dictatorships that devastated these countries during the 1970s and 1980s. Military interventions led to the persecution, disappearance, and death of teachers and students at the universities, thus creating a wide gap, which still remains, that slowed down the evolution of social medicine programs during the 1990s.

Also, this same period was characterized by the implementation of World Bank–recommended health system reform, which from its onset led to rigorous criticism by LASM workers and theoreticians.[36] Such neoliberal reform was implemented in the region on the basis of proposals of the World Bank, which, valuing efficiency and efficacy at the cost of equity, promoted the implementation of macroeconomic adjustment policies and reform of the public sector to enable such policies. In the health sector, measures implemented at a regional level included the extinction of policies oriented toward the values of universality and integrality by applying focused programs and creating a basic package of services as the only health care service guaranteed by the public sector to the whole population.[6,32] Another measure was the decentralization of national systems and services toward provincial or municipal areas.

Decentralization led to an increase in fragmentation of many health care systems, as well as an increase in quality differences because of the large economic disparities that exist between the provinces and municipalities in the regions characterized as having the greatest inequality in the world between rich and poor. This is described in a recent report by the Pan-American Health Organization,[42] which states that poverty in the Americas may be basically attributed to a poor income distribution, not to absolute poverty of the countries, as is the case of the countries of the Sub-Saharan Africa or some Asian countries where there is truly very little to distribute. If the distribution of wealth would be similar to that of European countries or the United States, our poverty level would only be a fourth of the one we currently have.[43]

The word "reform" encompasses different, sometimes opposing concepts. As an example, the Italian health care reform movement created a nationwide health system that tended toward equity, as did the Brazilian. Neoliberal reforms decentralize health care delivery but not real power or budgetary resources, as progressive reform did. They weaken the role of the state, short funds to emphasize the private sector, and tend toward social inequity.

More than a decade after the implementation of neoliberal health system reform, the general consensus (and not just voices from critical sectors)[36] is that this reform has not only failed to solve the problems that it aimed to solve, but has also created new ones: loss of leadership at the ministries of health; loss of financing of social security programs because of the decline in formal employment and the presence of corruption in management; and an increase in health care inequality and fragmentation.[44,45] One should note that during that decade when the public health care sector was being criticized for its inefficiency and lack of coverage, it continued to play—and even increased—its role as backup for the loss of coverage by the private sector and social security systems.[32]

One of the promises of neoliberal health system reform was to allow freedom of choice for users of the social security system by allowing the transfer of salary-linked health care contributions from the social security system to private health insurance companies.[46] What actually happened was a concentration of the market by the insurance companies and a setback in terms of the right to health care. Instead of improvements in the health care system, the result was the introduction of market logic into the whole system.[10]

Demystification of the processes of neoliberal health system reform has been one of the central pillars of the academic work of the LASM movement during this decade and has also been part of its social and political practice, as part of the agenda for the defense of health as citizen's right and a duty of the state.[32,36,44,45] Simultaneously, the LASM movement has expanded its areas of action to a wider span of issues that must be addressed for full implementation of citizens' right to health care[10–14]: violence,[35] gender,[47–49] human resources,[50] public policy,[31,36] decentralization,[51,52] health system reform,[44,45] globalization, epidemiology,[53] environment,[54] equity,[10] bioethics,[11] social participation,[13] ethnicity, multiculturalism, and human rights.[55,56]

Examples of the specific mode in which the LASM movement works in these areas are given in this issue in the commentaries by Saul Franco on violence and Cristina Laurell on the implementation of public policies. One good example related to gender, the field in which I work, is Angeles Garduño's thesis in progress (Metropolitan University of Mexico), a compilation of the ways in which LASM movement groups have focused on how the gender-based work conditions affect workers health. Another is the publication of 2 regional public forums co-organized by ALAMES on how to include gender perspectives in progressive public health policies. The forums were held in Rio de Janeiro, Brazil, in 1999[48] and San Jose de Costa Rica in 2002.[55]

This extensive agenda shows that in addition to its own subjects and methodology, the LASM movement represents a multidisciplinary ethical and ideological approach to health problems at the individual and collective level. This approach considers that health goes beyond health care per se[12] and is in a wider sense linked to quality of life and justice.

This approach has led to several internal changes in the LASM movement. From a group of physicians interested in "the poor," it has evolved to a group of health care workers from all disciplines, involved in health problems from a wider perspective as citizens. From an ideological vision of processes but using the classic methodology of public health, it has evolved to the creation of its own methodological models, which are tools to study an object that has been redefined.[6]

In the political arena, one of the lines of implementation of neoliberal health system reform in the region has been the decentralization of health management through the municipalization of services and actions in health. This opened an interesting scenario for the praxis of the LASM movement during the 1990s, because after the election of progressive local governments during this decade, several leaders of the LASM movement entered the political arena as municipal secretaries of health.

Realizing they could not achieve their whole program, they stuck to the areas under their control. This led to a change in the way state health policies

were conceived, as well as a change in the role of the LASM movement. Until then, the LASM movement's role consisted mainly of criticizing the state for reproducing conditions of dominance, and health management could only be imagined through a revolutionary process or radical change. In the 1990s, the political approach of many members of the LASM movement, then in power, might well have been considered not revolutionary enough, by the same actors in the past.

The coexistence of these 2 processes, decentralization and a change in how the political approach was viewed, caused a very characteristic praxis of this period, which was to engage government in the full local management of health, from the standpoint of training and research as well as direct political practice.

Brazilian health reform followed this trend and became a very important inspiration for the LASM movement. The Brazilian reform was undertaken during the 1980s in the spirit of the Italian health reform of the 1960s and 1970s, which—unlike World Bank–dictated reform—considered decentralization as a way of eliminating concentration of power. In both Italy and Brazil, this approach effectively promoted popular participation and the social control of health management, aiming at strengthening the public sector as a guarantor of citizens' rights.[58,59]

Guidance from Brazil was very inspiring and promoted political creativity among LASM movement members in other countries of the region. This is because decentralization processes in most other countries were implemented as part of the neoliberal reform process, to detach the state from its commitments in the area of health.

One should note that in contrast to the hegemonic neoliberal trend of the World Bank-promoted reform that encourages this kind of decentralization, many of these local health managers are genuinely interested in transforming the local health arena into a larger arena for implementing citizens' rights and in building up the public sector. Going against the neoliberal

thought that prevails in most countries at the national level, these managers took a chance on progressive reform.

Many of these managers belong to either counterhegemonic or progressive parties, such as Brazil's Workers Party; Mexico's Democratic Revolution Party; Argentina's Front for National Solidarity, Affirmative Movement for an Egalitarian Republic, and Popular Socialist Party; and Uruguay's Frente Amplio, which have had local victories. Many members of the LASM movement participate in these victories as managers, teachers, evaluators, and advisors. One example of key representatives of the LASM movement who now occupy management positions is Cristina Laurell, current municipal secretary of health of the Federal District of Mexico, whose commentary is published in this issue. Another is Maria Urbaneja, who is minister of health of Venezuela, formerly secretary of health of the Municipality of Caracas. The latter, drawing from her experience at the local level, now faces the challenge of implementing a new concept of the role of a national health manager who is committed to the public arena from a regulationist perspective and who guarantees citizens' rights, but without the centralizing perspective that the LASM movement promoted decades ago.

In this review of the political action of the LASM movement during the 1990s, I stress the movement's harmony with other social movements during that period and their emerging stress on political action in the joint fight against globalization. Many members of the LASM movement also belong to other movements; they include movements for the rights of young people, women, landless people (sin tierra), peasants, and indigenous people, and sexual rights and human rights. ALAMES has participated in the Social World Forum of Porto Alegre on 3 occasions and organized 2 international health forums during the 2 days before the forums.

CONCLUSION

Since its beginning, the LASM movement has been characterized by having established a critical framework and a proposal to change the classic form of public health in Latin America by transforming it into a tool for change and social justice. During the 1990s, the LASM movement offered alternative proposals for knowledge generation as well as political practice to the neoliberal model, through a new progressive way of working in health and by continuing to create an agenda that would not mimic the existing international cooperation organizations. Hence, the LASM movement is in an excellent position to offer theoretical and practical elements to colleagues from other regions of the world who are interested in building a public health practice that helps guarantee health as a right and a public good for all people.

Acknowledgments

This article was presented at the panel Latin American Social Medicine and the Quest for Social Justice and Public Health: Linking History, Data, and Pedagogy, 130th annual meeting of the American Public Health Association, November 9 to 13, 2002, Philadelphia, Pa. The meeting was organized by the Spirit of 1848 Caucus of the American Public Health Association and sponsored by the Pan-American Health Organization and ALAMES.

Thanks to Saul Franco and Jose Carlos Escudero for their helpful comments, to Juan Antonio Casas for his support to attend the American Public Health Organization's 2002 meeting, and to Ariel Zaltsman, Vivian Peisojovich, and Gabriela Hescht for the translation.

About the Authors

The author is with the Department of Psychology, University of Buenos Aires, Argentina and is a former president of ALAMES.

Correspondence: Requests for reprints should be sent to Débora Tajer, Av. Chenaut 1837 11°A (1426) Buenos Aires, Argentina (e-mail: dtajer@psi.uba.ar; deborat1@fibertel.com.ar).

References

1. Paim J. Medicina preventiva e social no Brasil: modelos, crises, perspectivas [Social and preventive medicine in Brazil: models, crisis, perspectives]. *Saúde em debate.*1981;11:57–59.

2. García JC. Entrevista Juan C García [Interview with Juan C García]. In: Nunes E, ed. *Ciencias Sociales y Salud en América Latina: Tendencias y Perspectivas [Social Sciences and Health in Latin America: Trends and Perspectives].* Montevideo, Uruguay: Pan-American Health Organization/CIESU; 1986:21–29.

3. Duarte E. Trayectoria de la medicina social en América Latina: elementos para su configuración [Trajectory of social medicine in Latin America: configuration elements]. In: Franco S, Nunes E, Breilh J, Laurell C, eds. *Debates en Medicina Social [Debates on Social Medicine].* 1st ed. Quito, Ecuador: Pan-American Health Organization–Asociación Latinoamericana de Medicina Social; 1991:17–137.

4. Arouca SO. *Dilema Preventivista: Contribuçao Para a Compreensao e Crítica da Medicina Preventiva [The Preventivist Dilemma: a Contribution to an Understanding and a Critique of Preventive Medicine]* [doctoral thesis]. Campinas, Brazil: Universidade de Campinas; 1975.

5. Testa M. *Pensar en Salud [Thinking on Health].* 1st ed. Buenos Aires, Argentina: Lugar; 1993.

6. Paim JS, Almeida NF. *A Crise da Saúde Pública e a Utopia da Saúde Colectiva. [Public Health Crisis and the Utopia of Collective Health].* 1st ed. Bahia, Brazil: Instituto de Saude Colectiva–Universidade Federal da Bahia; 2000.

7. Franco S, Nunes E, Breilh J, Laurell C, eds. *Debates en Medicina Social [Debates on Social Medicine].* 1st ed. Quito, Ecuador: Pan American Health Organization–Asociación Latinoamericana de Medicina Social; 1991.

8. Waitzkin H, Iriart C, Estrada A, Lamadrid S. Social medicine in Latin America: productivity and dangers facing the major national groups. *Lancet.*2001;358:315.

9. Waitzkin H, Iriart C, Estrada A, Lamadrid S. Social medicine then and now: lessons from Latin America. *Am J Public Health.*2001;91:1592–1601.

10. Plataforma Interamericana de Derechos Humanos. ¿Equidad? El Problema de la Equidad Financiera en Salud [Equity? Financial Equity Issue in Health]. Bogotá, Colombia: Antropos; 2001.

11. Mercado Martínez FJ, Robles Silva L, eds. *La medicina al final del milenio. Realidades y proyectos en la sociedad occidental [Medicine at the end of the century. Reality and projects in western society].* Guadalajara, Mexico: Universidad de Guadalajara and ALAMES; 1995.

12. Equity in Health Across the World: Neoliberalism or Welfare Policies? Proceedings of the 10th Conference of the International Association of Health Policy, Perugia, Italy, September 23–26, 1998. Perugia, Italy: International Association of Health Policy 1999.

13. ALAMES-IAHP Memorias de un encuentro. Globalización, Reformas y equidad en salud. Construyendo una agenda politca en defensa de la salud. [Memories of an encounter. Globlalization, Reform and Health Equity. Building a political agenda on health defense][CD-ROM]. 8th Latin American Social Medicine Congress and 11th Conference of the International Association of Health Policy. July 3–7, 2000; Havana, Cuba, 2000.

14. Sanchez Bayle M, Colomo C, Repeto I. Globalizacion y Salud [Globalization and Health]. Federacion de Asociaciones para la defensa de la Sanidad Publica. Madrid, Spain: In press.

15. Almeida Filho N. *Epidemiología sin Números [Epidemiology Without Numbers].* 1st ed. Buenos Aires, Argentina: Pan American Health Organization; 1992.

16. Laurell AC. El estudio social del proceso salud-enfermedad en América Latina [A social study of the health-disease process in Latin America]. *Cuadernos Médicos Sociales.*1985;37:43–48.

17. Breilh J, Granda E, eds. Investigación de salud en la sociedad [Health research in society]. Quito, Ecuador: Centro de Estudios y Asesorías en Salud; 1982.

18. Testa M. *Pensamiento Estratégico y Lógica de la Programación [Strategical Thinking and Programation Logic].* Buenos Aires, Argentina: Pan-American Health Organization; 1989.

19. De Sousa Campos GW, ed. *Reforma da Reforma. Repensando a Saúde [Reforming the Reform. Rethinking*

Health]. 2nd ed. Sao Paolo, Brazil: Huicitec; 1992.

20. Menendez E, Di Pardo R. El concepto de clase social en la investigación de la problematica de salud enfermedad [Social class in the health-disease process research]. *Revista Casa Chata.*1986;1:53–62.

21. Bloch C, Belmartino S, Troncoso M, Torrado S, Quintero Z, eds. El proceso de salud enfermedad en el primer año de vida [Health-disease process in the first year of life]. Rosario, Argentina: Centro de Estudios y Asesorías en Salud; 1984.

22. Navarro V, ed. *Salud e Imperialismo [Health and Imperialism]*. Mexico City, Mexico: Siglo XXI; 1983.

23. Escudero JC, Lopez S. La construcción de una hegemonía: el Banco Mundial en la salud Argentina [The building of an hegemony: the World Bank in Argentinian health issues]. *Salud Problema Debate.*1998;20:8–22.

24. Aricó J, ed. *La cola del diablo. Itinerario de Gramsci en America Latina [The Devil's tail. Gramsci's itinerary in Latin America]*. 1st ed. Buenos Aires, Argentina: Punto Sur; 1988.

25. Samaja J. *Epistemología y metodología [Epistemology and Methodology]*. 1st ed. Buenos Aires, Argentina: Universidad de Buenos Aires; 1994.

26. Breilh J. Nuevos conceptos y técnicas de investigación [New concepts and research techniques]. 3rd ed. Quito, Ecuador: Centro de Estudios y Asesorías en Salud; 1995.

27. De Souza Minayo MC, ed. *El desafío del conocimiento. Investigación cualitativa en salud [Knowledge's challenge. Qualitative research in health]*. 1st ed. Buenos Aires, Argentina: Lugar; 1997.

28. Varsavsky O, ed. *Ciencia, Política y Cientificismo [Science, Politics and Cientificism]*. 6th ed. Buenos Aires, Argentina: Centro Editor de América Latina; 1975.

29. Laurell AC. *Tendencias Actuales en Epidemiologia Social [Present Trends in Social Epidemiology]* [dissertation]. Cordoba, Argentina: Escuela de Salud Pública, Universidad Nacional de Córdoba. Presented at the 3rd Panamerican Congress of Epidemiology, Cordoba, Argentina; 1993.

30. Castellanos PL. O ecologico na epidemiologia [An ecological approach in epidemiology]. In: Almeida N, Barreto ML, Veras RP, Barata RB, eds. *Teoria Epidemiológica Hoje: Fundamentos, Interfaces e Tendência [Epidemiology Theory Today: Bases, Interfaces and Trends]*. 1st ed. Rio de Janeirio, Brazil: Fiocruz- Asociación Brasilera de Salud Colectiva; 1998:129–148.

31. Fleury S. *Estado sem Cidadãos [State Without Citizens]*. 1st ed. Rio de Janeiro, Brazil: Fiocruz; 1994.

32. Escudero JC. The Health Crisis in Argentina. *Int J Health Serv.* 2003 33(1):129–136.

33. ALAMES. *Proceedings of the 2nd Latin American Social Medicine Workshop.* Caracas, Venezuela: Venezuela Ediciones del Rectorado; 1991.

34. Lira E, ed. *Psicología y Violencia Política en América Latina [Psychology and Political Violence in Latin America]*. 1st ed. Santiago, Chile: Instituto Latinoamericano de Salud Mental y Derechos Humanos; 1994.

35. Franco S. *El Quinto: No Matar. Contextos Explicativos de la Violencia en Colombia [The Fifth: Don't Murder. Explanation of the Context of Violence in Colombia]*. 1st ed. Bogota, Colombia: Tercer Mundo; 1999.

36. Laurell AC, ed. *Estado y Politicas Sociales en el Neoliberalismo [State and Social Policies in Neo-Liberalism]*. 1st ed. Mexico City, Mexico: Fundacion Ebert; 1992.

37. Matus C. *Adeus Senhor Presidente [Good bye Mr. President]*. Recife, Brazil: Litteris; 1989.

38. Saidón O, Troianovski P, eds. *Políticas en Salud Mental [Policies in Mental Health]*. Buenos Aires, Argentina: Lugar; 1994.

39. Menendez E. *Cura y Control. La Apropiación de lo Social por la Práctica Psiquiátrica [Healing and Control. Psychiatric Practice and the Appropriation of the Social by Psychiatric Practice.* Mexico City, Mexico: Nueva Imagen; 1979.

40. Bourdieu P. *La Distinción. Criterio y Bases Sociales del Gusto [Distinction. Criteria and Social Bases of Taste]*. Madrid, Spain: Taurus; 1991.

41. *1st Pan American Conference on Education in Public Health. XVI ALAE-SP Conference, Final Report.* Rio de Janeiro, Brazil: Fiocruz; 1994.

42. *Equity and Health. Views from the Pan American Sanitary Bureau.* Washington, DC: Pan American Health Organization Occasional Publications; 2001.

43. Casas JA. La equidad como eje de la políticas públicas en salud [Equity as an axis of public policies in health]. In: Castillo A, ed. *Políticas Públicas y Equidad de Género en Salud: Desafíos para Centroamérica y Caribe [Public Policies and Gender Equity in Health: Challenges for Central America and Caribbean]*. San Jose, Costa Rica: Universidad de Costa Rica. In press.

44. Arroyo J. *Salud: La Reforma Silenciosa [Health: The Silent Reform]*. 1st ed. Lima, Peru: Universidad Peruana Cayetano Heredia; 2000.

45. Tavares L. *Ajuste Neoliberal e Desajuste Social na America Latina [Neoliberal Adjustment and Social Desadjustment in Latin America]*. 1st ed. Rio de Janeiro, Brazil: State University of Rio de Janeiro; 1999.

46. Mussot ML, ed. *Alternativas de Reforma de la Seguridad Social [Alternative Reforms of Social Security]*. 1st ed. Mexico City, Mexico: Metropolitan University of Mexico; 1996.

47. Tajer D, Ynoub R, Huggins M, eds. *Oficina de Género y Salud Colectiva [Gender and Collective Health Workshop]*. 1st ed. Buenos Aires, Argentina: Asociación Latinoamericana de Medicina Social–/International Development Research Center–Canada; 1997.

48. Costa AM, Merchán-Hamman E, Tajer D, eds. *Saúde, Eqüidade e Gênero. Um Desafio para as Políticas Públicas [Health, Equity and Gender. A challenge for Public Policies]*. 1st ed. Brasilia, Brazil: Ed Universidad Nacional de Brasilia /Asociación Brasilera de Salud Colectiva /Asociación Latinoamericana de Medicina Social; 2000.

49. Sarduy Sánchez C, Alfonso A, eds. *Género: Salud y Cotidianeidad. Temas de Actualidad en el Contexto Cubano [Gender: Health and Daily life. Current Events Themes Within the Cuban Context]*. Havana, Cuba: Científico Técnica; 2000.

50. Calderon R, Mendoza J. *Oficina de Recursos Humanos en Salud [Human Resources in Health Workshop].* 1st ed. Buenos Aires, Argentina: ALAMES–IDRC; 1997.

51. Borgia F, Brykman D. *Oficina de Gestión Local en Salud [Local Health Management workshop]*. 1st ed. Buenos Aires, Argentina:ALAMES–IDRC; 1997.

52. Luz M., Pinheiro R. Borgia F, eds. Descentralización y Nuevas Formas de Gestión Social [Decentralization and New Ways of Social Management]. Rio de Janeiro, Brazil: State University of Rio de Janeiro–Asociación

Latinoamericana de Medicina Social. In press.

53. Barata R, Barreto M, Almeida Filho, Peixoto R, eds. *Serie Epidemiologica 1-2-3-4 [Epidemilogical Series 1-2-3-4]*. 1st ed. Rio de Janeiro, Brazil: Fiocruz; 1997.

54. Escudero JC. The logic of the biosphere, theologic of capitalism: nutrition in Latin America.. *Review XIV Fernand Braudel Center.*1991;14:1–25.

55. Plataforma Colombiana de Derechos Humanos. Documento N° 5 para avivar la reflexión en torno al Congreso Nacional por la salud [Document Number 5 to revitalize the deliberation around the National Health Congress]. In: Torres M, ed. *Derecho a la Salud: Motor de Movilización Social [Right to Health: Social Mobilization Engine]*. Bogotá, Colombia; 2001.

56. Currea Lugo V, Hernández M, Paredes N. *La Salud Está Grave. Una Visión Desde los Derechos Humanos [Health is in Bad Shape. A Vision From the Human Rights Standpoint]*. Bogota, Colombia: Instituto Latinamerica de Servicio Legales Alternativos; 2000.

57. Castillo A, ed. *Políticas Públicas y Equidad de Género en Salud: Desafíos Para Centroamérica y Caribe [Public Policies and Gender Equity in Health: Challenges for Central America and Caribbean]*. San Jose, Costa Rica: Universidad de Costa Rica. In press.

58. Monteiro de Andrade LO. *SUS Passo a Passo. Normas, Gestão e Financiamento [SUS Step by Step. Regulations, Management and Financing]*. São Paulo-Sobral, Brazil: Huicitec-Universidade Estadual Vale do Acaraú; 2001.

59. Boletín Red Américas. *Publicación Semestral de la Red de Secretarios Municipales de Salud de las Americas [Red Americas Bulletin. Semiannual Publication of the Municipal Health Secretaries of the Americas]*. 2002;1(1). Available at: http://www.conasems .com.br/saudeamericas. Accessed March 2002.

Global Health and National Governance

| *Daniel Tarantola, MD, International Associate Editor*

The term *global* as applied to human development emerged in the 1960s at the time of the green revolution, when the World Bank advocated the need to "think globally, act locally." The terms *global, international,* and *intergovernmental* have different roots and translate differently in policy; institutional functions; and level of analysis, action, and accountability. They are not mutually exclusive. While the term *international* has framed much of the work in health across countries over the past decades, the term *global* has become more politically viable in that it elevates the vision of health to the whole planet, moving beyond geopolitical boundaries and including not only governments but nongovernmental stakeholders and actors.

The World Health Organization (WHO), created shortly after World War II as a specialized, intergovernmental agency, is intended to lead and coordinate the health actions of governments worldwide. The work of WHO is facilitated when consensus is reached among countries on global priorities, as was the case for malaria and smallpox eradication in the 1960s, primary health care and immunization in the 1970s, and the Global Program on HIV/AIDS in the 1980s. It is hampered when a few influential countries disagree with the majority, as illustrated by current controversies surrounding access to essential medicines in developing countries. Differing emphases on equitable access to life-saving products versus protection of the global pharmaceutical market impede consensus on the interpretation of the agreement on Trade-Related Intellectual Property Rights. WHO's work is also hampered when controversy is fueled by cultural and religious differences, as in the area of reproductive health.

Today, health is heralded as both a source and a product of economic development that necessitates the coalition of governmental and nongovernmental actors. Accordingly, an impressive and growing number of global health initiatives intended to move beyond the confines of intergovernmental efforts have been launched over the last decade. To cite only some, the Global Alliance for Vaccines and Immunization; the Global Tuberculosis Partnership; and the Global Fund on HIV/AIDS, Tuberculosis and Malaria all represent coalitions of a range of concerned actors. These global ventures offer structured responses to the most significant causes of mortality and morbidity in low- and medium-income countries. They stimulate the transfer of unprecedented amounts of financial resources by bringing together governmental and nongovernmental stakeholders, including the private commercial sector, under what are now commonly referred to as public–private partnerships. Yet these global initiatives raise important issues for the autonomy of recipient countries, in relation to both investment priorities and governance. While laudable in their goals, they carry with them the risk of further distancing poor countries from choices made by donors on their behalf. Indeed, both the magnitude and strategic priorities of these initiatives are strongly influenced by external funding, be it from donor governments or foundations, and they are often placed under the oversight of makeshift governing bodies with unquestioned legitimacy and accountability.

The short-term gains offered to countries through these sorts of efforts must be balanced against the long-term benefits to be derived from stronger national self-reliance. The success and sustainability of these initiatives will depend on the capacity of states—all states—to determine the course of their future health within and beyond negotiated international agreements, treaties, and programs of action that bring into focus the obligations of states to improve the health of all people, and thereby global health.

Global Trade and Public Health

| Ellen R. Shaffer, PhD, MPH, Howard Waitzkin, MD, PhD, Joseph Brenner, MA and Rebeca Jasso-Aguilar, MA

ABSTRACT

Global trade and international trade agreements have transformed the capacity of governments to monitor and to protect public health, to regulate occupational and environmental health conditions and food products, and to ensure affordable access to medications. Proposals under negotiation for the World Trade Organization's General Agreement on Trade in Services (GATS) and the regional Free Trade Area of the Americas (FTAA) agreement cover a wide range of health services, health facilities, clinician licensing, water and sanitation services, and tobacco and alcohol distribution services.

Public health professionals and organizations rarely participate in trade negotiations or in resolution of trade disputes. The linkages among global trade, international trade agreements, and public health deserve more attention than they have received to date.

INTRODUCTION

Global trade and international trade agreements have transformed governments' ability to monitor and to protect public health (box p24). They have also restricted the capacity of government agencies to regulate occupational and environmental health conditions and food products and to ensure affordable access to medications and water. Pending proposals cover a wide range of health services, health facilities, clinician licensing, and distribution of tobacco and alcohol.

Public health organizations are only beginning to grapple with trade-related threats to global health, including emerging infectious diseases and bioterrorism. Although economic globalization has attracted wide attention, its implications for public health remain poorly understood.

In this article, we analyze key global trade issues that affect public health, briefly tracing the history of international trade agreements and describing the forces shaping agreements such as the North American Free Trade Agreement (NAFTA). The recent shift to treating services as tradable commodities is of particular importance; we analyze the General Agreement on Trade in Services (GATS) as a case in point. We also discuss the implications for public health of the Agreement on Trade-Related Aspects of Intellectual Property Rights (TRIPS) and the proposed Free Trade Area of the Americas (FTAA) agreement. Although many agreements contain implications for public health, as we summarize in Table 1 and the box on page 26, we emphasize those features of agreements currently under negotiation that warrant attention by public health practitioners and organizations.

EMERGENCE OF INTERNATIONAL TRADE AGREEMENTS

Historical Origins

Although trade across nations and continents dates back centuries, the framework for current international trade agreements began after World War II with the "Bretton Woods"

accords. These accords sought to generate economic growth in the reconstruction of Europe and Japan after World War II, in part by stabilizing currency rates and trade rules. Between 1944 and 1947, the Bretton Woods negotiations led to the creation of the International Monetary Fund and the World Bank and to the establishment of the General Agreement on Tariffs and Trade (GATT). GATT aimed to reduce tariffs and quotas for trade among its 23 participating nations and also established such general principles as "most favored nation treatment" (according to which the same trade rules were applied to all participating nations) and "national treatment" (which required no discrimination in taxes and regulations between domestic and foreign goods).[1] GATT also established ongoing rounds of negotiations concerning trade agreements.

During the 1980s and 1990s, these international financial institutions embraced a set of economic policies known as "the Washington consensus." Advocated primarily by the United States and the United Kingdom, these policies involved deregulation, privatization of public services, measures designed to achieve low inflation rates and stable currencies, and mechanisms enhancing the operations of multinational corporations. As the pace of international economic transactions intensified, facilitated by technological advances in communications and transportation, the World Trade Organization (WTO) in 1994 replaced the loose collection of agreements subsumed under GATT.

TABLE 1— Summary of International Trade Agreements and Trade Organizations Pertinent to Public Health and Their Principal Implications for Public Health

Treaty, Organization, or Law	Focus and Implication	Ratification or Negotiation Status	Examples of Cases Relevant to Public Health
Summary of key multilateral agreements			
General Agreement on Trade and Tariffs (GATT)	Part of Bretton Woods accords at end of World War II; reduced tariffs as financial barrier to trade	Applies to all 148 nations that now participate in WTO	Venezuela won a challenge to the US Clean Air Act of 1990, weakening regulation of gasoline contaminants that contribute to pollution.
World Trade Organization (WTO)	Emerged in 1994 from the "Uruguay round" of GATT negotiations; created a stable organization with staff; aims to remove tariff and nontariff barriers to trade	Includes all WTO member nations	See below under separate trade agreements.
General Agreement on Trade in Services (GATS)[a]	Opens services to participation by foreign private corporations; services may include health care services, national health programs, public hospitals and clinics, professional licensure, water, and sanitation systems	Applies to WTO member nations; commitments by countries currently under negotiation	Country requests have targeted US professional licensing requirements and restrictions on corporate involvement in drinking water and wastewater systems.
Agreement on Trade-Related Aspects of Intellectual Property Rights (TRIPS)[a]	Protects patents, copyrights, trademarks, and industrial designs across national boundaries; limits governments' ability to introduce medication programs and to restrict the availability and reimbursement of medications under publicly funded programs	Applies to WTO member nations; rules concerning medications for conditions such as AIDS under negotiation	On behalf of pharmaceutical corporations, the United States has challenged attempts by South Africa, Thailand, Brazil, and India to produce low-cost antiretroviral medications effective against AIDS.
Agreement on Technical Barriers to Trade (TBT)[a]	Reduces barriers to trade that derive from technical standards and regulations applying to the safety and quality of products; covers tobacco and alcohol, toxic substances and waste, pharmaceuticals, biological agents, foodstuffs, and manufactured goods	Applies to WTO member nations	In its challenge of France's ban on asbestos imports, Canada argued that international standards require the "least trade restrictive" regulations; a WTO tribunal approved the challenge, although an appeal tribunal rejected Canada's claim after international pressure.
Agreement on the Application of Sanitary and Phyto-Sanitary Standards (SPS)[a]	Reduces barriers to trade that derive from governments' regulations and laws designed to protect the health of humans, animals, and plants; covers food safety provisions	Applies to WTO member nations	On behalf of the beef and biotechnology industries, the United States successfully challenged the European Union's ban on beef treated with artificial hormones.
Summary of key US regional agreements			
North American Free Trade Agreement (NAFTA)[b]	Removed most restrictions on trade among the United States, Canada, and Mexico	Ratified and implemented in 1994	Under Chapter 11, the US Metalclad Corporation successfully sued Mexico in regard to toxic waste restrictions; the Methanex Corporation of Canada challenged the United States over California's ban of a carcinogenic gasoline additive.
Free Trade Area of the Americas (FTAA)[b]	Extends NAFTA to all countries of the Western hemisphere except Cuba	Under negotiation	This agreement would open public sector health care services and institutions to corporate participation.
Central American Free Trade Agreement (CAFTA)[b]	Applies NAFTA-like trade rules to the United States, the 5 Central American countries and the Dominican Republic	Agreed by trade negotiators, signed by US president, awaiting consideration by US Congress	This agreement would interfere with the ability of Central American generic drug industry to produce and sell affordable prescription drugs.

[a]WTO trade agreement (applies to all WTO member nations).
[b]Regional trade agreement (applies only to signatory nations).

Trade Rules

The WTO and regional trade agreements have sought to remove both tariff and nontariff barriers to trade. Tariff barriers involve financial methods (e.g., taxes on imports) of protecting national industries from competition by foreign corporations. Nontariff barriers refer to laws and regulations affecting trade, including those that governments use to ensure accountability and quality. In more than 900 pages of rules, the WTO set criteria for permissible and impermissible nontariff barriers, for example domestic policies governing environmental protection, food safety, and health services. These rules aim to increase cross-border trade under the assumption that increased trade may enhance nations' wealth or well-being. While aiming to achieve "free" trade across borders, the rules in trade agreements limit governments' regulatory authority over trade and enhance the authority of international financial institutions and trade organizations.[2]

Examples of Actions Under International Trade Agreements That Affect Public Health

- Under Chapter 11 of the North American Free Trade Agreement (NAFTA), the Metalclad Corporation of the United States successfully sued the government of Mexico for damages after the state of San Luis Potosí prohibited Metalclad from reopening a toxic waste dump. The Methanex Corporation of Canada sued the government of the United States in a challenge regarding environmental protections against a carcinogenic gasoline additive, methyl tertiary butyl ether (MTBE), banned by the state of California. The Free Trade Area of the Americas (FTAA), currently under negotiation, would extend such investor's rights to all countries in the Western hemisphere except Cuba.

- Acting on behalf of pharmaceutical corporations, the US government invoked the Agreement on Trade-Related Aspects of Intellectual Property Rights (TRIPS) of the World Trade Organization (WTO) in working against attempts by South Africa, Thailand, Brazil, and India to produce low-cost antiretroviral medications effective against AIDS.

- Canada challenged France's ban on asbestos imports under WTO's Agreement on Technical Barriers to Trade. Although a WTO tribunal initially approved Canada's challenge, an appeal tribunal reversed the decision after international pressure.

- On behalf of the beef and biotechnology industries, the United States successfully challenged the European Union's ban of beef treated with artificial hormones under the WTO Agreement on the Application of Sanitary and Phyto-Sanitary Standards.

- Currently under negotiation, the WTO General Agreement on Trade in Services (GATS) targets the removal of restrictions on corporate involvement in public hospitals, water, and sanitation systems. GATS could affect state and national licensing requirements for professionals and may raise challenges to national health programs that limit participation by for-profit corporations.

- In the first trade dispute decided under GATS, a WTO tribunal rejected Mexico's defense of its telecommunications regulations. The tribunal found that charges including a contribution to the development of Mexico's telecommunications infrastructure were not "reasonable." Mexico had argued that GATS provisions appeared to give flexibility to governments in achieving development objectives, including Mexico's policy goal of promoting universal access to basic telecommunications services for its population.

Although the WTO (under general exceptions of GATT, Article XX) permits national and subnational "measures necessary to protect human, animal or plant life or health," other provisions make this exception difficult to sustain in practice. For example, a country can be required to prove that its laws and regulations represent the alternatives that are least restrictive in regard to trade and that they are not disguised barriers to trade.[3] Such rules also can restrict public subsidies, including those designated for domestic health programs and institutions, labeling them potentially "trade distortive." Requiring that such subsidies apply equally to domestic and foreign companies that provide services under public contracts can preempt public policies directing subsidies to domestic corporations.

Of particular relevance to public health, 1 WTO provision requires "harmonization," that is, reducing variations in nations' regulatory standards for goods and services. Proponents have noted that harmonization can motivate less developed countries to initiate labor and environmental standards where none had previously existed.[4] However, harmonization also can lead to erosion of existing standards, because it requires uniform global standards at the level *least* restrictive to trade.[5] The WTO encourages national governments to harmonize standards on issues as diverse as truck safety, pesticides, worker safety, community right-to-know laws regarding toxic hazards, consumer rights regarding essential services, banking and accounting standards, informational labeling of products, and pharmaceutical testing standards.

Trade Enforcement and National Sovereignty

WTO and regional agreements such as NAFTA supersede member countries' internal laws and regulations, including those governing public health. Under these agreements, governments at all levels are facing loss of sovereignty in policymaking pertinent to public health and health services. Technically, nations apply voluntarily to become WTO members. However, most less developed countries perceive that they will experience disadvantages in trade relations if they do not join.[6]

Traditionally, government agencies at the federal, state, county, and municipal levels have been responsible for protecting the public's health, for example by ensuring safe water supplies, controlling environmental threats, and monitoring industries in regard to occupational health conditions. Trade agreements can reduce or eliminate such governmental activities to the extent that they represent barriers to trade.

Glossary of Key Terms

"Bretton Woods" accords

Agreements negotiated mainly at Bretton Woods, NH, at the end of World II; sought to generate economic growth for the reconstruction of Europe and Japan, partly by stabilizing currency rates and rules for trade.

Commitment

A country's decision to cover specified services under certain General Agreement on Trade in Services (GATS) rules (market access and national treatment). When a country commits to a specific type of service (for instance, health services, insurance services, public health services), the country must include all of those services under these GATS rules. Later reversal of commitments is extremely difficult because of a requirement of compensation to all countries whose companies have incurred losses after beginning to provide the service in question.

Compulsory license

Under Trade-Related Aspects of Intellectual Property Rights (TRIPS), a country may require that a pharmaceutical company receive a government license to market a needed medication under patent at a lower price than the company could charge under usual market conditions. Low-income countries with AIDS epidemics have considered using compulsory licensing to enhance access to the newer generation of effective but expensive medications for AIDS.

Domestic regulation rule

Provision under World Trade Organization (WTO), adopted in other regional and bilateral agreements, that government regulations and standards regarding services are "not more burdensome than necessary to ensure the quality of the service" (the "necessity test") and do not constitute barriers to trade.

Harmonization

Principle that seeks to reduce variation in nations' regulatory standards for goods and services; requires uniform global standards in health and safety at the level least restrictive to trade.

International Monetary Fund (IMF)

International financial institution initiated after World War II as part of Bretton Woods accords. The IMF's mission is to "to promote international monetary cooperation, exchange stability, and orderly exchange arrangements; to foster economic growth and high levels of employment; and to provide temporary financial assistance to countries to help ease balance of payments adjustment" (see http://www.imf.org/external/about.htm).

Investor's rights

Mechanism under Chapter 11 of North American Free Trade Agreement (NAFTA) by which individual foreign investors or corporations can directly sue any of the 3 participating national governments.

Market access

Principle that prohibits governments from restricting the number or type of providers for a specific good or service within a country.

Most favored nation treatment

Principle that applies the same trade rules to all countries participating in a trade agreement.

Multilateral, regional, bilateral agreements

Defines which group of countries are signatories and which sets of rules apply. Multilateral WTO agreements apply to all 148 WTO member countries. Countries can negotiate regional agreements or bilateral (country-to-country) agreements. There is debate on whether WTO rules act as a floor or a ceiling for regional and bilateral agreements.

National treatment

Principle that requires no discrimination in taxes and regulations between domestic and foreign goods and services.

Non-tariff barriers to trade

Laws and regulations affecting trade, including those used by governments to ensure accountability and quality in such areas as environmental protection, food safety, and health services.

Tariff barriers to trade

Financial methods of protecting national industries from competition by foreign corporations, such as taxes on imports.

Trade Promotion Authority ("Fast Track")

US Congress delegates authority for negotiation of trade agreements to the president; permits only approval or disapproval without amendment by Congress.

Washington consensus

Set of economic policies that favor deregulation, privatization of public services, measures to achieve low inflation and stable currencies, and mechanisms that enhance the operations of multinational corporations.

World Bank

International financial institution initiated after World War II as part of Bretton Woods accords. The World Bank's Mission was initially to contribute through loans to the economic reconstruction of Europe and Japan. Its current mission is "to fight poverty and improve the living standards of people in the developing world" (see http://web.worldbank.org/WBSITE/E XTERNAL/EXTABOUTUS/0,,pagePK :43912~piPK:36602~theSitePK:297 08,00.html).

In cases of dispute, an appointed 3-member WTO tribunal, rather than a local or national government, determines whether a challenged policy conforms to WTO rules. This tribunal includes experts in trade but not necessarily in the subject matter of the cases in question (e.g., cases involving health or safety) or in the laws of the contesting countries.[3] Documents and hearings are closed to the public, the press, and state and local elected officials; the WTO considers only federal governments as members.

When a tribunal finds that a domestic law or regulation does not conform to WTO rules, the tribunal orders that the contested transaction in question must proceed. If a country fails to comply, the WTO can impose financial penalties and authorize the "winning" country to apply trade sanctions against the "losing" country in whatever sector the winner chooses until the other country complies. In challenges decided by WTO or NAFTA tribunals, corporations and investors have caused governments to suffer financial consequences and trade sanctions because of governments' efforts to pursue traditional public health functions (box p24). Losing countries in these cases experience pressure to eliminate or to change the legislation in question and not to enact similar new laws.

TRADE AGREEMENTS AND PUBLIC HEALTH

A set of international trade agreements applies to all WTO member countries (currently 148). WTO agreements pertinent to public health include GATS, TRIPS, the Agreement on the Application of Sanitary and Phyto-Sanitary Standards, and the Agreement on Technical Barriers to Trade. In addition, regional agreements and nation-to-nation (bilateral) agreements are proliferating, with provisions based on the WTO and NAFTA.

North American Free Trade Agreement (NAFTA)

Initiated in 1994, NAFTA focuses on expanding opportunities for new investments, acquiring property, and opening services to competition by private corporations in the United States,

Canada, and Mexico. NAFTA provisions have proven controversial, in that numerous US-based manufacturing industries have moved to Mexico, where environmental and occupational health standards are less strict and most companies pay lower wages. Unemployment and cuts in benefits for workers remaining employed in the United States have resulted in a growing number of uninsured workers and families.[7] Overall, NAFTA did not create the new jobs in the United States that proponents predicted and has contributed to increasing inequality of wages.[8]

In Mexico, NAFTA's impact has proven more dramatic. Jobs lost in agriculture owing to the increases in imports have far outweighed the jobs created by export manufacturing. Unemployment has increased most dramatically in rural areas.[8] After NAFTA lowered tariffs on US agricultural products, crop prices dropped, and even Mexican subsistence farmers could not compete with US agribusiness, which receives large government subsidies. Between 1994 and 2003, 9.3 million workers entered Mexico's labor market, but only 3 million new jobs were created during that period; in the same time span, real wages lost approximately 20% of their purchasing power.[9] NAFTA also has led to widespread environmental damage as agriculture has seen a shift to large-scale, export-oriented farms that rely on water-polluting agrochemicals and more use of water for irrigation.[8] Chronic public health problems along the border between the United States and Mexico persist.[10]

Chapter 11 of NAFTA, concerning investments, includes a unique "investor's rights" mechanism by which individual foreign corporations (referred to as "investors") can directly sue any of the 3 participating national governments. Before the establishment of NAFTA, trade agreements permitted only country-to-country enforcement by governments. However, companies can now sue for loss of current or future profits, even if the loss is caused by a government agency's prohibiting the use of a toxic substance.[11]

Several landmark cases filed under Chapter 11 have dealt with environmental laws or regulations. For example, a NAFTA tribunal awarded the US-based Metalclad Company $16.7 million in its suit against Mexico. The state of San Luis Potosí had refused permission for Metalclad to reopen a waste disposal facility after a geological audit showed that the facility would contaminate the local water supply and after the local community opposed the reopening. Metalclad claimed that this local decision constituted an expropriation of its future potential profits and filed a successful suit against the country of Mexico.[12,13]

In addition, the Methanex Corporation of Canada initiated an approximately $1 billion suit against the United States after the state of California banned the use of methyl tertiary butyl ether (MTBE), a gasoline additive, because of its demonstrated carcinogenicity. Methanex produces methanol, a component of MTBE. This case remains under consideration by a closed appeal tribunal, while MTBE remains in use in California.

Such cases can exert a chilling effect on environmental protection efforts. For instance, several other states have deferred their planned bans on MTBE as a result of the threat posed by the pending Methanex case.[14] Similar investor's rights provisions have appeared in other regional and bilateral agreements, such as those recently negotiated by the United States with Singapore and Chile.

Free Trade Area of the Americas (FTAA)

The FTAA proposes that most provisions of NAFTA be extended to all 31 of the remaining nations in the Western hemisphere with the exception of Cuba.[15] Ongoing negotiations include efforts to introduce an investor's rights clause, similar to NAFTA's, as well as to replicate features of GATS and other WTO agreements. If completed on schedule, negotiations will conclude in early 2005.

The FTAA agreement would foster participation of multinational corporations in administering programs and institutions, such as public hospitals and community health centers, currently managed in the public sector. US-based insurance companies have expressed their interest in delivering services now provided by public sector social security systems throughout Latin America,[16] as indicated in their testimony on the FTAA (Washington, DC, March 28, 2000): "public ownership of health care has made it difficult for U.S. private-sector health care providers to market in foreign countries. . . . Existing regulations . . . present serious barriers . . ., including restricting licensing of health care professionals, and excessive privacy and confidentiality regulations."[17]

Proponents of privatization emphasize the inefficiencies and corruption that have occurred in some countries' public sector programs. However, in many countries privatization and the participation of multinational corporations in public services have led to problematic effects. Such changes in Latin America have resulted in barriers to access stemming from copayments, private practitioners' refusal to see patients because corporations have not paid professional fees, and bureaucratic confusion in the assignment of private providers; public sector expenditures increasingly have covered the higher administrative costs and profits of investors as clinical services have decreased for the poor at public hospitals and health centers.[16,18,19] Similar trends have occurred in Africa and Asia.[20,21]

Although, at present, countries are free to privatize public services, the FTAA would impose the threat of a trade challenge against countries' decisions to maintain or to expand public services, as well as costly trade sanctions if privatized services were to be returned to the public sector. FTAA chapters directly related to public health cover trade in services such as health care, water, education, and energy; intellectual property, which addresses access to affordable medications; standards for plant and food safety; and rules regarding governments' allocation of subsidies and procurement of goods and services. Also important to public health, the FTAA's language on financial investments adopts Chapter 11 of NAFTA as a model, and rules on trade in products could restrict governments' regulation of product safety.

The FTAA process is entirely "top down"; all services are covered by all FTAA rules unless a country takes action affirmatively to exclude specific services. The Central American Free Trade Agreement (CAFTA), awaiting final review by Congress as of late 2004, and recently concluded US bilateral agreements with Chile, Singapore, Vietnam, and Jordan contain similar provisions.

General Agreement on Trade in Services (GATS)

Recognizing the increasing proportion of economic activities worldwide devoted to services, this WTO agreement encourages private investment and deregulation in terms of a wide spectrum of services. GATS treats human services such as health care, water and sanitation, energy, and education as commodities subject to trade rules. According to its stated aims, GATS will progressively cover an increasing number of services over time. The current round of GATS negotiations is scheduled to conclude in 2005.

A majority of GATS rules, including "most favored nation," are "top down" (Table 2). That is, they already apply to all services in all WTO member countries. For example, according to the domestic regulation rule, government regulations regarding services should not be "more burdensome than necessary to ensure the quality of the service," and qualification requirements and procedures for service providers, technical standards, and licensing requirements should not constitute unnecessary barriers to trade in services.[1] When the process of minimizing trade restrictions comes into conflict with health standards, trade tribunals under WTO usually have decided that the former take priority.[22] GATS sections on subsidies and government procurement, described subsequently, also apply to all services offered.

Because many countries have opposed expanding WTO rules to the service sector, GATS operates, to some extent, according to a stepwise approach. Through a "bottom-up" process, nations negotiate with each other to "commit" to covering (or adding to the list of) services falling under 2 trade rules (Table 3). One of these rules, referred to as "market access," prohibits governments from restricting numbers or types of service providers. As an example, this rule could undermine local laws restricting the number of liquor stores on a city block. Under the second rule, "national treatment" (described earlier), a country must treat foreign companies in the same manner as domestic companies.[23] Programs designed to achieve social goals, such as measures aimed at ensuring accountability in regard to national privacy regulations by restricting medical transcription services to domestic companies, could violate this rule by "discriminating" against foreign corporations.

Within these 2 rules, GATS specifies 4 service modes to which a country can commit particular services[24]: (1) delivery of services based in 1 country to consumers based in another country (e.g., telemedicine), (2) delivery of services to foreign consumers within the provider's country (e.g., "niche" specialty medical services that patients travel to receive), (3) investment in the services of another country, and (4) temporary migration by workers. For example, covering a service such as hospitals under Mode 3 can restrict nations' or states' ability to limit or control foreign investments in their health care systems. Covering nurses under Mode 4 can accelerate the migration of trained clinicians.

There is no formal process for public debate in GATS decisions about committing services; countries make confidential requests regarding services that they would like other countries to commit, and the respondents can agree or disagree. Regarding public health, the European Union has requested that the United States drop restrictions on private corporate involvement in water and sanitation

TABLE 2- Major Provisions and "Top-Down" Rules Relevant to Public Health in the General Agreement on Trade in Services (GATS)

Rule	Content	Issues Relevant to Public Health
Disclosure (Article III)	Each nation shall publish all current laws, regulations, or administrative guidelines related to GATS and at least annually inform the WTO's Council for Trade in Services of the introduction of any new measures, or any changes to existing measures, which significantly affect trade in services covered by its specific commitments under this agreement.	Rule imposes an administrative burden on local, state, and federal governments. International involvement in domestic rule making is costly.
Domestic regulation (Article VI)	The WTO's Council for Trade in Services shall establish any necessary disciplines to ensure that measures relating to qualification requirements and procedures, technical standards, and licensing requirements do not constitute unnecessary barriers to trade in services. Such measures should be based on objective and transparent criteria, such as competence and the ability to supply the service, and should not be more burdensome than necessary to ensure the quality of the service. Licensing procedures should not in themselves constitute a restriction on the supply of the service.	Trade tribunals without expertise in health can determine that laws and regulations that protect health are more burdensome than necessary and are unnecessary barriers to trade in services. Criteria for this determination have not been specified. "Overly burdensome" measures could include training and licensing for health professionals, privacy of information, patient protection, health and safety, alcohol and tobacco control, equitable services for vulnerable populations, and access to affordable medications.
Monopolies and exclusive service suppliers (Article VIII)	Nations must ensure that any monopoly supplier of a service subject to a GATS commitment does not compete to supply that service outside the scope of its present monopoly rights. If a member grants new monopoly rights regarding the supply of a service covered by its specific commitments, it shall notify the WTO's Council for Trade in Services no later than 3 months before the intended implementation.	Some public health systems are monopoly suppliers of health care and insurance. Since the United States has made a GATS commitment for health insurance, legislation to create a nationally or state-funded health insurance system would have to be reported 3 months in advance to the WTO to ensure that the program would not prevent competition among private insurance companies.
Government procurement (Article XIII)	Procurement of services by governmental agencies can be exempt from GATS if the services are purchased for governmental purposes and not with a view to commercial resale or use in the supply of services for commercial sale.	Some public payments could be considered purchases for commercial sale and therefore could be challenged under GATS. For example, Medicaid payments to private hospitals and nursing homes that are then used to reimburse temporary employment agencies could be considered commercial sales.
Subsidies (Article XV)	Members recognize that, in certain circumstances, subsidies may have distortive effects on trade in services. Members shall enter into negotiations with a view to developing the necessary multilateral disciplines to avoid such trade-distortive effects.	Government subsidies for many health services at the local, state, and federal levels could be challenged as distortions to trade, including disproportionate share hospital payments and community health center allocations.

Note. "Top-down" GATS rules apply to all services. The exact wording of some provisions is under negotiation.

TABLE 3— Selected Health-Related Services Currently Covered by the United States Under the "Bottom-Up" Rules of the General Agreement on Trade in Services (GATS)

Service Category That the United States Has Agreed to Cover	GATS Rules and Modesa That the United States Has Agred to Apply	US Measuresb and Programs Subject to Challenge	Measures and Services Currently Excluded From Bottom-Up Rules; Pending Requests to Remove Exclusions
Hospital and community health center services	Market access: mode 2	Prioritization of resources for domestic populations vs foreigners who travel to the United States to receive services	No exclusions or requests
	Market access: mode 3	Limits on establishment of hospital services based on need, outcomes, or other criteria (e.g., coronary care or neonatal intensive care units)	Need-based limits on new hospitals, medical equipment, or medical procedures "may" be excluded
			New York rules limiting corporate ownership of hospitals, nursing homes, or diagnostic and treatment centers excluded
			Michigan and New York laws on licensing of managed care organizations excluded
	National treatment: modes 2 and 3	Public sector support for domestic safety net providers	Mexico and Paraguay have requested removing restriction of federal or state government reimbursement to licensed facilities in the United States
	National treatment: mode 4	Training and residency requirements for non-professional health personnel (e.g., technicians, clerical workers)	No stated exclusions or requests
Health insurance	Market access: modes 1, 2, and 3	Limits on number of competing insurers	State laws limiting foreign life, accident, and health insurance companies excluded
			Tax exemptions for employee benefit trusts excluded
			European Union has requested removal of exclusion that grants tax exemptions for employee benefit trusts
	National treatment: modes 1, 3, and 4	Government subsidies and procurement under Medicare and Medicaid	Worker's compensation excluded
		New government programs to extend coverage Patient protection laws	
		Restrictions on genetic and gender discrimination Privacy protections	
Environmental services: sanitation, sewage, nature and landscape protection	Market access: modes 1, 2, and 3	Rules and decisions regarding standards for delivery of services	European Union has requested that the United States cover drinking water and wastewater treatment, which would facilitate privatization
	National treatment: modes 1, 2, 3, and 4		
Distribution of goods, including tobacco and alcohol products	National treatment: modes 1, 2, 3, and 4	State run liquor stores	Wholesale distribution of alcohol and tobacco products is currently covered by national treatment but not by market access rules
			Retail distribution of alcohol and tobacco products is currently not covered by market access and national treatment rules
			European Union has requested that the United States cover retail distribution of alcohol under market access rules. This could challenge state laws and regulations restricting retail distribution of alcohol products and communities' efforts to limit liquor stores in neighborhoods

Note. Under "bottom-up" rules, countries can choose whether and how particular services are covered. The major bottom-up rules are (1) market access rules, which prohibit government limitations on the amount or type of services supplied by foreign private service providers, and (2) national treatment rules, which grant foreign private service providers the same treatment as domestic service providers.

aMarket access and national treatment rules can be applied to cover services in any or all of the following "modes" of trade: mode 1 (cross-border supply: provision of services to consumers located abroad [e.g., telemedicine]), mode 2 (consumption abroad: provision of services in the provider's home country to foreign consumers [e.g., "niche" specialty medical services that patients travel to receive]), mode 3 (commercial presence: foreign direct investment [e.g., European hospital chain ownership of hospitals in the United States]), and mode 4 (presence of natural persons: temporary immigration of personnel [e.g., health professionals, nonprofessional health workers])

bMeasures refer to laws, regulations, and governmental funding arrangements.

systems, as well as in the retail distribution of alcohol products.[25] While the European Union has announced that it will not commit further any of its own human services, both the EU and the United States seek removal of barriers to trade in other countries covering health services, energy services, higher education, and environmental services.[26]

Several countries have submitted GATS requests with important implications for US health services (Table 4). For instance, India has asked that the United States recognize foreign licensing and other certified qualifications of medical, nursing, and dental professionals. Mexico has requested that the United States no longer limit foreign direct investment in hospitals and health facilities. Both Mexico and Paraguay have asked the United States to eliminate the "restriction of federal and state reimbursement to licensed, certified [health] facilities in the United States or a U.S. state."[25]

Although the technical language of GATS has generated controversy about the extent of its eventual effects,[27] GATS will probably affect public sector health programs in several ways. First, GATS will facilitate greater participation by private corporations within public health care institutions. For instance, the United States currently includes hospitals and health insurance coverage (within GATS, the latter falls under financial services rather than health services) in its commitments. Under GATS rules on public subsidies and government procurement, subsidies awarded to institutions for treatment of the underserved, graduate medical education, or research may be discontinued if challenged by other countries, or they could be directed to foreign private corporations that offer competing services. Municipal and county governments that reject bids or attempt to discontinue contracts with foreign companies could become liable to challenge.

Although GATS proponents emphasize that countries' commitments remain voluntary, policy analysts have expressed concern that WTO rules will permit a variety of challenges to countries with national health programs.[28–30]

Nations' commitments under GATS so far have varied.[4,31] The European Union has committed to including medical, dental, nursing, and hospital services, but not health insurance coverage, which therefore would remain in the public sector. Canada has not committed in regard to any health services. Although the United States has committed for hospital services, health facility services, and health insurance coverage and proposes to expand its commitment under "environmental services" to include wastewater, it has not made commitments in regard to professional licensing, alcohol and tobacco distribution, or drinking water. If the GATS objective of eventually including all services is achieved, however, these lim-

TABLE 4— US Services for Which Other Countries Have Requested Future Coverage Under the "Bottom-Up" Rules of the General Agreement on Trade in Services (GATS)

Service Category	Pending Requests to Extend Coverage	US Laws, Regulations, and Funding Arrangements Subject to Future Challenge Under GATS if the US Trade Representative and Congress Agree to Extend Coverage
Physicians, dentists, veterinarians, midwives, nurses, physiotherapists, and paramedical personnel	India has requested that the United States extend recognition for clinicians trained in India	Immigration and licensing standards for clinicians
Research and development in the natural sciences, social sciences, humanities, and engineering	European Union has requested inclusion of these services	Standards for and allocation of funding; rules concerning conflicts of interest with corporations and other funding sources
Energy: exploration, production, distribution, trading, brokering	European Union has requested inclusion of these services	Regulations protecting safety of workers and the public
Exploration, production, and bulk storage of liquids or gases	European Union has requested inclusion of these services and removal of a Michigan law requiring that contractors maintain an in-state monitoring office	Measures that protect the safe storage of these potentially hazardous materials
Small Business Administration loans	European Union has requested that the United States remove restriction of federal Small Business Administration loans to US nationals	Federal small business loan programs that restrict loans to US citizens would be opened to foreign applicants; similar state programs could also be challenged, including those that restrict loans to categories such as veterans (Maine), socially disadvantaged populations (Maryland), dislocated timber workers (Oregon), and minority-owned businesses (Pennsylvania)

its will prove temporary.[32–34] Tables 2–4 presents health-related services in the United States now covered by GATS, and those that could be covered in the future.

Agreement on Trade-Related Aspects of Intellectual Property Rights (TRIPS)

The TRIPS agreement protects patents, copyrights, trademarks, and industrial designs across national boundaries. On the basis of the argument that such protections enhance economic incentives for creativity and invention, this agreement covers patented medications and equipment, textbooks and journals, and engineering and architectural innovations for health institutions, as well as computer technologies and entertainment products. TRIPS rules mandate that all WTO member countries implement intellectual property protections that provide 20-year monopoly control over patentable items. Entry into the WTO required that the United States extend patents from 17-year terms to the WTO's 20-year standard.

TRIPS can limit governments' ability to provide generic medications under publicly funded programs. For instance, federal and state government health programs such as Medicare and Medicaid have paid substantially higher drug prices as a result of these patent extensions. Overall, TRIPS has adversely affected US health care cost containment efforts by extending the period during which purchasers have had to pay higher prices for medications covered by patents.[3,35]

Provisions of TRIPS also could block proposals to reimport affordable prescription drugs from Canada into the United States.[36] Similar provisions have appeared in bilateral agreements such as the Australia Free Trade Agreement.[37]

TRIPS especially affects access to medications for life-threatening conditions in low-income countries. TRIPS rules required most developing countries to change their rules by 2001, while the "least developed countries" must do so by 2016. One policy tool designed to deal with this problem in low-income countries, permissible under TRIPS rules, involves "compulsory licensing." Under this provision, a country may require that a pharmaceutical company obtain a government license to market a needed medication under patent at a lower price than the company could charge under usual market conditions. The US government has supported efforts under TRIPS to prevent the governments of South Africa, Thailand, and Brazil from initiating compulsory licenses for production of generic alternatives to patented AIDS medications.[38–40]

As a result of concerns among professionals, legislators, and advocates, the Doha round of WTO negotiations in 2001 involved a proposal to relax some of TRIPS's most severe rules regarding patent protection for medications useful in treating AIDS.[41,42] Partly by threatening to impose compulsory licensing, Brazil's government obtained low prices from pharmaceutical companies; this change has facilitated improvements in the country's AIDS morbidity and mortality outcomes.[43] In August 2003, the US pharmaceutical industry abandoned its insistence that the relaxed rules apply only to medications for AIDS, tuberculosis, and malaria.[44] The resulting agreement has led to WTO control over a complex process for approving lowered medication prices under limited circumstances and leaves the issue of accessible medications in less developed countries unresolved.[45–47]

ACTIONS TAKEN BY PUBLIC HEALTH PRACTITIONERS

Concern about trade policies that cause adverse effects on public health has increased worldwide.[48,49] Specific instances of organized resistance have shown that such policies can be blocked or reversed. For instance, as already described, the coordinated international efforts to expand the availability of AIDS medications in Africa despite TRIPS restrictions led to major changes in trade policies, and, partly by threatening to impose compulsory licensing, Brazil's government helped improve AIDS outcomes through low medication prices.[41] In addition, the campaign to eliminate users' fees in public sector health services and education led to a major change in the World Bank's policies in regard to enhancing privatization and corporate trade in services. Communities in Bolivia have succeeded in reversing the privatization of water supplies. Finally, through a series of protests, a coalition of health professionals, nonprofessional health workers, and patients in El Salvador has repeatedly blocked the privatization of public hospitals.

Alternative projects favoring international collaboration have countered some of the adverse effects of global trade on public health. For instance, the Brazilian Workers Party, which won the country's presidency in late 2002, has emphasized expansion of public hospitals and clinics at the municipal level. Adopting the principle of community participation in municipal budgets, the new government has encouraged strengthening municipal public services and has attempted to limit the participation of multinational corporations in the area of public health. Such efforts have occurred in the context of a growing network of organizations that emphasize a strengthened public sector, critically assess the corporatization in health care that international trade agreements encourage, and express concern about the impact of global trade on public health, health services, and democracy.[50,51]

Because critical trade negotiations are taking place now and in the near future, we recommend that public health practitioners engage in several actions to address the growing challenges of global trade:

- Participate in national and international networks that conduct research, surveillance, and advocacy concerning global trade and public health.
- Engage in educational outreach to encourage more informed decisions about the relationships between global trade and public health and to influence the direction of international trade agreements; outreach activities should target (1) professional associations in the areas of public health, clinical medicine, health policy, and allied

health professions; (2) state, county, and local health departments; (3) local communities and civic organizations; and (4) elected officials at the federal, state, county, and municipal levels.

- Engage in efforts to introduce the themes just mentioned into the public media.
- Conduct further research on the public health implications of existing and pending trade agreements.
- Gain public health representation on advisory committees to the US Congress and the US Trade Representative.

The Center for Policy Analysis on Trade and Health maintains a listserve on globalization and health and also has posted on its Web site (available at: http://www.cpath.org) brief descriptions and contact information for key organizations attempting to address the public health effects of global trade.

CHALLENGES FOR PUBLIC HEALTH

The changing conditions of global trade have raised important challenges for public health, including privatization and reduction of public services; reduced sovereignty of governments in regulating services, medications, equipment, and economic activities that affect occupational and environmental health; and enhanced power of multinational corporations and international financial institutions in policy decisions. Processes that link global trade and health often occur silently, with little attention or representation by legislators, the public media, and health professionals.[18]

Linkages between global trade and public health deserve more critical attention. A growing number of advocacy organizations and professional associations have drawn attention to such linkages.[52–56] Those concerned with health and security worldwide cannot afford to ignore the profound changes generated by global trade.

About the Authors

Ellen R. Shaffer and Joseph Brenner are with the Center for Policy Analysis on Trade and Health, San Francisco, Calif. Howard Waitzkin is with the Department of Family and Community Medicine, and Rebeca Jasso-Aguilar is with the Department of Sociology, University of New Mexico, Albuquerque.

Correspondence: Requests for reprints should be sent to Ellen R. Shaffer, PhD, MPH, Center for Policy Analysis on Trade and Health, 98 Seal Rock Dr, San Francisco, CA 94121 (e-mail: ershaffer@cpath.org).

Acknowledgments

This research was supported in part by grants from the National Library of Medicine (grant 1G08 LM06688), the New Century Scholars Program of the US Fulbright Commission, the John Simon Guggenheim Memorial Foundation, the Roothbert Fund, the US Agency for Healthcare Research and Quality (grant 1R03 HS13251), the National Institute of Mental Health (grants 1R03 MH067012 and 1 R25 MH60288), the United Nations Research Institute for Social Development, and the Unitarian Universalist Veatch Program at Shelter Rock.

Ellen R. Shaffer and Joseph Brenner thank Alicia Yamin, Erica Frank, and Kristen Smith for their contributions to this work. Howard Waitzkin and Rebeca Jasso-Aguilar are grateful to Ron Voorhees, Carolyn Mountain, Celia Iriart, Angela Landwehr, Francisco Mercado, and Lori Wallach for their contributions to this project.

Note. The views expressed in this article do not necessarily represent those of the funding agencies.

Contributors

E.R. Shaffer and H. Waitzkin originated and designed the research and drafted the article. All of the authors participated in data acquisition and interpretation, provided administrative and technical contributions, and contributed to revising the article for content. E.R. Shaffer and H. Waitzkin obtained funding for the study.

References

1. World Trade Organization. General agreement on trade in services. Available at: www.wto.org/english/docs_e/legal_e/26-gats.doc. Accessed May 28, 2004.
2. Kickbusch I. The development of international health policies—accountability intact? *Soc Sci Med.* 2000;51:979–989.
3. Wallach L, Woodall P. *Whose Trade Organization?: A Comprehensive Guide to the WTO.* New York, NY: New Press; 2004.
4. Drager N, Vieira C, eds. *Trade in Health Services: Global, Regional, and Country Perspectives.* Washington, DC: Pan American Health Organization; 2002.
5. Wallach L. Accountable governance in the era of globalization: the WTO, NAFTA, and international harmonization of standards. *University Kansas Law Review.* 2002;50:823–865.
6. Bello W. Reforming the WTO is the wrong agenda. In: Danaher K, Burbach R, eds. *Globalize This!* Monroe, Maine: Common Courage Press; 2000:103–119.
7. Anderson S. *Seven Years Under NAFTA.* Washington, DC: Institute for Policy Studies; 2003.
8. Carnegie Endowment for International Peace. NAFTA's promises and realities: lessons from Mexico for the hemisphere. Available at: http://www.ceip.org/files/pdf/NAFTA_Report_ChapterOne.pdf. Accessed May 28, 2004.
9. Nadal A, Aguayo F, Chávez M. Los siete mitos del TLC: lecciones para América Latina. Available at: http://www.jornada.unam.mx. Accessed November 18, 2003.
10. Homedes N, Ugalde A. Globalization and health at the United States–Mexico border. *Am J Public Health.* 2003;93:2016–2022.
11. Epstein R. *Takings: Private Property and the Power of Eminent Domain.* Cambridge, Mass: Harvard University Press; 1985.
12. US Dept of State. Metalclad Corporation v. United Mexican States. Available at: http://www.state.gov/s/1/c3752.htm. Accessed May 28, 2004.
13. Sforza M. MAI and the Metalclad case. Available at: http://www.canadianliberty.bc.ca/relatedinfo/metalclad.html. Accessed May 28, 2004.
14. Greider W. The right and U.S. trade law: invalidating the 20th century. *The Nation.* October 15, 2001:21–29.
15. Free Trade Area of the Americas. Available at: www.ftaa-alca.org. Accessed May 28, 2004
16. Stocker K, Waitzkin H, Iriart C. The exportation of managed care to Latin America. *N Engl J Med.* 1999;

340:1131–1136.

17. Coalition of Service Industries. Response to Federal Register notice of March 28, 2000. Available at: http://www.uscsi.org/publications/papers/CSIFedReg2000.pdf. Accessed May 28, 2004.

18. Iriart C, Merhy E, Waitzkin H. Managed care in Latin America: the new common sense in health policy reform. *Soc Sci Med.* 2001;52:1243–1253.

19. Waitzkin H, Iriart C. How the United States exports managed care to third world countries. *Monthly Rev.* 2000;52(1):21–35.

20. Turshen M. *Privatizing Health Services in Africa.* New Brunswick, NJ: Rutgers University Press; 1999.

21. Rao M, ed. *Disinvesting in Health: The World Bank's Prescriptions for Health.* New Delhi, India: Sage; 1999.

22. Hilary J. *The Wrong Model: GATS, Trade Liberalization and Children's Right to Health.* London, England: Save the Children; 2001.

23. US International Trade Commission. U.S. schedule of commitments under the General Agreement on Trade in Services, May 1997. Available at: ftp://ftp.usitc.gov/pub/reports/studies/GATS98.pdf. Accessed May 28, 2004.

24. Adlung R, Carzaniga A. Health services under the General Agreement on Trade in Services. *Bull World Health Organ.* 2001;79:352–364.

25. Trade Observatory, Institute for Agriculture and Trade Policy. GATS requests by state. Available at: http://www.tradeobservatory.org/library/uploadedfiles/GATS_Requests_By_State.pdf. Accessed May 28, 2004.

26. Office of the United States Trade Representative. Trade facts: free trade in services. Opening dynamic new markets, supporting good jobs. Available at: http://www.ustr.gov/sectors/services/2003-03-31-services-tradefacts.pdf. Accessed May 28, 2004.

27. Belsky L, Lie R, Mattoo A, Emanuel EJ, Sreenivasan G. The General Agreement on Trade in Services. *Health Aff.* 2004;23:137–145.

28. Pollock AM, Price D. Rewriting the regulations: how the World Trade Organisation could accelerate privatisation in health-care systems. *Lancet.* 2000; 356:1995–2000.

29. Commission on the Future of Health Care in Canada. Final report. Available at: http://www.hc-sc.gc.ca/english/care/romanow/hcc0023.html. Accessed May 28, 2004.

30. Pollock AM, Price D. The public health implications of world trade negotiations on the General Agreement on Trade in Services and public services. *Lancet.* 2003;362:1072–1075.

31. Ranson MK, Beaglehole R, Correa CM, Mirza Z, Buse K, Drager N. The public health implications of multilateral trade agreements. In: Lee K, Buse K, Fustukian S, eds. *Health Policy in a Globalising World.* Cambridge, England: Cambridge University Press; 2002:18–40.

32. World Trade Organization. General Agreement on Trade in Services, Part IV, progressive liberalization. Available at: http://www.wto.org/english/docs_e/legal_e/26-gats.doc. Accessed May 28, 2004.

33. Sanger M. *Reckless Abandon: Canada, the GATS and the Future of Health Care.* Ottawa, Ontario, Canada: Canadian Centre for Policy Alternatives; 2001.

34. Grieshaber-OttoJ, Sinclair S, Schacter N. Impacts of international trade, services and investment treaties on alcohol regulation. *Addiction.* 2000; 95(suppl 4):S491–S504.

35. Schondelmeyer SW. *Economic Impact of GATT Patent Extension on Currently Marketed Drugs.* Minneapolis, Minn: PRIME Institute, College of Pharmacy, University of Minnesota; 1995.

36. Agreement on Trade-Related Aspects of Intellectual Property Rights, Article 28. Available at: http://www.wto.org/english/docs_e/legal_e/27-trips.doc. Accessed October 20, 2004.

37. Becker E, Pear R. Trade pact may undercut inexpensive drug imports. *New York Times,* July 12, 2004, p. 1.

38. Annas GJ. The right to health and the nevirapine case in South Africa. *N Engl J Med.* 2003;348:750–754.

39. Barnard D. In the high court of South Africa, case no. 4138/98: the global politics of access to low-cost AIDS drugs in poor countries. *Kennedy Inst Ethics J.* 2002;12:159–174.

40. Supakankunti S, Janjaroen WS, Tangphao O, Ratanawijitrasin S, Kraipornsak P, Pradithavanij P. Impact of the World Trade Organization TRIPS agreement on the pharmaceutical industry in Thailand. *Bull World Health Organ.* 2001;79:461–470.

41. Correa CM. *Implications of the Doha Declaration on the TRIPS Agreement and Public Health.* Geneva, Switzerland: World Health Organization; 2002.

42. Henry D, Lexchin J. The pharmaceutical industry as a medicines provider. *Lancet.* 2002;360:1590–1595.

43. Brazil fights for affordable drugs against HIV/AIDS. *Pan Am J Public Health.* 2001;9:331–337.

44. World Trade Organization. Decision of 30 August 2003: WT/L/540. Available at: http://www.wto.org/english/tratop_e/trips_e/implem_para6_e.htm. Accessed May 28, 2004.

45. Doctors without Borders. Doha derailed: a progress report on TRIPS and access to medicines. Available at: www.doctorswithoutborders.org/publications/reports/2003/cancun_report.pdf. Accessed May 28, 2004.

46. Barton JH. TRIPS and the global pharmaceutical market. *Health Aff.* 2004;23:146–154.

47. Attaran A. How do patents and economic policies affect access to essential medicines in developing countries? *Health Aff.* 2004;23:155–166.

48. Labonte R. From the global market to the global village: "free"trade, health and the World Trade Organization. *Promo Educ.* 2003;10(1):23–27, 33–39, 46.

49. Checa N, Maguire J, Barney J. The new world disorder. *Harvard Bus Rev.* 2003;81(8):70–79, 140.

50. Call for health accountability in trade negotiations. Available at: www.cpath.org. Accessed May 28, 2004.

51. Armada F, Muntaner C, Navarro V. Health and social security reforms in Latin America: the convergence of the World Health Organization, the World Bank, and transnational corporations. *Int J Health Serv.* 2001;31:729–768.

52. Bettcher DW, Yach D, Guindon GE. Global trade and health: key linkages and future challenges. *Bull World Health Org.* 2000;78:521–534.

53. Kim JY, Millen JV, Irwin A, Gershman J, eds. *Dying for Growth: Global Inequality and the Health of the Poor.* Monroe, Maine: Common Courage Press; 2000.

54. World Trade Organization Secretariat, World Health Organization. *WTO Agreements and Public Health: A Joint Study by the WHO and the WTO Secretariat.* Geneva, Switzerland: World Trade Organization; 2002.

55. Shaffer ER, Brenner JE. International trade agreements: hazards to health. *Int J Health Serv.* 2004;34:467–481.

56. Fort M, Mercer MA, Gish O, eds. *Sickness and Wealth: The Corporate Assault on Global Health.* Cambridge, Mass: South End Press; 2004.

The Changing Role of the WORLD BANK in Global Health

| Jennifer Prah Ruger, PhD

ABSTRACT

The World Bank began operations on June 25, 1946. Although it was established to finance European reconstruction after World War II, the bank today is a considerable force in the health, nutrition, and population (HNP) sector in developing countries. Indeed, it has evolved from having virtually no presence in global health to being the world's largest financial contributor to health-related projects, now committing more than $1 billion annually for new HNP projects. It is also one of the world's largest supporters in the fight against HIV/AIDS, with commitments of more than $1.6 billion over the past several years.

I have mapped this transformation in the World Bank's role in global health, illustrating shifts in the bank's mission and financial orientation, as well as the broader changes in development theory and practice. Through a deepened understanding of the complexities of development, the World Bank now regards investments in HNP programs as fundamental to its role in the global economy.

INTRODUCTION

June 25, 2004, marked the 58th anniversary of the World Bank, which opened its doors in Washington, DC, in 1946. The International Bank for Reconstruction and Development, as it was initially called, was created at the Bretton Woods Conference in July 1944, along with its sister institution, the International Monetary Fund. At the outset, the bank's dual roles were reconstruction and development, as implied by its original name. Its primary function was to reconstruct Europe after World War II. However, unlike other specialized United Nations (UN) agencies the bank raised funds through private financial markets and received donations on a regular basis from the world's wealthiest countries.[1] With these funds, it provided interest-bearing and interest-free loans, credits, grants, and technical assistance to war-damaged and economically developing countries that could not afford to borrow money in international markets. These activities are ongoing, making the bank the "world's premier economic multilateral"[2] institution.

Over the course of more than 50 years, the bank's priorities and development philosophy—along with its role in the world—have changed from reconstructing Europe to alleviating poverty in developing countries. Perspectives on development also have changed dramatically during that time. New theories and evidence have deepened and transformed the international development debate and have influenced the bank's development practices and policy decisions. In particular, the bank now has a more sophisticated view of well-being, living standards, and poverty. In addition, evidence on the primary means of poverty reduction and development has accumulated throughout the bank's history, and the bank now has an improved, though still evolving, understanding of how to achieve development objectives. In the 1950s and 1960s, for example, when the prevailing wisdom was that economic growth was the key to development, the bank focused primarily on large investments in physical capital and infrastructure, because such investments were viewed as the most likely to increase national income.

However, in the 1960s through 1980s development theory shifted to encompass more than economic growth; it aimed at meeting individuals' "basic needs," because the objective was to provide all human beings with the opportunity for a "full life." This approach appealed to bank staff and especially to Robert McNamara, then president of the bank. Consequentially, the World Bank's focus began to slowly shift to investments in family planning, nutrition, health, and education. In the 1990s, the "Washington Consensus," which emphasized macroeconomic stability, privatization, trade liberalization, and public sector contraction, dominated development thinking, and the bank focused on open markets and economic management. However, lessons learned from this period of market-oriented reforms demonstrated that good governance, strong institutions, and human capital are critical for eradicating global poverty. Today, the bank views development as a holistic and multidimensional process that focuses on people in the societies in which it operates. This "comprehensive development framework" now gives health, nutrition, and population (HNP) programs a central place in the bank's work and mission.

The World Bank is now the world's largest external funder of health, committing more than $1 billion annually in new lending to improve health, nutrition, and population in developing countries.

The World Bank has gone from having virtually no presence in global health to being one of the leading global health institutions. Over time, its loans, credits, and grants to fund HNP programs have become substantial. The largest shift occurred over the past 20 years: World Bank support for social services such as health, nutrition, education, and social security grew from 5% of its portfolio in 1980 to 22% in 2003.[3]

The World Bank is now the world's largest external funder of health,[4] committing more than $1 billion annually in new lending to improve health, nutrition, and population in developing countries.Moreover, it is one of the worlds' largest external funders of the fight against HIV/AIDS, with current commitments of more than $1.3 billion, 50% of that to sub-Saharan Africa.[5] Because it allows long repayment periods (up to 35–40 years and a 10-year grace period), it provides the time and resources to address special problems, such as widespread disease epidemics.

THE EARLY YEARS: BRETTON WOODS

In July 1944, delegates from 45 national governments convened in Bretton Woods, NH, to adopt the Articles of Agreement for the World Bank and the International Monetary Fund, establishing the 2 entities in international law.[6] The nascent bank was the first "multilateral development bank," a uniquely public sector institution created in a post-World War II era of intergovernmental cooperation. The International Monetary Fund, by contrast, was created to stabilize the international monetary system and monitor world currencies. A year later, the UN General Assembly convened in San Francisco, Calif, to draft the UN charter. A new era of multilateralism and intergovernmental cooperation had emerged.

By December 31, 1945, 29 governments had ratified the bank's

Articles of Agreement. In March 1946, the board of governors of the World Bank and the International Monetary Fund were inaugurated in Savannah, Ga, where they adopted the institutions' bylaws and elected the bank's executive directors.[7] The board first met on May 7, 1946. The bank's first president, Eugene Meyer, took office on June 18, and the bank opened its world headquarters at 1818 H Street, NW, Washington, DC, on June 25 (Figure 1).[8]

The job of being the first bank president was challenging. In the 10th anniversary issue of *International Bank Notes*, Mr. Meyer noted that, "Finding the proper path for this new experiment in international cooperation was not easy. We had only the Articles of

Agreement to guide us, and they provided only the sketchiest of outlines."[9]

Meyer resigned after 6 months and was succeeded by John McCloy, who held the position for 2 years, a period that initiated a rapid change in the World Bank's work and geographic orientation.

FROM RECONSTRUCTION TO DEVELOPMENT

McCloy helped shift the bank's focus from postwar reconstruction to economic development. On May 9, 1947, the bank authorized its first loan: $250 million to France for postwar reconstruction. By August 1947, it had authorized reconstruction loans to The Netherlands ($195 million),

FIGURE 1— 1818 H Street, NW, Washington, DC. The World Bank opened for business on the 10th floor of this building on June 25, 1946 (World Bank Group Archives).

Denmark ($40 million), and Luxembourg ($12 million).[10] These first loans were for "reconstruction" (compared with project-specific loans), and they launched the nascent bank into international capital markets. However, the international community soon realized that, instead of piecemeal loans, European and Japanese reconstruction would require a full-fledged effort by international leaders. Hence, the Marshall Plan was established in June 1947.[11] Relieved of the reconstruction burden, the bank's directors turned their full attention to development.

In the postwar era, the prevailing wisdom in development theory was that economic growth (increasing gross national product or growth rates) was the key to development. Therefore, during this era the bank focused primarily on large investments in physical capital and heavy infrastructure. From 1948 to 1961, for example, 87% of its loans to less developed countries were for power and transportation. The remaining commitments provided for other forms of economic overhead, such as industry and telecommunications, and a small fraction (4%) was invested in agriculture and irrigation.[12] Moreover, from January 1949 through April 1961, the bank provided $5.1 billion to 56 countries for 280 different loans, primarily for economic development.[13] The first development loan ($13.5 million), effective on April 7, 1949, was to Chile's Corporacion de Fomento de la Produccion for 4 electric power projects and incidental irrigation.[14] The second development loan ($2.5 million), effective the same day, focused on machinery for Chilean agriculture. Education, health, and other social sectors were not provided for in the loans.[15]

This development theory and investment philosophy remained constant for most of the bank's first 2 decades, espousing the idea that public utility and transportation projects, financial stability, and a strong private sector were the primary means to development.[16] These types of projects were also easier to finance and were considered more appropriate for bank financing.[17] During this time, the World Bank shunned public investments in sanitation, education, and health.[18] One reason for this neglect, as previously mentioned, was the prevailing development paradigm that public utility investments and other economic infrastructure were the key to economic growth. Another reason related to the bank's culture as a "financial institution," because "by the early 1950s the bank's operations and development thinking had been set into a banker's mold."[19] This financial "mold" valued investments that showed a measurable and direct monetary return. As Edward Mason and Robert Asher explain in their book, *The World Bank Since Bretton Woods*,

The contribution of social overhead projects to increased production . . . is less measurable and direct than that of power plants. . . . Financing them, moreover, might open the door to vastly increased demands for loans and raise hackles anew in Wall Street about the "soundness" of the bank's management. It therefore seemed prudent to the management . . . to consider as unsuitable in normal circumstances World Bank financing of projects for eliminating malaria, reducing illiteracy, building vocational schools, or establishing clinics. . . .[20]

Some bank staff and advisors disagreed with this view. E. Harrison Clark, chief of the 1952 Survey Mission to Nicaragua, returned from that country with strong recommendations. The mission reported that expenditures to improve sanitation, education and public health should, without question, be given first priority in any program to increase the long-range growth and development of the Nicaraguan economy . . . high disease rates, low standards of nutrition, and low education and training standards are the major factors inhibiting growth of productivity. . . .[21]

Despite these recommendations, none of the 11 loans Nicaragua received from the World Bank between 1951 and 1960 covered water, sanitation, health, or education.[22]

By virtually ignoring the social sectors, the World Bank charted a different course from the US government and other development institutions. From 1951 to 1954, more than 30% of US foreign aid to South Asia was for health, agriculture, and education.[23] In particular, US bilateral aid to Thailand for public health was a significant priority.[24] Although the primary motivation for US bilateral human resource lending in South Asia appeared to stem from the fear that poverty and ill health bred communist ideology,[25] such investments were consistent with the US post-war emphasis on individualism and human capacity and its confidence in science and medicine.[26] Other development institutions, such as the US Agency for International Development; Food and Agriculture Organization, UN Educational, Science, and Cultural Organization; United Nations Children's Fund (UNICEF); and especially the World Health Organization (WHO), also focused on improving public health.

The rationale for the bank's independent course was both academic and financial. Academic development dialogue at the time emphasized that economic growth was the principal tool for reducing poverty in developing countries and that social services investments would be counterproductive. Davesh Kapur et al. wrote, "Such measures would be temporary palliatives, at the expense of savings and productive investment; direct and immediate attacks on mass poverty would only squander limited national resources."[27]

This "trickle down" economic approach was reinforced by the idea that industrialization and urbanization were necessary for economic growth,[28] a view dominating bank thinking during most of the 1950s and 1960s.[29] Sociologists and economists agreed that urbanization was an inevitable component of development,[30] that income inequality was inevitably linked to economic growth,[31] and that growth, not distribution, should be the focus of development.[32]

The World Bank's financial interests were equally at odds with lending policies that favored social and human resources. Robert Cavanaugh, the bank's chief fundraiser and a bridge between the New York stock market—the bank's primary funding source—and the bank's lending instruments during this period, stated in 1961, If we got into the social field . . . then the bond market would definitely feel that we were not acting prudently from a financial standpoint. . . . If you start financing schools and hospitals and water works, and so forth, these things don't normally and directly increase the ability of a country to repay a borrowing.[33]

Cavanaugh's statement reflected how the World Bank was influenced by potential financial market reactions, especially when it was trying to build a strong reputation within financial markets and development circles. Even if some bank officials thought health and education were important to development, academic and financial influences swayed the bank to put aside welfare matters for the first 25 years of its existence.

INVESTMENTS IN HEALTH, NUTRITION, AND POPULATION PROGRAMS

On April 1, 1968, Robert S. McNamara became president of the World Bank. During his long tenure (ending June 1981), he transformed the bank by moving poverty reduction to center stage. He sought to redefine the bank as a bona fide "development agency" and not just a financial institution[34] and was a forceful agent of change.

McNamara's arrival coincided with a shift in academic thinking and research about development. This shift began in the 1950s, when orthodox views of development[35]—focusing on economic growth—were questioned, and studies found that physical capital played a smaller-than-expected role in economic growth. Moreover, it appeared that a "residual factor" existed in macroeconomic statistical models.[36] This residual factor was believed to be investment in education, innovation, entrepreneurship, and, later,

health.[37] The concepts of "human capital" and "human development"—investments in people—also gained acceptance.[38] The basic needs approach to development influenced the way academics and policymakers viewed development,[39] later forming the cornerstone of the US Agency for International Development program.[40]

These development ideas made sense to McNamara. They both appealed to him personally and were consistent with his own personal history, prior loyalties, and experience with the US government and the private sector. Moreover, internal bank studies and country mission reports revealed that hundreds of millions of people in developing countries were living in extreme poverty and lacking health clinics, primary and secondary schools, and safe drinking water.[41] Such conditions of "underdevelopment" were key barriers to productivity, economic growth, and poverty reduction, and poverty was a direct result of insufficient investments in health and education. Dragoslav Avramovic, acting head of the bank's economics department just before McNamara's arrival, was a strong critic of prevailing orthodox views. His critique of trickle-down economics later provided key aspects of McNamara's attack on poverty.[42] Although shifts in academic thinking about development influenced some bank staff in the 1960s, they did not take root in the bank's policies and institutional ethos until after McNamara arrived in 1968.

The bank's gradual shift toward more social sector lending began with an emphasis on population control, which McNamara regarded as the first step to alleviating poverty. In a landmark speech at the University of Notre Dame in 1969, he urged the international community to address population growth, the "most delicate and difficult issue of our era, perhaps of any era in history."[43] Population control was a major focus for other development agencies at the time, particularly the Ford Foundation and US Agency for International Development. By 1970, McNamara had established the Population Projects Department in the

World Bank and continued to advocate population control in speeches and dialogue with governments. In June 1970, the bank approved its first family planning loan ($2 million)—to Jamaica.[44] By the end of fiscal year (FY) 1973, the bank's lending in family planning totaled $22 million, less than 10% of that given for electric power ($322 million) and telecommunications ($248 million). It was an even lower fraction of that given for agriculture ($938 million) and transportation ($682 million).[45] On August 26, 1974, the report *Population Policies and Economic Development*, which analyzed the effect of rising populations on poverty, was published.[46] However, population control failed to develop into a strong lending program, perhaps because it could not meet the bank's interest in projects that were both acceptable to borrowers and attractive to bank shareholders.[47]

McNamara's attention then turned to nutrition, motivated in part by the International Conference on Nutrition, National Development, and Planning at Massachusetts Institute of Technology in 1971 and the International Nutrition Planning Program established in 1972 at the university and funded by the Rockefeller Foundation and US Agency for International Development.[48] In November 1970, biochemist James Lee became the bank's scientific advisor and was responsible for nutrition policy along with other areas of science.[49] In his speech at the bank's 1971 annual meeting, McNamara emphasized that "malnutrition is widespread and it limits the physical, and often the mental growth of hundreds of millions and it is a major barrier to human development."[50] By January 1972, the World Bank report *Possible Bank Actions on Malnutrition Problems* led to the establishment of a bank nutrition unit. In 1973, Alan Berg's book *The Nutrition Factor* and a 1973 nutrition policy paper, which called for a more active role in nutrition, reinforced McNamara's support for eventual bank lending in that area.[51] However, the

FIGURE 2— Villagers being examined by a member of the Onchocerciasis Control Program (World Bank Group Archives).

bank did not approve its first loan for nutrition (to Brazil for $19 million) until 1976.[52]

Since 1970, McNamara had been advocating bank support of health and nutrition programs, as in speeches at Columbia University (1970) and the bank's annual general meetings (1972). In June 1973, he requested a health policy paper from bank staff.[53] The resulting 1975 *Health Sector Policy Paper* was 1 of the bank's first efforts to generate and disseminate knowledge on health policy issues. In 1974, 1 of the bank's most successful programs, the Onchocerciasis Control Program (OCP), was created to eliminate onchocerciasis (river blindness) and enhance country and regional control of the disease (Figure 2). This health initiative involved 11 countries in West Africa and was sponsored, along with the World Bank, by United Nations Development Program (UNDP), Food and Agriculture Organization, and WHO. It also involved the private sector and nongovernmental organizations. Onchocerciasis is caused by a parasitic worm and is spread by black flies that breed in fast-flowing water. The group determined they could stop flies from transmitting the disease by treating the

water flow. The OCP also established a program of insecticide application to prevent the growth of black flies.[54]

Because the bank was not notably engaged in health issues at the time, its decision to tackle river blindness was a turning point. The program, which continued for some 30 years, protected an estimated 34 million people from river blindness and cleared nearly 25 million hectares of land for agricultural use.[55] The OCP gave the bank a boost in the health sector. In 1979, the bank established a health department and a policy to consider funding stand-alone health projects, as well as health components in other projects.[56]

These efforts in the health arena were influenced by the growing recognition in academic and policymaking development discourse that the basic needs approach was essential to poverty reduction.[57] McNamara, in particular, engaged with this dialogue. In his 1976 address to the annual general meeting of the board of governors in Manila, the Philippine Islands, he underscored the need to reexamine trickle-down economics and to focus on the unmet basic human needs of hundreds of millions of people in developing countries.[58] Over the ensuing years, he called for further

research within the bank before endorsing a full-scale lending program for basic needs.

Despite its failure to become fully institutionalized in World Bank culture and policy, the basic-needs approach laid the foundation for further expansion in the bank's HNP sector. Official recognition of this shift came most publicly in the *World Development Report, 1980* which demonstrated that malnutrition and ill health were 2 of the worst symptoms of poverty and that both could be addressed by direct government action, with bank assistance. The report also suggested that improving health and nutrition would likely accelerate economic growth. After a series of research papers suggested that health and education were directly productive, these findings were incorporated in the *World Development Report, 1980* to argue for greater emphases on social sector lending.[59]

Because the bank was not notably engaged in health issues at the time, its decision to tackle river blindness was a turning point. The program, which continued for 30 years, protected an estimated 34 million people from river blindness and cleared 25 million hectares of land for agricultural use.

The bank translated development theory and research into action by creating the Population, Health, and Nutrition Department in October 1979 and allowing stand-alone health loans. A 1980 *Health Sector Policy Paper* was 1 of the first attempts to provide a rationale for stand-alone investments in the health sector.[60]

In 1980, the bank approved another nutrition loan—to the India Tamil Nadu Nutrition project. In 1984, it provided a $2 million grant for social emergency programs, and, in 1985, it gave a $3 million grant to the World Food Program for emergency food supplies to sub-Saharan Africa.[61] The creation of the Population, Health, and Nutrition Department became a landmark in the World Bank's involvement in health.

On February 10, 1987, the bank cosponsored—with WHO and United Nations Population Fund—a conference in Nairobi, Kenya, on safe motherhood.[62] This conference launched the bank's Safe Motherhood initiative, which was its first global commitment to health issues of this nature; the program is now in its 17th year. This initiative solidified the bank's commitment to family planning and maternal and child health. The public and financial commitments resonating from this initiative became important pillars of the bank's health sector work. Safe motherhood projects increased from 10 in 1987 to 150 in 1999, with an annual commitment of $385 million between 1992 and 1999—30% of total bank HNP lending.[63] Between 1987 and 1998, the bank supported safe delivery activities in 29 countries.[64] In 1987, it loaned $10 million for Zimbabwe's Family Health Project and $11 million to Malawi for its Second Family Health Project. In 1990, it supported a $267 million loan to Brazil's Second Northeast Basic Health Services Project.[65]

A second global health conference on safe motherhood, sponsored by the World Bank, WHO, UNICEF, and United Nations Population Fund, took place on January 30, 1989, in Niamey, Nigeria. A November 1989 bank report, *Sub-Saharan Africa: From Crisis to Sustainable Growth*, followed and called for doubling expenditures on human resource development.[66] Together, these events provided further momentum for investments in family planning and child and maternal health. In 1998, the bank loaned $300 million for India's Women and Child Development Project and $250 million for Bangladesh's Health and Population Program Project.[67] The bank's family planning work was not without controversy, however. Its *World Development Report, 1984: Population and Development* which emphasized governments' role in reducing fertility and mortality,[68] was criticized, as were its family-planning projects (drawn into abortion politics) in Latin America and elsewhere (Figure 3).[69]

Other noteworthy early HNP activities included the first loan in 1981 to Tunisia to expand basic health services, the 1987 study *Financing Health Services in Developing Countries: An Agenda for Reform*, and the bank's seminal *World Development Report, 1993: Investing in Health*.[70] The 1987 document, in particular, underscored the need for improved health sector financing and included user fees/charges, which are highly controversial, as 1 instrument for mobilizing resources. The *World Development Report, 1993* was a watershed in international health, giving the World Bank greater exposure and legitimacy in the health sector. The first *World Development Report* devoted entirely to health (signaling the bank's commitment), its overall aim was to make the case to the broader development community for investing in health. The *World Development Report, 1993* identified several major problems in international health systems, in particular, inefficient use of funds and human resources, inequitable access to basic heath care, and rising health care costs. As a result, the bank advocated several key recommendations for improving health: educating girls and empowering women, reallocating government resources from tertiary facilities to primary care, investing in public health and essential clinical services, and promoting private and social insurance and competition in health services delivery. Although generally well received, the report was criticized for introducing disability-adjust-ed life years (DALYs), for lacking a strong evidence base, and for promoting privatization.[71]

THE WORLD BANK'S INCREASING INVOLVEMENT IN GLOBAL HEALTH

The *World Development Report, 1993* has been supplemented over the past decade with bank operational research and analysis, including the bank's Special Program of Research, Development and Training in Human Reproduction, the WHO/United Nations Development Program/World Bank Tropical Diseases Research Program, and the Global Micronutrient Initiative.[72] Since 1993, the bank has also increased its support of country-specific research and analysis of HNP issues, primarily through bank loans and credits, which has resulted in significant external HNP research funding in developing countries.[73] The World Bank's own Policy Research Department has also grown its interest in HNP issues and now spends $1 million annually (8% of the department's total research budget) on HNP studies.[74] Such policy research builds on the bank's comparative advantage in economic and intersectoral analysis related to health issues. Other areas of bank involvement in global health knowledge include training and semi-

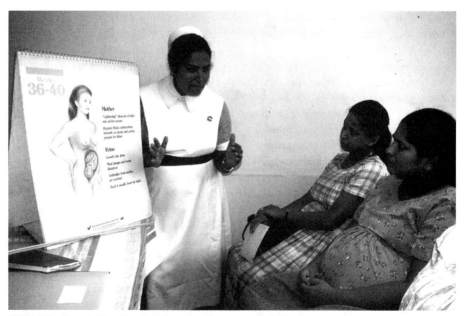

FIGURE 3— Prenatal health education class for women in Sri Lanka Dominic Sansoni/The World Bank).

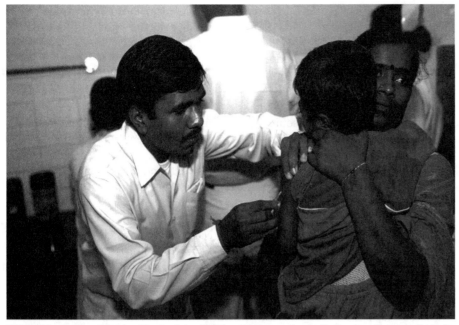

FIGURE 4— Doctor giving health check to child from slum area in charity-run hospital in India (John Isaac/The World Bank).

nars on HNP topics for policymakers in developing countries. Over the past several years, the bank has produced 210 country-specific HNP sector studies and staff appraisal reports and hundreds of country strategy documents on HNP topics,[75] including, for example, a study in Morocco on health financing and insurance.[76]

Although the bank's role in generating and disseminating global health knowledge is important, its main advantage compared with other international institutions is its ability to mobilize financial resources. By far the most dramatic change in its role in global health has been its increased financial support for HNP through loans, credits, and grants. Indeed, it is now the "single largest external source of HNP financing in low- and middle-income countries."[77] In contrast to approving only 1 HNP loan in 1970, it had financed 154 active and 94 completed projects in 1997 with a total of $13.5 billion.[78] From 1987 to 1992 alone, it tripled its HNP lending, and the average number of new projects per year increased from 8 in FY 1987–1989 ($317 million annually) to 21 in FY 1990–1992 ($1.2 billion annually).[79] HNP projects grew from less than 1% of total World Bank lending in 1987 to nearly 7% in

1991.[80] By the end of FY 1996, the World Bank's new annual lending was $21 billion, and 24% of that was directed to HNP (11% or $2.4 million), education (8%), and social protection (5%).[81]

The types of HNP activities pursued by the bank also have changed over the past several years. Early projects focused primarily on strengthening countries' basic HNP infrastructure and services, specific diseases (e.g., OCP), and certain populations (e.g., rural development). However, a late-1990s review by the bank's Operations Evaluation Development Department of 120 projects conducted between FY 1970–1995 found that the narrow focus on capital investment failed to achieve the significant institutional and systematic changes necessary for project effectiveness. It also found that the bank's HNP portfolio was fragmented and of uneven quality.[82] This assessment has led the bank to shift its HNP activities away from basic health services toward broader policy reforms.[83] The Operations Evaluation Development Department review also called for a strategic policy direction and for lending supported by rigorous analysis and research. The bank responded with its 1997 *HNP Sector Strategy Paper*.[84]

The review also recommended enhanced selectivity, involving a focus on country needs and an analysis of the costs, benefits, and risks (including political, institutional, and economic) of all planned HNP activities (Figure 4).

The World Bank also tried to tune into the international dialogue on the need to improve the effectiveness of development assistance through cooperation among agencies. A key lesson learned over the past decades is that institutions acting alone cannot meet complex HNP challenges. Thus, the bank has been working to strengthen its collaboration with other international organizations. In Brazil, Uganda, and Ghana, it collaborated with other donors through its sector-wide approach programs, which aim to bring multiple donors together to fund an entire sector, develop comprehensive sector-wide policies, and pursue similar policy objectives. Sector-wide approach programs are an improvement on the previously fragmented approach of multiple donors funding ad hoc projects without coordination, but they have not been without controversy.[85]

However, the World Bank recognizes that it must do more to strengthen its partnerships with client countries, civil society, stakeholders, and other agencies. Recently, it entered into collaborative agreements with WHO that will provide technical assistance for improving the design, supervision, and evaluation of bank-supported projects. The WHO and the World Bank are collaborating to advance international understanding of HNP issues, as was done, for example, through the recent Framework Convention for Tobacco Control, through which the bank worked with WHO to establish the evidence base on effective methods of curbing the prevalence and consumption of tobacco products.

CRITICISMS OF THE WORLD BANK

The World Bank and its policies are among the most hotly debated and highly criticized in the global development community. With regard to health sector policies, key concerns involve user fees, structural adjustment, use of DALYs, and privatization.

In its 1987 report on financing, the bank highlighted user fees as an instrument for mobilizing resources. However, empirical evidence demonstrates that user fees reduce the demand for both necessary and unnecessary care and that they disproportionately affect poor and sick people. Evidence also suggests that such fees have not been overwhelmingly successful in raising revenue or enhancing efficiency. In its 1997 sector strategy, the bank claimed that it does not support user fees; however, it maintained that such fees are 1 tool for mobilizing resources. By contrast, critics prefer the bank to reject user fees entirely, a policy the World Bank has yet to pursue.

In the 1980s and 1990s, the bank pressured countries to adopt "structural adjustment" programs for their economies and to follow many prescriptions of the "Washington Consensus" by emphasizing economic management, macroeconomic stability, privatization, trade liberalization, and public sector contraction. This involved opening markets (trade liberalization), reducing government expenditures (in some cases for health), and privatizing state-owned enterprises. Critics argue that such programs reduce health care spending and have deleterious health effects.[86] UNICEF estimated that structural adjustment programs may have been associated with 500 000 deaths of young children in a 12-month period,[87] even though a 1998 study of the effect of structural adjustment operations on health expenditures and outcomes and the World Bank's own research[88] found no negative impact.[89] Still, much concern remains both within and outside the bank on the efficacy and negative effect of such programs, and the bank has moved away from endorsing them.

The bank also was criticized for introducing DALYs to global health assessments. It described DALYs in the *World Development Report, 1993* as a way to conceptualize and measure the global disease burden and to associate this burden with health and other social policies. Critics argue that DALYs lack a sound theoretical framework and are inequitable because they value years saved for the able-bodied more than for the disabled, the middle-aged more than the young or old, and the currently ill more than those who will be ill tomorrow.[90] By introducing DALYs, the bank contends it improved analysis of international health systems. Critics remain concerned with its use in global health, and the debate continues.

Critics also have been concerned about the negative effects of the World Bank's support for privatization in general and the health sector specifically.[91] Research focused on private markets in the health sector has demonstrated that a strong government is necessary to address market failures that occur in financing, consuming, and providing both personal and public health services. Insurance market failures, credit shortages, information asymmetries, and insufficiencies, in particular, can inhibit people from realizing economic benefits that accrue from collective risk reduction through risk pooling.[92] However, although the bank now admits that open markets and economic management are insufficient and that good governance and strong institutions are critical for eradicating poverty, in the health sector, more specifically, critics argue the bank needs to present a clearer position on the trade-offs between public and private financing and delivery of health services.[93]

CONCLUSION

The World Bank today is very different from the organization conceived at Bretton Woods in 1944. Its mission has changed from post–World War II reconstruction and development to worldwide poverty alleviation. Although the bank invested almost exclusively in physical infrastructure in its early days, its focus has broadened to include significantly more social sector lending. A major expansion of the bank's work in HNP took place between the late 1980s and late 1990s, and the bank is now the world's largest external funder of health and one of the largest supporters in the fight against HIV/AIDS.

The World Bank's role in global health has evolved through a better understanding of development, which the bank now sees as a holistic, integrated, and multidimensional task that should balance the strengths of the market and other institutions and focus on people in client countries.[94] This approach reflects, in part, a new paradigm of academic thought that development is the process of expanding the real freedoms people enjoy,[95] a concept set forth by Amartya Sen. Lessons learned from 50 years of development experience and theory suggest that economic growth, investments in infrastructure and physical capital, macroeconomic stability, liberalization, and privatization still matter, but that development is multifaceted and our understanding of it must be broad and inclusive. A number of key elements, including economic growth and stability, a thriving private sector, investment in people and physical assets, a sustainable environment, and sound institutions and policies are necessary to promote prosperity, reduce poverty, and improve the human condition.

In the late 1990s, the bank's *Voices of the Poor* study, which provided detailed interviews of impoverished people in developing countries,[96] showed that the experience and determinants of poverty are multidimensional. Poor people require not only higher incomes but also security and empowerment, opportunities for education, jobs, health and nutrition, a clean and sustainable environment, a well-functioning judicial and legal system, civil and political liberties, and a rich cultural life. Reflecting these views, the Bank's *World Development Report, 2000–2001* on Poverty[97] identified good health and nutrition and effective reproductive policies and health services as critical for allowing countries to break the vicious circle of poverty, high fertility, poor health, and low economic growth.

All of these changes in the bank's mission, leadership, research, and philosophy have made health, nutrition, and population programs priorities for its work and for the wider development community. The World Bank's evolution, like development research and thinking, has been slow and steady, suggesting that health's importance to development[98] is a concept with long-lasting implications.

About the Author

At the time of writing the author was with Washington University School of Medicine in St. Louis, Mo.

Correspondence: Requests for reprints should be sent to Jennifer Prah Ruger, PhD, Yale University School of Medicine, Department of Epidemiology and Public Health, 60 College Street, P.O. Box 208034, New Haven, CT (e-mail: jennifer.ruger@yale.edu).

Acknowledgments

The author is supported in part by a Career Development Award from the US National Institutes of Health (grant 1K01DA01635810).

The author thanks Kimberly Hannon and Susan Gatchel for administrative assistance, Linda Sage for editing assistance, and Washington University Center for Health Policy and School of Medicine for support.

Human Participant Protection

No human participants were involved with this study

Footnotes

The author worked previously as a health economist in the health, nutrition, and population sector and as speechwriter to James D. Wolfensohn, president of the World Bank.

References

1. World Bank, "What is the World Bank," http://web.worldbank.org/WBSITE/EXTERNAL/EXTABOUTUS/0,,contentMDK:20040558~menuPK:34559~pagePK:34542~piPK:36600~the-SitePK:29708,00.html (accessed February 27, 2004).

2. D.Kapur, J. P. Lewis, and R. Webb, *The World Bank. Its First Half Century, Volume 1: History* (Washington, DC: Brookings Institution, 1997), 2.

3. World Bank, "Ten Things You Never Knew About the World Bank," http://www.worldbank.org/tenthings/index.html (accessed March 5, 2004).

4. The Human Development Network, *Health, Nutrition, & Population*, World Bank Sector Strategy Paper (Washington, DC: World Bank, 1997).

5. World Bank, "What is the World Bank."

6. World Bank, "World Bank Group Historical Chronology 1944–1949," http://web.worldbank.org/WBSITE/EXTERNAL/EXTABOUTUS/EXTARCHIVES/0,,contentMDK:20035657~menuPK:56307~pagePK:36726~piPK:36092~the-SitePK:29506,00.html (accessed February 27, 2004).

7. Ibid.

8. World Bank, "Pages from World Bank History—Bank's 57th Birthday Retrospective," http://web.worldbank.org/WBSITE/EXTERNAL/EXTABOUTUS/EXTARCHIVES/0,,contentMDK:20116771~pagePK:36726~piPK:36092~theSitePK:29506,00.html (accessed February 25, 2004).

9. World Bank, *International Bank Notes*, June 1956, quoted in World Bank, "Pages for World Bank History—Bank's 57th Birthday Retrospective."

10. World Bank, "Pages from World Bank History: Bank's First Development Loans," May 30, 2003, http://web.worldbank.org/WBSITE/EXTERNAL/EXTABOUTUS/EXTARCHIVES/0,,contentMDK:20113929~pagePK:36726~piPK:36092~theSitePK:29506,00.html (accessed February 25, 2004); World Bank, "World Bank Group Historical Chronology 1944–1949."

11. Kapur, Lewis, and Webb, *The World Bank. Its First Half Century.*

12. Ibid, 85–86, 109–110.

13. Ibid, 85–86, 109–110.

14. World Bank, "Pages from World Bank History: Bank's First Development Loans."

15. Kapur, Lewis, and Webb, *The World Bank. Its First Half Century*, 82; World Bank, "Pages from World Bank History: Bank's First Development Loans."

16. E. S.Mason and R. E. Asher, *The World Bank Since Bretton Woods* (Washington, DC: Brookings Institution, 1973.)

17. L.Currie, *The Role of Economic Advisors in Developing Countries* (Seattle, WA: Greenwood Press, 1981).

18. Kapur, Lewis, and Webb, *The World Bank. Its First Half Century.*

19. Ibid, 85.

20. Mason and Asher, *The World Bank Since Bretton Woods*, 151–152.

21. World Bank, *The Economic Development of Nicaragua*, (Baltimore, MD: Johns Hopkins University Press, 1953), 22–23, quoted in Kapur, Lewis, and Webb, *The World Bank. Its First Half Century*, 111.

22. Kapur, Lewis, and Webb, *The World Bank: Its First Half Century.*

23. C.Wolf, *Foreign Aid: Theory and Practice in Southern Asia* (Princeton, NJ: Princeton University Press, 1960).

24. R. J.Muscat, *Thailand and the United States: Development, Security, and Foreign Aid* (New York: Columbia University Press, 1990).

25. Kapur, Lewis, and Webb, *The World Bank. Its First Half Century.*

26. R. A.Pastor, *Congress and the Politics of U.S. Foreign Economic Policy, 1929–1976* (Berkeley: University of California Press, 1980).

27. Kapur, Lewis, and Webb, *The World Bank. Its First Half Century*, 115.

28. J.Morris, *The Road to Huddersfield* (New York: Pantheon, 1963).

29. H. B.Chenery, "The Role of Industrialization in Development Programs," *American Economic Review* 45 (1955): 40; W.A. Lewis, "Economic Development with Unlimited Supplies of Labour," *Manchester School of Economic and Social Studies* 22 (1954): 131–191; W.A. Lewis, *Theory of Economic Growth* (London: George Allen and Unwin, 1955); B. F. Johnston and J. W. Mellor, "The Role of Agriculture in Economic Development," *American Economic Review* 51 (1961): 566–93; Kapur, Lewis, and Webb, *The World Bank. Its First Half Century.*

30. C. D. H.Cole, *Introduction to Economic History, 1750–1950* (London: Macmillan, 1952).

31. S.Kuznets, "Economic Growth and Income Equality," *American Economic Review* 45 (1955): 1–28.

32. Lewis, *Theory of Economic Growth.*

33. R. W.Cavanaugh, interview, World Bank Oral History Program, July 25, 1961, 63–64, quoted in Kapur et al., *The World Bank. Its First Half Century*, 119–120.

34. Kapur, Lewis, and Webb, *The World Bank. Its First Half Century.*

35. Lewis, *Theory of Economic Growth.*

36. M.Abramovitz, *Resource and Output Trends in the United States Since 1870*, Occasional Paper 52 (New York:

National Bureau of Economic Research, 1956).

37. S.Enke, *Economics for Development* (London: Dennis Dobson, 1963).

38. T.W. Shultz, "Investment in Human Capital," *American Economic Review* 51 (1961): 11.

39. P.Streeten, *The Distinctive Features of a Basic Needs Approach to Development*, Basic Needs Paper 2, World Bank Policy Planning and Program Review Department, Washington, DC, August 10, 1977.

40. R. H.Sartorius and V. W. Ruttan, "The Sources of the Basic Needs Mandate," *Journal of Developing Areas* 23 (1989): 331–62.

41. Kapur, Lewis, and Webb, *The World Bank: Its First Half Century.*

42. Memorandum, Dragoslav Avramovic to George D. Woods, February 13, 1964, cited in Kapur, Lewis, and Webb, *The World Bank. Its First Half Century*, 208.

43. World Bank, "Pages from World Bank History—Bank Pays Tribute to Robert McNamara," March 21, 2003, http://web.worldbank.org/WBSITE/EXTERNAL/EXTABOUTUS/EXTARCHIVES/0,,contentMDK:20100171~pagePK:36726~piPK:36092~theSitePK:29506,00.html (accessed February 25, 2004).

44. World Bank, "World Bank Group Historical Chronology 1970–1979," http://web.worldbank.org/WBSITE/EXTERNAL/EXTABOUTUS/EXTARCHIVES/0,,contentMDK:20035661~menuPK:56317~pagePK:36726~piPK:36092~theSitePK:29506,00.html (accessed February 27, 2004).

45. World Bank, "Pages from World Bank History: Excerpts from the 1973 Annual Report," http://web.worldbank.org/WBSITE/EXTERNAL/EXTABOUTUS/EXTARCHIVES/0,,contentMDK:20108747~pagePK:36726~piPK:36092~theSitePK:29506,00.html (accessed November 10, 2004).

46. World Bank, "World Bank Group Historical Chronology 1970–1979."

47. Kapur, Lewis, and Webb, *The World Bank. Its First Half Century.*

48. Ibid, 253.

49. Ibid.

50. World Bank, "Pages from World Bank History—Bank Pays Tribute to Bob McNamara."

51. Kapur, Lewis, and Webb, *The World Bank. Its First Half Century*, 253–254.

52. World Bank, "World Bank Group Historical Chronology 1970–1979,"

53. Kapur, Lewis, and Webb, *The World*

Bank. Its First Half Century.*

54. World Bank, "Pages from World Bank History: The Fight Against Riverblindness," March 14, 2003, http://web.worldbank.org/WBSITE/EXTERNAL/EXTABOUTUS/EXTARCHIVES/0,,contentMDK:20098846~pagePK:36726~piPK:36092~theSitePK:29506,00.html (accessed February 25, 2004).

55. Ibid.

56. Kapur, Lewis, and Webb, *The World Bank. Its First Half Century*, 345.

57. P.Streeten with Shahid Javed Burki, et al., *First Things First: Meeting Basic Human Needs in Developing Countries*, (Oxford: Oxford University Press, 1981).

58. R. S.McNamara, "To the Board of Governors, 1976, Manila, Philippines, October 4, 1976," in McNamara, *The McNamara Years at the World Bank*, 337, quoted in Kapur, Lewis, and Webb, *The World Bank. Its First Half Century*, 266.

59. World Bank, *World Development Report, 1980* (New York: Oxford University Press, 1980).

60. The Human Development Network, *Health, Nutrition, and Population.*

61. World Bank, "World Bank Group Historical Chronology 1980–1989," http://web.worldbank.org/WBSITE/EXTERNAL/EXTABOUTUS/EXTARCHIVES/0,,contentMDK:20035663~menuPK:56318~pagePK:36726~piPK:36092~theSitePK:29506,00.html (accessed February 27, 2004).

62. Ibid.

63. The Human Development Network, *Safe Motherhood and the World Bank: Lessons From 10 Years of Experience*, (Washington, DC: The World Bank, 1999), 5.

64. Ibid, 33.

65. Ibid, 25.

66. World Bank, "World Bank Group Historical Chronology 1980–1989."

67. The Human Development Network, *Safe Motherhood and the World Bank*, 30.

68. World Bank, *World Development Report, 1984: Population and Development* (New York: Oxford University Press, 1984).

69. World Bank, "World Bank Group Historical Chronology 1990–1999."

70. World Bank, *World Development Report, 1993: Investing in Health* (New York: Oxford University Press, 1993).

71. K.Abbasi, "The World Bank and World Health: Under Fire," *British Medical Journal* 318 (1999), 1003–6.

72. The Human Development Network, *Health, Nutrition, & Population.*

73. Ibid, 11.

74. Ibid, 11.

75. Ibid, 13.

76. G. J.Schieber, J. P. Ruger, N. Klingen, A. M. Pierre-Louis, and Z. E. Driss, *Morocco Health Financing Brief*, World Bank Document (Washington, DC: World Bank, 1999); J. P. Ruger. "Health Financing and Insurance in Morocco" (paper presented at the Symposium on Health Sector Financing in Morocco, jointly sponsored by the Government of Morocco and the World Bank, Rabat, Morocco, June 1999).

77. The Human Development Network, *Health, Nutrition, & Population*, ix.

78. Ibid, ix.

79. World Bank, *World Development Report, 1993*, 169.

80. Ibid, 169.

81. The Human Development Network, *Health, Nutrition, & Population*, 69.

82. Ibid, 15.

83. Ibid.

84. The Human Development Network, *Health, Nutrition, & Population.*

85. Abbasi, "The World Bank and World Health: Under Fire."

86. M.Rao (ed.), *Disinvesting in Health: The World Bank's Prescriptions for Health* (Thousand Oaks, CA: Sage Publications, 1999).

87. UNICEF. *The State of the World's Children* (New York: Oxford University Press, 1989), 16–7.

88. World Bank, *Adjustment Lending: Policies for Sustainable Growth* (Washington DC: World Bank, 1990), 11; Abbasi, "The World Bank and World Health: Under Fire."

89. J.Van der Gaag and T. Barham, "Health and Health Expenditures in Adjusting and Non-Adjusting Countries," *Social Science and Medicine* 46 (1998): 995–1009.

90. Abbasi, "The World Bank and World Health: Under Fire"; S. Anand and K. Hanson, "DALYs: Efficiency Versus Equity," *World Development* 26 (1998): 307–10.

91. M.Turshen, *Privatizing Health Services in Africa* (New Brunswick, NJ: Rutgers University Press, 1999).

92. J. P.Ruger, D. Jamison, D. Bloom, "Health and the Economy," in *International Public Health: Disease, Programs, Systems, and Policies*, ed. M. Merson, R. Black, A. Mills, 617–66 (New York: Aspen Publishers, 2001); J. P. Ruger, "Catastrophic health

expenditure" *Lancet* 2003 Sep 20; 362: 996–7.

93. K.Abbasi, "The World Bank and World Health: Interview with Richard Feachem," *British Medical Journal* 318 (1999): 1206–8; A. Wagstaff, "Economics, Health and Development: Some Ethical Dilemmas Facing the World Bank and the International Community," *Journal of Medical Ethics* 27(2000): 262–7.

94. World Bank, Comprehensive Development Framework, http://web.worldbank.org/WBSITE/E XTERNAL/PROJECTS/STRATE-GIES/CDF/0,,pagePK:60447~theSite PK:140576,00.html (accessed March 5, 2004).

95. A. K.Sen. *Development as Freedom* (New York: Knopf, 1999); J. P. Ruger, "Health and Development," *Lancet* 362 (2003): 678; J. P. Ruger, "Combating HIV/AIDS in Developing Countries," *British Medical Journal* 329 (2004): 121–2; J. P. Ruger, "Health and Social Justice," *Lancet* 2004; 364:1075–80; J. P. Ruger, "Ethics of the Social Determinants of Health," *Lancet* 2004; 364: 1092–97; J. P. Ruger, "Aristotelian Justice and Health Policy: Capability and Incompletely Theorized Agreements" (Ph.D. thesis, Harvard University, 1998).

96. D.Narayan, R. Patel, K. Schafft, A. Rademacher, and S. Koch-Schulte. *Voices of the Poor: Can Anyone Hear Us?* (New York: Oxford University Press, 2000); D. Narayan, R. Chambers, M. K. Shah, P. Petesch. *Voices of the Poor: Crying Out for Change* (New York: Oxford University Press, 2000).

97. World Bank, *World Development Report, 2000–2001: Attacking Poverty* (New York: Oxford University Press, 2001).

98. Ruger JP. Millennium development goals for health: building human capabilities. *Bulletin of the World Health Organization.* 2004;82(12):951–952.

Ethics in Public Health Research: A Research Protocol to Evaluate the Effectiveness of Public–Private Partnerships as a Means to Improve Health and Welfare Systems Worldwide

| Donald A. Barr, PhD, MD

ABSTRACT

Public–private partnerships have become a common approach to health care problems worldwide. Many public–private partnerships were created during the late 1990s, but most were focused on specific diseases such as HIV/AIDS, tuberculosis, and malaria.

Recently there has been enthusiasm for using public–private partnerships to improve the delivery of health and welfare services for a wider range of health problems, especially in developing countries. The success of public–private partnerships in this context appears to be mixed, and few data are available to evaluate their effectiveness.

This analysis provides an overview of the history of health-related public–private partnerships during the past 20 years and describes a research protocol commissioned by the World Health Organization to evaluate the effectiveness of public–private partnerships in a research context.

INTRODUCTION

In November 2002, the World Health Organization (WHO) Centre for Health Development in Kobe, Japan, convened the Global Symposium on Health and Welfare Systems Development. Participants concurred that strategies to improve the availability of health and welfare services in developing countries should include an increased emphasis on ". . . partnerships among communities, civil societies, the private sector and government."[1(p15)] The report from this symposium recommended that WHO member states explore ways of adopting the public–private partnership model for the delivery of health and welfare services. At the same time, though, the conference report acknowledged that there is a lack of scientific evidence regarding the effectiveness of these partnerships.

In 2003, the WHO Centre for Health Development asked researchers at Stanford University to assist in the development of a research protocol to evaluate the effectiveness of the public–private partnership model. From the development of this protocol it became evident that there is tremendous enthusiasm internationally for use of the public–private partnership model to improve health care, but no common understanding about what precisely constitutes a public–private partnership. In addition, there is a lack of firm evidence of the circumstances under which a public–private partnership approach is preferable to more traditional models. I provide an overview of the history of the public–private partnership worldwide movement and propose criteria by which the effectiveness of public–private partnerships might be assessed.

PUBLIC AND PRIVATE SECTOR INVOLVEMENT IN HEALTH SERVICES

Article 25 of the United Nations' Universal Declaration of Human Rights[2] affirms that all people have a right to what Amartya Sen referred to as "social opportunities," which he described as "the arrangements that society makes for education, health care, and so on, which influence the individual's substantive freedom to live better."[3(p39)] On the basis of these principles, established at the time of the founding of the United Nations, responsibility for maintaining systems to promote health and welfare was situated primarily within the public sector. During the 1980s, political and economic disruptions in many areas of the world led to a reassessment of this reliance on the public sector. Both national governments and global economic organizations began to shift to an increasing reliance on the private sector for improvements in health and welfare systems. The restructuring of the British National Health Service under Prime Minister Margaret Thatcher and the restructuring of the Mexican health care system as part of the international response to its economic crises were examples of the movement toward privatization and increased reliance on market forces that became increasingly widespread.

William Hsiao of Harvard University published an analysis of the effects of these marketization efforts in the health care systems of 4 countries. Calling marketization "the illusory magic pill," Hsiao concluded that "neither pure centrally planned nor free-market health systems can achieve maximum efficiency. A complex mixed system seems to be the answer."[4(p356)] Hsiao called for a collaborative effort by public and private sectors to confront the health care challenges of developing countries. The effort would emphasize an incremental approach, evaluate demonstration sites on an experimental basis, and eventually expand the model based on evidence of its efficacy.

Around the same time Hsiao published his analysis, perceptions about the role of the private sector in providing health and welfare services were rapidly shifting. Rather than adopting a pure privatization model, increased emphasis was placed on establishing partnerships between the public sector and various organizations in the private sector.[5] The term "public–private partnership" became common and was typically referred to simply by its acronym "PPP." Before 1990, the term public–private partnership rarely appeared in articles abstracted in PubMed. Figure 1 shows that between 1990 and 2004 there has been a steady increase in the use of the term.

The enthusiasm for the public–private partnership approach to global health problems was evident in a series of articles published in 2000 and 2001. One article suggested that, "through the emerging new paradigm of public– private partnerships . . . the challenges of the myriad unmet health needs of developing nations can begin to be fulfilled."[6(p65)] Two articles described "the proliferation of public–private partnerships [that] is rapidly reconfiguring the international health landscape."[7(p549),8] An editorial in the *British Medical Journal* referred

to public–private partnerships as "essential" for getting vaccines and new medicines to the world's poorest populations.[9] One author emphasized the advantages of the public–private partnership model and issued a "global call for action."[10(p5)]

Despite increased attention to the public–private partnership model, there has been no consistent definition of what, precisely, constitutes a public–private partnership. WHO has acknowledged the diversity of arrangements subsumed under the public–private partnership moniker: "The term public–private partnerships covers a wide variety of ventures involving a diversity of arrangements, varying with regard to participants, legal status, governance, management, policy-setting prerogatives, contributions and operational roles."[11]

The enthusiasm for a public–private partnership approach to global health problems arose in response to the convergence of a number of forces during the mid- and late 1990s. The first was the growing skepticism directed at a private sector approach. A second force was a growing pattern of collaboration in the United States between the federal government, private universities, and private pharmaceutical companies in the development and marketing of new pharmaceutical

products; a collaboration initiated by the Bayh–Doyle Act that was passed by Congress in 1980.[12] The third force was the decision by the Rockefeller Foundation, the Bill and Melinda Gates Foundation, and other organizations to rely extensively on the public–private partnership model when funding efforts to address the growing worldwide crises of HIV/AIDS, malaria, tuberculosis, and other major diseases.

Not all observers shared the enthusiasm of early public–private partnership proponents. Muraskin described the experience of establishing the global Children's Vaccine Initiative, citing "the political problems caused by organizational and national rivalries that the new [public–private partnership] venture faced from its inception."[13(p1721)] In a similar vein, Birn cited the "political obstacles to decentralizing fiscal power, redistributing resources in an equitable fashion, and eliminating the inefficiencies of separate but unequal health systems,"[14(p81)] that plagued Mexico's attempt to improve health and welfare systems through the integration of public and private sectors.

In 2001 the Bill and Melinda Gates Foundation provided a grant of $1 million in support of the worldwide Initiative on Public–Private Partnerships for Health (IPPPH).[16] As part of this effort, IPPPH cataloged and categorized new and existing major public–private partnership efforts in health. Figure 2 shows that there was a dramatic increase in the formation of health-related public–private partnerships in the late 1990s. Of the 90 public–private partnerships identified by IPPPH, 72 (80%) were focused on specific diseases such as HIV/AIDS, malaria, and tuberculosis (Table 1). Only 1 was focused on improving health systems beyond specific illnesses or conditions. This pattern of successful public–private partnerships in a disease-specific context is reflected by recent published reports.[17–22] However, the public–private partnership model in a disease-specific context has not been uniformly successful. A review of the experi-

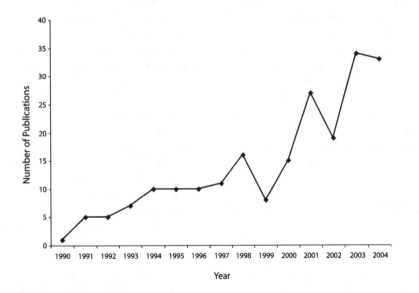

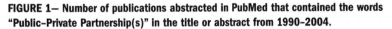

FIGURE 1— Number of publications abstracted in PubMed that contained the words "Public–Private Partnership(s)" in the title or abstract from 1990–2004.

ence with public–private partnerships cautioned that, although such partnerships may be able to produce the desired outcome, they also bring their own problems. . . . [W]e know little about the conditions when partnerships succeed . . . but considerable skepticism exists about the motives of private firms that engage in partnerships, even when the efforts have substantial public health benefits.[23]

Roy Widdus, the project manager for IPPPH, reviewed the record of public–private partnerships for health and concluded, "These partnerships should be regarded as social experiments; they show promise but are not a panacea."[24(p713)]

Few reports address the use of a public–private partnership approach to improve health delivery systems for a wider range of health problems, but 1 that does described an effort in the city of São Paulo, Brazil, to create a partnership between the city government and private physicians to provide health care for the poor residents of 2 São Paulo neighborhoods.[25] The plan ended after 5 years amid controversy and evidence of poor administration and financial irregularities.[26]

In the absence of research that established the effectiveness of the public–private partnership model, and in the face of expanded efforts to apply the public–private partnership approach beyond a disease-specific context, concerns began to arise about the appropriate role of public–private partnerships. Buse and Waxman suggested that public–private partnerships

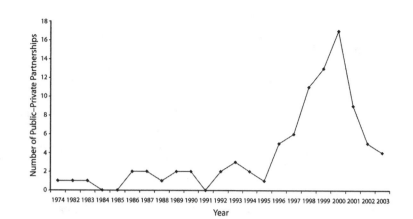

FIGURE 2— Number of new public–private partnerships in health created from 1974–2003.
Source. Initiative on Public-Private Partnerships for Health.[15]

have potential risks as well as benefits and recommended that before investing more deeply in the public–private partnership model, "WHO should promote and support research aimed at identifying good partnership practice and leveraging private sector contributions to health development."[27(p752)] It was in the context of these recommendations that the WHO Centre for Health Development commissioned a research protocol.

A PROTOCOL TO ASSESS PUBLIC–PRIVATE PARTNERSHIPS

In 2004, a panel of 9 scholars from around the United States, each with expertise in a discipline relevant to international health, convened for a 2-day meeting. Each scholar contributed his or her perspective on the optimal methodology to establish a

protocol to evaluate the effectiveness of public–private partnerships in improving health and welfare systems worldwide. There are 8 principal aspects of the protocol.

The Relationship Between Public and Private Sectors

When evaluating public–private partnerships, 1 of the first issues to be confronted was the difficulty establishing a clear, consistent, and reasonable division between which organizations should be considered in the "public sector" and which organizations should be considered in the "private sector." In the research that preceded the development of the protocol, it became apparent that there was no common understanding of what precisely constitutes the public or the private sectors. Some individuals considered only for-profit, market-based

TABLE 1— Number of Public-Private Partnerships Identified by the Initiative on Public-Private Partnerships for Health: 1974-2003

Public-Private Partnership Focus	Number of Partnerships
HIV/AIDS and other sexually transmitted diseases	21
Malaria/dengue	16
Tuberculosis	6
Other specific diseases	29
Vaccines for preventable diseases	5
Reproductive health	4
Syringe distribution	4
Other miscellaneous	2
Drug safety/counterfeit and substandard drugs	2
Health policy/health systems	1

organizations to be within the private sector; private, not-for-profit organizations were considered to be in the public sector. Others, including representatives from the WHO Centre for Health Development, believed that only governments and government agencies were in the public sector, and all nongovernmental organizations, whether for profit or not for profit, were in the private sector.

Although it was not necessary for the purposes of the protocol to establish a universally acceptable division between the public and private sectors, it was nonetheless important for methodological consistency to establish such a distinction as it pertains to the research on the effectiveness of public–private partnerships. Accordingly, the consultants who participated in this project concurred on the following distinction between public and private sectors:

For purposes of evaluating public–private partnership efforts, we include government agencies and nongovernmental organizations that have multilateral approval by formal state governments (e.g., treaties, charters) in the public sector, and those organizations, either for-profit or nonprofit, that act independently of formal multilateral state agreements in the private sector.

A key aspect of characterizing the involvement of the public sector was describing the administrative structure of the public sector organization(s) that were involved in the public–private partnership effort. This included indicating whether the public sector agency was part of the central government or organization (e.g., a ministry or principal agency) or part of a local government or organization (e.g., a local health department or branch agency).

It was equally important to accurately characterize the nature of the private sector involvement. Private sector participation can take many forms, ranging from international nongovernmental organizations to local nonprofit organizations to market-based for-profit firms. One or more of these organizational forms may participate in a public–private partnership. It was important to identify the structure of

the participating entities to fully appreciate the extent to which market forces affect the outcomes of the public–private partnership. If more than 1 organizational type participated in the public–private partnership, it was important to identify the hierarchical decisionmaking process among or between the private sector participants (i.e., does 1 organization have more decisionmaking authority than the other[s]). Finally, in those cases in which market-based organizations participated in the public–private partnership, it would be important to characterize the market system in which the public–private partnership operates. The effects of a public–private partnership in a highly regulated market may be quite different than those in a more loosely regulated market.

The Nature of the Partnership Between Public Sector and Private Sector Participants

It will be important for methodological consistency to describe in some detail the partnership relationship between the 2 sectors. In some cases, that relationship may be a loose one, with little in the way of formalized agreements. In other cases, that relationship may be or may approximate a formal partnership. For the purposes of the protocol, the concept of partnership, " . . . implie[d] a commitment to a common goal through the joint provision of complementary resources and expertise, and the joint sharing of the risks involved . . . [that was] directed from the outset."[28(p694)]

Although such a formal definition of partnership arrangements may describe many public–private collaborative efforts, there could be other arrangements that are neither as formally structured nor as specifically focused as this definition implies. Accordingly, research that addresses the effectiveness of public–private partnership efforts need not require that a formal partnership agreement exist between public and private sector participants in order for a case study to be undertaken.

In describing the partnership arrangement between public and pri-

vate sectors, it will also be important to address the following question: why is each participant there? Partnership arrangements involve shared benefits for both partners. In some cases, the expected benefits for each participant might be spelled out clearly as part of a partnership agreement. Alternatively, the benefits to 1 partner may be more indirect and may accrue in various ways or at various times. Clarifying the expected benefits of the partnership relationship will be an important part of the analysis of the effectiveness of a public–private partnership.

The Financial Arrangements of the Public–Private Partnership Project

There are a number of ways a public–private partnership project can operate in an effort to improve health and welfare services. These include (1) establishing direct service provision by a new public or private entity with joint funding; (2) expanding existing private sector service provision through increased public sector funding, or conversely, expanding existing public sector service provision through increased private sector funding; and (3) establishing new private sector service provision through new public sector funding, or conversely, establishing new public sector service provision through new private sector funding.

The ability to understand the effectiveness of a public–private partnership project will depend on an accurate description of the form and financing of enhanced service provision. Of particular importance is clarifying whether the project represents a new investment from the private sector in public sector service programs, or, alternatively, a new public sector investment in private sector service programs. Placing this analysis in the context of the history of financing health and welfare systems in the country or region under study also will be important.

The Structure, Scope, and Functions of Enhanced Health and Welfare Services

Once the administrative structure of a public–private partnership project has been established, the actual manner of the service provision must be carefully detailed. Differing organizational forms can have quite different outcomes within the same market context. Characteristics of the enhanced service programs that should be included in the public–private partnership analysis can be seen in the box on this page.

Characteristics of the Enhanced Service Programs to Be Evaluated in a Public–Private Partnership

- Types of services provided: medical care, social support, public health
- Formalized management system, including processes for decision-making, resource allocation, and fiscal oversight
- Administrative linkages between public and private sectors; ongoing management process
- Centralization versus decentralization of services
- Hospital-based versus central facility-based versus community-based
- Emphasizes facilities versus emphasizes labor-intensive services
- Operational linkages between public and private sectors for activities such as training, research, conferences, and collaborative project planning
- Level of professional activities involved: physicians, nurses, other certified providers
- Extent to which pharmaceutical treatments are involved, and the policy for pharmaceutical choice, pricing, distribution
- Mechanism of payment for services: budget, capitation, fee-for-service, user fees
- Types and degrees of risk involved and which partner was most susceptible to risk

Government Policy Enacted to Promote Partnership Efforts

Research on the effectiveness of public–private partnerships needs to clarify the policy process by answering questions such as: were new multilateral treaties or compacts required? Were new national laws required? Were new national regulations (without the enactment of new laws) required? If so, were they national or regional? Were new public sector regulatory or oversight agencies or processes required? Were any legal or regulatory changes made by executive decision or legislative action? Did any international organization impose needed legal or regulatory changes?

Measuring the Effectiveness of the Public–Private Partnership

A crucial aspect of public–private partnership research is the ability to identify and quantify outcomes and to establish that changes in these measures that coincide with public–private partnership efforts were actually the result of public–private partnership activities. Addressing questions such as the following should use both qualitative and quantitative methods of analysis, as appropriate to the situation:

1   What were the intended outcomes of the public–private partnership effort?
2   Did the effort target specific aspects of health and well-being for improvement?
3   Did the effort identify specific, measurable indicators of the intended outcomes?
4   Did the effort identify specific target levels to be attained for these indicators?
5   Are the methods used to measure the outcome indicators reliable and consistent over time?
6   Did the indicators change during the period of the effort under study? If so, in the desired direction? Did they attain the target levels?
7   Are there sufficient longitudinal or comparison data to support the conclusion that identified changes in the indicators were the result of the programs and activities under study?
8   Were there any outcomes from the effort (either beneficial or detrimental) that were not expected to occur?

Assessing Issues of Equity

A crucial aspect of WHO programs is to enhance equity in health and well-being. Accordingly, research on the effectiveness of public–private partnership efforts should include specific data regarding the effect of the public–private partnership efforts on equity for vulnerable groups as an outcome distinct from the assessment of overall effectiveness described above. The examination of equity will include addressing several key questions.

1   Do target outcomes and indicators adequately reflect outcomes specific to vulnerable groups (e.g., maternal and child health for gender equity) as well as general population outcomes (e.g., mortality rates)?
2   In selecting target levels of outcome indicators, are group-specific levels set so as to reduce previous inequities?
3   How did the public–private partnership effort affect the bottom 20% of the population, based on measures of socioeconomic status or health status, in comparison to the results for the population overall?
4   Was there a reduction in preexisting inequities coincident with the effort under study?

Identifying Potential Weaknesses of the Analysis

As is the case in all carefully done research, if the members of a study team identify weaknesses in their analysis that may limit the ability to generalize from their study to other contexts, it is incumbent on those members to identify and characterize those weaknesses. The weaknesses may be the result of factors beyond their control (e.g., missing data) or may be because of factors specific to the case study (e.g., inconsistencies in the way data were gathered). Identifying potential weaknesses in a study does not detract from the quality of the study. On the contrary, the quality of the study may be enhanced by a frank discussion of potential weaknesses in the study methodology and by including suggestions on how to improve it.

RESPONSE TO THE PROPOSED PROTOCOL

In March 2004, this research protocol was presented to a global consultative meeting convened at the WHO Centre for Health Development. Representatives from several member states as well as representatives from WHO regional offices provided feedback and suggestions for revision. The feedback focused on 2 principal points. First, a number of member states wanted a more loosely structured definition of what constitutes a public–private partnership to include in the analysis existing efforts at privatization that do not involve a true partnership. Second, a number of states emphasized the need to have analyses rapidly available to meet local political objectives, even at the expense of loss of methodological rigor or consistency.

It was clear from the discussions at the consultative meeting that there is continued confusion within the WHO as to the distinction between creating structured public–private partnerships and efforts at local privatization that do not involve partnership efforts. Some participants voiced substantial resistance to excluding from the analysis programs that follow historical market-based privatization models of the type described by Hsiao.[4] This resistance of certain member states is despite the statement by WHO headquarters that, "Public–private partnerships for health should be distinguished from privatization."[11] Nevertheless, it was the firm recommendation of the consulting scholars who helped develop the protocol that efforts that involve privatization exclusively, without efforts at forming new, cross-sector partnerships, should not be included in the analysis of public–private partnership effectiveness.

Similarly, a core assumption in developing the protocol is the need for methodological rigor and consistency. As such, the analysis of public–private partnership effectiveness must exclude considerations of local political needs or exigencies.

CONCLUSIONS

During the 1990s, public–private partnerships evolved into a very popular means of addressing a number of serious diseases in the developing world. Although there has been substantial success in using the public–private partnership approach, the record of success for public–private partnerships is still mixed. There has been recent enthusiasm within the WHO and elsewhere for extending the public–private partnership model to the delivery of health and welfare services for a wider range of health problems. There are few available data about the success or problems of using a public–private partnership approach to improve the delivery of health and welfare services, because few published case studies of successful public–private partnerships of this type are available. Further research on the effectiveness of public–private partnerships, using standardized research protocols, is needed before substantial resources are invested in the expansion of public–private partnership efforts.

About the Author

Donald A. Barr is with the Department of Sociology, Stanford University, Stanford, Calif.

Correspondence: Requests for reprints should be sent to Department of Sociology, Stanford University, Stanford, CA 94305–2047 (e-mail: barr@stanford.edu).

Acknowledgments

I acknowledge the invaluable assistance of the following consultants in developing this protocol: Ben Crow, Norman Daniels, Anjini Kochar, Donald Light, Harold Luft, Mark Peterson, Debra Satz, and Julia Walsh. In addition I acknowledge the valuable assistance of Kamba Tshionyi and Andrada Tomoaia-Cotisel as research assistants on this project.

References

1. World Health Organization. *Health and Welfare Systems Development in the 21st Century: Proceedings of the Third Global Symposium.* Kobe, Japan: Centre for Health Development; 2002.
2. United Nations. Universal Declaration of Human Rights. Available at: http://www.un.org/Overview/rights.html. Accessed July 19, 2005.
3. Sen, A. *Development as Freedom.* New York, NY: Random House, Inc.; 1999. p. 39.
4. Hsiao „ WC. 'Marketization'– the illusory magic pill. *Health Economics* 1994;3:351–357.
5. Frenk J. The public/private mix and human resources for health. *Health Policy Plan.* 1993;8:315–326.
6. Ahn M, Herman A, Damonti J. Public-private partnerships in health care for developing countries: a new paradigm for change. *Manag Care Q.* 2000;8:65–72.
7. Buse K, Walt G. Global public-private partnerships. Part I: A new development in health? *Bull World Health Organ.* 2000;78:549–561.
8. Buse K, Walt G. Global public-private partnerships. Part II: What are the health issues for global governance? *Bull World Health Organ.* 2000;78:699–709.
9. Smith R. Vaccines and medicines for the world's poorest. *BMJ.* 2000;320:952–953.
10. Nishtar S. Public-private 'partnerships' in health—a global call to action. *Health Res Policy Syst.* 2004;2:5.
11. World Health Organization. Public-Private Partnerships for Health. Available at: http://www.who.int/trade/glossary/story077/en/index.html. Accessed December 29, 2005.
12. The University and Small Business Patent Procedures Act of 1980. Pub. L. No. 96–517, 6(a), Dec. 12, 1980, 94 Stat 3018 (35 U.S.C. 200 et seq.).
13. Muraskin W. Origins of the Children's Vaccine Initiative: the political foundations. *Soc Sci Med.* 1996;42:1721–1734.
14. Birn AE. Federalist flirtations: the politics and execution of health services decentralization for the uninsured population in Mexico, 1985–1995. *J Public Health Policy.* 1999;20:81–108.
15. Initiative on Public–Private Partnerships for Health. Partnerships database, by date established. Available at http://www.ipph.org/index.cfm?page-/ipph/partnerships/date_established. Accessed November 13, 2006.

16. Bill and Melinda Gates Foundation. Bill & Melinda Gates Foundation awards $1 million to Geneva-based Initiative to Promote Global Health Partnerships. Available at: http://www.gatesfoundation.org/GlobalHealth/InfectiousDiseases/Vaccines/Announcements/Announce-349.htm. Accessed July 20, 2005.

17. Ramiah I, Reich MR. Public-private partnerships and antiretroviral drugs for HIV/AIDS: lessons from Botswana. *Health Aff.* 2005;24:545–551.

18. Collins K. Profitable gifts: a history of the Merck Mectizan donation program and its implications for international health. *Perspect Biol Med.* 2004; 47:100–109.

19. Newell JN, Pande SB, Baral SC, Bam DS, Malla P. Control of tuberculosis in an urban setting in Nepal: public-private partnership. *Bull World Health Organ.* 2004;82:92–98.

20. Ridley RG. Product R&D for neglected diseases. Twenty-seven years of WHO/TDR experiences with public-private partnerships. *EMBO Rep.* 2003; 4(Spec No):S43–S46.

21. Caines K, Bataringaya J, Lush L, Murindwa G, N'jie H. Impact of public-private partnerships addressing access to pharmaceuticals in low income countries. Uganda pilot study. Geneva, Switzerland: Initiative on Public Private Partnerships for Health, Global Forum for Health Research; 2003.

22. Schwartz JB, Bhushan I. Improving immunization equity through a public-private partnership in Cambodia. *Bull World Health Organ.* 2004;82: 661–667.

23. Reich MR. Public-private partnerships for public health. *Nat Med.* 2000; 6:617–620.

24. Widdus R. Public-private partnerships for health: their main targets, their diversity, and their future directions. *Bull World Health Organ.* 2001;79: 713–720.

25. Csillag C. São Paulo's medical market. *The Lancet.* 1995;345:1168.

26. Csillag C. São Paulo's controversial public–private partnership ends. *The Lancet.* 2001;358:47.

27. Buse K, Waxman A. Public-private health partnerships: a strategy for WHO. *Bull World Health Organ.* 2001;79: 748–754.

28. Ridley R. Putting the partnership into public-private partnerships. *Bull World Health Organ.* 2001;79:694.

Overview of HIV/AIDS Section
The Global AIDS Pandemic: Failures and Opportunities at Home and Abroad

| *Neal Nathanson, MD, Associate Dean for Global Health Programs, University of Pennsylvania*

How are we doing in our efforts to control the global pandemic of HIV/AIDS? In brief, not well, either at home or abroad. The publication of this set of reprints provides an opportunity to evaluate successes, failures, and opportunities. Although these articles make no attempt to cover all aspects of HIV/AIDS, they do provide some trenchant insights about critical aspects of the field.

Ultimately, our success in dealing with the AIDS pandemic must be assessed by several outcome measures: new cases of AIDS, deaths from AIDS, and, most important, new HIV infections. The communicable nature of HIV infections provide both opportunities and challenges that are fundamentally different from the control of non-infectious health problems. Viewed from a worldwide perspective, HIV/AIDS continues to spread, with an annual increase in all of these outcome measures (see UNAIDS website). Arguments about the accuracy of the data should not obscure the judgement that public health successes are few and far between in the international effort to control HIV/AIDS.

Even more troublesome is the situation in the United States (Kates et al, 2002), where our national resources make failure less excusable. It is sad that after all these years, CDC has little confidence in its ability to measure the annual number of new infections. The best available estimates suggest that annual incidence of new HIV infections in the United States has been constant at about 40,000 annually (see CDC website). Most shocking, this number has not decreased since

about 1990. In my view, this represents a public health failure of deplorable proportions, which reflects the weakness of national leadership and lack of political will. If our national policies had been guided by science and good public health practice, rather than by stigma, apathy, and misguided libertarian advocates, the outcome might have been different. A cynical view is that HIV/AIDS has been pushed off our national radar screen because it preferentially impacts less powerful and under-represented minority communities.

SCIENCE, NOT POLITICS
(See articles by Quinn, Pawinski and Lalloo; Castro and Farmer)

Research has made some outstanding contributions to the control of the AIDS epidemic. Lest we overlook them, it is useful to list these advances: (1) identification of HIV as the causal agent and proof beyond question of its relationship to AIDS; (2) a detailed dissection of the molecular and biochemical steps in HIV replication that provided multiple drugable targets for development by the pharmaceutical industry; (3) an in depth understanding how HIV persists and destroys the immune system, which now equals or exceeds our understanding of the pathogenesis of any infectious disease; (4) the development of multiple tests for diagnosing infection and the stages of the disease, including rapid, inexpensive, simple antibody assays that are practical to use in any corner of the globe; (5) the ability to screen the blood supply with the potential to reduce blood transmis-

sion to the vanishing point; (6) the introduction of an armamentarium drugs that can reduce HIV replication in humans to a minimum level and have converted an inevitably fatal disease into a potentially controllable chronic illness, capable of restoring moribund patients to a high degree of health and function; (7) the ability to anticipate and prevent mother-to-child transmission of HIV, and—under optimal conditions—to almost eliminate pediatric AIDS; (8) the identification of risk factors for the sexual transmission of HIV such as partner number, contact with sex workers, concurrent sexually transmitted diseases (STDs), and absence of circumcision; (9) the identification of effective methods to reduce sexually transmitted risk, such as use of male and female condoms, circumcision, treatment of STDs; (10) the demonstration of the effectiveness of methods to reduce needle transmission such as exchange of needles and syringes, and treatment programs for injecting addicts.

It is also important to emphasize the contribution of research in the social and behavioral sciences to the control of HIV/AIDS. It is self evident that altering human behavior could play a significant role in controlling transmission of HIV. However, there has been a paucity of research focused on understanding issues such as the nature and source of HIV/AIDS stigma, the impact of stigma on treatment or prevention, and how to destigmatize the disease (Castro and Farmer). Other behavioral interventions has shown some degree of success and justify a major investment in relevant research.

At another level in the war on HIV/AIDS, it is important to base public health policies upon scientific evidence. As Quinn points out, too often policies are dictated by political and moral judgments (and, I would add, stigma). A recent trenchant discussion by Coovadia et al (2007) of the role of breast feeding in the transmission of HIV/AIDS illustrates the proper use of evidence to frame public health policies.

However, there have been some notable research failures in HIV/AIDS. In spite of an enormous investment and efforts of outstanding investigators, an AIDS vaccine eludes the scientific community. I am deeply pessimistic that a safe and effective AIDS vaccine will be developed within the foreseeable future, unless some unexpected scientific breakthrough is achieved. All our successful viral vaccines act by ameliorating rather than preventing infection, which is sufficient for the control of acute viral diseases. Unfortunately, it appears that candidate HIV vaccines that down-modulate infection will – at best – prolong the incubation period to AIDS rather than protecting against disease. It appears that HIV/AIDS falls into the category of persistent infections such as malaria and tuberculosis, where the search for an effective vaccine is still ongoing.

Microbicides are another potential addition to the prevention armamentarium that have been touted to empower women to reduce their risk of HIV acquisition. Unfortunately, the rush to develop products has bypassed microbicide science, leading to expensive human efficacy trials of ineffective or (in some cases) dangerous products. Fortunately, there are many promising compounds that might be incorporated into a microbicide, and a variety of delivery systems that could make a microbicide more practical and user friendly. An expanded investment in microbicide science is badly needed, coupled with a disinterested and rational approach to evaluation of potential products. Clearly, it will be a decade or more before an effective microbicide will be available for general use.

TREATMENT
(see articles by McCoy et al, Galvao; Berkman et al, Desvarieux et al, McCough et al)

A significant new development in global AIDS interventions has been the effort to deploy antiretroviral treatment in low income countries. This initiative has been fueled by several sources: first, the availability of significant funding from the United States via the President's Emergency Plan for AIDS Relief (PEPFAR) and from other governments and NGOs such as the Global Fund; and second, the ethical mandate for more global equity in drug access.

The therapeutic initiative has important potential for the control of HIV/AIDS. (1) In low income countries with high prevalence of HIV/AIDS, a large segment of the adult population is seriously handicapped by AIDS which renders them unable to maintain productive employment or to care for children. Interventions that seek to rescue family units must undertake treatment of infected young adults (15-45 years of age). (2) If properly administered, an infusion of funds for diagnosis and treatment of HIV/AIDS could be used to underpin primary care systems, which are marginal at best in many poor countries. (3) For HIV/AIDS, treatment and prevention are closely linked, since effective ARV therapy dramatically reduces infectiousness. Furthermore, properly exploited, a treatment program can significantly improve the health status and political will of a community, vastly facilitating the effort to engage in prevention at an individual and group level.

Several reprints in this collection deal with these subjects. Two articles (Galvao, Berkman et al) examine Brazil, a large middle income country that decided to make free ARV treatment available to all infected citizens. Admittedly, Brazil cannot be considered a model that can "exported" to other countries, but it does illustrate what can be accomplished if there is the political will to implement widespread ARV. To my mind, the Brazil

experience teaches two very important 'take home' lessons. First, the savings from reduced medical care costs are estimated to be four times the cost of the ARV program. Second, concomitant with the implementation of the ARV rollout, the incidence of new HIV infections is estimated to have fallen drastically.

Three articles (McCoy et al, Desvarieux et al, McGough et al) deal with the challenges that confront ARV programs in low income countries. Although donors may succeed in obtaining expensive drugs at markedly reduced prices, most of their investment may be exhausted in payment for large drug supplies. This alone constitutes a problem, by diverting funding away from delivery systems which are crucial to successful ART rollout. A central concern is that independent ARV programs will compete with and undermine existing health care systems. Even though donors are sensitive to this problem, they may be tempted to set up parallel ARV treatment centers because of the frustrations with any attempt to integrate ARV into existing marginal health care. Another challenge is that the expensive and sophisticated laboratory tests to monitor therapy may not be available, leading to poor patient management and the circulation of drug resistant HIV strains. These concerns lead to difficult choices: is it better use a high standard to treat a subset of patients, and if so, which patients? (McGough et al), or attempt a mass therapy approach (Desvarieux et al)? These challenging problems in health systems management are well illuminated by the reprinted articles.

PREVENTION AND PUBLIC HEALTH
(see articles by Kates et al, Dworkin and Ernhardt, Thielman et al, Kerrigan et al)

Prevention has to be the core of any HIV/AIDS control program for several reasons. First, even with ready unrestricted access to the best treatment, AIDS is a terrible lifelong burden no matter how measured. Second, prevention is—in theory—a much more efficient and cost effective approach

Table 1. Projection of new infections and infections averted by applying a full treatment, prevention, and care package, Sub-Saharan Africa, 2005-2015 (after Stover at al, 2006)

	CURRENT EFFORT	EXPANDED PREVENTION: INFECTIONS NOT AVERTED	EXPANDED PREVENTION: INFECTIONS AVERTED
Number of HIV infections	38.6 million new infections	19.2 million new infections	19.4 million infections averted
Cost in dollars Per person	$ 3,469 treatment	$ 3,469 treatment	$ 2,109 prevention
Cost in dollars Total	$ 133.9 billion treatment	$ 67.0 billion treatment	$ 40.9 billion prevention

than is ARV treatment. Third, and most important, the negative multiplier effect of prevention is the only viable strategy for control of the global pandemic.

The good news is that there are many proven interventions to reduce the risk of transmission, which include: (1) safe sex practices, including postponed sexual debut, oral or manual sex, reduced number of partners, avoidance of commercial sex workers, male and female condoms, and the like; (2) management of sexually transmitted diseases; (3) male circumcision; (4) antiretroviral treatment of HIV infected patients; (5) prevention of mother-to-child transmission; (6) needle exchange and addiction treatment; and (7) screening of the blood supply.

The inference is clear: the problem is under-utilization of proven preventive interventions. Various aspects of that challenge are addressed by these articles. Thelman et al discuss the facilitation of voluntary counseling and testing to identify HIV-infected persons for referral and followup. Kerrigan et al review an initiative to increase the use of condoms by com-

mercial sex workers. Dworkin and Ehrhardt propose an extension of "ABC" (abstinence, be faithful, condoms) by a focus on gender relations, economics, and migration. Finally, Kates et al discuss the critical policy changes that might expand effective prevention efforts both in the United States and abroad.

CONCLUDING COMMENT

In my view, there is an important concluding message. We now possess an armamentarium of tools to treat AIDS and to prevent transmission of HIV. UNAIDS has made a calculation of the potential benefit of a scale up of proven interventions (Stover et al, 2006). It was concluded that over a 10-year period, it would be possible to save millions of lives in the high prevalence regions such as sub-Saharan Africa (Table 1). The cost in billions would be more than offset by the savings computed for treatments that would no longer be necessary. Our past failure and our present challenge is to utilize the opportunities provided by this armamentarium of interventions.

About the Author

Dr. Nathanson is Associate Dean for Global Health Programs at the University of Pennsylvania School of Medicine. His former positions include Director of the Office of AIDS Research at the National Institutes of Health.

References
1. UNAIDS website. http://www.unaids.org/en/HIV_data/default.asp
2. CDC website. http://www.cdc.gov/hiv/topics/surveillance/basic.htm#hivest.
3. Kates J, Sorian R, Crowley JS, Summers TA. Critical policy challenges in the third decade of the HIV/AIDS epidemic. *American J Public Health* 2002; 92; xx-xx.
4. Coovadia HM, Rollins NC, Bland, RM, et al. Mother-to-child transmission of HIV-1 infection during exclusive breastfeeding the first 6 months of life: an intervention cohort study. *Lancet* 2007; 369: 1107-1116.
5. Stover J, Bertozzi S, Gutierrez J-P, et al. The global impact of scaling up HIV/AIDS prevention programs in low- and middle-income countries. *Science* 2006; 311: 1474-1476.

We Must Fight HIV/AIDS with Science, not Politics

| Sandra Crouse Quinn, PhD

Stall and Mills[1] speculated on how future historians will view our efforts to combat the global catastrophe of HIV/AIDS. In 1989, Victoria Harden interviewed Anthony Fauci, asking him to speculate on how biomedical researchers would have responded to HIV/ AIDS in 1955. Fauci said,

> I think it would have been much more frightening than it is now, and it is frightening now. . . . I think we would not have a clue as to how to combat this disease from a basic scientific standpoint. . . . So within the framework of the catastrophe of AIDS, we're lucky, in the sense that it came at a time when retrovirology, molecular biology, molecular immunology, and immune system studies were at the stage where we could very quickly identify the agent, how it works, the pathogenic mechanisms, its effect on the immune system, etc. If it had happened in 1955, we would have been in very serious trouble.[2(p37)]

Unfortunately, we are in very serious trouble, owing to something that Fauci may not have considered: our refusal to use science-based knowledge that has been shown to prevent new HIV infections. As a society, we have too frequently substituted political and moral judgments about prevention for science. In 2006, we continue to place intravenous drug users at risk by failing to ensure access to clean syringes through pharmacy sales or needle exchanges. Our government's insistence on abstinence-only education places our youths at risk. Public health professionals must become more skilled at combating the substitution of politics for true science.

As an educator in a school of public health, I call upon my colleagues to ensure that we are training a new generation of public health professionals with all the necessary competencies and passion to address the issues catalogued by Stall and Mills. Are we preparing our students to recognize that science does not occur in a vacuum? Will they be ready to answer political challenges to scientific evidence? Are they competent in the use of meta-analyses to examine the evidence from multiple studies, and are they able to make the case when the evidence points us toward effective interventions? Are we training our students to fully understand political forces, the policymaking process, and strategies for advocacy to advance sound public health policies? Are we grounding our students in the values and ethics of public health, which demand that we use our expertise to advance effective, science-based prevention programs and policies? Finally, are we as faculty and administrators modeling for our students the use of scientific evidence to advocate healthy public policies?

Stall and Mills's editorial should prompt schools and programs of public health to assess to what extent they will be part of the solution to the challenges of HIV/AIDS. With true commitment to using science to foster the most effective prevention and treatment, we can change the course of the history of the HIV/AIDS epidemic.

About the Author

Correspondence: Requests for reprints should be sent to Sandra Crouse Quinn, PhD, Department of Behavioral and Community Health Sciences, Graduate School of Public Health, University of Pittsburgh, 230 Parran Hall, 130 DeSoto St, Pittsburgh, PA 15261 (e-mail: squinn@pitt.edu).

Acknowledgments

The author is supported by the EXPORT Health Center at the Center for Minority Health, University of Pittsburgh (National Institutes of Health grant P60 MD–000–207–02).

References

1. Stall R, Mills T. A quarter century of AIDS. *Am J Public Health.* 2006;96:959–961.

2. Harden V. The biomedical response to AIDS in historical perspective. In: Harden V, Risse G, eds. *AIDS and the Historian.* Bethesda, Md: National Institutes of Health; 1991. NIH publication 91–1584.

Critical Policy Challenges in the Third Decade of the HIV/AIDS Epidemic

| Jennifer Kates, MPA, MA, Richard Sorian, Jeffrey S. Crowley, MPH and Todd A. Summers

ABSTRACT

Numerous policy challenges continue to face the United States in the third decade of the HIV/AIDS pandemic, in both the health and foreign policy arenas. They include long-standing questions about care, treatment, prevention, and research, as well as new ones introduced by the changing nature of the epidemic itself and the need to balance demands for limited resources.

These challenges concern the United States not only in its role as a world leader in combating a global epidemic, but in its decisions and focus at home, where the epidemic continues to take a toll.

INTRODUCTION

The XIV international aids Conference will take place in Barcelona, Spain, in July 2002. This year's conference is notable on several fronts: it follows the Durban Conference, the first international AIDS conference to be held in a developing country deeply affected by the epidemic; it comes one year after an unprecedented special session of the United Nations General Assembly on HIV/AIDS; and it is the first international conference to take place since the events of September 11, 2001.

The policy challenges facing the United States in the third decade of the pandemic are both long-standing—such as questions about care, treatment, prevention, and research—and new—including the challenges introduced by the changing nature of the epidemic itself and the need to balance demands

for limited resources. The United States must meet these challenges both at home, where the epidemic continues to take a toll, and on the global front, where US leadership is needed to help combat the epidemic.

THE US EPIDEMIC

Since the beginning of the epidemic in the United States, close to 800 000 AIDS cases have been reported, and more than 450 000 people have died.[1] Nationally, 850 000 to 950 000 Americans are estimated to be living with HIV/AIDS.[2] While HIV/AIDS is a national epidemic, it has had an especially severe impact on certain groups, including gay and bisexual men, injection drug users and their sexual partners, young people, and racial and ethnic minorities. The epidemic is also increasingly affecting women and economically disadvantaged communities.[3] In addition, recent data suggest that the era of sharp declines in AIDS deaths and new AIDS diagnoses, brought on by the introduction of better therapies in the mid-1990s, may have come to an end.[4] Within this context, there are several critical challenges.

Reducing New Infections

Efforts to raise awareness about HIV/AIDS and change risky behaviors have helped to slow the number of new HIV infections in the United States from more than 150 000 per year in the mid-1980s to 40 000 today. Yet the United States has continued to experience about 40 000 new infections each year since the early

1990s.[5] The recent stabilization in the number of AIDS cases and deaths is also cause for concern.

A key aspect of HIV prevention is the frequent collision between politics and public health science. Prevention interventions have historically been mired in controversy, owing in part to the fact that HIV transmission involves sex and drugs, subjects with which many—policymakers included—are uncomfortable. This discomfort, and the absence of a national consensus, has affected the use of proven strategies for reducing the number of new infections, including targeting at-risk populations and those who are HIV-positive with tailored, culturally specific interventions[6]; reducing stigma, given that stigma may contribute to risky behavior and affect individuals' willingness to get tested or seek care[5,7–10]; integrating prevention into the clinical care setting[11]; and implementing syringe exchange as part of comprehensive prevention programs for injection drug users.[12] There is also a need for continued research to develop new behavioral and clinical prevention strategies, including topical microbicides and vaccines.

Increasing the Number of People Who Know Their Status

About 400 000 to 500 000 people with HIV/AIDS in the United States remain undiagnosed, untreated, or both, and are therefore not receiving the treatments that could forestall disease progression or the prevention supports needed to avoid passing the virus to others.[2] Many continue to face economic barriers to care, lacking insurance coverage to help them afford the high cost of HIV care, which can average as much as $20 000 a year. Increasingly, HIV affects those who are poor, are outside the workforce, and have a history of barriers to access. Even among individuals who have some resources, the high cost of HIV care can quickly exhaust their assets and leave them impoverished.[13]

As a result, people with HIV/AIDS increasingly rely on the public sector for care, primarily Medicaid, Medicare, and the Ryan White CARE Act.[14] One major barrier to Medicaid coverage is a catch-22 in eligibility—most low-income people with HIV must wait until they become disabled by AIDS to be eligible for coverage of treatments that can prevent disability.

Strategies for addressing these issues include increasing the number of people who know their HIV status by providing more information to the public and at-risk populations about voluntary HIV counseling and testing; using new testing technologies, such as rapid testing, to better target those most at risk; furthering efforts to reduce stigma and discrimination; and increasing access to care and coverage for people with HIV/AIDS through expansions of public and private coverage. For example, Congress is considering the Early Treatment for HIV Act, which would address Medicaid's catch-22 by creating a new state option to expand Medicaid coverage to lowincome people with HIV who are not yet disabled.[15,16]

Addressing the Impact of HIV in Minority Communities

HIV/AIDS disproportionately affects racial and ethnic minorities, as it has since the beginning of the epidemic. HIV is the leading cause of death for African Americans between the ages of 25 and 44 years and the third leading cause of death for Latinos in this age group.[17] People of color now represent the majority of new HIV infections (74%) and people living with AIDS (62%).[1]

The increasing concentration of the epidemic among minority Americans is due to many complex factors, including social inequalities related to income and race and stigma associated with being gay or bisexual, which exists within minority communities as well as in the larger society. These contextual forces may operate at the individual level to increase high-risk behaviors or at the societal level by compromising community infrastructure for responding to the epidemic. There is a critical need to better understand where and why these disparities occur, what factors affect receptivity to prevention messages and health care access, and whether public programs, particularly Medicaid and the Ryan White CARE Act, are adequately serving people of color. Understanding the views of minority leaders and communities toward HIV/AIDS is essential to an informed response.[18–20] The Minority HIV/AIDS Initiative, adopted by Congress in 1999 after much community pressure, has been one attempt to enhance community capacity to respond to HIV/AIDS.[21]

Addressing Rising Drug Costs

Spending on prescription drugs is one of the fastest growing components of US health care spending,[22] and spending on HIV-related therapies is no exception. Because access to medications is critical for people with HIV/AIDS and these drugs are expensive, concerns have been raised about rising expenditures and the price of prescription drugs. Policymakers are faced with several questions: Are there mechanisms for purchasing drugs at lower prices, such as purchasing in bulk or through rebate programs? Should government be involved in limiting or controlling drug prices? Should the public and private sectors' respective investments in drug research be considered in determining drug pricing? Are there ways to use existing resources more efficiently, such as purchasing or continuing private insurance coverage for people with HIV?

Stimulating Research and Development

Despite significant public investment and progress in HIV research, there is still no cure for HIV and no vaccine against the virus, and available treatments, while effective for many, do not help everyone and often have severe side effects. There is a great deal to learn about how to use existing pharmaceuticals safely and appropriately; about long-term toxicities of the multiple medications that are being prescribed for people living with HIV; and about the development of drug resistance. Priority research areas include vaccine development, prevention, microbicides, and therapeutic research.

Policymakers are faced with a complex array of decisions and choices concerning research and development: What is the role of the federal government in conducting therapeutics research vis-à-vis private pharmaceutical and biotechnology companies? What is the best way to allocate public research dollars for basic science research vs clinical research? Are public dollars—or public policies—leading to research that can answer some of the questions about long-term toxicities, resistance, and so forth? Since barriers prevent private firms from aggressively conducting vaccine research, should federal policymakers fund this research directly or provide incentives for private research (e.g., through tax credits)?

Maintaining Attention to the US Epidemic

After 2 decades of fighting the HIV/AIDS epidemic in the United States, it is not surprising that there may be some signs of "AIDS fatigue." For example, although Americans still rate AIDS as a top health concern for the nation, the proportion who see it as the number one health problem has declined over the past few years.[8] In addition, a recent report on the role of private philanthropy in responding to the epidemic found that while philanthropic support of global AIDS efforts is on the rise, support for domestic efforts has not grown.[23] Yet as the US epidemic continues to exact an increasing toll on racial and ethnic minority communities, maintaining attention to the epidemic at home remains critical, even as the global response gains attention.

THE GLOBAL EPIDEMIC

Worldwide, more than 60 million people have been infected with HIV, and 20 million have died. HIV is now the leading cause of death in Africa and the fourth leading cause of death worldwide. Most of the impact has been felt in the developing world. Young people and women are increasingly at risk.[24,25] In addition, it is estimated that more than 40 million children will have lost one or both parents to HIV/AIDS by 2010, and these children will also be at increased risk for HIV.[26] The United States faces several challenges in addressing this global epidemic.

Identifying Appropriate Forms of US Assistance

The United States allocates funding and other resources used to address the global epidemic in several ways, including direct financial assistance to other countries, support for multilateral organizations such as the Joint United Nations Program on HIV/AIDS (UNAIDS), and broader forms of development assistance. This assistance goes toward a variety of activities, including direct prevention, care, treatment, and support services and, increasingly, impact mitigation efforts that address the larger societal consequences of the pandemic.

To date, the bulk of US foreign assistance in the fight against the global pandemic has been in the form of bilateral assistance to other nations. While the level of spending and other resources made available is clearly a fundamental component of the US response, it is also important to assess the mechanisms by which resources are allocated and their effect on recipient countries and programs. These mechanisms include US agency activity; direct assistance through government-to-government agreements and bilateral aid; contributions to multilateral programs; loans to developing countries; debt relief; and direct assistance to nongovernmental organizations. For example, since foreign debt is one of the major barriers facing developing nations' ability to respond to the epidemic, grants and debt relief may represent more viable options than loans.[27]

Shaping the Global Fund to Fight AIDS, TB, and Malaria

Total resources for addressing the HIV/AIDS epidemic in the developing world are estimated to be at least $7 to $10 billion annually.[28] In April 2001, UN Secretary-General Kofi Annan issued a call to action to create a Global Fund to fight HIV/AIDS as a mechanism for mobilizing and coordinating additional resources toward this goal. The scope of the fund was expanded to include tuberculosis and malaria and plans for the fund began later that year.[29] The first round of grants were announced in April 2002. The United States has pledged $300 million to date and has earmarked an additional $200 million for fiscal year 2003, which is awaiting congressional approval.[30]

The US government has played a critical role in shaping decisions concerning the fund, working with other governments, research and community organizations, foundations, and other private sector players. Continued leadership from the United States is needed to address ongoing challenges including mobilizing larger and sustained contributions (and articulating the appropriate role of US commitments in this regard); expediting disbursements without sacrificing oversight and accountability; establishing executive leadership and appropriate staffing; and clarifying the role of the Global Fund in the context of other global AIDS efforts (the fund is intended to represent new resource commitments, rather than funding redirected from other health and international development efforts).[29,31]

Balancing Priorities

Research, care and prevention are integral components of an effective global or national HIV/AIDS strategy, and understanding the often complex relationships between them is critical. To date, the majority of US government spending on HIV/AIDS in developing countries has been for prevention, with few resources allocated to care.[32] As the United States seeks to promote an integrated approach to the global pandemic, it will need to look at ways to foster public–private partnerships that support prevention and care, including the provision of antiretroviral therapies (to prevent mother-to-child transmission and to treat those who are living with HIV) and research in developing countries.

The issue of health care infrastructure is fundamental to these considerations. Definitions of infrastructure include such elements as the availability of health centers, facilities such as laboratories, and trained personnel; roads, equipment, supply systems, and water; security; and stability of government. There has been some reluctance on the part of the United States, other nations, and the private sector to provide increased or new support for certain interventions in developing countries because of concerns about existing infrastructure. There is a need to improve the understanding of the definition and role of infrastructure in delivery of prevention and treatment interventions in resource-poor settings and to identify ways to support infrastructure enhancements. It will be important to gain experience in implementing infrastructure development initiatives, assessing the level of infrastructure needed for different types of interventions and insuring the capacity of indigenous institutions.

Promoting Access to Treatment

The last couple of years have witnessed important progress in removing barriers to access to treatment for people living with HIV in developing countries. Nonetheless, the cost of antiretroviral and other medications far exceeds what is affordable for most individuals in these countries, raising concerns about the need to balance intellectual property rights protections with greater access to medications and propelling the discussion into the realm of US and global trade policy. Within this context, several strategies are being explored to enhance access to treatment, including the purchasing of generic drugs, bulk purchasing, parallel importation, compulsory licensure, and tiered pricing. In addition, UNAIDS and individual nations have worked with several pharmaceutical manufacturers to forge price reduction arrangements for antiretroviral and other HIV-related medications.[33]

CONCLUSION

Taken together, these challenges are formidable. Meeting them will require resources and leadership. Resources for the epidemic have always competed with other national priorities but generally have fared well on Capitol Hill. Still, total US support for international AIDS efforts represents a smaller proportion of gross national product for the United States than for many other wealthy nations.[34] In addition, the President's fiscal year 2003 budget proposes flat funding for US prevention efforts and the Ryan White CARE Act.[30] Resources, then, remain a key, overriding challenge, underscoring the need to demonstrate that a response to HIV/AIDS is connected to numerous other areas, including national security.

There are no easy choices. Yet, as UNAIDS' Peter Piot recently noted, "the AIDS epidemic is different from any other epidemic the world has faced, and as such, requires a response from the global community that is broader and deeper than has ever before been mobilized against a disease."[35] The United States continues to be in a position to provide critical leadership to such a response.

About the Authors

Jennifer Kates is with the Henry J. Kaiser Family Foundation, Washington, DC. At the time of writing, Richard Sorian was with the Institute for Health Care Research and Policy, Georgetown University, Washington, DC. Jeffrey S. Crowley is with the Institute for Health Care Research and Policy, Georgetown University, Washington, DC. Todd A. Summers is with Progressive Health Partners, Washington, DC.

Correspondence: Requests for reprints should be sent to Jennifer Kates, MPA, MA, Kaiser Family Foundation, 1450 G St, NW, Suite 250, Washington, DC 20005 (e-mail: jkates@kff.org).

Acknowledgments

We would like to acknowledge the contributions to our thinking of Drew Altman, PhD; Diane Rowland, ScD; and Marsha Lillie-Blanton, DrPh, of the Kaiser Family Foundation, Christopher Collins of the AIDS Vaccine Advocacy Coalition, amd David Winters of the Ford Foundation.

References

1. Centers for Disease Control and Prevention. *HIV/AIDS Surveillance Report*, 2001; 13 (1).

2. Fleming PL, Byers RH, Sweeney PA, Daniels D, Karon JM, Janssen RS. HIV prevalence in the United States, 2000. In: Proceedings of the 9th Conference on Retroviruses and Opportunistic Infections; February 24-28, 2002; Seattle, Wash. Abstract 11, Oral Abstract Session 5.

3. Karon JM, Fleming PL, Steketee RW, De Cock KM. HIV in the United states at the turn of the century: an epidemic in transition. *Am J Public Health.* 2001;91:1060–1068.

4. AIDS cases and deaths hold stable for second year [press release]. Atlanta, Ga: Centers for Disease Control and Prevention; August 13, 2001.

5. *HIV Prevention Strategic Plan Through 2005.* Atlanta, Ga: Centers for Disease Control and Prevention; 2001.

6. *Compendium of HIV Prevention Interventions With Evidence of Effectiveness.* Atlanta, Ga: Centers for Disease Control and Prevention; 1999.

7. Centers for Disease Control and Prevention. HIV incidence among young men who have sex with men—seven U.S. cities, 1994–2000. *MMWR Morb Mortal Wkly Rep.* 2001;50(21).

8. *The AIDS Epidemic at 20 Years: The View From America.* Menlo Park, Calif: Kaiser Family Foundation; 2001.

9. Valdiserri RO. HIV/AIDS stigma: an impediment to public health. *Am J Public Health.* 2002;92:341–342.

10. Herek GM, Capitanio JP, Widaman KF. HIV-related stigma and knowledge in the United States: prevalence and trends, 1991–1999. *Am J Public Health.* 2002;92:371–377.

11. Institute of Medicine. *No Time to Lose: Getting More From HIV Prevention.* Washington DC: National Academy Press; 2000.

12. *Evidence-Based Findings on the Efficacy of Syringe Exchange Programs: An Analysis for the Assistant Secretary for Health and Surgeon General of the Scientific Research Completed Since April 1998.* Washington, DC: US Dept of Health and Human Services; 2000.

13. *Financing HIV/AIDS Care: A Quilt With Many Holes.* Menlo Park, Calif: Kaiser Family Foundation; 2000.

14. *Federal HIV/AIDS Spending: A Budget Chartbook, FY 2000.* Menlo Park, Calif: Kaiser Family Foundation; 2000.

15. Early Treatment for HIV Act of 2001, 107th Cong, 1st sess, HR 2063 IH and S 987 IS (introduced June 5, 2001).

16. Kahn JG, Haile B, Kates J, Chang S. Health and federal budgetary effects of increasing access to antiretroviral medications for HIV by expanding Medicaid. *Am J Public Health.* 2001;91:1464–1473.

17. National Center for Health Statistics. Deaths: leading causes for 1999. *Natl Vital Stat Rep.* October 12, 2001;49(11).

18. Friday JC, Lee DH, Lillie-Blanton M, Weinstock B, Kates J. A survey of black elected officials on HIV/AIDS in the African American community. *Minority Health Today.* April 2002(suppl).

19. *African Americans' Views of the HIV/AIDS Epidemic at 20 Years: Findings From a National Survey.* Menlo Park, Calif: Kaiser Family Foundation; 2001.

20. *Latinos' Views of the HIV/AIDS Epidemic at 20 Years: Findings From a National Survey.* Menlo Park, Calif: Kaiser Family Foundation; 2001.

21. About the initiative. Available at: http://www.omhrc.gov/omh/aids/about/abt_toc.htm. Accessed March 6, 2002.

22. *Prescription Drug Trends: A Chartbook Update.* Menlo Park, Calif: Kaiser Family Foundation; 2001.

23. Funders Concerned About AIDS. Voices from the field: remobilizing HIV/AIDS philanthropy for the 21st century. 2001. Available at: http://www.fcaaids.org/spotlight/010622.html. Accessed May 6, 2002.

24. *AIDS Epidemic Update.* Geneva, Switzerland: UNAIDS; 2000.

25. *AIDS Epidemic Update.* Geneva, Switzerland: UNAIDS; 2001.

26. *Children on the Brink.* Washington, DC: US Agency for International Development; 2000.

27. Phillips M. Treasury's O'Neill pushes plan to give grants to poor nations. *Wall Street Journal.* February 21, 2002.

28. *Fact Sheet: HIV/AIDS Financing Gap.* Geneva, Switzerland: UNAIDS; February 2002.

29. The Global Fund to Fight AIDS, Tuberculosis, and Malaria. Available at: http://www.globalfundatm.org/.

Accessed March 6, 2002.

30. HHS budget for HIV/AIDS increases 8 percent [press release]. Washington, DC: US Dept of Health and Human Services; February 4, 2002.

31. *The Global Fund to Fight AIDS, TB, and Malaria: Successes and Challenges.* Washington, DC: Center for Strategic and International Studies; 2002.

32. USAID combatting HIV/AIDS: a record of accomplishment [press release]. June 22, 2001. Available at: http://www.usaid.gov/press/releases/2001/fs010420.html. Accessed March 6, 2002.

33. UN efforts broaden availability of anti-retrovirals: accelerating access initia-

tive moving forward; 72 countries worldwide express interest [press release]. Geneva, Switzerland: UNAIDS/WHO; December 11, 2001.

34. *Global Spending on HIV/AIDS: Tracking Public and Private Investments in AIDS Prevention, Care, and Research.* Menlo Park, Calif: Kaiser Family Foundation; 2001.

35. *Hearings Before the Committee on Foreign Relations of the United States Senate,* 107th Cong, 2nd sess (February 13, 2002) (testimony of Peter Piot, "Halting the Global Spread of HIV/AIDS: the Future of US Bilateral and Multilateral Responses").

Expanding Access to Antiretroviral Therapy in Sub-Saharan Africa: Avoiding the Pitfalls and Dangers, Capitalizing on the Opportunities

| David McCoy, DrPH, BMed, Mickey Chopra, MSc, BMed, Rene Loewenson, PhD, Jean-Marion Aitken, MA, Thabale Ngulube, PhD, MBChB, Adamson Muula, MPH, MBBS, Sunanda Ray, MPH, MBBS, Tendayi Kureyi, MPhil, Petrida Ijumba, MPH and Mike Rowson, MSc

ABSTRACT

We describe a number of pitfalls that may occur with the push to rapidly expand access to antiretroviral therapy in sub-Saharan Africa. These include undesirable opportunity costs, the fragmentation of health systems, worsening health care inequities, and poor and unsustained treatment outcomes. On the other hand, AIDS "treatment activism" provides an opportunity to catalyze comprehensive health systems development and reduce health care inequities.

However, these positive benefits will only happen if we explicitly set out to achieve them. We call for a greater commitment toward health activism that tackles the broader political and economic constraints to human and health systems development in Africa, as well as toward the resuscitation of inclusive and equitable public health systems.

INTRODUCTION

The global movement to reduce the price of medicines and expand access to antiretroviral therapy (ART) continues to gather momentum. In sub-Saharan Africa (SSA), the region with the highest number of people living with AIDS, millions of dollars are being directed at this cause through governments as well as through the Global Fund to Fight AIDS, Tuberculosis and Malaria, the World Bank, and bilateral overseas development aid. Private foundations such as the Gates and Clinton Foundations, and nongovernmental organizations

such as Médecins Sans Frontières, are providing additional funds and technical support.

The World Health Organization (WHO) has further catalyzed efforts by announcing its aim to help put 3 million people in developing countries on ART by the end of 2005. It currently estimates that only 100 000 people out of 4.1 million who need it in Africa are receiving ART.[1] The plans to expand access to ART are therefore bold and ambitious and are a testament to a campaign that has challenged the indifference of governments and societies to people living with AIDS and the "profiteering" of pharmaceutical companies. Just as important, the campaign around treatment access has helped motivate health workers and mobilize civil society in Africa around a struggle for health.

However, there are a number of inadequately acknowledged pitfalls associated with the push to rapidly expand access to ART in SSA. Unless the push to expand access to ART is placed within the context of a response to comprehensive health systems development, it will fail to avoid the pitfalls and undermine the desired aim of reducing AIDS-related mortality.

THE HEALTH CARE SYSTEMS CONTEXT OF SUB-SAHARAN AFRICA

Underlying our concern is the fact that treatment expansion plans and programs are being implemented without adequate investment in strengthening the weak, and in some cases collapsing, health systems in SSA.[2] A large number of health care systems in

SSA are currently grossly underresourced. Thirty-one African countries had total annual per capita health expenditures of $20 or less in 2001.[3] The available number and skills of doctors, nurses, and other health workers fall short of what is required to deliver an adequate health service, a problem that threatens to get worse as a consequence of the international brain drain of health workers to developed countries, and the effect of HIV/AIDS itself on health workers.[4] In Malawi, for example, there is only 1 physician for approximately every 50 000 to 100 000 people (by contrast, a developed country may have 1 physician for every 500 people).[5]

The effects of this situation are clear to see in the deterioration of a number of health care indicators. The lifetime risk of a woman dying in pregnancy is now 1 in 16 in SSA.[6] In Malawi, the 2000 Demographic and Health Survey estimated the maternal mortality rate to be 1120 per 100 000 live births, nearly double the rate of 620 per 100 000 live births estimated in 1992.[7] In several countries, immunization coverage has deteriorated.[8] African children still die from diarrheal disease and upper respiratory tract infections, and yet the simple health care services to manage these problems remain inadequate.[9,10]

The additional funding to combat HIV/AIDS and increase access to ART will not change the fact that most SSA health systems have inadequate resources. In Malawi, for example, the projected addition of approximately $40 million per annum from Global Fund grants would increase total per capita health care expenditures by less than $4, which would still leave annual per capita health expenditures about $10 short of the estimated $30 required to provide full coverage for a package of essential health services, excluding ART.

In addition to enforcing public sector budget cuts, structural adjustment programs and health sector reforms imposed on many developing countries by the World Bank and the International Monetary Fund have encouraged liberalization, privatization, and the outsourcing of health care services, which has weakened public sector capacity and resulted in increasingly disorganized and fragmented health systems.[2,11,12] Poorly coordinated donor programs also contribute to fragmentation of the health system and undermining of public sector stewardship.[13] Patients, especially the poor, are increasingly vulnerable to exploitation and bad practice in an unregulated market.[14]

THE PITFALLS

With an average adult HIV prevalence of 13.7% in southern Africa, we clearly need a bold and ambitious response to the HIV/AIDS epidemic. There are, however, pitfalls associated with setting overoptimistic and unrealistic targets for ART coverage without similarly bold investments in the health systems to reach these targets. One pitfall is that the expansion of access to ART can come at the expense of other vital health care services, such as maternal and child health care services, or lead to an unintended diversion of attention and resources away from HIV prevention.

There may also be opportunity costs related to development actions in other sectors. For example, it has been reported that there has been a decrease in country requests for nutrition support because of the attention being focused on HIV/AIDS.[15] We also note a growing tendency to blame chronic household food insecurity and malnutrition on HIV/AIDS, at the expense of drawing attention to the more fundamental problems of global trade imbalances, the dismantling of public support for subsistence and smallholding farmers, and chronic poverty.

Within the health care sector, the current focus on ART could also overmedicalize the response to HIV/AIDS, and divert attention and funds away from the more fundamental political, social, and economic determinants of poverty and the AIDS epidemic. Although the attraction toward a "magic bullet" or technological solution is understandable, the goal of addressing AIDS and improving health in Africa will require a broad, multisectoral response to the disease *and* its underlying social and economic causes.

A second pitfall is that ART programs may take inappropriate shortcuts to achieve ambitious coverage targets and compromise the quality and sustainability of care. Insufficient community and patient preparation, erratic and unsustainable drug supplies, and inadequate training and support of health care providers could result in low levels of treatment adherence and an increased threat of the development of drug resistance.[16] If the existing batch of generic antiretrovirals becomes ineffective because of the development of viral resistance, the need to use more expensive second-line treatment regimens could result in fewer people having access to treatment in the longer run. However, governments and international agencies are increasingly being held accountable to ambitious targets, which may promote treatment coverage at the expense of effective, long-term outcomes.

A third pitfall, arising out of the pressure to achieve quick results, is the use of inappropriate "vertical" treatment programs (i.e., the establishment of separate and parallel supply and delivery systems for ART). One manifestation of this is the use of nongovernmental personnel to deliver treatment because of their ability to set up projects quickly.[17] Apart from the burden of having to coordinate and monitor multiple nongovernmental treatment services, this approach threatens to further weaken the capacity of the public health system by draining skilled personnel into the (often)

better-paid independent sector. At Lilongwe Central Hospital, a 970-bed facility in Lilongwe, Malawi, authorized to employ 520 nurses, currently only 169 nurses are available for clinical care. Many have left to work on nongovernmental AIDS projects.[18]

Although a degree of single-focus and dedicated systems and structures will be necessary to catalyze the scale-up of treatment access for AIDS, the dangers of over verticalization (whereby ART is provided through a system that stands apart from other services) are that the opportunity costs of ART programs will be magnified; that the potential to lever broader health systems development will be lost; and that the risk of unsustainable treatment will be heightened.

Furthermore, dismantling the social barriers to voluntary counseling and testing; ensuring the existence and accessibility of a functional laboratory service; establishing efficient and reliable medical supply and distribution systems; providing geographically accessible service points; and ensuring long-term follow-up of patients receiving complex treatment clearly require a health care infrastructure that cannot be effectively or efficiently sustained through multiple, stand-alone projects. It requires a coherent, countrywide health systems approach.

In addition, the many calls for public-private partnerships to increase the coverage and speed of ART delivery are being made with little discussion about the broader implications of a shift in the public-private mix of health care systems. For example, plans to engage the private sector in the delivery of ART do not make policy distinctions between independent private for-profit health care services, the occupational health sector of the corporate sector, private medical insurance schemes, drug manufacturers and suppliers, and the nonprofit health care sector. Other plans submitted for the delivery of ART make little reference to pre-existing policy intentions to delegate state authority to semi-independent hospital boards, or to devolve health care responsibilities to local government, and reveal a disconnection between treatment objectives and a broader health systems development agenda.

Concerns about verticality and multiple nongovernmental delivery systems echo the experience and debates in the 1970s and 1980s about the shortcomings of selective primary health care and verticalized child survival programs.[19–21] However, little seems to have been learned from this history. In contrast, some commentators have even called for the establishment of centralized "incident command systems" modeled on disaster-response experiences and the control of severe acute respiratory syndrome.[22] This makes an inappropriate comparison between the multifaceted components of a comprehensive AIDS program (which is inherently unsuited to vertical programs) with the control of an acute communicable disease outbreak, and reveals the tension between an "emergency response" to AIDS with a longer-term, sustainable public health and systems development approach.

The pitfalls highlighted in this article also include a number of threats to equity. Although the rationing of treatment is inevitable in many SSA countries, ambitious targets may lead to a preferential targeting of easier-to-reach, higher-income groups, typically living in urban areas. Without an investment in the social and economic requirements of the poor and marginalized sections of society to access treatment, ART programs could widen the inequitable health outcomes of social and geographic disparities in access to health care. A treatment-focused approach that inadequately addresses the basic needs of households, such as food security and access to water, will also limit the capacity of the poor to benefit from ART. Finally, not paying due attention to the opportunity costs of expanding access to ART could result in unintended inequities within the health care system between different patient groups.

THE WAY FORWARD

Highlighting the pitfalls associated with the global movement to expand

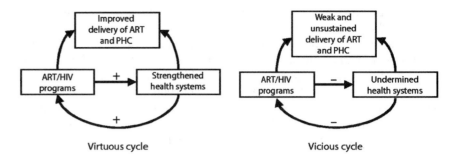

FIGURE 1— The virtuous and vicious cycles of rapid ART expansion.
Note. ART = antiretroviral therapy; PHC = primary health care.

access to treatment can draw criticism for reflecting an overly pessimistic attitude and undermining the campaign to expand access to treatment. Treatment activists may also dismiss these concerns because they echo the expressions of pharmaceutical companies wanting to block the use of generic medicines, or of scientists and politicians who continue to deny the existence of AIDS, or who block the justified call for antiretroviral treatment to poor communities.

However, genuine public health concerns about worsening health care inequities, undesirable opportunity costs, sustainability, and the development of drug resistance must not be construed as an obstacle to the aim of ensuring universal access to ART. Unless we acknowledge these concerns, we risk doing more harm than good. Furthermore, underplaying the challenges to equitable and sustainable ART may undermine the very health system on which the long-term success of ART programs is dependent.

On the other hand, the mobilization of resources and health activism around treatment for people living with AIDS provides an opportunity to strengthen health systems and catalyze action in a number of other vital areas of development. However, these spin-off benefits will only be realized if ART programs are constructed in a way that *explicitly* seeks to do this.

Instead of distorting the health system to quickly deliver ART (thereby weakening it further), the momentum around the expansion of ART should rather be used to build strong, integrated and effective public health systems,

in particular, the human resource capacity of public health systems. This will require the Global Fund and WHO's 3-by-5 initiative to review *how* they position themselves vis-à-vis national health systems, and to promote efforts to build health systems capacities for the delivery of comprehensive primary health care, and not just selected treatments. This will allow the treatment agenda and the health systems development agenda to exist in a virtuous cycle of mutual development rather than in a vicious cycle that undermines both (Figure 1).

An explicit health systems development agenda implies the need for a much clearer vision of health systems. Such a vision must incorporate the resuscitation of health systems through sustained funding to ensure an adequate health care infrastructure of health workers, accessible facilities, and health management systems. A critical threshold of sustained investment in health systems must be met in all countries.

African governments can contribute to this by fulfilling the pledge of the Abuja Declaration to commit 15% of their budgets to health.[23] However, multilateral and bilateral donors will need to come up with medium-term commitments to complement domestic financing. This would include raising official development assistance levels to 0.7% of the donor country gross national product (a target set by the United Nations decades ago[24]) and mitigating the effects of outflows of skilled health personnel from Africa to wealthier countries, possibly through some form of recompense.

There are also sources for revenue generation that can be sought at the global level, such as through the legitimate taxation of multinational corporation profits that currently escape national tax systems,[25] or through a levy placed on global financial transactions (for example, the proposed Tobin tax).[26] These suggestions are now being raised within the United Nations system and by civil society and deserve as much attention from the public health community as the effects of patents on medicine prices. The establishment of a global fund for health systems, which would complement funds raised specifically for disease programs or vaccines, should be considered.

At the same time, the cancellation of SSA's unfair debt burden[27] and the reform of the global trade and economic architecture that keeps poor countries and poor people poor needs to be tackled.[28] This will help promote other essential poverty-alleviating interventions and development priorities such as household food security, access to water and sanitation, and education. It is only by incorporating broader political and economic factors that African health policy-makers and public health practitioners will escape the reality of unacceptable trade-offs and opportunity costs associated with HIV/AIDS programs.

Such proposals will require the mobilization of civil society, particularly in wealthy countries, to convince governments and global decisionmakers that debt cancellation and a doubling of the development aid budget is both feasible and just, especially in the context of rising military expenditures and growing global inequalities in wealth.[29]

A clear health systems vision is also needed to bring to the surface a number of policy contradictions, such as those that exist between World Bank grants for treatment programs and macroeconomic prescriptions on governments to reduce their social sector budgets. Inappropriate public sector budget ceilings imposed on poor governments by the International Monetary Fund must be challenged

vigorously by institutions such as the World Health Organization. The contradictions between the US government's international AIDS program and its trade policy that inhibits the production of generic essential medicines and undermines the regulatory capacity of governments to implement national essential drug programs must be exposed.

Finally, a clear health systems vision needs to incorporate an unambiguous rebuttal of neoliberal health policy prescriptions that have undermined public health systems, commercialized health care, and worsened inequity. This would include reasserting and promoting the responsibility of governments to provide health care for all as a social right; progressive, equitable, and risk-sharing health-financing mechanisms; and nonsegmented health systems. A coherent form of decentralization based on the principles of the District Health System needs to be rediscovered to create an organizational framework to allow for comprehensive, bottom-up planning; appropriate health care prioritization; the functional integration of the public, nonprofit, and private health care sectors; and the involvement of communities in public health actions.

In conclusion, we believe that AIDS treatment activism needs to be balanced by 2 other forms of public health activism. First, a "macroactivism" that tackles the broader political and economic causes of poverty and impoverished health systems. Second, a "health systems activism" to ensure that health systems are capacitated to provide comprehensive health care effectively, efficiently, and equitably. In order to achieve the just demand for comprehensive health care for all, we need a different 3-by-5: one that entails the 3 prongs of macro, health systems, and treatment activism.

About the Authors

Petrida Ijumba is with the Health Systems Trust, Durban, South Africa. Mickey Chopra is with the University of Western Cape School of Public Health, Cape Town, South Africa. Rene Loewenson is with the Training and Research Support Centre, Harare, Zimbabwe. Thabale Ngulube is with the Centre for Health, Science & Social Research, Lusaka, Zambia. Adamson Muula is with the University of Malawi, Lilongwe. Sunanda Ray and Tendayi Kureyi are with the Southern Africa AIDS Network in Harare, Zimbabwe. Mike Rowson is with Medact, London, United Kingdom. At the time of writing, David McCoy was with the Health Systems Trust, Durban South Africa; Sunanda Ray was with the Southern Africa AIDS network, Harare, Zimbabwe, and Jean-Marion Aitken was an independent consultant in Lilongwe, Malawi.

D. McCoy, M. Chopra, and R. Loewenson developed the initial draft of this article. All other authors helped to further refine the ideas and review drafts of the article.

Correspondence: Requests for reprints should be sent to Petrida Ijumba, Health Systems Trust, PO Box 808, Durban 4000, South Africa (e-mail: petrida@hst.org.za).

Acknowledgments

This article drew on research coordinated by EQUINET (southern Africa) and Oxfam (Great Britain), with support from the International Development Research Centre (Canada) and the Department for International Development (United Kingdom).

References

1. *Treating 3 Million by 2005: Making It Happen.* Geneva, Switzerland: World Health Organization; 2003.
2. Simms C, Rowson M, Peattie S. *The Bitterest Pill of All: The Collapse of Africa's Health Systems.* London, England: Save the Children and Medact; 2001.
3. *World Health Report 2004.* Geneva, Switzerland: World Health Organization; 2004.
4. Padarath A, Chamberlain C, McCoy D, Ntuli A, Rowson M, Loewenson R. Health personnel in southern Africa: confronting maldistribution and brain drain. EQUINET Discussion Paper No. 4; 2003. Available at: http://www.equinetafrica.org/bibl/docs/DIS3hres.pdf. Accessed March 6, 2004.

5. Aitken JM, Kemp J. HIV/AIDS, Equity and health sector personnel in southern Africa. EQUINET discussion paper No. 12; 2003. Available at: http://www.equinetafrica.org/bibl/docs/DISC12aids.pdf. Accessed March 6, 2004.

6. *Maternal Mortality in 2000: Estimates Developed by WHO, UNICEF and UNFPA.* Geneva, Switzerland: World Health Organization; 2001. Available at: http://www.who.int/reproductive-health/publications/maternal_mortality_2000/. Accessed June 20, 2004.

7. *Malawi Demographic and Health Survey 2000.* Zomba, Malawi, and Calverton, Md: National Statistical Office [Malawi] and ORC Macro; 2001.

8. WHO, UNICEF, and the World Bank. *State of the World's Vaccines and Immunisations.* Geneva, Switzerland: WHO; 2002. Available at: http://www.who.int/vaccines-documents/. Accessed January 20, 2004.

9. Walker N, Schwartlander B, Bryce J. Meeting international goals in child survival and HIV/AIDS. *Lancet.* 2002; 360:284–289.

10. Black RE, Morris SS, Bryce J. Where and why are 10 million children dying every year? *Lancet.* 2003;361: 2226–2234.

11. Pollock A, Price D. Re-writing the regulations: how the World Trade Organisation could accelerate privatisation in health-care systems. *Lancet.* 2000; 356:1995–2000.

12. Breman A, Shelton C. *Structural Adjustment and Health: A Literature Review of the Debate, Its Role Players and the Presented Empirical Evidence.* Geneva, Switzerland: World Health Organization; 2001. WHO Commission on Macroeconomics and Health Working Paper WG 6:6.

13. Pfeiffer J. InternationalNGOs and primary health care in Mozambique: the need for a new model of collaboration. *Soc Sci Med.* 2003;56:725–738.

14. Brugha R, Zwi A. Antiretroviral treatment in developing countries: the peril of neglecting private providers. *BMJ.* 2003;326:1382–1384.

15. Kisanga P, Latham M. *Impact of Policy on Breastfeeding and MTCT in Four Countries* [consultant report for UNICEF ESARO]. Nairobi, Kenya: UNICEF; 2001.

16. Stevens W, Kaye S, Corrah T. Antiretroviral therapy in Africa. *BMJ.* 2004; 328:280–282.

17. Kemp J, Aitken JM, LeGrand S, Mwale B. *Equity in ART? But the Whole Health System Is Inequitable. Equity in Health Sector Responses to HIV/AIDS in Malawi* [paper produced for EQUINET/Oxfam]. Bulawayo, Zimbabwe: Hunyani Printers; 2003. EQUINET discussion paper no 6. Available at: http://www.equinetafrica.org/Resources/downloads/eqser6.pdf. Accessed January 20, 2004.

18. Kushner AL, Mannion SJ, Muyco AP. Secondary crisis in African health care [letter]. *Lancet.* 2004;363:1478.

19. Smith DL, Bryant JH. Building the infrastructure for primary health care: an overview of vertical and integrated approaches. *Soc Sci Med.* 1988;26: 909–917.[ISI][Medline]

20. Mills A. Vertical versus horizontal programmes in Africa:idealism, pragmatism, resources and efficiency. *Soc Sci Med.* 1983;26:1971–1981

21. Rifkin S, Walt G. Why health improves: defining the issues concerning "comprehensive primary health care" and selective primary health care. *Soc Sci Med.* 1986;23:559–566.

22. Stabinski L, Pelley K, Jacob ST, Long JM, Leaning J. Reframing HIV and AIDS. *BMJ.* 2003;327:1101–1103.

23. *Abuja Declaration on HIV/AIDS, Tuberculosis and Other Related Infections Diseases.* Addis Ababa, Ethiopia: Organisation of African Unity; 2001. OAU/SPS/ABUJA/3.

24. German T, Randel J, Ewing D. *Reality of AID.* Manila, Philippines: Ibon Press; 2002

25. World Commission on the Social Dimension of Globalisation. *Fair Globalisation: Creating Opportunities for All.* Geneva, Switzerland: International Labour Organisation; 2004.

26. Michalos AC. *Good Taxes: The Case for Taxing Foreign Currency Exchange and Other Financial Transactions.* New York, NY: Duncan Press; 1997.

27. Greenhill R, Sisti E. *Real Progress Report on HIPC.* London, England: New Economics Foundation; 2003. Available at: http://www.jubileeplus.org/analysis/reports/realprogressHIPC.pdf (PDF file). Accessed January 20, 2004.

28 Labonte R, Schrecker T, Sanders D, Meeus W. *Fatal Indifference: The G8, Africa and Global Health.* Cape Town, South Africa: UCT press; 2004.

29. Jubilee Research. *Can the World Bank and IMF cancel 100% of Poor Country Debts?* Available at: http://www.jubilee2000uk.org. Accessed January 20, 2004.

Multisectoral Responses to HIV/AIDS: Applying Research to Policy and Practice

| *Robert A. Pawinski and Umesh G. Lalloo*

ABSTRACT

The KwaZulu-Natal Enhancing Care Initiative is a program developed by a consortium of members who represent 4 sectors: academia, government, nongovernmental and community-based organizations, and the business sector. The Initiative was formed to develop a plan for improved care and support for people with HIV/AIDS and who live in resource-constrained settings in the province of KwaZulu-Natal, South Africa. A needs analysis helped to determine the following priorities in prevention, treatment, care, and support: training, grant-seeking, prevention, and care and treatment, including provision of antiretroviral therapy. A partnership approach resulted in better access to a wider community of people, information, and resources, and facilitated rapid program implementation. Creative approaches promptly translated research into policy and practice.

INTRODUCTION

The countries that make up sub-Saharan Africa have the largest burden of HIV/AIDS worldwide.[1] Most of the health care systems in this region have ranked among the 50 worst health systems in the world[2] and are under significant human resource constraints, aggravated by the exodus of health care professionals to countries with more economic resources.[3,4] The HIV/AIDS pandemic has most severely affected South Africa, where an estimated 6 million of its 44.8 million citizens are living with the disease

(29.5% antenatal seroprevalence in 2004[5]).

In 2000, the South African National Department of Health released the HIV/AIDS/STD Strategic Plan for South Africa 2000–2005,[6] which focused on prevention and provided a framework for a multisectoral (also known as *multidisciplinary*) response to HIV/AIDS. It was only in November 2003, after prolonged controversy, that the NDoH launched the Comprehensive HIV and AIDS Care and Treatment Plan for South Africa to address the wide-scale provision of antiretroviral therapy in the public sector.[7–9]

METHODS

A multidisciplinary and multisectoral team was assembled in KwaZulu-Natal, South Africa, to develop an HIV/AIDS prevention and support program. Members represented academia, government, nongovernmental and community-based organizations, people living with HIV/AIDS, and the Durban Chamber of Commerce and Industry. The team received seed funding from the Harvard School of

Public Health's AIDS Initiative, and launched the KwaZulu-Natal Enhancing Care Initiative (ECI KZN).

Figure 1 illustrates the process this team followed,[10] which culminated in the implementation of a proposal based on the results of operational research[11] and funded by the Global Fund to Fight AIDS, Tuberculosis, and Malaria (GFATM). The ECI KZN team used research to help shape policies that led to implementation of one of the largest HIV/AIDS prevention, care, and support programs in sub-Saharan Africa.

Rapid assessment is a recognized practice that helps policymakers formulate new health interventions.[12–14] The ECI KZN team, and KwaZulu-Natal Department of Health representatives developed an ongoing rapid assessment tool (a questionnaire) to identify the priorities in HIV/AIDS prevention, treatment, and support. This questionnaire was administered to 795 patients and 188 health care providers at 6 research sites, and to 220 health professionals in the private sector. A follow-up appraisal was administered to 483 public health care workers who represented more

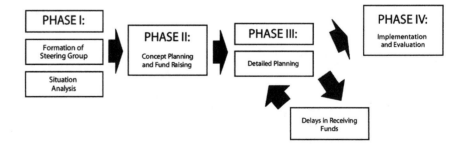

FIGURE 1— Process from acceptance of funds to implementation

TABLE 1— Survey Responses of HIV-Positive Patients Visiting Health Facilities in KwaZulu-Natal, South Africa

	Response
Average age, y	
Men	32.8
Women	31.7
Marriage status, %	
Single	71.4
Married	20.0
"Labola" paid[a]	96.0
Average no. children with each patient	4
Lost job due to HIV/AIDS-related illness, %	50.9
Used traditional healer prior to utilizing health facility, %	50.0
Had not disclosed their HIV-positive status to anyone, %	
Men	49.0
Women	36.0
Not disclosed their HIV-positive status to previous partners, %	87.5
Sexually active respondents that had not disclosed their HIV-positive status, %	61.0
Person to whom HIV-positive status most often disclosed, %	
Mother	43.0
Sister	42.0
Most common reasons for nondisclosure, %	
Fear of violence	43.0
Uncomfortable talking about these issues with partner	16.0
Fearful partner would leave them	12.0
100% adherence to current medication (self-report), %	87.9
Most common problems encountered in taking or obtaining medicine, %	
No problems	71.2
Side effects of medication	10.8
Financial problems	10.7
Distance traveled to obtain medication	2.9
Most common problems in accessing care, %	
Ignorance of care available	28.8
Not able to access facilities	17.4
Afraid of stigma	13.0
Priority needs for patients in community care, %	
Financial assistance	21.2
Drugs, including antiretroviral therapy	14.5
Food	10.8

Note. n = 795 for all 6 sites in KwaZulu-Natal.

[a]"Labola" is a traditional payment made to in-laws for a wife's hand in marriage; usually money or cows, etc.

TABLE 2— Survey Responses of Private-Sector Health Professionals Attending a Medicines Update Session in KwaZulu-Natal, South Africa

	Response
See patients who have	
HIV/AIDS-related diseases and who lack private insurance	73.8 (SD = 30.4)
Provide referral service	74.7
Prescribe antiretroviral therapy	56.8
Attended a course in HIV/AIDS management	66.4
Top priority for private-sector health professionals	
Free drugs for patients	18.5
Information and education about HIV/AIDS and	12.3
antiretroviral therapy	
Access to counseling facilities	7.5

Note. n = 146 (66.4% of sample returned surveys).

than 70 health facilities. The follow-up assessment confirmed the results of the health care providers' evaluation beyond the original research sites. Questions covered demographics, access to care, priority needs, awareness of services, stigma and discrimination, and constraints to care. Priorities that were identified (e.g., training needs, funding, other resource needs, and drugs) (Tables 1–3), were jointly addressed and solutions to resolve them were implemented.

The ECI KZN team was able to directly influence practice and indirectly influence policy for the provision of antiretroviral therapy. The first strategy was to implement the first province-wide comprehensive HIV and antiretroviral therapy training program, which reached more than 1000 health professionals in over 50 health institutions.[15,16] The second strategy was to initiate fundraising. The result of these efforts was that the Global Fund to Fight AIDS, Tuberculosis and Malaria approved a proposal entitled "Enhancing the Care of HIV/AIDS Infected and Affected Patients in Resource-Constrained Settings in KwaZulu-Natal."[17] The proposal, submitted by the ECI KZN team, included the development of a pilot infrastructure to provide antiretroviral therapy, which was not part of government policy at that time.

RESULTS

The partnerships formed by the ECI-EZN enabled the team to accomplish their goals effectively and efficiently. The involvement of stakeholders at the outset meant that programs throughout KwaZulu-Natal could be implemented and expanded soon after evaluation.[18] Access to policymakers throughout the process also facilitated rapid implementation and scale-up of programs. The ECI team learned about successful projects and best practices from each other, which enabled them to obtain assistance with program implementation. Fundraising was perceived as the most difficult and most important achievement, and yet the multidisciplinary team was able to collectively obtain funds to ensure medium-term sustainability of the program. For example, one nongovernmental organization (NGO) involved in hospice and home-based care was enabled to scale up their resource-intense activities from district-wide to province-wide with additional funds and logistic support from government and academia.

Partners were privileged to be part of a team, and perceived that international collaborators, such as the Harvard School of Public Health, helped to raise the profile of their program and their contributions at a community level. In one case, an exercise to budget for scaling-up of antiretroviral therapy also helped an ECI KZN partner to prepare a successful grant proposal to the President's Emergency Plan for HIV/AIDS. A small NGO partner linked to a rural government hospital collaborated with the local medical school and the Yale AIDS Program to provide antiretroviral therapy to tuberculosis patients undergoing DOTS (directly-observed treatment, short-course) in one of the first strategies successfully implemented in a rural district (using GFATM funds and other foundation grants).[19,20] This program expanded its provincial services more rapidly than any other site in KwaZulu-Natal after the antiretroviral therapy program began. The academic team at the medical school was also able to set up one of the largest clinical HIV/AIDS postgraduate training programs in sub-Saharan Africa[21] to meet the training needs of the province. Thus, the team's priorities changed from immediate funding and training needs to provide a sustained continuing education strategy to meet ever increasing human capacity needs.

DISCUSSION

During the era of no treatment interventions, international collaboration proved critical to identifying prior-

TABLE 3— Survey Responses of Public Health Workers at 6 Health Institutions in KwaZulu-Natal, South Africa

	Response
Most important area of achievement in improving access to care for patients	
Home-based care	20.0
Drop-in centers	18.0
Management of opportunistic infections	17.6
HIV/AIDS awareness campaigns	14.9
Involving communities	14.9
Prevention of mother-to-child transmission and all voluntary counseling and testing	9.0
Health institutions lack the capacity to deal with HIV/AIDS	83.0
Proportion of all hospital deaths perceived to be from HIV/AIDS	> 50.0
Stigma and discrimination	
Women are stigmatized and disadvantaged	37.0
HIV+ and HIV– patients are treated the same	54.0
Women are disadvantaged in accessing health facilities	37.0
Top priority for management of HIV/AIDS	
Financial assistance	35.0
More staff	27.0
Training	14.0
More space	6.0
Institutional services	
Institution has HIV/AIDS action team	2.1
Institution provides dedicated HIV/AIDS clinic services	< 3
Institution provides services for dying patients	3.0
HIV/AIDS training program is available in KwaZulu-Natal	1.1
Institution offers comprehensive care for HIV/AIDS patients	6.0
Institution lacks a training course on HIV/AIDS patient management	96.3

Note. n = 188 (80% of sample returned surveys).

ities and best practices. Seed funding provided a springboard to expand successful initiatives and activities after new policies were developed (i.e., provision of antiretroviral therapy).

The opportunity to develop research tools facilitated a partnership for joint implementation of subsequent strategic initiatives. The successful proposal and unfortunate 2-year delay of the grant[21] had the indirect effect of publicizing and highlighting the lack of antiretroviral drugs in public health policy, which stimulated an intensification of community mobilization to lobby government to provide antiretroviral therapy. Once the Comprehensive HIV and AIDS Care and Treatment Plan for South Africa[17] was approved, funds from GFATM to KwaZulu-Natal enabled the team to implement key strategies to provide a comprehensive package of prevention, care, and support, which included infrastructure for the provision of antiretroviral therapy. As of March 2006, there are over 30000 patients undergoing antiretroviral therapy in KwaZulu-Natal.

Acknowledgments

This work was supported by Merck Company Foundation through the Harvard School of Public Health.

The authors thank Noddy Jinabhai, Raziya Bobat, Vindoh Gathiram, and Ann Strode, University of KwaZulu-Natal, South Africa; Ronald Green-Thompson, Daya Moodley, Thilo Govender, Khumbu Mtinjana, Rosemary Mthethwa, Gay Koti, Khetiwe Mfeka, Mnguni Mabuyi, Caroline Armstrong, Paul Kocheleff, Jayshree Ramdeen, and TS Makatini, Department of Health, KwaZulu-Natal, SA. They also thank field workers Zethu Gwamande (field manager), Sikhumbuza Kheswa, Philani Made, Victoria Matisilza, Nosipo Mbanjwa, Virginia Mgenga, and Marjorie Njeje.

Participants from the nongovernmental organization/ community-based organization groups were Tony Moll, Kath Defilippi, Lucky Barnabas, and Duma Shange, and from the Harvard School of Public Health were Richard Marlink and Sofia Gruskin.

Human Participant Protection

This study was approved by the research ethics committee of the University of KwaZulu-Natal.

About the Authors

Robert Pawinski and Umesh Lalloo are with the Enhancing Care Initiative, KwaZulu-Natal, Nelson R. Mandela School of Medicine, University of KwaZulu-Natal, Congella, KwaZulu-Natal, South Africa.

Correspondence: Requests for reprints should be sent to Robert Pawinski, Enhancing Care Initiative, KwaZulu-Natal, Nelson R. Mandela School of Medicine, University of KwaZulu-Natal, Umbilo Road, Congella, KwaZulu-Natal (e-mail: pawinskir@ukwazulu-natal.ac.za).

Contributors

R.A. Pawinski developed and conducted the research, captured and analyzed the data, and wrote the article. U.G. Lalloo supervised and contributed substantially to the research and analysis, and assisted with reviewing the article.

References

1. *2004 Report on the Global AIDS Epidemic.* Geneva, Switzerland: Joint United Nations Programme on HIV/AIDS; 2004. Available at: http://www.unaids.org/bangkok2004/report.html. Accessed March 06, 2006.

2. *The World Health Report 2000: Health Systems: Improving Performance.* Geneva, Switzerland: World Health Organization; 2000. Available at: http://www.who.int/whr/2000/en/whr00_en.pdf. Accessed 06 March 06.

3. Raviola G, Machoki M, Mwaikaimboi E, et al. HIV, disease plague, demoralisation, and "burnout": resident experience of the medical profession in Nairobi, Kenya. *Cult Med Psychiatry.* 2002; 26:55–86.

4. Padarath A, Ntuli A, Berthiaume L. Human Resources. In: *South African Health Review 2003/2004.* Cape Town, South Africa: Health Systems Trust. Available at: http://www.hst.org.za/generic/29. Accessed March 6, 2006.

5. *National HIV and Syphilis Aantenatal Ssero-Prevalence Survey in South Africa (2004).* Pretoria, South Africa: South African Department of Health; 2004.

Available at http://www.doh.gov.za/aids/index.html. Accessed March 6, 2006.

6. *HIV/AIDS/STD Strategic Plan for South Africa 2000–2005.* Pretoria, South Africa: National Department of Health; 2000. Available at: http://www.gov.za/documents/2000/aidsplan2000.pdf. Accessed March 6, 2006.

7. Baleta A. Questioning of HIV theory of AIDS causes dismay in South Africa. *Lancet.* 2000; 355:1167.

8. Baleta A. South Africa stalls again on access to HIV drugs. *Lancet.* 2003; 361:9360.

9. Stewart GT, de Harvey E, Fiala C, Hexheimer A, Kohntein K. The debate on HIV in Africa. *Lancet.* 2000; 355:2162–2163.

10. Gruskin S, Ayres JR, Khamranksi B, Lalloo U, Marlink R. GAVI, the first steps: lessons for the Global Fund. *Lancet.* 2002; 360:176

11. Pawinski RA. *Developing Enabling Mechanisms to Enhance a Multi-Sectoral Response to HIV/AIDS.* SA-AIDS Conference; August 3–6, 2003; Durban, South Africa.

12. Rhodes T, Stimson GV, Fitch C, Ball A, Renton A. Rapid assessment, injecting drug use, and public health. *Lancet.* 1999; 354:68–68.

13. Ong BN, Humphris G, Annett H, Rifkin S. Rapid appraisal in an urban setting, an example from the developed world. *Soc Sci Med.* 1991; 32:909–915.

14. Smith GS. Development of rapid epidemiologic assessment methods to evaluate health status and delivery of health services. *Int J Epidemiol.* 1989;18(4 suppl 2): S2–S15.

15. Pawinski R. *Report on the KwaZulu-Natal HIV/ AIDS Training Program, South Africa 2001/2002.* Durban, South Africa: University of KwaZulu-Natal. Available at: http://www.uKwaZulu-Natal.ac.za/eciKwaZulu-Natal.

Accessed March 6, 2006.

16. Lalloo U, Pawinski R, Bobat R, Moodley D, Jinabhai C, Amod F, Conway S, Friedland G. *A Comprehensive HIV/AIDS Training Course to Meet the Needs of Public Sector Health Care Workers in the Province of KwaZulu-Natal, South Africa.* XVI International AIDS Conference, July 7–12, 2002; Barcelona, Spain; MoPeB3234.

17. Hope for South Africa—at last. *Lancet.* 2003; 362:501.

18. Mbali M, Pawinski R. *Report on the ECI KZN PLUS Rapid Qualitative Impact Assessment. 2004.* Durban, South Africa: University of KwaZulu-Natal. Available at: http://www.ukzn.ac.za/eciukzn. Accessed March 6, 2006.

19. Gandi N, Moll A, Pawinski R, et al. Initiating and providing antiretroviral therapy for TB/HIV co-infected patients in a rural tuberculosis directly observed therapy program South Africa: the Sizonqoba study. Paper presented at: XV International AIDS Conference, July 11–16, 2004. Bangkok, Thailand; MoOrB1014.

20. Pawinski R, Moll T, Gandi N, Lalloo U, Jack C, Fried-land G. Strategies and Clinical Outcomes of Integrating the Provision of Antiretroviral Therapy to TB Patients Using DOTS in High TB and HIV Prevalence Rural Settings: the Sizonqoba Study. 2nd South African AIDS Conference; 7–10 June, 2005; Durban, South Africa. Abstract 490.

21. Pawinski RA, Pillay S, Abdool Karim Q, et al. *Utilizing Video-Conference Facilities for Wide-Spread Postgraduate Clinical HIV/AIDS Training Throughout KwaZulu-Natal.* 2nd South African AIDS Conference; 7–10 June, 2005; Durban, South Africa. Abstract 459. 22. Baleta A. Global Fund dispute in KwaZulu-Natal. *Lancet Infect Dis.* 2002; 2:510.

Brazil and Access to HIV/AIDS Drugs: A Question of Human Rights and Public Health

| Jane Galvão, PhD

ABSTRACT

I explore the relationship between public health and human rights by examining the Brazilian government's policy of free and universal access to anti-retroviral medicines for people with HIV/AIDS.

The Brazilian government's management of the HIV/AIDS epidemic arose from initiatives in both civil society and the governmental sector following the democratization of the country. The dismantling of authoritarian rule in Brazil was accompanied by a strong orientation toward human rights, which formed the sociopolitical framework of Brazil's response to the HIV/AIDS epidemic.

Even if the Brazilian experience cannot be easily transferred to other countries, the model of the Brazilian government's response may nonetheless serve as inspiration for finding appropriate and lifesaving solutions in other national contexts.

INTRODUCTION

For several years I have studied Brazil's management of the HIV/AIDS epidemic and the ways in which Brazil's policies have contributed to the global fight against the HIV/AIDS epidemic.[1–7] In this article, I analyze the links between public health and human rights, using the Brazilian government's policy of free and universal access to anti-retroviral medicines (ARVs) for people with HIV/AIDS as an example. Although I refer to the production of generic versions of AIDS drugs as well as the role of international pharmaceutical companies, both topics are explored in greater detail elsewhere.[8–15]

Globally, ARVs remain beyond the reach of the majority of people with HIV/AIDS.[16–18] Of the 6 million people worldwide who needed ARVs in 2003, fewer than 8% were receiving them.[18] Although Brazil is considered a middle-income country,[19] its government provides ARVs to its constituents free of charge. To make such a policy viable, the government has limited the drugs' high cost by producing some ARVs domestically and by negotiating with international pharmaceutical companies to import other ARVs[2,20]; of the 15 ARVs utilized in the country in 2002, 7 were produced in local laboratories, either public or private, and the remainder were purchased on the international market.[2,21]

The relative success of the ARV program in Brazil reflects a somewhat privileged position compared to lower-income countries, some of which have higher levels of HIV infection. In turn, using the Brazilian government's management of HIV/AIDS as a model may not transfer easily to other nations.[22] However, Brazil's experience offers inspiration for finding appropriate and life-saving solutions in other contexts.[23] To gain a wider perspective on Brazil's HIV/AIDS policy—and in particular the synergy between health and human rights—I solicited comments from several individuals, quoted in this article, who work for Brazilian and international organizations that are currently at the forefront of the struggle against HIV/AIDS. By reviewing Brazil's policies and relating other people's experiences, I hope to demonstrate the importance of community mobilization, political will, international solidarity, and financial commitment in the fight against HIV/AIDS.

HIV/AIDS IN BRAZIL

In 1980, the first case of AIDS in Brazil was registered. By December 2003, 310 310 cases had been reported in the country, comprising 220 783 men and 89 527 women[24]; of this total, approximately 48% have died.[24] The epidemic is spreading, particularly among the poor, women, and those living outside the urban centers.[25] In people aged 15 to 49 years, the estimated prevalence of HIV is 0.65%, with approximately 600 000 people infected with HIV.[21] Of this total, approximately 200 000 know their HIV status,[26,27] the majority of which are registered in the public health system and are receiving treatment. According to figures from 2003, of those individuals in the public health system, 135 000 were undergoing highly active antiretroviral therapy.[28]

LIMITING THE COSTS OF ARV THERAPY

Although other countries in Latin America have established programs to improve access to treatment for people with HIV/AIDS,[29] Brazil's program is the most far reaching.[30] The program provides state-of-the-art ARV treatment to people in need, free of charge, through the public health system, and the government controls the costs of the program by encouraging local laboratories to produce ARVs, which decreases Brazil's need to import vital drugs from foreign countries. During his tenure as director of Brazil's National AIDS Program, Paulo Teixeira understood that the success and sustainability of Brazil's policy of access to ARVs depended on effective strategies to control costs. He believes that maintaining political will while fostering new international alliances for more favorable regulations on pharmaceutical-related trade and intellectual property will continue to be central. According to Teixeira,

The biggest challenge for the future of the Brazilian National AIDS Program is the maintenance and the sustainability of the policy of free and universal access to ARVs. This is directly linked to a change in the world economic order with regard to medicines. It will depend not only on a firm position by Brazil, in the defense of its policy of production and distribution of ARVs, but also on the strengthening of international alliances that are beginning to form with the World Health Organization, the World Trade Organization, the United Nations Special Session on HIV/AIDS, and the Global Fund to Fight AIDS, Tuberculosis and Malaria. It is extremely important that these alliances are maintained and intensified to guarantee the conquests already achieved.

Increased local production of ARVs has been integral to the Brazilian strategy. According to Eloan Pinheiro, former director of Far-Manguinhos, a Brazilian Ministry of Health (MOH) laboratory that produces ARVs, "the local production of AIDS drugs made access to ARV therapy possible for the Brazilian population. Without it, the price of the drugs would be beyond Brazil's reach."

The Brazilian government's strategy for controlling the costs of AIDS medicines has not been without challenges and obstacles. In 2001, the country was involved in international disputes about its program of access to AIDS medicines.[2] In that year, the

World Trade Organization (WTO) accepted a request for a panel by the United States, which was challenging Brazil's patent laws, laws that permit the compulsory license of patents under special conditions. At its heart, the US challenge questioned Brazil's commitment to producing ARVs nationally; explicitly, however, the United States was challenging the prospective patent violations that would occur as a result of Brazil's program. In June 2001, the United States withdrew its complaint before the WTO. To date, Brazil has not produced any of its medicines under compulsory licensing, and the ARVs that are currently produced are those medications whose introduction predated Brazil's signing of the Trade-Related Aspects of Intellectual Property Rights (TRIPS) agreement. In September 2003, a presidential decree was issued that facilitated the importation of generic medicines.[31] At the time, according to Brazil's MOH, 3 imported name-brand ARVs—nelfinavir, lopinavir, and efavirenz—were consuming 63% of the budget for acquiring ARVs.[28,32] The possibility of importing generic medicines improved Brazil's bargaining position with the patent-holding companies that manufacture those medicines. As a result, in January 2004, the National AIDS Program announced that it had successfully negotiated reduced prices for those drugs and other related medicines, thereby anticipating savings of almost US$100 million for 2004.[33,34] Because of these price reductions, the estimated costs of ARV treatment in 2004 were around US$170 million.[33]

Concern for human rights combined with the urgent need for access to treatment by people with HIV/AIDS has bolstered wider efforts to lower the costs of ARVs. Peter Piot, executive director of the Joint United Nations Programme on HIV/AIDS (UNAIDS), recognized the role of Brazil's HIV/AIDS policies in facilitating this development, saying,

The Brazilian experience has played a key part in changing expectations in the interpretation of the World Trade Organization's TRIPS (Trade-

Related Aspects of Intellectual Property Rights) Agreement. When the Doha Ministerial Meeting of the World Trade Organization at the end of 2001 declared that the TRIPS Agreement ought not stand in the way of AIDS responses, it in effect acknowledged the ethical and practical imperatives represented by Brazil's generic anti-retroviral industry.

AIDS AND HUMAN RIGHTS

Globally, violating the human rights of people with HIV/AIDS—through stigmatization, discrimination, and violence—is increasingly recognized as a central problem that is impeding the fight against AIDS.[35–38] AIDS NGOs and human rights advocates have linked HIV/AIDS to human rights and have demonstrated that human rights violations increase the spread of HIV.[39–42] For example, people affected by HIV/AIDS who are living in areas where discrimination, stigmatization, and threats against individuals with HIV/AIDS are high are less inclined to seek testing, thereby postponing treatment if available, which means that opportunities to decrease HIV transmission are lost.

Gruskin et al. described 3 stages through which the relationship between HIV/AIDS and human rights has proceeded.[42] In the first stage, 1981–1986, human rights advocates pitted themselves against public health officials who proposed measures such as mandatory testing and quarantine to counter the emerging epidemic. In the second stage, beginning around 1987, officials openly acknowledged that mandatory testing and quarantine undermined the efficacy of prevention programs. In the third phase, which started in the late 1980s, research developed from the idea that vulnerability was a key to infection. This research was then developed and disseminated by human rights activists such as the late Jonathan Mann, a central figure for and staunch defender of human rights for people living with HIV/AIDS, and by groups such as the Global AIDS Policy Coalition, which was founded and led by Mann. During this phase, Gruskin et al. argued, "it became clear that a lack of respect for human rights and dignity was a major contributor to the HIV/AIDS problem."[42(p326)] With the advent of more effective treatments for controlling the effects of AIDS, a fourth phase in the relation between human rights and HIV/AIDS began: the promotion of access to treatment.

Today, access to treatment increasingly is being advocated as a human right, a viewpoint that is playing a prominent role in developments to counter the HIV/AIDS pandemic.[43–48] For example, at the April 2001 57th Session of the Commission on Human Rights, the United Nations High Commissioner for Human Rights approved a resolution that makes access to medical drugs in cases of pandemics such as HIV/AIDS a basic human right.[49] Although this resolution did not have the power of law, it was nonetheless an important step toward establishing the right of people living with HIV/AIDS to receive the medicine and treatment they need. Also in 2001, a declaration was approved at the Fourth World Trade Organization Ministerial Conference[50] that allowed countries to apply for compulsory licensing in order to produce necessary medicines in cases of national public health emergencies.[51] In 2003, UNAIDS reaffirmed the relevance of human rights to HIV/AIDS by establishing a Global Reference Group on HIV/AIDS and Human Rights.[52]

HIV/AIDS AND HUMAN RIGHTS IN BRAZIL

In the early 1980s, after a military dictatorship that lasted almost 20 years, Brazil went through a process of democratization, gradually reconstructing civil society[53] and formulating a new social agenda for areas such as education and health. During this period, campaigns such as the Movement for Sanitary Reform, which sought to democratize health policy and establish health care as a right for all Brazilians, began.[20,54] At this time, Brazilian newspapers also began

describing the emergence of a new disease, as the first AIDS cases in the country were being reported.[3,6]

In Brazil, the early HIV/AIDS movement relied on experienced activists who had organized against the military regime; some of these individuals helped create the first nongovernmental organizations (NGOs) and some came to assume roles in local, state, and federal government. Not surprisingly, this first generation of Brazilian activists approached the government about the new disease using strategies they had implemented against the dictatorship, strategies that included the demand for the democratization of access to information and the defense of human rights.[4] In Brazil, the response to the HIV/AIDS pandemic arose from initiatives in both civil society and the government and followed the process of democratization[4,55]—a context with a strong orientation toward human rights.

In 1988, with the reorganization of Brazil's public health system[56] and the adoption of Brazil's new constitution, access to health care, including access to medicines, improved in the country. At that time, the Unified Health System (Sistema Único de Saúde [SUS]) was established.[54,56,57] The SUS offered free comprehensive health care to the entire population, regardless of employment status or access to other forms of health insurance.[2] However, prior to the establishment of the SUS, the national agenda had included local production of some medicines by state laboratories and free distribution of certain medicines by the public health system.[58]

People with HIV/AIDS were among those who benefited from the new health system; they began to receive drugs for opportunistic infections, and in 1991 began to receive zidovudine (AZT).[3,4,59] In November 1996, the access to medicines policy became firmly established when the president of the republic signed a law[60] that guaranteed free distribution of medicines to people with HIV/AIDS throughout the public health system.[2,3,21,29,59] ARVs, along with medicine for malaria, Hansen dis-

ease, cholera, hemophilia, diabetes, schistosomiasis, trachoma, leishmaniasis, and filariasis, form the category of medicines the MOH has deemed "strategic" for treating endemic diseases; these medicines in turn are purchased by the federal government.[5,61]

The government's commitment to provide AIDS medicines resulted, in part, from pressure from civil society, where people with HIV/AIDS sought to force the health system to provide them with the needed medications by suing state or municipal governments.[62,63] In these struggles, the judiciary proved to be an important ally. The judges often ruled favorably, citing Brazil's constitution, which guaranteed that every citizen had a right to health and the state had a duty to ensure every citizen's health. Brazilian lawyer Miriam Ventura pointed to the codification of the policy as the "successful result of a model of action adopted by organized civil society." This mobilization, she continued, "utilized the language of human rights and the strategic application of national laws . . . [and] succeeded in placing on the political agenda questions that affect the life of people living with HIV/AIDS, and in so doing altered public and state policies regarding health care."

In 1989, Ventura helped to establish *Pela VIDDA*—which means "For the Valorization, Integration and Dignity of People with AIDS"—the legal AIDS service for the first group of Brazilian people with HIV/AIDS. Herbert Daniel, founder and first president of the group, denounced the denial of the rights of people with HIV/AIDS, which he termed "civil death."[64] Daniel was a writer and a militant of the gay movement who also fought against the dictatorship in Brazil before being forced into exile; he died of AIDS in 1992.

In Brazil, the participation of civil society had a key role in bringing about and sustaining the Brazilian government's ARV distribution policy.[1,7,62,63] The importance of this contribution was highlighted by Veriano Terto, Jr, executive director of the Brazilian Interdisciplinary AIDS

Association (ABIA), an NGO founded in 1986 in Rio de Janeiro:

The participation of organized civil society in access to AIDS treatment goes back to the eighties, when popular pressure and progressive political forces were fundamental in creating a unified public health system based on the principles of universal access, comprehensiveness, and participatory decision making. If currently we have a system for the distribution of medicines in the public health network, and legislation that guarantees this system, this is based in the values of universality and equality in access to treatment for all epidemics contemplated in the health system, and in public participation, which underlies and accompanies the Brazilian public health policies.

Terto continued, saying,

The participation of civil society also was fundamental for including solidarity, respect for human rights, and the struggle against prejudice and discrimination to the response against AIDS. These points were fundamental for amplifying the notion of health beyond the search for physical well-being, and technical measures focused only on the treatment of individuals. In this sense, the demand for universal and free access to medicines should be seen as a question of making real the right to life, and respect of the basic human rights of people living with HIV/AIDS in Brazil.

Piot made a similar observation:

The HIV epidemic is aided by social exclusion—marginalized populations are the most vulnerable to HIV infection, whether through sex or needle sharing, and people living with HIV/AIDS, however they acquired infection, are tarred with the same brush of stigma. Breaking the vicious cycle of social exclusion is therefore crucial both to interrupting transmission and to maximizing the care and support available to people living with HIV/AIDS. This is perhaps the key to the tremendous impact of Brazil's 1996 decision to guarantee constitutionally access to ARV therapy. Not only has this decision led to the quadrupling of the number of Brazilians accessing these drugs, it also sent the signal that people living with HIV/AIDS were valued citizens, whose care was a matter of entitlement, not of privilege.

ABIA was the first Brazilian AIDS NGO to have as its president and founder someone who disclosed his HIV positive status. Herbert de Souza—known by the nickname Betinho—was a former political exile. He was a hemophiliac, as were his 2 brothers; all 3 became infected with HIV through blood transfusions in the mid 1980s. One of the first important struggles carried out by ABIA was the promotion of blood safety, a tremendous problem at that time in Brazil. After the approval of the Brazilian constitution in 1988, it was forbidden to sell blood in Brazil. Betinho's brothers died in the mid 1980s, and Betinho died in 1997.[4,7]

LINKING TREATMENT AND PREVENTION

In Brazil, there are at least 2 important arguments from an economic perspective for maintaining free access to AIDS medicines: the impact of ARVs in reducing deaths and the significant reduction in hospitalization and treatment costs associated with opportunistic infections.[2,21,29] However, beyond the biomedical and economic arguments for treatment, a rights-based approach focused on the inequality that fueled the virus's spread.[65,66] Current ABIA president Richard Parker, chair of the Department of Sociomedical Sciences in the Mailman School of Public Health at Columbia University, stated

By affirming universal access to treatment for all those infected with HIV, Brazilian policy has simultaneously reaffirmed the rights and citizenship of those who otherwise would be defined primarily by their broader exclusion in Brazilian society. Because of this, prevention becomes possible, not just as a technical exercise in public health, but as itself the right to health of all citizens. While the broader social inequalities that shape the epidemic have only become more extreme over time, the strategic approach to AIDS in Brazil has thus been able, in a targeted way, to mitigate their worst effects, to respond to the stigma and discrimination so often generated by the epidemic, and to recover the simple idea of human dignity, guaranteed by civil rights, as the most powerful way of responding to the reality of AIDS-related vulnerability.

Providing better access to HIV/AIDS therapy in resource-poor countries is not only a humanitarian imperative[67] but also a viable and financially justified course of action in terms of economic costs and social benefits. This is apparent when considering the Brazilian initiative of distributing ARVs—with savings in both lives and financial resources—along with studies elsewhere that suggest socioeconomic levels of patients do not interfere with adherence to treatment.[68–71]

Providing better access to HIV/AIDS therapy has become a global initiative as well. In 2003, the World Health Organization launched its "3 by 5" strategy,[18,43,47,72] which aims to extend access to ARV therapy to an additional 3 million people with HIV/AIDS living in developing countries by the end of 2005.[72] The theme for the XV International AIDS Conference, held in Bangkok, Thailand, in July 2004 was "Access for all," an assertion that it is time to deliver the message, the medicine, the help, and the hope to all.[73] In this manner, Brazil, whose human rights advocates lobbied for health rights and whose government placed human rights at the center of its HIV/AIDS policy, has been a vital role model.

Resources allocated to disease treatment are often seen as competing with resources available for disease prevention, a dichotomy leading to a debate regarding priorities in the fight against the HIV/AIDS pandemic.[74] In the 1990s, The World Bank, for example, did not favor a policy of providing AIDS medicines to developing countries,[75] including Brazil.[76] At the time, the World Bank believed that, with limited resources, funds should be directed to prevention in order to limit new infections. More recently, however, the World Bank has come to emphasize the importance of combining prevention and treatment.[77,78] According to Piot, "[there is an] inextricable link between prevention and care, which operate together as twin pillars of a comprehensive AIDS response." He added that "Brazil is perhaps the world's leading example of the synergies available between prevention and care." But even with Brazil's success at offering treatment to people with HIV/AIDS, an assessment is needed to determine how the nation—which is devoting financial and human resources to both prevention and treatment—is or is not succeeding in preventing new infections.

In order to adequately analyze the public health system in Brazil[54,56,57] and explain how Brazil's AIDS program was developed, I would need to write another entire article. However, even in Brazil, when deciding how to first proceed against the HIV/AIDS pandemic, there was great internal conflict within Brazil's government, as sectors that wanted to prioritize HIV/AIDS were opposed by sectors that wanted money and resources allocated elsewhere.[79] Even today, despite international recognition and growing internal support, the Brazilian government's HIV/AIDS policy occasionally receives criticism at home from those who believe Brazil should spend more money in other areas and less money on HIV/AIDS.[80]

There are 3 points to consider regarding Brazil's HIV/AIDS policy, lest the positive lessons described herein give a simplistic image of a genuinely complex reality. First, the Brazilian program in response to the HIV/AIDS epidemic has been successful even though the country is still marked by profound socioeconomic inequalities.[81] Second, the Brazilian policy regarding access to ARVs needs to be analyzed in terms of the program's sustainability and potential transferability to other countries.[2,22,82] Third, Brazil must continue to strive for positive results. The experience of other countries such as Thailand demonstrates that it is not easy to sustain a successful response against the HIV/AIDS pandemic.[83–85] In Thailand, severe police repression against injection drug users has threatened prevention measures directed at that particular population. In any national program, it is essential to prevent past success from turning into complacency and inaction and to remain vigilant in regard to human rights, particularly for the rights of those people who are made most vulnerable.[85]

New developments linking HIV to national, international, and human security,[86–89] together with a growing human rights orientation toward people with HIV/AIDS, have contributed to new recommendations from organizations such as the World Health Organization[90] and others[91] to combine prevention, support, treatment, and care in responding to the HIV/AIDS pandemic. Although the Brazilian experience has helped move access to treatment as a basic human right beyond abstract discussion, this approach still poses immediate and practical challenges, particularly in terms of maintaining political will and sustaining financial support. To respond to some of these challenges, UNAIDS recently announced the establishment of an International Centre for Technical Cooperation on AIDS in Brazil to help developing countries strengthen their responses to HIV/AIDS.[92] Placing this center in Brazil is not likely coincidental—UNAIDS hopes to draw from Brazil's rich experience in responding to the HIV/AIDS pandemic.

Brazil's experience and related initiatives will merit continued attention as the world confronts the growing HIV/AIDS pandemic. Providing access to lifesaving medicines and transferring technologies will be challenges, not only for those involved with HIV/AIDS but also for the field of public health as a whole, posing practical and theoretical questions that will need to be answered in the years to come.[93]

About the Authors

At the time of the study, Jane Galvão was with the Institute for Global Health, University of California, San Francisco, and the School of Public Health, University of California, Berkeley.

Correspondence: Requests for reprints should be sent to Jane Galvão, PhD, International Planned Parenthood Federation/Western Hemisphere Region, 120 Wall St, 9th Fl, New York, NY 10005-3902 (e-mail: jgalvao@ippfwhr.org).

Acknowledgments

The first draft of this article was supported by the Fogarty International AIDS Training Program (grant 1-D43-TW00003) (School of Public Health, University of California, Berkeley) from February 2001 to November 2002.

I thank Daniel Hoffman for his comments and for translating the original text from Portuguese, and Kate MacLaughlin for further editing the text. I especially wish to thank Richard Parker, Eloan Pinheiro, Peter Piot, Paulo Teixeira, Veriano Terto, Jr, and Miriam Ventura for contributing comments that have enriched this article.

References

1. Galvão J. *AIDS no Brasil: A Agenda de Construção de uma Epidemia.* São Paulo and Rio de Janeiro, Brazil:

Editora 34, Associação Brasileira Interdisciplinar de AIDS; 2000.

2. Galvão J. Access to antiretroviral drugs in Brazil. *Lancet.* 2002;360: 1862–1865.

3. Galvão J. Brazilian policy for the distribution and production of antiretroviral drugs: a privilege or a right? [in Portuguese.] *Cad Saúde Pública.* 2002; 18:213–219.

4. Galvão J. Brazil and access to AIDS medication: public health as a human right issue. In: Sydow E, Mendonça ML, eds. *Human Rights in Brazil 2002.* São Paulo, Brazil: Social Network for Justice and Human Rights and Global Exchange; 2002:181–188.

5. Galvão J, Passarelli CA, Reingold AL, Rutherford GW. Acesso a medicamentos para AIDS: lições da iniciativa brasileira. *Divulg Saúde Debate.* 2003; 29:11–22.

6. Galvão J. Community mobilization and access to medicines: the Brazilian nongovernmental responses for the HIV/AIDS epidemic. Text presented at: Harvard Forum on Human Rights in Brazil, Brazil Human Rights Series: Rights to Health; November 3, 2003; Boston, Mass.

7. Galvão J. O modelo brasileiro na promoção ao acesso aos medicamentos para AIDS. Sociedad Iberoamericana de Información Científica [online database]; March 11, 2004. Available at: http://www.siicsalud.com/dato/dat03 6/04309001.htm. Accessed April 4, 2005.

8. Attaran A, Gillespie-White L. Do patents for antiretroviral drugs constrain access to AIDS treatment in Africa? *JAMA.* 2001;286:1886–1892.

9. Chien CV. Cheap drugs at what price to innovation: does the compulsory licensing of pharmaceuticals hurt innovation? *Berkeley Technol Law J.* 2003; 18(1)1–57.

10. Patently robbing the poor to serve the rich [editorial]. *Lancet.* 2002;360: 885.

11. Kapczynski A, Crone ET, Merson M. Global health and university patents. *Science.* 2003;301:1629.

12. Prusoff W. The scientist's story. *New York Times.* March 19, 2001:A4.

13. Shanker D. Brazil, the pharmaceutical industry and the WTO. *J World Intellect Prop.* 2002;5(1):53–104.

14. Vianna JMN. Intellectual property rights, the World Trade Organization and public health: the Brazilian perspective. *Conn J Int Law.* 2002;17:311–318.

15. McNeil D Jr. Plan to battle AIDS worldwide is falling short. *New York Times.* March 28, 2004:A1;A14.

16. Attawell K, Mundy J. *Provision of Antiretroviral Therapy in Resource-Limited Settings: A Review of Experience Up to August 2003.* London, England: Health Systems Resource Centre, Department for International Development; 2003. Available at: http://www.who.int/3by5/publications/documents/en/ARTpaper_DFID _WHO.pdf. Accessed April 4, 2005.

17. International HIV Treatment Access Coalition. *A Commitment to Action for Expanded Access to HIV/AIDS Treatment.* Geneva, Switzerland: World Health Organization; 2002. Available at: http://www.who.int/hiv/pub/ arv/who_hiv_2002_24.pdf. Accessed April 4, 2005.

18. World Health Organization, Joint United Nations Programme on HIV/AIDS. *Treating 3 Million by 2005: Making It Happen. The WHO Strategy.* Geneva, Switzerland: World Health Organization; 2003. Available at: http://www.who.int/3by5/publications/documents/en/3by5StrategyMak ingItHappen.pdf. Accessed April 4, 2005.

19. World Bank. *World Development Indicators 2003.* Washington, DC: World Bank; 2003.

20. Teixeira PR, Vitória MAA, Barcarolo J. The Brazilian experience in providing universal access to antiretroviral therapy. In: Moatti J-P, Coriat B, Souteyrand Y, Barnett T, Dumoulin J, Flori Y-A, eds. *Economics of AIDS and Access to HIV/AIDS Care in Developing Countries, Issues and Challenges.* Paris, France: Agence Nationale de Recherches sur le Sida; 2003:69–88.

21. Levi GC, Vitória MA. Fighting against AIDS: the Brazilian experience. *AIDS.* 2002;16:2373–2383.

22. Oliveira-Cruz V, Kowalski J, McPake B. Viewpoint: the Brazilian HIV/AIDS 'success story'—can others do it? *Trop Med Int Health.* 2004;9: 292–297.

23. Médecins Sans Frontières (MSF). 8,000 deaths a day [editorial]. *Washington Post.* March 26, 2004:A22.

24. Ministry of Health. *Boletim Epidemiológico AIDS.* Brasília, Brazil: Ministry of Health; 2004. Available at: http://www.aids.gov.br/final/biblioteca/boletim_dezembro_2003/bol_ dezem-bro_2003.pdf. Accessed April 4, 2005.

25. Ministry of Health. *Response: The Experience of the Brazilian AIDS Programme.* Brasília, Brazil: Ministry of Health; 2002. Available at: http://www.aids.gov.br/final/biblioteca/resposta/resp_ingles.pdf. Accessed April 4, 2005.

26. Ministério da Saúde lança campanha com o objetivo de incentivar os testes de HIV. *Folha de S. Paulo.* January 18, 2003:C3.

27. Kaisernetwork.org. Brazil Launches Free HIV Testing Campaign. Menlo Park, Calif: Henry J. Kaiser Family Foundation; November 3, 2003. Available at: http://www.kaisernetwork.org/daily_reports/rep_index.cfm ?hint=1&DR_ID=20647. Accessed April 4, 2005.

28. Programa Nacional de DST e AIDS. *O perfil da AIDS no Brasil e metas de governo para o controle da epidemia.* Brasília, Brazil: National AIDS Program; 2003. Available at: http://www.aids.gov.br/final/biblioteca/metas/metas.pdf. Accessed April 4, 2005.

29. Chequer P, Cuchí P, Mazin R, Calleja JMG. Access to antiretroviral treatment in Latin American countries and the Caribbean. *AIDS.* 2002;6(suppl 13):S50–S57.

30. Antirretrovirales: esfuerzos de América Latina y el Caribe hacia el acceso universal [information about access to ARV treatment in the Latin American region]. Pan American Health Organization Web site. Available at: http://www.paho.org/Spanish/AD/FC H/AI/antiretrovirals_HP.htm. Accessed April 4, 2005.

31. Decreto Número 4.830. *Diário Oficial da União.* September 5, 2003; 140(172):1. Available at: http://www.aids.gov.br/imprensa/pdf/ DECRETO%20N%204.830%20DE %2005.09.2003.pdf. Accessed April 4, 2005.

32. Governo cria instrumento que facilita importação de medicamentos genéricos [press release]. Brasília, Brazil: National AIDS Program; September 4, 2003. Available at: http://www.aids.gov.br/imprensa/noticiasimpressao.asp?notcod=49511. Accessed April 4, 2005.

33. Saúde fecha acordo com laboratórios de anti-retrovirais [press release]. Brasília, Brazil: National AIDS Program; January 15, 2004. Available at: http://www.aids.gov.br/imprensa/noti-

ciasimpressao.asp?notcod=53234. Accessed April 4, 2005.

34. Kaisernetwork.org. *Brazil's National STD/AIDS Programme Announces Largest Drug Price Reduction Deals in Five Years.* Menlo Park, Calif: Henry J. Kaiser Family Foundation; January 20, 2004. Available at: http://www.kaisernetwork.org/daily_r eports/print_report.cfm?DR_ID=2175 1&dr_cat=1. Accessed April 4, 2005.

35. Farmer P. *AIDS and Accusation: Haiti and the Geography of Blame.* Berkeley: University of California Press; 1992.

36. International Council of AIDS Service Organizations. *The International Guidelines on HIV/AIDS and Human Rights: How Are They Being Used and Applied?* Toronto, Canada: International Council of AIDS Service Organizations; 2002.

37. Parker R, Aggleton P. HIV and AIDS-related stigma and discrimination: a conceptual framework and implications for action. *Soc Sci Med.* 2003;57: 13–24.

38. Sabatier R. *Blaming Others: Prejudice, Race and Worldwide AIDS.* London, England: The Panos Institute; 1988.

39. Mann JM. AIDS and human rights: where do we go from? *Health Hum Rights.* 1998;3:143–149.

40. Mann J, Tarantola D. Responding to HIV/AIDS: a historical perspective. *Health Hum Rights.* 1998;2:5–8.

41. Mann J, Gruskin S, Grodin MA, Annas GJ. *Health and Human Rights: A Reader.* London, England: Routledge; 1999.

42. Gruskin S, Hendriks A, Tomasevski K. Human rights and responses to AIDS. In: Mann J, Tarantola D, eds. *AIDS in the World II.* New York, NY: Oxford University Press; 1996: 326–340.

43. Coutinho A. Pills and promises—a personal account from Uganda. *Lancet.* 2004;363:1073.

44. Easley CE, Marks SP, Morgan RE Jr. The challenge and place of international human rights in public health. *Am J Public Health.* 2001;91: 1922–1925.

45. Farmer P. Political violence and public health in Haiti. *N Engl J Med.* 2004;350:1483–1486.

46. Gruskin S, Tarantola D. *Health and Human Rights.* Boston, Mass: François-Xavier Bagnoud Center for Health and Human Rights; 2000. Working Paper 10. Available at: http://www.hsph.har-vard.edu/fxbcen-ter/FXBC_WP10-Gruskin_and_Tarantola.pdf. Accessed April 4, 2005.

47. Mukherjee J. Basing treatment on rights rather than ability to pay: 3 by 5. *Lancet.* 2004;363:1071–1072.

48. Tarantola D. *Building on the Synergy Between Health and Human Rights: A Global Perspective.* Boston, Mass: François-Xavier Bagnoud Center for Health and Human Rights; 2000. Working Paper 8. Available at: http://www.hsph.harvard.edu/fxbcen-ter/FXBC_WP8-Tarantola.pdf. Accessed April 4, 2005.

49. United Nations High Commissioner for Human Rights. *Access to Medication in the Context of Pandemics Such as HIV/AIDS. Commission on Human Rights Resolution 2001/33.* Geneva, Switzerland: United Nations High Commissioner for Human Rights; 2001. Available at: http://www.unhchr.ch/huridocda/huri doca.nsf/framepage/docs+chr?open-document. Accessed April 4, 2005.

50. World Trade Organization. *Declaration on the TRIPS Agreement and Public Health.* Geneva, Switzerland: World Trade Organization; 2001. WT/MIN(01)/DEC/2. Available at: http://www.wto.org/english/thewto_e /minist_e/min01_e/mindecl_trips_e.p df. Accessed April 4, 2005.

51. Correa CM. *Implications of the Doha Declaration on the TRIPS Agreement and Public Health.* Geneva, Switzerland: World Health Organization; 2002. Available at: http://whqlibdoc.who.int/hq/2002/w ho_edm_par_2002.3.pdf. Accessed April 4, 2005.

52. Joint United Nations Programme on HIV/AIDS. *Public Report: First Meeting of the UNAIDS Global Reference Group on HIV/AIDS and Human Rights, January 23–24, 2003, Geneva, Switzerland.* Geneva, Switzerland: Joint United Nations Programme on HIV/AIDS; 2003. Available at: http://www.unaids.org/html/pub/UN A-docs/HRrefgroup_0103mtg_en_pdf.ht m. Accessed April 4, 2005.

53. Skidmore T. *The Politics of Military Rule in Brazil, 1964–85.* New York, NY: Oxford University Press; 1988.

54. Mattos RA. Os sentidos da integral-idade: algumas reflexões acerca dos valores que merecem ser defendidos. In: Pinheiro R, Mattos RA, eds. *Os Sentidos da Integralidade na Atenção e no Cuidado à Saúde.* Rio de Janeiro, Brazil: IMS/UERJ/ABRASCO; 2001: 39–64.

55. Galvão J. Access to antiretrovirals: where South Africa, China, and Brazil meet. *Lancet.* 2004;363:493.

56. Elias PE, Cohn A. Health reform in Brazil: lessons to consider. *Am J Public Health.* 2003;93:44–48.

57. Souza RR. *O Sistema Público de Saúde Brasileiro.* Brasília, Brazil: Ministry of Health; 2002. Available at: http://dtr2001.saude.gov.br/editora/p rodutos/livros/pdf/02_0784_M.pdf. Accessed April 4, 2005.

58. Orsi F, Hasenclever L, Fialho B, Tigre P, Coriat B. Intellectual property rights, anti-AIDS policy and generic drugs: lessons from the Brazilian public health program. In: Moatti J-P, Coriat B, Souteyrand Y, Barnett T, Dumoulin J, Flori Y-A, eds. *Economics of AIDS and Access to HIV/AIDS Care in Developing Countries, Issues and Challenges.* Paris, France: Agence Nationale de Recherches sur le Sida; 2003:109–135.

59. Ministry of Health. *Terapia Antiretroviral e Saúde Pública: Um Balanço da Experiência Brasileira.* Brasília, Brazil: Ministry of Health; 1999.

60. Dispõe sobre a distribuição gratuita de medicamentos aos portadores do HIV e doentes de AIDS. November 13, 1996. Law 9.313. Available at: http://www.aids.gov.br/assistencia/lei 9313.htm. Accessed April 4, 2005.

61. Negri B. *Política Federal de Assistência Farmacêutica, 1990–2002.* Brasília, Brazil: Ministry of Health; 2002. Available at: http://dtr2001.saude.gov.br/editora/p rodutos/livros/pdf/03_0049_M.pdf. Accessed April 4, 2005.

62. Bastos FI, Kerrigan D, Malta M, Carneiro-da-Cunha C, Strathdee SA. Treatment for HIV/AIDS in Brazil: strengths, challenges, and opportunities for operations research. *AIDScience.* 2001;1(15). Available at: http://www.aidscience.org/Articles/aid science012.pdf. Accessed April 4, 2005.

63. Passarelli C, Terto V Jr. Good medicine: Brazil's multifront war on AIDS. *NACLA Report on the Americas.* 2002; 35(5):35–37,40–42.

64. Daniel H. *Vida Antes da Morte [Life Before Death].* Rio de Janeiro, Brazil: Tipografia Jaboti; 1989.

65. Farmer P. *Pathologies of Power: Health, Human Rights and the New War on the Poor.* Berkeley: University of California Press; 2003.

66. Parker R. The global HIV/AIDS pan-

demic, structural inequalities, and the politics of international health. *Am J Public Health.* 2002;92:343–346.

67. Mukherjee JS, Farmer PE, Niyizonkiza D, et al. Tackling HIV in resource poor countries. *BMJ.* 2003;327: 1104–1106.

68. Grubb I, Perriëns J, Schwartländer B. *A Public Health Approach to Antiretroviral Treatment: Overcoming Constraints.* Geneva, Switzerland: World Health Organization; 2003. Available at: http://www.who.int/ hiv/pub/prev_care/en/PublicHealthApproach_E.pdf. Accessed April 4, 2005.

69. Laurent C, Diakhaté N, Gueye NF, et al. The Senegalese government's highly active antiretroviral therapy initiative: an 18-month follow-up study. *AIDS.* 2002;16:1363–1370.

70. Mukherjee JS. HIV-1 care in resource-poor settings: a view from Haiti. *Lancet.* 2003; 362:994–995.

71. Orrell C, Bangsberg DR, Badri M, Wood R. Adherence is not a barrier to successful antiretroviral therapy in South Africa. *AIDS.* 2003;17:1369–1375.

72. World Health Organization. *Emergency Scale-Up of Antiretroviral Therapy in Resource-Limited Settings: Technical and Operational Recommendations to Achieve 3 by 5.* Geneva, Switzerland: World Health Organization; 2003. Available at: http://www.who.int/3by5/publications/documents/en/zambia_doc_final .pdf. Accessed April 4, 2005.

73. XV International AIDS Conference Bangkok Web site. Available at: http://www.aids2004.org. Accessed April 4, 2005.

74. Marseille E, Hofmann PB, Kahn JG. HIV prevention before HAART in sub-Saharan Africa. *Lancet.* 2002;359: 1851–1856.

75. World Bank. *Confronting AIDS: Public Priorities in a Global Epidemic.* New York, NY: Oxford University Press; 1997.

76. Mattos RA, Terto V Jr, Parker R. World Bank strategies and the response to AIDS in Brazil. *Divulg Saúde Debate.* 2003;27:215–227.

77. World Bank. *Project Information Document (PID), Appraisal Stage: Regional HIV/AIDS Treatment Acceleration.* Washington, DC: World Bank; 2004. Report AB892. Available at: http://www-wds.worldbank.org/servlet/WDSContentServer/WDSP/IB/2004/05/24/000104615_20040525112142/Rendered/PDF/PID0TAP.pdf. Accessed April 4, 2005.

78. Piot P, Feachem RG, Lee JW, Wolfensohn JD. Public health. A global response to AIDS: lessons learned, next steps. *Science.* 2004;304:1909–1910.

79. Parker R. Building the foundations for the response to HIV/AIDS in Brazil: the development of HIV/AIDS policy, 1982–1996. *Divulg Saúde Debate.* 2003;27:143–183.

80. Frei Betto condena AIDS ter mais verba que fome. *O Globo.* October 14, 2003:11.

81. Instituto Brasileiro de Geografia e Estatística. *Sintese de indicadores sociais 2003.* Rio de Janeiro, Brazil: Instituto Brasileiro de Geografia e Estatística; April 13, 2004. Available at: http://www.ibge.gov.br/home/presidencia/noticias/pdf/13042004sintese2003.pdf. Accessed April 4, 2005.

82. Decosas J. HIV prevention and treatment in South Africa: affordable and desirable [published correction appears in *Lancet.* 2003;362:84]. *Lancet.* 2003;361:1146–1147.

83. United Nations Development Programme. *Thailand's Response to HIV/AIDS: Progress and Challenges.* Bangkok, Thailand: United Nations Development Programme; 2004. Available at: http://www.undp.or.th/documents/HIV_AIDS_FullReport_ENG.pdf. Accessed April 4, 2005.

84. United Nations Population Fund. *Investing in People: National Progress in Implementing the ICPD Programme of Action 1994–2004.* New York, NY: United Nations Population Fund; 2004. Available at: http://www.unfpa.org/upload/lib_pub _file/284_filename_globalsurvey.pdf. Accessed July 9, 2004.

85. Human Rights Watch. *Not Enough Graves: The War on Drugs, HIV/AIDS, and Violations of Human Rights.* New York, NY: Human Rights Watch; 2004. Available at: http://hrw.org/reports/2004/thailand0704/thailand0704.pdf. Accessed April 4, 2005.

86. Elbe S. *Strategic Implications of HIV/AIDS.* New York, NY: Oxford University Press; 2003.

87. Price-Smith AT. *The Health of Nations: Infectious Disease, Environmental Change, and Their Effects on National Security and Development.* Cambridge, Mass: MIT Press; 2002.

88. Galvão J. More money for AIDS. *Lancet.* 2003;361:1569–1570.

89. International Crisis Group. *HIV/AIDS as a Security Issue.* Brussels, Belgium: International Crisis Group; June 19, 2001. Available at: http://www.crisisweb.org//library/documents/report_archive/A400321_19062001.pdf. Accessed April 4, 2005.

90. World Health Organization. *The World Health Report 2004: Changing History.* Geneva, Switzerland: World Health Organization; 2004.

91. Global HIV Prevention Working Group. *HIV Prevention in the Era of Expanded Treatment Access.* Global HIV Prevention Working Group; 2004. Available at: http://www.gatesfoundation.org/nr/downloads/globalhealth/aids/PWG2004Report.pdf. Accessed April 4, 2005.

92. Brazil and UNAIDS join forces in the global fight against AIDS [press release]. Geneva, Switzerland: Joint United Nations Programme on HIV/AIDS–Brazil; September 1, 2004. Available at: http://www.unaids.org/NetTools/Misc/DocInfo.aspx?href=http://gva-docowl/WEBcontent/Documents/pub/Media/Press-Releases02/PR_Brazil_01Sep04_en.pdf. Accessed April 4, 2005.

93. Beaglehole R, Bonita R, Horton R, Adams O, McKee M. Public health in the new era: improving health through collective action. *Lancet.* 2004;363: 2084–2086.

Understanding and Addressing AIDS-Related Stigma: From Anthropological Theory to Clinical Practice in Haiti

| Arachu Castro, PhD, MPH and Paul Farmer, MD, PhD

ABSTRACT

For the past several years, diverse and often confused concepts of stigma have been invoked in discussions on AIDS. Many have argued compellingly that AIDS-related stigma acts as a barrier to voluntary counseling and testing. Less compelling are observations regarding the source of stigma or its role in decreasing interest in HIV care.

We reviewed these claims as well as literature from anthropology, sociology, and public health. Preliminary data from research in rural Haiti suggest that the introduction of quality HIV care can lead to a rapid reduction in stigma, with resulting increased uptake of testing. Rather than stigma, logistic and economic barriers determine who will access such services. Implications for scale-up of integrated AIDS prevention and care are explored.

INTRODUCTION

Most of those involved in the movement to slow the spread of AIDS and to improve the quality of life of those living with HIV view stigma and discrimination as human rights violations requiring redress. Both organizations and individuals have taken various actions to address stigma; however, these actions often have not been grounded in a broad biosocial understanding of stigma and AIDS-related discrimination. The Joint United Nations Programme on HIV/AIDS (UNAIDS) often refers to the need to fight stigma in order to combat HIV/AIDS,[1] but the definition of stigma remains unclear.

Stigma undoubtedly poses several challenges, but the mechanisms by which it is at the heart of the AIDS pandemic need to be explored. Stigma and discrimination are part of complex systems of beliefs about illness and disease that are often grounded in social inequalities. Indeed, stigma is often just the tip of the iceberg; because it is visible and generally accepted in public health discourse without further qualification, the term has frequently served as a means of giving short shrift to powerful social inequalities (for example, in Valdiserri[2]) that are much harder to identify and conceptualize.

In addition, the tendency to use "rapid" methodologies has generated a wealth of information regarding people's knowledge and attitudes about AIDS-related stigma in different situations, but this information is often "desocialized"—decontextualized from larger social processes that are both historically rooted and linked to persons and processes that are not visible to the survey researcher. Such desocialized and disparate approaches have hindered the advancement of a theoretically sound understanding of AIDS-related stigma and have slowed effective actions to counter stigma.

Similar confusion surrounds debate over stigma as a barrier to introducing antiretrovirals to poor countries or to making voluntary HIV tests accessible. Again, such comments are insufficiently grounded in broader social analyses. The AIDS literature is rife with surveys that offer completely discrepant views on how stigma is related to events and processes as varied as sexual comportment, care-seeking behavior, and adherence to antibiotic regimens.[3–5] Without reference to any particular experience in delivering AIDS care in the world's poorest nations, 1 recent review claimed that

in many countries hardest hit by HIV, the stigma of this disease is at least as powerful, if not more so, than in wealthy nations. Although the prospect of access to treatment may encourage individuals to determine their HIV status, the linkage of treatment to directly observed HIV therapy may paradoxically lower the use of counseling and testing services due to confidentiality concerns.[6(p1385)]

Elsewhere, we have termed those assertions "immodest claims of causality,"[7] since they are advanced authoritatively but may be readily countered by contrary claims.

Our concern in this review is to question the understanding of AIDS-related stigma and to assess its relationships to integrated HIV prevention and care. That AIDS-related stigma exists and needs redress is not debated. But where is the evidence that stigma stands as a ranking obstacle to treatment in poor countries when less than 5% of people with advanced AIDS in these countries have access to highly active antiretroviral therapy (HAART)?[8] Instead, some recent studies conducted in Botswana,[9] Senegal,[10] and Côte d'Ivoire[11] showed that the cost of medications borne by patients is the main stated reason for lack of adherence to therapy.

Still, "stigma" has become, in the popular press, one more argument used to walk a slow walk to fight the pandemic. A study conducted in Zambia claims that "despite increasing access to prevention of mother-to-child transmission initiatives, including antiretroviral drugs, the perceived disincentives of HIV testing, particularly for women, largely outweigh the potential gains from available treatments."[12] (p347) A closer look at the study shows that the use of antiretrovirals was limited to the prevention of mother-to-child transmission of HIV and did not include HAART to treat women (or any other adults) outside of pregnancy. What conclusions might be reached if proper therapy and a more equitable distribution of that therapy were introduced? A study conducted in Kenya showed that lack of access to drugs is the main factor compromising medical residents' ability to provide care to AIDS patients.[13]

On a more hopeful note, the evaluation of a mother-to-child transmission program in the Dominican Republic suggested that implementation of effective therapy for mothers has helped diminish the stigmatization of patients, in part because health professionals focused on pregnant women as potential conduits of antiretrovirals destined to prevent transmission to unborn children.[14] An AIDS program in rural Haiti also reported a sharp decline in AIDS-related stigma since the introduction of HAART.[15]

THEORETICAL FRAMEWORK

Our theoretical framework for the understanding of AIDS-related stigma has been developed over a decade of ethnographic research in rural Haiti. Our interpretations of the relevant literature are informed by more recent experience providing clinical services in rural Haiti.[15] Although the first references to the association between stigma and health in the social science literature date back to the 1880s,[16] sociologist Erving Goffman, beginning with his work in psychiatric hospitals in the late 1950s, developed what has become the benchmark social theory of the association between stigma and disease.[17,18] Goffman defined stigma as the identification that a social group

creates of a person (or group of people) based on some physical, behavioral, or social trait perceived as being divergent from group norms. This socially constructed identification lays the groundwork for subsequent disqualification of membership from a group in which that person was originally included. Although Goffman emphasized the importance of analyzing stigma in terms of relationships rather than individual traits or attributes,[18] many subsequent interpretations of stigma have focused on individual attributes and are divorced from broader social processes, especially from relations of power.

Key anthropological and sociological contributions to our understanding of AIDS have introduced new components to Goffman's definition of stigma and offer the promise of novel conceptual frameworks.[19–22] Others have used a similar approach to understanding stigma associated with diseases such as hookworm, tuberculosis, cancer, polio, and sexually transmitted infections and the association of these diseases with racist ideology in the United States[23,24] or with cholera-related stigma in Venezuela.[25] Further contributions of anthropological work to the understanding of AIDS stigma have been obtained through research conducted in Zambia,[26] South Africa,[27] the Philippines,[28] Haiti,[29] and Puerto Rico and the United States.[30]

The field of social psychology has clarified the cognitive processes that lead to labeling and stereotyping. However, most psychological research focuses more on individualistic perceptions and attitudes than on the broader social context in which such perceptions are grounded. Most of these studies discuss the implications of these beliefs—in terms of misunderstandings, misinformation, and negative attitudes—as far as efforts to change the perceptions of the stigmatizers are concerned. Examples from Jamaica[31] and Mexico[32] are illustrative. Such approaches seek to improve HIV/AIDS education and to enhance sensitivity and empathy training or tolerance through personal contact with people living with HIV.[4,33–35]

However, these laudable efforts have placed little emphasis on the larger economic and political processes in which stigma is grounded.

More recently, some anthropologists[20,36–39] have challenged approaches that emphasize cognitivist explanations of stigma rather than the structural violence that generates the social inequalities in which stigma is invariably rooted. According to Parker and Aggleton, the desocialization of stigma is not drawn directly from Goffman, who, on the contrary, was very much concerned with issues of social change. . . . Yet the fact that Goffman's framework has been appropriated in much research on stigma (whether in relation to HIV/AIDS or other issues), as though stigma were a static attitude rather than a constantly changing (and often resisted) social process has seriously limited the ways in which stigmatization and discrimination have been approached in relation to HIV and AIDS.[20(p14)]

These authors proposed that stigma be analyzed within frameworks drawing on concepts of power, dominance, hegemony, and oppression.[40,41] They further proposed interventions that have deeper social, political, and economic roots, because "stigma is deployed by concrete and identifiable social actors seeking to legitimize their own dominant status within existing structures of social inequality."[20(p18)] This resocialized view of stigma defines discrimination, one of the consequences of stigma, as "when, in the absence of objective justification, a distinction is made against a person that results in that person's being treated unfairly and unjustly on the basis of belonging or being perceived to belong, to a particular group."[42] Other anthropologists have been scrupulous in ensuring that their interpretations of stigma are informed by the lived experience of those who suffer from it.[22,29,43–47]

A useful definition of AIDS-related stigma comes from the field of sociology:

In our conceptualization, stigma exists when the following interrelated components converge. In the first component, people distinguish and label human differences. In the second, dominant cultural beliefs link labeled persons to undesirable characteristics—to negative stereotypes. In the third, labeled persons are placed in distinct categories so as to accomplish some degree of separation of "us" from "them." In the fourth, labeled persons experience status loss and discrimination that lead to unequal outcomes. Finally, stigmatization is entirely contingent on access to social, economic, and political power that allows the identification of differentness, the construction of stereotypes, the separation of labeled persons into distinct categories, and the full execution of disapproval, rejection, exclusion, and discrimination.[48(p367)]

These authors noted that stigma is a "persistent predicament" and sought to understand "why the negative consequences of stigma are so difficult to eradicate."[48,49(p379)] The fundamental causes of stigma need to be addressed, they argued, by targeting multiple mechanisms to bring about change. Yet these authors limited the depth of required transformations to changing "deeply held attitudes and beliefs of powerful groups" and confining "the power of such groups to make their cognitions the dominant ones."[48(p381)] In acknowledging the centrality of social, economic, and political power differentials—emphasizing that cognitive processes are necessary but not sufficient causes for the production of stigma—they concluded that a better understanding of stigma requires an understanding of how these power differentials, along with issues of constraint and resistance, exert their impact on stigma.[48]

We propose *structural violence* as a conceptual framework for understanding AIDS-related stigma. Every society is shaped by large-scale social forces that together define structural violence. These forces include racism, sexism, political violence, poverty, and other social inequalities that are rooted in historical and economic processes that sculpt the distribution and outcome of HIV/AIDS. Structural violence predisposes the human body to pathogenic vulnerability by shaping risk of infection and also rate of disease progression.[7,50–53] Structural violence also determines who has access to counseling, diagnostics, and effective therapy for HIV disease. Finally, structural violence determines, in large part, who suffers from AIDS-related stigma and discrimination.

In societies marked by profound racism, it is expected that people of color with AIDS will be more stigmatized than in societies where racism is more attenuated. Similarly, gender inequality determines the extent to which sexism will mark the course of HIV disease. In highly sexist settings, the disclosure of HIV infection is more likely to provoke stigma and threat of domestic violence than in environments where women enjoy gender equity. Class often trumps both racism and sexism. The poor almost invariably experience violations of their social and economic rights. We can therefore conclude that poverty, already representing an almost universal stigma, will be the primary reason that poor people living with HIV suffer from greater AIDS-related stigma. Racism, sexism, and poverty exacerbate one another, especially where political violence and social inequalities are added to the equation. Together, social forces determine not only risk of HIV infection but also risk of AIDS-related stigma.

To improve our understanding of AIDS-related stigma, it is necessary to focus on a series of variables readily discernible across different societies; these include the experience of people living with HIV, public perceptions of AIDS, local experiences of stigma and discrimination and their influence in care-seeking activities, varied degrees of stigma over the course of HIV disease, impact of stigma on quality of life, and structural sources of stigma and discrimination (B. J. Good, written communication, May 2003). The understanding of these experiences and the analysis of these processes permit a better understanding of how different strategies, ranging from legal recourse to the introduction of HAART, can alter the course of AIDS-related stigma.

RESULTS

Public health experts prescribing health policies for poor countries believe that stigma, the high cost of treatment, the lack of infrastructure, and poor patient adherence to treatment constitute insurmountable barriers to effective AIDS control. From our experience providing health and social services in rural Haiti, this is not the case.[15,52,54,55] Haiti is by far the most impoverished country in Latin America and, not coincidentally, the hemisphere's most HIV-affected country, with an adult prevalence of around 5.6%.[56] To illustrate how structural violence is embodied and generates stigma, we explored the history of one of our patients in rural Haiti. Because the "texture" of dire affliction is better felt in the gritty details of biography, and since any example begs the question of its relevance, we argue that the story of our patient is anything but anecdotal. In the eyes of the epidemiologist as well as the political analyst, Samuel has suffered in exemplary fashion.

In 2001, Samuel Morin was dying of AIDS. Until then, Samuel, 40 years old, had farmed a small plot of land and had a tiny shop—which sold everything from matches to soap—in a town in central Haiti. He considered himself poor but was able to send his 4 children to school. Samuel was an active member of his church and sometimes used his meager earnings to help neighboring families in crisis, providing food if their crops failed, or helping with school fees. He also supported his sister and her 3 children after his brother-in-law died of AIDS.

When Samuel became ill in the mid-1990s, his wife had to assume all responsibility for the farming, although he could still sit and mind the shop. But after a while, Samuel recalled, "the disease transformed me. I looked like a stick." He continued to lose weight and then developed visible skin infections and thrush; he had difficulty swallowing food and began to cough. It was at this time, he felt, that people stopped coming to his shop. His children had to leave school because they

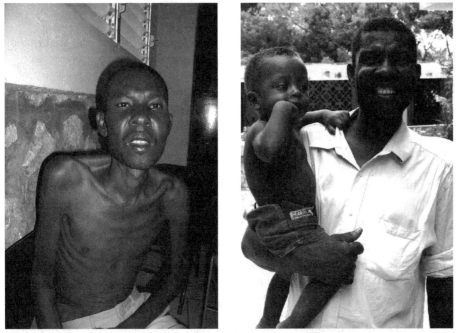

FIGURE 1— Samuel Morin, (a, left) in July 2001 before receiving HAART and (b, right) 1 year later, after a year of therapy.

were needed to help in the fields and because Samuel and his wife could no longer afford the school fees. Eventually, the shop failed completely. His wife left him and returned to her parents' home in Portau-Prince.

In July 2001, when Samuel weighed only 80 pounds (Figure 1a), he decided to use his last 10 Haitian dollars to pay for a truck ride to the Clinique Bon Sauveur in Cange, a 6-hour walk from his home. Since then, Samuel has been receiving HAART under the supervision of an *accompagnateur* (community health worker), free of charge. In almost 3 years of therapy, Samuel stated, he has not missed a dose; he has responded clinically—he has gained 30 pounds, has normal skin color, and feels "great"—and has an undetectable viral load (Figure 1b shows Samuel a year after initiation of therapy). Moreover, his family has returned to him, his children are back in school, and he has reopened his shop. He also volunteers with the local Partners In Health team in HIV-prevention efforts. Of his recovery, Samuel said, "I was a walking skeleton before I began therapy. I was afraid to go out of my house and no one would buy things from my shop. But now I am fine again. My wife has returned to

me and now my children are not ashamed to be seen with me. I can work again."

In reflecting on Samuel's experience, it is possible to argue that AIDS treatment can spark a "virtuous social cycle." Access to comprehensive AIDS care[57] saved Samuel's life; returning to work and securing school fees for his children has allowed him to surmount some of the miserable conditions faced by the majority of Haitians. It is also possible to discern direct links between access to care and stigma. There are the links mentioned by Samuel: proper HIV care can transform a disfiguring and consumptive disease into a manageable condition that is invisible to one's consociates. Integrating people living with HIV into the workforce of a community health program—around 5% of our current staff are persons living with HIV—permits them to receive comprehensive care, send their children to school, and earn steady wages. Further, the demonstrably favorable response of Samuel and others to HAART has sparked interest in voluntary counseling and testing. Together, these processes have contributed to lessening the impact of the AIDS stigma.

Years ago, before the advent of

effective therapy for AIDS, anthropologists noted that the introduction of such therapy may alter profoundly the social interpretations of the disease.[43,58] Other social scientists have shown that stigma is aggravated by an undefined etiology and the lack of an effective treatment.[59] AIDS has afforded ample possibilities to study the social construction of stigma. Exposure to a new disease, as occurred with AIDS in Haiti in the 1980s, generates new cultural models of the etiology and expected course of disease.[29,60,61] These models change with time because diseases have a social course—that is, pathology is embedded in social experience.[42,60] The social experience of AIDS is affected profoundly by the advent of effective therapy.

The Haiti project already demonstrates that individuals who can access effective care are the most likely to get an HIV test,[15] which supports social theories on the social course of illness. The introduction of antiretrovirals has had a profound and positive impact on the demand for voluntary counseling and testing. It is possible to chart the rise in demand for testing and counseling in rural Haiti by following laboratory registers and daily reports. Since 1998, when we introduced the first free and comprehensive AIDS program in rural Haiti at the Clinique Bon Sauveur,[15] demand for such services has more than quintupled.

Samuel Morin was diagnosed and treated initially in Cange. But looking at his home-town of Thomonde, where community-based AIDS care was introduced only in 2003, is instructive. Figure 2 shows how rapidly voluntary counseling and testing may increase when comprehensive prevention and care are introduced. In Thomonde, voluntary counseling and testing sessions per month have skyrocketed from 0 to an average of 869 in the second quarter and up to 1450 in the fourth quarter; at the Clinique Bon Sauveur in Cange, the number of voluntary counseling and testing sessions are stable, averaging 2118 per month.

As so many of our patients have noted, what is the motivation for learning one's serostatus when there is no possibility of being treated for opportunistic infections or of access to prevention of mother-to-child transmission during pregnancy, much less of being treated with antiretrovirals when needed? Can we blame these public health failures on stigma alone?

DISCUSSION

The Haiti experience suggests that improving clinical services can raise the quality of prevention efforts, boost staff morale, and reduce AIDS-related stigma. As 1 of the first donor-supported treatment projects in a very poor country, our team's experience suggests that the full participation of community health workers will be required if HIV prevention and care are to reach the poorest and most vulnerable communities. Adjuvant social services must also be part of a comprehensive project, as must attention to tuberculosis and primary health care needs. Only a biosocial framework drawing on both qualitative and quantitative methods can hope to assess the epidemiological, social, and economic impact of both the epidemic and responses to it.

The last 2 decades have taught us a great deal about failure and how it is best measured; new HIV infections and AIDS deaths are the grim yardsticks. A lack of decent medical care and effective prevention strategies (including the absence of a vaccine and inadequate women-controlled barrier methods) frustrates public health efforts. However, a broad range of other events and processes are markers for failure: AIDS-related stigma and discrimination, unsafe blood transfusions, unattended childbirths, unclean water, and a lack of social services for HIV-affected individuals and families would figure high on this list of indirect markers.

And there's the analytic rub: we don't know how best to analyze such a diverse set of inextricably related problems. What evaluative framework might guide us as we attempt to measure phenomena as varied as HIV incidence and AIDS-related stigma and discrimination? How might we assess

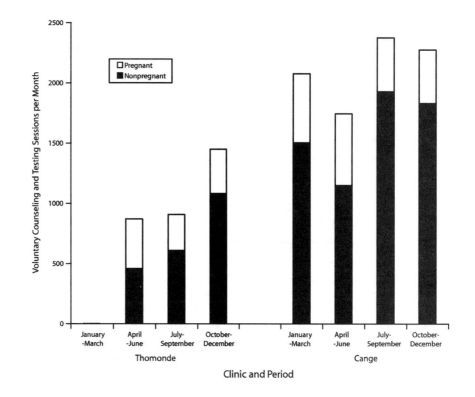

FIGURE 2— Average monthly uptake of voluntary counseling and testing in a new (Thomonde) and an ongoing (Cange) AIDS clinic: rural Haiti, 2003.

the impact of new projects? How do we address poverty and gender inequality in AIDS prevention and care, if they are so manifestly related to HIV transmission and outcomes? The best framework for analysis and evaluation would need to be robustly biosocial, since the phenomena it attempts to describe are nothing if not both biological and social. The framework would draw on conventional epidemiology, certainly, but also on complementary resocializing disciplines in which patients' voices and experiences are heard and documented. Anthropology and sociology are among these disciplines, as is the sociology of science. Unfortunately, ethnographic inquiry and community health worker reports are not often regarded, within public health, as reliable sources of information.

Could this evaluative framework be anything other than biosocial? It must not only assess the impact of stigma on morbidity and mortality but also address questions of stigma and equity; it must offer a resocialized understanding of how inequalities

come to take their toll through disparities of risk for infection, radically different courses of disease, and disparities of access to proven therapies. Some of the indicators that we suggest be used include the number of patients with access to effective care, serosurveys in sentinel populations (e.g., prenatal clinics), HIV prevention checklists (sex education, condom distribution), number of person-hours of prevention through information and education campaigns, number of sites offering prevention of mother-to-child transmission of HIV, number of community health workers supervising therapy, reinforcement of public health infrastructures, creation of coalitions to expand and "harmonize" prevention and care services, transparent reporting of expenditures, and avoidance of drug stock depletions. We need, now, a novel synthesis of complementary methodologies, both quantitative and qualitative. We need to value the input of community groups, including community health workers and others who deliver services directly to those in greatest need.

TABLE 1— Assessing the Impact of a Comprehensive AIDS Program: Possible Data Points

Indicators	Sources of Information Needed to Evaluate Indicators
Impact on patient outcomes	Patient charts, weight, activities of daily living
Impact on burden of disease	Prenatal screening
Response to local calls for equity	Community forums, focus groups
Reduced mortality	Chart review, community health workers' reports
Reduced rates of hospitalization	Daily reports, chart review
Reduced stigma	Ethnographic inquiry, case histories
Improved staff morale	Staff meetings, ethnographic study
Increased demand for voluntary counseling and testing	Laboratory registers, daily reports
Meeting public health goals	External Ministry of Health evaluation

The transformation of AIDS from an inevitably fatal disease to a chronic and manageable one has decreased stigma dramatically in Haiti, as Samuel's story shows. Our own experience in Haiti suggests that it is clear that the impact of a "low-tech" HIV prevention-and-care project could be measured without importing a new and costly "evaluation infrastructure." Table 1 lists some indirect indices of positive impact and the potential sources of data that might be made available in even the poorest communities. The most daunting challenges for which scale-up projects must be prepared are those having to do with the poverty of patients.

AIDS, stigma, and blame have been intertwined since the start of the epidemic. One of the characteristics of AIDS stigma is that, from the onset, this disease has been associated with lifestyles that society attributes, with little evidence, to being shaped by "voluntary acts." In America and Europe, where in the 1980s the epidemic ravaged groups of homosexuals and heroin addicts, there was very little solidarity with infected people because they were blamed for having "opted" for sexual practices or for addiction and reproached by society as immoral. The stigma that already existed toward these groups was amplified by AIDS.[62] This type of social discrimination was extended to poor countries where cases of HIV infection began to be diagnosed[29] and to other groups of vulnerable people, including poor women.

Some of these prejudices were reflected within universities, international organizations, foundations, bilateral organizations, governments, financing institutions, and pharmaceutical companies—institutions key to effective responses to the pandemic. A general hostility to people living with HIV is suggested by the fact that, until recently, AIDS prevention, not treatment, was the leitmotiv of international AIDS work; treatment was the privilege of those able to pay for it. These are powerful fora, and their position set the agenda for both funding and action. Freire might say that such positions are "sectarized": "Sectarization . . . transforms reality into something false that, thus, cannot be transformed."[63(p30)] By ignoring or giving short shrift to visible evidence of structural violence in the transmission of HIV and in the stigma that it generates, these "fora of knowledge" may perpetuate, sometimes by inaction, both stigma and discrimination.

Since the 1980s, blaming the victim has been a powerful current in the social experience of AIDS. Victim blaming helps to explain the lack of solidarity in providing appropriate care to people living with HIV; discrimination in the arenas of housing, employment, and education has been documented in the Caribbean[64–68] and in other parts of the world. The only people not often blamed for their own misfortune are those deemed infected by mechanisms considered unrelated to "personal choices in lifestyles." These exceptions include health professionals who, by occupational accident, are exposed to HIV-infected blood and hemophiliacs and other recipients of blood products infected by medical and political negligence, as occurred in France in 1985.[69] Additionally, children who contract HIV in utero or during birth or breastfeeding are also often exempt from blame (as noted in Puerto Rico[70]). These same children may face, as they grow older, discrimination when attending school (as in Mexico[71]). Even women infected through rape are often blamed or the violence of which they are victims.[53]

Exemptions from blame may be reflected at the national level within systems of social security or of private insurance that cover antiretroviral therapy for exempted groups but not for others. In the international arena, the division of people living with HIV into "blameworthy" and "blameless" categories reinforces the lack of will on the part of rich countries to finance AIDS treatment in poor countries. The funding gap, which reflects social inequalities between and among countries, is itself a reflection and source of structural violence contributing to AIDS-related stigma. Stigma and human-rights violations deriving from it are often the only visible part of deep-rooted social inequality. Addressing the root causes of stigma will require addressing structural violence, including the symbolic violence perpetuated by shallow theories about AIDS-related stigma. These theories may lead to inaction. To assess AIDS-related stigma and declare it a cause rather than both cause and consequence of inequality will probably weaken efforts to address AIDS among those with heightened risk of HIV because of poverty, racism, and gender inequality.

About the Authors

The authors are with the Program in Infectious Disease and Social Change, Department of Social Medicine, Harvard Medical School; Partners In Health; and the Division of Social Medicine and Health Inequalities, Department of Medicine, Brigham and Women's Hospital, Boston, Mass.

Correspondence: Requests for reprints should be sent to Arachu Castro, PhD, MPH, Program in Infectious Disease and Social Change, Department of Social Medicine, Harvard Medical School, 641 Huntington Ave, Boston, MA 02115 (e-mail: arachu_castro@hms.harvard.edu).

Acknowledgments

We acknowledge the Wilbur Marvin Fund of the David Rockefeller Center for Latin American Studies at Harvard University for the award of a 2003 Faculty Grant to the authors to work on the project "HIV/AIDS in the Caribbean: The Impact of Effective Therapy on Stigma." The scale-up of AIDS care in central Haiti has been made possible by the Global Fund to Fight AIDS, Tuberculosis and Malaria.

We are grateful to Yasmin Khawja, Haun Saussy, Joan Paluzzi, Alice Yang, and Rob Stavert for their contributions. We are most indebted to the Haitian clinical team, led by Dr Fernet Léandre, for its efforts to implement integrated AIDS prevention and care under very difficult circumstances.

Contributors

Both authors conceptualized the article, interpreted findings, and wrote the article.

References

1. Piot P. From planning to implementation: success against AIDS in the region. Opening speech at: 2nd Latin American Forum on HIV/AIDS and STIs; April 8, 2003; Havana, Cuba.

2. Valdiserri RO. HIV/AIDS stigma: an impediment to public health. *Am J Public Health.* 2002;92: 341–342.

3. Fortenberry JD, McFarlane M, Bleakley A, et al. Relationships of stigma and shame to gonorrhea and HIV screening. *Am J Public Health.* 2002;92:378–381.

4. Herek GM, Capitanio JP, Widaman KF. HIV-related stigma and knowledge in the United States: prevalence and trends, 1991–1999. *Am J Public Health.* 2002;92:371–377.

5. Egger M, Pauw J, Lopatatzidis A, et al. Promotion of condom use in a high-risk setting in Nicaragua: a randomised controlled trial. *Lancet.* 2000;355: 2101–2105.

6. Liechty C, Bangsberg D. Doubts about DOT: antiretroviral therapy for resource-poor countries. *AIDS.* 2003;17:1383–1387.

7. Farmer P. *Infections and Inequalities: The Modern Plagues.* Berkeley: University of California Press; 1999.

8. *Scaling Up Antiretroviral Therapy in Resource-Limited Settings.* Geneva, Switzerland: World Health Organization; 2002.

9. Weiser S, Wolfe W, Bangsberg D, et al. Barriers to antiretroviral adherence for patients living with HIV infection and AIDS in Botswana. *J Acquir Immune Defic Syndr.* 2003;34(3):281–288.

10. LanièceI, Ciss M, Desclaux A, et al. Adherence to HAART and its principal determinants in a cohort of Senegalese adults. *AIDS.* 2003;17(suppl 3):S103–S108.

11. Delaunay K, Vidal L, Msellati P, Moatti J-P. La mise sous traitement antirétroviral dans l'Initiative: l'explicite et l'implicite d'un processus de sélection. In: Msellati P, Vidal L, Moatti J-P, eds. *L'accès aux traitements du VIH/sida en Côte d'Ivoire. Aspects économiques, sociaux et comportementaux.* Paris, France: Agence Nationale de Recherches sur le Sida; 2001:87–113.

12. Bond V, Chase E, Aggleton P. Stigma, HIV/AIDS and prevention of mother-to-child transmission in Zambia. *Eval Program Plann.* 2002;25:347–356.

13. Raviola G, Machoki MI, Mwaikambo E, Good MJD. HIV, disease plague, demoralization and "burnout": resident experience of the medical profession in Nairobi, Kenya. *Cult Med Psychiatry.* 2002;26: 55–86.

14. Cáceres Ureña FI, Duarte I, Moya EA, Pérez-Then E, Hasbún MJ, Tapia M. *Análisis de la situación y la respuesta al VIH/SIDA en República Dominicana.* Santo Domingo, Dominican Republic: Instituto de Estudios de Población y Desarrollos (IEPD) and Asociación Dominicana Pro-Bienestar de la Familia (PROFAMILIA); 1998.

15. Farmer P, Léandre F, Mukherjee J, et al. Community-based approaches to HIV treatment in resource-poor settings. *Lancet.* 2001;358:404–409.

16. Tuke DH. The Cagots. *J Anthropol Instit Great Britain Ireland.* 1880;9:376–385.

17. Goffman E. *Asylums: Essays on the Social Situation of Mental Patients and Other Inmates.* Garden City, NY: Anchor Books; 1961.

18. Goffman E. *Stigma: Notes on the Management of Spoiled Identity.* Garden City, NY: Anchor Books; 1963.

19. Weiss MG, Ramakrishna J. Stigma interventions and research for international health. Paper presented at: Stigma and Global Health: Developing a Research Agenda; September 5–7, 2001; Bethesda, Md.

20. Parker R, Aggleton P. HIV and AIDS-related stigma and discrimination: a conceptual framework and implications for action. *Soc Sci Med.* 2003;57:13–24.

21. Das V. Stigma, contagion, defect: issues in the anthropology of public health. Paper presented at: Stigma and Global Health: Developing a Research Agenda; September 5–7, 2001; Bethesda, Md.

22. Alonzo AA, Reynolds NR. Stigma, HIV and AIDS: an exploration and elaboration of a stigma trajectory. *Soc Sci Med.* 1995;41(3):303–315.

23. Wailoo K. Stigma, race, and disease in 20th century America: an historical overview. Paper presented at: Stigma and Global Health: Developing a Research Agenda; September 5–7, 2001; Bethesda, Md.

24. Brandt A. *No Magic Bullet: A Social History of Venereal Disease in the United States Since 1880.* Oxford, England: Oxford University Press; 1985.

25. Briggs C, Mantini-Briggs C. *Stories in the Time of Cholera: Racial Profiling During a Medical Nightmare.* Berkeley: University of California Press; 2003.

26. Gausset Q. AIDS and cultural practices in Africa: the case of the Tonga (Zambia). *Soc Sci Med.* 2001; 52(4):509–518.

27. Wojcicki JM, Malala J. Condom use,

power and HIV/AIDS risk: sex-workers bargain for survival in Hillbrow/Joubert Park/Berea, Johannesburg. *Soc Sci Med.* 2001;53(1):99–121.

28. Simbulan NP, Aguilar AS, Flanigan T, Cu-Uvin S. High-risk behaviors and the prevalence of sexually transmitted diseases among women prisoners at the women state penitentiary in Metro Manila. *Soc Sci Med.* 2001;52(4):599–618.

29. Farmer P. *AIDS and Accusation: Haiti and the Geography of Blame.* Berkeley: University of California Press; 1992.

30. Finlinson HA, Robles RR, Colón HM, et al. Puerto Rican drug users experiences of physical and sexual abuse: comparisons based on sexual identities. *J Sex Res.* 2003;40(3):277–285.

31. Hue LE. Children's [*sic*] involvement in HIV/AIDS support initiatives help reduce stigma and discrimination. Paper presented at: 14th International AIDS Conference; July 7, 2002; Barcelona, Spain.

32. McCauley A, Stewart H, Baker S, et al. HIV prevention programs can reduce stigma among students. Paper presented at: 14th International AIDS Conference; July 9, 2002; Barcelona, Spain.

33. Devine PG, Plant EA, Harrison K. The problem of "us" versus "them" and AIDS stigma. *Am Behav Sci.* 1999;42(7):1208–1224.

34. Herek GM. Illness, stigma, and AIDS. In: Costa P, Vanden GR, eds. *Psychological Aspects of Serious Illness.* Washington, DC: American Psychological Association; 1990:103–150.

35. Pryor JB, Reeder GD, Landau S. A social-psychological analysis of HIV-related stigma. *Am Behav Sci.* 1999;42(7):1189–1207.

36. Parker R, Camargo KR Jr. Pobreza e HIV/AIDS: aspectos antropológicos e sociológicos. *Cad Saúde Pública.* 2000;16(suppl 1):89–102.

37. Farmer P. Introducing ARVs in resource-poor settings. Plenary lecture. Paper presented at: 14th International AIDS Conference; July 10, 2002; Barcelona, Spain.

38. Castro A. Determinantes socio-políticos de la infección por VIH: violencia estructural y culpabilización de la víctima. Conferencia plenaria [Socio-political determinants of HIV: structural violence and the blaming of the victim. Plenary lecture]. Paper presented at: 2nd Latin American Forum on HIV/AIDS and STIs; April 10, 2003; Havana, Cuba.

39. Abadía-Barrero C. *"I Have AIDS but I Am Happy": Children's Subjectivities, AIDS, and Social Responses in Brazil.* Boston, Mass: Harvard School of Dental Medicine; 2002.

40. Foucault M. *Histoire de la sexualité* [*The History of Sexuality*]. Paris, France: Gallimard; 1976.

41. Bourdieu P. *La distinction: Critique sociale du jugement* [*Distinction: A Social Critique of the Judgment of Taste*]. Paris, France: Minuit; 1979.

42. Maluwa M, Aggleton P, Parker R. HIV- and AIDS-related stigma, discrimination, and human rights. *Health Hum Rights.* 2002;6(1):1–18.

43. Kleinman A, Wang W-Z, Li S-C, et al. The social course of epilepsy: chronic illness as social experience in interior China. *Soc Sci Med.* 1995;40(10):1319–1330.

44. Good BJ, Good M-JDV. In the subjunctive mode: epilepsy narratives in Turkey. *Soc Sci Med.* 1994;38(6):835–842.

45. Kleinman A, Kleinman J. Suffering and its professional transformation. *Cult Med Psychiatry.* 1991;15(3):275–301.

46. Farmer P, Kleinman A. AIDS as human suffering. *Dædalus.* 1989;118(2):135–160.

47. Whittaker AM. Living with HIV: resistance by positive people. *Med Anthropol Q.* 1992;6(4):385–390.

48. Link B, Phelan J. Conceptualizing stigma. *Annu Rev Sociol.* 2001;27:363–385.

49. Link BG, Phelan J. On stigma and its public health implications. Paper presented at: Stigma and Global Health: Developing a Research Agenda; September 5–7, 2001; Bethesda, Md.

50. Castro A, Farmer P. Anthropologie de la violence: la culpabilisation des victimes. *Notre Librairie: Revue des Littératures du Sud.* 2002;148:102–108.

51. Farmer P. *Pathologies of Power: Health, Human Rights, and the New War on the Poor.* Berkeley: University of California Press; 2003.

52. Castro A, Farmer P. El sida y la violencia estructural: la culpabilización de la víctima. *Cuadernos de Antropología Social.* 2003;17:31–49.

53. Farmer P, Connors M, Simmons J, eds. *Women, Poverty, and AIDS: Sex, Drugs, and Structural Violence.* Monroe, Me: Common Courage Press; 1996.

54. Farmer P, Castro A. Un pilote en Haïti: de l'efficacité de la distribution d'antiviraux dans des pays pauvres, et des objections qui lui sont faites. *Vacarme.* 2002;19:17–22.

55. Castro A, Farmer P. Infectious disease in Haiti: HIV/AIDS, tuberculosis, and social inequalities. *EMBO Rep.* 2003;4(6 suppl):S20–S23.

56. *Report on the HIV/AIDS Epidemic.* Geneva, Switzerland: UNAIDS; 2004.

57. Castro A, Farmer P, Kim JY, et al., eds. *Scaling Up Health Systems to Respond to the Challenge of HIV/AIDS in Latin America and the Caribbean.* Washington, DC: Pan American Health Organization; 2003.

58. Lévi-Strauss C. *Anthropologie structurale* [*Structural Anthropology*]. Paris, France: Plon; 1958.

59. Sontag S. *Illness as Metaphor.* New York, NY: Farrar, Straus and Giroux; 1978.

60. Farmer P. Sending sickness:sorcery, politics, and changing concepts of AIDS in rural Haiti. *Med Anthropol Q.* 1990;4(1):6–27.

61. Farmer P. AIDS-talk and the constitution of cultural models. *Soc Sci Med.* 1994;38(6):801–809.

62. Altman D. *AIDS in the Mind of America.* Garden City, NY: Doubleday; 1986.

63. Freire P. *Pedagogía del oprimido* [*The Pedagogy of the Oppressed*]. Madrid, Spain: Siglo XXI; 1970.

64. Bacchus R. Legal and ethical dimensions of HIV/AIDS. In: Howe G, Cobley A, eds. *The Caribbean AIDS Epidemic.* Kingston, Jamaica: University of the West Indies Press; 2000:151–185.

65. Walrond ER. Regional policies in relation to the HIV/AIDS epidemic in the Commonwealth Caribbean. In: Howe G, Cobley A, eds. *The Caribbean AIDS Epidemic.* Kingston, Jamaica: University of the West Indies Press; 2000:57–70.

66. Trotman L. HIV/AIDS in the workplace: the workers' perspective. In: Howe G, Cobley A, eds. *The Caribbean AIDS Epidemic.* Kingston, Jamaica: University of the West Indies Press; 2000:139–150.

67. Francis CR. The psychological dynamics of the AIDS epidemic in the Caribbean. In: Howe G, Cobley A, eds. *The Caribbean AIDS Epidemic.* Kingston, Jamaica: University of the West Indies Press; 2000:186–201.

68. Royes H. *A Cultural Approach to HIV/AIDS Prevention and Care: Jamaica's Experience.* Kingston,

Jamaica: UNESCO, Cultural Policies for Development Unit; 1999. Studies and Reports, Special Series 8.

69. Sultan Y. Épidémiologie de l'infection par le virus LAV/HTLVIII chez les hémophiles polytransfusés en France. Résultats d'une enquête menée par 28 centres d'hémophiles. *Nouv Rev Fr Hematol.* 1986;28(5): 327–329.

70. Susser I, Kreniske J. Community organizing around HIV prevention in rural Puerto Rico. In: Bond GC, Kreniske J, Susser I, Vincent J, eds. *AIDS in Africa and the Caribbean.* Boulder, Colo: Westview Press; 1997:51–64.

71. Aggleton P, Parker R, Maluwa M. *Stigma, Discrimination and HIV/AIDS in Latin America and the Caribbean.* Washington, DC: Inter-American Development Bank; February 2003.

Going Beyond "ABC" to Include "GEM": Critical Reflections on Progress in the HIV/AIDS Epidemic

| Shari L. Dworkin, PhD, MS and Anke A. Ehrhardt, PhD

ABSTRACT

A considerable number of studies have sought to identify what factors accounted for substantial reductions in HIV seroprevalence after several countries deployed "ABC" (abstinence, be faithful, condom use) strategies. After much public discourse and research on ABC success stories, the Joint United Nations Programme on HIV/AIDS 2004 epidemic report indicated that nearly 50% of infected people worldwide were women, up from 35% in 1985.

In light of the feminization of HIV/AIDS, we critically assess the limitations of ABC strategies. We provide 3 additional prevention strategies that focus on gender relations, economics, and migration (GEM) and can speak to the new face of the epidemic. Pressing beyond ABC, GEM strategies provide the basis for a stronger central platform from which national efforts against HIV/AIDS can proceed to reduce transmission risks.

INTRODUCTION

Many studies have sought to identify what factors accounted for substantial reductions in HIV seroprevalence in Uganda, Thailand, and other countries. A shared characteristic of these HIV/AIDS "success stories" is that these countries deployed specific combinations of "ABC" (abstinence, be faithful, condom use) strategies.[1–13] After much public discourse and research that emphasized the positive outcomes of ABC strategies, the Joint United Nations Programme on

HIV/AIDS published its 2004 epidemic report.[14] The report revealed a new face of HIV/AIDS; nearly 50% of infected people worldwide were women, up from 35% in 1985. In nearly every region of the world, the number of women living with HIV/AIDS has risen, and, in most regions of the world, women and adolescent girls represent an increasing proportion of people living with HIV/AIDS.

The Joint United Nations Programme on HIV/AIDS report also detailed that in several countries, 50% of new infections were occurring between spouses and that women were most often at risk from their main male partner. In the 1970s and 1980s, there was the "feminization of poverty," a phrase used by researchers to convey that women disproportionately lived in poverty[15–17]; similarly, we now have a "feminization of HIV/AIDS." The evidence from these studies reinforces the necessity of placing comprehensive, long-term efforts that focus on gender relations in the forefront of the fight against HIV/AIDS.

Given that the populations being affected by infection are shifting, it is more urgent than ever to press forward with approaches that are long term and gender specific and that attempt to fundamentally change the contexts in which risk occurs. In this article, we first provide a critical analysis of the limitations of ABC approaches. Next, to counter the limitations of ABC, we offer 3 additional prevention strategies that focus on gender, economics, and migration and will assist

with the long-term minimization of HIV/AIDS risks. These 3 strategies provide the basis for a stronger central platform from which national efforts against HIV/AIDS can proceed to reduce transmission risks. These prevention strategies are better able to take the new face of the epidemic into account.

LIMITATIONS OF ABC

It is instructive to examine ABC success stories from a gendered perspective. In Uganda, for example, there were significant reductions in overall HIV seroprevalence from 1997 to 2001. However, in 2002, persistent differences remained between young women and men, with 2.4% of young men and 5.6% of young women aged 15 to 24 years affected by the virus. Furthermore, although there were significant reductions in incidence during the same period, the male-to-female ratio for new HIV infections in 2002 was 1:5 in Uganda. There are numerous other examples of regional specificities that underscore gender differences.[14] One must therefore ask several key questions to facilitate rigorous examinations of the success of ABC. When HIV/AIDS prevention successes are attributed to some combination of ABC strategies, who actually enjoyed the benefits of success? For how long does a region actually maintain success? If successes begin to recede, what are the reasons for these changes? Do these changes tell us about which strategies we should consider successful in the fight against HIV/AIDS? To be considered successful, HIV/AIDS intervention strategies should critically engage with the reasons for the differences in rates of infection that are found between heterosexually active females and males.

The data just presented underscore the first clear limitation of ABC approaches: the underlying assumption that individual decisionmaking is the key site for risk minimization.[18–22] This assumption ignores or negates the gendered contexts in which individuals attempt to enact behavioral change. Recent research confirms that women's relationship power level plays a vital role in facilitating or hindering protected sexual intercourse.[23,24] Women's lack of property rights, differential access to literacy and education, lower wages, and lack of assets also shape their HIV/AIDS risks.[25–28] Research also confirms that sexual double standards, harmful cultural practices (e.g., widow cleansing, a practice that involves a widow having sexual relations with a relative of her late husband), and sexual violence structure women's HIV/AIDS risks.[25–35] Echoing numerous researchers, the executive director of the United Nations Population Fund, Thoraya Obaid, argued

Abstinence is meaningless to women who are coerced into sex. Faithfulness offers little protection to wives whose husbands have several partners or were infected before marriage. And condoms require the cooperation of men. The social and economic empowerment of women is key.[18(p2)]

A second success story reveals a second limitation of ABC strategies. Thailand experienced much initial success with its structural intervention that enforced 100% condom use in collaboration with brothel owners, sex workers, clients of sex workers, and the police.[1,12,36–39] But the Asian financial crisis caused widespread unemployment, which worsened the economic situation, particularly for women and youths.[37,38] Because of waning economic opportunities, girls and women—particularly sex workers—found it difficult to insist on condom use. Further more, there is evidence

that women and girls facing economic duress are more likely to acquiesce to sexual intercourse with no condoms when men offer more money for condomless sexual intercourse.[36,38] In this context, HIV incidence levels began to rise among new sex workers.[37] ABC approaches do not take into account economic contexts at all, even though prevention researchers have identified the critical intersection of poverty and women's HIV/AIDS risks.[40,41]

A third clear limitation of ABC strategies is that these approaches are for individuals who face static conditions and unchanging geographic locations. However, research clearly underscores that HIV/AIDS risks can be exacerbated by economic destabilization and migration flows in particular. Such movements entail separation from partners and provide opportunities for more sexual interactions, thereby enabling transfer of infection from high seroprevalence areas to lower ones.[42–47] Although dominant migration patterns involve men acquiring HIV when away from home and then returning to rural female partners, there is evidence that women with absent migrant male partners also become infected outside of their primary relationship.[48] The ABC strategies fail to recognize the massive increases in migration around the world—both cross-border and internally.[49–51] Instead, the solutions the ABC approaches offer are reduced to static individualized behaviors and morality (e.g., "be faithful").

THE WAY FORWARD

To move beyond the limitations of ABC, and to emphasize longer-term, comprehensive, and gender-focused HIV/AIDS prevention, we propose 3 additional prevention strategies—gender relations, economic contexts, and migration (GEM)—and add these to the current prevention discourse.

Gender-Specific and Gender-Empowering HIV Prevention Interventions

Researchers made early calls for gender-specific interventions, but it is only over the past decade that HIV

prevention programs have recognized and incorporated this perspective. Since then, a crucial transition has occurred from gender-neutral to gender-focused and gender-empowering interventions.[25,28]

Research first pressed beyond the rationalist assumption that women can simply and freely enact condom use, emphasizing that its use is embedded in gender relations and women's relationships with male partners.[25,29,52] Prevention researchers designed interventions to improve women's safer sex negotiation skills and to increase awareness that women's own monogamy does not guarantee the safety of their partners.[53–58] Researchers also sought to understand the relationship between traditional gender roles and risk, examining how men were socialized to initiate and expect sexual intercourse, whereas women tended to be centered on 1 partner and oriented their sexuality toward their partners' needs.[59–60] By applying the knowledge gained from an understanding of relationship contexts, researchers began to successfully intervene directly at the individual and couple level.[53,54,61]

A second key component of gender-specific interventions included an expansion of women's repertoire of methods and skills beyond the male condom to include female-initiated methods (female condom); nonpenetrative sexual contact, or outercourse; and refusal skills. Several of these gender-specific interventions at the group and couple level were successful and have been reviewed extensively elsewhere.[25,34,56] Gender-focused interventions also identified the dilemmas that arise from the competing wishes of preventing HIV/AIDS and other sexually transmitted diseases and having children, particularly because condoms do not adequately speak to this tension.[25,29]

A third wave of successful interventions, based on Robert Connell's structural theory of gender and power,[56–58] elaborated on how the interrelated domains of labor (both paid and unpaid), power (authority and decisionmaking), and cathexis (emotional investments) shape HIV/AIDS risks.[23,24,56] Most recently, gender-specific prevention interventions have moved beyond an emphasis on women and femininity to theorize about how gender relations and masculinities contribute to risk, targeting heterosexually active men. These types of programs are ongoing and examine how masculinities contribute to risk by focusing on the costs of masculinity, i.e., the harm caused to both men and women when men adhere to narrow and constraining definitions of masculinity, and aim to create more gender-equitable norms while reducing violence against women.[62–64]

Economic and Educational Contexts and Structural Interventions

Governments, nongovernmental organizations, and community groups are increasingly recognizing evidence suggesting that the relative economic disadvantage of females compared with males significantly increases the likelihood of unsafe sexual contact.[40,65–69] In response, and in combination with an emphasis on poverty reduction, several governments (e.g., Thailand, India) and nongovernmental organizations have embraced efforts to keep girls in school—or to pay for their fees for school—as a way to diminish the chances of early pregnancies, increase safer sex practices, minimize HIV/AIDS and other sexually transmitted disease risks, and keep girls out of sex work.[65–66]

Worldwide, as many as 100 million children and teenagers—almost two thirds of which are girls—do not attend school at any point in their lives.[67] This shortage of girls in school is often because families give boys priority over girls when allocating their scarce resources for education. Families generally pull girls out of school before boys when families are affected by the impact of HIV/AIDS because girls are responsible for helping families when household crises strike. Some researchers, nongovernmental organization leaders, and community groups argue that eliminating school fees could provide a much-needed structural HIV/AIDS prevention intervention that

would contribute to reductions in risk.[65–67]

Although governments and research organizations are slowly incorporating gender-specific structural innovations into their programs,[68,70,71] HIV/AIDS intervention research lags behind in this area.[20,72,73] In "Gender-Specific and Gender-Empowering HIV Prevention Interventions," we noted several successful interventions that drew upon Connell's structural theory of gender and power. Although this tripartite theory (labor, power, and cathexis) has certainly aided understandings of HIV/AIDS risks, only 2 of the 3 domains of Connell's theory of gender and power have been operationalized and validated to form a scale that formally measures relationship power, called the Sexual Relationship Power Scale. High sexual relationship power has been found to be associated with consistent condom use and is negatively associated with relationship abuse. The first domain of Connell's theory—labor (both paid and unpaid)—was not included in the measurement of relationship power. Connell's second domain, power, is defined as decision-making dominance in the Sexual Relationship Power Scale, and the third domain, cathexis, has been defined as relationship control.[23,24] The omission of labor is surprising, as the relationship between economic disenfranchisement and HIV/AIDS risks is already well established.[40,73] New efforts that seek to further define and detail the important connections between resources, women's empowerment, and health outcomes are promising and sorely needed.[74,75]

Simultaneously, there is growing interest in merging economic interventions with gender equity and HIV/AIDS prevention interventions.[75–79] Such structural approaches are vital, because increased access to financial independence has been linked to bargaining power in relationships, status in the community, and decision-making in the family and can offer alternatives to sex work,[72,78,79] all of which may help to minimize HIV/AIDS risks. However, economic (or educational) interventions alone

may not assist women in changing male sexual behavior or enforcing monogamy. This fact points to the simultaneous need for educational, economic, domestic violence, and gender-specific HIV/AIDS prevention interventions that are culturally specific.[70]

Migration and Population Movements

Few countries explicitly include migrants in their national strategic plan for HIV/AIDS. Protecting the health of migrants will require multisectoral leadership across multiple segments of society and sound policies for workplaces, borders, and informal market activities. As long as national and sectoral policies do not include mobile populations, research and programmatic efforts to assist these populations will surely fall short.[43,80]

To date, HIV/AIDS prevention interventions for migrants have largely focused on men who are truck drivers, sea farers, uniformed servicemen, and traders, assuming that they are the ones who engage in risky sexual behaviors. However, massive numbers of women workers also flow into large industrial centers, particularly for work in domestic service, other service-oriented jobs, or entertainment industries. Some of these women travel to multiple destinations within and across countries; this continual cycling between higher and lower HIV seroprevalence locations can increase women's and men's risk of becoming infected. Several program reports clearly delineate how reductions in HIV/AIDS risks for migrants must come from targeting not only the destination points but also the multiple points of entry and return paths of the migration process.[43,45,46]

Programs that attend to migrants are especially needed because globalization and policies of liberalization did not simply open up global trade markets, they necessitated that countries had to contend with structural adjustment programs. Structural adjustment programs were programs that governments followed to receive International Monetary Fund and World Bank loans that allowed poor nations to substantially increase participation in global trade. Many governments in poor nations tended to respond to structural adjustment programs by spending much of their assets on paying back high-interest debt, leaving little money for health care and education. Structural adjustment resulted in massive migration flows as women and men left economically destabilized areas to search for work. Researchers believe women's HIV/AIDS risks are exacerbated by structural adjustment programs because poor women in particular suffer even greater economic vulnerability under these policies. Some researchers argue that structural adjustment depressed income among the lowest socioeconomic sectors of the population, where women were often disproportionately located, and increased women's vulnerability to HIV/AIDS.[81-85] Recently, researchers have theorized that "sexual opportunity structures," i.e., structural factors that create increased possibilities for sexual interaction, result at the intersection of poverty, migration, and gender relations, leading to unique environments of risk, especially for heterosexually active married women.[86-89]

HIV/AIDS researchers can bolster efforts to help migrants by furthering their understandings of the structural properties of migrant social networks (e.g., size, density, geographies of space) and the networks' relationship to HIV/AIDS risk.[86,89-91] Evidence suggests that there may also be value in providing migrants with HIV/AIDS information and negotiation skills and offering additional supports, such as job skills, credit and financial assistance, and integrating sexual and reproductive health needs with HIV/AIDS prevention for both men and women.[38,46,92] Calls for abstinence and faithfulness are largely out of touch with these needs, which require gender-focused and multisectoral strategies to shape individual or group behaviors over time.

CONCLUSIONS

In a context of burgeoning discourse on stories of ABC success and renewed emphasis on abstinence-only approaches,[19,22] there have also been recent calls from senior HIV/AIDS researchers for the research community to look to the important role that ABC strategies can play, embrace the ABC strategies, end the polarizing debate, and urge the international community to unite around an "inclusive evidence-based approach."[93(p1913)] These authors[93] offer numerous important strategies to slow the spread of HIV/AIDS. But the face of HIV/AIDS is undoubtedly changing. The virus is no longer confined to high-risk populations; it is becoming increasingly feminized and it is clearly linked to cumulative patterns of gender inequality, economic disruption, and population movements. Around what "inclusive" strategy shall the international community unite?

If the research community moves to rally further around the need for ABC strategies, what will undergird this rallying point? The driving principle underlying ABC strategies is that of scaling individual behavioral interventions to fit the population level. Just as individually focused HIV/AIDS prevention interventions first ignored gender relations, gender inequality, and the broader forces that shape behavior, ABC is facing similar limitations.[20,21,28,87,94] In the third decade of the epidemic, it remains vital to not just emphasize how individuals need to change and maintain their own behaviors. Rather, we must also emphasize how successful prevention strategies need to take into account gender relations, other relations of social inequality, economic contexts, and migration movements. These strategies will best sustain behavioral changes in the contexts that drive risk. The breadth and the maintenance of success rely on united work in these areas. The new face of the epidemic speaks strongly to the urgency of these efforts.

About the Authors

Shari L. Dworkin and Anke A. Ehrhardt are with the Department of Psychiatry, Columbia University, New York, NY and the HIV Center for Clinical and Behavioral Studies, New York State Psychiatric Institute and Columbia University, New York.

Correspondence: Requests for reprints should be sent to Dr. Shari L. Dworkin, HIV Center for Clinical and Behavioral Studies, New York State Psychiatric Institute and Columbia University, 1051 Riverside Drive Unit 15, New York, NY 10032 (e-mail: sld2011@columbia.edu).

Acknowledgments

This research was supported by center grants to Anke A. Ehrhardt from the National Institute of Mental Health (P50-MH43520 and P30-MH43520), HIV Center for Clinical and Behavioral Studies, and by a National Research Service Award training grant to Behavioral Sciences Research Training in HIV Infection (T32-MH19139).

The authors gratefully acknowledge comments provided by anonymous reviewers. We are also grateful for generous insights and comments provided by Susie Hoffman, Theresa Exner, Jenny Higgins, Rogerio Pinto, and postdoctoral research fellows at the HIV Center. We thank Vanessa Haney for incisive comments and editing.

Contributors

S. L. Dworkin originated the article, carried out the research, and led the writing. A. A. Ehrhardt supervised all aspects of the manuscript process and contributed ideas to all drafts and final versions.

Accepted for publication June 5, 2006.

References

1. Celentano DD, Nelson KE, Lyles CM, et al. Decreasing incidence of HIV and sexually transmitted diseases in young Thai men: evidence for success of the HIV/AIDS control and prevention program. *AIDS.* 1998;12:F29–F36.

2. Konde-Lule JK. The declining HIV seroprevalence on Uganda: what evidence? *Health Transit Rev.* 1995;S5: 27–33.

3. Stoneburner RL, Low-Beer D. Population-level HIV declines and behavioral risk avoidance in Uganda. *Science.* 2004;304:714–718.

4. UNAIDS. Evaluation of the 100%

Condom Programme in Thailand. Available at: http://data.unaids.org/Publications/IRC-pub01/JC275-100pCondom_en.pdf. Accessed April 22, 2005.

5. USAID. Phase I Report of the ABC Study: summary of HIV prevalence and sexual behavior findings. Available at: http://www.usaid.gov/our_work/global_health/aids/News/ph1abcjan04.pdf. Accessed April 14, 2005.

6. Hogle JA, ed. *What Happened in Uganda? Declining HIV Prevalence, Behavior Change, and the National Response.* Washington, DC: USAID; 2002.

7. USAID. The "ABCs" of HIV prevention: report of a USAID technical meeting on behavior change approaches to primary prevention of HIV/AIDS. Available at: http://www.usaid.gov/our_work/global_health/aids/TechAreas/prevention/abc.pdf. Accessed March 15, 2005.

8. Low-Beer D, Stoneburner RL. Behaviour and communication change in reducing HIV: is Uganda unique? *Afr J AIDS Res.* 2003;2:9–21.

9. Shelton JD, Halperin DT, Nantulya V, Potts M, Gayle HD, Holmes KK. Partner reduction is crucial for balanced "ABC" approach to HIV prevention. *BMJ.* 2004;328:891–894.

10. Asiimwe-Okiror G, Opio AA, Musinguzi J, Madraa E, Tembo G, Caraël M. Change in sexual behavior among young pregnant women in urban Uganda. *AIDS.* 1997;11:1757–1763.

11. Kilian AH, Gregson S, Ndyanabangi B, et al. Reductions in risk behavior provide the most consistent explanation for declining HIV-1 prevalence in Uganda. *AIDS.* 1999;13:391–398.12. Punpanich W, Ungchusak K, Detels R. Thailand's response to the HIV epidemic: yesterday, today, and tomorrow. *AIDS Educ Prev.* 2004;16: 119–136.

13. Ehrhardt AA, Dworkin S, White MA. Blueprint for action: progress in the global fight against AIDS. Paper presented at: The Institute of Journalism and Communication; May 12, 2004; Hanoi, Vietnam.

14. UNAIDS, Word Health Organization. AIDS epidemic update. Available at: http://www.unaids.org/wad2004/report.html. Accessed January 10, 2005.

15 Fuchs VR. *The Feminization of Poverty?* Cambridge, Mass: National Bureau of Economic Research; 1986. Working Paper 1934.

16. Pearce D. The feminization of poverty: women, work, and welfare. *Urban Soc Change Rev.* 1978;11:128–136.

17. McLanahan SS, Sorenson A, Watson D. Sex differences in poverty, 1950–80. *Signs.* 1989;15:102–122.

18. UNAIDS, Word Health Organization. Action against AIDS must address epidemic's increasing impact on women, says UN report [press release]. Bangkok, Thailand; July 14, 2004. Available at: http://data.unaids.org/Media/Press-Releases02/PR_Women-AIDS_14Jul04_en.pdf. Accessed January 10, 2005.

19. Cohen J, Tate T. The less they know, the better: abstinence-only HIV/AIDS programs in Uganda. *Hum Rights Watch.* 2005;17(4A). Available at: http://hrw.org/reports/2005/uganda0305/uganda0305.pdf. Accessed May 5, 2005.

20. Kmietowicz Z. Women are being let down in efforts to stem HIV/AIDS. *BMJ.* 2004;328:305.

21. Coates TJ, Szekeres G. A plan for the next generation of HIV prevention research: seven key policy investigative challenges. *Am Psychol.* 2004;59: 747–757.

22. US House of Representatives Committee on Government Reform—Minority Staff Special Investigations Division. The content of federally funded abstinence-only education programs, prepared for Rep. Henry A. Waxman. Available at: http://www.democrats.reform.house.gov/Documents/20041201102153-50247.pdf. Accessed May 5, 2005.

23. Pulerwitz J, Amaro H, De Jong W, Gortmaker SL, Rudd R. Relationship power, condom use, and HIV risk among women in the USA. *AIDS Care.* 2002;14:789–800.

24. Pulerwitz J, Gortmaker SL, De Jong W. Measuring sexual relationship power in HIV/STD research. *Sex Roles.* 2000;42:637–660.

25. Exner T, Hoffman S, Dworkin S, Ehrhardt AA. Beyond the male condom: the evolution of gender-specific HIV interventions for women. *Annu Rev Sex Res.* 2003;14:114–136.

26. Gupta GR, Weiss E. Women's lives and sex: implications for HIV prevention. *Cult Med Psychiatry.* 1993;17: 399–412.

27. *Testimony on Women and HIV/AIDS to the US House of Representatives Committee on International Relations,* 109th Cong, 2nd Sess (April 13, 2005) (testimony of Geeta Rao Gupta, PhD, president, International Center for Research on Women).

28. Gupta GR. Gender, sexuality and HIV/AIDS: the what, the why and the how. *SIECUS Rep.* 2001;29:6–12.

29. Amaro H. Love, sex, and power: considering women's realities in HIV prevention. *Am Psychol.* 1995;50: 437–447.

30. Jewkes RK, Levin JB, Penn-Kekana LA. Gender inequalities, intimate partner violence and HIV preventive practices: findings of a South African cross-sectional study. *Soc Sci Med.* 2003;56:125–134.

31. Maman S, Mbwambo JK, Hogan NM, et al. HIV-positive women report more lifetime partner violence: findings from a voluntary counseling and testing clinic in Dar es Salaam, Tanzania. *Am J Public Health.* 2002;92:1331–1337.

32. El-Bassel N, Gilbert L, Golder S, et al. Deconstructing the relationship between intimate partner violence and sexual HIV risk among drug-involved men and their female partners. *AIDS Behav.* 2004;8:429–439.

33. Wingood GM, DiClemente RJ. The effects of an abusive primary partner on the condom use and sexual negotiation practices of African-American women. *Am J Public Health.* 1997;87: 1016–1018.

34. Logan TK, Cole J, Leukefeld C. Women, sex, and HIV: social and contextual factors, meta-analysis of published interventions, and implications for practice and research [published correction appears in *Psychol Bull.* 2003;129(2):following 334]. *Psychol Bull.* 2002;128:851–885.

35. Hoffman S, O'Sullivan L, Harrison A, Dolezal C, Monroe-Wise A. HIV risk behaviors and the context of sexual coercion in young adults' sexual interactions: results from a diary study in rural South Africa. *Sex Transm Dis.* 2005;33: 52–58.

36. Ainsworth M, Beyrer C, Soucat A. AIDS and public policy: the lessons and challenges of "success" in Thailand. *Health Policy.* 2003;64:13–37.

37. Kilmarx PH, Palanuvej T, Limpakarnjanarat K, et al. Seroprevalance of HIV among female sex workers in Bangkok: evidence of ongoing infection risk after the "100% condom program" was implemented. *J*

Acquir Immune Defic Syndr. 1999;21: 313–316.

38. Marten L. Commercial sex workers: victims, vectors, or fighters of the HIV epidemic in Cambodia. *Asia Pacific Viewpoint.* 2005;46:21–34.

39. Phoolcharoen W. HIV/AIDS prevention in Thailand: success and challenges. *Science.* 1998;280:1873–1874.

40. Hallman K. *Socioeconomic Disadvantage and Unsafe Sexual Behaviors Among Young Women and Men in South Africa.* New York, NY: Population Council; 2004. Policy Research Division Working Paper 190.

41. Parker R, Easton D, Klein C. Structural barriers and facilitators in HIV prevention: a review of international research. *AIDS.* 2000;14:S22–S32.

42. Stoneburner RL, Carballo M. *An Assessment of Emerging Patterns of HIV Incidence in Uganda and Other East African Countries. Final Report of Consultation for Family Health International, AIDS Control and Prevention Project (AIDSCAP).* Geneva, Switzerland: International Centre for Migration and Health; 1997.

43. Family Health International. HIV prevention in mobile populations. Available at: http://www.fhi.org/en/HIVAIDS/pub /fact/mobilepop.htm. Accessed May 19, 2005.

44. Hirsch JS, Higgins J, Bentley ME, Nathanson CA. The social constructions of sexuality: marital infidelity and sexually transmitted disease—HIV risk in a Mexican community. *Am J Public Health.* 2002;92:1227–1237.

45. UNAIDS. Population mobility and AIDS: UNAIDS technical report. Available at: http://data.unaids.org/ Publications/IRC-pub02/JC513-PopMob-TU_en.pdf. Accessed March 25, 2005.

46. UNAIDS, International Organization for Migration. Mobile populations and HIV/AIDS in the southern African region: recommendations for action. Available at: http://www.sarpn.org.za/ documents/d0000365/P348-HIV_SouthAfrica_report.pdf. Accessed March 25, 2005.

47. Macdonald DS. Notes on the Socioeconomic and cultural factors influencing the transmission of HIV in Botswana. *Soc Sci Med.* 1996;42: 1325–1333.

48. Lurie MN, Williams BG, Zuma K, et al. 2003. Who infects whom? HIV-1 concordance and disconcordance among migrant and non-migrant couples in South Africa. *AIDS.* 2003;17: 2245–2252.

49. Population Division/DESA. United Nations. International migration trends 1960–2000. Available at: http://www.un.org/esa/population/pu blications/ittmigdev2005/Population DivI_pp.pdf. Accessed October 2006.

50. Population Reference Bureau. Transitions in world population. *Popul Bull.* 2004;59(1). Available at http://www.prb.org/Template.cfm?Sect ion=PRB&template=/ContentManage ment/ContentDisplay.cfm&ContentID =12488. Accessed February 20, 2006.

51. International Organization for Migration. *World Migration.* Geneva, Switzerland: International Organization for Migration; 2003.

52. Ehrhardt AA, Exner TM. Prevention of sexual risk behavior for HIV infection with women. *AIDS.* 2000; 14:S53–S58.

53. Ehrhardt AA, Exner TM, Hoffman S, et al. A gender-specific HIV/STD risk reduction intervention for women in a health care setting: short- and long-term results of a randomized clinical trial. *AIDS Care.* 2002;14:147–161.

54. Ehrhardt AA, Exner TM, Hoffman S. HIV/STD risk and sexual strategies among women family planning clients in New York: Project FIO. *AIDS Behav.* 2002;6:1–13.

55. Wingood GM, DiClemente RJ. Application of the theory of gender and power to examine HIV-related exposures, risk factors, and effective interventions for women. *Health Educ Behav.* 2000;27:539–565.

56. Wingood GM, DiClemente RJ. HIV sexual risk reduction interventions for women: a review. *Am J Prev Med.* 1996; 12:209–217.

57. Wingood GM, DiClemente RJ, Mikhail I, et al. A randomized controlled trial to reduce HIV transmission risk behaviors and sexually transmitted diseases among women living with HIV: the WiLLOW program. *J Acquir Immune Deific Syndrm.* 2004;37:S58–S67.

58. DiClemente R, Wingood GM, Harrington KF, et al. Efficacy of an HIV prevention intervention for African American adolescent girls. *JAMA.* 2004; 292:171–179.

59. Seal DW, Ehrhardt AA. Masculinity and urban men: perceived scripts for courtship, romantic, and sexual inter-actions with women. *Cult Health Sex.* 2003;5:295–319.

60. Ortiz-Torres B, Williams SP, Ehrhardt AA. Urban women's gender scripts: implications for HIV. *Cult Health Sex.* 2003;5:1–17.

61. El-Bassel N, Witte S, Gilbert L, et al. The efficacy of a relationship-based HIV/STD prevention program for heterosexual couples. *Am J Public Health.* 2003;93:963–969.

62. Hutchinson S, Weiss E, Barker G, Sagundo M, Pulerwitz J. Involving young men in HIV prevention programs: operations research on gender-based approaches in Brazil, Tanzania, and India. *Horizons Rep.* 2004; December. Available at: http://www.popcouncil.org/horizons/n ewsletter/horizons(9)_1.html. Accessed May 23, 2005.

63. Pulerwitz J, Barker G, Sagundo M. Promoting healthy relationships and HIV/STI prevention for young men: positive findings from an intervention study in Brazil. *Horizons Rep.* 2004; April. Available at: http://www.pop-council.org/pdfs/horizons/brgndrnrm-sru.pdf. Accessed May 23, 2005.

64. Peacock D. The men as partners program in South Africa: reaching men to end gender-based violence and promote HIV/STI prevention. Available at: http://www.engenderhealth.org/ ia/wwm/pdf/map-sa.pdf. Accessed March 22, 2005.

65. UNAIDS. Reducing girls' vulnerability to HIV/AIDS: the Thai approach. Available at: http://data.unaids.org/ Publications/IRC-pub05/JC466-GirlsVuln_en.pdf. Accessed April 20, 2005.

66. Grown C, Gupta GR, Kes A. *Taking Action: Achieving Gender Equality and Empowering Women.* Sterling, Va: Earth-scan; 2005.

67. The Global Coalition on Women and AIDS. "Educate girls, fight AIDS." Available at: http://data.unaids.org/ GCWA/GCWA_FS_GirlsEducation_Se p05_en.pdf. Accessed March 22, 2005.

68. United Nations Development Programme. HIV/AIDS and poverty reduction strategies: policy note. Available at: http://www.undp.org/ hiv/docs/alldocs/hivprsEng25oct02.p df. Accessed May 22, 2005.

69. Smith S, Cohen D. Gender, development, and the HIV epidemic. Available at: http://www.undp.org/ hiv/publications/gender/gendere.htm. Accessed January 15, 2005.

70. Vun MC. Fighting HIV/AIDS on all fronts: Cambodia's multisectoral approach. Available at: http://www1.worldbank.org/devoutreach/july04/article.asp?id=248. Accessed February 22, 2005.

71. The Government of Uganda AIDS Commission, Joint United Nations Programme on AIDS. The national strategic framework for HIV/AIDS activities in Uganda: 2000/1–2005/6. Available at: http://hivaidsclearinghouse.unesco.org/ev_en.php?ID=2533_201&ID2=DO_TOPIC. Accessed May 22, 2005.

72. Blankenship K, Friedman S, Dworkin S, et al. Structural interventions: challenges and opportunities for interdisciplinary research. *J Urban Health.* 2006;83:59–72.

73. Farmer P. Women, poverty, and AIDS. In: Farmer P, Conners M, Simmons J, eds. *Women, Poverty, and AIDS: Sex, Drugs, and Structural Violence.* Monroe, Me: Common Courage Press; 1996; 3–38.

74. Kabeer N. Resources, agency, and achievements: reflections on the measurement of women's empowerment. *Dev Change.* 1999;30:435–464.

75. Measham DM. *Gender-Based Power and Susceptibility to Sexually Transmitted Infections Among Women in Karnataka State, India* [dissertation]. Berkeley: University of California; 2004.

76. Costigan A, Odek WO, Ngugi EN, Oneko M, Moses S, Plummer FA. Income generation for sex workers in Nairobi, Kenya: business uptake and behavior change. Paper presented at: XIV International AIDS Conference; July 7–12, 2002; Barcelona, Spain.

77. Davison J, Strickland J. *Leveling the Playing Field: Promoting Women's Economic Capabilities and Human Rights.* Washington, DC: International Center for Research on Women and the Centre for Development and Population Activities; 2000.

78. Hashemi SM, Schuler SR. Rural credit programs and women's empowerment in Bangladesh. *World Dev.* 1996; 244:635–653.

79. Nyanzi B, Nyanzi S, Wolff B, Whitworth J. Money, men and markets: economic and sexual empowerment of market women in southwestern Uganda. *Cult Health Sex.* 2005;7:13–26.

80. UNAIDS, UNESCO. Migrant populations and HIV/AIDS: the development and implementation of programmes: theory, methodology and practice. Available at: http://www.unesco.org/education/educprog/pead/GB/AIDSGB/AIDSGBtx/immcont.pdf. Accessed March 22, 2005.

81. Baden S. *The Impact of Recession and Structural Adjustment on Women's Work in Selected Developing Countries.* Brighton, UK: Institute of Development Studies; 1993. Report 15.

82. Cagatay N, Ozler S. Feminization of the labor force: the effects of long-term development and structural adjustment. *World Dev.* 1995;23:1883–1894.

83. Cagatay N, Elson D, Grown C. Introduction. *World Dev.* 1995;23: 1827–1836.

84. Chang G. Global exchange: the World Bank, "welfare reform," and global trade in Filipina workers. In: Coontz S, Parson M, Raley G, eds. *American Families: A Multicultural Reader.* New York, NY: Routledge; 1999:305–317.

85. Lingham L. *Structural Adjustment, Gender, and Household Survival Strategies: Review of Evidences and Concerns.* Ann Arbor: Center for the Education of Women, University of Michigan; 2005.

86. Hirsch J. You get tired of eating beans every day: social, cultural, and economic aspects of married women's HIV risks in rural Mexico. Paper presented at: Annual Public Health Association Meeting; December 14, 2005; Philadelphia, Pa.

87. Parikh S. Be faithful: cultural, social, and economic contradictions of the ABC message and married women's HIV risk in Uganda. Paper presented at: Annual Public Health Association Meeting; December 14, 2005; Philadelphia, Pa.

88. Phinney H. Rice is essential but tiresome, you should get some noodles: social, cultural, and economic aspects of married women's HIV risks in Hanoi, Vietnam. Paper presented at: Annual Public Health Association Meeting; December 14, 2005; Philadelphia, Pa.

89. Smith D. Modern marriage, extramarital sex, and HIV risk in southeastern Nigeria. Paper presented at: Annual Public Health Association Meeting; December 14, 2005; Philadelphia Pa.

90. Youm Y, Laumann E. Social networks and sexually transmitted diseases. In: Laumann E, Ellingson S, Mahay J, Paik A, eds. *The Sexual Organization of the City.* Chicago, Ill: University of Chicago Press; 2003;264–283.

91. Liljeros F, Edling CR, Amaral LA. Sexual networks: implications for the transmission of sexually transmitted infections. *Microbes Infect.* 2003; 189–196.

92. Berer M. HIV/AIDS, sexual and reproductive health: intersections and implications for national programmes. *Health Planning Policy.* 2004;i62–i70.

93. Halperin DT, Steiner MJ, Cassell MM, et al. The time has come for common ground on preventing sexual transmission of HIV. *Lancet.* 2004;364: 1913–1914.

94. Gupta G. Luncheon remarks on women and AIDS. Available at: http://womenandaids.unaids.org/GCWA_SP_Gupta_02Jun05_en.pdf. Accessed March 22, 2005.

Cost-Effectiveness of Free HIV Voluntary Counseling and Testing Through a Community-Based AIDS Service Organization in Northern Tanzania

| Nathan M. Thielman, MD, MPH, Helen Y. Chu, MD, Jan Ostermann, PhD, Dafrosa K. Itemba, BA, Anna Mgonja, Sabina Mtweve, MD, MHP, John A. Bartlett, MD, John F. Shao, MD, PhD and John A. Crump, MB, ChB, DTM&H

ABSTRACT

Objectives. We evaluated the cost-effectiveness of fee-based and free testing strategies at an HIV voluntary counseling and testing (VCT) program integrated into a community-based AIDS service organization in Moshi, Tanzania.

Methods. We waived the usual fee schedule during a 2-week free, advertised VCT campaign; analyzed the number of clients testing per day during prefree, free, and postfree testing periods; and estimated the cost-effectiveness of limited and sustained free testing strategies.

Results. The number of clients testing per day increased from 4.1 during the prefree testing interval to 15.0 during the free testing campaign ($P<.0001$) and remained significantly increased at 7.1 ($P<.0001$) after resumption of the standard fees. HIV seroprevalence (16.7%) and risk behaviors were unchanged over these intervals. Modeled over 1 year, the costs per infection averted with the standard fee schedule, with a 2-week free VCT campaign, and with sustained free VCT year-round were $170, $105, and $92, respectively, and the costs per disability-adjusted life year gained were $8.72, $5.40, and $4.72, respectively.

Conclusions. The provision of free VCT enhances both the number of clients testing per day and its cost-effectiveness in resource-limited settings.

INTRODUCTION

In sub-Saharan Africa, HIV voluntary counseling and testing (VCT) is a cost-effective method of reducing high-risk sexual behavior and preventing HIV transmission. A large multicenter study conducted in Kenya, Trinidad, and Tanzania demonstrated that VCT reduced unprotected sexual contact with a nonprimary partner by 35% among men and 39% among women (vs 13% and 17% reductions, respectively, among those who received health information only).[1] It has been estimated that VCT offered to 10000 Tanzanians would avert 895 HIV infections at a cost of $346 per infection averted and $17.78 per disability-adjusted life year (DALY) saved.[2]

Universal voluntary testing with individual informed consent and confidentiality protection in Africa has been advocated.[3,4] The World Health Organization and Joint United Nations Programme on HIV/AIDS have recently endorsed moving from client-initiated requests for VCT to provider-initiated approaches.[5] In addition to promoting behavior change, VCT can serve as a point of referral for preventive services, including the prevention of mother-to-child transmission and as an entry point for treatment programs for sexually transmitted infections, prophylaxis of opportunistic infections, diagnosis and treatment of tuberculosis,[6] and, increasingly, initiation of highly active antiretroviral therapy,[7] thereby further enhancing its cost-effectiveness. Greater access to VCT has been facilitated through cheaper, rapid, and simple HIV testing kits, which reduce the cost per test performed.[8]

Despite these considerations, VCT is vastly underutilized, particularly in poor countries, where the current overall coverage is estimated to be less than 1% to 10% of those at risk for HIV infection.[9] In a population-based nationally representative survey in Tanzania, approximately 7% of women and 12% of men reported ever having received an HIV test.[10] In the Kilimanjaro Region, even in a hospital setting, 44% of those found to be HIV infected in a systematic serosurvey were previously unaware of their infection.[11]

Barriers to accessing VCT services include stigmatization (with abandonment and abuse being common, particularly among women who test positive), geographic accessibility, lack of social promotion, inefficient counseling and testing practices, and cost.[12] We describe a newly established VCT program in Moshi, Tanzania, designed to overcome many of these barriers and in particular focus on testing uptake before, during, and after a free VCT campaign.

METHODS

Location and Context

A new VCT program was integrated into a well-established HIV service organization, Kikundi cha Wanawake Kilimanjaro Kupambana na UKIMWI (KIWAKKUKI; Women Against AIDS in Kilimanjaro) at their easily accessible AIDS Information Centre in downtown Moshi, Tanzania. This nongovernmental organization, established in 1990 with strong community ties, supports persons living with HIV/AIDS by providing home-based care, counseling, and information about HIV infection, and orphan care and assistance. The

KIWAKKUKI VCT program set charges of 1000 Tanzania shillings (TSh; US $0.95 at the 2003 exchange rate) for VCT, except for clients aged 24 years or younger and KIWAKKUKI members (the latter estimated to receive less than 5% of all tests).

The VCT program was initiated in March 2003, and data collection to analyze socio-demographic and clinical characteristics of clients began on May 19, 2003. These characteristics are described in detail elsewhere[13]; 52% were female, and the median age was 29 years (13 to 80 years). A stable number of clients testing per day of 4.1 was observed for 1 month before initiating a free VCT campaign from July 8 through July 21, 2003, during which KIWAKKUKI waived all VCT fees. The free VCT campaign was advertised on national radio in a series of 4 announcements. Posters advertising the availability of free testing were posted in Moshi municipality, and public announcements were made throughout the district.

VCT Procedures and Costs

Clients presenting for VCT received confidential pre- and post-test counseling with a trained counselor according to Tanzanian Ministry of Health Guidelines.[14] The protocol and prevention messages of the KIWAKKUKI VCT service have been outlined previously.[13] Test results were typically received within 30 to 40 minutes. Those testing positive were invited to participate in a KIWAKKUKI-sponsored peer support group and to join the KIWAKKUKI home-based care program that provided trimethoprim-sulfamethoxazole prophylaxis, weekly visits by a trained home care worker, food supplements, and treatment of some opportunistic infections. In addition, all such patients were referred to the zonal hospital HIV clinic, where antiretroviral therapy was available. Sociodemographic data, risk behaviors, and general medical information were recorded on standard questionnaires, and daily numbers of persons testing were tabulated.

Trained counselors were paid approximately $3 (all dollar amounts

are in US dollars) per day. HIV testing was accomplished using Capillus (Trinity Biotech PLC, Bray, County Wicklow, Ireland) and Determine (Abbott Laboratories, Abbott Park, Ill) HIV1/ 2 rapid antibody tests. Every 20th blood sample or any blood sample yielding discrepant rapid testing results was sent to the zonal referral hospital for confirmatory testing using Vironostika HIV (Organon Teknika, Charlotte, NC).

The costs associated with testing were estimated to be $2700 per year for a laboratory technician, $1 per person for each rapid test, $5 for each validation sample sent for confirmatory testing, and $360 per year for laboratory consumables. Additional costs for the program included $500 per year for building space for the program, $600 per year for telephone, $150 per year for electricity consumption, $500 for consumables such as paper forms and copying fees, and $3700 per year for program coordination. During the free VCT campaign, additional costs included hiring a second counselor, advertising (estimated at $40), and proportional increases in consumables, including laboratory supplies and HIV test kits. No additional rental, telephone, or electricity costs were incurred.

Analysis

Data from questionnaires were entered into an electronic database constructed with Epi-Info 2002 software (Centers for Disease Control and Prevention, Atlanta, Ga). Data were validated by randomly sampling 10% of the questionnaires, with an acceptable error rate being less than 1 error per 5 forms. Data were analyzed with EpiInfo 2002 and Stata 8.0 (Stata Corp, College Station, Tex). Differences in daily number of persons testing during and after the free testing period relative to the prefree testing period were analyzed with t tests. Rates of seropositivity in the tested population, published estimates of the effectiveness of VCT in preventing HIV infections,[2] and estimates of DALYs saved/ gained from prevention and treatment[15] were combined with KIWAKKUKI cost data

to estimate the cost per DALY saved/gained because of free testing, with and without subsequent treatment of those testing positive.

RESULTS

Observed Number of Clients Testing per Day in Relation to the Free VCT Campaign

More than 99% of the 813 individuals presenting to KIWAKKUKI for testing from May 19 to November 23, 2003, consented to participate in a study describing the sociodemographic and clinical characteristics of such clients.[13] The number of clients testing per day was considered in relation to the free testing campaign and divided into the prefree testing period from May 19 to July 7, 2003, during which a modest fee (1000 Tsh, approximately $0.95 at the 2003 exchange rate) was charged for clients older than 24 years; the free testing period from July 8 to July 21, 2003; and the postfree testing period from July 22 to November 13, 2003, during which the usual fee schedule was resumed. The secular trends in the number of clients testing per day for all age groups are shown in Figure 1. The periods of peak attendance corresponded to the days when testing was offered free, increasing from mean ±SD of 4.1 ±2.5 clients per day in the prefree testing period to 15.0 ±4.8 and 7.1 ±2.6 clients per day, respectively, during free and postfree testing periods ($P < .0001$ compared with prefree period for each).

Because fees are usually waived for clients younger than 25 years, we considered the number of clients testing per day by age strata as well. The mean daily number of tested persons aged 25 years and older quadrupled during the free testing period relative to the period before free testing (11.4 ±3.5 vs 2.7 ±2.1 clients per day; $P<.0001$). After free testing ended, the number of persons testing declined to 4.6 ±2.2 clients per day but remained significantly higher than before free testing ($P=.0004$). During the free testing period, the daily number of clients testing increased for persons younger than 25 years who received free testing throughout the study period (3.6

±1.8 vs 1.4 ±1.2) clients per day; *P*= .0003). As with the older group, the daily number of clients testing per day remained at a higher level after the free VCT campaign than during the prefree testing period (2.5 ±1.8 clients per day; *P*=.0091). The magnitude of the differences between the 3 periods was smaller for this group of clients than for the older group. There were no significant differences among study subjects in demographic characteristics, knowledge of HIV/AIDS, prevalence of symptoms, or seropositivity between any of the 3 periods.

Annualized Models of Cost-Effectiveness

During the free VCT campaign, 109 excess clients than would have been predicted (based on the prefree testing rate of 4.1 clients per day) presented for testing, and in the following 80 days, 238 excess clients were tested. We used the HIV seroprevalence and postfree period number of persons testing per day seen over the latter 29 weeks of observation to develop a

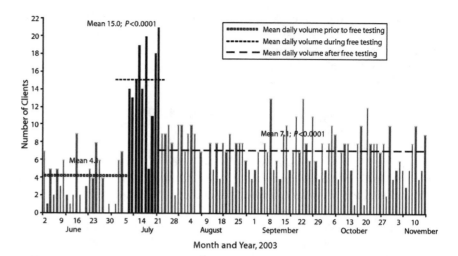

FIGURE 1— Number of persons testing per day before (gray bars to the left), during (black bars), and after (gray bars to the right) the free voluntary HIV counseling and testing campaign at KIWAKKUKI (n = 813).

model annualizing these data in order to perform cost-effectiveness analyses. Over 1 year, without a free VCT campaign, 966 individuals would be tested at a net cost of $11 518 ($11.92 per client tested) (Table 1). With the addition of a 2-week free VCT campaign, 1864 persons would be tested for $13 771 ($7.38 per client tested) over 1 year, assuming no increases in fixed costs since the number of persons testing per day in our circum-

TABLE 1— One-Year Estimated Testing Volumes and Costs in US Dollars Without Free VCT, With a Free VCT Campaign, and With Sustained Free VCT: Moshi, Tanzania, May through November, 2003

Economic parameters	No Free VCT, n = 966[a]		Free VCT Campaign, n = 1864[b]		Sustained Free VCT, n = 3915[c]	
	Cost	Cost per Client	Cost	Cost per Client	Cost	Cost per Client
Building rent	500.00	0.52	500.00	0.27	1000.00	0.26
Telephone	600.00	0.62	600.00	0.32	1200.00	0.31
Power	150.00	0.16	150.00	0.08	600.00	0.15
Advertising[d]	0.00	0.00	40.00	0.02	1040.00	0.27
Labor[e]	8036.80	8.32	8102.80	4.35	9759.40	2.49
Lab supplies	360.00	0.37	694.51	0.37	1458.16	0.37
HIV test kits	2021.63	2.09	3900.13	2.09	8188.46	2.09
Other consumables	500.00	0.52	964.60	0.52	2025.22	0.52
Total cost	12 168.43	12.59	14 952.05	8.02	25 271.23	6.45
Estimated income from VCT charges[f]	650.06		1181.44		0.00	
Net cost	11 518.37	11.92	13 770.61	7.38	25 271.23	6.45

Note. VCT = voluntary counseling and testing.
[a]Applies prefree VCT campaign daily client volumes to 261 testing days in a calendar year.
[b]Applies free VCT daily client volumes to 10 days and postfree VCT daily client volumes to 251 testing days in calendar year.
[c]Applies free VCT daily client volumes to 251 testing days in a calendar year.
[d]Radio advertisements, gasoline for car during free VCT campaign.
[e]Laboratory technician, VCT program director, counselors.
[f]Assumes fees are waived for those aged < 25 years per Tanzanian Ministry of Health guidelines.

stance had not reached the capacity of the VCT center. A third scenario applied the free VCT daily client testing number to the entire year with appropriate cost increases in rent, telephone, power, testing supplies, and consumables, including adding 2 additional counselors for $6.60 per day. Under these conditions, the cost of sustained free VCT over 1 year would be reduced further to $6.45 per client.

We applied the previous estimates of Sweat et al.,[2] stratified by gender and serostatus, for HIV infections averted by VCT among individuals in Tanzania. Without free VCT, we estimated that, over 1 year, 68 HIV infections would be prevented at a cost of $169.69 per infection averted and $8.72 per DALY gained (Table 2). The increased daily testing number and cost-efficiency of testing afforded by the addition of a free VCT campaign would avert 63 additional HIV infections, at a cost of $105.12 per infection averted, reducing the cost per DALY saved to $5.40, and a model of sustained free VCT program would reduce the cost per infection averted further to nearly $92 and a cost per DALY saved of $4.72.

Assuming that 30% of those presenting for testing would receive antiretroviral therapy at a cost of $420 per year (on the basis of current retail pricing for fixed dose combination stavudine/lamivudine/nevirapine in retail pharmacies in the Kilimanjaro Region) and that 50% would receive tuberculosis prophylaxis with isoniazid for 6 months at a cost of $25 (on the basis of estimates from Creese et al.[15]), we calculated that a total of 1381 DALYS would be gained at a cost of $24.52 per DALY without free VCT. With the free VCT campaign, 2666 DALYS would be gained at a cost per DALY of $21.34, and with the sustained free VCT program, 5597 DALYS would be gained at a cost per DALY of $20.69. Sensitivity analyses included in Table 2 varied assumptions of HIV seroprevalence and rates of treatment. At an HIV seroprevalence of 25%, there is marked improvement in the cost-effectiveness of VCT, particularly with a free VCT

campaign. Holding HIV seroprevalence constant and varying rates of treatment with antiretrovirals and tuberculosis prophylaxis shows small improvements in cost-effectiveness.

DISCUSSION

We have demonstrated that a period of free VCT significantly increases the number of persons testing per day and enhances cost-effectiveness of VCT when offered as an integrated program within an existing AIDS service-oriented nongovernmental organization. Modeled over a 1-year time horizon, a policy of sustained free VCT would likely further enhance the cost-effectiveness of this intervention.

Previous work in Tanzania estimated the cost of VCT per infection prevented to be $346, and that of per DALY saved, $17.78.[2] Even without a free VCT campaign or sustained free services for all clients, we have shown standard VCT practices in our setting to be nearly twice as cost-effective as these estimates.

Several factors likely explain these differences. First, our VCT program was integrated into an existing, community-based, volunteer AIDS service organization, minimizing startup costs and costs for counselors (who were motivated women from the community paid approximately $3.30/day). Second, testing costs were reduced by the use of onsite rapid HIV antibody testing, which is the method of choice in this region. Others have shown this approach to increase the number of patients receiving their results, making it both more convenient and economical in comparison with conventional enzyme-linked immunosorbent assay testing.[8] Third, operating costs may be lower in Moshi municipality, compared with larger urban settings in Tanzania.

Surprisingly little research has focused on strategies to enhance testing uptake and cost-effectiveness at community-based VCT programs. Gresenguet et al.[16] described increased testing volumes in Bangui, Central African Republic, at a VCT site during annual AIDS day free testing events, which attracted mostly asymptomatic

students, but they did not note the effect of this campaign on subsequent testing.

A survey assessing willingness to pay among VCT clients in Kenya suggested that more people are reluctant to access VCT services as the costs approach $1 to $2.[17] In our study, after the introduction of a free VCT campaign, increases in the number of clients testing per day were sustained and cost increases were limited primarily to excess testing supplies. The costs per infection averted and per DALY gained decreased by 38% to $105 and $5.40, respectively. If free VCT were offered year-round, assuming sustained client testing numbers of around 15 clients per day, the costs per infection averted and per DALY gained would decrease by 46%. The provision of free VCT, only if for a brief campaign, thus renders VCT an even more effective intervention, on the order of single-dose nevirapine for the prevention of mother-to-child transmission.[15] When VCT is considered as an entry point for care of the HIV-infected and is included in the summary cost per DALY calculation, it contributes around 96% of the DALYS gained and substantially reduces the cost per DALY.

Why did more clients present for testing in the interval following the free testing campaign? The free VCT testing period was promoted soon after the initiation of VCT at KIWAKKUKI, raising the possibility that the increase in daily testing numbers reflected growing awareness of this new service by the community. Against this, the VCT program was initiated 2 months before data collection for this study, and a stable daily testing pattern was observed before the free VCT campaign. It is possible that some clients presented thinking VCT was still offered free at KIWAKKUKI, but this seems unlikely several months after the campaign, when daily testing numbers remained sustained and clients were asked to pay before testing.

It is likely that the combination of a simple, inexpensive advertising campaign helped to increase the social acceptability and awareness of VCT.

TABLE 2— Cost-Effectiveness and Sensitivity Analyses Without Free VCT, With a Free VCT Campaign, and With Sustained Free VCT

	No Free VCT						Free VCT Campaign						Sustained Free VCT					
	Number Treated	New Diagnoses	Infections Averted	Cost Per Infection Averted[a]	DALYs Gained	Cost Per DALY, US$	Number Treated	New Diagnoses	Infections Averted	Cost Per Infection Averted[a]	DALYs Gained	Cost Per DALY, US$	Number Treated	New Diagnoses	Infections Averted	Cost Per Infection Averted[a]	DALYs Gained	Cost Per DALY, US$
Prevention																		
HIV Prevalence																		
Observed (16.7%)	...	...	67.9	169.69	1321	8.72	...	...	131.0	105.12	2549	5.40	...	653.8	275.0	91.89	5352	4.72
Low (8%)	...	...	40.0	288.04	778	14.80	...	...	77.2	178.47	1502	9.17	...	313.2	162.0	156.00	3152	8.02
High (25%)	...	...	95.0	121.24	1848	6.23	...	...	183.3	75.12	3567	3.86	...	978.8	384.9	65.66	7490	3.37
New Diagnoses																		
HIV Prevalence																		
Observed (16.7%)	...	161.4	...	...	...	...	...	311.3	...	...	...	...	...	...	...	...	...	...
Low (8%)	...	77.3	...	...	...	...	...	149.1	...	...	...	...	...	...	...	...	...	...
High (25%)	...	241.5	...	...	...	...	...	466.0	...	...	...	...	...	...	...	...	...	...
Antiretroviral treatment[b]																		
Rates of Treatment																		
Medium (30%)	48.4	...	...	...	48.4	420.00[c]	93.4	48.4	...	...	93.4	420.00	196.1	...	...	...	196.1	420.00
Low (10%)	16.1	...	...	...	16.1	420.00[c]	31.1	16.1	...	...	31.1	420.00	65.4	...	...	...	65.4	420.00
High (50%)	80.7	...	...	...	80.7	420.00	155.6	80.7	...	...	155.6	420.00	326.9	...	...	...	326.9	420.00
Tuberculosis prophylaxis[b]																		
Rates of Treatment																		
Medium (50%)	80.7	...	...	...	12.1	166.67[d]	155.6	80.7	...	...	23.3	166.67	326.9	...	...	...	49.0	166.67
Low (30%)	48.4	...	...	...	7.3	166.67[d]	93.4	48.4	...	...	14.0	166.67	196.1	...	...	...	29.4	166.67
High (70%)	112.9	...	...	...	16.9	166.67[d]	217.9	112.9	...	...	32.7	166.67	457.7	...	...	...	68.6	166.67
Tuberculosis prophylaxis[b]																		
Rates of Treatment																		
Medium treatment	...	...	...	1381.4	...	24.52	...	...	...	...	2666.0	21.34	...	...	...	...	5,597.2	20.69
Low treatment	...	...	...	1344.3	...	14.51	...	...	...	...	2594.4	11.25	...	...	...	...	5,446.9	10.58
High treatment	...	...	...	1418.5	...	34.00	...	...	...	...	2737.6	30.90	...	...	...	...	5,747.6	30.28

Note. VCT = voluntary counseling and testing; DALY = disability-adjusted life year.
[a] Based on previous estimates in Tanzania.[2]
[b] With an observed HIV infection prevalence of 16.7%.
[c] Assumes cost for antiretroviral therapy of $35 per month and does not include cost for monitoring and care.
[d] Based on an estimated cost of $25 for 6 months of preventive therapy.[15]

Further, the provision of free testing removed a cost barrier to VCT, making it accessible to less wealthy clients. From a health policy point of view, including an inexpensive promotional campaign is necessary to create awareness of the free service.

There were limitations to this study. Although the calculations for the numbers of HIV infections averted and cost-effectiveness of this intervention were based on data from Tanzania,[2] these data may not necessarily be representative of our population. In addition, our study was observational. Without formal hypothesis testing in which clinics are randomized to free VCT campaigns or their standard fee schedule, we cannot rigorously infer that free VCT campaigns lead to increased participation. Clearly a large, multisite, longer-term, randomized trial would help to refine the magnitude of the impact and cost-effectiveness of free VCT campaigns, but only after several years.

We used daily testing numbers obtained over a 2-week free testing period to estimate the cost-effectiveness of free VCT offered over a 1-year time horizon but did not demonstrate whether such daily testing numbers can be sustained. In response to these analyses, KIWAKKUKI has implemented a free VCT service and has sustained daily testing numbers of 13 persons per day over 6 months. Furthermore, there was no change in HIV seroprevalence among VCT clients over the same 6-month period. Our data suggest that VCT with free campaigns or the provision of sustained free VCT should be adopted into national HIV control policies.

In some instances, governments and nongovernmental organizations offer free VCT,[18,19] but at least partial cost recovery through client charges is more typical. In resource-limited settings, sustained provision of universal free VCT may be unrealistic given the multiple demands on the resources allocated for HIV/AIDS prevention and care services.

An approach of strengthening existing health infrastructure by investing enough funds to maximize testing capacity within stable community-based organizations rather than the creation of new services would also be beneficial in terms of the relative ease of implementation. Similarly, costs could be reduced by integrating VCT into other health services, such as those for tuberculosis, sexually transmitted infections, hospital inpatient and outpatient services, and antenatal clinics.

The integration of this VCT program within a volunteer-based AIDS service organization in Moshi, Tanzania, was highly cost-effective. Our study suggests that the provision of free VCT not only results in a prolonged increase in daily testing number but also optimizes testing throughput and efficiency. The enhanced cost-effectiveness of this intervention was reflected in potential disability averted by preventing new HIV infections and facilitating access to expanding HIV treatment programs. In addition to further operational research aimed at optimizing VCT in other settings, policy-makers should support the small investment necessary to underwrite free VCT, particularly when integrated into existing community-based AIDS service organizations.

About the Authors

At the time of the study, Nathan M. Thielman, John A. Bartlett, John A. Crump, and Helen Y. Chu were with the Division of Infectious Diseases and International Health at Duke University Medical Center, Durham, NC. Jan Ostermann is with the Health Inequalities Program, Terry Sanford Institute of Public Policy, Duke University. Dafrosa K. Itemba, Anna Mgonja, and Sabina Mtweve are with KIWAKKUKI (Kikundi cha Wanawake Kilimanjaro Kupambana UKIMWI; Women Against AIDS in Kilimanjaro). John F. Shao is with Tumaini University, Moshi, Tanzania. Sabina Mtweve and John A. Crump are also with Kilimanjaro Christian Medical Centre and Kilimanjaro Christian Medical College of Tumaini University, Moshi.

Correspondence: Requests for reprints should be sent to John A. Crump, Division of Infectious Diseases and International Health, Duke University Medical Center, Box 3867, Durham, NC 27701 (e-mail: crump017@mc.duke.edu).

Acknowledgments

This study was supported in part by Roche Laboratories. Additional investigator support was obtained from AIDS Clinical Trials Group (U01 AI-39156, J.A. Bartlett and N.M. Thielman) and mid-career investigator (K24 AI-0744–01, J. A. Bartlett) awards from the National Institutes of Allergy and Infectious Diseases and from the US Department of State Fulbright Program (N.M. Thielman and H.Y. Chu).

We are grateful to the staff of KIWAKKUKI AIDS Information Centre for their collaboration, and in particular to the VCT counselors Beatrice Mandao, Eliakesia Shangali, Anna Msuya, Anna Mchaki, Agatha Chuwa, Alexia Mella, Awaichi Malle, B. Haule, E. Kiwla, Grace Gumbo, Lillian Mtui, Naomi Ringo, Magdalena Lyimo, Sylvia Mlay, and Yesusia Mariki.

We thank the clients of the KIWAKKUKI VCT program for their participation.

Human Participant Protection

Ethical approval for the study was granted by the Kilimanjaro Christian Medical Centre Research Ethics Committee, the institutional review board of Duke University Medical Center, and the Tanzania National Institute of Medical Research National Medical Research Coordinating Committee.

Contributors

N.M. Thielman and J.A. Bartlett originated the study. N.M. Thielman wrote the final article. They received assistance in designing the survey instrument from S. Mtweve and D. Itemba. A. Mgonja enrolled clients at KIWAKKUKI. H.Y. Chu performed initial data analysis and wrote an early draft of the article. J. Ostermann oversaw statistical analyses and performed the final cost-effectiveness calculations. J.A. Crump contributed to study implementation, data management and analysis, interpretation, and article editing. J.F. Shao facilitated critical administrative support. All authors contributed to the final version of the article.

References

1. The Voluntary HIV-1 Counseling and Testing Efficacy Study Group. Efficacy of voluntary HIV-1 counselling and testing in individuals and couples in Kenya, Tanzania, and Trinidad: a randomised trial. *Lancet.* 2000;356:103–112.

2. Sweat M, Gregorich S, Sangiwa G, et al. Cost-effectiveness of voluntary HIV-1 counselling and testing in reducing sexual transmission of HIV-1 in Kenya and Tanzania. *Lancet.* 2000;356:113–121.

3. De Cock KM, Marum E, Mbori-Ngacha D. A serostatus-based approach to HIV/AIDS prevention and care in Africa. *Lancet.* 2003;362:1847–1849.

4. Ammann AJ. Preventing HIV. *BMJ.* 2003;326: 1342–1343.

5. *UNAIDS/WHO Policy Statement on HIV Testing.* Geneva, Switzerland: UNAIDS/WHO; 2004.

6. Godfrey-Faussett P, Maher D, Mukadi YD, Nunn P, Perriens J, Raviglione M. How human immunodeficiency virus voluntary testing can contribute to tuberculosis control. *Bull World Health Organ.* 2002;80: 939–945.

7. De Cock KM, Mbori-Ngacha D, Marum E. AIDS in Africa, V: shadow on the continent: public health and HIV/AIDS in Africa in the 21st century. *Lancet.* 2002;360:67–72.

8. Ekwueme DU, Pinkerton SD, Holtgrave DR, Branson BM. Cost comparison of three HIV counseling and testing technologies. *Am J Prev Med.* 2003;25: 112–121.

9. Jha P, Mills A, Hanson K, et al. Improving the health of the global poor. *Science.* 2002;295:2036–2039.

10. HIV/AIDS Survey Indicators Database: Tanzania Country Report. Available at: http://www.measuredhs.com/hivdata/reports/start.cfm?L0.1&char_urban=0&char_age=0&char_ed=0&report_action=view. Accessed May 29, 2004.

11. Ole-Nguyaine S, Crump JA, Kibiki GS, et al. HIV-associated morbidity, mortality, and diagnostic testing opportunities among inpatients at a referral hospital in northern Tanzania. *Ann Trop Med Parasitol.* 2004;98: 171–179.

12. Vermund SH, Wilson CM. Barriers to HIV testing-where next? *Lancet.* 2002;360:1186–1187.

13. Chu HY, Crump JA, Osterman J, Oenga RB, Itemba DK, Mgonja A, Mtweve S, Bartlett JA, Shao JF, Thielman NM. Sociodemographic and clinical characteristics of clients presenting for HIV voluntary counseling and testing in Moshi, Tanzania. *Int J STD AIDS.* 2005;16:691–696.

14. The United Republic of Tanzania Ministry of Health. *National Guidelines for Clinical Management of HIV/AIDS.* Dar es Salaam, Tanzania: United Republic of Tanzania Ministry of Health; 2002.

15. Creese A, Floyd K, Alban A, Guinness L. Cost-effectiveness of HIV/AIDS interventions in Africa: a systematic review of the evidence. *Lancet.* 2002;359: 1635–1642.

16. Gresenguet G, Sehonou J, Bassirou B, et al. Voluntary HIV counseling and testing: experience among the sexually active population in Bangui, Central African Republic. *J Acquir Immune Defic Syndr.* 2002;31: 106–114.

17. Forsythe S, Arthur G, Ngatia G, Mutemi R, Odhiambo J, Gilks C. Assessing the cost and willingness to pay for voluntary HIV counselling and testing in Kenya. *Health Policy Plan.* 2002;17:187–195.

18. Kawichai S, Celentano DD, Chaifongsri R, et al. Profiles of HIV voluntary counseling and testing of clients at a district hospital, Chiang Mai Province, northern Thailand, from 1995 to 1999. *J Acquir Immune Defic Syndr.* 2002;30:493–502.

19. Peck R, Fitzgerald DW, Liautaud B, et al. The feasibility, demand, and effect of integrating primary care services with HIV voluntary counseling and testing: evaluation of a 15-year experience in Haiti, 1985–2000. *J Acquir Immune Defic Syndr.* 2003;33: 470–475.

Environmental–Structural Interventions to Reduce HIV/STI Risk Among Female Sex Workers in the Dominican Republic

| Deanna Kerrigan, PhD, MPH, Luis Moreno, BA, Santo Rosario, BA, Bayardo Gomez, MD, Hector Jerez, MA, Clare Barrington, MPH, Ellen Weiss, MA and Michael Sweat, PhD

ABSTRACT

Objectives. We assessed the effectiveness of 2 environmental–structural interventions in reducing risks of HIV and sexually transmitted infections (STIs) among female sex workers in the Dominican Republic.

Methods. Two intervention models were implemented over a 1-year period: community solidarity in Santo Domingo and solidarity combined with government policy in Puerto Plata. Both were evaluated via preintervention–postintervention cross-sectional behavioral surveys, STI testing and participant observations, and serial cross-sectional STI screenings.

Results. Significant increases in condom use with new clients (75.3%–93.8%; odds ratio [OR]=4.21; 95% confidence interval [CI]=1.55, 11.43) were documented in Santo Domingo. In Puerto Plata, significant increases in condom use with regular partners (13.0%–28.8%; OR=2.97; 95% CI=1.33, 6.66) and reductions in STI prevalence (28.8%–16.3%; OR = 0.50; 95% CI = 0.32, 0.78) were documented, as were significant increases in sex workers' verbal rejections of unsafe sex (50.0%–79.4%; OR=3.86; 95% CI=1.96, 7.58) and participating sex establishments' ability to achieve the goal of no STIs in routine monthly screenings of sex workers (OR=1.17; 95% CI=1.12, 1.22).

Conclusions. Interventions that combine community solidarity and government policy show positive initial effects on HIV and STI risk reduction among female sex workers.

INTRODUCTION

Efforts to reduce female sex workers' vulnerability to HIV have frequently relied on individual-level interventions such as condom promotion and management of sexually transmitted infections (STIs).[1–4] Increasingly, HIV prevention programmers are focusing their attention on "environmental–structural" interventions that seek to alter the physical and social environments in which individual behavior takes place.[5,6] Two environmental–structural approaches have emerged in the context of female sex work—community mobilization initiatives such as the "Sonagachi project" in Calcutta, India,[7–9] and government policy initiatives such as the Thai "100% condom program"[10,11]—and program evaluations of each have documented increases in condom use and decreases in STI prevalence. Several countries have sought to adopt or adapt either the community mobilization[12–14] or government policy approach[15–18] to prevent HIV and STIs among sex workers and their partners; however, few have sought to integrate the strengths of both approaches.

In 1995, 2 Dominican nongovernmental organizations (NGOs), *Centro de Orientación e Investigación Integral* (COIN), based in Santo Domingo, and *Centro de Promoción y Solidaridad Humana* (CEPROSH), based in Puerto Plata, began exploring the possibility of adapting elements of the Thai 100% condom program to the Dominican context, where peer education among sex workers began in the late 1980s.[19] Both qualitative and quantitative research was conducted in Santo Domingo from 1996 to 1998 to help inform the process of adapting elements of the Thai model to the Dominican context.[20,21] On the basis of the results of these studies, and through consultations with the local sex worker organization, Movimiento de Mujeres Unidas (MODEMU), 2 environmental–structural intervention models were developed. Our primary objective was to assess the effectiveness of each of these models in reducing HIV and STI risks among female sex workers.

METHODS

Study Design

We primarily relied on a pretest–posttest design to evaluate the interventions over a period of 1 year. The intervention was implemented in 68 female sex establishments (34 per city) in 2 cities: Santo Domingo, the capital, and Puerto Plata, the fifth largest city, located in the northeastern section of the country. We also accessed serial cross-sectional data from government health clinics to complement the preintervention–postintervention data. Within each city, the geographic areas where commercial sex was most prevalent were purposively selected. Selection criteria for participating sex establishments were based on the potential acceptability and feasibility of implementing the intervention research and included establishments employing more than 5 women and those where a set fee was paid by the client to the establishment.

The managers of all 68 sex establishments selected agreed to participate in the intervention activities.

Intervention Components

Over the course of the study, an average of 15 sex workers worked in each of the participating sex establishments, and all sex workers were invited and encouraged to participate in all of the intervention components implemented in their city. Components 1–4, discussed next, were implemented in both cities, while component 5 was implemented in Puerto Plata only. The reason we chose to implement component 5 in Puerto Plata was that the political leadership necessary to implement a policy-level intervention was present in that city at the time of the study.

1. Solidarity and collective commitment. Quarterly workshops and monthly follow-up meetings were implemented with sex workers, establishment owners and managers, and other establishment employees. The purpose of these encounters was to encourage and strengthen a sense of solidarity and collective commitment toward HIV and STI prevention, and discussion included the role that each actor could play in supporting sex workers to use condoms with their partners. Population-specific educational materials were used to reinforce responsibilities and benefits pertinent to each group. An additional focus of the workshops and materials was the role of trust and intimacy associated with condom use among sex workers and regular-paying and nonpaying partners.

2. Environmental cues. Establishment owners were asked to post 100% condom posters and stickers, as well as to make available glass bowls filled with condoms. They were also asked to maintain a stock of at least 100 condoms at all times. Additional cues implemented on a quarterly basis in each establishment included disc jockey messages regarding safe sex, information booths, educational materials, and interactive theater presentations engaging male clients in HIV prevention themes, facilitated by sex worker peer educators and NGO staff.

3. Clinical services. At the time the intervention began, female sex workers in the Dominican Republic were required by the Ministry of Health to attend monthly STI checks at government clinics, and government health inspectors were mandated to monitor their attendance. This system was not implemented in a standardized or consistent manner. Our intervention sought to overcome these barriers by providing clinicians and inspectors in both cities with training in the areas of basic HIV/AIDS information, data collection and monitoring, and ethical procedures. In addition, sex worker peer educators from the project were given private offices in government clinics to provide pretest–posttest STI counseling.

4. Monitoring and encouraging adherence. In both cities, establishment owners were notified of their status in terms of adherence to 5 study elements on a monthly basis: presence of posters, visible condoms, stocks of at least 100 condoms, attendance of sex workers at monthly STI checks, and lack of positive STI diagnoses among the establishment's sex workers. These elements were evaluated each month by government health inspectors accompanied by NGO staff. No individual STI results were shared with establishment owners. At the end of each month, establishments that were not in adherence with these elements were the focus of intensified educational efforts. On a quarterly basis, award certificates were given to establishments adhering to all elements.

5. Policy and regulation. In Puerto Plata, information on a regional government policy requiring condom use between sex workers and clients was communicated to all participating sex establishment owners in a meeting that took place at the beginning of the study and was jointly sponsored by the regional health department and the implementing NGO. Owners were told that they, not the sex workers, would be responsible for ensuring that their establishment complied with the policy and associated program activities. NGO staff and regional public health officials in Puerto Plata met with establishment owners on a quarterly basis to encourage adherence to the policy and discuss barriers to implementation.

In addition to intensified educational efforts, establishments that were not in adherence in Puerto Plata were subject to a graduated sanction system targeted to establishment owners, including notifications, fines, and closings. During the course of the intervention in Puerto Plata, 113 notifications, 18 fines, and 1 temporary closing were levied on participating sex establishments as a result of nonadherence to the 5 monitoring elements assessed on a monthly basis.

Data Collection Procedures

Evaluation data were collected at baseline, between September and December 1999, and again toward the end of the 12-month intervention period, during November and December 2000. At both preintervention and postintervention, structured behavioral surveys were administered and nonroutine STI testing conducted among cross-sectional samples of approximately 200 female sex workers older than 18 years working in participating sex establishments in each city. An average of 6 sex workers from each of these establishments participated in the survey and underwent nonroutine STI testing at preintervention and postintervention. There was minimal overlap (less than 5%) of the cross-sections of sex workers recruited at preintervention and postintervention within each city.

All potential survey and nonroutine STI testing participants were recruited from government health clinics. On days selected for recruitment, our NGO study team approached every third woman from a participating establishment attending the monthly clinical consultations. All potential participants were given detailed information about the objectives, procedures, and risks and benefits of the study. Those who agreed to participate provided written consent to be interviewed and undergo nonroutine STI screening. The consent rate was 95%. Consenting participants were asked to provide urine samples for gonorrhea and chlamydia testing and vaginal swabs for trichomoniasis testing. All STI testing was confidential, and all participants testing positive for STI were treated promptly. All survey interviews were anonymous and were conducted by trained interviewers recruited from local health NGOs. Participants received approximately US$3 for completing the survey and undergoing nonroutine STI screenings.

Preintervention and postintervention participant observations were also conducted among a random sample of sex workers recruited from participating sex establishments in each city. Approximately 2 observations were conducted at each of the 34 establishments in each city at both preintervention and postintervention, with a minimum of 64 observations per city and data collection period. After selecting a woman according to established criteria, NGO staff followed a strict research protocol whereby they talked with the participant for approximately 30 minutes and then asked whether she would be willing to have sex without a condom, providing up to 4 reasons why a condom should not be used. After the sex worker gave her final response, the NGO staff member excused himself from the interaction and paid the bill for his table, compensating the sex worker with a tip of approximately US$6 for her time. All interactions were anonymous and took place within the confines of the sex establishments. After leaving the establishment, NGO staff documented the interaction in a private setting.

The local MODEMU sex worker organization was consulted on and approved of the use of the partici-

pant–observation methodology. We suggest that other researchers interested in adopting this methodology refer to the *International Ethical Guidelines for Biomedical Research Involving Human Subjects*[22] and consult with a bioethicist, as we did, to ensure that the ethical rights of the human participants involved are duly protected.

Measures

Condom use was assessed via participants' self-reports of the percentage of sex acts in which condoms were used in the past month with new clients, regular partners, and all partners. New clients were defined as people with whom sex workers had engaged in sex only once or twice in exchange for money. Regular partners were defined as people with whom they had engaged in sex at least 3 times or people they considered "trusted" partners, whether they directly paid for sex or not. These categories were developed on the basis of previous qualitative research.[20] In the case of new clients and regular partners, a 5-point Likert scale (1=*always*, 5=*never*) was used to measure condom use. Participants were also asked the total number of partners with whom they had had sex in the past month and the number of those partners with whom they had always used condoms during that time. All condom use variables were dichotomized into consistent versus inconsistent use.

Rejection of unsafe sex was measured through participant observations of female sex workers conducted by NGO staff. Four common reasons mentioned by a male client in order not to use condoms were selected on the basis of findings from previous qualitative studies: not wanting to use a condom simply because he does not like condoms, not needing to use a condom because he is a "serious guy who is married and has kids," offering 50% more money than the sex worker's asking rate, and offering 100% more money than the sex worker's asking rate. These 4 scenarios were posed sequentially to the sex worker, who was not offered the next scenario

unless she rejected unsafe sex in response to all previous scenarios. The NGO worker recorded whether the sex worker accepted any of these offers or whether she verbally rejected unsafe sex throughout the encounter.

We documented *STIs* by measuring the prevalence of each of 3 infections—gonorrhea, chlamydia, and trichomoniasis—among individual sex workers also completing the preintervention and postintervention cross-sectional behavioral surveys. We constructed a dichotomized measure of whether participants had any of these 3 STIs. Chlamydia and gonorrhea were detected via Ligase chain reaction DNA tests, while the presence of trichomoniasis was established through culture-based tests.

In addition, we documented the number of establishments that achieved the goal of no STIs in a given month, per city, over the 1-year intervention. This establishment-level information was collected from local public health clinics that serve female sex workers; these clinics provide routine monthly checks using the syndromic management approach for detection of STIs.[23] We also calculated 2-month averages of the percentage of establishments with no STIs per month and city over the year.

We measured *exposure* to the intervention using a 13-item scale (Cronbach =0.80) that included items focusing on sex workers' exposure to key intervention components, such as solidarity and collective commitment, environmental cues, monitoring, and policy and regulation, in the past month. The scale was dichotomized at the median into high (more than 11 positive responses out of a possible total of 13) versus low. In addition, an observed measure of *adherence* to 4 intervention elements—presence of 100% condom posters, visible condoms in glass bowls, stocks of at least 100 condoms, and attendance of all sex workers at monthly STI checks—was calculated for each establishment over the course of the intervention. The 4-point adherence score was dichotomized at the median into high (3–4) versus low (0–2).

Data Analysis

Chi-square tests of association were conducted to identify differences in sociodemographic characteristics of the participants from preintervention to postintervention. Preintervention to postintervention changes in HIV-and STI-related outcomes such as condom use and STI prevalence were assessed via multivariate logistic regression analyses controlling for the 5 demographic variables for which significant differences were observed in either of the 2 cities over the course of the study (Table 1). Changes in sex workers' rejection of unsafe sex did not allow for adjusted analyses, because no sociodemographic information was collected from participating sex workers during these observations. Using serial cross-sectional data, we conducted bivariate logistic regression analyses to assess preintervention to postintervention changes, both within and across cities, in adherence to the

intervention and the ability of establishments to achieve the goal of no STIs. Our serial cross-sectional data were collected at the level of the clinic and the sex establishment, and hence no sociodemographic data were available to use as controls in these analyses.

Multivariate logistic regression analyses were conducted among sex workers participating in the posttest survey to assess the relationship between exposure and adherence to the intervention and consistent condom use with all sex partners in the past month and prevalence of STIs; only variables found to be significant in the bivariate analyses were included in these multivariate analyses. Standard errors from all of the regression analyses were adjusted for potential clustering, or nonindependence of study outcomes, among women from the same sex establishment via the Huber–White robust variance

estimator.[24] Regression analyses were limited to cases involving no missing data.

The original sample size calculation was based on our ability to detect significant (i.e., odds ratio [OR] of 2.0) preintervention to postintervention changes in participating establishments' adherence to the intervention, including establishment-level decreases in STI prevalence observed in routine monthly screenings across cities, with 80% power and 95% confidence. Calculating our power to test preintervention–postintervention changes in individual-level HIV- and STI-related outcomes among our feasibility-based samples, we found that we had approximately 80% power to detect an odds ratio of 2.5 or greater with 95% confidence in the case of within-city analyses.

TABLE 1– Sociodemographic and Behavioral Characteristics of Female Sex Workers, Preintervention and Postintervention, by Site: Dominican Republic, 1999–2000

	Santo Domingo			Puerto Plata		
	Preintervention (n = 210), %-	Postintervention (n = 206), %-	P	Preintervention (n = 200), %-	Postintervention (n = 200), %-	P
Age, y			.916			.607
18–25	60.8	61.3		54.0	56.6	
≥ 26	39.2	38.7		46.0	43.4	
Education, y			.167			.008
0–8	69.0	62.6		73.0	83.9	
≥ 9	31.0	37.4		27.0	16.1	
Civil status			.006			.562
Single	72.1	59.0		71.5	68.8	
Married	27.9	41.0		28.5	31.2	
Regular partner			.104			.004
Yes	68.6	75.7		64.0	77.3	
No	31.4	24.3		36.0	22.7	
No. of client dates in past week			.880			.022
< 2	56.5	55.7		44.7	33.5	
≥ 2	43.5	44.3		55.3	66.5	
Total no. of sexual partners in past month			.0001			.040
< 3	75.1	48.8		50.3	40.0	
≥ 3	24.9	51.2		49.7	60.0	
Average fee per client date, US $			.685		67.8	.423
0–18	57.1	59.1		71.5		
≥ 19	42.9	40.9		28.5	32.2	

RESULTS

Characteristics of the Sample

The majority of the female sex workers participating in the study were younger than 26 years (Table 1). Most did not have any secondary school education (i.e., more than 8 years of schooling). While most participants reported being single in terms of their civil status, nearly two thirds, from both cities and at both preintervention and postintervention, reported having a regular sexual partner. Median numbers of dates with paying clients in the past week were relatively low, 1.0 in Santo Domingo and 2.0 in Puerto Plata at baseline. Participants from both cities charged a median average amount per client date of US$18 at baseline. Sample sociodemographic characteristics that differed significantly from preintervention to postintervention included civil status and number of sexual partners in the past month in Santo Domingo and education level, reports of a regular partner, and number of sexual partners in the past month in Puerto Plata.

Changes in HIV/STI Risk

Consistent condom use. As can be seen in Table 2, reported consistent condom use with new clients in the past month increased significantly in preintervention to postintervention adjusted analyses in Santo Domingo, from 75.3% to 93.8% (OR=4.21; 95% confidence interval [CI]=1.55, 11.43). The rate of consistent condom use with new clients was already quite high in Puerto Plata at the start of the study, at 96.5%, and the rate increased to 98.6% at postintervention (OR=2.27; 95% CI=0.47, 10.84). In the case of regular paying and nonpaying partners, the rate of consistent condom use rose significantly in Puerto Plata only, from 13.0% to 28.8% (OR=2.97; 95% CI=1.33, 6.66).

Rejection of unsafe sex. Sex workers' observed verbal rejection of unsafe commercial sex increased significantly from preintervention to postintervention in Puerto Plata only. The percentage of sex workers who rejected unsafe sex after hearing all 4 reasons offered increased from 50.0% to 79.4% (OR=3.86; 95% CI=1.96, 7.58).

STIs. In adjusted preintervention–postintervention analyses, significant decreases in the percentage of women with 1 or more STIs (gonorrhea, trichomoniasis, or chlamydia) were documented in Puerto Plata only (28.8% to 16.3%; OR = 0.50; 95% CI = 0.32, 0.78). STI prevalence decreased from 25.5% to 15.9% in Santo Domingo from preintervention to postintervention, but this decrease was not significant in adjusted analyses (OR = 0.60; 95% CI = 0.35, 1.03).

Table 3 shows the percentages of participating establishments per city that achieved the goal of no STIs among sex workers at 2-month intervals during the 1-year intervention period. We found significant increases in the ability of sex establishments to achieve this goal from preintervention to postintervention in Puerto Plata only (OR=1.17; 95% CI=1.12, 1.22). Examining the interaction between city and time, we found that there was a significant city-specific difference (greater in Puerto Plata) in the odds of establishments achieving the goal of no STIs at preintervention versus postintervention (OR=1.20; 95% CI=1.09, 1.31).

TABLE 2— Changes in Condom Use Behaviors and Sexually Transmitted Infections Among Female Sex Workers, Preintervention and Postintervention, by Site: Dominican Republic, 1999–2000

	Santo Domingo			Puerto Plata		
	Preintervention, %	Postintervention, %	Adjusted OR (95% CI)	Preintervention, %	Postintervention, %	Adjusted OR (95% CI)
Reported condom use per partner type						
New clients	75.3	93.8	4.21** (1.55, 11.43)	96.5	98.6	2.27 (0.47, 10.84)
Regular partners	14.6	17.6	1.29 (0.62, 2.70)	13.0	28.8	2.97** (1.33, 6.66)
Verbal ability to reject unsafe sex[a]						
Stated he did not like condoms	76.1	78.5	1.17 (0.57, 2.39)	79.7	94.1	4.08* (1.32, 12.60)
Stated he was a "serious guy"	71.6	76.9	1.35 (0.71, 2.58)	64.1	91.2	5.80*** (2.03, 16.57)
Offered 50% more money	67.2	73.8	1.42 (0.75, 2.64)	54.7	83.8	4.29*** (1.97, 9.35)
Offered 100% more money	64.2	72.3	1.49 (0.81, 2.73)	50.0	79.4	3.86*** (1.96, 7.58)
STI prevalence						
Gonorrhea	2.3	1.9	0.63 (0.17, 2.38)	6.6	3.9	0.59 (0.24, 1.46)
Trichomoniasis	9.1	6.1	0.58 (0.24, 1.38)	9.6	3.9	0.36** (0.17, 0.75)
Chlamydia	16.4	9.3	0.63 (0.34, 1.15)	14.6	9.8	0.70 (0.38, 1.28)
1 or more of 3 STIs	25.5	15.9	0.60 (0.35, 1.03)	28.8	16.3	0.50** (0.32, 0.78)

Note. OR = odds ratio; CI = confidence interval; STI = sexually transmitted infection. Sample sizes varied owing to missing data. Adjusted ORs controlled for significant variables shown in Table 1: education, civil status, regular partner, number of client dates, and number of sexual partners.
[a]Cumulative percentage at each level.
* P < .05; **P < .01; ***P < .001.

TABLE 3— Percentages of Participating Establishments Achieving the Goal of No Sexually Transmitted Infections During the 1-Year Intervention Period: Dominican Republic, 1999–2000 (n = 68)

	Establishments With No STIs at Preintervention, %-	Average of Months 1 and 2, % (Range)-	Average of Months 3 and 4, % (Range)-	Average of Months 5 and 6, % (Range)-	Average of Months 7 and 8, % (Range)-	Average of Months 9 and 10, % (Range)-	Average of Months 11 and 12, % (Range)-
Santo Domingo	6	47 (44–50)	29 (. . .)	25 (20–30)	6 (4–8)	21 (. . .)	29 (23–35)
Puerto Plata	25	46 (9–83)	8 (3–13)	75 (62–87)	55 (31–79)	69 (67–71)	65 (45–86)

Intervention effects on condom use and STI outcomes. Multivariate logistic regression analyses controlling for adherence to the intervention, city, civil status, and presence of a regular partner showed that participants who reported a high level of exposure to the intervention were significantly more likely than participants without such exposure to use condoms consistently with all sex partners in the past month (OR=1.90; 95% CI=1.12, 3.21). Participants working in establishments with higher adherence to the intervention were not significantly more likely to have used condoms with all sex partners in the past month after control for exposure to the intervention, city, civil status, and presence of a regular partner. Only observed adherence to the intervention was significantly associated with STI prevalence among postintervention participants in the bivariate analyses, and in turn it remained the only variable in the final regression model (OR=0.52; 95% CI=0.35, 0.78).

Individual reports of exposure to the intervention increased from preintervention to postintervention in both cities (both Ps=.000), while establishment-level adherence to the intervention increased in Puerto Plata only (OR=1.14; 95% CI=1.07, 1.21). Examining the interaction between city and time, we found that there was a significant city-specific difference in the odds of establishment adherence (greater in Puerto Plata) at preintervention versus postintervention (OR= 1.20; 95% CI=1.11, 1.30).

DISCUSSION

The majority of significant preintervention to postintervention changes in key study outcomes were documented in Puerto Plata, where an intervention model that combined the strengths of community solidarity and government policy was implemented. The only significant preintervention to postintervention changes documented in Santo Domingo involved condom use with new clients. In contrast, condom use rates in Puerto Plata increased significantly with regular paying as well as nonpaying partners. While the median number of client dates per week was found to be relatively low, our data indicate that the most common types of client in the present context were regular paying partners. Hence, the increase in condom use with regular partners documented in Puerto Plata takes on additional importance. Many programs have cited lower condom use rates among sex workers and their regular paying and nonpaying partners as a key HIV prevention challenge,[25–28] suggesting the global relevance of the changes observed in this study.

In addition to reported behavioral risk indicators such as condom use, our study also documented, in Puerto Plata but not in Santo Domingo, preintervention to postintervention changes in participants' observed verbal rejection of unsafe sex and STI outcomes. Here it is important to emphasize the scope of the changes that occurred. The preintervention to postintervention decline in individual-level STI prevalence in Puerto Plata was almost 43% (from 28.8% to 16.3%). While a similar trend was found in Santo Domingo, only in Puerto Plata did decreases in STI prevalence remain significant in multivariate analyses.

It is also important to highlight that the only significant predictor of STI prevalence at postintervention was establishment-level adherence to the intervention and that adherence increased significantly over the course of the intervention in Puerto Plata only. While adherence was significantly associated with STI prevalence at postintervention, it was not significantly related to consistent condom use with all types of partners in the past month after control for exposure to the intervention. This finding suggests the need for further research regarding the potential pathways by which the significant declines in individual-level STI outcomes documented in Puerto Plata were achieved.

Our study was originally powered to test the difference in preintervention to postintervention changes across cities for establishment-level STI outcomes only. Hence, we can definitively state that participating sex establishments in Puerto Plata were significantly more effective in achieving the goal of no STIs from preintervention to postintervention. In the case of our other study outcomes, we are able to document only within-city preintervention to postintervention effects. In addition, because of our study design, we cannot establish causality regarding exposure and adherence to the intervention and changes in individual-level study outcomes. However, it is noteworthy that the broad-based, significant changes that occurred in Puerto Plata were not paralleled in Santo Domingo, which indicates that an integrated approach mobilizing both communities and governments to confront HIV- and STI-related vulnerability in the context of female sex work merits further study and application.

About the Authors

Deanna Kerrigan, Clare Barrington, and Michael Sweat are

with the Johns Hopkins Bloomberg School of Public Health, Baltimore, Md. Luis Moreno and Santo Rosario are with the Centro de Orientación e Investigación Integral, Santo Domingo, Dominican Republic. Bayardo Gomez and Hector Jerez are with the Centro de Promoción y Solidaridad Humana, Puerto Plata, Dominican Republic. Ellen Weiss is with the International Center for Research on Women, Washington, DC.

Correspondence: Requests for reprints should be sent to Deanna Kerrigan, PhD, Johns Hopkins Bloomberg School of Public Health, 615 N Wolfe St, Room 5523A, Baltimore, MD 21205 (e-mail: dkerriga@jhsph.edu).

Acknowledgments

The research was supported by the Horizons Program of the Population Council under funding from the US Agency for International Development (USAID) (contract HRNA00970001200). Additional support was received from the AcciónSIDA Project of the Academy for Educational Development and the Fogarty International Center of the National Institutes of Health through a grant to Johns Hopkins University (2D43TW000010-18-AITRP). Finally, Deanna Kerrigan was supported by a Career Development Award (K01MH3491) from the National Institute of Mental Health during the analysis and write-up phase of the research.

We would like to thank all of the intervention and research participants and the entire staff of the Centro de Orientación e Investigación Integral (COIN) in Santo Domingo and the Centro de Promoción y Solidaridad Humana (CEPROSH) in Puerto Plata for their time, dedication, and insight during the entire study process. We would also like to thank Martha Butler de Lister, director of the National STD and AIDS Control Program at the time the study began, for her help in making this research a reality, as well as Jonathan Ellen of the Johns Hopkins School of Medicine for his input and suggestions during the analysis.

Note. Any opinions expressed are those of the authors and do not necessarily reflect the views of USAID.

Human Participant Protection

The research and informed consent protocols for this study were reviewed and approved by the institutional review boards of the Johns Hopkins Bloomberg School of Public Health and the Population Council.

Contributors

D. Kerrigan, L. Moreno, S. Rosario, B. Gomez, H. Jerez, E. Weiss, and M. Sweat worked together to conceptualize and design the study. L. Moreno, S. Rosario, B. Gomez, and H. Jerez oversaw the implementation of the intervention research. D. Kerrigan, C. Barrington, and M. Sweat analyzed the data collected, and all authors assisted in interpreting the data.

References

1. Laga M, Alary M, Nzila N, et al. Condom promotion, sexually transmitted diseases treatment, and declining incidence of HIV-1 infection in female Zairian sex workers. *Lancet.* 1994;344:246–248.
2. Bhave G, Lindan CP, Hudes ES, et al. Impact of an intervention on HIV, sexually transmitted diseases, and condom use among sex workers in Bombay, India. *AIDS.* 1995;9(suppl 1):S21–S30.
3. Ngugi EN, Wilson D, Sebstad J, Plummer FA, Moses S. Focused peer-mediated educational programs among female sex workers to reduce sexually transmitted disease and human immunodeficiency virus transmission in Kenya and Zimbabwe. *J Infect Dis.* 1996;174 (suppl 2):S240–S247.
4. Ford K, Wirawan DN, Fajans P, Meliawan P, MacDonald K, Thorpe L. Behavioral interventions for reduction of sexually transmitted disease/HIV transmission among female commercial sex workers and clients in Bali, Indonesia. *AIDS.* 1996;10:213–222.
5. Sweat M, Denison J. Reducing HIV incidence in developing countries with structural and environmental interventions. *AIDS.* 1995;9(suppl A):S251–S257.
6. Sumartojo E, ed. Structural factors and HIV prevention. *AIDS.*

2000;14(suppl 1):S3–S10.
7. Bandopadhyay N, Ray K, Banerjee A, et al. Operationalizing an effective community development intervention for reducing HIV vulnerability in female sex work: lessons learned from the Sonagachi project in Kolkata, India. In: Programs and abstracts of the International Conference on AIDS, July 2002, Barcelona, Spain. Abstract ThOrF1478.
8. Jana S, Bandyopadhyay N, Mukherjee S, Dutta N, Basu I, Saha A. STD/HIV intervention with sex workers in West Bengal, India. *AIDS.* 1998;12(suppl B): S101–S108.
9. Jana S, Singh S. Beyond medical model of STD intervention—lessons from Sonagachi. *Indian J Public Health.* 1995;39:125–131.
10. Hanenberg RS, Rojanapithayakorn W, Kunasol P, Sokal DC. Impact of Thailand's HIV-control programme as indicated by the decline of sexually transmitted diseases. *Lancet.* 1994;344:243–245.
11. Rojanapithayakorn W, Hanenberg R. The 100% condom program in Thailand. *AIDS.* 1996;10:1–7.
12. Dias PR, Longo P, Torres H, Szterenfeld C, Castle C, Kerrigan D. Beyond health promotion: the role of community capacity building and social inclusion in reducing HIV vulnerability among Brazilian female sex workers. In: Programs and abstracts of the International Conference on AIDS, July 2002, Barcelona, Spain. Abstract ThPeD7672.
13. Williams EE. Women of courage: commercial sex workers mobilize for HIV/AIDS prevention in Nigeria. *Aidscaptions.* 1994;1:19–22.
14. Williams E, Lamson N, Efem S, Weir S, Lamptey P. Implementation of an AIDS prevention program among prostitutes in the Cross River State of Nigeria. *AIDS.* 1992;6:229–230.
15. *Strategic Plan for the Promotion of the 100% Condom Use Programming, Asia, 2000–2003.* Geneva, Switzerland: Joint United Nations Programme on HIV/AIDS; 2000.
16. Morisky DE, Pena M, Tiglao TV, Liu KY. The impact of the work environment on condom use among female bar workers in the Philippines. *Health Educ Behav.* 2002;29:461–472.
17. Morisky DE, Tiglao TV, Sneed CD, et al. The effects of establishment practices, knowledge and attitudes on condom use among Filipina sex workers. *AIDS Care.* 1998;10:213–220.

18. Tiglao TV, Morisky DE, Tempongko SB, Baltazar JC, Detels R. A community PAR approach to HIV/AIDS prevention among sex workers. *Promotion Educ.* 1996; 3:25–28.

19. Moreno L, Kerrigan D. The evolution of HIV prevention strategies among female sex workers in the Dominican Republic. *Res Sex Work.* 2000;3:8–10.

20. Kerrigan D, Moreno L, Rosario S, Sweat M. Adapting the Thai 100% condom programme: developing a culturally appropriate model for the Dominican Republic. *Cult Health Sexuality.* 2001;3:221–240.

21. Kerrigan D, Ellen J, Moreno L, et al. Environmental-structural factors significantly associated with consistent condom use among female sex workers in the Dominican Republic. *AIDS.* 2003;17:415–423.

22. Council for International Organizations of Medical Sciences. *International Ethical Guidelines for Biomedical Research Involving Human Subjects.* Geneva, Switzerland: World Health Organization; 2002.

23. *Manual para el Manejo Sindromico de las Enfermedades de Transmision Sexual para Tratantes.* Santo Domingo, Dominican Republic: AIDS Control and Prevention Project, Family Health International; 1995.

24. Rogers W. Regression standard errors in clustered samples. *Stata Tech Bull.* 1993;13:19–23.

25. Pickering H, Quigley M, Hayes RJ, Todd J, Wilkins A. Determinants of condom use in 24,000 prostitute/client contacts in The Gambia. *AIDS.* 1993;7:1093–1098.

26. Mgalla Z, Pool R. Sexual relationships, condom use and risk perception among female bar workers in northwest Tanzania. *AIDS Care.* 1997;9:407–416.

27. Morris M, Pramualratana A, Podhisita C, Wawer MJ. The relational determinants of condom use with commercial sex partners in Thailand. *AIDS.* 1995;9:507–515.

28. Walden VM, Mwangulube K, Makhumula-Nkhoma P. Measuring the impact of a behaviour change intervention for commercial sex workers and their potential clients in Malawi. *Health Educ Res.* 1999;14:545–554.

A Critical Analysis of the Brazilian Response to HIV/AIDS: Lessons Learned for Controlling and Mitigating the Epidemic in Developing Countries

| Alan Berkman, MD, Jonathan Garcia, BA, Miguel Muñoz-Laboy, DrPH, Vera Paiva, PhD and Richard Parker, PhD

ABSTRACT

The Brazilian National AIDS Program is widely recognized as the leading example of an integrated HIV/AIDS prevention, care, and treatment program in a developing country. We critically analyze the Brazilian experience, distinguishing those elements that are unique to Brazil from the programmatic and policy decisions that can aid the development of similar programs in other low- and middle-income and developing countries.

Among the critical issues that are discussed are human rights and solidarity, the interface of politics and public health, sexuality and culture, the integration of prevention and treatment, the transition from an epidemic rooted among men who have sex with men to one that increasingly affects women, and special prevention and treatment programs for injection drug users.

INTRODUCTION

For those concerned about the HIV/AIDS pandemic, we are living through the best of times and the worse of times. Since the 13th International AIDS Conference in Durban, South Africa, there has been growing international attention to the scope and nature of the catastrophe, increased political will in a number of countries, and a substantial, albeit insufficient, increase in available resources. At the same time, the epidemic continues to grow, reversing decades of development in a number of African countries and promoting the very economic and social conditions that facilitate its spread to yet another generation of young people.

A consensus formed at the Durban Conference was that a strategic approach to the HIV epidemic must integrate prevention with care, treatment, and mitigation. This was an implicit rejection of the dominant international paradigm that poor and developing countries must focus only on prevention. Because the demand for treatment has become such a contentious topic, advocates, policy-makers, and researchers have focused special attention on Brazil's successful program for providing universal access to free antiretroviral therapy.[1,2]

Many national governments are now developing new, strategic AIDS plans that incorporate enhanced care and treatment for those infected with HIV. The challenge to develop such a program in the context of poorly developed health systems is profound, and there is an understandable and urgent need for direction. "Best practice" strategies have been one answer; however, while inspiring, they are often small-scale projects that focus on a single element of a comprehensive plan (treatment, care, prevention) with limited heuristic value for those charged with formulating an integrated national plan.[3] There is also a temptation to decontextualize such programs and mechanically transplant them to radically different settings. Yet, the need to learn from others' experiences so that mistakes can be minimized and scarce resources allocated correctly remains critical.

With this environment in mind, we present a critical analysis of the development of the Brazilian National AIDS Program (NAP), a widely recognized, leading example of the feasibility and effectiveness of an integrated approach to the epidemic in the setting of a middle-income country characterized by significant levels of social inequality. Even though United Nations indices of human development have consistently placed Brazil around 70th place, the impact of the Brazilian response to AIDS has been impressive: incidence rates of HIV are much lower than projected a decade ago, and mortality rates have fallen by 50% and inpatient hospitalization days by 70% to 80% over the past 7 years.[4] While implementation of this program required the commitment of significant resources, it is now estimated that by 2001 an investment of US $232 million resulted in a total savings of US $1.1 billion.[5]

We do not believe that the Brazilian NAP can serve as a "model" that can be uncritically implemented in other countries; in fact, the most basic lesson from the Brazilian experience may well be that there is no homogeneous HIV/AIDS epidemic nor a prepackaged approach to dealing with it. The way in which a nation responds to the social, political, economic, and human stress (and distress) caused by HIV/AIDS will be shaped by that country's unique history, culture, governmental institutions, and economic resources and the diverse social forces and institutions that get lumped together as "civil society." However, we believe there is value in looking at Brazil as a case study, briefly examining the unique Brazilian context and then focusing on specific policy decisions that may be helpful to those grappling with their own national realities.

THE BRAZILIAN CONTEXT

As a consequence of the deep inequalities and regional differences that exist in Brazilian society, the spread of HIV infection has been complex, characterized by a number of diverse patterns in different regions of the country.[6,7] In spite of regional differences, however, the Brazilian epidemic is currently characterized by 3 major, interrelated, epidemiological trends that are evident in all regions of the country, which are described by Brazilian researchers as (1) *heterosexualization*, (2) *feminization*, and (3) *pauperization*.[8,9]

Although the epidemic began in Brazil in the early 1980s primarily through sexual transmission between men, heterosexual transmission has gradually become the major mode of HIV infection (Figure 1).[6] Increased heterosexual transmission has resulted in substantial growth of HIV infection and AIDS cases among women, and the male-to-female ratio of reported cases has shifted from 23.5 to 1 in 1985 to 1.7 to 1 in 2002 (Figure 2).[6] When level of education is used as a proxy for socioeconomic status, the increasing proportion of cases among people with lower education levels indicates a trend of pauperization in the epidemic (Figure 3).[6] These patterns are important in revealing the key challenges that must still be overcome to control the epidemic.

Nonetheless, the effectiveness of Brazil's response to HIV/AIDS has been demonstrated through Brazil's historical epidemiological profile, with a clear trend toward the stabilization of the epidemic over time.[8] In 1990, the World Bank predicted that within 10 years there would be 1.2 million people infected with HIV in Brazil unless an effective, nationally based intervention was mounted.[2] Fourteen years later, this scenario has yet to materialize. On the contrary, an estimated 600 000 people in Brazil are

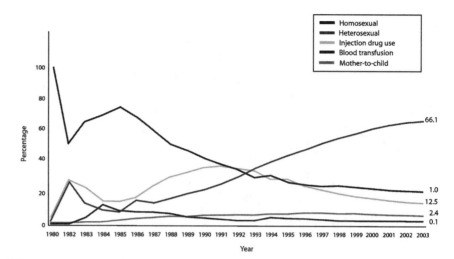
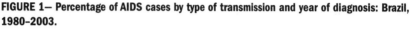

FIGURE 1— Percentage of AIDS cases by type of transmission and year of diagnosis: Brazil, 1980–2003.

Source. National AIDS Program, Brazilian Ministry of Health.
Note. Notified cases up to December 31, 2003.

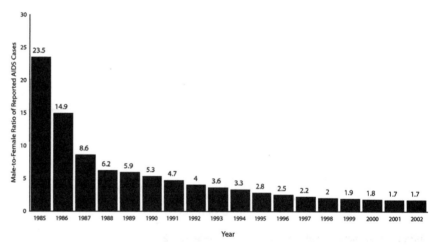

FIGURE 2— Gender ratio (male to female) of notified AIDS cases: Brazil, 1985–2002.

Source. National AIDS Program, Brazilian Ministry of Health.

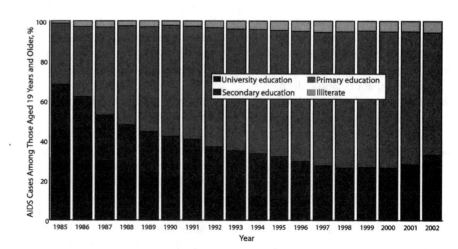
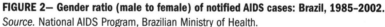

FIGURE 3— Percentage of AIDS cases among those aged 19 years and older, by level of education: Brazil, 1985–2002.

Source. National AIDS Program, Brazilian Ministry of Health.

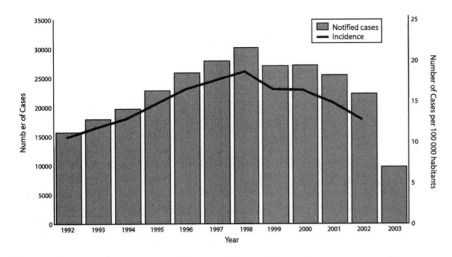

FIGURE 4— Number of AIDS cases and incidence rate, by year of diagnosis: Brazil, 1992–2003.

Source. National AIDS Program, Brazilian Ministry of Health.

Note. Notified cases up to December 31, 2003.

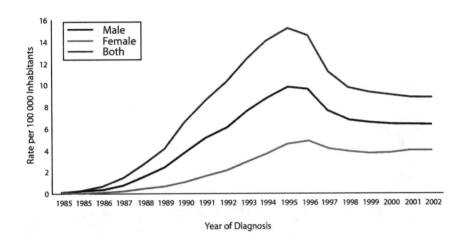

FIGURE 5— AIDS mortality rate, by gender: Brazil, 1984–2002.

Source. National AIDS Program, Brazilian Ministry of Health.

infected with HIV and 362 364 have AIDS.[6] Incidence rates of HIV infection are much lower than projected a decade ago (Figure 4), and mortality rates have fallen by roughly 50% (Figure 5). Inpatient hospitalization days have been significantly reduced, resulting in lower hospital expenses owing to the investment in treatment access.[1,2,4]

Aspects of the Brazilian response to HIV/AIDS have been described and analyzed by a number of the outstanding activists, social scientists, and public health officials who helped shape that response. There is widespread agreement among these analysts that the Brazilian mobilization against HIV must be viewed in the context of the larger social mobilization of Brazilians confronting the military dictatorship and demanding democracy and a return to civilian rule.[10–12]

Citizenship, Solidarity, and Social Mobilization

Two key concepts that underlay the social mobilization for democracy (and that would, in turn, prove to be central to the Brazilian response to HIV/AIDS) were "citizenship" and "solidarity." Citizenship defined the relationship between the Brazilian people and the state (through its democratic institutions); solidarity, and respect for human rights, defined the relationship among the people.[10,13,14]

In asserting their rights as citizens in the new constitution of 1988, Brazilians were demanding that the city, state, and national administrations enter into a dialog with civil society about the future of the country.[15–17] This redemocratization movement built political parties, trade unions, and nongovernmental organizations (NGOs) throughout the country in the 1980s, culminating in a demand for elections for a new and free Congress. Democratic elections were initially held only at the municipal and state levels. The negotiation and promulgation of the new "democratic" constitution, passed in 1988, included the reinstitution of free national elections as of 1990.

One strong player in this national mobilization for democracy was the "sanitary reform movement," a loose affiliation of health care workers, collective health academics,[18] trade unions, Catholic and Christian churches, and new political parties, who demanded a public health system responsive to and controlled by the public and who defended the right to health as a fundamental human right to be guaranteed by the constitution. The sanitary reform movement[19,20] was particularly strong in São Paulo state and city, and when opposition parties won the first state elections, members of that movement were appointed to senior positions in the health department. São Paulo was the epicenter of the AIDS epidemic, and the São Paulo State Health Department led the response to the emergence of the first reported cases of AIDS (in 1983). It later became the model for the National Unitary Health System, typically referred to by its acronym in Brazilian Portuguese, SUS (*Sistema Único de Saúde*).[12,21,22]

This mobilization process, in which many diverse social movements made up of Brazilian citizens came together in a common struggle for democracy, was the basis for a sense of social solidarity across many traditional societal divisions.[10] This should not be idealized or romanticized: Brazil was and is a nation with great disparities of wealth, a long history of social discrimination based on skin color, and oppressive gender relationships, all of which had (and continue to have) a longstanding negative impact on the health of the Brazilian population.[23,24] Despite these very real differences in power and prestige, however, social solidarity built up out of common suffering and the struggle for democracy and citizenship became a countervailing force to the stigma surrounding the emergence of HIV.[14,24,25]

What were the factors that effectively mitigated the worst aspects of the stigma surrounding both HIV and homosexuality? A critical number of gay men and human rights activists, as well as men and women infected or affected by HIV, openly confronted the stigma, demanding that the rights of people living with AIDS be respected by the government and by their fellow citizens. These developments were particularly important in São Paulo, where opposition to the military regime had been deeply rooted and where opposition political parties had come to power as soon as democratic elections had been restored. In 1983, in response to demands from gay activists, the São Paulo State Secretariat of Health founded the first governmental AIDS program in the country. In 1985, an alliance of gay men, human rights activists, and health professionals came together to form GAPA (the AIDS Prevention and Support Group), the first nongovernmental AIDS service organization, which became an important model for similar organizations in cities around the country.[25–28] Similarly, in Rio de Janeiro (like São Paulo, an important center for political opposition), researchers, health professionals, and activists came together to form ABIA (the Brazilian Interdisciplinary AIDS Association) in 1986, and the Grupo Pela Vidda (the Group for Life), the first self-identified HIV-positive advocacy group in the country, was founded in 1989.

Throughout the late 1980s and early 1990s, a vibrant rebirth of civil society[29] led to the formation of NGOs (described in Brazil as *ONGs/AIDS* or AIDS NGOs) in other key cities and states around the country. Working together with progressive state and municipal health departments, they would pressure the federal government to create a national AIDS program. These factors combined to create an early response to HIV that was based on solidarity and inclusion rather than stigma and exclusion, which in turn provided the foundation for the later development of the national response to AIDS, as discussed under the section heading "Culture."[13,24,25]

The political crisis of military rule that precipitated the social mobilization of large numbers of Brazilians cannot be artificially recreated in other countries. Yet there may be important lessons for other countries in the Brazilian experience. The issue of political leadership is often put forward as critical to an effective response to HIV. While that may be true in Uganda and certain other frequently cited examples, political leadership is not necessarily synonymous with governmental leadership. The situation in Brazil (and this is true of many other countries) was that leadership emerged from civil society.[13] This is not to downplay the critical role of government in confronting HIV; it was the sometimes tense dialog between civil society and the government in Brazil that resulted in an effective national response. One only has to examine the painful situation in South Africa over the past several years to understand the impact of a government that is unresponsive or too slow to answer and collaborate with civil society initiatives.[30,31]

Big State, Little State

Attempts to take lessons from the Brazilian experience and use them in developing national AIDS programs in sub-Saharan Africa must take into account the relative strength of the Brazilian public health care system. Its strength is not solely a function of Brazil's economic standing as a middle-income country; South Africa's per capita gross national product is also considered middle income by international standards. Brazil and South Africa share similarly high levels of economic polarization—both have a GINI Index of 59.[32] In Brazil, as in any other country, political decisions as well as economic resources shape the health care system.

The SUS has unquestionably been a qualitative advance in the history of public health in Brazil.[21] Its core principles of integrality (prevention and treatment), public accountability, and public funding distinguish it from early versions of governmental health systems and make it a proper vehicle for comprehensive management of HIV. While recognizing the unique aspects of the SUS, it is equally important to recognize that it emerged from a long tradition of advocacy for governmental responsibility for the health of the nation, albeit a tradition frequently marred by inefficiency, waste, and corruption.[22]

This social pact was challenged by the embrace of the macroeconomic policies of the International Monetary Fund and the World Bank as a solution to problems such as inflation and the debt crisis. These policies, often called "the Washington Consensus," encouraged foreign capital investment in finance and industry and prioritized fighting inflation through currency devaluation and restricted governmental expenditures on social services. Financing for the public health system was slashed, and the privatization of health services grew rapidly. It was in this context that the movement for redemocratization in Brazil made public health and the human right to health central demands on government (see the section "Health Care as a Human Right").[5,33]

South Africa and most other sub-Saharan African countries have a much different political history. The progressive colonization of the continent by European powers was formalized in 1885. Colonial governments were primarily charged with maximizing extraction of raw materials and profits for the colonizing country; health care was largely limited to those interventions necessary to control epidemics that might affect Europeans and to do the minimum necessary to maintain a stable work force. This policy resulted in a stunted public health care system centered in large cities with the greatest European populations, and a health system for African workers in the extractive industries that was under the control of mining companies. Colonial governments (with the exception of some coastal West African countries) reserved administrative and professional positions in the health care system for Europeans and limited access to higher education for Africans. Perhaps the most extreme, but not unrepresentative, example was the Belgian Congo, which had a total of 8 university graduates at the time of independence in 1960.

Political decolonization in most of Africa occurred during the period 1960 to 1970 and was often accompanied by the emigration of the European administrators and physicians responsible for the health care system. A number of newly independent countries made attempts to develop primary health care systems in the decade after independence, but such efforts were often handicapped by insufficient funds and human resources. In other countries, the functions of the state apparatus were never reoriented to serve the needs of the citizenry.[34–36]

Attempts to strengthen public health systems during this period met strong opposition from the International Monetary Fund and the World Bank. Rather than promote public health, structural adjustment programs forced governments to cut spending on health care and institute users' fees in the public system. To make a reasonable salary, professionals in the public health system often sought work in the private health care system. The weak health systems that now plague efforts to control HIV in sub-Saharan Africa must be seen as the product of both colonial history and the "small government" model promoted by the Washington consensus.[33,37]

The AIDS epidemic may force African governments to make public health a priority. African heads of state meeting in Abuja, Nigeria, in 2001 pledged to increase spending on health to 15% of their national budgets. Not one has yet achieved that goal. Correspondingly, promises by the United States and its major European allies to eliminate debt repayment and increase development aid to 0.7% of gross national product have not been implemented.[38]

The lesson that one can reasonably draw from the Brazilian experience is that governments must acknowledge that health care is as much a central responsibility as national defense and that international agencies cannot merely lament weak health care systems but should take steps to change those macroeconomic policies that hamstring governmental efforts to strengthen those systems.

Health Care as a Human Right

Health care is recognized in the Brazilian constitution as a fundamental right of all citizens and a fundamental responsibility of the government. This status as a fundamental right creates an obligation on the part of the government to take all reasonable steps to actualize that right.

The Brazilian constitution created both a moral and a legal basis for the demand for comprehensive treatment for people living with HIV/AIDS (PLWHA). However, it must be recognized that, at least until the mid-1990s, the government itself rarely took the initiative to expand services for PLWHA.[26] AIDS advocacy groups developed legal aid programs and brought a series of successful class action suits focused on specific programmatic issues (e.g., free viral-resistance testing, an expanded drug formulary) that have operationalized the constitutional right to health. These law suits, in turn, created a public venue where PLWHA can assert their rights as Brazilian citizens and function as protagonists in their own struggle for life.[29,39]

Many countries recognize health care as a human right, but in relatively few instances have legal strategies been as fruitful as in Brazil. The Treatment Action Campaign and the AIDS Law Project in South Africa have pursued a similar strategy in the South African courts with some success. Within Latin America and the Caribbean, a number of organizations representing PLWHA have demanded antiretroviral treatment in suits filed against their respective governments before the InterAmerican Court of Human Rights. This court has ruled in favor of the plaintiffs, but it has no direct authority to force governments to comply with its orders.[40] What seems to distinguish the Brazilian situation from that of many other countries is that the Brazilian government acts in a timely and appropriate manner to implement court rulings.

Health care as a fundamental right has been operationalized in the SUS. The SUS was founded on and developed from 4 key principles: (1) universal access, (2) integral care, (3) social control, and (4) public funding.

Integral care was a core concept of the sanitary reform movement in Brazil before the debate about the need for linking treatment and prevention emerged within the international AIDS movement.[41] Integrality recognizes that the governmental responsibility to health is not limited to the basic prevention measures (e.g., vaccines) found in maternal and child health programs. It asserts that prevention must be integrated with care and treatment. The right to health extends to those already ill and in need of treatment, and there is recognition that having people access the health system will improve the whole range of public health initiatives. Integrality also is based on a commitment to the human rights of those afflicted: a prevention-only approach to health violates those rights and the dignity of those in need of care, devalues their lives, and adds to the stigma that may accompany illness.[42,43] This lesson was learned during the development of a plan for Hansen's disease (leprosy) in São Paulo years before the first case of AIDS in Brazil.[12]

Social control refers to the direct role that civil society plays in setting the priorities for the SUS. Public health councils with elected community representatives exist at all levels of the SUS: municipal, state, and federal.[44] Planning is the responsibility of the federal and state levels, while implementation is done through the municipalities. Over 120 000 people serve on these health councils, setting local programmatic and budgetary priorities within the overall national health plan.

Every 4 years, there is a structured debate at the local and state levels about national health planning; the SUS uses input from this debate to present a plan to a national health conference. This system of *controle social* or "social control" (as it is described by health activists and government officials alike) is still in the process of being constructed and can still be vulnerable to changing political priorities, as was the case during the Collor government in the early 1990s. Nonetheless, this process has been extended steadily over the course of the past decade, and it starkly contrasts with the bureaucratic nature of public health in many other countries.[15] Involvement of PLWHA and other sectors of society is still contentious or only given lip service in many countries; however, such involvement existed in the state of São Paulo and in other regions of Brazil from the very beginning of the AIDS epidemic, eventually becoming the model for the NAP and the proactive response to HIV/AIDS within the SUS.

Centralization vs Decentralization

The balance between centralized functions such as planning, standards, and budgeting, and decentralized functions, primarily implementation, is a problem all national health systems confront. In most countries, the ministry of health initiates programs, issuing directives to state or provincial health departments responsible for regional planning. These regional ministries then direct local health departments to implement the programs. Financing, unfortunately, often does not follow the same direction as the directives.

The SUS and, particularly, the NAP have a different dynamic. As discussed in the section "Health Care as a Human Right," members of the sanitary reform movement were appointed to a number of large municipal and state health departments in the late 1970s and began to reorganize public health along democratic principles. Dialog, responsiveness, and cooperation characterized the relationship between the health department and civil society groups. In 1983, when the first cases of AIDS were reported in São Paulo, the Brazilian government's response to demands from gay rights groups was rapid and positive, and strong links were forged between the health department and NGOs.[13,20] The program that emerged combined prevention, treatment, surveillance, and support for human rights. While treatment and surveillance remained governmental functions, NGOs increasingly took the lead in the prevention of HIV and the promotion of human rights. The São Paulo AIDS program became the model for other states and ultimately helped shape the NAP.[13]

The Brazilian response to AIDS thus emerged from the bottom up. It has been characterized by an active collaboration between government and NGOs, as well as by mobilization of activist political support and commitment within the machinery of the state itself, particularly on the part of local service providers in the public health system. While the dynamic between centralization and decentralization within the NAP has fluctuated over time, there remains room for local initiatives, and the alliance with NGOs remains strong.

Equally important, through a succession of different presidential administrations, is that the Brazilian AIDS Program has managed to sustain a consistent commitment to strengthening previously marginalized communities, to defending their rights, and to articulating respect for diversity as a key component of official government policy. Organizations representing sex workers; drug users; gay and lesbian, bisexual, and transgender populations; PLWHA; and other groups affected by the epidemic have received significant funding from the government.[25] Support has been provided for more than a decade now for legal aid work carried out by NGOs working on behalf of PLWHA.[29] Projects have been funded for lesbian organizations, independent of the relatively low epidemiological risk of HIV infection in this population, precisely because strengthening sexual rights has been understood as central to a broader effective response to the epidemic. Even the annual Gay Pride Parade in São Paulo, which has grown in recent years to draw up to 1 million people from all over the country, has received regular financial support from the Brazilian Ministry of Health. In short, the battle against stigma and discrimination has been understood as central to the response to HIV and AIDS, and it has been waged consistently through the development of partnerships between government and civil society.[45]

The experience in most other countries differs from that of Brazil. Centralization is dominant in most health ministries, and it is not uncommon for regional and municipal departments to be responsible for implementing programs without receiving funding to deliver the services. It is less common for governments to welcome the input and involvement of NGOs, although a nominal NGO presence is required by almost all international funding agencies. Even fewer governments accept their responsibility to promote and defend the human rights of PLWHA; on the contrary, governments often contribute to civil and human rights abuses through criminalization of risk behaviors (sodomy laws, drug laws, prostitution) and punitive policies toward PLWHA in prisons.

Culture

The commitment to human rights and the early emphasis placed on solidarity as central to the response to HIV/AIDS in Brazil, while articulated as a response to the military authoritarian regime and social inequality, also is clearly deeply rooted in a longstanding emphasis on solidarity in Brazilian culture. Principles of solidarity and reciprocity have long been understood as central to the moral economy of the poor in Brazilian society.[46] Solidarity among family members and neighbors is a key element of the survival strategies traditionally employed by poor people with little access to services and social welfare benefits in Brazil. These same principles have been extremely important to critical societal institutions, such as the Catholic Church and the Brazilian state apparatus.[47,48] This same principle of solidarity has clearly resonated in response to the plight of PLWHA.

Just as moral principles of solidarity in Brazilian culture have been central to the foundation of a national response to HIV and AIDS, sexuality and sexual expression are also an integral part of Brazilian culture and have facilitated the development of an effective response to the epidemic.[10,45,49] Certainly there is more than 1 discourse about sexuality in Brazil—some sectors of the religious community may make moral judgments, just as some in the medical professions may reduce sexuality to decontextualized risk behaviors—but there is a capacity for HIV prevention programs to address sexuality more openly than in most other countries.[14] It is notable that condom sales and distribution have risen dramatically in the general population, and there are data that suggest that condom use among HIV-positive people has increased as well.[50] Openness about sexuality and the diversity of gender and sexual identities have helped to break down the stigma surrounding both homosexuality and HIV.

Nowhere is the importance of sexual culture in Brazil as clear as in the ways in which prevention programs have been able to address sexuality, focusing on condom promotion while also combating stigma and discrimination. The public service announcements sponsored by the NAP have been among the most explicit of any governmental information campaign in the world. Condom use has been promoted relentlessly, female as well as male condoms have been widely distributed by the Brazilian government, and studies of sexual behavior have demonstrated significant increases in

the adoption of condom use across population groups (especially among young people).[50] Public information campaigns also have focused on the need to combat stigma and support sexual diversity, with 1 recent campaign focusing on the need for parents to accept and support children who are homosexual. These mass media approaches have been accompanied by significant levels of government support for community-based prevention programs among men who have sex with men, sex workers, young people, and other populations perceived to be at elevated risk of HIV infection.

Just as Brazil has confronted the international community around issues of treatment access, it has also resisted international pressure with regard to prevention programs. While the Brazilian NAP has acknowledged that reducing the number of sexual partners can decrease an individual's risk of infection, it has also recognized that many people, especially women, are not always able to control the multiple relations of their primary partners. The NAP has therefore been firm in putting condom use at the center of its program.[51] This position has caused tension with some international agencies, such as USAID, which came close to closing its AIDS prevention activities in Brazil because of the Brazilian refusal to adopt USAID's "ABC" (Abstinence, Be faithful, Condoms) prevention strategy, a strategy that explicitly prioritizes both abstinence and fidelity over and above an emphasis on promoting condom use.[52–54]

Culture cannot be reduced to "best practices" and transferred from one social reality to another. In many countries, AIDS prevention efforts have been blocked by societal and governmental leaders claiming that discussion of sexuality is antithetical to traditional culture. This position assumes that culture is static, unresponsive to changing conditions or focused intervention. The Brazilian experience, as well as that of Uganda, Senegal, and a number of other countries, disproves that generalization.[55,56]

Harm Reduction

Finally, building on many of the same principles discussed earlier, Brazil's response to injection drug users provides another key example of the important ways in which the government's approach has differed from the responses of other governments and yet has still achieved positive results. Injection drug use was limited in Brazil prior to the 1980s; however, as international drug control efforts in the highland Andean region intensified over the course of that decade, Brazil's largely uncontrolled border became an attractive route for drug trafficking. Subsequently, rates of HIV infection linked to injection drug use began to rise. By the mid-1990s, almost 30% of HIV infections in the country were estimated to be the result of needle sharing and related sexual transmission.[57]

In Brazil, as elsewhere, the initial response of the public health system was constrained by criminal justice authorities who sought to interpret the issue as the province of the justice system rather than the public health system. Early attempts to implement needle exchange programs in the city of Santos and the state of São Paulo were met with extreme resistance, including threats to imprison public health officials promoting needle exchange programs. By the early 1990s, however, a process of negotiation had begun that involved representatives of the Ministry of Health and the Ministry of Justice, with behind-the-scenes support from a number of United Nations agencies. The result was the establishment of a task force to develop a national policy to respond to HIV and injection drug use. As part of the more general program of prevention initiatives developed for support from the World Bank, a set of pilot needle exchange and harm reduction programs were established and implemented in key cities across the country.[1]

In 1998, the state of São Paulo passed legislation authorizing the health department to buy and distribute sterile needles and syringes. The success of this publicly sponsored program led to similar legislation in other states, culminating in modifications to the Brazilian Law on Drugs that authorized the Ministry of Health to implement national harm reduction programs. Input from injection drug users has helped shape these programs. Whether as a direct result of these policies and programs or not, the percentage of AIDS cases linked to injection drug use had declined to 11% in 2003.[6]

It was a longer and more difficult process to build a public and governmental consensus that drug use should be addressed as a public health rather than criminal justice problem. As with other aspects of the NAP, certain themes and processes underlie that change: local initiatives at the municipal and state levels shaped the national program, a strong emphasis on human rights was the context for reaching out to an extremely marginalized population, free and universal HIV treatment was an incentive for injection drug users to access and stay in care, and active input from the target group itself helped create an effective program.[1]

PROGRAMMATIC LESSONS

While national and local context will fundamentally shape a country's response to its AIDS epidemic, there are programmatic elements that public health planners must address in all countries. A critical analysis of the Brazilian approach, both its strengths and weaknesses, may give insights helpful to others.

Prevention

The SUS, for all its accomplishments, has not been the primary vehicle for HIV prevention efforts in Brazil. From the earliest days of the epidemic, civil society organizations (CSOs), in alliance with local governmental AIDS programs, have led the development and implementation of most prevention programs. The national government was slow to respond throughout the 1980s, and CSOs, primarily the newly formed AIDS NGOs, emerged as the most vocal and active critics of the federal government's HIV policies. It was only as redemocratiza-tion proceeded and key personnel from some of the progressive state and municipal public health departments were brought into the Federal Health Ministry that collaborations at the national level developed.[58] The lessons from the local initiatives based on nondiscrimination and solidarity began to shape the NAP.[13]

Perhaps the most crucial development in HIV control efforts in Brazil emerged from the prolonged (1992–1994) negotiation between Brazil and the World Bank over the terms of a large loan to help finance its response to the HIV epidemic. The successful negotiation of the US $160 million loan required active collaboration across many governmental ministries, active participation of CSOs through the NAP, and support from a wide range of political parties; it also required US $90 million in matching funds from the Brazilian Treasury. (Throughout this process, Brazil refused to conform to the World Bank demands that it halt the free distribution of azidothymidine, or AZT, a program it had started several years before.) The total program of US $250 million over 5 years financed a large-scale control effort capable of a major impact throughout much of the country.[25,59]

There are important lessons to be drawn from the experience of the first World Bank loan, as well as 2 subsequent loans.

Broad-based political support. Key individuals in government committed to an aggressive response to HIV were politically adept enough to use the loan negotiation process to build support for the HIV control program across a wide range of governmental and nongovernmental sectors. Control of HIV became a national priority, even if implementation efforts largely remained within the Ministry of Health.

Adequate funding. A large-scale prevention program capable of a major impact on the epidemic requires equally large-scale funding. As in many other areas of AIDS programming, half-hearted and inadequately funded programs are destined to fail.

Human resources. Not only financial resources, but also human resources have been essential. There was a successful training program for human resources in and out of government, which had begun even before the World Bank loans but was intensified and expanded dramatically after the loans. There is an emphasis on health educators and a particular focus on peer educators, who serve as a natural link between the most vulnerable communities and the health system.

CSO involvement. CSOs were involved throughout the process and helped shape a prevention program that funded a wide range of NGO-led initiatives. While there is some concern that governmental funding of NGOs compromises their willingness and capacity to criticize the government, there is little question that it has made it possible to reach many of the most vulnerable people in Brazil.[43]

HIV control efforts in Brazil are decentralized and multifaceted, but there are some significant generalizations, both positive and negative, about the prevention program. For example, the mass media (press, radio, television) has played a positive role in control efforts. Generally, stigma and stereotyping have been avoided, and there is an openness about sexuality and condom use that is not present in many other countries. However, the prevention program has not succeeded in stopping increasing rates of HIV infection among the poorest strata of society, particularly poor women. HIV prevention programs have not yet been integrated into other aspects of women's health programs, such as family planning, treatment of sexually transmitted infections, and routine gynecological care. Programs for the prevention of mother-to-child transmission have inadequate coverage for pregnant women despite the availability of testing and treatment.[60] Perhaps most important, at least in terms of long-term sustainability, while the overall NAP addresses prevention, care, and treatment, the SUS has continued to view its primary responsibility as care and treatment. Prevention efforts have still not been fully integrated with care and treatment at the programmatic level in the SUS, and there is still not an effective interface between the SUS and the CSOs involved in prevention efforts.

Treatment

The Brazilian program of free, universal access to antiretroviral treatment has had a dramatic impact on morbidity and mortality from AIDS in Brazil and has gained considerable international recognition for its efforts. Since the Durban International AIDS Conference, the Brazilian government has offered free technical assistance to other countries developing similar programs. The following sections provide a few lessons that may be of value to other countries.

Integration of treatment and prevention. The integration of care and treatment was fundamental to the Brazilian program even before the development of effective antiretroviral treatment. When AZT became available in the late 1980s, the state of São Paulo made small quantities available at no cost. The promise of treatment gave an incentive for more at-risk individuals to be tested and gave doctors an incentive to report AIDS cases, thus improving surveillance and prevention programs. The success of the São Paulo free drug program led to its adoption by other states and ultimately by the federal government. While AZT monotherapy was of limited value, it did create the principle that PLWHA have the right to free treatment.[25,41]

Universal access. That Brazil's treatment program is free has received considerable attention, but less publicized is the fact that it is universal. Universal distribution, in contrast to free medication solely in the public health sector, created many more points of access to treatment and allowed more rapid scale-up. Quite intentionally, it also eliminated the financial incentive for such corrupt practices as theft from central supplies or resale of medication by individuals. Free and universal distribution became a proactive solution to the potential

development of a domestic black market for antiretrovirals.

Local manufacture. The Brazilian program of universal, free access is financially viable in large measure because of Brazil's capacity for local manufacture of pharmaceuticals. Local manufacture, particularly but not exclusively of generics, creates systemic downward pressure on patented drug prices and, importantly, avoids the currency fluctuations that make it extremely difficult for importing countries to project drug costs effectively. The domestic pharmaceutical manufacturing capacity strengthens the government's hand in its negotiations with the multinational pharmaceutical companies by enabling the government to issue a compulsory license if companies abuse their patent monopoly by pricing the drug out of the range of the Brazilian market.

Capacity to use complex therapies. The Brazilian program is proof that health care systems outside the wealthy countries can effectively use complex therapies such as anti-retroviral treatment. Although less tangible than the manufacture of generic drugs, using complex therapies is as important a lesson for other countries with weak health care systems. The Brazilian treatment program was initiated as a vertical program guided by the NAP with its own administration, staff, logistical systems, and budget. This has resulted in ongoing difficulties in creating horizontal linkages within the SUS, but realistically it was the only way to rapidly establish and scale up the program. One of the major challenges in the last 4 to 5 years has been to decentralize this program within the SUS and at the state and municipal levels—a challenge that is accentuated owing to the continental size of the country.[61]

Creating international alliances. The Brazilian government has acted proactively and strategically to protect the NAP from international pressures. As mentioned previously, Brazil firmly resisted World Bank demands that it drop its free distribution of AZT as a condition of the first loan agreement; it subsequently resisted threats from the

United States to challenge Brazil's generic manufacture of some antiretrovirals before the World Trade Organization. The NAP has also resisted pressure to change its open approach to the prevention of sexual transmission. Brazil has allied itself with other developing and poor countries to create a global consensus more favorable to health initiatives; these countries have led efforts to challenge the restrictive interpretation of the TRIPS (Trade Related Aspects of Intellectual Property) agreement, succeeded in having the United Nations Human Rights Commission declare access to treatment part of the human right to health, and helped forge a bloc of nations that made the right to treatment a prominent part of the Consensus Statement from the UN General Assembly Special Session on AIDS.

Like Brazil's prevention record, Brazil's success in integrating care and treatment into a unified approach to the control and mitigation of the HIV/AIDS epidemic is thus impressive. No one, not even the greatest supporters of the Brazilian program, would suggest that these achievements have come easily or that there is not still much important work to be done to strengthen existing programs and to ensure their sustainability over time. Political tensions that sometimes threaten to disrupt service provision are still all too common, particularly when different political parties or factions control municipal, state, and national health programs in Brazil's federalist system of government.[24] Logistics in relation to the distribution of medications is still often uneven, sometimes requiring aggressive interventions on the part of CSOs as well as the NAP.[58] At least thus far, however, these challenges have been met with consistent success, in large part through partnership and collaboration between the Brazilian government and civil society. Brazil's response to HIV and AIDS at every level has increasingly emerged as a model program that other health programs in Brazil seek to emulate and that other countries look to for inspiration as they seek to develop their own unique responses to the challenges posed by the epidemic.

Conclusions

Controlling the HIV/AIDS pandemic will likely be the greatest challenge to public health in the 21st century. HIV is a minuscule bit of RNA, but this viral event causes a profoundly human phenomenon. Modifying intimate experiences, changing established social relationships, and challenging global inequalities are all part of the response to HIV.

Brazil has done all of these things with some success; insights into the process can hopefully be of some value to all of us grappling with these concerns. There is a final lesson from Brazil that is worthy of notice: the NAP has become a source of national pride for the Brazilian people. It is "owned" by the government, civil society, the media, and, most importantly, people living with HIV. Solidarity and pride, it seems, may be the most effective counter to stigma. To control HIV, we must first admit that the problem belongs to all of us.

Acknowledgments

This article draws on data collected with support from the National Science Foundation (grant 1025–0440; principal investigator, R. Parker) and analyses developed with support from the Ford Foundation (grant BCS-9910339; principal investigator, R. Parker). Additional support for writing and analysis was provided through the International Core of the HIV Center for Clinical and Behavioral Studies at the New York State Psychiatric Institute and Columbia University (supported by center grant P30 MH43520 from the National Institute of Mental Health; principal investigator and center director, A. A. Ehrhardt; international core director, R. Parker).

About the Authors

The authors are with the Department of Sociomedical Sciences and the Center for Gender, Sexuality and Health, Mailman School of Public Health, Columbia University, and the International Core of the HIV Center for Clinical and Behavioral Studies, New York State Psychiatric Institute and Columbia University, New York, NY. Alan Berkman is also with the Department of Epidemiology, Mailman School of Public Health, Columbia University. Vera Paiva is also with NEPAIDS, the Nucleus for AIDS Prevention Studies, Institute of Psychology, University of São Paulo, São Paulo, Brazil. Vera Paiva and Richard Parker are also with the Brazilian Interdisciplinary AIDS Association, Rio de Janeiro, Brazil.

Correspondence: *Requests for reprints should be sent to Richard Parker, PhD, Department of Sociomedical Sciences, Mailman School of Public Health, Columbia University, 600 West 168th St, New York, NY 10032 (e-mail: rgp11@columbia.edu).*

Contributors

A. Berkman and R. Parker developed the initial draft of this article. All other authors helped to further refine the ideas and contributed to drafts of the article.

Accepted for publication January 3, 2005.

References

1. National Coordination for STD and AIDS. *The Brazilian Response to HIV/AIDS.* Brasília, Brazil: Ministry of Health; 2000.
2. Parker R, Passarrelli CA, Terto V, Pimenta C, Berkman A, Muñoz-Laboy M. The Brazilian response to HIV/AIDS: assessing its transferability. *Divulgação em Saúde para Debate.* 2003;27:140–142.
3. Ministry of Health of Brazil, National Coordination for STD and AIDS. Drugs and AIDS. *The Brazilian Response to HIV/AIDS: Best Practices.* Brasilia, Brazil: Ministry of Health; 2000:116–130.
4. World Health Organization. The World Health Report 2004: changing history. Available at: http://www.who.int/whr/2004/en/report04_en.pdf. Accessed October 7, 2004.
5. Antonio de Ávila VitóriaM. The experience of providing universal access to ARV drugs in Brazil. *Divulgação em Saúde para Debate.* 2003;27:247–264.
6. Coordenação Nacional de DST/AIDS. *Boletim Epidemiológico AIDS,* Ano XVIII. No. 01–01a–26a semanas epidemiológicas. Brasília, Brazil: Ministério da Saúde; January–June 2004.
7. *Epidemiological Fact Sheets on HIV/AIDS and Sexually-Transmitted Infections, 2004, Update: Brazil.* Geneva, Switzerland: Joint United Nations Programme on HIV/AIDS; 2004.
8. Barreira D. *Números e Tendências Atuais da Epidemia do HIV e AIDS.* Brasília, Brazil: Ministério da Saúde; July 2004.
9. Parker R, Rochel de Camargo K Jr. Pobreza e HIV/AIDS: aspectos antropológicos e sociológicos. *Cadernos de Saúde Pública.* 2000;16(suppl 1):89–102.
10. Daniel H, Parker R. *Sexuality, Politics and AIDS in Brazil: In Another World?* London, England: Falmer Press; 1993.
11. Parker R. Introdução. In: Parker R, ed. *Políticas, Instituições e AIDS: Enfrentando a Epidemia no Brasil.* Rio de Janeiro, Brazil: ABIA; 1997:7–15.
12. Teixeira PR. Políticas públicas em AIDS. In: Parker R, ed. *Políticas, Instituições e AIDS: Enfrentando a Epidemia no Brasil.* Rio de Janeiro, Brazil: ABIA; 1997:43–68.
13. Galvão J. AIDS e activismo: o surgimento e a construção de novas formas de solidariedade. In: Parker R, Bastos C, Galvão J, Stalin Pedrosa J, eds. *A AIDS No Brasil.* Rio de Janeiro, Brazil: ABIA; 1994:341–350.
14. Paiva V. Beyond magic solutions: prevention of HIV and AIDS as a process of psychosocial emancipation. *Divulgação em Saúde para Debate.* 2003;27: 192–2003.
15. Weyland K. Social movements and the state: the politics of health reform in Brazil. *World Dev.* 1995; 23(10):1699–1712.
16. Weyland K. Obstacles to social reform in Brazil's new democracy. *Comp Polit.* 1996;29(1):1–22.
17. Weyland K. The Brazilian state in the new democracy. *J Interamerican Stud World Aff.* 1997;39(4): 63–94.
18. Waitzkin H, Iriart C, Estrada A, Lamadrid S. Social medicine in Latin America: productivity and dangers facing the major national groups. *Lancet.* 2001; 358:315–323.
19. Paiva V, Ayres JR, Buchalla CM, Hearst N. Building partnerships to respond to HIV/AIDS. *AIDS.* 2002;16(suppl 3):76–83.
20. Arretche M. *Decentralização das*

Políticas Sociais no Estado de São Paulo. São Paulo, Brazil: Edições Fundap; 1998.

21. Monteiro de Andrade LO. *SUS Passo a Passo: Normas, Gestão e Financiamento.* São Paulo, Brazil: Editora Hucitec Ltda; 2001.

22. Elias PE, Cohn A. Health reform in Brazil: lessons to consider. *Am J Public Health.* 2003;93:44–48.

23. Bastos FI. *A Feminização da Epidemia de AIDS no Brasil: Determinantes Estruturais e Alternativas de Enfrentamento.* Rio de Janeiro, Brazil: ABIA; 2001. Coleção ABIA: Saúde Sexual e Reprodutiva publication no. 3.

24. Parker R. Building the foundations for the response to HIV/AIDS in Brazil: the development of HIV/AIDS policy, 1982–1996. *Divulgação em Saúde para Debate.* 2003;27:143–183.

25. Galvão J. *AIDS no Brasil.* São Paulo, Brazil: Editora 34; 2000.

26. Galvão J. As respostas das organizações não-governamentais brasileiras frente à epidemia de HIV/AIDS. In: Parker R, ed. *Políticas, Instituições e AIDS: Enfrentando a Epidemia no Brasil.* Rio de Janeiro, Brazil: ABIA; 1997:67–108.

27. Paiva V. *Em tempos de AIDS.* São Paulo, Brazil: Summus; 1992.

28. Parker R. *Políticas, Instituições e AIDS: Enfrentando a Epidemia no Brasil.* Rio de Janeiro, Brazil: Zahar/ABIA; 1997.

29. Ventura M. Strategies to promote and guarantee the rights of people living with HIV/AIDS. *Divulgação em Saúde para Debate.* 2003;27:239–246.

30. Heywood M. Current developments: preventing mother-to-child transmission in South Africa. *S Afr J Health.* 2003;19:278–315.

31. Barnett T, Whiteside A. *AIDS in the Twenty-First Century: Disease and Globalization.* New York, NY: Pal-grave Macmillian; 2002.

32. World Bank. World development indicators, GINI Index. 2004. Available at: http://www.worldbank.org/data/wdi2004. Accessed October 10, 2004.

33. Araújo de Mattos R, Terto V Jr, Parker R. World Bank strategies and the response to AIDS in Brazil. *Divulgação em Saúde para Debate.* 2003;27:215–246.

34. Mamdani M. *Citizen and Subject: Contemporary Africa and the Legacy of Late Colonialism.* Princeton, NJ: Princeton University Press; 1996.

35. Young C. *The African Colonial State in Comparative Perspective.* New Haven, Conn: Yale University Press; 1994.

36. Amin S. Underdevelopment and dependence in black Africa: origins and contemporary forms. *J Modern Afr Stud.* 1972;10(4):503–524.

37. Deng L, Kostner M, Young C. *Democratization and Structural Adjustment in Africa in the 1990s.* Madison: University of Wisconsin Press; 1991.

38. Smith M. False hope or new start? The Global Fund to Fight HIV/AIDS, TB and Malaria. Oxfam Briefing Paper, 2002. Available at: http://www.oxfam.org/eng/pdfs/pp0206_false_hope_or_new_start.pdf. Accessed May 12, 2005.

39. Raupp Rios R. Legal responses to the HIV/AIDS epidemic in Brazil. *Divulgação em Saúde para Debate.* 2003;27:228–238.

40. Latin American and Caribbean Council of AIDS Service Organizations (LAC-CASO). *Report on Access to Comprehensive Care, Antiretroviral Treatment (ARVs) and Human Rights of People Living With HIV/AIDS in Latin America.* Washington, DC: Inter-American Commission on Human Rights; October 2002.

41. Pinheiro R, Araújo de Mattos R. *Os Sentidos da Integralidade: Na Atenção e no Cuidado à Saúde.* Rio de Janeiro, Brazil: UERJ; 2001.

42. Pinheiro R, Araújo de Mattos R. *Construção da Integralidade: Cotidiano, Saberes e Práticas em Saúde.* Rio de Janeiro, Brazil: UERJ; 2003.

43. Passarelli CA, Terto V Jr. Non-governmental organizations and access to antiretroviral treatments in Brazil. *Divulgação em Saúde para Debate.* 2003;27: 252–264.

44. Arretche M. Graus de descentralização na municipalização do atendimento básico. In: Arretche M, ed. *Estado Federativo e Políticas Sociais: Determinantes de Descentralização.* Rio de Janeiro, Brazil: Revan; 2000: 197–239.

45. Parker R. *Na Contramão da AIDS: Sexualidade, Intervenção, Política.* Rio de Janeiro, Brazil: ABIA; 2000.

46. Zaluar AM. Exclusion and public policies: theoretical dilemmas and political alternatives. *Revista Basileira de Ciências Sociais.* 2000;1:25–42.

47. Zaluar AM. *Condomínio do Diabo.* São Paulo, Brazil: Editora Brasiliense; 1996.

48. Fonseca C. Mãe é uma só? Reflexões em torno de alguns casos brasileiros. *Psicologia USP.* 2002;13(2): 49–68.

49. Parker R. *Bodies, Pleasures and Passions: Sexual Culture in Contemporary Brazil.* Boston, Mass: Beacon Press; 1991.

50. Berquó E . *Comportamento Sexual da População Brasileira e Percepções do HIV/AIDS.* Brasília, Brazil: Ministério da Saúde; 2000.

51. *Project Appraisal Document on a Proposed Loan in the Amount of US $165 Million.* Washington, DC: World Bank; 1998. Report 18338-BR.

52. US–Brazil Joint Venture on HIV/AIDS in Luso-phone Africa. Available at: http://www.whitehouse.gov/news/releases/2003/06/20030620-14.html. Accessed June 20, 2003.

53. Girard F. *Global Implications of US Domestic and International Policies on Sexuality.* New York, NY: International Working Group on Sexuality and Social Policy; June 2004. Working paper no. 1.

54. Agência nacional de AIDS. Estados Unidos cancelam grande programa de combate à AIDS no Brasil. Available at: http://www.agenciaaids.com.br. Accessed September 2003.

55. Stoneburner RL, Low-Beer D. Population-level HIV decline and behavioral risk avoidance in Uganda. *Science.* 2004;304:714–718.

56. Rosenfield A, Figdor E. Where is the M in MTCT? The broader issues in mother-to-child transmission of HIV. *Am J Public Health.* 2001;91:703–704.

57. Castilho EA, Chequer P. Epidemiologia do HIV/AIDS no Brasil. In: Parker R, ed. *Políticas, Instituições e AIDS: Enfrentando a Epidemia no Brasil.* Rio de Janeiro, Brazil: ABIA; 1997:17–42.

58. Passarelli CA, Parker R, Pimenta C, Terto V Jr. *AIDS e Desenvolvimento: Interfaces e Políticas Públicas.* Rio de Janeiro, Brazil: ABIA; 2003.

59. World Bank. *Acordo de Empréstimo (Projeto de Controle da AIDS e das DST) entre a República Federativa do Brasil e o Banco Mundial, 16 March 1994.* Brasília, Brazil: Brazilian Ministry of Health; 1994.

60. Barbosa RM, Di Giacomo do Lago T. AIDS e direitos reprodutivos: para além da transmissão vertical. In: Parker R, ed. *Políticas, instituições e AIDS: Enfrentando a Epidemia no Brasil.* Rio de Janeiro, Brazil: ABIA; 1997:163–175.

61. Westphal MF. *Gestão de Serviços De Saúde: Descentralização, Municipalização do SUS.* São Paulo, Brazil: Editora da Universidade de São Paulo; 2001.

Antiretroviral Therapy in Resource-Poor Countries: Illusions and Realities

| Moïse Desvarieux, MD, PhD, Roland Landman, MD, Bernard Liautaud, MD, Pierre-Marie Girard, MD, PhD
for the INTREPIDE Initiative In Global Health

ABSTRACT

The prospects for antiretroviral therapy in resource-poor settings have changed recently and considerably with the availability of generic drugs, the drastic price reduction of brand-name drugs, and the simplification of treatment. However, such cost reductions, although allowing the implementation of large-scale donor programs, have yet to render treatment accessible and possible in the general population.

Successfully providing HIV treatment in high-prevalence/high-caseload countries may require that we redefine the problem as a public health mass therapy program rather than a multiplication of clinical situations. The public health goal cannot simply be the reduction of morbidity and mortality *for those treated* but must be the reduction in morbidity and mortality *for the many,* that is, at a population level.

INTRODUCTION

The prospects for antiretroviral (ARV) therapy in Africa and other resource-poor settings have changed so drastically over the last few years that it is almost embarrassing to realize that it could have changed much earlier. Prices of drugs from pharmaceutical giants have fallen 10- to 40-fold, and the emergence of generic drugs as well as the simplification of treatment has made care possible in these countries.[1]

However, often overlooked is the fact that such reductions in costs, if they allow the implementation of large-scale donor programs, have yet to render treatment economically

accessible to or possible for the general population. Indeed, even with these substantial cost reductions, like those negotiated via the United Nations Global Fund,[2] the US president's initiative,[3] and the Clinton Foundation, or even the advent of generics, treatment remains beyond the reach of all but the upper classes in numerous countries.[4] It is indeed the paradox of lower ARV therapy costs that these reductions brought with them a cortege of pressures that must be recognized with wide-open eyes. In order for lower ARV therapy costs to truly usher in the era of "global treatment" beyond pilot or research programs, a realistic discussion of attainable goals of ARV treatment in resource-poor countries is necessary.[5]

The debate is peculiar in that the necessity of making ARV therapy available in resource-poor countries has been justified for its population benefits (namely, maintenance of economic capacity, distributive justice, and curbing of the HIV epidemic) as much as for the immediate public health goals of reduced morbidity and mortality. As a consequence, these larger population benefits are sometimes seen as primary, with the public health objectives considered a vehicle toward accomplishing these larger goals. But are those goals always in harmony? Or might some of those goals be better attained in other ways? If so, which objectives are the most important?

We review the population goals implicit in ARV treatment programs, assess their feasibility, and contrast them with the vehicle that is supposed to bring them to fruition—access to

ARV care for the many—before proposing a paradigm shift anchored in today's reality.

POPULATION OBJECTIVES OF ARV DRUG THERAPY PROGRAMS

Objective 1: Maintaining Economic Stability

It is often assumed that treating HIV patients will automatically result in economic benefits. That is not necessarily the case. The interplay between effectiveness, benefit, and cost varies across settings. For example, the Brazilian National AIDS Control Program, emboldened by a federal law mandating free drugs through the public health system, recorded that US $954 million was spent on providing free ARV drugs from 1997 to 2001 with an estimated savings of over US$1 billion, mostly in hospitalization costs.[6] Senegal's government recently announced that it will cover costs for all patients, (initially drug costs, but now expanding to hospitalization costs), the first African country to do so. Although the relatively modest seroprevalence in Senegal no doubt renders such an approach possible, it is not clear that it will have immediate economic benefit. Direct savings will be attained only if AIDS patients would otherwise be hospitalized for care, a proposition often absent in Africa, where many die from their initial opportunistic infections.[7] Alternatively, South Africa has recently chosen an approach that most directly leads to an economic impact by engaging large companies and the military in the HIV-related care of their employees, thus preserving the workforce and the security apparatus.

Of course these observations ignore the intangible economic impact of the patients' lost contributions to society and those of family members drawn to their care. Nevertheless, immediate economic gains would be better guaranteed in settings where patients would have received a certain level of care leading to prolonged life and its attendant hospitalization costs. Thus, at a population level, economic stability is likely to be a benefit of untargeted treatment only if the HIV prevalence cuts across social groups to such an extent that a substantial portion of the productive workforce is affected and if the population reached by treatment is large enough to encompass a significant portion of the untargeted workforce. Conversely, a siphoning of resources from other health priorities may increase economic instability: for example, if malaria mortality or morbidity were to increase as an unintended result of increased attention to HIV/AIDS, the impact across social classes might be greater. In the end, the long-term economic (and social) impact of raising generations of orphans may be the most staggering, albeit delayed, draw on resources.

Nevertheless, the strict goals of economic benefits might be more surely attained with *targeted* treatment of the critical workforce rather than the general population; this possibly conflicts with the larger public health goals.

Objective 2: Achieving Distributive Justice

The issue of distributive justice between rich and poor countries often obscures the fact that distributive injustices within a country may be compounded by the availability of treatments to only the privileged segments of resource-poor countries. Also—and this is often overlooked—distributive justice encompasses the reciprocal obligation between neighboring countries to ensure that drug resistance emergence is minimized. This illustrates the difficulty of having neighboring countries with and without access to ARV therapy and the dis-

junction in responsibility that ensues. This is also true for prevention efforts; for example, an excellent Population Services International social marketing program promoting Kapot Pantè (a condom brand) in Haiti but not in the Dominican Republic led to substantial trans-border transportation of condoms, draining condoms away from the intended Haitian population, and Population Services International recently had to launch a new distribution program in the Dominican Republic. This could again happen with ARV therapy, because drugs are presently more widely accessible in Haiti than in the Dominican Republic. Thus, the availability of ARV therapy might paradoxically further the injustices within and across resource-poor countries.

Objective 3: Curbing the HIV Epidemic

Treatment of severely symptomatic patients, as currently recommended in resource-poor countries, is unlikely to affect the epidemic transmission significantly, because most transmission occurs via patients with high viremia who are well enough to engage in sexual activities.[1] The latter generally represent the larger pool, especially in countries where survival is limited once AIDS is diagnosed. Curbing the epidemic would thus entail treatment of most HIV patients, including the asymptomatic ones with a high viral load, thereby shifting the incidence and seroprevalence curve to lesser values.[5] This naturally presupposes effective large-scale screening and individualized CD4 count and viral load assessments to select those asymptomatic people eligible for treatment. This approach would be most similar to that used in resource-rich countries where all at-risk individuals are encouraged to be tested. Even in these countries, however, this strategy is only marginally successful in identifying eligible patients. Thus, although laudable, this objective is realistically unattainable in most resource-poor countries for the foreseeable future.

Therefore, to summarize the 3 objectives mentioned previously, the population goal of economic stability

might be more immediately achieved through targeted treatment of the privileged or productive workforce. The quest for distributive justice might paradoxically lead to a furthering of the gap within and across resource-poor countries, and epidemic containment is unattainable in most settings. Thus, these population objectives should not be seen as primary, because they may indeed conflict with the immediate public health goal of reduced morbidity and mortality for the many; this goal must stand on its own as a primary objective rather than as a vehicle to other goals.

Objective 4: Reducing Morbidity and Mortality

At an individual level, the objectives of reduced morbidity and mortality are naturally the ones directly sought when ARV treatment is initiated. These individual objectives entail an eminently clinicobiological approach to care that originated in resource-rich countries, with the consecrated mainstays of treatment initiation: CD4 counts and the viral load. It has now become clear that viral load assessment is not necessary to initiate treatment,[8,9] as reflected in World Health Organization guidelines.[9] However, the CD4 count guidelines of resource-rich countries remain a prominent goal.[10] In an attempt to replicate resource-rich countries' treatment guidelines, efforts have been directed toward greater availability or affordability of CD4 counts, cheaper ways to determine viral loads, or substitutes for CD4 counts.[11,12]

At a population level, however, the goal of reduced morbidity and mortality can be achieved only if a large number of patients receive care. In the collective attempt to do so, HIV health providers have struggled to transpose an individualized, highly biological approach to care onto a massive public health problem. We have ourselves experimented with these approaches in countries with varied seroprevalence rates, for example, in Senegal, Côte d'Ivoire, or Haiti. Indeed, it is the difficulties we have encountered in these various seroprevalence settings that have led us to realize that current approaches, based on model transposition, neglect one singularly important factor: the actual patient load. For example, HIV seroprevalence rates in the United States and in France are estimated to be around 0.25%, leading to a national caseload of 800 000 (Centers for Disease Control and Prevention) to 950 000[13] in the United States and 150 000 in France.[13] As a comparison, an estimated 250 000 to 400 000 people live with HIV/AIDS in Haiti, a larger patient load than in France, where the population is nearly 8 times larger. India, with the largest number of people living with HIV outside South Africa, has 5.1 million seropositive people,[13] and Nigeria, with a relatively low HIV seroprevalence of 5.8%, still yields a caseload of 7 million, nearly 10 times the number of seropositive people in the entire United States.[13]

A 5% to 10% HIV seroprevalence in the United States or France would translate to a 20-to 40-fold increase in current caseloads. Because of this reality, it is extremely doubtful that current extensive biological monitoring approaches would be either used or simply feasible, even within the United States or France, given the multifold increase in labor, personnel, and infrastructure that such approaches require. As an example, Cohen et al.[14] projected that 5.1 million additional patient visits per year would be required to provide routine HIV care in western Kenya alone with the current treatment paradigms. Thus, in spite of improvements in cost and technical requirements for CD4 counts,[15,16] replicating the individual monitoring of resource-rich countries remains illusory. It is not simply a matter of cost.

Therefore, addressing the global problem of HIV treatment in high-prevalence/high-caseload (HPHC) countries may require that health decisionmakers first specifically recognize that the public health goal cannot simply be the reduction of morbidity and mortality for *those treated* but must be the reduction in morbidity and mortality for *the many*, that is, at a population

level. Once that goal is clearly stated, the HIV seroprevalence or caseload constitutes the major operational factor, necessitating that we redefine the problem in the most affected regions as a public health mass therapy program rather than simply a multiplication of clinical situations. Therefore there is a need for a paradigm shift in delivering, monitoring, and assessing success of ARV therapy programs in HPHC settings.

PROPOSAL FOR A NEW PROGRAM-BASED STRATEGY

Not so long ago, it was widely perceived that ARV treatment was impossible in resource-poor countries. After publication of our 1997 consensus guidelines on ARV therapy in Africa[17] and the first studies of efficacy and acceptability,[18–21] the pendulum swung sharply in the opposite direction, with some people successfully introducing ARV drugs in resource-poor countries with only clinical evaluation.[22] Between these 2 poles is, of course, a middle ground. We submit for discussion a shift from a clinical to a public health approach to HIV treatment prioritizing large-scale programs rigorously evaluated for their population impact, rather than on a patient-by-patient basis. Such an approach presumes that we should not await data establishing the relative contribution of CD4 counts or viral loads before initiating treatment for HIV-positive patients in resource-poor settings. Rather, treatment would be initiated quickly, focused on HIV-seropositive symptomatic patients[22] in accordance with the goal of a population-wide reduction in morbidity and mortality. Similarly, treatment would be monitored on the basis of improvement in clinical symptoms and possibly limited laboratory tests (cell blood count, liver function tests, and creatinine). The urgency of initiating treatment is reinforced by reports showing lower survival rates with delayed treatment initiation among symptomatic patients in Africa.[21]

Initially, from a pragmatic point of view, programs need to be implemented around existing centers (generally,

but not always, urban centers because seroprevalence is generally higher in urban centers, populations are more accessible and have more access to care, and tailored training is easier) and radiate outward. In this programmatic approach, extensive evaluation would move away from the individual but would utilize the population as the unit of analysis. Such a programmatic approach implies a small number of specific requirements.

Immediate Planning of First- (ARV) and Second-line (ARV-plus) Drug Supply

Unlike tuberculosis therapy, in which programs have been built largely on first-line treatments, with second-line treatments (directly observed therapy [DOT]-plus) recommended only in settings with established DOT programs,[23] ARV-plus programs would need to be planned concurrently because, at a population level, HIV develops resistance to ARV drugs faster than tuberculosis bacilli do to antibiotics.

Program Evaluation in Concordance with the Principles of Mass Therapy

We should abandon individual efficacy in favor of population efficiency as tenets of program success. We propose the following criteria for annual or semiannual population-based evaluation of program success: (1) death rate (overall and HIV-related); (2) incidence of major opportunistic infections, for example, tuberculosis; (3) magnitude of CD4 changes among a sample of treated individuals; (4) proportion of patients with undetectable viral loads among a sample of treated individuals; (5) rates of drug resistance among a sample of treated individuals; and (6) rates of drug resistance among a sample of untreated individuals to estimate the diffusion in the population. Sequential data on CD4 counts, viral loads, and drug resistance, collected on a representative sample of the population, would thus assess treatment efficiency at the population level and inform changes in recommended regional or national treatment guidelines. This is somewhat similar to tuberculosis and malaria therapy, in which treatment guidelines are informed by prevalent drug resistance rates in several countries that do not actually have the effective capacity for individual drug susceptibility testing.

The annual rates of HIV infection among women with first pregnancies also may be incorporated to monitor the continuation of prevention in a comprehensive program.[24] Well-integrated prevention programs may benefit from the availability of ARV therapy. Like the "combination prevention" advocated by the Gates Foundation,[25] "combination outcomes" should primarily measure program success. Utilizing—and adapting—these proposed criteria across countries and regions should allow more direct comparisons and improve experience sharing.

Simple Schemes for Community-Level HIV Treatment

In a second phase, treatment should move from hospital- and clinic-based to community-based programs with staff at each level trained for appropriate referral dictated by clinical worsening or side effects. This approach would differ from that of resource-rich countries. Moving from well-equipped health care centers in urban sites to ill-equipped suburban or rural areas is an undeniable challenge in HIV care. All personnel should be trained in recognizing adverse outcomes and among them those requiring treatment interruption. Clear referral guidelines should be created and taught.

We must state candidly that in advocating this approach, we recognize that treatment may not be as effective for every patient as that provided by the biological approach. However, this public health approach recognizes reality. Indeed, we wonder whether the difficulties in adapting to the reality dictated by high caseloads are a remnant of the exceptionalism that has historically characterized policy in resource-rich countries, wherein HIV was exempted from traditional public health practices such as contact tracing and partner notification.[26] To be frank, in the context of resource-poor countries, this reluctance to implement public heath measures is compounded by the

fear of being accused of advocating a 2-tiered system, lesser for the poor and disenfranchised. This fear clouds the reality that even the scaling up of facilities and staff will not change the impossibility of meeting the challenges with the traditional approach.

However, we do advocate scaling up. First, 1 central national or regional reference laboratory must be improved for *population-based* evaluation of program success (CD4 levels, viral loads, drug-resistance). Second, general laboratories must be improved for *individual* monitoring of toxicity that will impact overall public health. HIV programs should therefore be linked to primary care,[25,27,28] including existing mother–infant programs as well as tuberculosis programs. More specialized treatment can be only at the tertiary care level with training at these levels done accordingly. The demise of exceptionalism can be a good thing.[26–28] Naturally, improvements in laboratory techniques and logistics (including personnel training) should be monitored for adaptation of the population-based/individual-based ratio of laboratory tests.

A Plan for Adherence Monitoring

Preliminary data[17–19,29] show adherence to be high in several African settings. Careful monitoring of clinic visits to replenish drug supplies, questioning by friendly staff, and validated clinical signs and symptoms might be acceptable surrogate markers of adherence. Regions should be able to reasonably tailor adherence monitoring to their reality with supervision from funding agencies and health authorities. Is universal DOT necessary? In spite of the attractiveness of DOT for ARV therapies, it seems doubtful that in HPHC settings, strict DOT will be practical or possible.[30] It would entail the lifelong mobilization of huge numbers of "accompagnateurs" if one were to replicate the successful program of Farmer et al.[22] in central Haiti or those of Médecins sans Frontières.[31] However, programs should clearly define and integrate their plans for treatment adherence monitoring at the time of initiation of therapy, and fund-

ing agencies should insist on those plans and link continued funding to their effective implementation. Black markets for ARV therapies as well as counterfeit drugs are major concerns in countries with poor capacity for pharmacological control, and specific policies must be in place. From a programmatic standpoint, investing in such efforts seems more efficient than investing in large-scale individual immunologic monitoring.

Finally, public health principles require donor agencies to ensure that drugs are not simply delivered to countries and allowed to disappear into the local distribution system. Donor agencies that engage solely in ARV distribution must guard against the illusion of a policy of treatment. Without programs, a narrow policy of drug distribution may simply lead to a policy of drug disappearance masquerading as a policy of treatment. Now that drugs are being made available to countries, both recipients *and* donors have new responsibilities. Some would argue that a program of drug delivery is better than no program at all. They might further argue that our position of requiring an effective program of drug treatment is equal to advocating that drugs not be delivered at all. This point of view clouds the debate. From a population perspective, if it is morally untenable that drugs be withheld from those regions most in need to prevent resistance in those regions least in need, it is equally ethically impermissible to abdicate the dual responsibility of ensuring that the drugs reach the intended patients and of protecting the efficacy of these drugs. An example of the potentially deleterious effects of unbridled drug delivery without this assurance is provided by nevirapine, distributed largely to pregnant women in certain areas; its use has even been advocated for *all* women in highly HIV endemic countries.[32] Even the brief use of nevirapine in mother-to-child transmission prevention leads to increased resistance to the entire class of drugs, possibly erasing the efficacy of 1 of the 3 major drug classes available for HIV treatment.[33] Therefore, preserving the future for both local populations and neighboring countries should be a primary objective.

ARV Therapy Deliverers as Primary Care Deliverers

The dual role of ARV deliverer and primary care deliverer will reduce the stigmatization of HIV and minimize resources and personnel drain. This principle also recognizes reality: a public health problem affecting a substantial number of the population is a primary care issue. The appellation "HIV doctors" should be discouraged.

Of course, easier treatments, with fewer side effects, would make things simpler. We still need the innovation of pharmaceutical companies to develop these better treatments, as much as we needed generic drugs to render the current debate even possible. The superb advocacy of individuals and groups like Médecins Sans Frontières, the Clinton Foundation, or the United Nations, as well as the availability of generic drugs, clearly has to be credited for persuading the pharmaceutical companies to lower their prices. Delaporte's recent evaluation of a fixed-drug combination pill,[34] regrouping generic ARV drugs from different manufacturers, may be seen as a telling illustration of the cooperation that is both possible and needed. However, contrary to popular belief, generic drugs are not always cheaper than patented drugs.[35] Therefore, the debate should not be cast in terms of good versus evil, in spite of the obvious temptation to do so.

CONCLUSIONS

The argument often advanced by those who strongly oppose anything less than unfettered delivery of ARV therapy to high-prevalence settings in Africa and resource-poor countries is that to do otherwise is a breach of human rights.[36] The argument advanced by those advocating more research and the adapted transposition of northern clinical standards is that we should not allow a lower standard of care in resource-poor countries. We note logical and ethical inconsistencies

that undermine the feasibility of programs that would emanate from these high-minded notions. We propose a new strategy: (1) realistically recognize the diversity of situations and the truly attainable goals of any program; (2) in the HPHC countries, treat HIV as the public health crisis that it is, with massive programs evaluated at the population level: only strict program evaluation can ensure that a policy of drug disappearance does not masquerade as a policy of treatment; (3) on an individual level, focus on adherence monitoring, clinical evaluation, and toxicity evaluation rather than on immunologic evaluation; (4) make strategies for preserving the future a common ethical issue for all neighboring countries, as well as donor programs.

The urgency of the need to rush HIV treatment to resource-poor countries underscores a true public health emergency, and the achievement of public health goals requires access to the many. However, the understandable fear of rushing in with eyes shut may now lead to the pursuit of laudable yet disproportional responses to an outsized reality. Only a public health approach will allow a timely and proportional impact, with eyes wide open to the dangers and to the responsibilities of all health providers and decisionmakers.

About the Authors

Moïse Desvarieux is with the Department of Epidemiology, Mailman School of Public Health, Columbia University, New York, NY. Roland Landman is with the Service de Maladies Infectieuses, Centre Hospitalier Universitaire, Bichat Claude Bernard, Université de Paris, Paris, France, and the Institut de Médecine et d'Épidémiologie Appliquée (IMEA), Paris. Bernard Liautaud is with the Hôspital de Jour en Maladies Infectieuses, Centre Hospitalier Universitaire de Fort-de-France, Fort-de-France, Martinique, and Groupe Haitien d'Études du Sarcome de Kaposi et des Infections Opportunistes, Port-au-Prince, Haiti. Pierre-Marie Girard is with the Service de Maladies Infectieuses et Tropicales, Centre Hospitalier Universitaire de Saint-Antoine, Université de Paris, Paris, and the Institut de Médecine et d'Épidémiologie Appliquée, Paris.

Correspondence: Requests for reprints should be sent to Moïse Desvarieux, MD, PhD, Department of Epidemiology, Mailman School of Public Health, 722 W 168th St, New York, NY 10032 (e-mail: md108@columbia.edu).

Acknowledgments

Financial support for INTREPIDE was provided in part by the Institut de Médecine et d'Epidémiologie Appliquée Paris, France, and the University of Minnesota School of Public Health and Division of Epidemiology, Minneapolis, Minn.

Members of the International Training and Research Program in Infectious Disease Epidemiology (INTREPIDE) include Olivier Bouchaud, MD, Anke Bourgeois, MD, Marc Brodin, MD, Jean-Pierre Coulaud, MD, Eric Delaporte, MD, Philippe Deloron, PhD, Moïse Desvarieux, MD, PhD, Arnaud Fontanet, MD, DrPH, Pierre-Marie Girard, MD, Roland Landman, MD, Bernard Larouzé, MD, Jacques Lebras, PhD, Bernard Liautaud, MD, and Sophie Matheron, MD, from the Université de Paris, the Université de Montpellier, the Institut Pasteur de Paris, the Centre Hospitalo-Universitaire de Martinique.

This article is dedicated to Professor Jean-Pierre Coulaud, who in 1997 chaired the first international meeting Guidelines in the Use of Antiretroviral Drugs in Africa in Dakar, Senegal, and remains a fervent advocate for, and an inspiration to, many.

Contributors

M. Desvarieux and P.-M. Girard wrote the original article with substantial input and editing from R. Landman and B. Liautaud.

References

1. World Health Organization. Accelerating access to HIV/AIDS care and treatment in developing countries. *Antiretroviral Newsletter*. June 2001:1–5.

2. The Global Fund to Fight AIDS, Tuberculosis and Malaria Web page. Available at: http://www.theglobal-fund.org/en. Accessed April 6, 2005.

3. United States Leadership Against HIV/AIDS, Tuberculosis, and Malaria Act of 2003. Pub L No. 108–125.

4. HIV/AIDS: not one epidemic but many [editorial]. *Lancet.*2004;364:1–2.

5. Rose G. Sick individuals and sick populations. *Int J Epidemiol.* 2001;30:427–432 (discussion 433–434).

6. Levi GC, Vitoria MA. Fighting against AIDS: the Brazilian experience. *AIDS.*2002;16:2373–2383.

7. Lucas SB, Hounnou A, Peacock C, et al. The mortality and pathology of HIV infection in a west African city. *AIDS.*1993;7:1569–1579.8. Yeni PG, Hammer SM, Carpenter CC, et al. Antiretroviral treatment for adult HIV infection in 2002: updated recommendations of the International AIDS Society-USA Panel. *JAMA.*2002;288:222–235.

9. *Scaling Up Antiretroviral Therapy in Resource-Limited Settings: Guidelines for a Public Health Approach.* Geneva, Switzerland: World Health Organization; 2002.

10. Rabkin M, El-Sadr W, Katzenstein DA, et al. Antiretroviral treatment in resource-poor settings: clinical research priorities. *Lancet.*2002;360:1503–1505.

11. Mekonnen Y, Dukers NH, Sanders E, et al. Simple markers for initiating anti-retroviral therapy among HIV-infected Ethiopians. *AIDS.*2003;17:815–819.

12. Didier JM, Kazatchkine MD, Demouchy C, et al. Comparative assessment of five alternative methods for CD4 T-lymphocyte enumeration for implementation in developing countries [letter]. *J Acquir Immune Defic Syndr.*2001;26:193–195.

13. UNAIDS 2004 report on the global AIDS epidemic. Available at: http://www.unaids.org/bangkok2004/report.html. Accessed July 8, 2004.

14. Cohen J, Kimaiyo S, Winstone N, et al. Addressing the educational void during the antiretroviral therapy rollout [letter]. *AIDS.*2004;18:2105–2106

15. Diagbouga S, Chazallon C, Kazatchkine M, et al. Successful implementation of a low-cost method for enumerating CD4 T-lymphocytes in resource-limited settings: the ANRS 12–26 study. *AIDS.*2003;17:2201–2208.

16. Balakrishnan P, Dunne M, Kumarasamy N, et al. An inexpensive, simple and manual method of CD4 T-cell quantitation in HIV-infected individuals for use in developing countries. *J Acquir Immune Defic Syndr.* 2004;36:1006–1010.

17. Place of antiretroviral drugs in the treatment of HIV-infected people in Africa. International AIDS Society. *AIDS.* 1999;13:IAS1–IAS3.

18. Laurent C, Diakhate N, Gueye NF, et al. The Senegalese government's highly active antiretroviral therapy initiative: an 18-month follow-up study. *AIDS.*2002;16:1363–1370.

19. Landman R, Schiemann R, Thiam S, et al. Once-a-day highly active antiretroviral therapy in treatment-naive HIV-1-infected adults in Senegal. *AIDS.*2003; 17:1017–1022.

20. Agence Nationale de Recherche sur le Sida. Institut de Médecine et d'Epidémiologie. Use of antiretroviral drugs in the management of HIV-infected persons. Updated Recommendations. 2000. Available at: http://www.imea.fr. Accessed April 20, 2005.

21. Coetzee D, Hildebrand K, Boulle A, et al. Outcomes after two years of providing antiretroviral treatment in Khayelitsha, South Africa. *AIDS.*2004; 18:887–895.

22. Farmer P, Leandre F, Mukherjee J, Gupta R, Tarter L, Kim JY. Community-based treatment of advanced HIV disease: introducing DOT-HAART (directly observed therapy with highly active an-tiretroviral therapy). *Bull World Health Organ.*2001;79:1145–1151.

23. DOTS-Plus and the Green Light Committee. World Health Organization Web site. Available at: http://www.who.int/tb/dots/dot-splus/management/en. Accessed April 19, 2005.

24. Quinn TC, Wawer MJ, Sewankambo N, et al. Viral load and heterosexual transmission of human immunodeficiency virus type 1. Rakai Project Study Group. *N Engl J Med.*2000;342:921–929

25. Gayle HD. Curbing the global AIDS epidemic. *N Engl J Med.*2003; 348:1802–1805.

26. Bayer R. Public health policy and the AIDS epidemic. An end to HIV exceptionalism? *N Engl J Med.*1991;324:1500–1504.

27. Reynolds SJ, Bartlett JG, Quinn TC, Beyrer C, Bollinger RC. Antiretroviral therapy where resources are limited. *N Engl J Med.*2003;348:1806–1809.

28. De Cock KM, Mbori-Ngacha D, Marum E. Shadow on the continent: public health and HIV/AIDS in Africa in the 21st century. *Lancet.*2002;360:67–72.

29. Weidle PJ, Malamba S, Mwebaze R, et al. Assessment of a pilot antiretroviral drug therapy program in Uganda: patients' response, survival, and drug resistance. *Lancet.*2002;360:34–40.

30. Liechty CA, Bangsberg DR. Doubts about DOT: antiretroviral therapy for resource-poor countries. *AIDS.*2003; 17:1383–1387.

31. Poole C, Chesney MA, Mdani L, Dzazela N, Nyatela N, Kasper T. Patient-centered approaches to adherence to highly-active antiretroviral therapy in resource-poor settings [abstract ThPeF8195]. In: Program and abstracts of the XIV International AIDS Conference; July 7–12, 2002; Barcelona, Spain.

32. Stringer JS, Rouse DJ, Sinkala M, et al. Nevirapine to prevent mother-to-child transmission of HIV among women of unknown serostatus. *Lancet.*2003;362:1850–1853.

33. Jourdain G, Ngo-Giang-Huong N, LeCoeur S, et al. for the Perinatal HIV Prevention Trial Group. Intrapartum exposure to nevirapine and subsequent maternal responses to nevirapine-based antiretroviral therapy. *N Engl J Med.*2004;351:229–240.

34. Laurent C, Kouanfack C, Koulla-Shira S, et al. for the ANRS 1274 study group. Effectiveness and safety of a generic fixed-dose combination of nevi-rapine, stavudine, and lamivudine in HIV-1 infected adults in Cameroon: open-label multicentre trial. *Lancet.*2004;364:29–34.

35. Médecins sans Frontières. Untangling the web of price reductions: a pricing guide for the purchase of antiretrovirals for developing countries. Available at: http://www.accessmed-msf.org/upload/ReportsandPublications/91220021653552/Final.pdf. Accessed April 17, 2005.

36. Hogg R, Cahn P, Katabira ET, et al. Time to act: global apathy towards HIV/AIDS is a crime against humanity. *Lancet.* 2002;360:1710-1711.

Which Patients First? Setting Priorities for Antiretroviral Therapy Where Resources Are Limited

| Laura J. McGough, PhD, Steven J. Reynolds, MD, MPH, Thomas C. Quinn, MD, MS and Jonathan M. Zenilman, MD

ABSTRACT

The availability of limited funds from international agencies for the purchase of antiretroviral (ARV) treatment in developing countries presents challenges, especially in prioritizing who should receive therapy. Public input and the protection of human rights are crucial in making treatment programs equitable and accountable. By examining historical precedents of resource allocation, we aim to provoke and inform debate about current ARV programs.

Through a critical review of the published literature, we evaluate 4 precedents for key lessons: the discovery of insulin for diabetes in 1922, the release of penicillin for civilian use in 1943, the development of chronic hemodialysis programs in 1961, and current allocation of liver transplants. We then describe current rationing mechanisms for ARVs.

INTRODUCTION

Currently, at least 5.8 million people in developing countries urgently need antiretroviral (ARV) therapy, but only approximately 12% are receiving it.[1] Although the number of people receiving ARV therapy worldwide increased from 440 000 in June 2004 to approximately 700 000 in December 2004, ARV therapy is still reaching only a fraction of the people who need it, especially in countries such as India (4%), the Russian Federation (3%), and many sub-Saharan African countries (Ethiopia, 5%; South Africa, 7%).[2] The delivery of ARV treatment in developing countries through programs such as the Global Fund to Fight AIDS, Tuberculosis and Malaria; President Bush's US Emergency Plan for AIDS Relief (PEPFAR); and other private sector or nongovernmental organization programs presents tremendous challenges and opportunities, especially in prioritizing who should receive therapy. The World Health Organization's (WHO's) goal of treating 3 million people by 2005 would reach only half of those who urgently need medication[3] and an even smaller fraction of those who could potentially benefit.

WHY IS PATIENT SELECTION A PROBLEM?

Developing countries now face the challenge of implementing these ARV delivery programs. Open, public discussions about patient selection—or rationing—have largely been avoided in recipient countries. It is possible that government officials fear the potentially divisive consequences of open discussions about who receives access to a lifesaving medication available in only limited quantities.[4] However, avoiding a decision about rationing does not mean that decisions are not made. "Passive decisions"—that is, limiting access to patients who have already tested HIV positive or live near a clinic site—favor those with economic, political, or social power.[5] Trust and social capital (trust demonstrated by mutual reciprocity and cooperation among members of society) have been identified as key elements in the successful implementation of major public health interventions. Resources that benefit only 1 group, or 1 subset of patients, have the potential to disrupt community relations, promote conflict, and undermine public health programs.

Because the limited ability to provide care raises ethical issues about patient selection, Dr Peter Piot, executive director of the Joint United Nations Programme on HIV/AIDS, has called for the establishment of national ethics panels in recipient countries,[6] while WHO has commissioned a series of background papers and a guidance document on ethics, equity, and access to ARV therapy.[7] In order for beneficiary countries to implement these suggestions, however, it is important for donors to recognize patient selection as part of the process of introducing or expanding access to ARV therapy and long-term strategic planning.

Decisionmaking occurs in specific historical and cultural contexts: each recipient country faces a unique set of challenges in deciding how to allocate resources. Because of these widely disparate contexts, both the Global Fund and PEPFAR have given recipient countries the responsibility for patient selection. We do not disagree with the decision to assign responsibility for patient selection to recipient countries. Instead, we recognize the complex responsibilities and burdens that countries face in expanding access to ARV treatment. Patient selection is a difficult issue involving competing demands between equity, urgency, efficiency, and other factors.

In order to facilitate discussion about patient selection in recipient countries, we have critically analyzed the history of patient selection for scarce medical resources in the US context. Our goal is not to provide a one-size-fits-all model based on experiences unique to the United States, but rather to use these historical experiences as an entry into the complex issues regarding resource allocation. Policymakers in other countries may want to evaluate their own histories of patient selection and scarce resource allocation, since current reactions to ARV patient selection will be shaped partially by each country's historical experiences.

METHODOLOGY

We evaluated the following 4 historical precedents of rationing of a scarce medical resource: the discovery of insulin for diabetes in 1922, the release of penicillin for civilian use in 1943, the development of chronic hemodialysis programs in 1961, and current approaches to allocating liver transplants. Each of these cases involved the availability of new therapies for formerly fatal diseases.

The limiting factor for both insulin and penicillin was the ability to manufacture large quantities of the medication. With hemodialysis, however, the constraint was limitations of financial resources to pay for the therapy, similar to the constraints related to delivery of ARV therapies. Pharmaceutical companies are able to manufacture sufficient quantities of ARVs; the limitation is the amount of money available for these medications in addition to the limitations of infrastructure and health personnel to treat patients in developing countries. Both diabetes and kidney disease are chronic illnesses which were not "cured" by insulin and hemodialysis, similar to the case with HIV/AIDS, where ARV therapies do not provide a cure but a way to manage the disease.

We critically review the published, peer-reviewed literature on these medical discoveries, specifically concentrating on identifying the approach to resource allocation decisions and the key determinants of those decisions. We then compare these case studies with the situation of AIDS and ARV therapy.

DECISIONS CANNOT BE AVOIDED

Between 1921 and 1922, Fredrick Banting and Charles Best discovered insulin as treatment for diabetes mellitus and learned how to produce it from livestock pancreas. With this discovery, diabetes was transformed from a fatal illness into a chronic, manageable disease. As scientists and researchers, Banting and Best never anticipated that they would be in the position of allocating medications. Consequently, they developed no concrete plan until a crisis developed. Flooded by requests for the limited quantities of the new drug, Banting himself decided which terminally ill patients would receive insulin.[8]

With neither experience in health policy nor any reliable precedents for guidance, Banting resorted to subjective criteria in deciding whom to treat. One third of the insulin went to his own private practice, another one third to his clinic, and the remaining one third to Toronto General Hospital and the Hospital for Sick Children. Because the discovery was well publicized, patients' families and physicians within Canada and from the United States flooded Banting's laboratory with requests for insulin. Emotional, political, and personal appeals often influenced who received treatment; the patient of a doctor who served in the Army with Banting, as well as the politically well-connected daughter of the US secretary of state, received insulin while others were denied treatment.[9]

THE PROCESS IS AS IMPORTANT AS THE CRITERIA

The therapeutic value of penicillin against a variety of infections was recognized in the period 1941 to 1943, when war provoked renewed research into the drug's efficacy. Initially, the drug was limited to military use.

Determined to avoid the problems connected with insulin rationing, a panel of experts developed medical criteria to handle rationing. Rationing for the military was handled separately from civilian rationing according to 2 sets of criteria: (1) the efficacy of the drug against the disease in question and (2) the speed of treatment in returning soldiers to active duty. Since penicillin was effective against gonorrhea and patients recovered quickly, gonorrhea patients in military service received priority. As production increased, it was released to the civilian sector under strict control.[10]

From January 1942 to May 1944, the Committee on Chemotherapeutic and Other Agents (COC) handled the rationing of penicillin to civilians. The COC was responsible for investigating the clinical uses of penicillin, especially the application of the drug for wound infections. Officially independent of government, the committee was composed of leading academic physicians responsible for developing clinical guidelines for penicillin use. Civilian demand for penicillin skyrocketed during the summer of 1943, when the public became aware of the drug's usefulness. The COC's allocation decisions were made according to severity and type of infection, with priority given to acute illnesses caused by sulfonamide-resistant streptococci, gonococci, and staphylococci, which had proven responsive to penicillin in clinical trials.[11]

Research value was also part of the criteria for patient selection. For rare diseases, data on penicillin's efficacy did not exist, but treatment of patients with rare diseases could potentially advance knowledge. One patient suffering from what was regarded as a rare form of blood disease was offered penicillin to evaluate the drug's efficacy against this infection, thereby possibly advancing the war effort.[12]

Unlike researchers' rationing of insulin, the COC's decisionmaking about which patients received penicillin remained uninfluenced by criteria such as a patient's political ties, media attention, or number of letters written on behalf of the patient. The potential for clinical efficacy overrode patients' political, financial, or social status. Despite this apparent success, the committee nonetheless endured a barrage of criticism from the media and the public, which often viewed the committee's chairman, Dr Chester Keefer, who served as chief of medicine at Boston University, as coldhearted and unresponsive.

The public became angry with the COC and Dr Keefer for 2 reasons. First, the public regarded rationing as a political process from which it had been excluded. Although the COC was a civilian committee independent of both the military and the government, it was perceived by the public as being either the army or the federal government, which had unnecessarily intruded into civilian life.[13] Many members of the public disagreed with the criteria established, since civilian needs came second to military needs. When Norris Higgins, a 29-year-old physician from Connecticut, became sick and then died in the fall of 1943, family and friends criticized the committee for having denied him penicillin. In a letter written October 22, 1943, former Congressman William Fitzgerald expressed his frustrations that a worthy young man would die while soldiers who contracted syphilis or gonorrhea had access to penicillin: "I think it is a crime that the Health Department in Washington [sic] refused to release any of this drug for his benefit, and then I read in the paper this drug is available for men who have been careless in their lives and have contracted a dreadful disease. . . ."[14]

Although Fitzgerald misunderstood which agency was responsible for rationing penicillin, he did understand that the public had exercised no authority in establishing criteria for the allocation of penicillin. Not all members of the public agreed that every soldier's right to medication preceded the right of any civilian.

The second reason for dissatisfaction with the COC was that the public did not always understand the criteria for patient selection. Seriously ill patients who suffered from a variety of diseases, such as cancer, hoped that this new wonder drug would cure them. The COC denied access to penicillin on clinical grounds, but the media and the public did not clearly understand why access was granted in some cases but not others. Media attention focused on dramatic cases of sick young children who had been denied penicillin and followed their cases with attention-grabbing headlines, such as "7 hours to live" in the case of a 2-year-old girl.[15]

The highly centralized structure and scientific focus of the COC alienated civilians, who had already been asked to make sacrifices during wartime.[16] This model of expert centralized decisionmaking remained politically unacceptable after the war, as the case of the drug cortisone, discovered in 1949, demonstrates.[17] Experts from the "disease foundations" (which focus on particular diseases, such as arthritis) successfully challenged the authority of a committee at the National Academy of Sciences to control the allocation of scarce supplies of corisone.[17(p420)] The COC failed to realize that rationing of a scarce medical resource is an inherently political process. Despite the development of clinical criteria, nonmedical criteria were part of the rationing process simply by giving priority to the military and by including speed in returning soldiers to active duty as part of the criteria. Even during a critical national emergency such as World War II, it was difficult to sustain public confidence in rationing decisions because the public had no voice in how those decisions were made. Ensuring that the decisionmaking body for patient selection is accepted as politically legitimate and accountable to the public is as important as agreeing on a system of criteria for patient selection.

MEDICAL CRITERIA ARE NOT "NEUTRAL"

In 1960, hemodialysis, which had been limited to treating acute renal failure, became feasible for chronic, end-stage kidney disease when Belding Scribner and his colleagues at the University of Washington developed a shunt that allowed patients to be easily treated 3 times a week.[18] (Although other medical centers in the United States soon began offering chronic hemodialysis, we focus on Seattle's experience because it was the first and most widely publicized example of priority setting for dialysis.) It quickly became apparent to Seattle's Artificial Kidney Center that, given the scarcity of the dialysis machines and trained personnel, choices would need to be made about which patients would have access to this life-long and expensive treatment. While the doctors in charge were willing to determine which kidney patients qualified medically for dialysis, they soon decided that choosing "who shall live" among these patients was a task better left to others, and in 1961 a 9-member committee composed of 7 lay people and 2 physicians was appointed to recommend patients for treatment.[19]

The physicians had already made a few "medical decisions" about who should receive treatment. They excluded children as candidates on the grounds that it would be a mistake to accept children and reject heads of households who might be supporting several children.[20] The logic was utilitarian: the greatest number of children, they reasoned, could benefit from allocation of resources to heads of households rather than directly to children. Although the decision to exclude children was presented as a medical one, in fact it involved a moral decision about overall benefit to society. Even these rules still left several candidates for just one slot, and hence the necessity for the 9-member committee to decide who would receive treatment.

The committee members were aware of the impact of disease not just on health and mortality but also on the social and economic lives of households and the surrounding community. Their decisions reflected their understanding of disease as social and economic phenomena, and public money for treatment as a kind of collective good for the benefit of society as a whole. Their first requirement was therefore residence within the state of Washington (since the program was supported by the state's tax revenues). The committee then chose according to 2 other sets of criteria: who had the largest number of dependents requiring state financial assistance if that patient could not work and who "deserved" treatment because of their social worth. "Social worth" criteria included a patient's marital status, occupation, income, education, emotional stability, and future potential, along with the patient's gender and age.[21]

As guardians of a public resource, the committee evaluated patients' eligibility to receive medication according to their value to society as a whole: their contributions as workers, family members, and volunteers versus the loss to society if they died, especially in leaving dependent children. The committee's first selection was a 33-year-old electrician with 7 dependents who would require state financial assistance if he were unable to work. Generally speaking, preferred candidates for dialysis were those who were successful at work but possessed limited monetary savings, had numerous children, and were actively involved in church and community affairs. The importance placed upon the male head of household's responsibilities to his family created gender inequality in the selection of patients and was weighted heavily in favor of males: a car salesman (male), a physicist (male), an engineer (male), and a homemaker (female) were among the earliest patients. The committee's decisionmaking process reflected the values and biases of White, middle-class Protestant American society: the committee chose patients most like themselves.[22]

After a critical article by reporter Shana Alexander appeared in *Life* magazine in 1962, the committee received widespread criticism for its reliance on social criteria in selecting patients.[18] The subsequent controversy induced changes in the process. The committee no longer assessed the "social worth" of candidates, but

nonetheless relied on interviews with patients and patients' family members; psychological assessments; and detailed employment, educational, and personal histories, all of which reinforced the committee's bias in favor of middle-class Americans who conformed to the committee's ideals about proper behavior and norms. Furthermore, the composition of the committee changed so that it no longer included members from the surrounding community. Two physicians, along with the center's administrative director and 2 board members, served on the new committee, which relied heavily on reports by experts in psychology and social work.

The emphasis changed from judging a patient's overall contribution to society to judging a patient's "psychological suitability" for dialysis, a demanding treatment that required patients' commitment to their own care. The committee was trying to ensure that scarce resources would not be wasted on patients who were unmotivated or unlikely to succeed in therapy, an understandable concern. But the committee's definition of psychological suitability reveals how difficult it is to disentangle factors that contribute to a patient's ability to benefit from medical therapy contrasted with social prejudices about desirable and undesirable behavior that may or may not affect patient survival.

For example, one candidate for dialysis, an unemployed 22-year-old truck driver (referred to here as Mr A), received critical remarks from committee members because his common-law wife was obese and apparently critical of medical authorities.[23] Subsequent discussion of Mr A's case focused on the management problems his common-law wife would present. Mrs A clearly failed to meet the committee's definition of a suitable wife, because she was obese, defensive about her weight, and emotional. It is not clear, however, whether these traits would have impeded her ability to support her husband's dialysis program. Under the earlier system, 1 committee member voted for a candidate with strong church involvement because the com-

mittee member thought religious belief was a reliable indicator of commitment to undergo a difficult therapeutic regimen.[24] In practice, it was difficult to isolate traits that predicted potential for clinical success from socially desirable, but clinically irrelevant, factors.

The Seattle experience illustrates the difficulty decisionmakers face in trying to make efficient use of scarce resources, especially when the therapy is lifelong and difficult. Even before the civil rights movement's emphasis on human rights and equality, Americans were uncomfortable with defining the "social worth" of patients to determine access to therapy. The reaction was 2-fold. First, the new committee tried to make its moral choices sound as medical—and therefore morally neutral—as possible. Evaluating a candidate as "psychologically unfit" made the decisionmaking process sound like a technical, scientific decision, even if it actually involved disguising what amounted to moral choices as medical ones.

Second, to prevent difficult choices about which patients to treat, the US Congress approved legislation in 1972 to provide funding for all patients with end-stage renal disease who could not afford to pay for dialysis themselves. This legislation dramatically increased resources available for kidney dialysis but, by removing selection criteria, led to a higher rate of poor health outcomes since sicker patients were now being treated.[25] Ironically, the legislation introduced a new kind of inequality: between patients with end-stage renal disease and patients with other chronic, fatal conditions not covered by national legislation. Furthermore, the legislation compromised the goal of using scarce resources efficiently—sick patients not only received dialysis but a range of support services, despite their slim chances of long-term survival and recovery.

BALANCING COMPETING DEMANDS FOR ACCESS

The trend toward relying on "neutral" medical criteria for patient selection is especially evident in decisionmaking about organ transplants. By using seemingly neutral criteria, policymakers can avoid fundamental conflicts over ethical choices in patient selection, since an appeal to medical criteria masks the ethical choices that are often involved. Defining the "most good" is itself a controversial process involving value judgments about the relative importance of urgency, chances for survival, or quality and quantity of life. In choosing to do the most "good" with a scarce resource, should priority be given to a patient who faces death more immediately, or to a patient who is not as sick but stands a better chance of survival if given treatment? "Doing good" with a limited resource could mean not only averting death but factoring in the quality of life after treatment, as well as expected years of survival.[26] Medical criteria are not completely "value-free" but often incorporate decisions about whether to give priority to the most urgent cases, to those with the best chance of survival, or to those with the best chances of quality and length of life outwards.

Liver transplant allocation, for example, moved from a system that prioritized the potential for clinical efficacy to a system that prioritized urgency, partly because of public pressure over the underlying values embedded in different medical scoring systems. Before 1998, liver transplant patients received organs according to their score on the Child–Turcotte–Pugh system[27] and their position on a waiting list. Allowing patients to receive liver transplants on a first-come-first-served basis (if they met clinical criteria) produced a conflict between the principle of fairness and the problem of urgency. Patients with more severe disease would not receive a transplant if a less sick person were "ahead in line."

This method of establishing priorities was especially vulnerable to the criticism that it systematically discriminated against those with less access to the health care system, such as the poor and minorities. Opponents of the system feared that the poor and minorities were more likely to have

clinically advanced stages of disease when they were placed on waiting lists. In addition to fears about systematic (even if unintended) discrimination about waiting lists, the public also voiced concerns about the use of predictors of clinical efficacy in selecting patients for transplants. One 1996 study showed that the public valued giving "everyone a chance" and allocating livers according to a first-come-first-served basis, rather than linking organ allocation to patient prognosis so that those most likely to survive according to clinical criteria would receive priority.[28]

In response to these 2 different criticisms, in 1998 the US Department of Health and Human Services adopted a policy that prioritizes urgency rather than potential for clinical efficacy and time on waiting lists. The new system stratifies patients according to their score on the Model for End-Stage Liver Disease, with priority given to the more seriously ill patients.[29] Even medical criteria often incorporate a decision to prioritize clinical efficacy versus urgency; public debate about and input into these 2 often-competing values is necessary. Furthermore, seemingly fair criteria such as waiting lists can also incorporate significant inequalities, if certain groups have limited access to health care and therefore cannot get their names entered on waiting lists as quickly as others.

ACCESS TO ANTIRETROVIRAL THERAPY

With the rapid expansion of ARV therapy under new programs such as the Global Fund and PEPFAR—especially, but not only, in sub-Saharan Africa—more patients are now or will be receiving ARV therapy. These programs have established treatment targets that are widely regarded as ambitious and challenging, but will nonetheless reach only about 50% of those urgently needing ARV therapy.[30] However, if the Global Fund does not receive adequate funding, even these targets will be difficult to reach, making the issue of patient selection more pressing. As treatment programs are

being implemented over the next 1 to 3 years, it will be necessary to focus initial efforts in limited areas. Step-by-step implementation means that patient selection will be the reality for the next several years, even if ideal targets are met.

On a country-by-country basis, the percentage of patients receiving ARV therapy out of the estimated population in urgent need of ARV therapy varies tremendously. In sub-Saharan Africa, for example, where coverage of the population that needs medication averages 8%, the figure ranges from 1% in the Central African Republic to a high of 50% in Botswana.[31] Table 1 shows the numbers of patients receiving ARV therapy in 4 countries, the first 2 eligible for PEPFAR funds (Ethiopia and Uganda) and the following 2 ineligible (India and Malawi) and hence dependent on the Global Fund and other donors. Although many governments, such as that of Uganda, have announced plans to provide free ARV therapy to all patients,[32] the reality for the present and the next several years is that medications will be rationed.

Several rationing mechanisms exist at the international, national, and local levels. It is worth evaluating these rationing mechanisms in light of the historical experiences described here. Several important differences exist between those historical examples and the current ARV programs, however. First, the ARV treatment programs take place within the context of global development, international health, and trade regulations, unlike the previous examples of rationing within the United States. Some of the decision-making occurs by donors, such as the decision to select 15 specific countries as recipients of PEPFAR funds.[33] Recipient countries are more constrained in the kinds of decisions they can make than if these programs were initiated and funded by themselves; they cannot shift their own national health budget from HIV/AIDS to other diseases, but must use both Global Funds money and PEPFAR money as additions to their current spending on HIV/AIDS. These treat-

Country	No. of Patients
Ethiopia	
HIV positive[a]	1 500 000
Therapy urgently needed[b]	211 000
Receiving therapy[c]	10 000–13 000
Uganda	
HIV positive[a]	530 000
Therapy urgently needed[b]	114 000
Receiving therapy[c]	40 000–50 000
India	
HIV positive[a]	5 100 000
Therapy urgently needed[b]	770 000
Receiving therapy[c]	20 000–36 000
Malawi	
HIV positive[a]	900 000
Therapy urgently needed[b]	140 000
Receiving therapy[c]	10 000–12 000

[a]For adults and children.[1]
[b]For ages 15–49.[31]
[c]For adults and children.[31]
Source. "3 by 5" Progress Report December 2004 and UNAIDS/WHO Epidemiological Fact Sheet–2004 Update (see endnotes 1 and 31).

ment programs exist within the wider political economy of international relations, where health care in general and HIV/AIDS in particular are only part of a complex relationship between developing countries, donors, and international agencies.

Furthermore, the weak health infrastructure, limited availability of trained medical personnel to deliver and monitor ARV therapy, and widespread prevalence of HIV present serious challenges not faced by the previous historical examples. The feasibility of ARV treatment programs has been such a serious concern that issues of equity and fairness have received comparatively less attention. That said, treatment programs nonetheless face the problem of having more patients medically eligible for ARV therapy than resources permit, and hence have developed a variety of exclusion criteria to ration treatment.[34]

POSSIBLE ARV SELECTION FACTORS

In the sections that follow, I explain the current or proposed patient selection criteria at the national and local levels.

Selection at the Clinical Stage

Selecting patients at the clinical stage involves (1) prioritization of WHO-defined stage IV patients whose prognosis suggests that they are urgently in need of ARV therapies or (2) prioritization of WHO-defined stage III patients who are more likely to survive, and to survive free of long-term complications, than stage IV patients.

Prioritization of stage IV patients has been the explicit recommendation of at least 2 studies[35] and has been the de facto experience of pilot projects providing ARVs, simply because most patients seeking care have been

critically ill patients—desperate enough for access to ARVs to overcome the stigma of being identified as AIDS patients.[36] The decision is reminiscent of the choices outlined in the example of liver transplants: how to balance the conflicting values of fair chances at access versus best outcomes.

The argument in favor of prioritizing stage IV patients combines aspects of fair chances and best outcomes. Stage IV patients face imminent death and do not have the luxury of waiting for treatment programs to begin, while presumably stage III patients may survive until treatment programs are fully operational. Selection of stage IV patients still offers the possibility that stage III patients will be treated in the future, especially as they progress to clinical stage IV. This scenario depends on the continuing expansion of ARV therapy; otherwise, if funds remain fixed, stage III patients may never have access to treatment. Selection of stage IV patients also produces "good outcomes" in that it maximizes the number of deaths averted and may reduce the stigma associated with HIV/AIDS mortality.

Like the problem of liver transplants, however, the definition of "best outcomes" is not as simple as averting deaths. What about long-term chances of survival and overall quality of life? The problem with prioritizing stage IV patients is that they require more intensive and specialized care, which both costs more and requires medical expertise not readily available. Patients with low CD4 cell counts at the initiation of highly active anti-retroviral therapy (HAART) are less likely to survive for 5 years[37] and may develop (or have already developed) long-term disabilities that make a full recovery difficult to achieve.

Adherence Criteria

Whether to include estimations of a patient's ability to adhere to therapy as 1 of the criteria for patient selection is an important question to consider when determining who will receive necessary treatment.

Accounting for the crucial importance of adherence in the success of HAART, it is potentially useful to screen patients for their ability and willingness to adhere to a demanding medical regimen. The problem, however, is that it is difficult to predict accurately which individuals will adhere to ARV therapy, as evidence from the United States has shown.[38] One of the principal reasons for nonadherence in Senegal and Botswana has been the cost of drugs; treatment interruptions occurred because of financial difficulties, which presumably would not have occurred had the drugs been provided free of charge.[39] Once cost is removed as an obstacle, socioeconomic status is not a reliable predictor of adherence.

The situation is similar to the decision faced in the case of kidney dialysis, since this chronic disease necessitated patients' willingness to adhere to a diet and rigorous treatment regimen. In practice, however, selecting patients

according to perceived psychological, emotional, and social strengths introduced significant, unnecessary social biases into the selection process. It is not clear how a "family support network" is defined or its existence determined, again leaving a lot of room for discrimination. Second, no evidence yet exists that shows a clear link between social factors such as socioeconomic status and an individual patient's ability to adhere to ARV therapy.

However, because the issue of adherence is so important to the success of ARV treatment, a number of pilot projects have developed ways of trying to ensure that patients have the commitment to adhere to therapy. Medecins Sans Frontières, for example, requires that patients enroll in support programs, attend clinics regularly for a period of 3 months prior to receiving ARV therapies, and be open about their HIV status.[40] Other programs require a treatment support partner or patient commitment to safe sex practices.[41] The advantage of these approaches is that they depend on an individual's actual behavior, rather than on predictions of behavior based on factors beyond the patient's control. It is important to recognize that even these criteria can be influenced by unconscious biases and potentially unnecessary social criteria (the availability of a treatment support partner, for example).

Age

Whether to prioritize certain age groups, such as children or people with dependents, is another factor to consider in determining access to ARV therapies.

The government of India announced its decision to offer as of April 2004 free ARV therapy to all new parents who are HIV-positive, all children aged younger than 15 years, and eventually all patients with AIDS in the 6 states with the highest prevalence of HIV/AIDS.[42]

Prioritizing children younger than 15 years is meant to save both the next generation and "innocent victims," since most of these children become infected from their mothers rather than

from sexual intercourse. It is critically important to distinguish between the provision of ARV therapy to HIV-positive children and prevention of mother-to-child transmission. Preventing mother-to-child transmission of HIV involves a limited-duration course of medications to prevent primary infection. But the issue of providing lifelong ARV therapy to children is complex and is similar to the decisions initially faced in Seattle regarding dialysis. The Seattle committee excluded sick children from treatment on the grounds that more children would benefit by providing treatment to their parents.

More than virtually any other disease, AIDS has a serious economic and social impact because its victims are working-age and reproductive-age adults.[43] In a recent study, Ugandans apparently unwittingly share the same concerns as the Seattle dialysis policymakers in prioritizing the health care needs of income-producing adults over those of children. Stakeholders (community leaders) in rural and urban Uganda ranked lifelong provision of ARV therapy to adults above short-term prevention of mother-to-child transmission of HIV so that income-generating adults could care for children.[44] If governments are trying to mitigate the social and economic impact of the AIDS epidemic by providing treatment, it will be difficult to sort out which groups should be the primary beneficiaries of treatment programs. The potential for gender discrimination exists, because male heads of households contribute significantly to household wealth.

Occupation

Prioritizing patients with certain occupations is another possible criterion that needs to be considered.

The major argument for favoring a certain occupation is that the skills possessed by that group are vital to the survival of the society as a whole, such as the need for health care workers to protect the population as a whole, the need for teachers to train the next generation, and the need for soldiers to defend society against attack. However, as the experience with penicillin during

World War II suggests, giving priority to a certain group can create considerable conflict. Although American society was fairly united behind the military during World War II, even in these circumstances the public did not always agree that the military deserved priority in access to medications, especially if the soldiers had acquired gonorrhea or syphilis through "immoral means." Some members of the public even questioned the legitimacy of the decisionmaking body. For ARV therapy, policy-makers should therefore anticipate conflict if only 1 occupational group is given priority of access to medications.

Widespread public input into the selection criteria will not eliminate conflict, but it will at least give the public some voice and lend political legitimacy to the selection criteria. In a paper commissioned by WHO, Norman Daniels described the central features of a fair process for distributing ARV therapy; WHO has also issued guidelines on ethical and equitable access to care.[45] One of the significant advantages of this process is that it allows for local communities to have a voice in patient selection. Each country will have the flexibility to adopt policies relevant to its own situations.

Other methods of selecting patients are not carefully thought-out selection criteria but passive systems that make treatment available to the small numbers of people who have been tested (partly owing to the stigma surrounding HIV/AIDS) and to those living near clinic sites who request treatment.[46] The advantage of this system is that it is cost-effective since it requires no investments in infrastructure. The major problem is that it does not provide a fair chance of access for all, because those who have not been tested are more likely to live in rural areas, experience poverty, and have inadequate access to health care.

Furthermore, socially marginalized groups also have the most difficulty in mitigating the effects of stigma.[47] Relying on a system that selects patients according to access to testing sites and absence of stigma exacerbates existing social inequalities,

although it is a feasible and cost-effective method of delivering therapy. This system bears some similarity to the experience of insulin rationing, where no carefully thought-out criteria were in place and access was restricted to certain clinics and hospitals. Furthermore, this system was especially vulnerable to unfairness, as personal and political connections to the physicians and researchers brought access to medications.

The success of ARV programs rests at least partially on their public acceptance as fair programs accountable to local communities. Patient selection is a potentially divisive issue that could aggravate tensions between ethnic groups, religious groups, and social classes.[48] To avoid systematic discrimination—or even the perception that certain individuals or groups are favored at the expense of others— broad public participation in the process of establishing criteria for patient selection should be encouraged. It is also important to operate within a human rights framework to prevent the systematic discrimination in access to treatment according to such factors as sex, ethnicity, and sexual orientation.

Countries will no longer face the tough decisions regarding which patients receive ARV therapy first if prevention efforts are successful, developing countries' productivity and incomes expand as a result of greater international investment, and the costs of treatment continue to decline. Meanwhile, lessons learned from earlier experiences of patient selection can make the process more efficient, equitable, accountable, and legitimate in the eyes of the public. At a minimum, we hope policymakers are aware that patient selection is not a technical problem best solved by experts. Open, public debate will not resolve all conflict, but it will be an important part of the process of building local ownership of AIDS treatment programs, a critical element for their sustained success.

About the Authors

At the time this article was written, all authors were with the Department of Infectious Diseases, Johns Hopkins University, Baltimore, Md. Laura J. McGough is also with the Department of the History of Medicine, Johns Hopkins University. Steven J. Reynolds and Thomas C. Quinn are also with the National Institute of Allergy and Infectious Diseases, National Institutes of Health, Bethesda, Md.

Correspondence: Requests for reprints should be sent to Jonathan M. Zenilman, MD, Infectious Diseases Division, Johns Hopkins Bayview Medical Center, 4940 Eastern Ave, B-3 North, Baltimore, MD 21224 (e-mail: jzenilma@jhmi.edu).

Acknowledgments

Research for this article was supported by a fellowship from the Association of Teachers of Preventive Medicine.

We acknowledge Harry Marks, Nancy Kass, Randall Packard, Khalil Ghanem, Chris Beyrer, and the Journal's anonymous reviewers for their comments on earlier drafts of this article.

Contributors

L. J. McGough conceived the study and led the research and writing. S. J. Reynolds and T. C. Quinn offered technical advice and analysis. J. M. Zenilman supervised the entire process of analysis and article preparation. All authors helped to conceptualize ideas, interpret findings, and revise drafts of the article.

Accepted for publication January 30, 2005.

References

1. World Health Organization, " '3 by 5' Progress Report December 2004," 2005, available at http://www.who.int/3by5/progressreport05/en, accessed January 27, 2005.
2. Ibid.
3. Ibid; "Treating 3 Million by 2005: Making It Happen: The WHO Strategy," available at http://www.unaids.org, accessed April 1, 2005.
4. R. B. Cheek, "Playing God With HIV: Rationing HIV Treatment in Southern

Africa," *African Security Review,* 2001, available at http://www.iss.co.za/PUBS/ASR/10-No4/Cheek.html, accessed May 23, 2005.

5. L. Rosen, J. L. Simon, A. Collier, and I. M. Sanne, "Hard Choices: Rationing Antiretroviral Therapy for HIV/AIDS in Africa," *Lancet* 365 (2005): 354–356.

6. P. Piot, "Defeating HIV/AIDS: Africa Is Changing Gear," speech presented at closing ceremony of the International Conference on AIDS and STD in Africa, Nairobi, Kenya, September 26, 2003, available at http://www.unaids.org/Unaids/EN/About+UNAIDS+executive+director/unaids+executive+director/unaids+executive+directors+speeches+.asp?StartRow=20, accessed May 23, 2005.

7. R. Macklin, "Ethics and Equity in Access to HIV Treatment—3 by 5 Initiative," background paper for the Consultation on Equitable Access to Treatment and Care for HIV/AIDS, World Health Organization, 2004, available at http://www.who.int/ethics/en/background-macklin3.pdf, accessed March 29, 2005; N. Daniels, "How to Achieve Fair Distribution of ARTs in 3 by 5: Fair Process and Legitimacy in Patient Selection," background paper for the Consultation on Equitable Access to Treatment and Care for HIV/AIDS, World Health Organization, 2004, available at http://www.who.int/ethics/en/background-daniels3.pdf (accessed March 29, 2005); Pro-Poor Health Policy Team, " '3 by 5,' Priority in Treatment, and the Poor," background paper for the Consultation on Equitable Access to Treatment and Care for HIV/AIDS, World Health Organization, 2004, available at http://www.who.int/ethics/en/background-pro-poor3.pdf (accessed March 29, 2005); World Health Organization, "Guidance on Ethics and Equitable Access to HIV Treatment and Care," 2004, available at http://www.who.int/ethics/en/ethics_equity_HIV_e.pdf (accessed March 29, 2005).

8. For historical background on the discovery of insulin and its treatment of diabetes, see M. Bliss, *The Discovery of Insulin* (Chicago: University of Chicago Press, 1982); C. Feudtner, *Bittersweet: Diabetes, Insulin, and the Transformation of Illness* (Chapel Hill:

University of North Carolina Press, 2003).

9. Ibid, 135,144,146,151.

10. For the history of penicillin rationing during World War II, see D.P. Adams, *"The Greatest Good to the Greatest Number": Penicillin Rationing on the American Home Front, 1940–1945* (New York: Peter Lang, 1991).

11. Ibid, 70.

12. From the records of the Committee on Medical Research General Correspondence Files, quoted in Adams, *"The Greatest Good to the Greatest Number,"* 71.

13. Adams, *"The Greatest Good to the Greatest Number,"* 75.

14. Quoted in Adams, *"The Greatest Good to the Greatest Number,"* 86.

15. Ibid, 74.

16. M. Leff, "The Politics of Sacrifice on the American Home Front in World War II," *Journal of American History* 77 (1991): 1296–1318.

17. H.M. Marks, "Cortisone, 1949: A Year in the Political Life of a Drug," *Bulletin of the History of Medicine* 66 (1992): 419–439.

18. For a historical background of hemodialysis, see Albert Jonsen, *The Birth of Bioethics* (Oxford: Oxford University Press, 1998); S. Alexander "They Decide Who Lives, Who Dies," *Life* 53 (November 9, 1962): 102–125; R.C. Fox and J.P. Swazey, *The Courage to Fail: A Social View of Organ Transplants and Dialysis,* 2nd ed (Chicago: University of Chicago Press, 1978).

19. The lay members were a minister, a lawyer, a homemaker, a banker, a labor leader, a surgeon (who was not an expert in kidney disease), and a state government official. See Alexander, "They Decide Who Lives, Who Dies."

20. Ibid, 106.

21. Quoted in Fox and Swazey, *The Courage to Fail,* 232.

22. Alexander, "They Decide Who Lives, Who Dies," 106; and R. C. Fox and J. P. Swazey, *The Courage to Fail: A Social View of Organ Transplants and Dialysis* (Chicago: University of Chicago Press, 1974), 245–246.

23. Fox and Swazey, *The Courage to Fail,* 241.

24. Quoted in Alexander, "They Decide Who Lives, Who Dies," 123.

25. R.W. Evans and C.R. Blagg, "Lessons Learned From the End-Stage Renal Disease Experience: Their Implications for Heart

Transplantation," in *Organ Substitution Technology: Ethical, Legal, and Public Policy Issues,* ed. D. Mathieu (Boulder, Colo: Westview Press, 1988), 175–197.

26. D.W. Brock, "Ethical Issues in Recipient Selection for Organ Transplantation," in *Organ Substitution Technology,* 86–99.

27. For the Child-Turcotte-Pugh classification, see P.S. Kamath, R.H. Wiesner, M. Malinchoc, et al., "A Model to Predict Survival in Patients With End-Stage Liver Disease," *Hepatology* 33 (2001): 464–470.

28. P.A. Ubel and G. Loewenstein, "Distributing Scarce Livers: The Moral Reasoning of the General Public," *Social Science and Medicine* 42 (1996): 1049–1055.

29. A.J Muir, L.L. Sanders, M.A. Heneghan, P.C. Kuo, W.E. Wilkinson, and D. Provenzale, "An Examination of Factors Predicting Prioritization for Liver Transplantation," *Liver Transplantation* 8 (2002): 957–961; P.A. Ubel, R.M. Arnold, and A.L. Caplan, "Rationing Failure: The Ethical Lessons of the Retransplantation of Scarce Vital Organs," *Journal of the American Medical Association* 270 (1993): 2469–2474.

30. "Treating 3 Million by 2005," 31.

31. UNAIDS/WHO epidemiological fact sheet—2004 update; country-by-country search engine with HIV prevalence and incidence data available at http://www.who.int/GlobalAtlas/PDFFactory/HIV/index.asp (accessed March 29, 2005).

32. C. Wendo, "Uganda Begins Distributing Free Antiretrovirals," *Lancet* 363 (2004): 2062.

33. The countries are Botswana, Côte d'Ivoire, Ethiopia, Kenya, Mozambique, Namibia, Nigeria, Rwanda, South Africa, Tanzania, Uganda, Zambia, Guyana, Haiti, and Vietnam.

34. M. Rabkin, B. Tonwe-Gold, and W. El-Sadr, "Non-Medical Eligibility Criteria for Pilot HIV/AIDS Treatment Programs in Resource-Poor Settings: The Columbia University MTCT-Plus Experience," oral presentation, XV International AIDS Conference, July 14, 2004, Bangkok, Thailand, abstract WeOrB1278.

35. Christopher Kenyon, Jolene Skordis, Andrew Boulle, and Karrisha Pillay, "The ART of Rationing—The Need for a New Approach to Rationing Health

Interventions," *South African Medical Journal* 93 (2003): 56–60; M. Badri, L.G. Bekker, C. Orrell, J. Pitt, F. Cilliers, and R. Wood, "Initiating Highly Active Antiretroviral Therapy in sub-Saharan Africa: An Assessment of the Revised World Health Organization Scaling-Up Guidelines," *AIDS* 18 (2004): 1159–1168.

36. Louisana Lush and Ernest Darkoh, "HIV and Health Systems: Botswana," paper presented at 6th International Conference on Healthcare Resource Allocation for HIV/AIDS: Healthcare Systems in Transition, October 13–15, 2003, Washington, DC.

37. Ard van Sighem, Mark van de Wiel, Azra Ghani, et al., "Mortality and Progression to AIDS After Starting Highly Active Antiretroviral Therapy," *AIDS* 17 (2003): 2227–2236.

38. R. Murri, A. Antinori, A. Ammassari, et al., "Physician Estimates of Adherence and the Patient–Physician Relationship as a Setting to Improve Adherence to Antiretroviral Therapy,"

Journal of Acquired Immune Deficiency Syndrome 31 (2002): S158–S162.

39. I. Lanièce, M. Ciss, A. Desclaux, et al., "Adherence to HAART and Its Principal Determinants in a Cohort of Senegalese Adults," *AIDS* 17 supplement 3 (2003): S103–S108; S. Weiser, W. Wolfe, D. Bangsberg, et al., "Barriers to Antiretroviral Adherence for Patients Living With HIV Infection and AIDS in Botswana," *Journal of Acquired Immune Deficiency Syndrome* 34 (2003): 281–288.

40. T. Kasper, D. Coetzee, F. Louis, A. Boulle, and K Hilderbrand, "Demystifying Antiretroviral Therapy in Resource-Poor Settings," available at http://www.msf.org/content/page.cfm?articleid=3EC42CE5-ADDB-4384-BC25F9F03313DC04, accessed May 23, 2005.

41. Wendo, "Uganda Begins Distributing Free Antiretrovirals."

42. A. Waldman, "India Plans Free AIDS Therapy, But Effort Hinges on Price Accord With Drug Makers," *New York Times,* December 1, 2003. Available at http://www.aegis.com/news/ads/2003/AD032491.html, accessed May 23, 2005.

43. C. Bell, S. Devarajan, and H. Gersbach, "Thinking About the Long-Run Economic Costs of AIDS," in *The Macroeconomics of HIV/AIDS,* ed. M. Haacker (Washington: International Monetary Fund, 2004), 96–133.

44. L. Kapiriri, B. Robbestad, and O.F. Norheim, "The Relationship Between Prevention of Mother to Child Transmission of HIV and Stakeholder Decision Making in Uganda: Implications for Health Policy," *Health Policy* 66 (2003): 199–213.

45. Daniels, "How to Achieve Fair Distribution"; World Health Organization, "Guidance on Ethics and Equitable Access."

46. *Stepping Back From the Edge: The Pursuit of Antiretroviral Therapy in Botswana, South Africa, and Uganda*

Overview of Tobacco Section

| *Dr. John Seffrin, President and Chief Executive Officer, American Cancer Society*

Tobacco is a scourge that rivals the most destructive diseases, wars, and famines of human history. It killed 100 million people over the course of the 20th century and now kills more than five million people every year. If current trends continue, tobacco is expected to kill one billion people in the 21st century. This pandemic is perpetuated by a ruthless and unconscionable industry that has infiltrated every corner of the globe to market addictive and carcinogenic consumer products. Today, about one in 12 deaths worldwide is attributable to tobacco, and an increasing proportion of these deaths (about 70 percent of the 10 million annual tobacco deaths expected in 2025) will occur in low- and middle-resource countries.

To counter this public health disaster, tobacco control advocates have united behind the Framework Convention on Tobacco Control (FCTC), the world's first and only public health treaty. By demanding that governments ratify and implement the treaty, public health advocates have achieved remarkable success in curtailing tobacco's insidious spread. The articles presented in this section highlight both the victories to date and the important work that remains to be done in the long and challenging battle against the global scourge of tobacco.

The FCTC is designed to arrest the global toll of tobacco-related death and disease, but not all countries have ratified it. Developing countries that fail to ratify the treaty are prime targets for the tobacco industry's continued assault. There is a clear need for concerted global tobacco control meas-ures that can transcend borders in the same way that multinational tobacco companies operate across political boundaries. For example, Nadel, Rees, and Connolly describe how Altria (Philip Morris), the world's most profitable tobacco company, is exploiting weak tobacco control laws in countries such as Indonesia: "PM's involvement in the Indonesian tobacco market emphasizes the need for public health advocates to pressure multinational tobacco companies to support the principles of the Framework Convention on Tobacco Control. We welcome this momentous initiative. Nevertheless, a truly unified global tobacco control treaty must also have the capacity to prevent transnational tobacco companies from continuing to undermine public health in the developing world."

The FCTC's principles are built upon a vast record of tobacco control research that has produced mounting evidence about the devastating health effects of tobacco as well as the policies that can control it. Research is the foundation upon which good policy and progress are made. Stillman, et al., describe how the Global Tobacco Research Network (GTRN) unites organizations and individuals involved in tobacco control research: "The Global Tobacco Research Network (GTRN) was developed to enhance global tobacco control research through information sharing and collaboration among researchers. The formation of the GTRN is timely because of the need to ratify, implement, and track the Framework Convention on Tobacco Control. While the spectrum of international tobacco control research continues to expand, resources to support these efforts are still quite limited. As an issue-specific network focused on information sharing and capacity building associated with tobacco control research, the GTRN will provide an opportunity for enhancing the effectiveness of tobacco control initiatives."

Lando, et al., challenge researchers in developing countries not only to initiate more tobacco control research, but also to translate and implement research findings from both developed countries and developing countries to promote effective tobacco control policy changes. Better translation of research into practice will help foster the policies necessary to promote tobacco control in developing countries. According to the authors, "In low- and middle-income countries, translating research into practice and policy is integral for tobacco control."

Research provides the evidence base for promoting and implementing sound tobacco control policies. As Hammond, et al., point out, health hazard warnings and graphic labels on cigarette cartons and boxes are visible and effective regulations for reducing cigarette consumption: "Policymakers should not be reluctant to introduce vivid or graphic warnings for fear of adverse outcomes."

Regulating tobacco is imperative for countries where smoking prevalence rates are alarmingly high – and getting higher. Gu, et al., report that more smoking prevention and intervention efforts are desperately needed in China, the world's largest tobacco consumer. Multinational tobacco companies attempting to penetrate the Chinese market heavily promote smoking, especially among women, a group whose smoking prevalence rates have been historically low. The authors underscore the urgency of China's tobacco problem: "The high prevalence of cigarette smoking and environmental tobacco smoke exposure in the Chinese population indicates an urgent need for smoking prevention and cessation efforts"

Gilmore, et al., report that nations of the former Soviet Union are also suffering the disastrous effects of the encroaching tobacco plague. "Smoking rates among men … have been high for some time and remain among the highest in the world. Smoking rates among women have increased from previous years and appear to reflect transnational tobacco company activity."

To combat this plague that knows no borders, Kassel and Ross advocate culturally sensitive tobacco control policy implementation that is cognizant of global cultural diversity. Policies should be implemented in ways that are relevant to countries with different social and cultural values. They point out, "There are several conceptual training models, all of which emphasize communicative partnerships and multidisciplinary approaches. It also is important to take cultural background and specificity into account when shaping research and training agendas. We present a number of successful training initiatives and address both the strengths and the pitfalls of these endeavors."

Similarly, Bayer and Stuber report that understanding the underlying public values and perceptions regarding tobacco and how stigmas against smoking are formed can be useful for developing tobacco control messages. As knowledge about tobacco's adverse health effects becomes more widespread, smoking is less frequently regarded as glamorous and is increasingly stigmatized as disgusting and unhealthy. The authors assert that researchers must understand how this paradigm shift takes place: "Only when we understand the circumstances under which stigmatization transforms behaviors linked to disease and early death and are able to distinguish these from the circumstances in which stigmatization has negative impacts on public health will it be possible to weigh the competing moral claims of population health and the burdens that policy may impose on the socially vulnerable."

The tobacco industry has gone to great lengths to avoid such stigmatization and to whitewash its nefarious and mercenary activities. However, Wander and Malone warn that negotiating with the tobacco industry is not only a mistake, but that it could produce an effect opposite to that intended by public health advocates: "Tobacco companies can appear to accommodate public health demands while securing strategic advantages. Negotiating with the tobacco industry can enhance its legitimacy and facilitate its ability to market deadly cigarettes without corresponding benefits to public health."

Humanity faces catastrophic consequences unless organized, concerted, informed action is taken against tobacco. Tobacco control advocates and researchers are working worldwide to prevent the worst case of avoidable loss of life in human history. The enlightening articles in this section provide the public health community with critical information and key resources to fuel lifesaving tobacco control efforts in countries around the world.

References

1. Nadel J, Rees V, Connolly GN. Disparities in global tobacco harm reduction. *Am J Public Health*. 2005 Dec;95(12):2120.

2. Stillman FA, Wipfli HL, Lando HA, Leischow S, Samet JM. Building capacity for international tobacco control research: the global tobacco research network. *Am J Public Health*. 2005 Jun;95(6):965-8.

3. Hammond D, Fong GT, McDonald PW, Brown KS, Cameron R. Canadian cigarette warning labels and adverse outcomes: evidence from Canadian smokers. *Am J Public Health*. 2004 Aug;94(8):1442-5.

4. Bayer R, Stuber J. Tobacco control, stigma, and public health: rethinking the relations. *Am J Public Health*. 2006 Jan;96(1):47-50. Epub 2005 Nov 29.

5. Wander N and Malone RE. Making Big Tobacco Give In: You Lose, They Win. *Am J Public Health* 2006; 96: 2048-2054.

6. Lando HA, Borrelli B, Klein LC, Waverley LP, Stillman FA, Kassel JD, and Warner KE. The Landscape in Global Tobacco Control Research: A Guide to Gaining a Foothold. *Am J Public Health* 2005; 95: 939-945.

7. Kassel JD and Ross H. The Role of Training in Global Tobacco Control Research. *Am J Public Health* 2005; 95: 946-949.

8. Gu D, Wu X, Reynolds K, Duan X, Xin X, Reynolds RF, Whelton PK, He J for the InterASIA Collaborative Group. Cigarette Smoking and Exposure to Environmental Tobacco Smoke in China: The International Collaborative Study of Cardiovascular Disease in Asia. *Am J Public Health* 2004; 94: 1972-1976.

9. Gilmore A, Pomerleau J, McKee M, Rose R, Haerpfer CW, Rotman D, and Tumanov S. Prevalence of Smoking in 8 Countries of the Former Soviet Union: Results from the Living Conditions, Lifestyles and Health Study. *Am J Public Health* 2004; 94: 2177-2187.

Disparities in Global Tobacco Harm Reduction

| Jonathan Nadel, BS, Vaughan Rees, PhD and Gregory N. Connolly, DMD, MPH

In "Origins of the WHO Framework Convention on Tobacco Control," Roemer et al. present a compelling argument for a unified global approach to tobacco control.[1] However, the Framework Convention on Tobacco Control will not benefit nonsignatory countries, which tend to have few or no existing tobacco control measures in place. Indonesia is the only Asian country that failed to sign the treaty. Significantly, Indonesia is also one of the largest tobacco markets in the world, with smoking rates in excess of 60% for adult males and 20% for 10-year-old males.[2] Altria, the parent company of US cigarette giant Philip Morris (PM), recently acquired Sampoerna, Indonesia's second-largest cigarette manufacturer, and appears poised to exploit the virtual absence of tobacco industry regulation in that country.

In the United States, where more rigorous tobacco control measures are in effect, PM appears to be making some progress toward reducing the harms associated with tobacco use. Positive initiatives such as harm reduction, youth smoking prevention, and adult cessation programs are part of a strategy employed by PM in the United States in response to public health initiatives. PM recently announced plans to construct a US$300 million facility in Richmond, Va, to develop "reduced exposure" tobacco products and introduced Marlboro UltraSmooth, a cigarette with a carbon filter designed to reduce toxic gas phase smoke constituents, in test markets.

In Indonesia, more than 90% of cigarettes smoked are *kretek*, or clove cigarettes. These often unfiltered cigarettes contain a blend of ground clove buds and tobacco and deliver significantly higher levels of tar, nicotine, and carbon monoxide than a conventional US cigarette and much higher levels still than Marlboro UltraSmooth (Table 1).

Unfortunately, it is difficult to reconcile PM's expressed commitment to harm reduction with the company's investment in a product with such questionable health implications in a country with little or no regulation of marketing and sales to minors. PM's actions in Indonesia cast serious doubt on the company's purported reforms. PM's involvement in the Indonesian tobacco market emphasizes the need for public health advocates to pressure multinational tobacco companies to support the principles of the Framework Convention on Tobacco Control. We welcome this momentous initiative. Nevertheless, a truly unified global tobacco control treaty must also have the capacity to prevent transnational tobacco companies from continuing to undermine public health in the developing world.

About the Authors

The authors are with the Harvard School of Public Health, Boston, Mass.

Correspondence: Requests for reprints should be sent to Vaughan Rees, PhD, Harvard School of Public Health, Landmark Bldg 3rd Floor E, 677 Huntington Ave, Boston, MA 02115 (e-mail: vrees@hsph.harvard.edu).

References
1. Roemer R, Taylor A, Lariviere J. Origins of the WHO framework convention on tobacco control. *Am J Public Health*. 2005;95:936–938.
2. Reynolds C. The fourth largest market in the world. *Tob Control*. 1999;8:89–91.
3. Malson JL, Lee EM, Murty R, Moolchan ET, Pickworth WB. Clove cigarette smoking: biochemical, physiological and subjective effects. *Pharmacol Biochem Behav*. 2003;74;739–745.
4. Philip Morris USA. Product facts: tar and nicotine numbers. Available at: http://www.philipmorrisusa.com/en/product_facts/tar_nicotine/tar_nicotine_numbers.asp. Accessed June 29, 2005.

TABLE 1— Smoke Chemistry Data for an Indonesian Kretek (Clove Cigarette), a Conventional US Cigarette, and Marlboro UltraSmooth

	Kretek[a]	Conventional Cigarette[a]	Marlboro UltraSmooth[b]
Tar, mg	46.8	16.3	5.0
Nicotine, mg	2.2	1.1	0.4
Carbon monoxide, mg	28.3	15.5	NA

[a]Data for the popular brand Djarum Special, taken from Malson et al.[3]
[b]Data taken from Philip Morris USA[4]; however, an independent laboratory test found 5.5 mg of tar and 6.6 mg of carbon monoxide in one Marlboro UltraSmooth prototype test marketed (GN Connolly DMD, MPH, et al., unpublished data, 2005).

Building Capacity for International Tobacco Control Research: The Global Tobacco Research Network

| Frances A. Stillman, EdD, EdM, Heather L. Wipfli, MA, Harry A. Lando, PhD, Scott Leischow, PhD and Jonathan M. Samet, MD, MS

ABSTRACT

The Global Tobacco Research Network (GTRN) was developed to enhance global tobacco control research through information sharing and collaboration among researchers. The formation of the GTRN is timely because of the need to ratify, implement, and track the Framework Convention on Tobacco Control.

While the spectrum of international tobacco control research continues to expand, resources to support these efforts are still quite limited. As an issue-specific network focused on information sharing and capacity building associated with tobacco control research, the GTRN will provide an opportunity for enhancing the effectiveness of tobacco control initiatives.

INTRODUCTION

Global tobacco control is at a crossroads. On the one hand, there is strong evidence about the health effects of active and passive smoking, and there has been considerable progress toward understanding what constitutes effective tobacco control strategies. Moreover, many evidence-based strategies have been included in the Framework Convention on Tobacco Control (FCTC).[1] On the other hand, diminishing returns, complacency, and failure to translate evidence into practice threatens to undermine much of the excellent tobacco control work undertaken to date, and many low- and middle-income countries lack the capacity to undertake tobacco-related research and imple-

ment tobacco control strategies.[2]

Warner[3] and Lando et al.[4] addressed key weaknesses in implementing effective and resource-efficient tobacco control research in low-and middle-income countries. First, while relevant research is being produced, mechanisms are not in place for synthesis and dissemination to ensure that important findings inform national policy development.[2] Second, there is no central clearinghouse that provides contact information for tobacco control researchers or brief descriptions of current tobacco control research efforts.[4] Finally, collaboration among researchers is not taking advantage of potential efficiencies through joint training, mentoring, and pooling of information.

In response to these needs, a Global Tobacco Research Network (GTRN) developed. The GTRN connects individuals and organizations collaborating to conduct, synthesize, manage, and disseminate of tobacco control research in support of a policy-relevant research agenda. The network's goal is to consolidate researchers and institutions involved in the broad range of research that is addressing the determinants, consequences, and control of tobacco production, promotion, and consumption and exposure to tobacco smoke. These researchers have both the knowledge and the skills to build and sustain future global tobacco control research efforts.

BACKGROUND

In 2002, the US National Cancer Institute (NCI) launched the Initiative for the Study of Innovative Systems to

better understand strategies for integrating science and practice. The initiative included broad consultation with tobacco control experts to map out the current extent of tobacco control activity and to identify tobacco control priorities. Leading experts in systems and network theory helped develop an integrated model of tobacco control that could lead to a better alignment of tobacco control activities at the national, state, and local levels.[5] The NCI also supported the development of the GTRN to practically apply network development principles. The Institute for Global Tobacco Control is responsible for the GTRN's practical operations. A steering committee composed of individuals who represent major institutions and networks involved in international tobacco research drives the GTRN's conceptual development. Initial committee members represented the NCI, the Centers for Disease Control and Prevention, the National Institutes of Health Fogarty International Center, the Society for Research on Nicotine and Tobacco, GLOBALink, the Campaign for Tobacco Free Kids, the American Cancer Society, and Canada's Institute for International Research on Tobacco Control. GTRN developers are currently expanding this committee to increase the number of low- and middle-income-country researchers and to ensure these researchers' perspectives inform the GTRN's evolution. Developers also are working with other international research institutions to ensure the global nature of the network and to ensure a diverse, multi-institutional investment in the GTRN's future.

RATIONALE

Tobacco research is well suited to experimenting with new approaches to global public health networking. The large and diverse tobacco research community is composed of individuals and institutions that have a broad range of expertise (e.g., public health, behavioral science, communications, economics, trade, globalization, corporate social responsibility, law, and agriculture). Mechanisms are needed for enhancing the ability of this group to work with each other and to influence one another and the larger policy and social environment. New approaches also are needed for linking and consolidating the increasingly global and multidisciplinary nature of the tobacco control evidence base. A plethora of research conducted in low- and middle-income countries has yet to be summarized and disseminated, and important combinations and linkages have yet to be made within the voluminous evidence produced by expert groups and governments throughout the world. The lack of an overarching infrastructure means that tobacco research efforts often overlap and fail to fill existing knowledge gaps. Moreover, the lack of institutionalized methods for the global management and transfer of information means that the current tobacco research system is at risk of losing important technical resources and expertise as individuals move in and out of tobacco control. The GTRN could and should provide a sustainable and self-sufficient network that can respond to these current weaknesses in the system.

A second reason for developing the GTRN is the urgent demand for research and technical assistance by countries that seek to ratify and implement the FCTC. Article 20 of the FCTC (Research, Surveillance, Monitoring and Exchange of Information) outlines the minimum amount of evidence needed in every country. To fulfill the treaty's research and surveillance obligations, each country must provide (1) estimates of the burden of disease caused by smoking, (2) data on tobacco prevalence and use, (3) standardized measures and methods for monitoring tobacco control policy, and (4) mechanisms for industry tracking.[1] The FCTC, which also emphasizes the need for cooperation among scientific, technical, and legal professionals, has been ratified by more than 40 countries and entered into force in February 2005. The GTRN should provide a platform for developing international research collaborations that tracks the treaty's implementation and the unintended consequences that will surely arise as new regulations are passed.

Perhaps the most valuable reason for creating a tobacco research network is in the lessons its development will provide to the broader public health community. Improved global communication, knowledge sharing, and information dissemination—for both communicable and noncommunicable diseases—are all timely public health issues. Global public health capacity will be greatly enhanced if methods are developed to effectively link research communities, synthesize large amounts of information, and adequately disseminate information and knowledge to stakeholders (advocates, researchers, policymakers) who work at the local, regional, and international levels. The extensive, experienced, and multidisciplinary global tobacco research community is well poised to develop a network that will improve public health practice and research.

Developing the GTRN: 6 Principles

Six principles drove the initial development of the GTRN: purpose, values, people, concept, structure, and practice (Table 1). GTRN developers had to answer fundamental questions: Who belongs in the network? What do they share? What resources do they possess? What are their needs? What can the network offer? How can the network be structured to ensure access and use? What technology and techniques are available?

Purpose, values, and people. The lack of an easily identifiable tobacco research system is evidence of the need for a defined hub for tobacco research networking. Potential GTRN members' training, skills, and areas of expertise will differ greatly. For example, a researcher who studies the biobehavioral effects of nicotine uses different methods and requires a different skill set than a more applied researcher who compares the impact of different policies on youth cigarette consumption. However, both types of

TABLE 1— Principles Guiding the Initial Development of the Global Tobacco Research Network

People	Multisectoral community of researchers and institutions involved in the broad range of research that addresses the determinants, consequences, and control of tobacco production, promotion and consumption, and exposure to tobacco smoke
Purpose	Enhance research with the goal of reducing the burden of disease and death caused by tobacco
Values	Research collaboration, knowledge sharing, and educational partnerships
Concept	Network consolidation, knowledge management, and knowledge sharing to improve the conduct and the application of tobacco research
Structure	Virtual web of individuals and organizations connected through the Internet
Practice	Research and organization directories, information databases, research-related resources and tools, and online discussions

research can influence the course of tobacco control and may inform the conclusions of the other's work. The GTRN serves all individuals and organizations that support or conduct research that addresses the determinants, consequences, and control of tobacco production, promotion, and consumption and exposure to tobacco smoke. This community of researchers also shares an overriding purpose: a commitment to reducing the burden of disease and death caused by tobacco. This purpose brings coherence and thus enables longevity and collective action within the network. Potential GTRN members also commit themselves to the network's shared values of research collaboration, knowledge sharing, and educational partnerships.

The developers of the GTRN have undertaken many activities to better understand how potential future members are working together, what resources they possess, and what they want and need to improve the conduct and the impact of their work. The Institute for Global Tobacco Control collected information from tobacco control researchers during the August 2003 World Conference on Tobacco or Health in Helsinki, Finland. A series of meetings were held to discuss the networking structure and functions, and a needs assessment was conducted with a convenience sample (n = 228) who were asked about

researcher demographics, research priorities, and perceived needs. Respondents were from both developing countries (42%) and developed countries (58%), and all 6 of the World Health Organization's geographical regions were represented.

Analysis of the meetings' minutes and the assessment results showed the researchers were most interested in improved information dissemination, increased collaborative partnerships, better access to tools and protocols for surveillance and evaluation, and increased opportunities for face-to-face and virtual training. Figure 1 shows a comparison of developing- and developed-country research priorities.

The needs assessment provided information that helped with the development of the GTRN's priorities; however, the results were limited because of the small convenience sample. A much larger assessment is being developed that will collect information on organizational expertise and priorities and ongoing tobacco control research activities.

Concept, structure, and practice. During the initial network analysis, the steering committee identified 3 key concepts that are driving the demand for the GTRN: network consolidation, knowledge management, and knowledge sharing. Once the GTRN's conceptual foundation had been determined, practical work on delivery began.

To date, Web-based networks and e-mail exchange offer the most effective and cost-efficient structures for linking researchers and advocates worldwide. However, it is recognized that barriers to both accessing the Internet and downloading files still exist in many low- and middle-income countries. Use of knowledge management principles is essential for the GTRN, because information must be synthesized and provided in a form that reduces technology limitations.[6]

In an effort to learn from past virtual tobacco control networking and to not reinvest in structures already available, the GTRN was developed within the structure of GLOBALink.[7] Active since 1992, GLOBALink has become a very large network that incorporates many different aspects of tobacco control. GLOBALink's home page is available in 8 languages, has news bulletins, electronic conferences, live interactive chat, and full-text databases (including news, legislation, directories). The home page and all its features were developed to facilitate use in areas where slow or expensive Internet services exist. GLOBALink does not provide any research-related services, and it was pleased to partner with the GTRN to develop a globally accessible platform dedicated specifically to research.

Many of the same approaches and technologies used by GLOBALink have been incorporated into the GTRN's home page. Priority has been given to developing a site that will be user friendly in low- and middle-income countries. The GTRN home page is available only in English; however, initial proposals for developing language-specific regional pages have been received. If an opportunity to expand the GTRN arises, GLOBALink's language resources will be available.

GTRN Resource Development

GTRN membership and organizational databases. The GTRN is working closely with GLOBALink to develop databases that have in-depth and searchable profiles of researchers and organizations. A major challenge fac-

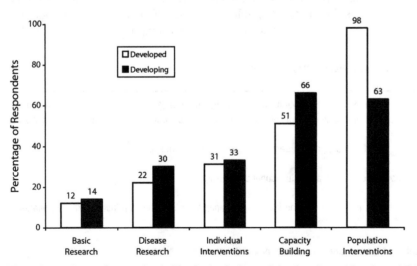

FIGURE 1— Comparisons of research priorities in developing and developed countries: August 5–7, 2003.

ing the GTRN is the way to systematically locate this information; however, once the data collection challenges are overcome, the databases will provide information that is searchable by region, country, research expertise, and institutional and network affiliations of the researchers and organizations involved. This database will allow funding agencies to identify qualified researchers who can undertake new research endeavors, and it will allow researchers to locate potential research partners.

GTRN informational databases. To facilitate information synthesis, the GTRN is developing several informational databases. The first is an Interactive Database of Tobacco Control Literature, which is the result of a systematic country-specific review of published tobacco control research. To date, the GTRN has completed literature reviews from more than 30 countries that were selected on the basis of these countries' involvement in ongoing Fogarty International Center tobacco control grant projects.[4] The literature was gathered from 10 electronic databases that collected articles, regardless of language, from internationally indexed journals (all of which provide abstracts in English). A previously developed tobacco research classification system (National Organization of Tobacco Use Research Funding) was used to categorize the articles and provided an organized framework and set of descriptors for cataloging tobacco-related research.[8] The initial literature review did not cover "gray literature," such as government reports on tobacco; however, the GTRN is now considering how such literature can be added to the database to provide a more comprehensive resource. The GTRN also is in the process of launching an interactive and updated form of the comprehensive *Tobacco Atlas,*[9] and the GTRN's Web site[10] provides links to other tobacco control online databases.

Research tools and training. The GTRN Web site also provides a repository of tobacco control research–related resources and tools. These tools should expand to include example pro-tocols, surveys, and grant applications; best practices and fact sheets; and certification exams. The GTRN also will play an important coordinating role in an international mentoring program that links experienced tobacco researchers with those in need of technical assistance.

Sustainability and Funding

The GTRN's first 2 years were supported with funding from the NCI. Funding for the next phase of the GTRN is currently being secured, with the possibility of additional organizations providing support. It is important to note that funding challenges are the norm for networks like the GTRN. Despite a membership of more than 4000 tobacco control professionals, GLOBALink continues to have significant funding restrictions and must seek new funding support for its operations each year. The GTRN and GLOBALink are working together to brainstorm new approaches to network resource mobilization. Membership dues, although effective in raising funds, cannot be seen as a viable method for fundraising for the GTRN or GLOBALink because, by definition, these networks seek to include members of the tobacco control community who have little or no resources. Another form of user fees—those that focus on the large organizations that use the networks to reach out to the global community—are under consideration. The GLOBALink–GTRN partnership is seen by both parties as a critical element of future fundraising efforts.

CONCLUSION

During its first 2 years, the GTRN developed a comprehensive understanding of current tobacco research system dynamics, built a strong coalition of global partners, and is in the process of developing a number of innovative resources. The GTRN is now poised to evolve into an effective information network that will (1) facilitate international research communication and collaboration; (2) manage, synthesize, and disseminate global tobacco control information; and (3) provide technical research–related resources.[10]

However, the next stage of GTRN's development faces many challenges. Better methods for including researchers from low-and middle-income countries are needed to ensure that the GTRN is more diverse and is not seen as an arrangement dominated by high-income countries. Although limited, the GTRN has experienced some organizational hesitation to fully participate in the networks' activities, particularly in terms of sharing resources and tools. Organizational turf battles must be anticipated as the network continues to grow. Whether or not the GTRN can truly provide a comprehensive global clearinghouse for training and employment opportunities still remains to be seen. Similar to other areas of tobacco control, the GTRN also is likely to suffer from limited resources and a lack of interested funding partners. Although the GTRN is being developed to be as self-sufficient as possible, quality networks require continued attention and resource support. However, this aspect of the GTRN's future may provide the most important lessons to the broader public health community. How can a publicly available information network that serves a global community without emphasizing any one specific organization or supporter be adequately developed and sustained over the long term?

About the Authors

Frances A. Stillman, Heather L. Wipfli, and Jonathan M. Samet are with the Institute for Global Tobacco Control, Johns Hopkins Bloomberg School of Public Health, Baltimore, Md. Harry A. Lando is with the Department of Epidemiology, University of Minnesota, Minneapolis, Minn. Scott Leischow is with the National Cancer Institute, Rockville, Md.

Correspondence: Requests for reprints should be sent to Frances A. Stillman, EdD, EdM, Institute for Global Tobacco Control, Johns Hopkins Bloomberg School of Public

Health, 615 N Wolfe St, Rm W6027, Baltimore, MD 21205 (email: fstillma@jhsph.edu).

Acknowledgments

We thank the Fogarty International Center of the National Institutes of Health for its continued support of our work (grant R01-HL-73699). Our study was also supported in part by National Cancer Institute Task Order number 10 (Public Service Contract number 282980019).

We also thank our research assistant, Wahid Maalouf, for his work in constructing the literature database.

Note. The views expressed are solely the responsibility of the authors and do not necessarily represent that of the National Cancer Institute.

Contributors

All authors contributed to the origination of the article. F.A. Stillman and H. L. Wipfli wrote the article. H. A. Lando, S. Leischow, and J. M. Samet reviewed and edited drafts of the article.

References

1. Framework Convention on Tobacco Control. World Health Organization. Available at: http://www.who.int/tobacco/fctc/text/en/fctc_en.pdf. Accessed August 31, 2004.
2. Research for International Tobacco Control (RITC). *Bridging the Research Gaps in Global Tobacco Control: Report on the Meeting in Ottawa, Canada, November 4–6, 2002.* Ottawa, Ontario, Canada: RITC; 2002.
3. Warner KE. The role of research in international tobacco control. *Am J Public Health*; 2005;95:976–984.
4. Lando HA, Borrelli B, Klein LC, et al. The landscape in global tobacco control research: a guide to gaining a foothold. *Am J Public Health*; 2005;95:939–945.
5. Best A, Tenkasi R, Trochim W, et al. Systemic transformational change in tobacco control: an overview of The Initiative for the Study and Implementation of Systems (ISIS). In: Casebeer A, Harrison A, Mark AE, eds. *Innovation in Health Care: A Reality Check.* New York, NY: Palgrave Macmillan. In Press.
6. Lau F. Toward a knowledge management framework in health. Available at: http://library.ahima.org/xpedio/groups/public/documents/ahima/bok1_024634.cfm. Accessed March 28, 2005.
7. GLOBALink home page. Available at: http://www.globalink.org. Accessed August 31, 2004.
8. Maule CO. Classifying tobacco-related research: development and use of a system to describe nonprofit extramural research funding in the United States and Canada, 1999. *Nicotine Tobacco Res.*

Graphic Canadian Cigarette Warning Labels and Adverse Outcomes: Evidence from Canadian Smokers

| David Hammond, MSc, Geoffrey T. Fong, PhD, Paul W. McDonald, PhD, K. Stephen Brown, PhD and Roy Cameron, PhD

ABSTRACT

Objectives. We assessed the impact of graphic Canadian cigarette warning labels.

Methods. We used a longitudinal telephone survey of 616 adult smokers.

Results. Approximately one fifth of participants reported smoking less as a result of the labels; only 1% reported smoking more. Although participants reported negative emotional responses to the warnings including fear (44%) and disgust (58%), smokers who reported greater negative emotion were more likely to have quit, attempted to quit, or reduced their smoking 3 months later. Participants who attempted to avoid the warnings (30%) were no less likely to think about the warnings or engage in cessation behavior at follow-up.

Conclusions. Policymakers should not be reluctant to introduce vivid or graphic warnings for fear of adverse outcomes.

INTRODUCTION

In recognition of the growing health and economic burden of tobacco use,[1,2] the World Health Organization recently adopted the world's first public health treaty, the Framework Convention on Tobacco Control. This requires nations to implement a range of tobacco control policies, including important provisions for package labeling. The Framework Convention on Tobacco Control calls for large, clear health warnings "that may be in the form of a picture" and cover between 30% and 50% of the pack.

Warning labels that meet and exceed these requirements were introduced on Canadian cigarette packages in December 2000. The Canadian labels feature 1 of 16 full-color, sometimes graphic, health warnings, covering more than 50% of the front and back of cigarette packages. Messages that provide more detailed health risk and cessation information appear on the inside of packages.

Graphic warnings have been criticized on 4 general grounds: they will cause unnecessary or excessive emotional distress; smokers will simply avoid the warnings; graphic labels will undermine the credibility of the message; and, most notably, graphic or "grotesque" labels will cause reactance, or *increases* in consumption.[3,4] However, at present, there are no published findings on the impact of graphic warning labels.

The present study sought to assess emotional reactions, avoidant behaviors, and self-report measures of impact in response to the new Canadian warning labels. The study also examined to what extent, if at all, emotional responses and avoidant behaviors predicted cessation behavior at a 3-month follow-up.

METHODS

Participants

Participants were 622 adult smokers living in southwestern Ontario. Adult smokers were aged 18 years or older, had smoked at least 100 cigarettes in their lifetime, and smoked at least 1 cigarette per day at the time of the survey.

Procedure

Baseline interviews were conducted during October and November 2001, approximately 9 months after the introduction of the graphic warnings. The sample was selected using a modified Mitofsky–Waksburg random-digit dialing technique.[5]

Eligible households were identified by asking respondents the number of adult smokers in the household, and the "most recent birthday" method[6] was used to select participants from households with more than 1 adult smoker. A total of 14% (n = 111) of eligible respondents refused or failed to complete the survey: 3% of potentially eligible households (it was assumed that 23% of households contained an eligible smoker, based on regional data from the Canadian Tobacco Use Monitoring Survey[7]) "broke off" before screening, and 11% of eligible respondents refused or terminated after screening. In addition, 10% (n = 80) of potentially eligible households were not reached, resulting in an American Association of Public Opinion Research No. 4 response rate of 76% (n = 616).[8] Participants completed a 3-month follow-up survey in January and February 2002.

Measures

Smoking Status and Demographic Variables. The baseline survey assessed daily cigarette consumption, number of years as a smoker, quitting history, and demographic variables. Intention to quit smoking was measured by asking participants whether they were seriously considering quitting in the next 30 days, 3 months, 6 months, 1 year, or not at all.

Perceived Impact of the Warning Labels. Participants were asked to what extent the warning labels had affected 4 cessation-related outcomes: daily cigarette consumption, how often they thought about the health risks of smoking, confidence in their ability to quit, and the likelihood they would quit smoking. Participants responded to these items on a 5-point bipolar Likert scale coded as negative impact (e.g., "I am a little/a lot less likely to quit as a result of the warnings"), no impact, and positive impact (e.g., "I am a little/a lot more likely to quit . . .").

Depth of Processing. A measure of *depth of processing* was developed to assess the salience of the warning labels and the extent to which smokers attended to the warnings. Nine items assessed how carefully smokers had looked at the warnings (e.g., "How closely have you ever read the messages on the outside of packages?") or reflected and elaborated on the warnings (e.g., "How often have you thought about the warnings on the inside of the pack?"). Responses were given on 5-point Likert scales and summed to create an index of depth of processing (Cronbach = 0.83).

Emotional Reactions, Avoidance, and Credibility. Participants were asked whether they had made any efforts to avoid the warnings by covering or hiding the labels, using a cigarette case of their own, or requesting a specific package to avoid a particular warning. Avoidance behaviors were analyzed as a dichotomous outcome, where 0 = no effort to avoid the warnings and 1 = any effort to avoid the warnings. Participants were also asked to what extent, if at all, they had felt fear or disgust as a result of the labels, using a 5-point Likert scale ranging from "not at all" to "extreme." An index of negative emotional reaction to the warnings was created by summing Likert responses for fear and disgust ($r = 0.034$, $P < .001$). Credibility of the warnings was measured by asking: "How accurately do you feel the warnings depict the risks to your health?" using a 5-point bipolar scale ranging from "very inaccurately" to "very accurately."

Follow-Up Survey. The 3-month follow-up survey assessed any changes in smoking behavior, including attempts to quit ("Have you made any attempts to quit smoking in the past 3 months that lasted at least 24 hours?") and reductions in daily consumption. A dichotomous variable was created for cessation-related outcomes, where 0 = no cessation behavior and 1 = participants who had either quit, made at least 1 attempt to quit, or reduced their smoking by at least 1 cigarette per day.

Statistical Analysis

Logistic regression analyses were used to predict cessation behaviors at follow-up. All odds ratios were adjusted for measures of cigarettes per day, years smoking, intentions to quit, prior attempts to quit, gender, age, and education. All analyses were conducted using SPSS, Version 10.0 (SPSS Inc, Chicago, Ill).

RESULTS

Characteristics of Sample

A total of 616 participants completed the baseline survey. Table 1 shows that the characteristics of the study participants were similar to those of a representative sample of Canadian smokers.[7] The 1 exception is that a greater proportion of study participants were female; however, gender was not associated with any of the predictors in the regression analyses, presented later. A total of 432 participants completed the 3-month follow-up survey, for a follow-up rate of 70%. There were no significant differences between completers and noncompleters on demographic variables or any explanatory variables, including measures of smoking status, emotional reaction, credibility, and avoidance.

Self-Report Impact

Figure 1 indicates that a substantial proportion of smokers perceived a cessationrelated benefit from the warning labels. Most important, 19% of smokers reported that the warnings had made them smoke less, in contrast

TABLE 1– Characteristics of Survey Respondents and of a Representative Sample of Canadian Smokers: Southwestern Ontario, October–November, 2001

Variable	Sample (n = 616)	Canada
Female, %	56.8	46.6*
Minimum of 12 years of education, %	52.1	51.3
Mean age, y	39.0	40.2
Cigarettes per day	16.2	17.0
Years smoking	20.7	21.4
Prior attempts to quit	3.5	. . .
Intentions to quit within 6 mo, %	41.2	42.5

Source. Data for Canadian smokers are from the Canadian Tobacco Use Monitoring Survey.[7]
*P < .05.

to only 1% who reported that they smoked more as a result of the labels ($^2 = 1334.6$, $P < .001$, $df = 1$). Overall, 63% of smokers reported at least 1 cessation benefit, whereas only 6% reported any negative impact ($^2 = 2462.2$, $P < .001$, $df = 1$).

Avoidance

A total of 36% of respondents reported making at least some effort to avoid the labels. Specifically, 19% had tried to cover or hide warnings, 21% had used a different case as a result of the warnings, and 17% had requested a specific package to avoid a particular warning label. Avoidance was not associated with either depth of processing of the warning labels at baseline (odds ratio [OR] = 0.97, 95% confidence interval [CI] = 0.93, 1.01) or cessation behaviors at follow-up (OR = 0.86, 95% CI = 0.56, 1.32).

Emotional Reactions

A substantial proportion of smokers reported experiencing at least some fear (44%) and disgust (58%). Smokers who reported greater fear and disgust in response to the labels were significantly more likely to have read and thought about the warnings at baseline (β_{stand} = .39, $P = .001$). Fear and disgust were also positively associated with each of the 4 self-report measures of perceived effectiveness at baseline. For example, smokers who reported greater fear were significantly more likely to indicate that the labels had reduced the amount they smoke (OR = 2.02, 95% CI= 1.59, 2.60), and increased their likelihood of quitting (OR = 1.82, 95% CI= 1.50, 2.22). Finally, a logistic regression was conducted to determine whether negative emotional reactions to the warnings at baseline predicted cessation behavior at follow-up. Smokers who reported greater fear and disgust were significantly more likely to have quit, made an attempt to quit, or reduced their smoking at follow-up (OR = 1.37, 95% CI = 1.15, 1.64). The results were similar when fear and disgust were analyzed as individual variables, rather than being combined in the index of negative emotion.

Credibility

Only 13% of smokers felt that the warnings were at all inaccurate in depicting the health risks of smoking. In addition, only 27% of smokers reported that the warnings contained "too much" health risk information, whereas 50% of all smokers wanted to see even more health information on cigarette packages.

DISCUSSION

The Canadian warning labels have elicited strong emotional reactions from smokers. However, these findings indicate that negative emotional reactions were associated with *greater* effectiveness of the warning labels. Most important, smokers who reported greater fear and disgust were more likely to either have quit, made an attempt to quit, or reduced their smoking at follow-up.

These results are consistent with the primary intent of the warning labels, which is to communicate health risks that are manifestly frightening and harsh. Warnings of lung cancer, for example, that fail to contain arousing information also fail to communicate these risks in a truthful, forthright manner. In this context, emotional reactions should be interpreted as a measure of effectiveness. In addition, although some respondents reported trying to avoid the warnings, those who avoided the warnings were no less likely to read and think about the warnings, and no less likely to engage in cessation behavior at follow-up.

Most important, this research provides no evidence of any reactance or boomerang effect in response to graphic pictorial warning labels. On the contrary, the findings suggest that the Canadian warnings may yield a public health benefit: approximately one third of smokers reported that the labels have increased their likelihood of quitting. Although the current study cannot speak directly to any public health benefit, the warnings may also act as a harm reduction measure, as 20% of smokers reported smoking less as a result of the warnings.

Finally, the graphic nature of the Canadian warnings does not appear to have compromised their credibility. Approximately 13% of smokers rated the warnings as inaccurate, only a 2% increase from the same question asked in 1999 of the previous text-only Canadian warning labels.[9] These findings add to the evidence that smokers perceive government-mandated cigarette warnings to be a credible source of health information.[9,10]

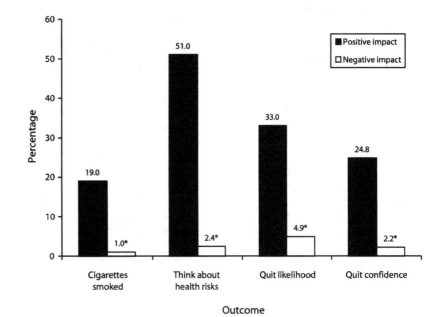

FIGURE 1— Self-reported outcomes of Canadian warning labels, at baseline (n = 616).
*P < .001.

This research has several limitations. First, in the absence of pre-post measurements, the current study was not able to assess changes in avoidance and emotional reactions from the previous generation of Canadian warning labels. Second, there is no control group against which to compare the impact of the Canadian warnings. However, the current findings are consistent with those from a quasi-experimental study of US and Canadian youth indicating a lack of adverse outcomes and greater impact for Canadian warning labels compared with US labels.[11]

Overall, the current research suggests that policymakers should not be reluctant to introduce graphic cigarette warning labels based on potential adverse outcomes. Rather, short of exaggerating the risks of smoking or crossing the bounds of public decency, warning labels should adopt vivid and striking features that increase their salience among smokers.

About the Authors

David Hammond and Geoffrey T. Fong are with the Department of Psychology at the University of Waterloo, Waterloo, Ontario. Paul W. McDonald and Roy Cameron are with the Department of Health Studies, and K. Stephen Brown is with the Department of Statistics and Actuarial Science at the University of Waterloo. Paul W. McDonald and K. Stephen Brown are also with the Ontario Tobacco Research Unit. Geoffrey T. Fong, Paul W. McDonald, Roy Cameron, and K. Stephen Brown are also with the Centre for Behavioural Research and Program Evaluation, University of Waterloo.

Correspondence: Requests for reprints should be sent to David Hammond, Department of Psychology, University of Waterloo, 200 University Avenue West, Waterloo, Ontario, N2L 3G1, Canada (e-mail: dhammond@uwaterloo.ca).

Acknowledgments

This research was supported by the National Cancer Institute of Canada (NCIC) with funds from the Canadian Cancer Society (CCS), the CCS/NCIC Centre for Behavioural Research and Program Evaluation, and the Ontario Tobacco Research Unit, and by a grant from the National Cancer Institute of the United States (R01 CA90955). We gratefully acknowledge the assistance of the Survey Research Centre and the Health Behavior Research Group at the University of Waterloo, Waterloo, Ontario. We also thank Jennifer Topham and 2 anonymous reviewers for their comments and suggestions on an earlier version of this article.

Human Participant Protection

This study was reviewed and approved by the office of research ethics at the University of Waterloo.

Contributors

D. Hammond conceived the study, conducted the analysis, and was the principal author of the article. G. T. Fong, P. W. McDonald, R. Cameron, and K. S. Brown contributed to the study design, analysis, and article preparation.

References

1. *Reducing Tobacco Use: A Report of the Surgeon General.* Atlanta, Ga: Centers for Disease Control and Prevention, National Center for Chronic Disease Prevention and Health Promotion, Office on Smoking and Health; 2000.
2. Gajalakshmi CK, Jha P, Ranson K, Nguyen S. Global patterns of smoking and smoking-attributable mortality. In: Jha P, Chaloupka FJ, eds. *Tobacco Control in Developing Countries.* Geneva, Switzerland: World Bank and World Health Organization; 1999.
3. Key Area Paper—Public Affairs: Smoking and Health-Health Warning Clauses. British-American Tobacco Company. May 28, 1992. Bates No. 502605183. Available at: http://www.library.ucsf.edu/tobacco/b atco/html/7000/7067/. Accessed December 22, 2002.
4. Ad Hoc Committee of the Canadian Tobacco Industry. A Canadian tobacco industry presentation on smoking and health: a presentation to the House of Commons Standing Committee on Health, Welfare and Social Affairs. House of Commons Standing Committee on Health, Welfare and Social Affairs. Minutes of Proceedings and Evidence, June 5, 1969; 1579–1689. Available from the Library and Archives Canada (Finding Aid: 14-27).
5. Waksberg J. Sampling methods for Random digit dialing. *J Am Stat Assoc.* 1978;73:40–46.
6. O'Rourke D, Blair J. Improving random respondent selection in telephone surveys. *J Marketing Res.* 1983;20:428–432.
7. Tobacco Control Program, Health Canada. *Canadian Tobacco Use Monitoring Survey, February–December 2001.* Ottawa, Ontario: Health Canada; 2002.
8. Standard Definitions: Final Dispositions of Case Codes and Outcome Rates for Surveys. Lenexa, Kan: American Association for Public Opinion Research; 2000.
9. Environics Research Group. *Baseline Surveys: The Health Effects of Tobacco and Health Warning Messages on Cigarette Packages: Report for Health Canada.* Ottawa, Ontario: Health Canada; 2001. Available at: http://www.hc-sc.gc.ca/hecs-sesc/tobacco/research/smoking-4774/index.html. Accessed December 21, 2002.
10. Centre for Behavioural Research in Cancer, Anti-Cancer Council of Victoria. *Health Warnings and Contents Labeling on Tobacco Products.* Carlton South, Victoria, Australia: Anti-Cancer Council of Victoria;1992.
11. Fong GT, Cameron AJR, Brown KS, Campbell HS, Zanna MP, Murnaghan D. Effects of the Canadian graphic warning labels among high school students: a quasi-experimental longitudinal survey. Paper presented at: 2002 National Conference on Tobacco or Health; November 20, 2002; San Francisco, Calif.

Tobacco Control, Stigma, and Public Health: Rethinking the Relations

| Ronald Bayer, PhD and Jennifer Stuber, PhD

ABSTRACT

The AIDS epidemic has borne witness to the terrible burdens imposed by stigmatization and to the way in which marginalization could subvert the goals of HIV prevention. Out of that experience, and propelled by the linkage of public health and human rights, came the commonplace assertion that stigmatization was a retrograde force.

Yet, strikingly, the antitobacco movement has fostered a social transformation that involves the stigmatization of smokers. Does this transformation represent a troubling outcome of efforts to limit tobacco use and its associated morbidity and mortality; an ineffective, counterproductive, and moralizing approach that leads to a dead end; or a signal of public health achievement? If the latter is the case, are there unacknowledged costs?

Long prohibited on trains, planes, and buses, smoking is increasingly barred in restaurants and bars. In 2004, 10 states had imposed total bans on smoking in restaurants, and 6 had extended such limits to bars.[1] Public beaches in California have enacted smoking prohibitions.[2] Although such restrictions have been imposed on the *act* of smoking, they have inevitably had profound impacts on smokers themselves and their social standing. In any city, smokers can be found huddled outside office buildings no matter how inclement the weather. Firms boldly announce that they will not employ and may even fire smokers because of the additional cost of their

medical care,[3] or because smoking does not project the "image" they wish to present to the public.[4]

Commenting on the rise and decline of the cigarette and smoker in America, medical historian Allan Brandt, who in the early 1980s, on the eve of the AIDS epidemic, so carefully examined the stigma associated with sexually transmitted disease, wrote,

> In the last half century the cigarette has been transformed. The fragrant has become foul. . . . An emblem of attraction has become repulsive. A mark of sociability has become deviant. A public behavior is now virtually private. Not only has the meaning of the cigarette been transformed but even more the meaning of the smoker [who] has become a pariah . . . the object of scorn and hostility.[5]

Has this transformation led to a decline in the prevalence of smoking in American society? If so, is this use of stigmatization justified or is it an ineffective—or even counterproductive—moralistic approach that leads to a dead-end?

The efforts propelling this transformation resonate with a long history of stigmatization in public health, especially involving the behavior of the poor, the foreign-born, and racial and ethnic minorities. But they run counter to a revisionist orthodoxy that had emerged during the last years of the 20th century that asserts that stigmatization of those who are already vul-

nerable provides the context within which disease spreads, exacerbating morbidity and mortality by erecting barriers between caregivers and those who are sick, and by constraining those who would intervene to contain the spread of illness. In this view, it is the responsibility of public health officials to counteract stigmatization if they are to fulfill the mission to protect the communal health.

Furthermore, because stigma imposes unfair burdens on those who are already at a social disadvantage, the process of stigmatization, it is argued, implicates the human right to dignity. Hence, to the instrumental reason for seeking to extirpate any stigma, a moral concern was added.

But is it true that stigmatization always represents a threat to public health? Are there occasions when the mobilization of stigma may effectively reduce the prevalence of behaviors linked to disease and death? And if so, how ought we to think about the human rights issues that are involved?

Although interest in how societies stigmatize outsiders and the impact of stigmatization on those marked by unacceptable differences was spurred by Erving Goffman's seminal *Stigma: Notes on the Management of Spoiled Identity*,[6] published more than 40 years ago, and although the sociologists of socially discordant behavior underscored the ways in which a stigma imposed burdens on those who were labeled "deviant,"[7,8] it was the AIDS epidemic both domestically and globally that provided the context for the articulation of a strong thesis linking stigmatization and public health.

Within the United States, discussions centered on the fact that those who were initially most vulnerable to HIV—gay and bisexual men and illegal drug users—were already stigmatized.[9] But even persons considered less culpable for their illness, such as children with HIV or persons infected through tainted blood products, were also the objects of fear, the targets of exclusionary impulses.[10] Globally, in nations where HIV was primarily transmitted heterosexually, a pattern of discrimination and even violence emerged.

Whenever stigmantization occurred, the negative consequences were predictable. Herek,[11] who has studied AIDS-related stigma, noted,

The widespread expectation of stigma combined with actual experiences with prejudice and discrimination exerts a considerable impact on [people with HIV], their loved ones and care-givers. It affects many of the choices [they] make about being tested and seeking assistance for their physical, psychological and social needs. . . . Fearing rejection and mistreatment many . . . keep their serostatus a secret.[11]

Stigmatization also functioned to buttress the social subordination of those who were already marginalized.[12]

Speaking before the UN General Assembly in 1987, Jonathan Mann, director of the World Health Organization's Global Program on AIDS, underscored the significance of stigmatization and the social and political unwillingness to face the epidemic as being "as central to the global AIDS challenge as the disease itself."[12] A year later, the world summit of health ministers adopted a declaration (as did the World Health Assembly) that underscored the obligation of governments to protect people with HIV from stigmatization. There was a "need in AIDS prevention programs to protect human rights and human dignity. Discrimination against, and stigmatization of HIV infected people and peo-

ple with AIDS . . . undermine public health and must be avoided."[12] At the beginning of the 21st century, the persistence of stigmatization and the need to confront it remained central concerns of international public health. Peter Piot, director of the Joint United Nations Programme on HIV/ AIDS, asserted that the "effort to combat stigma" was at the top of his list of "the five most pressing items on [the] agenda of the world community."[12]

Stigmatization represented a profound psychological and social burden on those with AIDS or HIV infection and it also fuelled the spread of the epidemic. Both these elements were central to asserting the link between public health and human rights. Writing some years after he had left the World Health Organization, Mann drew a conclusion about the need to fight stigmatization that was far broader than the pressing and immediate concern about AIDS. Indeed, it was Mann's central mission to extend to public health in general the lessons he had learned from his encounter with AIDS.

The evolving HIV/AIDS pandemic has shown a consistent pattern through which discrimination, marginalization, stigmatization and more generally a lack of respect for the human rights and dignity of individuals and groups heightens their vulnerability to being exposed to HIV. In this regard HIV/AIDS may be illustrative of a more general phenomenon in which individual and population vulnerability to disease, disability and premature death is linked to the status of respect for human rights and dignity.[13]

Against this backdrop, the course of antitobacco advocacy and policy seems all the more striking. Tobacco consumption accounts for close to 400 000 deaths a year in the United States. Globally, nearly 5 million deaths a year are attributed to cigarette smoking.[14] By any measure, tobacco-associated morbidity is a grave public health threat. Yet, in this instance, the concerns about the impacts of stigmatization have been given little consideration. In some public health circles, there has even been a return to an older public health tra-

dition, one that seeks to mobilize the power of stigmatization to affect collective behavior.

The 1964 surgeon general's report on smoking and health, a watershed in American public health, was issued at a moment when tobacco consumption was ubiquitous. In the United States, 50% of men and 35% of women smoked. Inadequate campaigns against the tobacco industry emerged, and those who smoked were warned weakly about the dangers of cigarettes. Some limits were imposed on advertising.[15] But it was the gradual framing of smoking as an environmental health issue by antismoking activists, even when scientific evidence was far from definitive, that began to transform the social context of smoking as normal adult behavior.[16]

By the end of the 1970s, evidence began to mount that smoking was increasingly being viewed as undesirable by significant proportions of nonsmokers. In 1 survey, a third of smokers agreed. In 1979, Markle and Troyer wrote, "In addition to being seen as harmful to health, smoking came to be seen as undesirable, deviant behavior and smokers as social misfits. In fact data shows that people increasingly view smoking as reprehensible."[17]

To confront such malefactors, some believed, anything that might work had to be considered, even heavy-handed moral opprobrium. In the *New York Times*, a psychiatrist wrote, "What we need is a national campaign that results in the stigmatization rather than the glorification of the smoker. This, in my opinion, would be the most effective way of reducing the number of smokers and confining their smoke to the privacy of their homes."[18(pA13)]

Under certain circumstances, parents who smoked in the presence of their children were accused of abuse and neglect.[19]

Responding to changing public attitudes, local lawmakers throughout the country began to impose restrictions on where smoking could occur. By the mid-1980s, 80% of the US population lived in states where some limits on public smoking had been imposed.[20] Research suggesting that passive smoking increases the risk of heart disease and cancer made it possible to assert that those who smoked in public were culpable of the deaths of innocents. Joseph Califano, former secretary of the US Department of Health, Education, and Welfare, if in a hyperbolic manner, gave voice to a mood that provided the impetus for such efforts. Cigarette smoking, he asserted, was

> America's top contagious killer disease. . . . Cigarette smoking is slow motion suicide. It is tragic when people do it to themselves. But it is inexcusable to allow smokers to commit slow motion murder.[21]

In an editorial commenting on research implicating passive smoke in the deaths of non-smoking spouses, the *New York Times* wrote of "Smoking Your Wife to Death."[22] Ironically then, the focus on the potential environmental impacts of smoking opened the way to a characterization of smokers that was more stigmatizing than had been the rationale of public policy, which is that tobacco use is self-harming.

As smoking rates declined in the 1980s and 1990s, and more importantly as the social class composition of smokers underwent a dramatic shift downward—those with more education were quitting, while those at the bottom of the social ladder continued to smoke—states with more aggressive antismoking campaigns moved beyond a focus on the deleterious consequences of public smoking for nonsmokers. Against a backdrop of massive advertising and promotion that linked cigarettes to athletic prowess, success, and sexual attraction, public health officials needed a powerful counterweight. And so they began to embrace a strategy of denormalization to further shift population norms about smoking—and that pits nonsmokers against smokers. Whether intentionally or inadvertently, this strategy provided fertile ground for stigmatization, at

once discouraging new smokers and prodding those who smoked into giving up their toxic habit.

The Massachusetts tobacco control program noted, "Norms that allow smokers to smoke in most venues, including while at work or *home,* provide little incentive to quit."[23] Florida's tobacco control efforts sought to "deglamorize" smoking, and the extent to which students were "less likely to buy into the allure of tobacco"[24] was viewed as a mark of their impact. California's campaign to "denormalize" tobacco consumption sought "to push tobacco use out of the charmed circle of normal desirable practice, to being an abnormal practice."[25] Lauding the efforts of the California Health Department, Gilpin et al. embraced the force of social conformity, noting, "In a society where smoking is not viewed as an acceptable activity, fewer people will smoke, and as fewer people smoke, smoking will become ever more marginalized."[26]

The social transformation of the smoker has occurred in other industrialized nations as well. In Germany, for example, the image of the smoker as a handsome, successful executive has been increasingly displaced by one that depicted smokers as asocial, irresponsible, and self-destructive.[27] Even in Denmark, which viewed itself as immune to the lures of moral crusades, there are indications that the aura surrounding tobacco has been transformed.[28]

The embrace of a strategy of denormalization by public health officials and antitobacco activists has been fueled by suggestions that the stigmatization of smoking has in fact had an impact on smoking behavior. One study noted in 2003, "Cigarette smoking is not simply an unhealthy behavior. Smoking is now considered a deviant behavior—smokers are stigmatized." Such stigmatization, the authors conclude, "may have been partly responsible for the decrease in the smoking population."[29] The advocacy group Americans for Non-Smokers' Rights noted that tobacco control advocates had stumbled onto the best strategy for reducing tobacco con-

sumption, "encouraging society to view tobacco use as an undesirable and antisocial behavior."[30]

What is most striking about these analyses is the extent to which they ignore without comment the overarching concerns raised in prior years about the relation between stigmatization and effective public health interventions. Certainly there are people within the public health community who believe that they are stigmatizing a behavior and not smokers themselves, and for them this distinction is crucial. However, whether it is in fact possible to make such a distinction is an empirical question.

Some commentators have also expressed concern about a process that seems to blame smokers rather than the industry that has ensnared them. Furthermore, critics have voiced concerns, well known from the literature on AIDS, that stigmatization may in the end be counterproductive. But there are also antitobacco advocates who believe that to the extent that stigmatization limits smoking behavior, it is to be deployed rather than eschewed. For them, the moral question of how to balance the overall public health benefit that may be achieved by stigmatization against the suffering experienced by those who are tainted by "spoiled identities" is virtually never addressed. The issue becomes all the more pressing as stigmatization falls on the most socially vulnerable—the poor who continue to smoke.

The AIDS epidemic bore witness to the terrible burdens imposed by stigmatization and to the way in which marginalization could subvert the goals of HIV prevention. Out of that experience and propelled by the linkage of public health and human rights, it became commonplace to assert that stigmatization was a retrograde force. Some might dismiss the parallel we have drawn between the role of stigmatization in the AIDS epidemic and its use by antitobacco advocates. Surely, the former case is more severe. But the experience of confronting AIDS stigmatization compels us to rethink these issues because many public health advocates have explicitly taken the experience of AIDS to draw a generalized lesson about the relation between stigmatization and public health.

If stigmatization does contribute to reducing the human costs of smoking by encouraging cessation or preventing the onset of tobacco use, are the personal burdens it creates morally justifiable? Although it provides a point of departure, the utilitarian calculus, so vital to public health thinking, is insufficient for answering the question.

Much will depend on the nature and the extent of stigma-associated burdens and on how the antitobacco movement deploys stigmatization as an instrument of social control. For example, policies and cultural standards that result in isolation and severe embarrassment are different from those that cause discomfort. Those that provoke a sense of social disease are not the same as those that mortify. Acts that seek to limit the contexts in which smoking is permitted are different from those that restrict the right to work, to access health or life insurance, or to reside in communities of one's choice.

The extent to which the deployment of stigmatization exacerbates already-extant social disparities or has long-term counterproductive consequences for the effort to confront the epidemic of smoking-related morbidity must also be considered. And what is true for smoking may have broader applicability for other individual behaviors deemed unhealthy such as "overeating" and illegal drug use.

Only when we understand the circumstances under which stigmatization transforms behaviors linked to disease and early death and are able to distinguish these from the circumstances in which stigmatization has negative impacts on public health will it be possible to weigh the competing moral claims of population health and the burdens that policy may impose on the socially vulnerable. Then it will be possible to make choices informed by hard evidence rather than wishful thinking.

About the Authors

Ronald Bayer is with the Center for the History and Ethics of Public Health, Department of Sociomedical Sciences, Mailman School of Public Health, New York, NY. Jennifer Stuber is a Robert Wood Johnson Health and Society Scholar at Columbia University, New York.

Correspondence: Requests for reprints should be sent to Jennifer Stuber, 420 W 118th Street, 8th Floor, Mail Code 3355, New York, NY 10027 (e-mail: js2642@columbia.edu).

Acknowledgments

J. Stuber's work is supported by the Health and Society Scholars Program.

Thanks to James Colgrove, Amy Fairchild, Gerald Oppenheimer, and Daniel Wolfe for their thoughtful reading.

Contributors

Both authors shared equally in the conceptualization, research, and writing of this article.

References

1. American Lung Association. State of tobacco control: 2002. Available at: http://www.lungaction.org/reports/tobacco-control.html. Accessed March 16, 2005.
2. Marshall C. San Francisco bans smoking in parks and other open spaces. *New York Times.* February 13, 2005;5:2.
3. Peters J. Company's smoking ban means off-hours, too. *New York Times.* February 8, 2005;C5.
4. Holt S. Saying no to smokers. *Seattle Times.* October 10, 2004:E1.
5. Brandt A. Blow some my way: passive smoking, risk and American culture. In: Lock S, Reynolds L, Tansey E, eds. *Ashes to Ashes: the History of Smoking and Health.* Amsterdam, The Netherlands: Rodopi BV; 1998:164–191.
6. Goffman E. *Stigma: Notes on the Management of Spoiled Identity.* Englewood Cliffs, NJ: Prentice Hall; 1963.
7. Becker H. *The Outsiders.* New York, NY: Free Press; 1963.
8. Schur E. *Labeling Deviant Behavior.* New York, NY: Harper & Row; 1971.
9. Poirier R. AIDS and traditions of homophobia. *Soc Res.* 1988;55:460–475.
10. Kirp DL, Epstein S. *Learning by Heart: AIDS and Schoolchildren in America's Communities.* New Brunswick, NJ: Rutgers University Press; 1989.
11. Herek G. AIDS and stigma. *Am Behav Scientist.* 1999;42:1102–1112.
12. Parker R, Aggleton P. HIV and AIDS-related stigma and discrimination: a conceptual framework and implications for action. *Soc Sci Med.* 2003; 57(1):13–24.
13. Mann J, Gostin J, Gruskin S. Health and human rights. *Health Hum Rights Int J.* 1994;1(1):1–14.
14. World Health Organization. Global tobacco treaty enters into force with 57 countries already committed. Available at: http://www.who.int/mediacentre/news/releases/2005/pr09/en. Accessed March 16, 2005.
15. McAuliffe R. The FTC and the effectiveness of cigarette advertising regulations. *J Public Policy Marketing.* 1988; 7:52.
16. Bayer R, Colgrove J. Children and bystanders first: the ethics and politics of tobacco control in the United States. In: Feldman EA, Bayer R, eds. *Unfiltered: Conflicts Over Tobacco Policy and Public Health.* Cambridge, Mass: Harvard University Press; 2004:9–37.
17. Markle G, Troyer R. Smoke gets in your eyes: cigarette smoking as deviant behavior. *Soc Problems.* 1979;26: 611–625.
18. Gardner R. Fatuous and futile road to self-esteem [letter to editor]. *New York Times.* July 30, 1977:A13.
19. Clark C. An argument for considered parental smoking in child abuse and neglect proceedings. *J Contemp Health Law Policy.* 2002;19:225–246.
20. *The Health Consequences of Involuntary Smoking.* Washington, DC: US Department of Health and Human Services; 1986.
21. Califano JA Jr. Testimony. In: *Hearings Before the Subcommittee on Civil Service, Post Office, and General Services of the Committee on Governmental Affairs, United States Senate.* Washington, DC: US Government Printing Office; 1985.
22. moking your wife to death [editorial]. *New York Times.* January 21, 1981:A22.
23. Commonwealth of Massachusetts Department of Public Health. Chapter 6: Changing Social Norms. Available at: http://www.mass.gov/dph/mtcp/reports/2000/aptrep_2000social.htm. Accessed September 24, 2005.

24. Bauer UE, Johnson TM, Hopkins RS, Brooks RG. Changes in youth cigarette use and intentions following implementation of a tobacco control program: findings from the Florida youth tobacco survey, 1998–2000. *JAMA.* 2000; 284:723–728.

25. *A Model for Change: The California Experience in Tobacco Control.* Sacramento, Calif: Tobacco Control Section, California Department of Health Services; 1998.

26. Gilpin E, Lee L, Pierce J. Changes in population attitudes about where smoking should not be allowed: California versus the rest of the USA. *Tob Control.* 2004;13:38–44.

27. Frankenberg G. Between paternalism and voluntarism: tobacco consumption and tobacco control in Germany. In: Feldman EA, Bayer R, eds. *Unfiltered: Conflicts Over Tobacco Policy and Public Health.* Cambridge, Mass: Harvard University Press; 2004:161–190.

28. Albaek E. Holy smoke, no more? Tobacco control in Denmark. In: Feldman EA, Bayer R, eds. *Unfiltered: Conflicts Over Tobacco Policy and Public Health.* Cambridge, Mass: Harvard University Press; 2004:190–218.

29. Kim SH, Shanahan J. Stigmatizing smokers: public sentiment toward cigarette smoking and its relationship to smoking behaviors. *J Health Commun.* 2003;8:343–367.

30. *Recipe for a Smoke Free Society.* Berkeley, Calif: Americans for Nonsmokers' Rights; 2003.

Making Big Tobacco Give In: You Lose, They Win

| Nathaniel Wander, PhD and Ruth E Malone, RN, PhD, FAAN

ABSTRACT

Objectives. To better understand how the tobacco industry responds to tobacco control activists, we explored Philip Morris's response to demands that consumers in developing countries be informed about smoking risks, and analyzed the implications of negotiating with a tobacco company.

Methods. We reviewed internal tobacco industry documents and related materials, constructed a case history of how Philip Morris responded to a shareholder campaign to require health warnings on cigarettes sold worldwide, and analyzed interactions between (1) socially responsible investment activists, (2) Philip Morris management, (3) institutional investors, and (4) industry competitors.

Results. After resisting for 11 years, Philip Morris unilaterally reversed direction, and proposed its own labeling initiative. While activists celebrated, Philip Morris's president detailed privately how the company would yield little and benefit disproportionately. Activists portrayed the tobacco industry as preying on the poor and uneducated and used delegitimization to drive a wedge between the industry and its financial and political allies. When Philip Morris "gave in" to their demands, it exchanged negative publicity for positive public relations and political credibility.

Conclusions. Tobacco companies can appear to accommodate public health demands while securing strategic advantages. Negotiating with the tobacco industry can enhance its legitimacy and facilitate its ability to market
deadly cigarettes without corresponding benefits to public health.

INTRODUCTION

The release of private, internal tobacco industry documents in 1998 disclosed "systematic and global efforts by the tobacco industry to undermine tobacco control policy."[1(p1)] Commenting on a report published in 2000 by the World Health Organization (WHO) about the tobacco industry,[2] Judith Mckay observed that it would be "premature to consider involving or consulting with the tobacco industry on [public health] policy issues."[3(p912)] In 2004, WHO recognized that the tobacco industry continued to use public relations campaigns to undermine tobacco control initiatives and explicitly warned governments and nongovernmental organizations: "Do NOT participate in industry-initiated dialogues—the industry portrays participation in these dialogues as endorsements for its programs."[4(p207)]

As the tobacco industry extends its global reach, some companies claim to have "turned over a new leaf." They provide tobacco-related health information, offer cessation guidance, coach parents regarding how to talk to children about smoking, and represent themselves as suitably responsible partners in tobacco control policymaking. Tobacco control advocates need to understand why WHO's exclusionary cautions remain warranted. We examined the resolution of a marketing controversy concerning developing countries to demonstrate how the tobacco

industry can appear to accommodate public health demands, while securing strategic advantages. Company documents are used to describe how Philip Morris "gave in" to demands from shareholder activists and restored its credibility with investors and policymakers, while undermining delegitimization as a key tobacco control strategy and ceding little of value to public health.

METHODS

This study originated from the discovery of a 1991 document in which Philip Morris management announced a new health warning label policy to its board of directors.[5] During the period December 29, 2003, to October 11, 2005, we searched previously undisclosed tobacco industry documents that were made public under *State of Minnesota v Philip Morris, Inc,*[6] and were posted electronically as a result of the 1998 Master Settlement Agreement between 46 state attorneys general and seven tobacco industry defendants.[7] We used multiple electronic archives, including the Legacy Tobacco Documents Library at the University of California, San Francisco (at: http://legacy.library.ucsf.edu); websites of tobacco industry defendants; and Tobacco Documents Online (at: http://tobaccodocuments.org).

We began with combinations of the key words *health, warning,* and *label,* and examined all documents containing these terms. This led to additional search terms, such as the acronym XWN for "export warning." Using XWN as a search term, we recovered additional documents concerning health warning issues in the former Soviet Union and in Africa. This process of iterative searching is called snowball sampling.[8,9] We further searched the "File Areas" of Philip Morris executives who were responsible for labeling-policy decisions, and searched for names of shareholder activists who raised the health warning issue. We also interviewed Father Michael Crosby, who led the activists, and searched Academic LexisNexis for contemporaneous news reports. Because the Philip Morris labeling policy involved industry-wide consultations, we also searched for documents from domestic competitors including RJ Reynolds and Brown & Williamson (now merged as Reynolds American), as well as transnational ones such as Rothmans and British American Tobacco. Relevant documents were retrieved from the University of California, San Francisco's British American Tobacco Company (BAT) document archive (at: http://bat. library.ucsf.edu), as well as the Legacy Tobacco Documents Library archive. We also reviewed relevant publications regarding European Community public policy directives.

We used approximately 600 retrieved documents as well as background materials to construct a case history. Within this case, we analyzed the strategic interactions of 4 sets of participants: (1) socially responsible investment activists, (2) Philip Morris management, (3) stakeholders including institutional stock investors, and (4) tobacco industry competitors.

RESULTS

Background

In 1979, spurred by a World Health Organization report,[10] tobacco control advocates began expressing concerns about the marketing of cigarettes in developing countries.[11–13] They saw that declining cigarette consumption in the United States was driving aggressively expanded promotion abroad. These same advocates protested that the tobacco industry was targeting people who had little

experience with commercial marketing or cigarettes engineered to deliver consistently high doses of nicotine and who could not afford additional health or financial burdens.[14–16]

In 1980, a coalition of religious organizations led by Father Michael Crosby[14] decided to intervene to protect the targets of "aggressive promotion tactics" by using the then novel tactic of a corporate shareholder resolution in order to obtain information about industry marketing practices.[17–19] (The US Securities and Exchange Commission [SEC] requires corporations to hold annual general meetings where stockholders vote on management proposals and may present resolutions of their own.[20]) Crosby's experience of widespread Marlboro advertising in Costa Rica led him to focus on Philip Morris,[17] although shareholder resolutions were also filed at R.J. Reynolds and possibly other US tobacco companies.[21]

At the Philip Morris April annual general meeting, shareholders decide resolutions submitted by the previous November. The Crosby coalition's 1980–1981 resolution called upon Philip Morris to: (1) describe the size and market share of the company's "Third World" markets; (2) report on advertising and promotion, "including projections for the next five years"; and (3) describe its policies with regard to 3 WHO recommendations[10]: (a) "banning promotions of tobacco"; (b) "limitation of cigarette tar and nicotine levels . . . to that in the United States"; and (c) "[i]nforming consumers of the risks of tobacco use in countries where there may be little or no regulations concerning health risks for smokers."[19]

Philip Morris management opposed the resolution,[22] and devoted a third of its 1981 executive preparation manual to the issue.[23] They denied any "causal connection" between smoking and disease,[22] and insisted that consumers worldwide were adequately informed of smoking "risks."[24] The company asserted that it was opposed in principle to intervening in the prerogatives of local governments,[25] but it also expressed commer-

cial concerns; namely, that sales would suffer if Philip Morris products were thought to be more dangerous than those without warning labels.[26]

The 1980–1981 resolution[18–20] won 3% of the shareholder votes,[27] enough by SEC rules to qualify for resubmission the following year.[17] However, despite a growing coalition of supporters,[16,28–31] the 1981–1982 resolution failed to win 6% of the votes required for further submission.[32] By SEC rules, the resolution could not be resubmitted for the balance of a 5-year period.[33] The 1981–1982 resolution, however, drew a critical, if ambivalent, response from institutional investors, which would have repercussions a decade later.[34–36] Yale University supported Philip Morris's refusal to release proprietary information, but criticized management for its unwillingness to cooperate with the socially responsible investment advocates.[37] Bryn Mawr College abstained from the vote because of similarly conflicted sentiments;[38] Connecticut Mutual Life Insurance voted for the resolution despite reservations.[39]

Shareholder activists kept the resolution alive for 11 years by focusing negative attention on the tobacco industry's behavior. A 1990–1991 resolution introduced at the April 1991 annual general meeting won 7% of the votes, which Philip Morris President and board vice chair R. William Murray acknowledged was "the largest favorable response ever to a proposal . . . not supported by management."[5] The April 1991 resolution, entitled "Establishing a Global Uniform Labeling Minimum," resolved: "that . . . users of our cigarettes throughout the world will be appropriately and clearly warned of the health hazards caused by smoking . . . based on similar warnings . . . demanded in the United States and the European Economic Community."[40] After 11 years of resistance and faced with the return of the shareholders' resolution in 1991–1992, Philip Morris introduced its own warning label initiative. Murray explained to Philip Morris's board how a "voluntary" initiative of management's devising would cost the company little, but would benefit it disproportionately.[5]

Turning Shareholder Activism Into Issues Management

Murray's December 1991 board presentation disclosed that Philip Morris had been considering a global health warning label policy for at least three years.[5] Privileged documents suggest that Philip Morris had been consulting with other tobacco companies regarding labeling,[41–44] in parallel with 1988–1989 European Community discussions about rationalizing tobacco warning labels. The European Community discussions were provoked by Ireland's 1986 passage of health warning regulations and its subsequent refusal of unlabeled cigarette imports. This resulted in a directive (89/622/EEC) which was issued in May 1989 that mandated health warnings throughout the European Community.[45,46]

As early as December 1988, an executive of the European branch of Burston-Marsteller, Philip Morris's public relations consultants, had queried Philip Morris International chief executive officer Geoffrey Bible regarding "whether the EEC [European Economic Community] approach might not make sense worldwide,"[47] but Philip Morris was also tracking opposition to the directive. In April 1989, for example, Philip Morris International had solicited a Belgian law firm's opinion regarding whether Directive 89/622/ EEC was legally defective.[48]

In September 1991, when Crosby notified Philip Morris of his intent to resubmit the resolution "Establishing a Global Uniform Labeling Minimum" at the 1992 annual general meeting,[49,50] chief executive officer Michael Miles queried top executives: "Should we preempt [Crosby] by just going ahead and doing it?"[51] For two months, memos circulated among Philip Morris executives analyzing the potential consequences of the preemptive action.[52–57] By November, Philip Morris International senior vice president Dinyar Devitre was confident

enough to explore the idea with William Ryan, chief executive officer of Rothmans, a transnational tobacco competitor.[58] Devitre's confidence, however, would prove premature.

The December speech prepared for Murray to deliver to his directors announced:

"We have decided to print the US Surgeon General's health warning on all PM [Philip Morris] cigarette packs which currently have no labels . . .. Implementation is underway. We expect to convert approximately 60% . . . by April 1 [1992] and the remainder by the end of 1992."[5] Murray explained that Philip Morris had been waiting for "such time that we could use the initiative as a bargaining chip with Congress. That occasion did not materialize."[5]

But the health warning issue had become a source of "growing agitation among a number of . . . important constituencies," and specifically, was "contribut[ing] to the decision to divest Company stock."[5] Indeed, while Philip Morris publicly denied any effects of the Crosby group's activities[59,60] (although the company acknowledged them internally[61]), the campaign by responsible investment activists was fueling pressure on institutional investors to eliminate their tobacco stock investments.[34–36]

Transmuting Public Pressure into Strategic Advantage

According to Murray, Philip Morris planned to use its labeling initiative in 4 ways: (1) to eliminate shareholder activism, "We will inform Father Crosby of the initiative and ask him to withdraw his proxy proposal"; (2) to counteract university divestments, "We will use the initiative in future discussions related to divestment to demonstrate a moderate, sensitive and responsive posture"; (3) to promote a responsible corporate image, "We can cite the initiative to demonstrate Philip Morris' consistent track record on matters of corporate responsibility"; and (4) to restore influence with policymakers, "We will use the initiative in Washington, informing our friends and moderates in the

Congress and the Administration."[5]

The shareholder coalition attempted to negotiate details: languages to be used, whether the initiative would be extended to advertising, how it would be publicized;[62] however, by February 5, 1992, the coalition had apparently agreed to Philip Morris's policy on Philip Morris's terms.[63] In competing public statements, Father Crosby claimed a victory for his coalition's 11-year campaign and highlighted the "half trillion cigarette[s]" that would henceforth carry health warning labels.[64] Philip Morris emphasized that "less than 10% of [its] overall cigarette sales" would be affected.[59]

In March 1992, Philip Morris responded to concerns from institutional shareholders about overseas labeling. Chief counsel Murray H. Bring assured Stanford University President Donald Kennedy "that by the end of this year, the US Surgeon General's warnings, or some other appropriate warning, will appear on every Philip Morris cigarette package sold worldwide."[65,66] Stanford chose not to divest at the time.[67] A similar exchange ensued between Bring and the University of Scranton.[68–70]

Philip Morris planned to maintain this "low key approach," and "not attempt to 'go public' to make news." Instead, they planned to use the [labeling] "initiative as a tactical tool to address specific circumstances."[61] This may have conflicted with publicizing the initiative as a demonstration of corporate responsibility. A draft statement was intended to promote the initiative as "another in a number of steps taken by Philip Morris in recent years to respond to concerns related to its cigarette business."[61] However, we found no evidence of how, if at all, it was used.

Although we discovered no documents that describe how Philip Morris used its labeling initiative to restore influence in Washington, the company used it in other capitals to "establish a dialogue with the Ministry of Health to work out . . . a warning acceptable both in content and language. We have already followed this route in the Dominican Republic and in the

Philippines."[71] The language Philip Morris negotiated with the Philippines ("Warning: Cigarette Smoking is Dangerous to Your Health"[72]) was neither as explicit nor as informative as the US Surgeon General's warnings (e.g., "Smoking Causes Lung Cancer, Heart Disease, Emphysema, and May Complicate Pregnancy," or "Smoking by Pregnant Women May Result in Fetal Injury, Premature Birth, and Low Birth Weight"[73]), that the company was otherwise volunteering to provide.

According to Murray, the company conceded little to the activists' goal of informing people in developing countries about the health risks of smoking. "Approximately 90% of the Company's worldwide cigarette sales are already labeled," he told his board. The largest Philip Morris market still receiving unlabeled cigarettes was Italy, where government regulation was expected shortly, and much of the remainder were duty-free cigarettes sold in the West.[5]

The information content of the new warnings was also questionable. The Dominican Republic, for example, ended up with weaker warnings than the Philippines when Philip Morris negotiated a change to the Health Ministry's proposed language from "Fumar *es* perjudicial . . ." ("Smoking *is* hazardous . . .") to "Fumar *puede ser* perjudicial . . ." ("Smoking *may be* hazardous . . .") [italics added].[74,75] In addition, the labels would mostly be printed in English or French, languages possibly not well known by consumers, who might not even be able to read. "I checked the official languages of some of the countries where we already have warnings," Philip Morris marketing communications manager Leslie Greher reported to public affairs director Matt Winokur. "In many cases we do not use the first-listed or even second-listed language."[76]

Finally, as Greher observed to Winokur, consumers stood to gain little from even well-translated warnings. "The bottom line is that the probability of a consumer noticing and/or understanding the warning will not be substantially increased."[76] As a 1992

British American Tobacco Company assessment of the issue noted, "Smokers have a low level of awareness and recall with regard to pack health warnings . . . generally ignor[ing] the warning once it becomes a familiar sight."[77]

Murray's speech to the board suggested the labeling initiative's costs would be modest. The company would scrap about $1 million in obsolete packaging, and invest $4 million to develop new materials[5]: a fraction of Philip Morris's 1991 worldwide tobacco revenues of $6.5 billion.[78] Murray also minimized the potential for lost sales resulting from consumers being put off by the labels.[5] Some Philip Morris executives even predicted that US-style warning labels would give their cigarettes "a marketing advantage . . . set[ting] the product apart as truly American."[79] The company's African experience later confirmed this. The regional director had worried that warning labels "might have a negative impact on . . . sales, especially if the competition did not follow," but by December 1993, he reported, "There was no negative impact; on the contrary, in some places it may be a positive."[80] Philip Morris had also "carefully examined the potential legal ramifications," Murray noted, and determined that "the initiative would have no significant impact on litigation in the United States or overseas."[5]

Outcomes and Interests

According to executive coaching materials prepared for Philip Morris's 1994 shareholders' meeting, Philip Morris's initiative was essentially completed by the spring of 1994; Morocco was the sole exception.[81] Correspondence between Philip Morris and its Moroccan trading partner, the state monopoly Regie des Tabacs Marocaine (RTM), suggests that RTM was engaged in negotiations for language weaker than the US surgeon general's warning,[82,83] as had previously been accomplished in the Philippines and the Dominican Republic.[71,73–75]

Early predictions of unconditional support from competitors,[58,84] howev-

er, failed to materialize. Instead, James Seddon of Rothmans Legal Services Department wrote: "The implication of your Company's move for industry affairs and for lawyers are many and complex . . . The issue is so important that it merits a meeting of the various company principals, the worst position being that the various companies become divided on the treatment of this issue."[85]

At that London meeting in January 1992, "[e]very company opposed PM's decision."[86] They insisted on caucusing in Philip Morris's absence, and when the Philip Morris representative was invited back, he was presented with a list of objections, which began with disappointment "that PM did not consult with [us] before making this decision."[86] Seddon noted "that PM's unilateral decision . . . was a departure from the industry's tradition of consultation, especially on matters affecting liability litigation."[86]

The companies feared that voluntary concessions would give away "the defense that 'smokers are already informed,'" while "tempting further labeling initiatives . . . [and] demands for 'uniform practices' in other areas."[86] They worried the concessions would (1) give the Americans an unfair advantage over the British, who were debarred from making Health Ministry attributions comparable to the US surgeon general's warnings, (2) undermine Germany's court challenge to European Community labeling regulations, and (3) complicate European negotiations over labeling duty-free cigarettes.[86] Most of all, the other companies questioned Philip Morris's motives, and asserted that Philip Morris's "'real' reason [for the initiative was] 'the share price'," which they felt no need to support.[84] Philip Morris was accustomed to labeling in its domestic market (where warnings negotiated between Congress and the tobacco industry[87] were weaker than what had been recommended by the Federal Trade Commission[88]), and for the company, the numerous advantages of "giving in" clearly outweighed the costs of ongoing resistance to the activist coalition's efforts.

DISCUSSION

Although Philip Morris minimized it, continued pressure from the Crosby coalition prodded the company to offer a "voluntary" labeling initiative. Philip Morris acknowledged that the labeling controversy was feeding into sensitive matters, notably the academic tobacco stock divestment discussions of 1990–1992,[34] and the coalition was winning too many battles before the SEC, which expanded the terrain upon which shareholders could challenge corporate management.[89] It is important, however, to consider just what the company conceded and what it got.

As Murray predicted, Philip Morris's costs for enacting its global labeling initiative were outweighed by the returns. Philip Morris bolstered claims of corporate social responsibility, enhanced relationships with institutional investors and governmental allies, augmented sales, improved conditions for tobacco stocks by eliminating an argument for divestment, and sidelined activists. Little, however, was gained for the people the activists sought to protect. Labeling was extended to a few small markets, in possibly irrelevant languages, while the industry negotiated watered-down wording. Although the activists made what must have seemed at the time to be plausible assumptions about the value of extending labeling worldwide, the industry already knew that the then-current warning label standard—plain print in a box (tombstone labeling)—was of limited effectiveness. This has been substantiated by subsequent research.

Compared with other strategies (taxation, ad bans, counter-advertising), health warning labels have not been particularly effective for reducing cigarette consumption.[88] Until Canada introduced oversized, graphic warnings in the late 1990s,[90–93] neither the content, format, nor placement of cigarette package warnings had been designed with clear health communication objectives in mind.[87] The United States standard tombstone-style warnings fail all requirements of salient design: they are too small, do not stand out, are printed vertically and on the pack's narrowest section, and lack attention-getting icons or graphics.[88,94] The US Federal Trade Commission criticized the lack of saliency of warning labels as early as 1981,[95] and a 1990 study found continuing problems with even the 1984-updated US Surgeon General's warning labels. The 1990 study recommended improved wording, increased size, and bolder design,[96] the same features that Canadian studies show to be most salient.[90–92] (Philip Morris consistently supports FDA regulation of the "text of health warnings"[97] but never mentions size or design.)

If warning labels were so ineffective, why did Philip Morris resist the activists for more than a decade, and why did other tobacco companies continue to resist labeling even after Philip Morris conceded? In addition to a general unwillingness to bow to outside pressures, Philip Morris and other companies feared that voluntary labeling could be taken as a legal admission of their product's dangers, or as an acknowledgment of negligence for not warning sooner. As late as November 1990, Philip Morris outside counsel cautioned that "placing a warning on cigarettes sold in a particular country . . . might be seen as admitting liability."[98] Philip Morris's competitors objected to Philip Morris's unilateral action, which they believed created complications in their home markets.

Another possible explanation for Philip Morris's reluctance is that labels disrupt the seductiveness of package designs.[99] A Philip Morris spokesperson's guide from the period speaks of "package design" as "a valuable commercial asset" which "shareholders . . . have a right to insist that warnings not deface."[100] As recently as 2002, a Philip Morris spokesman worried that expanded package warnings would not leave room enough "for company trademarks and other brand information."[101]

Study Limitations

We cannot claim that we have retrieved every extant document that is potentially relevant to this case, because of the voluminous archives and their limited indexing at the time of this study. It is possible that there are other relevant documents that were destroyed or never released.[102] All archival research is fundamentally interpretive, and involves retrospective examination of documentary evidence; we made efforts to consider alternative interpretations and to position our account within the context of the time by examining other data sources.[103]

Conclusions

This case study illustrates that, although direct engagement with the industry can focus attention on tobacco control issues, negotiations or settlements may undermine delegitimization and provide the industry with opportunities to improve public relations, and in the end, garner relatively little for public health. The Philip Morris shareholder resolutions questioned the legitimacy of the tobacco industry's business practices, and was an effective strategy for influencing public opinion and disrupting the industry's relations with allies.[34–36,104,105] The industry-focused media campaign integral to California's highly effective tobacco control program, for example, delivers a strong delegitimizing message,[106] as do successful campaigns in Canada and elsewhere.[105]

The Crosby campaign furthered tobacco industry delegitimization by portraying an industry that preys upon vulnerable people in the developing world, a matter of concern for institutional tobacco stockholders already sensitized by the South African divestment movement.[34–36,67] As Philip Morris's Murray acknowledged, the labeling campaign's greatest impact on Philip Morris was that it drove a wedge between the company and its financial and political allies,[5] an observation seconded by Father Crosby's own assessment of the accomplishments of his shareholder campaigns.[107]

But Philip Morris moved from strategic disadvantage to advantage precisely when it finally "gave in" to the activists' demands. This case analysis suggests that negotiating or settling with the tobacco industry may potentiate more risks than rewards, a conclusion that is in line with earlier studies of tobacco industry boycott settle-ments.[104,108] Perhaps the only goal worth the risks of negotiating directly with the industry would be a plan to end the for-profit manufacture and marketing of tobacco products.

About the Authors

Nathaniel Wander and Ruth E. Malone are at the Department of Social and Behavioral Sciences and the Center for Tobacco Control Research and Education, University of California, San Francisco.

Correspondence: *Requests for reprints should be sent to Nathaniel Wander, PhD, Department of Social and Behavioral Sciences, University of California, 3333 California Street, Suite 455, San Francisco, CA 94143–0612 (e-mail: nathaniel.wander@ucsf.edu).*

Acknowledgments

This work was funded by the California Tobacco-Related Disease Research Program (grant 11RT–0139) and the National Cancer Institute (grant CA095989).

The authors thank Geraint Howells of Lancaster University School of Law for insight into European Community tobacco directives, and the members of their research team—Patricia McDaniel, Naphtali Offen, Elizabeth Smith—as well as the other co-presenters of the 2005 National Conference on Tobacco or Health panel "Co-Opting the Tobacco Control Movement: Philip Morris' 'Extreme Makeover'"—Stella Bialous and Anne Landman—for their feedback in the development of this paper.

Human Participant Protection

This study was approved by the committee on human research of the University of California, San Francisco.

Contributors

N. Wander conducted the research, performed the analysis, and was the principal author of this article. R. E. Malone designed the research, obtained the funding, collaborated on the analysis, and contributed substan-tially to the writing of this article.

References

1. World Health Organization. *WHO inquiry on tobacco industry influence.* Geneva, Switzerland: World Health Organization, 2000. Available at: http://www.who.int/tobacco/policy/who_inquiry/en/print.html. Accessed June 22, 2005.
2. Saloojee Y, Dagli E. Tobacco industry tactics for resisting public policy on health. *Bull World Health Org.* 2000;78:902–910.
3. Mackay J. Lessons from private state-ments of the tobacco industry. *Bull World Health Org.* 2000;78:911–912.
4. World Health Organization. WHO tobacco free initiative. *Building blocks for tobacco control: a handbook.* Geneva, Switzerland: World Health Organization, 2004. Available at: http://www.who.int/tobacco/resources/publications/general/HAND-BOOK%20Lowres%20with%20cover.pdf. Accessed September 7, 2006.
5. [Winokur MN], [Devitre D], [Murray GW]. *Presentation to the board Labelling initiative.* Available at: http://legacy.library.ucsf.edu/tid/olo24e00. Accessed December 29, 2003.
6. *The State of Minnesota v Philip Morris Incorporated.* (MN District Court 1998). Available at: http://www.library.ucsf.edu/tobacco/litigation/mn/mnsettlement.html. Accessed June 30, 2005.
7. National Association of Attorneys General. *Master settlement agreement.* Available at: http://www.naag.org/upload/1032468605_cigmsa.pdf. Accessed August 6, 2004.
8. Malone RE, Balbach ED. Tobacco industry documents: treasure trove or quagmire? *Tobacco Control.* 2000;9:334–338.
9. MacKenzie R, Collin J, Lee K. *The tobacco industry documents: an intro-ductory handbook and resource guide for researchers.* Available at: http://www.lshtm.ac.uk/cgch/tobac-co/Handbook%2030.06.pdf. Accessed July 21, 2005.
10. WHO Expert Committee on Smoking Control. *Controlling the smoking epi-demic.* Geneva, Switzerland: World Health Organization; 1979. Technical Report Series 636. Also available at: http://tobaccodocuments.org/lor/03732214-2221.html. Accessed September 7, 2006.
11. Anderson G. *The tobacco industry and the Third World now that the dangers of smoking have prompted western nations to impose, however reluctantly, restraints on cigarette advertising, manufacturers seek to exploit new markets abroad.* Available at: http://legacy.library.ucsf.edu/tid/kpm68e00. Accessed October 13, 2004.
12. [Commonwealth Institute]. *Tobacco and the Third World.* Available at: http://legacy.library.ucsf.edu/tid/gzm44e00. Accessed October 13, 2004.
13. [Simpson D]. *Invitation to press confer-ence launching of the new WHO report "Controlling the smoking epidemic" London, Thursday, May 24, 1979.* Available at: http://legacy.library.ucsf.edu/tid/axq78e00. Accessed May 25, 2005.
14. Crosby MH. [*Letter to George Weissman concerning Philip Morris marketing abroad*]. Available at: http://legacy.library.ucsf.edu/tid/lhf12a00. Accessed August 27, 2004.
15. Investor Responsibility Research Center. *Tobacco sales in developing countries: Philip Morris Inc.* Available at: http://legacy.library.ucsf.edu/tid/aif12a00. Accessed August 27, 2004.
16. Crosby MH. [*Letter to George Weissman concerning 1982 Third World marketing resolution*]. Available at: http://legacy.library.ucsf.edu/tid/dat37c00. Accessed October 13, 2004.
17. Crosby MH. [*Letter to George Weissman concerning shareholder pro-posal regarding Philip Morris' market-ing policies in the Third World*]. Available at: http://legacy.library.ucsf.edu/tid/shf12a00. Accessed May 23, 2005.
18. [Crosby MH]. [*Third World marketing resolution*]. Available at: http://legacy.library.ucsf.edu/tid/thf12a00. Accessed May 23, 2005.
19. Baker MJ. [*Letter from Episcopal Church Publishing Company accompa-nying shareholder resolution concerning Philip Morris' promotion policies in the Third World*]. Available at: http://legacy.library.ucsf.edu/tid/ohf12a00. Accessed August 27, 2004.
20. Domini Social Investments. *How the process works.* Available at: http://www.domini.com/shareholder-advocacy/how_it_works.doc_cvt.htm. Accessed January 18, 2005.
21. Flanagan EJT. [*Memo to George Weissman advising that RJ Reynolds had also received a Third World mar-keting resolution from Father Crosby*]. Available at: http://legacy.library.ucsf.edu/tid/fqb81f00. Accessed October 13, 2004.

22. [Philip Morris Incorporated]. *The board of directors recommends a vote against proposal (3).* Available at: http://legacy.library.ucsf.edu/tid/vhf12a00. Accessed August 27, 2004.

23. [Philip Morris Incorporated]. *Philip Morris Incorporated questions and answers in preparation for the annual meeting of stockholders 810000.* Available at: http://legacy.library.ucsf.edu/tid/hhf12a00. Accessed August 27, 2004.

24. Maxwell H. *Philip Morris Companies Inc. annual report 900000.* Available at: http://legacy.library.ucsf.edu/tid/shu66e00. Accessed October 13, 2005.

25. Fried D. *Notice of annual meeting of shareholders to be held Thursday, April 25, 1991.* Available at: http://legacy.library.ucsf.edu/tid/zdk47c00. Accessed February 18, 2005.

26. [Burson H]. *Shareholder proposals [company response to resolutions proposed for 1991 AGM].* Available at: http://legacy.library.ucsf.edu/tid/skr82e00. Accessed February 17, 2005.

27. Flanagan EJT. [*Memo conveying IRRC analysis of ICCR shareholder resolution on Philip Morris' Third World promotional policies*]. Available at: http://legacy.library.ucsf.edu/tid/zhf12a00. Accessed August 27, 2004.

28. Crosby M. [*Letter to George Weissman conveying 1982 Third World marketing resolution*]. Available at: http://legacy.library.ucsf.edu/tid/cat37c00. Accessed October 13, 2004.

29. Finnegan RK. *Premonstratensian Fathers letter to George Weissman attaching 1982 Third World marketing resolution.* Available at: http://legacy.library.ucsf.edu/tid/bat37c00. Accessed January 19, 2005.

30. Pawlikowski JT. *Eastern Province of Servites letter to George Weissman attaching 1982 Third World marketing resolution.* Available at: http://legacy.library.ucsf.edu/tid/aat37c00. Accessed January 19, 2005.

31. [Crosby MH]. *Philip Morris. 1982 Third World marketing resolution.* Available at: http://legacy.library.ucsf.edu/tid/zzs37c00. Accessed January 19, 2005.

32. [Kull JB]. *Philip Morris Incorporated annual meeting of shareholders Wednesday, April 28, 1982, 9:30 am. Richmond, Virginia [minutes].* Available at: http://legacy.library.ucsf.edu/tid/ire35e00. Accessed January 18, 2005.

33. Ortman DE. *What is a shareholder res-olution?* Available at: http://www.scn.org/earth/wum/2Whatsr.htm#What1. Accessed January 18, 2005.

34. Wander N, Malone RE. Selling off or selling out? Medical schools and ethical leadership in the divestment of tobacco stocks. *Academic Med.* 2004;79:1017–1026.

35. Wander N, Malone RE. Fiscal versus social responsibility: how Philip Morris shaped the public funds divestment debate. *Tobacco Control* 2006; 15:231–241.

36. Wander N, Malone RE. Keeping public institutions invested in tobacco. *J Bus Ethics*; In press.

37. Storrs DK. [*Letter to George Weissman explaining Yale's opposition to the 1982 Third World marketing resolution, but urging Philip Morris to voluntarily provide health hazards information in the Third World*]. Available at: http://legacy.library.ucsf.edu/tid/amd38e00. Accessed January 20, 2005.

38. Spaeth EJ. [*Letter to George Weissman explaining Bryn Mawr's abstention on 1982 Third World marketing resolution, but urging Philip Morris to standardize worldwide tar and nicotine levels and health warning labels*]. Available at: http://legacy.library.ucsf.edu/tid/zil54e00. Accessed January 20, 2005.

39. Bates EB. [*Letter to George Weissman explaining why Connecticut Mutual Life voted in favor of the 1982 Third World marketing resolution*]. Available at: http://legacy.library.ucsf.edu/tid/yil54e00. Accessed January 20, 2005.

40. [Fried DD]. *Shareholder proposals [Draft resolutions and company responses proposed for Philip Morris 1991 AGM annotated by Charles Wall*]. Available at: http://legacy.library.ucsf.edu/tid/vma72e00. Accessed October 14, 2004.

41. Pollak L. *Memorandum from counsel to counsel and employees providing comments to report regarding health warning label policy on export cigarettes.* Available at: http://legacy.library.ucsf.edu/tid/dfa98d00. Accessed March 2, 2005.

42. Parrish S. *Memorandum from Philip Morris counsel to Philip Morris employees and Philip Morris counsel conveying legal advice regarding health warnings in foreign countries.* Available at: http://legacy.library.ucsf.edu/tid/cla98d00. Accessed August 26, 2004.

43. Pollak L. *Draft memorandum prepared by counsel and sent to employee reflecting legal advice regarding health warning label requirements on export cigarettes.* Available at: http://legacy.library.ucsf.edu/tid/dla98d00. Accessed August 26, 2004.

44. Whidden R. *Memorandum containing legal advice from counsel to counsel and employees discussing foreign warning labels.* Available at: http://legacy.library.ucsf.edu/tid/zka98d00. Accessed August 26, 2004.

45. The ASPECT Consortium, European Commission. *Tobacco or health in the European Union past, present and future.* Available at: http://ec.europa.eu/health/ph_determinants/life_style/Tobacco/Documents/tobacco_fr_en.pdf. Accessed March 7, 2005.

46. Howells G. The European approach to tobacco regulation. *N Z Yearbook of Jurisprudence.* 2001;5:75–111.

47. [Lindheim JB]. [*Letter to Geoffrey Bible concerning Burson-Marsteller Ltd proposal to assert EEC "local law" approach concerning health warning labels on duty free cigarettes*]. Available at: http://legacy.library.ucsf.edu/tid/vag42e00. Accessed August 25, 2004.

48. Vandermeersch D. *Compatibility with the EEC Treaty of the draft tobacco labeling directive.* Available at: http://legacy.library.ucsf.edu/tid/jok17d00. Accessed February 9, 2005.

49. Crosby M. [*Memo to D. Fried covering "Global Uniform Labelling Minimum" resolution for 1992 annual meeting*]. Available at: http://legacy.library.ucsf.edu/tid/klh46e00. Accessed August 17, 2004.

50. [Crosby MH]. *Philip Morris establishing global uniform labelling minimum.* Available at: http://legacy.library.ucsf.edu/tid/llh46e00. Accessed August 17, 2004.

51. Fried D, [Miles MA]. *920000 annual meeting shareholder proposals.* Available at: http://legacy.library.ucsf.edu/tid/ozh84a00. Accessed August 17, 2004.

52. Pollak L. *Memorandum from Philip Morris counsel to Philip Morris employees regarding warning labels, legal and other issues; forwarded from Philip Morris employee to Philip Morris employee.* Available at: http://legacy.library.ucsf.edu/tid/vmm88d00. Accessed August 17, 2004.

53. Pollak L. *Outline of discussion regarding warning labels prepared by Philip Morris counsel, forwarded to Philip Morris employee and copied to Philip Morris employee by Philip Morris*

employee. Available at: http://legacy.library.ucsf.edu/tid/wmm88d00. Accessed August 17, 2004.

54. Bible G. *Memorandum from Philip Morris employee to Philip Morris counsel and Philip Morris employees regarding warning labels.* Available at: http://legacy.library.ucsf.edu/tid/xmm88d00. Accessed August 17, 2004.

55. Bring M. *Memorandum from Philip Morris counsel to Philip Morris employees forwarded to Philip Morris employee containing legal advice regarding warning labels.* Available at: http://legacy.library.ucsf.edu/tid/anm88d00. Accessed August 17, 2004.

56. Bible G. *Memorandum from Philip Morris employee to Philip Morris counsel and Philip Morris employees regarding warning label issues.* Available at: http://legacy.library.ucsf.edu/tid/tlh46e00. Accessed August 17, 2004.

57. Bible GC. *Export labelling [Fax to Devitre asking for meeting].* Available at: http://legacy.library.ucsf.edu/tid/xlh46e00. Accessed August 17, 2004.

58. Devitre D. *Phone discussion with Rothmans regarding labelling.* Available at: http://legacy.library.ucsf.edu/tid/emh46e00. Accessed August 17, 2004.

59. Wollenberg S. *Philip Morris, RJ Reynolds agree to put warnings on all cigarette packs.* Available at: http://legacy.library.ucsf.edu/tid/pck47c00. Accessed February 24, 2005.

60. [Johnson DC]. *Philip Morris Companies Inc annual meeting of stockholders* [April 23, 1992 transcript]. Available at: http://legacy.library.ucsf.edu/tid/www88e00. Accessed February 25, 2005.

61. [Philip Morris]. *[Draft manual re "global uniform labelling" initiative].* Available at: http://legacy.library.ucsf.edu/tid/ooh19e00. Accessed August 25, 2004.

62. Smith T. *[ICCR questions on Philip Morris global labeling initiative in anticipation of January 28, 1992 discussion].* Available at: http://legacy.library.ucsf.edu/tid/ome42e00. Accessed February 25, 2005.

63. Crosby MH. *[Letter withdrawing Province of Saint Joseph of the Capuchin Order shareholder proposal demanding warning labels on cigarettes sold abroad].* Available at: http://legacy.library.ucsf.edu/tid/qnh46e00. Accessed August 17, 2004.

64. [Interfaith Center on Corporate Responsibility]. *Cigarette company reverses position on warning labels eleven year church group challenge to Philip Morris pays off.* Available at: http://legacy.library.ucsf.edu/tid/hoi58e00. Accessed August 19, 2004.

65. Kennedy D. *[Letter from Stanford's Kennedy to Miles expressing concerns about marketing practices].* Available at: http://legacy.library.ucsf.edu/tid/irt82e00. Accessed April 7, 2004.

66. Bring MH. *[Letter to Stanford president Casper responding to Kennedy's letter to Miles of March 19, 1992].* Available at: http://legacy.library.ucsf.edu/tid/pnf34e00. Accessed April 7, 2004.

67. Cogan D, ed. *Tobacco divestment and fiduciary responsibility: a legal and financial analysis.* Washington, DC: Investor Responsibility Research Center; 2000.

68. Bring MH. *[Letter from Murray Bring to the University of Scranton making Philip Morris's arguments against divestment].* Available at: http://legacy.library.ucsf.edu/tid/kbd78e00. Accessed January 23, 2004.

69. Christiansen DE. *[Letter from University of Scranton to Philip Morris stating its Committee on Responsibility in Investing had recommended divestment, and offering Philip Morris the right of reply before any university action].* Available at: http://legacy.library.ucsf.edu/tid/vit71f00. Accessed January 23, 2004.

70. Committee on Responsibility in Investing. *Proposal for divestiture of University of Scranton stock holdings in Phillip Morris Inc, and American Brands Inc.* Available at: http://legacy.library.ucsf.edu/tid/gbd78e00. Accessed November 6, 2002.

71. [Philip Morris International Inc]. *ICCR questions [answers to].* Available at: http://legacy.library.ucsf.edu/tid/obg42e00. Accessed August 25, 2004.

72. [Philip Morris Corporate Affairs Department]. *[Report on Philippine Congress passage of a tobacco health warning label requirement].* Available at: http://legacy.library.ucsf.edu/tid/pbg42e00. Accessed August 25, 2004.

73. National Center for Chronic Disease Prevention and Health Promotion. *Warning label fact sheet.* Available at: http://www.cdc.gov/tobacco/sgr/sgr_2000/factsheets/factsheet_labels.htm. Accessed June 3, 2005.

74. Marranzini CHS. *Advertencia al fumador.* Available at: http://legacy.library.ucsf.edu/tid/tsy71c00.

Accessed February 25, 2005.

75. Marranzini CHS. *Smoker's warnings.* Available at: http://legacy.library.ucsf.edu/tid/rsy71c00. Accessed February 25, 2005.

76. Greher L. *Health warning project.* Available at: http://legacy.library.ucsf.edu/tid/zni58e00. Accessed August 19, 2004.

77. [Bingham PM]. *Pack health warnings duty free.* Available at: http://bat.library.ucsf.edu/tid/lfo30a99. Accessed June 3, 2005.

78. Miles MA, Murray W. *Philip Morris Companies Inc. 1992 annual report.* Available at: http://legacy.library.ucsf.edu/tid/gpz74e00. Accessed June 3, 2005.

79. [Winokur M], [Devitre DS]. *Fact sheet [supporting December 1991 statement to Philip Morris BOD on export labelling].* Available at: http://legacy.library.ucsf.edu/tid/plo24e00. Accessed August 17, 2004.

80. Greher L. *Health warnings Africa.* Available at: http://legacy.library.ucsf.edu/tid/zka02a00. Accessed August 25, 2004.

81. [Philip Morris Companies Inc]. *Q and Q 940000 AGM.* Available at: http://legacy.library.ucsf.edu/tid/acc15e00. Accessed October 11, 2005.

82. Carlson S. *HWL opposition, Morocco.* Available at: http://legacy.library.ucsf.edu/tid/kbg42e00. Accessed August 25, 2004.

83. Salhi A. *Avertissement preventif sur paquets Marlboro* [Prevention warning on Marlboro packages]. Available at: http://legacy.library.ucsf.edu/tid/gbg42e00. Accessed August 25, 2004.

84. Bring MH. *Health warning labels.* Available at: http://legacy.library.ucsf.edu/tid/pzh84a00. Accessed Aug 17, 2004.

85. Seddon J. *US health warnings ex-USA.* Available at: http://legacy.library.ucsf.edu/tid/fln87e00. Accessed February 25, 2005.

86. Winokur MN. *Competitor positions on voluntary labelling.* Available at: http://legacy.library.ucsf.edu/tid/kmh46e00. Accessed August 17, 2004.

87. Krugman DM, Fox RJ, Fischer PM. Do cigarette warnings warn? Understanding what it will take to develop more effective warnings. *J Health Communications.* 1999; 4:95–104.

88. Cummings KM. Programs and policies to discourage the use of tobacco products. *Oncogene.* 2002; 21:7349–7364.

89. Scherer R. SEC move helps tobacco foes. Available at: http://web.lexis-nexis.com/universe/document?_m=18 643902298f9cedeca0a710a91ab25 5&_docnum=1&wchp=dGLbVlb-zSkVb&_md5=6ee3690b8dc872584 227083d0667f4b1. Accessed September 22, 2005.

90. Créatec. Effects of increasing the area occupied by health warnings on cigarette packages. Quebec: Health Canada; 1999.

91. Hammond D, Fong GT, McDonald PW, Brown KS. Impact of the graphic Canadian warning labels on adult smoking behavior. *Tobacco Control.* 2003;12:391–395.

92. Hammond D, Fong GT, McDonald PW, Brown KS, Cameron R. Graphic Canadian cigarette warning labels and adverse outcomes: evidence from Canadian smokers. *AJPH.* 2004;94:1442–1445.

93. Senior K. Bigger and better tobacco warning labels. *Lancet.* 2000; 356:139.

94. Agostinelli G, Grube JW. *Alcohol counter-advertising and the media: a review of recent research.* Rockville, MD: National Institute for Alcohol Abuse and Alcoholism; 2002.

95. US Department of Health and Human Services. *Review of the research literature on the effects of health warning labels: a report to the United States Congress.* Rockville, MD: US Department of Health and Human Services; 1987.

96. Meyers C. Cigarette warning label hoax. *Priorities.* 1990:42–44.

97. *FDA and tobacco: why Philip Morris USA supports passage of legislation in the 107th Congress granting FDA regulatory authority over tobacco products.* [Press release]. Available at: http://www.altria.com/media/press_release/03_02_pr_2001_03_22_03.asp. Accessed September 22, 2005.

98. Whitson JE. *910000 Shareholder Proposals.* Available at: http://legacy.library.ucsf.edu/tid/zkr8 2e00. Accessed February 17, 2005.

99. *JTI-MacDonald v Attorney General of Canada.* "The Role of Packaging seen though Industry Documents," Defense Exhibit D116, prepared by R. W. Pollay, Faculty of Commerce, University of British Columbia, History of Advertising Archives, March 21, 2001. 2001. Supreme Court, Province of Quebec, Montreal, Canada.

100. [Philip Morris Companies Inc]. *Spokesperson's guide.* Available at: http://legacy.library.ucsf.edu/tid/xcr3 9e00. Accessed September 24, 2005.

101. Fairclough G. *US study supports graphic cigarette warnings, lawmakers seek to introduce labels in US.* Available at: http://legacy.library.ucsf.edu/tid/lwq6 2a00. Accessed September 24, 2005.

102. Hill M. *Archival strategies and techniques.* Newbury Park, CA: Sage; 1993.

103. Prior L. *Using documents in social research.* Thousand Oaks, CA: Sage; 2003.

104. Offen N, Smith EA, Malone RE. The perimetric boycott: a tool for tobacco control advocacy. *Tobacco Control.* 2005;14:272–277.

105. Thomson G, Wilson N. Directly eroding tobacco industry power as a tobacco control strategy: lessons for New Zealand. *N Z Med J.* 2005;118:1223.

106. Glantz SA, Balbach ED. *Tobacco war inside the California battles.* Berkeley: University of California Press; 2000.

107. Crosby MH. Religious challenge by shareholder actions: changing the behavior of tobacco companies and their allies. *BMJ.* 2000;321:375–377.

108. Offen N, Smith EA, Malone RE. From adversary to target market: the ACT-UP boycott of Philip Morris. *Tobacco Control.* 2003;12:203–207.

The Landscape in Global Tobacco Control Research: A Guide to Gaining a Foothold

| Harry A. Lando, PhD, Belinda Borrelli, PhD, Laura C. Klein, PhD, Linda P. Waverley, PhD, Frances A. Stillman, EdD, Jon D. Kassel, PhD and Kenneth E. Warner, PhD

ABSTRACT

Smoking prevalence is shifting from more- to less-developed countries. In higher-income countries, smoking surveillance data, tailored treatments, public health campaigns, and research-based policy implementation have led to a decrease in tobacco use. In low- and middle-income countries, translating research into practice and policy is integral for tobacco control.

We describe the landscape of existing resources, both financial and structural, to support global tobacco control research and strengthen research capacity in developing countries. We identify key organizations that support international efforts, provide examples of partnerships between developed and developing countries, and make recommendations for advancing global tobacco research.

There is a need for increased commitment from organizations to support global tobacco control research.

The decline in smoking prevalence in high-income countries is attributable to a large extent to coordinated tobacco control efforts that are research-based, involving regional and population-specific epidemiological surveillance and intervention strategies that lead to implementation of tobacco control policies.[1–4] An important first step to cultivating region-specific research is understanding the current landscape of resources available to support and strengthen research capacity as well as opportunities to foster collaboration among tobacco control researchers when appropriate. Researchers entering the tobacco control field often confront daunting challenges in identifying potential collaborators and gaining financial support for their projects. These challenges are multiplied when they undertake tobacco control efforts in developing countries in the face of cultural, political, and economic impediments.

ORGANIZATIONS SUPPORTING GLOBAL TOBACCO CONTROL RESEARCH

The first step in facilitating international collaboration and strengthening the capacity for research is to carefully assess the current landscape: to determine what resources are now available and what can be realistically accomplished with these resources. Toward this end, a list of organizations that currently support research in global tobacco control has been published in a report prepared by Research for International Tobacco Control (RITC), an international multidonor secretariat housed at the International Development Research Centre in Ottawa, Ontario.[5] Table 1 provides a brief summary of the missions of selected agencies involved in supporting global tobacco control and tobacco control research as of 2002. The landscape in global tobacco control is ever shifting, and hence this listing is not entirely up to date. However, it does provide a starting point for tobacco control researchers and health care providers who are interested in accessing funding for international research on tobacco.

It is difficult, if not impossible, to determine the amount of money available for tobacco control research per se. Although the list in Table 1 is impressive, not all these organizations are granting agencies, and funds directly allocated to tobacco control research are limited. A review of Table 1 would suggest that this amount is surely less than $10 million for the entire globe, and perhaps closer to $5 million annually. Compare this expenditure with the $12.47 billion spent by the tobacco industry in 2002 on promotion and advertising in the United States alone.[6] Researchers in basic tobacco science may have a particularly difficult time in securing funding given that the listed granting agencies generally emphasize applied and policy research.

Governmental and Institutional Support

The Fogarty International Center of the National Institutes of Health, with the support and collaboration of 5 institutes of the National Institutes of Health, the US Centers for Disease Control and Prevention, the Canadian Institutes of Health Research, and the World Health Organization's Tobacco Free Initiative, established the International Tobacco Health Research and Capacity Building Program.[7]

This Fogarty International Center funding program is unique in supporting both trans-disciplinary research, including basic tobacco science and research involving partnerships between primarily US tobacco scientists and scientists in developing countries. Fourteen grants were awarded in response to an initial request for applications issued in

TABLE 1— Selected Organizations Involved in Global Tobacco Control Research[a]

Organization and Web Site	Annual Budget, US $[b]	Geographic Coverage	Mission
American Cancer Society (ACS) http://www.cancer.org	Not available	All regions, especially middle- and low-income nations	ACS has launched an international tobacco control program in collaboration with the International Union Against Cancer and other key partners. Primary goals include development of a broad-based cadre of international tobacco control leaders, advocates, and researchers; support for targeted, small research grants; and development of broad-based international nongovernmental organization tobacco control coalitions.
Campaign for Tobacco-Free Kids http://www.tobaccofreekids.org	Not applicable	United States	The campaign aims to prevent tobacco use by children and youths. Although much of its efforts have focused on the United States, the campaign supports a Global Initiatives Program.
Department for International Development (DFID) http://www.dfid.gov.uk	Not applicable	Most regions of the world; the poorest countries in Asia and sub-Saharan Africa receive the bulk of DFID funding	DFID aims to promote development and reduce poverty through its commitment to achieving international development targets. Commitment to tobacco control has been primarily through support of WHO and the Tobacco Free Initiative.
Fogarty International Center (FIC) http://www.fic.nih.gov	3.5 million	Currently funded projects cover a broad geographic distribution of low- and middle-income countries	As a branch of the National Institutes of Health, FIC promotes and supports scientific research and training. FIC emphasizes international research aimed at reducing the disparities that exist in global health. FIC provides funding through institutional training grants, cooperative agreements, small research grants, fellowships, and multilateral initiatives with international organizations.
Institute for Global Tobacco Control, Johns Hopkins Bloomberg School of Public Health http://www.jhsph.edu/IGTC	1 million	Global	The institute's mission is to prevent death and disease from tobacco use around the world through research, education, and policy development. The institute collaborates on research projects that support the development of tobacco control policy and interventions, serves as an educational resource by collecting and disseminating materials and developing and offering educational programs, and synthesizes evidence in support of stronger tobacco control measures worldwide. The Institute now hosts the Global Tobacco Control Research Network.
International Tobacco Evidence Network (ITEN), University of Illinois, Chicago http://www.tobaccoevidence.net	400 000	Southeast Asia, South Africa, Latin America and the Caribbean, central and eastern Europe	ITEN was established as the result of a partnership between the World Bank and WHO. ITEN's primary aim is to maintain a formal network of economists, epidemiologists, social scientists, and other tobacco control experts to provide rapid, policy-relevant research on country-level, regional, or international tobacco control issues.
Office on Smoking and Health, Centers for Disease Control and Prevention (OSH) http://www.cdc.gov/tobacco	2.6 million[c]	All regions, with the focus on low- and middle-income countries and countries with a population of 1 billion or more	The OSH within the Centers for Disease Control and Prevention is the lead agency within the US federal government for tobacco use prevention and control. OSH oversees the Global Tobacco Prevention and Control Program and is a World Health Organization (WHO) Collaborating Center for Global Tobacco Prevention and Control.
Open Society Institute (OSI) http://www.soros.org	300 000	Central and eastern Europe	The OSI and its network of foundations seek to build free and open societies by supporting an array of activities dealing with the strengthening of civil society, economic reform, education at all levels, human rights, legal reform and public administration, media communications, and public health.
Pan American Health Association World Health Organization (PAHO) http://www.paho.org	Not applicable	Latin American and the Caribbean	Its governing bodies have mandated PAHO to move aggressively to reduce the use of tobacco, emphasizing the health aspect and the high cost to countries of tobacco use. PAHO has supported World No Tobacco Day. It also has worked to support the FCTC and the World Bank report on curbing the tobacco epidemic. PAHO has developed a number of technical reports and other resources addressing the impact of tobacco in the region and making recommendations for tobacco control policy.
Research for International Tobacco Control (RITC) http://www.idrc.ca/ritc	400 000	Main geographic focus on Latin America and the Caribbean; West Africa, East Africa, central and southern Africa; South Asia and Southeast Asia	RITC's mission is to create a strong research, funding, and knowledge base for the development of effective tobacco control policies and programs that will minimize the threat of tobacco production and consumption to health and human development in low- and middle-income countries.
Rockefeller Foundation http://www.rockfound.org	2 million	Southeast Asia (including Vietnam, Cambodia, Thailand, and Malaysia)	The aim of the Trading Tobacco for Health initiative is to support efforts to reduce the health burden of tobacco on the poor in developing countries. By building local research capacity, the initiative seeks to enable developing countries to respond to the challenge of tobacco on their own terms for the long term.

TABLE 1— (Continued)

Organization and Web Site	Annual Budget, US $[b]	Geographic Coverage	Mission
Society for Research on Nicotine and Tobacco (SRNT) http://www.srnt.org	600 000	Primarily North America, western Europe, and Australia, although membership is increasing in developing countries	SRNT's mission is to stimulate the generation of new knowledge concerning nicotine in all its manifestations—from molecular to societal. SRNT achieves this by sponsoring scientific meetings and publications fostering the exchange of information on the biological, behavioral, social, and economic effects of nicotine; by encouraging scientific research on public health efforts for the prevention and treatment of nicotine and tobacco use; and by providing the means by which various legislative, governmental, regulatory, and other public agencies and the ethical drug industry can obtain expert advice and consultation.
Swedish International Development Cooperation Agency (Sida) http://www.sida.se/Sida/jsp/Crosslink.jsp	320 000	South Africa (Women's Health Project), Brazil, Malawi, Macedonia, Turkey, China, Zimbabwe, India, Vietnam, and Nicaragua	Sida aims to raise the standard of living in the poorer countries of the world. Sida has provided support for tobacco-relevant programs and initiatives at Research for International Tobacco Control (RITC, previously known as the International Tobacco Initiative) the World Bank, and WHO. Sida is currently establishing a set of guidelines and priorities for tobacco activities.
WHO-TFI Eastern Mediterranean Regional Office http://www.emro.who.int/index.asp	150000[d]	East Mediterranean region	Tobacco control research priorities include surveys related to different aspects of the tobacco epidemic, economic studies, and legislation. Key initiatives have included the Global Youth Tobacco Survey, the Global Health Professional Survey, tobacco economic studies, and studies of tobacco smuggling.
WHO-TFI European Regional Office (Euro-TFI) http://www.who.dk/eprise/main/WHO/Progs/TOB/Home	250 000[e]	Focus on central and eastern Europe and central Asia	The Euro-TFI program works to ensure that governments, international agencies, and other partners are equipped to work together to control tobacco use by building regionwide political commitment for tobacco control and the FCTC; providing international support for building national capacity for tobacco control; strengthening international coordination; and facilitating information exchange, technical cooperation, and monitoring. Euro-TFI provides technical assistance, training, and development of guidelines on surveillance, research, legislation, economics, health promotion, smoking cessation, and advocacy through public policy.
WHO-TFI Regional Office for Africa (AFRO-TFI) http://www.afro.who.int	Not applicable	Africa	AFRO-TFI notes the increasing burden of tobacco-related diseases, especially in African countries, and the fact that African countries are experiencing the highest increase in the rate of tobacco use among developing countries at 4.3% per year. AFRO-TFI promotes World No Tobacco Day. A specific theme has been tobacco-free films and tobacco-free fashion.
WHO-TFI Western Pacific Regional Office http://www.wpro.who.int/tfi	1.8 million plus 801 000 in country budget of 9 member states	Western Pacific: 36 member states and territories	The emphasis of the Regional Action Plan on Tobacco or Health 2000–2004 is the development and implementation of National Plans of Action for Tobacco Control, the support for development and adoption of the FCTC, the timely use of health promotion and advocacy initiatives, the use of mass media campaigns for quitting tobacco use, and the improvement of coordination of tobacco or health activities at the regional and national levels.
World Bank Group http://www.worldbank.org	140 000	Low- and middle-income countries in much of the world; current projects in Africa, central and eastern Europe, and Asia	Tobacco falls under the topic area of public health. The World Bank is mandated to support tobacco control research in low- and middle-income countries. The economics of tobacco is the priority of the bank's tobacco work. More specifically, research focuses on demand, taxes, smuggling, employment, and poverty. All research is expected to be policy relevant.
World Health Organization Tobacco Free Initiative (WHO-TFI) http://www.who.int/tobacco	1 million	All regions	WHO-TFI is a cabinet project of WHO. TFI's global mission is to reduce tobacco prevalence and consumption in all countries and among all groups. A major focus of TFI was the negotiation of the Framework Convention on Tobacco Control (FCTC).

[a]Data collected June–August, 2002. Agencies were asked to provide the "current" figures at the time of data collection.
[b]Budget figures indicated are for tobacco control research and for tobacco control activities.
[c]For global work in 2001.
[d]Spent last biennium on tobacco-related studies.
[e]Extrabudgetary allocations range from $150 000 to $300 000.

2001. The goals of the program are to reduce the burden of tobacco consumption in low- and middle-income nations by conducting observational, interventional, and policy research of local relevance and to build capacity in epidemiological and behavioral research, prevention, treatment, communications, health services, and policy research. A brief description of these 14 projects is included in Table 2.

Several institutes of the National Institutes of Health have also supported global tobacco research through other initiatives. The National Cancer Institute, for example, supports the Global Tobacco Research Network.[8] The National Institute on Drug Abuse allows grantees to apply for administrative supplements to existing grants to add components focusing on international research. The institute also supports several types of programs for international scientists in collaboration with US grantees, including the possibility of bringing researchers from developing countries to the United States for pre- and postdoctoral training. The Environmental Protection Agency supported work in China to combat environmental tobacco smoke. Health Canada and the Canadian Institutes of Health Research support global tobacco research including the Canadian Tobacco Control Research Initiative.

RITC was established in 1995 and has had multiple funding partners, including the International Development Research Centre, Health Canada, the Swedish International Development Cooperation Agency, and the Canadian International Development Agency. RITC was invited to take the lead in developing tobacco control research strategies and global partnerships that would respond to tobacco as a major threat to equitable and sustainable development.

For the past 10 years, RITC has supported tobacco control research and has worked to strengthen research capacity in low- and middle-income countries. RITC accepts investigator-initiated research proposals that are based in developing country institutions. The RITC secretariat works closely with research proponents to refine research proposals and to provide technical support as needed. Priority is given to research that is policy relevant and multidisciplinary and includes a capacity-building component.

Private Foundations

Private foundations have provided support for tobacco control initiatives around the globe. The Trading Tobacco for Health initiative of the Rockefeller Foundation included developing a partnership between US researchers and the Thailand Health Promotion Foundation to support research capacity and skill development throughout Southeast Asia by providing seed funding to local investigators and by supporting workshops and training. The Open Society Institute focuses on central and eastern Europe, specifically former Soviet Union and satellite countries. The tobacco initiative is mandated to fund policy research in order to establish an evidence base for the development of advocacy strategies. Priorities include critical tobacco-related issues such as price policy, taxation, and smuggling.

International Organizations

The World Health Organization (WHO) and its regional offices have worked to support the Framework Convention on Tobacco Control, a momentous step for tobacco control in which nations have united around a treaty to protect public health by reducing the harmful impact of tobacco use. Countries that sign the treaty agree to design, implement, and periodically update their national tobacco control strategies and programs, including public education, product regulation, and taxation, in accordance with treaty requirements. WHO also implemented the Tobacco Free Initiative, which supports communication, media, and advocacy for policy change and works with countries to strengthen national capacity for the development of sustainable tobacco control activities. WHO regional offices have varied in their emphasis on tobacco control initiatives.

The World Bank has made critical contributions to global tobacco control research, especially through its emphasis on research on the economics of tobacco. The World Bank's widely disseminated report *Curbing the Epidemic: Governments and the Economics of Tobacco Control* [9] has become a major resource for tobacco control advocates and researchers worldwide.

CAPACITY-BUILDING ORGANIZATIONS THAT DO NOT PROVIDE RESEARCH GRANTS

The International Tobacco Evidence Network emphasizes both interdisciplinary collaboration and communication between researchers in low- and middle-income countries and international experts in tobacco control. The network conducts country-specific research; has established regional centers in South Africa, Mexico, and Poland; provides peer reviews of manuscripts submitted by researchers from developing countries; and organizes regional workshops to promote research capacity building.

The International Tobacco Evidence Network emphasizes the economic research of tobacco control–related issues and provides technical support for such research. It seeks to encourage colleagues in low- and middle-income countries to undertake interdisciplinary analyses of tobacco consumption, providing them with both technical and strategic advice and helping them to identify research priorities. The network seeks to disseminate existing research-based knowledge and to monitor tobacco control research activities with an international aspect to identify research gaps.

The research capacity–building efforts by the network in Southeast Asia have demonstrated knowledge transfer by a series of successful grant applications from the region and by influence on formulating tobacco control policies in participating countries. One such success story is Vietnam, where analyses produced by a participant were presented at the ministerial level and were followed by the decision to increase taxes on tobacco products nationwide.

TABLE 2— Fogarty International Center Tobacco Grants

No.	Principal Investigator and Affiliations	Project Description
1	David Brook, Mount Sinai School of Medicine	A collaborative epidemiological study of disease-related psychosocial determinants of tobacco use in a cohort of 700 South African adolescents from several ethnic groups and capacity-building in tobacco research in South Africa
2	Linda Ferry, Loma Linda University	A Global Tobacco Control Methods (28-unit) graduate certificate offered by Loma Linda University, Schools of Public Health and Medicine, for 16 Cambodian and Laotian health professionals who are mentored to conduct a national tobacco use prevalence study and subsequent interventions based on the prevalence data
3	Teh-Wei Hu, University of California, Berkeley	Studies of the impact of an additional tobacco tax, economic costs of smoking, and cost-effectiveness of tobacco-control interventions in China
4	Ebenezer Israel, University of Maryland School of Medicine	A project creating a new smoking prevention research institute in Egypt to establish research and research capacity-building projects to reduce tobacco use
5	Prabhat Jha, University of Toronto	The India SRS Study: a 6-year prospective study of 6 million Indians in 1 million households to document the mortality risks of smoking by age, gender, and socioeconomic group
6	Gary King, Pennsylvania State University	A study collaborating with universities in South Africa and Tanzania to investigate tobacco control among youths and to establish 2 centers of excellence, form regional networks of researchers, establish fellowships, and promote exchanges between centers of excellence
7	Harry Lando, University of Minnesota	A project building tobacco research capacity and promoting tobacco cessation in India and Indonesia
8	Deborah Ossip-Klein, University of Rochester	A program increasing tobacco awareness and cessation activities in the Dominican Republic through existing Little Intelligent Communities units that offer wireless Internet access to state-of-the-art health education, agricultural science, and global economic information
9	Eliseo Perez-Stable, University of California, San Francisco	A longitudinal school-based survey among youths aged 11 to 15 years of 2 ethnic groups (Kolla and European descent) in the province of Jujuy, Argentina, to assess the prevalence of smoking behavior, as well as the predisposing, reinforcing, and facilitating factors associated with smoking acquisition within this population
10	Cheryl Perry, University of Minnesota	A randomized multicomponent, community intervention trial in Delhi and Chennai (India) and 32 schools focused on preventing the onset and reducing the prevalence of tobacco use among adolescents in grades 6 to 9 using curricula, parent involvement, and peer leadership and activism
11	Richard Peto, Clinical Trial Service Unit in Oxford, United Kingdom	A study of death rates among approximately 2 million people in 6 large study populations in Russia, China, India, North Africa, and Central America with the goal of determining to what extent tobacco is causing deaths from particular diseases and to ensure that data from these studies are available to inform future public health strategies and other research strategies
12	Ken Resnicow, University of Michigan	A randomized trial comparing the effectiveness of 2 approaches to tobacco-use prevention in a multi-ethnic sample of South African youths in grades 8 to 10 and a comprehensive capacity-building initiative to enhance knowledge of tobacco control among South African educators, clinicians, researchers, and policymakers
13	Jonathon Samet, Johns Hopkins University	An intervention in China to reduce women's and children's environmental tobacco smoke exposure at home, a survey on determinants of youth smoking in Brazil, and a study of smoking-attributable deaths and diseases and the associated costs of smoking-related diseases in Mexico
14	Kenneth Ward, University of Memphis	A project establishing the Syrian Center for Tobacco Studies as a resource for tobacco-control efforts, including epidemiological study, clinical research, and prevention and cessation intervention development, and as a focal point for dissemination of information about tobacco-control efforts in the eastern Mediterranean region

Note. SRS = Sample Registration System.
Source. Adapted and updated September 2004 from Fogarty International Center.[7]

The Campaign for Tobacco-Free Kids primarily focuses on the United States and emphasizes policy and advocacy issues while providing technical assistance in these areas to both individuals and organizations. Moreover, the campaign synthesizes and disseminates the evidence-based literature to support important policy decisions. At this time, the campaign does not have a specific mandate to support international tobacco control research, but it was involved in assisting researchers from low- and middle-income countries to locate US partners to apply for funding from the Fogarty International Center. The campaign played a key role in drafting and gathering support for a concept statement identifying tobacco control research as a priority area for the Gates Foundation's "grand challenges" in global medical research. The campaign was also a major supporter of the Framework Convention on Tobacco Control treaty described previously, through its work with the Framework Convention Alliance, an international network of tobacco control nongovernmental organizations.

The Society for Research on Nicotine and Tobacco, more than any other single organization, has emphasized nicotine and tobacco research. One of its key missions is to stimulate the generation of new knowledge concerning nicotine in all areas, from molecular to societal. However, SRNT's membership and focus have been primarily on a relatively few high-income regions, namely, North America, Europe, and Australia, with only 15% of its membership from outside North America. More recently, SRNT has sought to expand its work and membership into other regions. The 2003 annual meeting included a preconference meeting led by H. A. L. that included scientists from North America and abroad reporting on progress made in international collaborative efforts in terms of country-specific research and on strengthening research capacity in developing countries.

The 2005 SRNT scientific meeting will be held in Prague; this is the first time the annual meeting will take place outside North America. SRNT is continuing to promote membership of international researchers, especially from developing countries, by waiving conference registration fees, sponsoring travel to conferences, offering a limited number of free memberships, and sponsoring receptions and scientific sessions at international conferences.

The Institute for Global Tobacco Control at the Johns Hopkins Bloomberg School of Public Health is another important resource that is helping to broaden and expand global tobacco control research. The institute has been a major source of training and technical assistance and has conducted survey research and convened a number of conferences and workshops focused on global tobacco control work. The institute, through funding from the Rockefeller Foundation, has been able to support a number of small seed projects, primarily in Southeast Asian countries, and is conducting research and infrastructure development in Mexico, Brazil, and China as part of its Fogarty Initiative.

The Global Tobacco Research Network, which is supported by funding from the National Cancer Institute, is now housed under the umbrella of the Institute for Global Tobacco Control. Stillman and colleagues describe the network in greater detail in this issue.[8]

GLOBALink is another critical resource that has unique potential for linking researchers and advocates internationally and for disseminating information on tobacco control. Since 1993, GLOBALink has been bringing together tobacco control professionals around the world with a view to providing them with the opportunity to network, exchange ideas, and share information. With a membership of more than 4000 tobacco control advocates, GLOBALink is a recognized catalyst for dialogue and collective action.

EXAMPLES OF SUCCESSFUL RESEARCH CAPACITY BUILDING

A few thousand dollars in developing countries can support substantial research projects that may include collection of extensive survey data, moderate-sized randomized clinical trials, and stipends for investigators. H. A. L., for example, has worked with a student to conduct a comparative assessment of Chinese and US college student attitudes and behaviors relevant to tobacco and alcohol. This work was funded by a $2500 graduate research award.[10] RITC has supported similar efforts with relatively modest funding. For example, RITC supported the fieldwork of master's and doctoral degree students from low-income countries such as Nepal and Turkey for less than Can $5000 each. RITC has funded small grant competitions in the southern Africa region and the Middle East for as little as Can $20 000. Researchers in South Africa contributed to the evidence base that spawned that country's tobacco control legislation. The resulting tobacco tax increases led to a decrease in smoking prevalence in South Africa. Most recently, RITC partnered with the Canadian Tobacco Control Research Initiative and the American Cancer Society on a research competition for small grants to support ratification, implementation, or enforcement of the Framework Convention on Tobacco Control.

RITC also promotes dissemination of research results, particularly to policymakers. A recent publication with the World Bank, *Tobacco Control Policy: Strategies, Successes and Setbacks*,[11] tells the stories of tobacco control policy-making in 6 diverse countries and demonstrates the varied and important roles played by activists, health practitioners, policymakers, researchers, nongovernmental organizations, politicians, and the press.

Training international tobacco researchers is a critical step to ensure international collaboration and solid science. Kassel and Ross consider training issues in an accompanying commentary in this issue.[12]

DISCUSSION: RECOMMENDATIONS FOR GAINING A FOOTHOLD

The global tobacco epidemic continues to grow and spread to less developed countries that do not have the resources or infrastructure for tobacco control. Partnerships between the research community and those who apply research findings (practitioners, advocates, and representatives of both nongovernmental organizations and governmental organizations) are essential for success. These partnerships can mobilize financial resources and can facilitate knowledge transfer both to policymakers who need an evidence base on which to build policy recommendations and to the general public to increase awareness of the consequences of tobacco use.

Financial Resources

Tobacco control researchers and advocates should encourage the organizations listed in Table 1 to increase their financial commitments to tobacco control, as well as target other organizations to add tobacco control to their portfolio.

The United Nations Children's Fund (UNICEF) has focused primarily on children's health globally and is thus well positioned to support global tobacco prevention efforts. Although UNICEF has indicated interest in tobacco control issues, it has not yet made a major financial commitment to tobacco control efforts directed at children. Development agencies, most notably the US Agency for International Development, could also increase attention to economic threats posed to poorer countries by tobacco production and consumption and could provide dramatically greater financial support for initiatives to reduce tobacco's adverse impact on health and society. Perhaps in the future, the Gates Foundation can be persuaded to recognize tobacco control research as a grand challenge in global health, especially given its partnership with the National Institutes of Health. In the Ottawa Declaration on Tobacco and Sustainable Development[13] resulting from the November 2002 RITC-hosted meeting, Bridging the Research Gaps in Global Tobacco Control,[5] participants called on the development community to recognize the enormous threat to human life and health and, more

broadly, to sustainable development and poverty reduction posed by tobacco use.

A key question is whether a sufficiently compelling case can be made to governments to devote tobacco tax monies to tobacco control efforts, including research. Thailand, for example, increased taxes on tobacco products, and the resulting revenues have been used to fund a comprehensive tobacco control program.[11] The message should be clearly communicated that research can help to inform and drive policy and that locally relevant research can be especially important in this regard (see Warner[14] in this issue). In Taiwan, for example, researchers estimate that tobacco-related disease is costing the government $571 million per year, with 20% of illnesses and deaths directly related to tobacco smoking. Nearly 48% of Taiwanese men smoke, compared with 5.1% of women, although the percentage of adolescent girls who smoke is on the rise.[15] Fortunately, Taiwanese officials have taken notice of these alarming data and, as a result, have passed various tobacco acts and Department of Health initiatives to promote tobacco control.[16]

International Linkages

Home to active and aggressive multinational tobacco industries, wealthier countries would appear to have an obligation to poorer regions of the world increasingly being targeted for tobacco sales. These developed countries also should be encouraged to build linkages with governing health organizations of less developed countries, working with them on ways to provide funding and resources to local tobacco control researchers and advocates. The May 2003 approval of the Framework Convention on Tobacco Control is an important first step in this direction.[17]

We hope that tobacco research will be viewed in developing countries as a worthwhile endeavor and that those individuals who engage in such research will have opportunities for appropriate academic and research appointments and professional

advancement. Organizations such as SRNT can play a critical role in bringing together diverse constituencies of researchers, practitioners, and advocates to identify common interests. Currently there may be little contact among professionals concerned with tobacco control even when they are operating in close physical proximity. Establishing closer linkages is especially important in developing countries where the tobacco control infrastructure may be extremely limited.

CONCLUSION

In less developed countries, even relatively modest financial resources can be parlayed into large tobacco control initiatives that have the potential to save millions of lives around the globe. It is our hope that the landscape for global tobacco control will improve dramatically in the future and that far more coordinated efforts, additional resources, enhanced infrastructure, and a substantially increased cadre of researchers across disciplines will focus on confronting the rising tobacco epidemic. The Framework Convention on Tobacco Control treaty is a momentous step that, among other things, legitimizes tobacco control efforts, enabling tobacco researchers to use the treaty as leverage for motivating their own countries to shift priorities and support tobacco control research and policy. The potential for success is great; the consequences of failure to act are literally millions of preventable deaths around the world, primarily in developing countries.

About the Authors

Harry A. Lando is with the Division of Epidemiology and Community Health, University of Minnesota, Minneapolis. Belinda Borrelli is with the Center for Behavioral and Preventive Medicine, Brown University, Providence, RI. Laura C. Klein is with the Department of Biobehavioral Health, The Pennsylvania State University, University Park, Pa. Linda P. Waverley is with Research for International Tobacco Control, Ottawa, Ontario.

Frances A. Stillman is with the Institute for Global Tobacco Control, Johns Hopkins Bloomberg School of Public Health, Baltimore, Md. Jon D. Kassel is with the Department of Psychology, University of Illinois at Chicago. Kenneth E. Warner is with the Department of Health Management and Policy, University of Michigan, Ann Arbor.

Correspondence: Requests for reprints should be sent to Harry A. Lando, Division of Epidemiology and Community Health, University of Minnesota, 1300 South Second St, Suite 300, Minneapolis, MN 55454–1015 (e-mail: lando@epi.umn.edu).

Acknowledgments

We acknowledge the contributions of Mary Leitschuh.

Contributors

All the authors were involved in the writing and conceptualization of this article. All authors reviewed and commented on successive drafts. H. Lando took the lead in preparing the drafts. L. P. Waverley contributed substantially to Table 1.

References

1. Guindon GE, Boisclair D. *Past, Current and Future Trends in Tobacco Use, March 2003.* 2nd ed. Washington, DC: The World Bank; 2003. Available at: http://www1.worldbank.org/tobacco/publications.asp. Accessed December 1, 2003.

2. Jha P, Chaloupka F. The economics of global tobacco control. *BMJ.*2000; 321:358–361.

3. Shafery O, Dolwick S, Guindon GE, eds. *Tobacco Control Country Profiles.* 2nd ed. Atlanta, Ga: American Cancer Society, World Health Organization, and International Union Against Cancer Control; 2003.

4. Yach D, Bettcher D. Globalisation of tobacco industry influence and new global responses. *Tob Control.*2000;9: 206–216.

5. Research for International Tobacco Control. Bridging the Research Gaps in Global Tobacco Control: Report on the Meeting in Ottawa, Canada, November 4–6, 2002. Available at: http://www.idrc.ca/tobacco/BridgingFinalReport.pdf. Accessed November 11, 2003.

6. Federal Trade Commission cigarette report for 2002. Federal Trade Commission. 2004. Available at: http://www.ftc.gov/reports/cigarette/041022cigaretterpt.pdf. Accessed February 17, 2005.

7. Fogarty International Center Announces First Awards for International Tobacco and Health Research and Capacity Building Program. National Institutes of Health news release. September 25, 2002. Available at: http://www.nih.gov/news/pr/sep2002/fic-25.htm. Accessed February 17, 2005.

8. Stillman FA, Wipfli HL, Lando HA, Leischow S, Samet JM. Building capacity for international tobacco control research: the Global Tobacco Research Network. *Am J Public Health.*2005;95: 965–968.

9. Jha P, Chaloupka FJ, Brown P, et al. *Curbing the Epidemic: Governments and the Economics of Tobacco Control.* Washington, DC: World Bank Publications; 1999. Available at: http://www1.worldbank.org/tobacco/book/html/cover2.htm. Accessed November 10, 2003.

10. Lee J, Wu R, Jones-Webb R, Lando H, Ando A. Alcohol and tobacco use among undergraduates at Suzhou University in China. Paper presented at: the annual meeting of the American Public Health Association; October 22, 2001; Atlanta, Ga. Available at: http://apha.confex.com/apha/129am/techprogram/paper_21657.htm. Accessed November 13, 2003.

11. De Beyer J, Waverley Brigden L, eds. *Tobacco Control Policy: Strategies, Successes and Setbacks.* Washington, DC: World Bank/Research for International Tobacco Control Washington; 2003.

12. Kassel JD, Ross H. The role of training in global tobacco control research. *Am J Public Health.*2005;95: 946–949.

13. International Development Research Center. Ottawa Declaration on Tobacco and Sustainable Development. November 6, 2002. Ottawa, Canada. Available at: http://www.idrc.ca/tobacco/Ottawa_Statement_E.htm. Accessed November 14, 2003.

14. Warner KE. The role of research in international tobacco control. *Am J Public Health.*2005;95:976–984.

15. Koong SL, Alison M, Nakashima AK. A prevalence survey of behavioural risk factors in Taipei City, Taiwan. *Int J Epidemiol.* 1990:19;154–156. Available at http://ije.oupjournals.org/cgi/content/abstract/19/1/154. Accessed May 6, 2005.

16. Jha P, Chaloupka F, eds. *Tobacco Control in Developing Countries.* Oxford, England: Oxford University Press; 2000.

17. The World Health Organization Framework Convention on Tobacco Control. World Health Assembly Resolution 56.1. May 21, 2003. Available at: http://fctc.org/about_FCTC/treaty_text.shtml. Accessed November 10, 2003.

The Role of Training in Global Tobacco Control Research

| Jon D. Kassel, PhD and Hana Ross, PhD

ABSTRACT

Despite the pandemic nature of the tobacco control problem, little attention has been given to the role of research training in stemming the global tide of tobacco use. Tobacco research plays a critical role in both shaping policy and saving lives, and training new tobacco researchers is an important part of the tobacco control agenda.

There are several conceptual training models, all of which emphasize communicative partnerships and multidisciplinary approaches. It also is important to take cultural background and specificity into account when shaping research and training agendas.

We present a number of successful training initiatives and address both the strengths and the pitfalls of these endeavors.

INTRODUCTION

In the broad context of global tobacco control, the critical role of research in both shaping policy and saving lives has been articulated by Warner.[1] Indeed, since the publication of the 1964 surgeon general's report on smoking and health,[2] it is clear that research has had a profound influence on public policy and smoking behavior, particularly in developed nations. However, during this same time period, tobacco use has escalated in many low-income countries (e.g., Southeast Asia, Eastern Europe) because of increased tobacco company marketing spurred on by economic incentives.

Research training in the global tobacco arena occurs in developed countries, developing countries, or both. The specifics of the jobs and the activities that are pertinent to tobacco control training efforts must be fully clarified. Moreover, the extent to which training initiatives may vary from country to country—in terms of a given country's particular research needs—also must be acknowledged. Hence, we considered several conceptual models that detail how research training can be conceived and implemented. We stress the importance of cultural appropriateness and specificity within the global arena of research training efforts and share some examples of what we view as successful (e.g., resulted in grants, presentations, publications, expert testimony, policy change) and innovative training initiatives.

TRAINING DOMAINS

As described by Warner,[1] the content of research on global tobacco control can vary from country-specific research to tobacco industry analysis to treatment. Indeed, the research arena is vast and varies widely in content, ranging from basic and applied science (e.g., cellular research, epidemiology, economics, anthropology, sociology, psychology) to tobacco control (e.g., primary prevention, treatment, harm reduction) to societal interventions (e.g., advocacy, policy, education). Hence, it is important to remember that these areas of research, including research training, should all inform one another. Unfortunately, this is often not the case. For example, it is commonplace to find basic scientists working independently of policymakers and vice versa. As a result, much of the information gleaned from each of these respective domains is never adequately communicated to the other. Future research and training efforts must include channels of communication through which tobacco control information can be conveyed to those who work in different disciplines (e.g., via multidisciplinary workshops and Web-based communications). Interestingly, in some developing countries, there is less separation between researchers and advocates, because the same individuals are often involved in both activities. For example, the South East Asia Tobacco Control Alliance (http://www.tobaccofreeasia.net) promotes both researchers' involvement in advocacy and advocates' active participation in research. This is a step in the right direction.

A major obstacle facing tobacco research initiatives is the weak national capacity for preventing and controlling noncommunicable disease, such as nicotine and tobacco addiction.[3] As asserted by Mittelmark, "The lack of trained public health professionals is a gadfly in the global response to growing threats from communicable and noncommunicable diseases."[4(pS235)] Moreover, unlike most other noncommunicable disease prevention and control, nicotine and tobacco researchers face a well-funded adversary (see Warner[1]).

PROCESS OF TRAINING DEVELOPMENT

Developing trained scientists in the global arena of tobacco control presents daunting—yet exciting—challenges. Such capacity development requires dedication, motivation, communicative partnerships, and, ultimately, financial resources. Moreover, experience shows that certain aspects of international tobacco control training are imperative, such as the ability to teach the "language" of research, software development, basic research methodologies, and research writing skills. Far less valuable is sole reliance on scientists in developed countries who work only in developed countries. One useful approach has been to train a few scientists from developing countries in institutions in developed countries and then have the trainers partner with these individuals to design training for others within the developing country. For example, the London School of Hygiene and Tropical Medicine (http://www.lshtm.ac.uk) provides training in tobacco industry document analysis.

Nchinda[5] outlined a series of principles that can be used to govern research partnerships between developed and developing countries, all of which have implications for the development of successful training initiatives. First, at least 1 of the scientists from the partner institution in the developing country should have demonstrable competence in the research subject area in order to have a balanced partnership and to minimize any superior-to-inferior relationships. As such, the research leaders of the 2 partnership groups should have similarly high scientific qualifications and should feel mutual respect for one another. Indeed, our own experience shows that the host country must possess a sense of shared intellectual ownership in order for such collaborations to succeed. Second, partnerships should focus on nurturing sustainable institutional capacities for quality research by scientists in the developing country to further research that is beneficial to both parties. Third, the research must address common themes identified by the partners, with clearly defined areas of research for each partner. The partners should hold frequent meetings to discuss progress, although limited financial resources may make this difficult.

Fourth, the scientists in the developing country should be the privileged beneficiaries of partnerships that provide opportunities for obtaining valuable experience through an association with both institutions. Shared and equal input from both parties is integral to successful training initiatives. Finally, training should remain the central focus of partnerships, with "learning by doing" and "hands-on training" of trainees from the developing country strongly emphasized and encouraged.

The importance of transdisciplinary approaches to the global tobacco problem has been given voice by numerous advocates. For instance, Taub,[6] who believes that public health professionals working across disciplines can exert a greater impact on the health of the public than they can by working independently, described a conceptual model for building the capacity of the public health workforce that draws upon health care services, education, research, and policy. Correspondingly, an Institute of Medicine report[7] recommended that professional education, research, and training embrace a transdisciplinary approach, which was defined as drawing upon broadly constituted teams of researchers who work across disciplines in the development of research questions to be addressed (see Morgan et al.[8] for a discussion about the Transdisciplinary Tobacco Use Research Centers initiative). Transdisciplinary approaches to tobacco control are particularly important because they can address the diverse influences (e.g., politics, economics, health, addiction) that underlie global tobacco use.

CULTURAL CONTEXT

To forestall and ultimately stem the inevitable rise in tobacco-related deaths in developing countries, training efforts must address the dilemma as a global one.[9] At the same time, however, the importance of cultural context cannot be overlooked. The development of effective training programs must carefully consider the cultural backdrop in which such endeavors will be undertaken. Therefore, the goals to which tobacco control training efforts must aspire are lofty. These goals call for consideration of the tobacco epidemic as global in nature, yet they also take into account the unique cultural training needs and issues as they differ across and within developed and developing countries. Experts from developed countries cannot simply barge into developing countries and purport to offer solutions to problems that may, in many important respects, be idiosyncratic to these regions. Indeed, failure to seek feedback from host country participants has likely hindered some capacity-building efforts to date. As such, the context in which the problem—tobacco use—occurs must be fully considered and understood. It is at this juncture in the research process where the trainers become the students of a new culture.

Nichter[10] pointed out that many critical aspects of tobacco use—motivations for use, constraints on use, social attitudes toward use, personal and reference group identity as a function of use, and the portrayal of tobacco use in the media—are shaped by the cultures in which they evolve. This realization has profound implications for both research and the resultant training efforts. For example, basic epidemiological data gathering may be necessary in some countries; in others, emphasis may be placed on economic analyses, treatment accessibility, or any 1 of a number of other important research domains. Correspondingly, and as noted by Warner,[1] the numerous forms of tobacco and the manners in which they are used vary tremendously across developed and developing countries alike. Well-validated measures of nicotine dependence that are suitable for use in the United States, for example, may not be suitable in India, where the importance of the first cigarette of the day does not necessarily serve as an index of overnight tobacco deprivation but rather is attributed to nicotine's laxative properties.[10] Simply put, training in research must be guided by the cultural context in which it occurs.

SUCCESSFUL TRAINING INITIATIVES

Numbers alone will not create the research necessary for addressing global tobacco control needs. Countries, especially poor countries, must have the internal resources—the people, institutional commitment, and money—to make research a viable and productive part of tobacco control efforts. Moreover, as observed by Nchinda, "Training of scientists, the key to capacity strengthening, should take place in a broad and coordinated manner through well-integrated activities ..."[4(p1703)] We agree that research training must be viewed as integral to all successful capacity-building efforts. Some of the most prominent efforts to date are outlined in the following paragraphs (also see Lando et al.[11]).

Building Research Capacity

Within the United States, the Fogarty International Center at the National Institutes of Health (http://www.fic.nih.gov/programs.html) has developed the Tobacco and Health Research and Capacity Building Program, a model that is intended to (1) foster collaborative efforts between US scientists and scientists in low- and middle-income countries and (2) build both substantive knowledge and research capacity in the latter. The program is focused on 5 key research areas—epidemiology and surveillance, susceptibility and risk for smoking uptake, biobehavioral and social research, intervention research, and policy-related research—and it serves as an exemplar of how cross-cultural tobacco research training initiatives and partnerships can be successfully implemented.

Global Communication

An important and innovative capacity-building resource has been the international networks of scientists and activists who can now communicate instantly (see Stillman et al.[12] for a discussion about the Global Tobacco Research Network). GLOBALink (http://www.globalink.org) is a resource for policy-oriented activists, but it has served as an international research dissemination resource as well. The member e-mail discussion list of the Society for Research on Nicotine and Tobacco (http://www.srnt.org) is used daily to exchange information on research questions. To date, discussions have primarily focused on developed-country concerns; however, as the international membership grows, the organization and its e-mail discussion list will become significant resources for future global tobacco control researchers. Moreover, plans are under way for developing a mentoring program within the Society for Research on Nicotine and Tobacco to disseminate expert advice across the globe.

Education

Training within medical schools is emerging as another potent resource in the armamentarium against the global tobacco epidemic. Although most of these efforts have been advanced in developed countries,[13] it is clear from a global perspective that there are widespread deficits in physician knowledge and motivation about counseling patients to quit smoking.[14] Richmond et al. recently developed an impressive medical education protocol that has been incorporated into numerous medical schools across the globe, including Africa, Asia, and the Middle East.[15] Research opportunities (e.g., assessment of efficacy) from such initiatives inevitably present themselves as well. Moreover, these medical and health professionals may emerge as opinion leaders who will prove influential in increasing both the visibility and the priority given to tobacco control efforts, including research.

Multilevel Strategies

Country- and region-specific consultations on economic analyses have been engineered through the efforts of the World Health Organization (WHO), the World Bank, and the Centers for Disease Control and Prevention (CDC). These consultations are intended to assist target-country economists learning how to undertake policy-relevant economic research. For instance, the CDC has established the Global Tobacco Control Program to support sustainable global tobacco prevention and control. Another CDC initiative, the Global Youth Tobacco Survey, promotes both surveillance capacity and research skills building in low- and middle-income countries. Furthermore, the CDC is developing tools for enhancing national capacity to promote tobacco prevention and control policies. Toward this end, the CDC organizes skill-building workshops that foster an in-depth understanding of strategic approaches to designing tobacco control programs and policies.

Economic and Advocacy Skills Training

Several leading US tobacco policy scholars from the International Tobacco Evidence Network (ITEN; http://www.tobaccoevidence.net) and Johns Hopkins University's Institute for Global Tobacco Control (http://www.jhsph.edu/IGTC) have been working with the Rockefeller Foundation to select appropriate regional partners for establishing a sustainable research capacity in Southeast Asia. This 4-year training and technical assistance program not only supports research on the economic and epidemiological aspects of tobacco use and tobacco control but also teaches advocacy skills to local tobacco control activists. These advocates thus serve as the "customers" for the kind of public policy–relevant research that is integral to the project. Training and capacity building are carried out via workshops that aspire to (1) cultivate mentor-to-mentee relationships between individual researchers and international tobacco control experts, (2) provide scholarships to talented individuals who have the potential to become national champions of the tobacco control movement, and (3) establish a research grant competition that provides the necessary resources for carrying out the research activities.

An important aspect of the ITEN project proved to be establishing both effective methods of knowledge transfer and efficient modes of communication. These objectives were attained over time and were supported, in great part, by creating an environment of mutual respect and trust. During the course of the project, partners learned how to both integrate cultural differences into training curriculums and develop an agenda with which all participants felt comfortable. Moreover, a governing principle was that ownership of both the process and the results must stay in the region.

Certain difficulties will inevitably present themselves during such collaborative efforts. For instance, sustained recruitment of researchers within the host country proved problematic. In response, the ITEN modified its focus from recruiting additional researchers to providing continuing mentoring and hands-on training to the initial cadre of researchers. In another instance, failure to include prayer time for Muslim workshop participants emerged as an oversight that, upon its recognition, was quickly rectified.

Cost Efficiency

It is worth noting that many of the training activities (e.g., workshops, Web-based databases) can be provided at a relatively low cost. Thus, although there are financial constraints that limit the global context of tobacco research training, there are some relatively inexpensive, yet viable, options available.

CONCLUSION

The tobacco problem is not going away soon. Research training initiatives are integral to all capacity-building efforts, particularly within developing countries. Although many promising inroads have been made already, much work lies ahead. The success of such initiatives is contingent upon collaborative efforts that acknowledge—and embrace—the differences in the cultural contexts in which tobacco use occurs. For public health to exact its science in areas that need it most, the cultural backdrop must ultimately inform and guide the content and the process of

research and training initiatives. Moreover, such endeavors must be steeped in transdisciplinary perspectives that take into account the multiple influences that govern tobacco use.

About the Authors

Jon D. Kassel is with the Department of Psychology, University of Illinois at Chicago. Hana Ross is with the Research Triangle Institute, Research Triangle Park, North Carolina.

Correspondence: Requests for reprints should be sent to Jon D. Kassel, PhD, Department of Psychology (MC 285), 1007 W Harrison St, University of Illinois at Chicago, Chicago, IL 60607 (e-mail: jkassel@uic.edu).

Acknowledgments

We thank the following individuals for their valuable assistance and guidance: Harry Lando, Ken Warner, Belinda Borrelli, Laura Klein, Fran Stillman, and Linda Waverly.

Contributors

J. D. Kassel and H. Ross wrote and revised the article.

References

1. Warner KE. The role of research international tobacco control. *Am J Public Health.*2005;95:976–984.
2. US Department of Health, Education, and Welfare. *Smoking and Health: A Report of the Surgeon General.* Washington, DC: Government Printing Office; 1964.
3. Alwan A, MacLean D, Mandil A. *Assessment of National Capacity for Noncommunicable Disease Prevention and Control.* Geneva, Switzerland: World Health Organization; 2001.
4. Mittelmark MB. The role of professional education in building capacity for health promotion in the global south: a case study from Norway. *Ethnicity Dis.*2003;13:S235–S239.
5. Nchinda TC. Research capacity strengthening in the South. *Soc Sci Med.*2002;54:1699–1711.
6. Taub A. Transdisciplinary approaches to building the capacity of the public health workforce. *Ethnicity Dis.*2003;13:S245–S247.
7. Gebbie K, Rosenstock L, Hernandez LM, Eds. *Who Will Keep the Public Healthy? Educating Public Health Professionals for the 21st Century.* Washington, DC: National Academy Press; 2003.
8. Morgan GD, Kobus K, Gerlach KK, et al. Facilitating transdisciplinary research: the experience of the transdisciplinary tobacco use research centers. *Nicotine Tob Res.*2003;5(suppl 1): S11–S19.
9. Yach D, Bettcher D. Globalisation of tobacco industry influence and new global responses. *Tob Control.*2000;9:206–216.
10. Nichter M. *Global Research on Tobacco: An Anthropological Perspective.* Paper presented at: the Society for Research on Nicotine and Tobacco: Preconference on Global Tobacco Control; February 19, 2003; New Orleans, La.
11. Lando HA, Borrelli B, Klein LC, et al. The landscape in global tobacco control research: a guide to gaining a foothold. *Am J Public Health.*2005;95:939–945.
12. Stillman FA, Wipfli HL, Lando HA, Leischow S, Samet JM. Building capacity for international tobacco control research: the Global Tobacco Research Network. *Am J Public Health.*2005;95:965–968.
13. Spangler JG, George G, Foley KL, Crandall SJ. Tobacco intervention training: current efforts and gaps in US medical schools. *JAMA.*2003;288:1102–1109.
14. Richmond RL, Debono DS, Larcos D, Kehoe L. Worldwide survey of education on tobacco in medical schools. *Tob Control.*1998;7:247–252.
15. Richmond RL. *Educating Medical Students About Tobacco: Translating Research into a Global Initiative.* Paper presented at: the Society for Research on Nicotine and Tobacco: Preconference on Global Tobacco Control; February 19, 2003; New Orleans, La.

Cigarette Smoking and Exposure to Environmental Tobacco Smoke in China: The International Collaborative Study of Cardiovascular Disease in Asia

| Dongfeng Gu, MD, MSc, Xigui Wu, MD, Kristi Reynolds, MPH, Xiufang Duan, MD, Xue Xin, MD, MSc, Robert F. Reynolds, ScD, Paul K. Whelton, MD, MSc and Jiang He, MD, PhD for the InterASIA Collaborative Group

ABSTRACT

Objectives. We estimated the prevalence of cigarette smoking and the extent of environmental tobacco smoke exposure (ETS) in the general population in China.

Methods. A cross-sectional survey was conducted on a nationally representative sample of 15540 Chinese adults aged 35–74 years in 2000–2001. Information on cigarette smoking was obtained by trained interviewers using a standard questionnaire.

Results. The prevalence of current cigarette smoking was much higher among men (60.2%) than among women (6.9%). Among nonsmokers, 12.1% of men and 51.3% of women reported exposure to ETS at home, and 26.7% of men and 26.2% of women reported exposure to ETS in their workplaces. On the basis of our findings, 147358000 Chinese men and 15895000 Chinese women aged 35–74 years were current cigarette smokers, 8658000 men and 108402000 women were exposed to ETS at home, and 19072000 men and 55372000 women were exposed to ETS in their workplaces.

Conclusions. The high prevalence of cigarette smoking and environmental tobacco smoke exposure in the Chinese population indicates an urgent need for smoking prevention and cessation efforts.

INTRODUCTION

Cigarette smoking is a major public health challenge worldwide. Whereas cigarette smoking caused an estimated 3 million annual deaths worldwide at the end of the 20th century, this number is predicted to soar to more than 10 million by 2020, with the burden of smoking-related mortality shifting from developed to developing nations.[1–3] By 2030, 70% of annual smoking-related deaths worldwide will occur in developing countries.[4]

With a population of 1.2 billion, China is the world's largest producer and consumer of tobacco.[5] Several epidemiological studies conducted in China have documented that cigarette smoking increases mortality from cancer and from respiratory and cardiovascular disease.[6–10] Two previous national surveys have reported a high prevalence of cigarette smoking in Chinese men.[5,11] However, detailed information on home and workplace exposure to environmental tobacco smoke (ETS) was not reported in these surveys.

The objectives of this study were to estimate the prevalence and number of cigarette smokers in the general adult population in China, to examine the extent of ETS exposure in China, and to investigate the contribution of home and workplace exposure to ETS.

METHODS

The International Collaborative Study of Cardiovascular Disease in Asia (InterASIA) was a cross-sectional study of cardiovascular disease risk factors in the general population aged 35–74 years in China and Thailand. Details of the study's design and methods have been published elsewhere.[12]

In brief, InterASIA used a 4-stage stratified sampling method to select a nationally representative sample in China. A total of 19012 persons were randomly selected and were invited to participate. A total of 15838 persons (83.3%) completed the survey and examination. The analysis reported in this article was restricted to the 15540 adults who were aged 35–74 years at the time of the survey.

Trained research staff administered a standard questionnaire including questions from the lifetime smoking questionnaire used in the US National Health and Nutrition Examination Survey.[13] The questionnaire was translated into Chinese and translated back into English independently by investigators who were fluent in both languages. Information about current and former cigarette smoking, including age at which smoking was initiated, years of smoking, and cigarettes smoked per day, was obtained. Cigarette smokers were defined as persons who smoked at least 100 cigarettes in their lifetime. Those who were smoking tobacco products at the time of the survey were classified as current smokers.

Reported exposure to ETS at home was assessed by asking study participants whether any household member smoked cigarettes in their home, and if so, how many cigarettes per day were smoked in this setting. Study participants were classified as having been exposed to ETS at home if any household member smoked. Study participants were also asked how many hours per day they were close enough in proximity to tobacco smoke at work that they could smell it. Study participants were classified as having exposure to ETS at work if they could smell tobacco smoke at least 1 hour per day at work. These ETS exposure questions have been validated by serum cotinine measures in the National Health and Nutrition Examination Survey III.[14]

The prevalence and mean levels were weighted to represent the total Chinese adult population aged 35–74 years. The weights were calculated based on the 2000 China Population Census data and the InterASIA sampling scheme and took into account several features of the survey including oversampling for specific age or geographic subgroups, nonresponse, and other demographic or geographic differences between the sample and the total population. Standard errors were calculated by a technique appropriate to the complex survey design. All data analyses were conducted using Stata 7.0 (Stata Corp, College Station, Tex) software.

RESULTS

Overall, 60.2%, or an estimated 147358000, Chinese men aged 35–74 years had smoked at least 100 cigarettes during their lifetime and were current cigarette smokers. An additional 10.6%, or an estimated 25872000, Chinese men in the same age range had smoked at least 100 cigarettes during their lifetime but were not current smokers at the time of the survey (Table 1). The prevalence of current and former cigarette smokers was much lower among women, at 6.9% (an estimated 15895000 women) and 2.0% (an estimated 4553000 women), respectively. The prevalence of current cigarette smokers was higher in younger than in older men, but the prevalence of former smokers was higher in older than in younger men. The prevalence of both current and former cigarette smokers increased with age among women. The age-standardized prevalence of current cigarette smokers was significantly higher among rural residents compared with male (61.6% vs

54.5%; $P < .001$) and female (7.8% vs 3.4%; $P < .001$) urban residents. The age-standardized prevalence of current smokers was similar among men in North and South China (58.6% vs 61.2%; $P = 0.08$) and was significantly higher among women in South China than in North China (7.8% vs 5.6%; $P < .01$).

Among current cigarette smokers, the average number of cigarettes smoked was 20 per day for men and 7 per day for women. Among current cigarette smokers, the average number of pack-years of cigarette smoking, an estimate of lifetime exposure (the product of packs of cigarettes per day and years of smoking), was 20 for men and 11 for women. As expected, pack-years of cigarette smoking increased with age. The mean age of starting cigarette smoking was 22.0 years for men and 23.7 years for women. Younger smokers reported an earlier age of initiation than did the older smokers.

Of the nonsmokers, 41.4%, or an estimated 117060000, Chinese men and women aged 35–74 years reported exposure to ETS at home (Table 2). The prevalence of persons who reported home exposure to ETS was much higher among women (51.3%) compared with men (12.1%). The prevalence of home exposure to ETS was higher in older age groups for men and in younger age groups for women. There were 26.3%, or an estimated 74443000, Chinese men and women aged 35–74 years who reported exposure to ETS at work. The prevalence of persons who reported workplace exposure to ETS was similar among men (26.7%) and women (26.2%). The prevalence of work-place exposure to ETS was higher in younger age groups compared with older age groups.

Among nonsmokers, 22.9% of Chinese men and women aged 35–74 years reported exposure to ETS at home only, 7.9% at work only, and 18.4% both at home and at work. Overall, 49.2%, or an estimated 139421000, Chinese men and women nonsmokers aged 35–74 years reported exposure to ETS at home or at work. The percentage of nonsmokers

who reported exposure to ETS at home only was much higher among women (29.0%) than among men (5.1%), whereas the percentage of nonsmokers who reported exposure to ETS at work only was much higher among men (19.7%) than among women (3.9%). The percentage of nonsmokers who reported exposure to ETS both at home and at work was much higher among women (22.3%) than among men (7.0%). The prevalence of exposure to ETS at home but not at work was higher in older age groups for men and in younger age groups for women (Figure 1). The prevalence of exposure to ETS at work but not at home was higher in younger age groups for both men and women.

The age-standardized prevalence of ETS exposure among nonsmoking men was significantly higher in urban compared with rural areas (39.8% vs 29.4%; $P < .001$) and in North compared with South China (37.4% vs 27.1%; $P < .001$), mainly because of a higher proportion of work-related ETS exposure in urban and North China. The age-standardized prevalence of ETS exposure among nonsmoking women was similar in urban and rural areas (53.3% vs 55.9%) as well as in North and South China (54.5% vs 55.9%).

Of the nonsmokers, 38.4% of Chinese men and women aged 35–74 years had 1 household member who smoked in their home, 5.0% had 2 household members who smoked in their home, and only 0.6% had 3 or more household members who smoked in their home (Table 3). The percentages of 1, 2, and 3 or more household members who smoked in their home were higher for women (47.7%, 6.1%, and 0.7%, respectively) than for men (11.0%, 1.8%, and 0.2%, respectively). Among nonsmokers, 9.8%, 12.2%, and 15.0% of Chinese men and women aged 35–74 years reported exposure to ETS at work for 1, 2 to 3, and 4 or more hours per day, respectively (Table 3). The percent distribution by number of hours per day of exposure to ETS at work was similar among men and women.

TABLE 1— Prevalence and Estimated Number of Cigarette Smokers Aged 35–74 Years by Gender and Age Group: China, 2000–2001

Age Group, years	Current[a]		Former[b]		Never[c]	
	% (SE)	No.[d] (SE)	% (SE)	No.[d] (SE)	% (SE)	No.[d] (SE)
MEN						
All	34.3 (0.5)	163 253 (2568)	6.4 (0.3)	30 425 (1244)	59.4 (0.5)	282 892 (2522)
35–74	60.2 (0.8)	147 358 (2522)	10.6 (0.5)	25 872 (1130)	29.2 (0.7)	71 491 (1878)
35–44	63.3 (1.2)	60 190 (1728)	7.0 (0.6)	6684 (584)	29.7 (1.1)	28 218 (1258)
45–54	62.3 (1.4)	46 557 (1729)	10.4 (0.9)	7793 (659)	27.3 (1.3)	20 442 (1087)
55–64	57.8 (1.6)	26 015 (1136)	12.8 (1.0)	5745 (482)	29.4 (1.5)	13 226 (783)
65–74	48.9 (2.3)	14 596 (942)	18.9 (1.7)	5650 (566)	32.2 (2.1)	9605 (771)
WOMEN						
35–74	6.9 (0.4)	15 895 (963)	2.0 (0.2)	4553 (540)	91.2 (0.5)	211 401 (2469)
35–44	4.7 (0.6)	4209 (526)	0.8 (0.2)	751 (207)	94.5 (0.6)	84 459 (1860)
45–54	6.6 (0.8)	4600 (605)	2.1 (0.5)	1486 (345)	91.3 (0.9)	64 138 (1733)
55–64	8.8 (0.9)	3691 (410)	2.5 (0.6)	1056 (243)	88.7 (1.1)	37 087 (1236)
65–74	11.2 (1.4)	3395 (451)	4.1 (0.9)	1259 (275)	84.7 (1.6)	25 718 (1251)

[a]Current cigarette smokers were those who smoked at the time of the survey and had smoked more than 100 cigarettes in their lifetimes.
[b]Former cigarette smokers were those who had smoked more than 100 cigarettes in their lifetime but were no longer smoking at the time of the survey.
[c]Never smokers were those who had never smoked or smoked fewer than 100 cigarettes in their lifetimes.
[d]Estimated population in thousands.

TABLE 2— Prevalence of Home or Workplace Exposure to Environmental Tobacco Smoke Among Nonsmokers, by Gender and Age Group: China, 2000–2001

Age Group, years	Home		Workplace	
	% (SE)	Estimated Population[a] (SE)	% (SE)	Estimated Population[a] (SE)
All	41.4 (0.7)	117 060 (2110)	26.3 (0.6)	74 443 (1809)
MEN				
35–74	12.1 (0.9)	8658 (700)	26.7 (1.2)	19 072 (961)
35–44	6.0 (1.1)	1685 (333)	31.1 (2.0)	8771 (667)
45–54	13.1 (1.9)	2664 (404)	29.9 (2.4)	6106 (562)
55–64	19.9 (2.4)	2634 (344)	22.9 (2.4)	3028 (359)
65–74	17.5 (3.1)	1674 (322)	12.2 (2.5)	1166 (257)
WOMEN				
35–74	51.3 (0.8)	10 8402 (2041)	26.2 (0.7)	155 372 (1620)
35–44	57.5 (1.2)	48 533 (1463)	33.8 (1.2)	28 521 (1184)
45–54	51.4 (1.4)	32 915 (1264)	25.0 (1.3)	16 017 (952)
55–64	49.7 (1.8)	18 437 (896)	20.9 (1.5)	7732 (634)
65–74	33.1 (2.3)	8516 (708)	12.1 (1.7)	3102 (463)

[a]In thousands.

CONCLUSIONS

This study indicates that, of Chinese adults aged 35–74 years, 60.2% (147358000) of men and 6.9% (15895000) of women were current cigarette smokers. In addition, 49.2% (139421000) of nonsmokers aged 35–74 years reported exposure to ETS at home or at work. Overall, more than 300 million Chinese adults aged 35–74 years were exposed to active or passive cigarette smoking. This number is very significant because cigarette smoking has become the leading cause of preventable death in China and the world.[6–10,15]

Two national surveys on the prevalence of cigarette smoking were conducted in China in 1984 and 1996.[5,11] In the 1984 national survey, a multistage randomly selected sample of 519600 Chinese men and women aged 15 years or older participated in the survey.[11] Overall, the prevalence of cigarette smoking, defined as persons who had ever smoked at least 1 cigarette daily for at least 6 months, was 61.0% among men and 7.0% among women. In the 1996 national survey, 120298 persons aged 15 to 69 years were selected from 145 disease surveillance populations in the 30 provinces in China, using a 3-stage cluster, random sampling method.[5] Using the same definition for cigarette smoking as the 1984 survey, the prevalence of current smoking was 63.0% among men and 3.8% among women.

Our study employed a multistage stratified random sampling method to select a representative national sample from the Chinese general population. Cigarette smokers were defined as persons who had smoked at least 100 cigarettes during their lifetime. Our findings cannot be directly compared with the 2 previous national surveys, because of differences in sampling methods and definitions of cigarette smoking. However, our study confirmed the previous findings that the prevalence of current cigarette smoking was extremely high among men. In addition, we found that the prevalence of cigarette smoking among women was higher than previously reported.

American Journal of Public Health | November 2004, Vol 94, No. 11

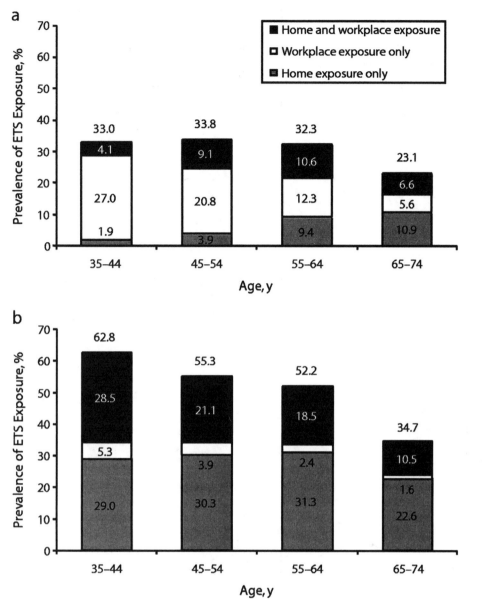

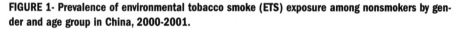

FIGURE 1- Prevalence of environmental tobacco smoke (ETS) exposure among nonsmokers by gender and age group in China, 2000-2001.

China, similar to what is seen in other countries.[4,6–10] Exposure to ETS has also been related to an increased risk of lung cancer and cardiovascular disease in Chinese population as well as in other populations.[21–25]

Our findings have important public health implications. The high prevalence of cigarette smoking in Chinese men indicates an urgent need for smoking prevention and cessation efforts. Smoking prevention efforts are also needed to further decrease the currently low prevalence of cigarette smoking among women. The large number of men and women being exposed passively to cigarette smoke in their workplace argues for legal prohibition of cigarette smoking in the workplace environment in China.

About the Authors

Dongfeng Gu, Xigui Wu, and Xiufang Duan are with the Division of Population Genetics and Prevention, Fuwai Hospital and Cardiovascular Institute, Chinese Academy of Medical Sciences and Peking Union Medical College, Beijing, People's Republic of China. Kristi Reynolds, Xue Xin, Paul K. Whelton, and Jiang He are with Department of Epidemiology, Tulane University School of Public Health and Tropical Medicine, New Orleans, La. Robert F. Reynolds is with Worldwide Safety Evaluation and Epidemiology, Pfizer Pharmaceuticals Group, New York, NY

Correspondence: Requests for reprints should be sent to Jiang He, MD, PhD, Department of Epidemiology, Tulane University School of Public Health and Tropical Medicine, 1430 Tulane Avenue SL18, New Orleans, LA 70112 (e-mail: jhe@tulane.edu).

Acknowledgments

The InterASIA study was funded by a contractual agreement between Tulane University and Pfizer Inc. Several researchers employed by Pfizer Inc. were members of the Study Steering Committee that designed the study. However, the study was conducted, analyzed, and interpreted by the investigators independent of the sponsor.

This study provides an opportunity to compare the prevalence of cigarette smoking in China with other countries because the survey instruments and definitions for cigarette smoking were identical to those used in other national surveys. The prevalence of cigarette smoking in Western populations was much lower for men and higher for women compared with that noted in China.[16–18] For example, the prevalence of current smokers was 26.4% among men and 22.1% among women in the 1997–1998 US National Health Interview Survey.[17]

The prevalence of cigarette smoking in China was similar to other economically developing countries in Asia.[19,20]

Our study is among the first surveys to provide detailed information on ETS in the general population in China. Our findings indicated that a high proportion of men and women are exposed to ETS smoke at work in China, which is cause for concern. Prohibition of cigarette smoking in the workplace is not required by law in China.

Epidemiological studies have documented that cigarette smoking is a leading preventable cause of death in

TABLE 3— Percentage of Nonsmokers, by Home Exposure (Number of Household Members Reported Smoking in Their Homes) and Workplace Exposure (Number of Hours Exposed to Cigarette Smoke at Work), Gender, and Age Group: China, 2000–2001

| | Exposed,[a] % (SE) | | | | | |
| | Smokers per Household | | | Hours of Exposure per Day | | |
Age Group, years	1	2	≥ 3	1	2–3	≥ 4
All	38.4 (0.7)	5.0 (0.3)	0.6 (0.1)	9.8 (0.5)	12.2 (0.5)	15.0 (0.6)
MEN						
35–74	11.0 (0.9)	1.8 (0.4)	0.2 (0.1)	9.1 (0.9)	11.0 (1.0)	14.4 (1.0)
35–44	6.1 (1.2)	0.5 (0.2)	0.02 (0.02)	8.2 (1.3)	10.9 (1.4)	17.5 (1.8)
45–54	12.0 (1.8)	1.5 (0.7)	0.4 (0.3)	11.5 (2.1)	11.4 (1.8)	14.8 (1.8)
55–64	16.7 (2.2)	4.0 (1.2)	0.3 (0.2)	10.6 (2.2)	12.5 (2.5)	10.6 (2.0)
65–74	14.8 (3.0)	3.2 (1.3)	0.0 (0.0)	4.1 (1.8)	8.4 (2.5)	6.8 (2.7)
WOMEN						
35–74	47.7 (0.8)	6.1 (0.4)	0.7 (0.1)	10.0 (0.6)	12.6 (0.6)	15.3 (0.7)
35–44	57.1 (1.2)	3.2 (0.5)	0.2 (0.1)	9.7 (0.8)	14.7 (1.0)	17.4 (1.0)
45–54	46.1 (1.5)	8.6 (0.9)	0.7 (0.2)	10.0 (1.1)	12.3 (1.2)	14.3 (1.3)
55–64	40.8 (1.8)	10.1 (1.1)	1.5 (0.4)	13.0 (1.7)	10.1 (1.6)	14.9 (1.8)
65–74	30.2 (2.3)	4.0 (1.1)	1.1 (0.5)	7.2 (1.9)	7.0 (1.7)	8.3 (2.0)

[a]Among those employed.

The InterASIA Collaborative Group: *Steering Committee*–Jiang He (Co-Principal Investigator), Paul K. Whelton (Co-Principal Investigator), Dale Glasser, Dongfeng Gu, Stephen MacMahon, Bruce Neal, Rajiv Patni, Robert Reynolds, Paibul Suriyawongpaisal, Xigui Wu, Xue Xin, and XinHua Zhang; *Participating Institutes and Principal Staff*–Tulane University, New Orleans, LA: Jiang He (Principal Investigator [PI]), Lydia A. Bazzano, Jing Chen, Paul Muntner, Kristi Reynolds, Paul K. Whelton, and Xue Xin; University of Sydney, Sydney, Australia: Stephen MacMahon (PI), Neil Chapman, Bruce Neal, Mark Woodward, and Xin-Hua Zhang. China: Fuwai Hospital and Cardiovascular Institute, Chinese Academy of Medical Sciences and Peking Union Medical College: Dongfeng Gu (PI), Xigui Wu, Wenqi Gan, Shaoyong Su, Donghai Liu, Xiufang Duan, and Guangyong Huang. Beijing: Yifeng Ma, Xiu Liu, Zhongqi Tian, Xiaofei Wang, Guangyong Fan, Jiaqiang Wang, and Changlin Qiu. Fujian: Ling Yu, Xiaodong Pu, Xinsheng Bai, Linsen Li, and Wei Wu. Jilin: Lihua Xu, Jing Liu, Yuzhi Jiang, Yuhua Lan, Lijiang Huang, and Huaifeng Yin. Sichuan: Xianping Wu, Ying Deng, Jun He, Ningmei Zhang, and Xiaoyan Yang. Shandong: Xiangfu Chen, Renmin Wei, Xingzhong Liu, Huaiyu Ruan, Ming Li, and Changqing Zhang. Guangxi: Naying Chen, Xiaoyu Meng, Fangqing Wei, and Yongfang Xu. Qinghai: Tianyi Wu, Jianjiang Ji, Chaoxiu Shi, and Ping Yang. Hubei: Ligui Wang, Yuzhi Hu, Li Yan, and Yanjuan Wang. Jiangsu: Cailiang Yao, Liangcai Ma, Jun Zhang, Mingao Xu, and Zhengyuan Zhou. Shanxi: Jianjun Mu, Zhexun Wang, Huicang Li, and Zirui Zhao.

Human Participant Protection

The institutional review board at the Tulane University Health Sciences Center approved the InterASIA study. In addition, ethics committees and other relevant regulatory bodies in China approved the study. Informed consent was obtained from each participant before data collection. During the study, participants with untreated conditions identified during the examination were referred to their usual primary health care provider.

Contributors

Dongfeng Gu participated in study design, data collection, and development. Xigui Wu, Xiufang Duan, and Xue Xin supervised data collection and quality control. Kristi Reynolds participated in data analysis and interpretation. Robert F. Reynolds and Paul K. Whelton participated in study design and interpretation of study findings. Jiang He participated in study design, supervised data collection and quality control, and wrote the article.

References

1. World Health Organization. Combating the tobacco epidemic. In: *World Health Report 1999*. Geneva: World Health Organization; 1999.
2. Houston T, Kaufman NJ. Tobacco control in the 21st century. Searching for answers in a sea of change. *JAMA*.2000;284:752–753.
3. Mackay J. Lessons from the conference: the next 25 years. In: Lu R, Mackay J, Nui S, Peto R, eds. *The Growing Epidemic: Proceedings of the 10th World Conference on Tobacco or Health*. Singapore: Springer; 1998.
4. Peto R, Lopez AD, Boreham J, et al. *Mortality from Smoking in Developed Countries 1950–2000*. New York, NY: Oxford University Press; 1994:103.
5. Yang G, Fan L, Tan J, et al. Smoking in China. Findings of the 1996 National Prevalence Survey. *JAMA*.1999;282:1247–1253.
6. Yuan JM, Ross PK, Wang XL, Gao YT, Henderson BE, Yu MC. Morbidity and mortality in relation to cigarette smoking in Shanghai, China. *JAMA*.1996;275:1646–1650.
7. Lam TH, He Y, Li LS, He SF, Liang BQ. Mortality attributable to cigarette smoking in China. *JAMA*.1997;278:1505–1508.
8. Chen ZM, Xu Z, Collins R, Li WX, Peto R. Early health effects of the emerging tobacco epidemic in China. *JAMA*.1997;278:1500–1504.
9. Liu BQ, Peto R, Chen ZM, et al. Emerging tobacco hazards in China: 1. Retrospective proportional mortality study of one million deaths. *BMJ*.1998;317:1411–1422.
10. Niu SR, Yang GH, Chen ZM, et al. Emerging tobacco hazards in China: 2. Early mortality results from a prospective study. *BMJ*.1998:317:1423–1424.
11. Weng XZ, Hong ZG, Chen DY. Smoking prevalence in Chinese aged 15 and above. *Chin Med J*. 1987;100:886–892.
12. He J, Neal B, Gu D, et al. for the InterASIA Collaborative Group. International Collaborative Study of Cardiovascular Disease in Asia: Design, Rationale and Preliminary Results. *Ethnicity Dis*.2004;14:260–268.
13. National Center for Health Statistics. Plan and operation of the Third National Health and Nutrition Examination Survey, 1988–94. Vital and Health Statistics, series 1, No. 32. Hyattsville, MD: U.S. Department of Health and Human Services, Public Health Service, Centers for Disease Control and Prevention, National Center for Health Statistics; 1994.
14. Pirkle JL, Flegal KM, Bernert JT, Brody DJ, Etzel RA, Maurer KR. Exposure of the US population to environmental tobacco smoke: the Third National Health and Nutrition Examination Survey, 1988 to 1991. *JAMA*. 1996;275:1233–1240.
15. Fellows JL, Trosclair A, Adams EK, Rivera CC. From the Centers for Disease Control and Prevention. Annual smoking attributable mortality, years of potential life lost and economic costs–United States, 1995–1999. *JAMA*. 2002;287:2355–2356.
16. Schoenborn CA, Vickerie JL, Barnes PM. Cigarette smoking behavior of adults: United States, 1997–98. Advance data from vital and health statistics; no 331. Hyattsville, MD; National Center for Health Statistics; 2003.
17. Office on Smoking and Health, National Center for Chronic Disease Prevention and Health Promotion, Centers for Disease Control and Prevention. Cigarette smoking among adults–United States, 1999. *MMWR*. 2001;50:869–873.
18. Primatesta P, Falaschetti E, Gupta S, Marmot MG, Poulter NR. Association between smoking and blood pressure: evidence from the health survey for England. *Hypertension*. 2001;37:187–193.
19. Jenkins CN, Dai PX, Ngoc DH, et al. Tobacco use in Vietnam. Prevalence, predictors, and the role of the transna-

tional tobacco corporations. *JAMA*. 1997;277:1726–1731.

20. Tatsanavivat P, Klungboonkrong V, Chirawatkul A, et al. Prevalence of coronary heart disease and major cardiovascular risk factors in Thailand. *Int J Epidemiol*. 1998;27:405–409.

21. Hackshaw AK, Law MR, Wald NJ. The accumulated evidence on lung cancer and environmental tobacco smoke. *BMJ*. 1997;315:980–988.

22. He J, Vupputuri S, Allen K, Prerost MR, Hughes J, Whelton PK. Passive smoking and risk of coronary heart disease: a meta-analysis of epidemiologic studies. *N Engl J Med*. 1999;340:920–926.

23. Zhong L, Goldberg MS, Gao YT, Jin F. A case-control study of lung cancer and environmental tobacco smoke among nonsmoking women living in Shanghai, China. *Cancer Causes Control*. 1999;10:607–616.

24. Wang L, Lubin JH, Zhang SR, et al. Lung cancer and environmental tobacco smoke in a non-industrial area of China. *Int J Cancer*. 2000;88:139–145.

25. He Y, Lam TH, Li LS, et al. Passive smoking at work as a risk factor for coronary heart disease in Chinese women who have never smoked. *BMJ*. 1994;308:380–384.

Prevalence of Smoking in 8 Countries of the Former Soviet Union: Results From the Living Conditions, Lifestyles and Health Study

| Anna Gilmore, MSc, MFPH, Joceline Pomerleau, PhD, MSc, Martin McKee, MD, FRCP, Richard Rose, DPhil, BA, Christian W. Haerpfer, PhD, MSc, David Rotman, PhD and Sergej Tumanov, PhD

ABSTRACT

Objectives. We sought to provide comparative data on smoking habits in countries of the former Soviet Union.

Methods. We conducted cross-sectional surveys in 8 former Soviet countries with representative national samples of the population 18 years or older.

Results. Smoking rates varied among men, from 43.3% to 65.3% among the countries examined. Results showed that smoking among women remains uncommon in Armenia, Georgia, Kyrgyzstan, and Moldova (rates of 2.4%–6.3%). In Belarus, Ukraine, Kazakhstan, and Russia, rates were higher (9.3%–15.5%). Men start smoking at significantly younger ages than women, smoke more cigarettes per day, and are more likely to be nicotine dependent.

Conclusions. Smoking rates among men in these countries have been high for some time and remain among the highest in the world. Smoking rates among women have increased from previous years and appear to reflect transnational tobacco company activity.

INTRODUCTION

In 1990, it was estimated that a 35-year-old man in the former Soviet Union had twice the risk of dying from tobacco-related causes before the age of 70 years as a man in the European Union (20% vs 10%).[1] In the former Soviet Union, 56% of male cancer deaths and 40% of all deaths are attributed to tobacco, compared with 47% and 35%, respectively, in the European Union.[1] Rates of circulatory disease among both men and women are approximately triple those in the European Union.[2] Moreover, tobacco-related mortality continues to increase in the former Soviet Union, while it has stabilized or declined in the European Union as a whole.[1]

Despite these deplorably high levels of tobacco-related mortality, relatively little is known about smoking prevalence rates in the region. Virtually no recent or reliable data exist for the central Asian countries (Kazakhstan, Kyrgyzstan, Tajikistan, Turkmenistan, and Uzbekistan),[2,3] and recent surveys conducted in Georgia have been limited to the capital, Tbilisi.[4,5] Data from elsewhere in the Caucasus (Armenia, Azerbaijan) are scarce,[6] and historical figures[7] are inconsistent with later findings, leading authors to rely on anecdotal reports of smoking rates.[8]

Historical[3] and more recent data, derived largely from Russia,[9] Ukraine,[10] Belarus,[11] and the Baltic states,[12] show—perhaps unsurprisingly, given the mortality figures just described—that smoking rates among men are high (45%–60%) while rates are far lower among women (1%–20%).[2] The higher rates previously seen among Estonian women are now being matched by rates among women in the other Baltic states[2,12,13] and by women in other urban areas.[9,10] Unfortunately, other than the Baltic states, few countries collect information using similar data collection tools, thereby precluding accurate between-country comparisons.

These issues underlie the need in the former Soviet Union for compara-ble and accurate data on smoking prevalence, given that such data are widely recognized as a prerequisite for the development of effective public health policies.[14–16] This need is made more urgent by the profound changes occurring as a result of the former Soviet Union's recent economic transition and, more specifically, by the changes taking place in its tobacco industry.[17] The latter were first felt as soon as these formerly closed markets opened, with a rapid influx of cigarette imports and advertising.[18–20] Later, as part of the large-scale privatization of state assets, most of the newly independent states privatized their tobacco industries, and the transnational tobacco companies established a local manufacturing presence, investing more than $2.7 billion in 10 countries of the former Soviet Union between 1991 and 2000.[21] Evidence from the industry's previous entry into Asia suggests that these changes are likely to have a significant upward impact on cigarette consumption.[22,23]

In response to these and other health and social issues facing the region, a major research project—the Living Conditions, Lifestyles and Health Study—was commissioned as part of the European Union's Copernicus program. This investigation involved surveys conducted in 8 of the 15 newly independent states: Armenia, Belarus, Georgia, Kazakhstan, Kyrgyzstan, Moldova, Russia, and Ukraine.[24] We present data on smoking prevalence, including age- and gender-specific smoking rates, age at initiation of smoking, and indicators of nicotine dependence.

METHODS

Study Population and Sampling Procedures

In autumn 2001, quantitative cross-sectional surveys were conducted in each country by organizations with expertise in survey research using standardized methods[25] (described in detail elsewhere[26]). In brief, each survey sought to include representative samples of the national adult population 18 years or older, although a few small regions had to be excluded as a result of geographic inaccessibility, sociopolitical situation, or prevailing military action: Abkhazia and Ossetia in Georgia, the Transdniester region and the municipality of Bender in Moldova, the Chechen and Ingush republics, and autonomous districts located in the far north of the Russian Federation.

Samples were selected via multistage random sampling with stratification by region and area. Within each primary sampling unit, households were selected according to standardized random route procedures; the exception was Armenia, where household lists were used to provide a random sample. Within each household, the adult with the birthday nearest to the date of the survey was selected to be interviewed. At least 2000 respondents were included in each country; 4006 residents of the Russian Federation and 2400 residents of Ukraine were interviewed, reflecting the larger and more diverse populations of these countries.

Questionnaire Design

The first draft of the questionnaire was created, in consultation with country representatives, from preexisting surveys conducted in other transition countries[9,10,12] and from New Russia Barometer surveys[27] adjusted to national contexts. It was developed in English, translated into national languages, back-translated to ensure consistency, and pilot tested in each country. Trained interviewers administered the questionnaire in respondents' homes.

Statistical Analyses

Stata (Version 6; Stata Corp, College Station, Tex) was used to analyze the data. As a means of reducing the skewness of their distribution, the continuous variables of age at smoking initiation and smoking duration were transformed, via log-normal transformations, before analyses were conducted; however, they were returned to their original units in computing results.

Current smokers were defined as respondents reporting currently smoking at least 1 cigarette per day. We calculated age- and gender-specific smoking prevalence rates for each country. Given the negative health effects of early initiation, we examined age at smoking initiation among current smokers, as well as number of cigarettes smoked. We assessed level of nicotine dependence, an indication of smokers' ability or inability to quit, by identifying the percentage of current smokers who smoked more than 20 cigarettes per day and smoked within an hour of waking. This level of use is equivalent to a score of 3 or more on the abbreviated Fagerstrom dependency scale[28,29] and indicates moderate (score of 3 or 4) to severe (score of 5 or above) dependency.

Within each country, gender differences in smoking habits were assessed with 2 tests and 2-sample t tests; variations according to age group were estimated via logistic regression analyses in which the 18- to 29-year age group was the reference category. Logistic regression analyses with Russia as the baseline were used in making between-country comparisons in likelihood of smoking, while analyses of variance combined with Bonferroni multiple comparison tests were used in comparing geometric mean ages at smoking initiation. To allow for the large number of comparisons, we used 99% confidence intervals and set the significance level at .01.

RESULTS

Response Rates

A total of 18428 individuals were surveyed. Response rates (calculated from the total number of households for which an eligible person could be identified) varied from 71% to 88% among the countries included. Rates of nonresponse for individual items were very low (e.g., 0.03% for current smoking and 0.5% for education level).

Sample Characteristics and Representativeness

The samples clearly reflected the diversity of the region and were broadly representative of their overall populations (Table 1). Comparisons of the present data and official data are potentially limited by the failure of some of the country data to fully capture posttransition migration and other factors,[30] but they suggest slight underrepresentations of men in Armenia and Ukraine, of the urban population in Armenia, and of the rural population in Kyrgyzstan. Age group comparisons among the respondents 20 years or older suggested a tendency for the oldest age group to be overrepresented at the expense of the youngest age group, particularly in Armenia, Moldova, and Ukraine.

Smoking Prevalence

Rates of male smoking were high. In many of the countries surveyed, almost 80% of male respondents reported a history of smoking (Table 2). Rates of current smoking were lowest in Moldova (43.3%) and Kyrgyzstan (51.0%) and highest in Kazakhstan (65.3%), Armenia (61.8%), and Russia (60.4%). Smoking rates in Russia were not distinguishable from those in Kazakhstan, Armenia, or Belarus but were significantly higher than those observed in Moldova, Kyrgyzstan, Ukraine, and Georgia ($P < .01$; data not shown).

Rates among women were far lower (gender comparisons were significant at the .001 level in all countries) and somewhat more variable, ranging from 2.4% to 15.5%; the lowest rates were seen in Armenia, Moldova, and Kyrgyzstan and the highest in Russia, Belarus, and Ukraine. Smoking among women in Russia was significantly more prevalent than among women in all of the other countries under study ($P < .01$) although adjusting for age

TABLE 1— Characteristics of Samples and Countries in the Living Conditions, Lifestyles and Health Study: 8 Countries of the Former Soviet Union, 2001

Characteristic	AR	BY	GE	KZ	KG	MD	RU	UA
Sample								
Response rate, %	88	73	88	82	71	81	73	76
Gender								
Male, %	40.3	44.1	45.7	44.4	45.0	45.1	43.5	38.8
Men aged ≥ 20 y, %	40.7	43.9	45.6	44.1	45.6	44.9	43.2	38.6
No.	2000	2000	2022	2000	2000	2000	4006	2400
Age group, y, %								
20–29	15.4	16.9	13.9	21.9	26.7	14.5	16.5	14.6
30–39	21.6	19.2	20.3	25.8	26.0	20.1	19.3	16.4
40–49	24.0	21.6	21.9	21.5	21.4	23.1	20.9	17.9
50–59	11.1	14.5	16.3	12.0	10.1	16.4	15.4	15.5
≥ 60	28.0	27.9	27.6	18.8	15.9	26.0	27.9	35.5
No. aged ≥ 20	1940	1922	1975	1890	1899	1945	3828	2324
No. aged 18–19	60	78	47	110	101	55	178	76
Interview location, %								
State/regional capital	44.0	33.9	41.4	27.0	27.5	30.4	35.7	31.5
Other city/small town	17.0	34.8	15.6	25.4	13.5	11.6	37.1	36.4
Village	39.0	31.4	43.0	47.6	59.0	58.1	27.3	32.1
No.	2000	2000	2022	1850	2000	2000	4006	2400
Reported nationality, %								
Nationality of countrya	97.3	80.1	90.2	36.3	68.6	76.7	82.4	77.7
Russian	0.8	12.1	1.3	41.5	18.0	7.7	. . .	16.5
Other	1.9	7.8	8.5	22.1	13.5	15.7	17.6	5.8
No.	2000	1979	2021	1979	1997	1980	3967	2371
Education, %								
Secondary education or less	49.1	49.4	33.8	35.7	48.3	52.2	43.2	44.2
Secondary vocational or some college	30.4	34.2	32.7	43.5	32.7	32.7	35.7	36.1
College	20.5	16.4	33.6	20.8	19.0	15.2	21.1	19.7
No.	1996	1984	1996	1995	1996	1984	4004	2381
Country data[b]								
Midyear population, 2001, thousands	3788	9971	5238	14821	4927	4254	144387	49111
Gross national product per capita, 2001, $	560	1190	620	1360	280	380	1750	720
Men aged ≥ 20 y, 2000, %	47.5	45.4	46.4	46.6	47.9	46.3	45.3	44.8
Urban population, 2001, %	67.3	69.6	56.5	55.9	34.4	41.7	72.9	68.0
Age group, y, % of total ≥ 20								
20–29	23.2	19.3	20.6	26.0	30.5	23.1	19.6	19.4
30–39	24.2	20.3	21.1	23.7	24.7	20.3	19.6	19.0
40–49	22.5	21.5	19.5	21.4	19.6	22.7	22.4	19.8
50–59	10.3	12.6	12.7	10.9	9.0	13.6	13.3	14.2
60	19.7	26.4	26.2	18.0	16.2	20.3	25.1	27.6
Unemployment rate, %[c]	11.7	2.3	11.1	2.9	3.2	2.0	13.4	5.8
Tobacco industry state owned (SO) or privatized (P)	P	SO	P	P	P	SO	P	P
Foreign direct investment in tobacco industry, end of 2000, $ millions[d]	8	0	0	440	. . .	0	1719	152.9
Foreign direct investment in tobacco industry per capita x 1000[d]	0.002	0.000	0.000	0.030	. . .	0.000	0.012	0.003

Note. AR = Armenia; BY = Belarus; GE = Georgia; KZ = Kazakhstan; KG = Kyrgyzstan; MD = Moldova; RU = Russia; UA = Ukraine.
[a]Mean Armenians in Armenia, Belarussians in Belarus, Georgians in Georgia, Kazakhs in Kazakhstan, Kirghiz in Kyrgyzstan, Moldovans/Romanians in Moldova, Russians in Russia, and Ukrainians in Ukraine.
[b]Data sources were European Health for All Database, January 2003; Population Division of the Department of Economic and Social Affairs of the United Nations Secretariat.
[c]In 1999 for Russia, 2000 for Armenia and Ukraine, and 2001 for the other countries.
[d]Data from Gilmore and McKee[21]; these are minimum investment figures.

TABLE 2— Smoking Prevalence Rates, by Country, Gender, and Age Group in 8 Countries of the Former Soviet Union, 2001

| | Male | | | | | | | | Female | | | | | | | | Gender Difference in |
| | All Age Groups | | | | | | | | All Age Groups | | | | | | | | Current Smoking, P[b] |
	No.	%	99% CI	18-29 y, %	30-39 y, %	40-49 y, %	50-59 y, %	≥60 y, %	18-29 y, %	30-39 y, %	40-49 y, %	50-59 y, %	≥60 y, %	No.	%	99% CI	
Armenia																	
Current Smoker	498	61.8	56.2, 67.4	62.5	76.8	68.3	67.1	44.4	0.9	3.1	3.9	2.9	1.0	28	2.4	-5.0, 9.7	
Former smoker	120	14.9	6.5, 23.3	8.3	5.5	14.2	17.1	25.1	0.9	0.4	0.4	0.7	0.7	7	0.6	-6.8, 8.0	
Never smoker	188	23.3	15.4, 31.3	29.2	17.7	17.5	15.8	30.5	98.1	96.5	95.7	96.4	98.4	1159	97.1	95.8, 98.3	
Odds of current smoking				1.00	1.98	1.29	1.22	0.48	1.00	3.43	4.3	3.15	1.05				
P					.006	.272	.499	.001		.121	.059	.19	.952				
Belarus																	<.001
Current Smoker	495	56.1	50.4, 61.9	58.2	65.3	59.8	60.2	40.3	30.4	18.5	12.7	3.1	0.9	135	12.1	4.9, 19.3	
Former smoker	125	14.2	6.1, 22.2	9.2	12.1	12.9	11.0	23.9	13.5	7.7	2.3	4.4	1.5	60	5.4	-2.1, 12.9	
Never smoker	262	29.7	22.4, 37.0	32.7	22.5	27.3	28.8	35.8	56.0	73.9	85.1	92.5	97.6	922	82.5	79.3, 85.8	
Odds of current smoking				1.00	1.35	1.07	1.08	0.49	1.00	0.52	0.33	0.07	0.02				
P					.159	.743	.726	<.001		<.001	<.001	<.001	<.001				
Georgia																	<.001
Current Smoker	491	53.3	47.4, 59.1	62.8	64.8	61.5	50.7	33.9	5.8	11.6	7.8	3.4	3.4	69	6.3	-1.2, 13.9	
Former smoker	71	7.7	-0.5, 15.9	2.0	4.4	4.5	10.4	14.5	2.3	1.4	1.3	0.0	0.0	10	0.9	-6.8, 8.7	
Never smoker	360	39.1	32.4, 45.7	35.1	30.8	34.0	38.9	51.6	91.9	87.0	90.9	96.6	96.6	1012	92.8	90.7, 94.9	
Odds of current smoking				1.00	1.09	0.94	0.61	0.30	1.00	2.13	1.38	0.58	0.57				
P					.707	.799	.037	<.001		.051	.426	.295	.219				
Kazakhstan																	<.001
Current Smoker	579	65.3	60.2, 70.4	66.0	72.7	65.9	64.2	50.0	16.1	10.9	11.2	3.4	0.4	103	9.3	1.9, 16.6	
Former smoker	119	13.4	5.4, 21.5	7.6	9.5	16.2	18.4	24.2	5.8	7.8	4.3	0.9	0.4	48	4.3	-3.2, 11.9	
Never smoker	189	21.3	13.6, 29.0	26.4	17.8	17.9	17.4	25.8	78.1	81.3	84.6	95.8	99.1	962	86.4	83.6, 89.3	
Odds of current smoking				1.00	1.37	1.00	0.92	0.52	1.00	0.64	0.66	0.18	0.02				
P					.111	.982	.744	.003		.087	.113	.002	<.001				
Kyrgyzstan																	<.001
Current Smoker	457	51.0	44.9, 57.0	56.2	60.4	49.8	50.0	25.0	4.2	5.4	6.0	4.9	1.7	49	4.5	-3.1, 12.1	
Former smoker	79	8.8	0.6, 17.0	4.9	5.5	8.3	6.8	25.8	2.7	1.8	2.5	0.0	1.7	22	2.0	-5.7, 9.7	
Never smoker	361	40.3	33.6, 46.9	39.0	34.1	42.0	43.2	49.2	93.1	92.8	91.5	95.1	96.7	1022	93.5	91.5, 95.5	
Odds of current smoking				1.00	1.19	0.77	0.78	0.26	1.00	1.31	1.45	1.18	0.39				
P					.353	.166	.313	<.001		.474	.357	.759	.140				

TABLE 2—Continued

	No.	%	95% CI						No.	%	95% CI						P
Moldova																	
Current Smoker	390	43.3	36.8, 49.8	62.6	52.4	44.9	38.3	24.7	43	3.9	-3.7, 11.5	6.0	7.7	2.5	3.6	1.1	<.001
Former smoker	125	13.9	5.9, 21.8	6.5	10.1	13.2	16.9	20.6	13	1.2	-6.5, 8.9	3.9	1.4	0.8	0.6	0.0	
Never smoker	386	42.8	36.4, 49.3	31.0	37.5	42.0	44.8	54.8	1043	94.9	93.1, 96.7	90.1	91.0	96.7	95.8	99.0	
Odds of current smoking	1.00	0.66		0.49	0.37	0.20			1.00	1.29		0.39	0.59	0.16				
P		.065		.001	<.001	<.001	<.001			.526		.070	.304	.006				
Russia																	
Current Smoker	1052	60.4	56.5, 64.3	66.4	69.7	68.4	59.9	42.3	348	15.5	10.5, 20.5	30.6	23.8	13.1	13.0	2.5	<.001
Former smoker	308	17.7	12.1, 23.3	10.1	13.6	11.6	18.5	31.9	135	6.0	0.7, 11.3	11.2	7.8	6.4	5.1	1.4	
Never smoker	381	21.9	16.4, 27.3	23.5	16.8	19.9	21.6	25.9	1768	78.5	76.0, 81.1	58.2	68.5	80.5	81.9	96.0	
Odds of current smoking	1.00	1.16		1.10	0.75	0.37			1.00	0.71		0.34	0.34	0.06				
P		.360		.558	.910	<.001	<.001			.025		<.001	<.001	<.001				
Ukraine																	
Current Smoker	488	52.5	46.7, 58.4	61.9	65.2	56.5	59.5	35.7	162	11.1	4.7, 17.4	32.9	15.3	9.2	8.7	1.0	<.001
Former smoker	157	16.9	9.2, 24.6	11.4	6.5	14.1	13.0	28.3	40	2.7	-3.9, 9.4	5.4	3.7	3.9	2.2	0.8	
Never smoker	284	30.6	23.5, 37.6	26.7	28.3	29.4	27.5	36.0	1261	86.2	83.7, 88.7	61.7	81.0	86.9	89.1	98.3	
Odds of current smoking	1.00	1.15		0.80	0.90	0.34			1.00	0.37		0.21	0.19	0.02				
P		.297		.549	.671	<.001	<.001			<.001		<.001	<.001	<.001				
Total[a]																	
Current Smoker	4417	55.5	53.5, 57.4	62.1	65.9	59.4	56.2	37.0	846	8.1	5.7, 10.5	15.9	12.0	8.3	5.4	1.5	<.001
Former smoker	1070	13.4	10.7, 16.1	7.5	8.4	11.9	14.0	24.3	301	2.9	0.4, 5.4	5.7	4.0	2.7	1.7	0.8	
Never smoker	2479	31.1	28.7, 33.5	30.4	25.7	28.7	29.8	38.7	9274	89.0	88.2, 89.8	78.4	84.0	89.0	92.9	97.7	
Odds of current smoking	1.00	1.19		0.91	0.76	0.36			1.00	0.70		0.45	0.34	0.08				
P		.018		.155	<.001	<.001	<.001			<.001		<.001	<.001	<.001				
Significance of between-country differences in current smoking[b]	<.001	.195		<.001	<.001	<.001	<.001		<.001	<.001		<.001	<.001	<.001	<.001	<.001	.032	

Note. CI = confidence interval.

[a] Average, assuming the same number of respondents in each country

[b] Results of χ^2 test on binary variable current versus never and former smokers.

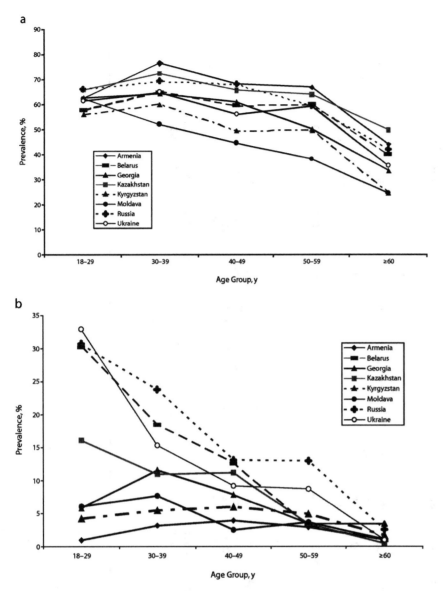

FIGURE 1— Current (a) male and (b) female smoking prevalence rates, by age group.

removed the difference between Russia and Belarus (data not shown).

The relationship between smoking and age varied by gender. Among men, with the exception of those residing in Moldova, smoking prevalence rates varied little between the ages of 18 and 59 years but then declined more markedly in men above the age of 60 years (Table 2, Figure 1). This decline with age was accounted for by increases in the older groups in terms of percentages of former smokers and never smokers. Among women, the overall trend was a decrease in reports of both current and former smoking with increasing age; very low smoking rates were observed in the oldest age group (rates of reported lifetime smoking varied from 0.8%–3.9%). However, closer inspection of the data suggested that the countries could be divided into 2 groups. In the first group (Russia, Belarus, Ukraine, and Kazakhstan), rates of current and ever smoking implied that initiation of smoking had increased rapidly between generations, especially in the youngest age group (Table 2, Figure 1). In the second group (Armenia, Georgia, Kyrgyzstan, and Moldova), the age trends were less obvious and were nonsignificant (with the exception of the comparison of the oldest and youngest age groups in Moldova).

Age at Initiation

The majority of male smokers reported that they began smoking before the age of 20 years, and, on average, a quarter reported that they began in childhood (Table 3). Far fewer women reported beginning in childhood, and sizable percentages began after the age of 20 years; for example, 86% of women residing in Armenia and more than 40% of women residing in Georgia, Kyrgyzstan, and Moldova reported that they initiated smoking after this age. These gender differences were significant in all of the countries under study.

Differences also were observed between countries; in Belarus, Kazakhstan, Russia, and Ukraine, geometric mean ages at smoking initiation were younger than 18 years among men and younger than 20 years among women, compared with older ages at smoking initiation elsewhere. Overall, between-country differences were significant for both women and men ($P < .001$); however, Bonferroni multiple comparisons showed that there were significant differences among women only in comparisons involving Armenia and countries other than Georgia and Moldova ($P < .01$; data not shown). Among men, significantly younger ages at initiation were observed in Russia and Ukraine versus Armenia, Georgia, Kyrgyzstan, and Moldova; in Belarus versus Armenia and Kyrgyzstan; and in Kazakhstan versus Kyrgyzstan (all $P < .01$; data not shown).

Amount Smoked and Nicotine Dependence

Men were found to smoke more cigarettes than women; the majority of men smoked 10 or more cigarettes per day, while most women smoked fewer than 10 per day. Between-gender differences in percentages of respondents smoking more than 20 cigarettes per day were significant only in the case of Belarus, Kazakhstan, Russia, and Ukraine ($P < .001$).

The majority of smokers reported smoking their first cigarette within an hour of waking, although, in all countries other than Georgia, a far higher proportion of men than women did so ($P < .01$). Thus, men were more likely to be moderately to severely dependent on nicotine, although gender differences were significant only for Belarus, Kazakhstan, Russia, and Ukraine.

DISCUSSION

The surveys conducted in this study provide important new data on the prevalence of smoking in 8 countries representing more than four fifths of the population of the former Soviet Union. In the case of some of these countries, these data represent the first accurate, countrywide smoking prevalence data reported. In addition, they provide some of the first truly comparative data for countries of the former Soviet Union other than the Baltic states,[31,32] and, because of the focus on obtaining accurate information on sample characteristics, they offer advantages over data available in public databases. Response rates were relatively high, and the samples were broadly representative of the overall country populations.

Study Limitations

The underrepresentation of men in Armenia and Ukraine should not have affected the gender-specific rates observed, but, as a result of the urban/rural differences in the composition of the sample, prevalence rates in Kyrgyzstan (where urban areas were overrepresented) may have been overestimated, and prevalence rates in Armenia (where urban areas were underrepresented) may have been underestimated. However, these discrepancies were likely to affect only the data relating to female respondents.[9–11] The age group disparities noted were minor but would tend to lead to underestimates of smoking prevalence.

In addition, the surveys were based on self-reported smoking status; there was no independent biochemical validation, and thus the smoking rates observed may have been affected by reporting bias. Although there is concern on the part of some that self-

reports of smoking status may produce underestimates of smoking levels, studies conducted in Western countries suggest that this technique is sensitive and specific; they also suggest that more accurate responses are provided in interviewer-administered questionnaires than in self-completed questionnaires.[33] The only study conducted in the former Soviet Union that has addressed this issue showed that, among individuals claiming to be nonsmokers, 13% (48/368) of women and 17% (12/375) of men in rural northwestern Russia were in fact, according to blood cotinine levels, likely to be smokers, compared with only 2% of men and women in Finland.[34] Given the far lower prevalence of smoking among women, this had disproportionately large effects on reported rates of smoking among women. Although our questionnaires were administered by interviewers in respondents' homes, potentially making it more difficult for respondents who smoked to deny doing so, we may have underestimated smoking prevalence rates, particularly in the case of women residing in areas where smoking remains culturally unacceptable.

A final shortfall of the present study was the failure to measure smokeless tobacco use, which is relatively common in parts of the former Soviet Union, mainly Azerbaijan, Tajikistan, and Turkmenistan. However, although chewing tobacco is used in some of the southern regions of Kyrgyzstan, cigarettes are the main form of tobacco used there as well as in all of the other countries in which surveys were conducted.[8,35]

Findings

The results of our study confirm that smoking rates among men in this region are among the highest in the world and higher than the maximum rates recorded in the United States at the peak of its epidemic; rates above 50% were observed in all countries other than Moldova and reached 60% or more in Armenia, Kazakhstan, and Russia. Elsewhere in Europe, rates above 50% are seen only in Turkey

(51%) and Slovakia (56%), and worldwide fewer than 20 countries report rates of more than 60%.[6]

In the case of men, the lower prevalence of current smokers and higher prevalence of never and former smokers among those 60 years or older probably reflect the disproportionate number of premature deaths among current smokers relative to never and former smokers. However, a cohort effect has been shown in the former Soviet Union, with those who were teenagers between 1945 and 1953 carrying forward lower smoking rates because cigarettes, like other consumer goods, were in short supply in the period of postwar austerity under Stalin.[36,37] This cohort effect is also thought to account for the unexpected current decline in male lung cancer deaths,[36] which must be set against the overall rise in male tobacco-related mortality[1] and, in particular, increases in the already staggeringly high number of cardiovascular deaths.[2]

In comparison with male smoking patterns, smoking among women is far less common, varies more between countries, and exhibits a different age-specific pattern. Although rates of lifetime smoking are below 4% among individuals older than 60 years in all 8 countries, in the 4 countries with the highest smoking rates among women (Belarus, Kazakhstan, Russia, and Ukraine), smoking is now significantly more common among members of the younger generations; risk ratios between the youngest and oldest age groups range from 12.2 to 37.3, compared with a range of 1.0 to 5.5 in the other 4 countries.

Lopez et al.[38] outlined a 4-stage model of the patterns of a smoking epidemic based on observations from Western countries. In this model, such an epidemic is described as involving an initial rise in male smoking followed by a rise in female smoking 1 to 2 decades later, after which each plateaus and then falls as a result of tobacco-related mortality, finally rising to a peak decades later. Our findings suggest that the former Soviet Union's tobacco epidemic may have developed differently. Male smoking has a long

TABLE 3— Smoking Characteristics of Current Smokers in 8 Countries of the Former Soviet Union, 2001

	AR, %	BY, %	GE, %	KZ, %	KG, %	MD, %	RU, %	UA, %	All,[a] %	Between-Country Comparison, P[b]
Age at smoking initiation, y										
Men										
Mean age	18.5	17.4	18.2	17.6	19.1	18.2	17.0	17.2	17.9	
Geometric mean age	17.8	16.6	17.7	17.1	18.6	17.6	16.2	16.2	17.2	<.001
< 16	22.2	32.8	18.0	27.9	14.7	22.8	36.4	35.2	26.2	
16–20	56.8	54.2	66.0	57.0	61.8	59.9	49.8	48.5	56.7	<.001
> 20	21.0	13.0	16.0	15.1	23.5	17.3	13.9	16.3	17.0	
No.	447	430	400	502	408	347	993	435	3962	
Women										
Mean age	28.0	18.9	22.7	20.7	21.5	23.0	20.9	21.2	22.1	<.001
Geometric mean age	27.0	18.5	21.3	19.9	20.7	21.5	19.8	19.9	21.1	
< 16	0.0	20.0	18.5	15.4	12.5	22.9	13.1	15.1	14.7	<.001
16–20	14.3	56.7	38.5	50.6	43.8	22.9	52.6	57.2	42.1	
> 20	85.7	23.3	43.1	34.1	43.8	54.3	34.4	27.6	43.3	
No.	28	120	65	91	48	35	329	152	868	
Between-gender comparison in geometric mean age[c]	<.001	.002	<.001	<.001	.002	<.001	<.001	<.001		
Number of cigarettes smoked daily										
Men										
1–2	1.8	13.4	1.9	4.5	15.4	8.2	2.4	4.6	5.3	
Up to 10	18.7	32.3	12.7	30.9	50.1	43.3	24.6	25.4	29.8	<.001
10–20	51.4	50.5	63.3	48.0	28.7	37.4	52.2	53.5	48.1	
> 20	28.1	13.7	22.2	16.6	5.8	11.0	20.8	16.5	16.9	
Odds ratio for likelihood of smoking >20 cigarettes per day	1.487	0.606	1.085	0.756	0.234	0.471	1.00	0.753		
P	.002	.001	.539	.038	<.001	<.001		.049		
No.	498	495	482	579	449	390	1052	484	4429	
Women										
1–2	32.1	23.7	1.9	4.5	15.4	8.2	2.4	4.6	5.3	
Up to 10	28.6	48.9	12.7	30.9	50.1	43.3	24.6	25.4	29.8	<.001
10–20	32.1	25.2	63.3	48.0	28.7	37.4	52.2	53.5	48.1	
> 20	7.1	2.2	22.2	16.6	5.8	11.0	20.8	16.5	16.9	
Odds ratio for likelihood of smoking > 20 cigarettes per day	1.50	0.44	1.085	0.756	0.234	0.471	1.00	0.753		
P	0.602	0.199	.539	.038	<.001	<.001		.049		
No.	28	135	482	579	449	390	1052	484	4429	
Between-gender comparison of % smoking >20 cigarettes per day[d]	.015	.000								
Time when usually smoke first cigarette										
Men										
First 30 minutes after awakening	63.5	47.9	52.9	442.8	39.0	44.1	56.5	55.8	50.3	
First hour after awakening	24.9	40.4	34.0	46.6	39.4	38.2	34.3	33.3	36.4	<.001
Before midday meal	4.6	6.9	5.0	5.0	7.1	6.7	4.7	6.0	5.7	
After midday meal or in the evening	7.0	4.9	8.1	5.5	14.5	11.0	4.6	5.0	7.6	
Odds ratio for likelihood of smoking in first hour	0.77	0.77	0.67	0.86	0.37	0.47	1.00	0.83		
P	.140	.129	.021	.394	<.001	<.001		.292		
No.	498	495	480	579	449	390	1051	484	4426	

TABLE 3—*Continued*

	AR, %	BY, %	GE, %	KZ, %	KG, %	MD, %	RU, %	UA, %	All,[a] %	Between-Country Comparison, P[b]
Women										
First 30 minutes after awakening	50.0	31.9	44.6	35.0	27.7	14.3	33.7	27.8	33.1	
First hour after awakening	14.3	28.9	30.8	27.2	31.9	38.1	32.0	32.1	29.4	.278
Before midday meal	3.6	19.3	12.3	13.6	12.8	11.9	13.5	17.3	13	
After midday meal or in the evening	32.1	20.0	12.3	24.3	27.7	35.7	20.8	22.8	24.5	
Odds ratio for likelihood of smoking in first hour	0.94	0.81	1.60	0.86	0.77	0.57	1.00	0.78		
P	.879	.307	.129	.505	.409	.092		.203		
No.	28	135	65	103	47	42	347	162	929	
Between-gender comparison in % smoking in first hour[d]	<.001	<.001	.014	<.001	.004	<.001	<.001	<.001		
Moderate to heavy nicotine dependence (> 20 cigarettes per day and smoking within first hour of awakening)										
Men	26.9	13.7	21.4	16.6	5.6	10.5	20.6	16.2	16.4	.000
Odds ratio for likelihood of moderate to severe dependency	1.42	0.62	1.05	0.77	0.23	0.45	1.00	0.74	0.8	
P	.005	.093	.142	.104	.000	.000		.042	.00	
No.	498	495	477	579	449	390	1051	483	4422	
Women	7.1	2.2	10.8	3.9	0.0	1.0	17.0	9.0	6.4	.139
Odds ratio for likelihood of moderate to severe dependency	1.49	0.44	2.34	0.78	...	0.47	1.00	1.14	1.0	
P	.605	.197	.071	.669	...	.473		.754	.3	
No.	28	135	65	103	47	42	347	162	929	
Between-gender dependency comparison[d]	.020	<.001	.045	.001	.097	.091	<.001	.001		

Note. AR = Armenia; BY = Belarus; GE = Georgia; KZ = Kazakhstan; KG = Kyrgyzstan; MD = Moldova; RU = Russia; UA = Ukraine.
[a]Average, assuming the same number of respondents in each country.
[b]Results of analyses of variance (geometric mean) and χ^2 tests (categorical variable) for mean age at smoking initiation; χ^2 test for no. of cigarettes smoked, time to first cigarette, and dependency.
[c]Results of *t* tests.
[d]Results of χ^2 tests.

history in this region. The first accounts of tobacco smoking in Russia date from the 17th century,[39] papirossi (a type of cigarette, popular in the former Soviet Union, characterized by a long, hollow mouthpiece that can be twisted before smoking) were first mentioned in 1844,[39] and cigarette factories were first constructed later in the 19th century.[40,41] Historical data on smoking[3] and high male tobacco-related mortality rates[1] suggest that smoking among men has been at a high level for some time and, contrary to the predictions of the 4-stage model just mentioned, has failed to exhibit a postpeak decline.

Smoking among women remains relatively uncommon, and rates have been far slower to rise than would be expected given male rates in the former

Soviet Union and trends observed in the West. Indeed, it appears that female rates began to increase only in the mid- to late 1990s, when transnational tobacco companies arrived with their carefully targeted marketing strategies.[18–20] Therefore, although the exact stage of the epidemic varies slightly between the countries of the former Soviet Union, overall we suggest that men have remained between stages 3 and 4, with high rates of both smoking and mortality, while women in some countries are at stage 1 and others at stage 2, the latter with more rapidly rising smoking rates. Although rates of cardiovascular disease have been increasing, this can largely be explained by risk factors other than tobacco (including diet and stress), and female lung cancer rates have yet to increase.

Comparisons between our results and previous data are problematic given that much of the information that exists is fragmentary, of uncertain quality, and rarely nationally representative. This is particularly the case in the central Asian and Caucasian states, although limited data from Armenia and Moldova gathered between 1998 and 2001 suggest few changes in smoking prevalence rates[2,6]; data from Kazakhstan suggest small increases from the 60% male and 7% female prevalence rates recorded in 1996.[2] More data are available for Belarus, Russia, and Ukraine. These data suggest that smoking rates in men have changed little,[2,10,11,42] although in Russia they appeared to rise between the 1970s and 1980s[2,3,7] and into the mid-1990s, with little subsequent change. Among women, rates appear to have increased in all 3 countries,[2,11] and Russian data suggest that although rates have been rising since the 1970s, increases were most notable during the 1990s.[3,7,9,43]

Between-gender and intercountry differences in smoking prevalence rates are reflected in other smoking indicators as well; for example, men are more likely than women to start smoking when they are young, to smoke more heavily, and to be nicotine dependent. Two separate groupings of countries appeared to emerge from the between-country comparisons: Belarus, Kazakhstan, Russia, and Ukraine, on one hand, and Armenia, Georgia, Kyrgyzstan, and Moldova, on the other. In addition to exhibiting higher smoking rates among women and more pronounced age-specific trends, the former group tended to show lower ages at smoking initiation (particularly in comparison with Armenia, Georgia, and Moldova) along with more marked gender differences in regard to number of cigarettes smoked per day and level of nicotine dependency.

The differences observed in this study suggest that smoking patterns in Armenia, Georgia, Moldova, and Kyrgyzstan are more traditional than those in Belarus, Kazakhstan, Russia, and Ukraine. This situation can be explained by the differing degree of transnational tobacco company penetration.[21,44] Industry in Moldova continues to be in the form of a state-owned monopoly; industry in Georgia and Armenia has been privatized, but this change was rather recent (occurring after 1997), and none of the major transnational tobacco companies have invested directly in those countries.[21] Kazakhstan, Russia, and Ukraine, by contrast, saw major investments from most major transnational tobacco companies beginning in the early 1990s. Belarus, which retains a state-owned monopoly system, and Kyrgyzstan, where the German cigarette manufacturer Reemtsma has invested, would therefore appear to be exceptions, with Belarus more typical of the countries with transnational

tobacco company investments and Kyrgyzstan more typical of the countries without such investments. In Belarus, however, the state tobacco manufacturer has only a 40% market share, with smuggled and counterfeit brands accounting for an additional 40% of this share. The importance the transnational tobacco companies attach to the illegal market in Belarus can be seen in the fact that, despite having little official market share,[44] British American Tobacco and Philip Morris have the highest outdoor advertising budgets and the 9th and 10th highest television advertising budgets of all companies operating in that country.[45] In Belarus, as in Ukraine and Russia, tobacco is the product most heavily advertised outdoors and the fourth most advertised product on television (there are now restrictions on television advertising in Ukraine and Russia).[45,46] Thus, it appears that with the continuing (if so far fruitless) discussions of possible reunification with Russia, the transnational tobacco companies treat Belarus as an important extension of the Russian market.[47]

Kyrgyzstan differs from the other countries in which there have been transnational tobacco company investments in that these investments occurred later (in 1998) and one company, Reemtsma, achieved a manufacturing monopoly.[44] However, Kyrgyzstan also differs from Belarus, Kazakhstan, Ukraine, and Russia in regard to its lower levels of development and industrialization and its larger rural and Muslim populations. Other potential explanations for the between-country differences observed cannot be excluded here, and such possibilities are explored in a separate article.[48] Whatever reasons emerge, the rising rates of smoking among women and the younger ages of smoking initiation are cause for concern in all of these countries.

Meanwhile, the present findings, combined with earlier data on disease burden,[1,37] confirm that high smoking rates among men continue unabated. Smoking among women in Armenia, Georgia, Kyrgyzstan, and Moldova

remains relatively uncommon and does not appear to have increased significantly, as can be seen in rates among the younger relative to older generations and in limited comparisons with previous data. By contrast, smoking rates among women in Belarus, Ukraine, Kazakhstan, and Russia showed an increase from previous surveys, and age-specific rates suggest an ongoing increase in tobacco use among members of the younger generations. It is probably not a coincidence that these higher rates were observed in the countries with the most active transnational tobacco company presence.

Conclusions

Concerted and urgent efforts to improve tobacco control must be made throughout the former Soviet Union to curtail current smoking and prevent further rises in smoking among women. Such efforts will require enactment and effective enforcement of comprehensive tobacco control policies, including a total ban on tobacco advertising and sponsorship, adequate taxation of both imported and domestic cigarettes, controls on smuggling, and restrictions on smoking in public places. The barriers to achieving these goals are considerable given the powerful influence of transnational tobacco companies and the limited development of democracy and civil society groups in much of the region.[21] The international community, cognizant of the role that international companies play in pushing the tobacco epidemic, should build on the work of the Open Society Institute (R. Bonnell, oral communication, September 2003) in strengthening the policy response to this threat.

About the Authors

Anna Gilmore, Joceline Pomerleau, and Martin McKee are with the European Centre on Health of Societies in Transition, London School of Hygiene and Tropical Medicine, London, England. Richard Rose is with the Centre for the Study of Public Policy, University of Strathclyde, Glasgow, Scotland. At the time of the study, Christian W. Haerpfer was with the Institute for Advanced Studies, Vienna, Austria. David Rotman is with the Center of Sociological and Political Studies, Belarus State University, Minsk, Belarus. Sergej Tumanov is with the Centre for Sociological Studies, Moscow State University, Moscow, Russia.

Correspondence: Requests for reprints should be sent to Anna Gilmore, MSc, MFPH, European Centre on Health of Societies in Transition, London School of Hygiene and Tropical Medicine, Keppel Street, London WC1E 7HT, England (e-mail: anna.gilmore@lshtm.ac.uk).

Acknowledgments

We are grateful to the members of the Living Conditions, Lifestyles and Health Study teams who participated in the coordination and organization of data collection for this study. The Living Conditions, Lifestyles and Health Study is funded by the European Community (contract ICA2-2000–10031). Support for A. Gilmore's and M. McKee's work on tobacco was also provided by the National Cancer Institute (grant 1 R01 CA91021-01).

Note. The views expressed in this article are those of the authors and do not necessarily reflect the views of the European Community.

Human Participant Protection

This study was approved by the ethics committee of the London School of Hygiene and Tropical Medicine. Verbal informed consent was obtained from all study participants at the beginning of the interviews.

Contributors

A. Gilmore contributed to questionnaire design and data analysis and drafted the article. J. Pomerleau and M. McKee contributed to questionnaire design, data analysis, and revisions of the article. R. Rose contributed to questionnaire design and generation of hypotheses. C. W. Haerpfer, D. Rotman, and S. Tumanov designed and supervised the conduct of the surveys. M. McKee, C. W. Haerpfer, D. Rotman, and S. Tumanov originated and supervised the overall study.

References

1. Peto R, Lopez AD, Boreham J, Thun M, Heath C. *Mortality From Smoking in Developed Countries 1950–2000.* Oxford, England: Oxford University Press Inc; 1994.
2. *Health for All Database.* Copenhagen, Denmark: World Health Organization, Regional Office for Europe; 2003.
3. Forey B, Hamling J, Lee P, Wald N. *International Smoking Statistics.* 2nd ed. Oxford, England: Oxford University Press Inc; 2002.
4. Grim CE, Grim CM, Petersen JR, et al. Prevalence of cardiovascular risk factors in the Republic of Georgia. *J Hum Hypertens.* 1999;13:243–247.
5. Grim CE, Grim CM, Kipshidze N, Kipshidze NN, Petersen J. CVD risk factors in Eastern Europe: a rapid survey of the capital of the Republic of Georgia [abstract]. *Am J Hypertens.* 1997;10:211A.
6. Corrao MA, Guindon GE, Sharma N, Shokoohi DF, eds. *Tobacco Control Country Profiles.* Atlanta, Ga: American Cancer Society; 2000.
7. Zaridze D, Dvoirin VV, Kobljakov VA, Pisklov VP. Smoking patterns in the USSR. In: Zaridze DG, Peto R, eds. *Tobacco: A Major International Health Hazard.* Lyon, France: International Agency for Research on Cancer; 1986. IARC Scientific Publication 74.
8. *Tobacco or Health: A Global Status Report.* Geneva, Switzerland: World Health Organization; 1997.
9. McKee M, Bobak M, Rose R, et al. Patterns of smoking in Russia. *Tob Control.* 1998;7:22–26.
10. Gilmore AB, McKee M, Telishevska M, Rose R. Smoking in Ukraine: epidemiology and determinants. *Prev Med.* 2001;33:453–461.
11. Gilmore AB, McKee M, Rose R. Smoking in Belarus: evidence from a household survey. *Eur J Epidemiol.* 2001;17:245–253.
12. Pudule I, Grinberga D, Kadziauskiene K, et al. Patterns of smoking in the Baltic Republics. *J Epidemiol Community Health.* 1999;53:277–282.
13. Raudsepp J, Rahu M. Smoking among schoolteachers in Estonia 1980. *Scand J Soc Med.* 1984;12: 49–53.
14. *Confronting the Epidemic: A Global Agenda for Tobacco Control Research.* Geneva, Switzerland: World Health Organization; 1999.
15. Baris E, Waverley Brigden L, Prindiville J, Da Costa e Silva VL, Chitanondh H, Chandiwana S. Research priorities for tobacco control in developing countries: a regional approach to a global consultative process. *Tob Control.* 2000;9:217–223.
16. Lopez AD. Epidemiologic surveillance of the tobacco epidemic. *Morb Mortal Wkly Rep.* 1992; 41(suppl):157–166.
17. Connolly GN. Tobacco, trade and Eastern Europe. In: Slama K, ed. *Tobacco and Health.* London, England: Plenum Press; 1996:51–60.
18. Prokhorov AV. Getting on smokin' Route 66: tobacco promotion via Russian mass media. *Tob Control.* 1997;6:145–146.
19. Hurt RD. Smoking in Russia: what do Stalin and Western tobacco companies have in common? *Mayo Clin Proc.* 1995;70:1007–1011.
20. Krasovsky K. Abusive international marketing and promotion tactics by Philip Morris and RJR Nabisco in Ukraine. In: *Global Aggression: The Case for World Standards and Bold US Action Challenging Phillip Morris and RJR Nabisco.* New York, NY: Apex Press; 1998: 76–83.
21. Gilmore AB, McKee M. Tobacco and transition: an overview of industry investments, impact and influence in the former Soviet Union. *Tob Control.* 2004;13: 136–142.
22. Bettcher D, Subramaniam C, Guindon E, et al. *Confronting the Tobacco Epidemic in an Era of Trade Liberalisation.* Geneva, Switzerland: World Health Organization; 2001.
23. Chaloupka FJ, Laixuthai A. *US Trade Policy and Cigarette Smoking in Asia.* Cambridge, Mass: National Bureau of Economic Research; 1996. Working paper 5543.
24. EU-Copernikus Project Living Conditions: Lifestyle and Health. Vienna, Austria: Institute for Advanced Studies, 2003. Available at: http://www.llh.at. Accessed October 19, 2004.
25. Living Conditions, Lifestyles & Health Project Partners. Methods. Available at: http://www.llh.at/llh_partners_start.html. Accessed September 20, 2004.
26. Pomerleau J, McKee M, Rose R, Balabanova D, Gilmore A. *Living Conditions Lifestyles and Health:*

Comparative health report, June 2003. London, England: London School of Hygiene and Tropical Medicine; 2003.

27. Centre for the Study of Public Policy, University of Strathclyde. New Europe Barometer Surveys. Available at: http://www.cspp.strath.ac.uk. Accessed September 20, 2004.

28. Heatherton TF, Kozlowski LT, Frecker RC, Fagerstrom KO. The Fagerstrom Test for Nicotine Dependence: a revision of the Fagerstrom Tolerance Questionnaire. *Br J Addict.* 1991;86:1119–1127.

29. Fagerstrom Test for Nicotine Dependence. Available at: http://www.fpnotebook.com/PSY81.htm. Accessed September 5, 2003.

30. Badurashvili I, McKee M, Tsuladze G, Meslé F, Vallin J, Shkolnikov V. Where there are no data: what has happened to life expectancy in Georgia since 1990? *Public Health Rep.* 2001;115:394–400.

31. Prattala R, Helasoja V, Finbalt Group. *Finbalt Health Monitor: Feasibility of a Collaborative System for Monitoring Health Behavior in Finland and the Baltic Countries.* Helsinki, Finland: National Public Health Institute; 1999.

32. Puska P, Helasoja V, Prattala R, Kasmel A, Klumbiene J. Health behaviour in Estonia, Finland and Lithuania 1994–1999. *Eur J Public Health.* 2003;13:11–17.

33. Patrick DL, Cheadle A, Thompson DC, Diehr P, Koepsell T, Kinne S. The validity of self-reported smoking: a review and meta-analysis. *Am J Public Health.* 1994;84:1086–1093.

34. Laatikainen T, Vartiainen E, Puska P. Comparing smoking and smoking cessation processes in the Republic of Karelia, Russia and North Karelia, Finland. *J Epidemiol Community Health.* 1999;53:528–534.

35. *World Tobacco File 1997–Cigars, Smoking Tobacco and Smokeless Tobacco.* London, England: DMG Business Media; 1999.

36. Shkolnikov V, McKee M, Leon D, Chenet L. Why is the death rate from lung cancer falling in the Russian Federation? *Eur J Epidemiol.* 1999;15:203–206.

37. Ezzati M, Lopez AD. Measuring the accumulated hazards of smoking: global and regional estimates for 2000. *Tob Control.* 2003;12:79–85.

38. Lopez AD, Collishaw NE, Piha T. A descriptive model of the cigarette epidemic in developed countries. *Tob Control.* 1994;3:242–247.

39. British American Tobacco Russia. History of tobacco in Russia. Available at: http://www.batrussia.ru/oneweb/sites/BAT_5FZF3V.nsf/vwPagesWebLive/DO5JVJYD?opendocument&SID=BAA08166A513AAEF3959A15BC3562EBC&DTC=20040920&TMP=1. Accessed September 20, 2004.

40. British American Tobacco Russia. BAT-Yava factory history. Available at: http://www.batrussia.ru/oneweb/sites/BAT_5FZF3V.nsf/vwPagesWebLive/DO5G2FWX?opendocument&SID=BAA08166A513AAEF3959A15BC35 62EBC&DTC=20040920&TMP=1. Accessed September 20, 2004.

41. Dragounski D. Well–this is the Russian market. *World Tob Russia Eastern Eur.* 1998;2:32–46.

42. Alcohol and Drug Information Center. Economics of tobacco control in Ukraine from the public health perspective. Available at: http://www.adic.org.ua/adic/reports/econ. Accessed September 20, 2004.

43. Molarius A, Parsons RW, Dobson AJ, et al. Trends in cigarette smoking in 36 populations from the early 1980s to the mid-1990s: findings from the WHO MONICA Project. *Am J Public Health.* 2001;91: 206–212.

44. *World Cigarettes 2001.* Vol. 1. Newmarket, England: ERC Group; 2001.

45. *Central and Eastern Europe Market and Mediafact.* London, England: Zenith Optimedia; 2000.

46. World Health Organization Regional Office for Europe. Tobacco control database. Available at: http://data.euro.who.int/tobacco/. Accessed September 20, 2004.

47. A tactical market. *Tob J Int.* 2003;1:68. Also available at: http://www.tobacco.org/articles/country/Belarus. Accessed September 20, 2004.

48. Pomerleau J, Gilmore A, McKee M, Rose R, Haerpfer CW. Determinants of smoking in eight countries of the former Soviet Union: results from the Living Conditions, Lifestyles and Health Study. *Addiction.* In press.

Overview of Vaccines Section

| *Dr. Stanley A. Plotkin, Executive Advisor to CEO, Sanofi Pasteur, Emeritus Professor of Pediatrics, University of Pennsylvania*

The articles on vaccines in this compendium prompt two reflections. The first is the opening line of Dickens' *A Tale of Two Cities*, which has become a cliché: "It was the best of times, it was the worst of times..." Vaccines have never been more talked about by both scientists and the public, nor has their impact ever been more evident than now, but there is also a distinct malaise caused by opposition to vaccination on all sorts of solipsistic grounds. The second reflection is about how fast the vaccine field is moving. The articles were timely when they were published in 2004 and 2005, but now suffer from being dated due to critical new developments. Nevertheless, they are still valuable beyond their historical interest.

Kieny et al wrote a "tour of the horizon" concerning new vaccines in research and development. At the time of writing, new rotavirus vaccines were under trial, and there was still concern about a possible repetition of the disastrous withdrawal of the first rotavirus vaccine owing to an association with intussusception of the intestines. Now there are abundant data that the new pentavalent bovine-human reassortant vaccine and the attenuated human virus vaccine do not cause that complication.

SARS was still a worry, particularly as the reservoir was unknown. Now it seems that the virus resides in bats, and research has shown that a vaccine based on the whole virus or its spike protein could be developed, if needed. Research on meningococcal Group B vaccines is mentioned, but not the reverse vaccinology genomic approach that has identified heretofore unknown potential vaccine proteins.

However, Kieny et al were right about RSV, in which live attenuated vaccines are still the most likely to succeed, about pneumococcus, where a 13 valent conjugated polysaccharide vaccine is in clinical trial for use in developing countries, and about the amazingly efficacious human papillomavirus vaccine. Unfortunately, they were also right about the difficulties in making an effective vaccine against HIV.

Vaccine safety has been a contentious subject ever since Jenner, but today the economic, medico-legal and public health implications are larger. Of course no substance given to humans is entirely without side effects, real or perceived. Folb et al tell us about the global approach to vaccine safety, very necessary in this day of globalization, when an incident or a rumor started in one country rapidly spreads to another through the Internet. Therefore, a scientific approach to vaccine safety issues by an international committee of experts is valuable both to identify real safety problems that might not be evident in small populations and contrariwise to put to rest accusations that have no merit. We have to admit that it took us over 200 years to realize that vaccinia could cause myopericarditis, whereas on the other hand the unwarranted allegations against MMR and thiomersal have caused significant public rejection of vaccination.

Aylward and Heymann describe the philosophy and practice of the polio eradication initiative. It is only fair to state that I am one who is critical of the WHO policy and that I have a conflict of interest (see below). Nevertheless, in the three years that have elapsed since their article, eradication has not happened. The reasons for this are complex, but the main point of disagreement is whether or not IPV immunization should be brought into play now to supplement OPV and also to protect populations during the discontinuation of OPV that is necessary to eliminate reverted vaccine strains. If wild poliovirus returns to an unvaccinated population after putative eradication, the consequences to individuals and to confidence in public health will be disastrous, and far more costly than the use of IPV in pediatric combination vaccines.

The last article, by Muraskin, concerns the Global Alliance for Vaccines and Immunization (GAVI) that currently plays a key role in financing vaccination in developing countries. He calls our attention to the negative aspect of GAVI funding: the implicit judgment that vaccination is more important than other public health measures, a judgment made without input from the countries themselves. Indeed, even the polio eradication program has been criticized for diverting money from other needs. Certainly Muraskin is right that measures such as provision of clean water have more impact than vaccination, and that perennial vaccine funding is not assured, but until economic studies prove otherwise it can be argued that vaccination is the lowest hanging fruit on the public health tree.

Research and Development of New Vaccines Against Infectious Diseases

| *Marie Paule Kieny, PhD, Jean-Louis Excler, MD and Marc Girard, DVM*

ABSTRACT

Infectious diseases are responsible for approximately 25% of global mortality, especially in children aged younger than 5 years. Much of the burden of infectious diseases could be alleviated if appropriate mechanisms could be put in place to ensure access for all children to basic vaccines, regardless of geographical location or economic status. In addition, new safe and effective vaccines should be developed for a variety of infections against which no effective preventive intervention measure is either available or practical.

The public, private, and philanthropic sectors need to join forces to ensure that these new or improved vaccines are fully developed and become accessible to the populations in need as quickly as possible.

INTRODUCTION

The implementation of large-scale and comprehensive national immunization programs, and the considerable successes that were achieved in the eradication of smallpox and the reduction of polio, measles, pertussis, tetanus, and meningitis, were among the most notable achievements of the 20th century. Even in the poorest countries, it has been possible to achieve significant progress in disease control by immunization.[1] There is good reason to expect that these advances will be sustained and will progress even further in the 21st century.[2]

However, the world's poorest regions are still suffering a heavy toll of premature deaths and disabilities from infectious diseases for which vaccines do not exist, or need to be improved.[3] Infectious diseases are still responsible for at least 15 million deaths per year, making them the largest contributors to the disparity in average life span between rich and poor countries (77 and 52 years, respectively). In addition to this high death toll, millions of children are suffering from disability and illness because they have not been properly immunized. The most effective way to reduce disease and deaths from infectious diseases is to vaccinate populations at risk. Unfortunately, vaccines are still missing for a number of pathogens, and some of the existing vaccines are not completely protective. For these diseases, it is of crucial importance that research and development of vaccines be a priority.

The following is an overview of a few selected fields of current vaccine development.

DIARRHEAL DISEASES

Conservative estimates place the death toll from diarrheal diseases at 4 million to 6 million per year, with most of these deaths occurring in young children. In the long term, access to clean water, better hygiene, and improvement of sanitation would have the greatest impact on diarrheal diseases, but immunization against specific pathogens is the best hope for the short term and medium term. The burden of diarrhea among children aged younger than 5 years in the developing world is estimated to be 1.5 billion episodes per year, leading to 3 million deaths. Enterotoxinogenic *Escherichia coli* is the most frequently isolated bacterial enteropathogen, followed by shigellas (*Shigella flexneri* and *S sonnei*) and cholera bacteria (*Vibrio cholerae*). Enterotoxinogenic *E coli* is also the most common cause of travelers' diarrhea. The development of new vaccines against viral diarrhea caused by rotavirus, present in countries with high and low levels of hygiene, is the focus of intense international efforts.

Rotavirus is the leading cause of severe diarrheal disease and dehydration of infants in both industrialized and developing countries. By age 3 to 4 years, virtually all children have had the disease. Rotavirus is responsible for 25% of deaths associated with diarrhea and for 6% of all deaths in children younger than 5 years of age.

Rotavirus is a double-stranded RNA virus belonging to the Reoviridae family. In the United States, an oral live tetravalent rhesus–human reassortant vaccine was licensed in 1998; recommended for the routine immunization of infants, it was administered to more than 900 000 children. Efficacy estimates were around 55% against all cases of rotavirus diarrhea and over 70% against severe disease. However, an increased frequency of a rare but severe vaccine-associated side effect, called intussusception, was demonstrated, leading to the vaccine's withdrawal from the market in 1999. Unfortunately, the vaccine, which was undergoing testing concomitantly in Asia and Africa, could not be evaluated in terms of risk-benefit for children in developing countries since the trials were stopped.

A lamb-derived monovalent live-attenuated oral vaccine is licensed in China, but the vaccine cannot be distributed on the international market at present. Several new vaccine approaches are currently being pursued:

- A human-derived monovalent live-attenuated oral vaccine is being tested in phase III trials in Latin America and Asia and has undergone extensive testing in Europe, the United States, South Africa, and Bangladesh.
- A bovine–human reassortant pentavalent live-attenuated oral vaccine is currently in late phase III trials, but large efficacy trials in developing countries remain to be conducted.
- A human neonatal vaccine and 2 human–bovine naturally occurring neonatal-derived strains are also under development.

It remains to be seen whether intussusception will be associated with any of these new rotavirus vaccines, and several alternative vaccine approaches have been proposed to avoid this potential adverse event.

ACUTE RESPIRATORY INFECTIONS

Both viruses and bacteria are a common cause of acute lower respiratory infection (LRI) in children worldwide. The commonest pathogens causing acute LRI are respiratory syncytial virus (RSV) and *Streptococcus pneumoniae*. Dual infections with viral and bacterial pathogens are frequent and seem to increase the severity of the disease.

The sudden emergence in early 2003 of an epidemic of atypical pneumonia originating in China led to the identification of the severe acute respiratory syndrome (SARS) virus, a coronavirus unrelated to previously known coronaviruses. The virus was later recovered from Chinese masked palm civets and raccoon dogs, which might have acted as an intermediate host between an as yet unidentified natural virus reservoir and man. The develop-

ment of a vaccine against SARS has been judged a global priority, but it is still only at the early clinical stage.

RSV

RSV infects nearly all children by age 2 years. The global annual infection and mortality figures for RSV are estimated to be 64 million and 160 000, respectively. The disease spectrum includes a wide array of respiratory symptoms, from rhinitis and otitis media to pneumonia and bronchiolitis, the latter 2 being associated with substantial morbidity. In industrialized countries, RSV is a well-documented cause of yearly winter and spring epidemics of bronchiolitis and pneumonia, which are responsible for 18 000 to 75 000 hospitalizations and 90 to 1900 deaths annually in the United States. Existing data clearly indicate that RSV also accounts for a high proportion (20% to 30%) of LRI cases in children aged 1 to 4 years in developing countries.

RSV belongs to the Paramyxoviridae family, genus Pneumovirus. Two subgroups, A and B, have been described, primarily based on differences in the antigenicity of the surface glycoprotein (G). Two factors have complicated the development of vaccines to prevent RSV infection. First, host immune responses appear to play a role in the pathogenesis of disease, as early studies with a Formalin-inactivated vaccine showed that vaccine recipients suffered from more severe disease. Second, naturally acquired immunity is neither complete nor durable and recurrent infections occur frequently. Purified fusion protein vaccines have been shown to be safe and immunogenic in 12- to 48-month-old children. A subunit vaccine containing the RSV F, G, and M proteins, now in phase II in Canada and Australia, has exhibited an excellent safety and immunogenicity profile. Another candidate vaccine is a synthetic peptide of the conserved region of the G protein administered intranasally. Live attenuated RSV vaccines based on temperature-sensitive, cold-adapted strains of the virus that

could be delivered to the respiratory mucosa are probably among the most promising approaches.

S pneumoniae

Infections caused by pneumococci are a major cause of morbidity and mortality all over the world. Pneumonia, febrile bacteremia, and meningitis are the most common manifestations of the disease. The highest rates of pneumococcal disease occur among young children and the elderly. Pneumococci are estimated to cause over 1 million deaths, most of which occur in developing countries, where they probably are the most important pathogen of early infancy. In Europe and the United States, pneumococcal pneumonia is the most common community-acquired bacterial pneumonia, estimated to affect approximately 100 adults per 100 000 each year. In developing countries, infants aged younger than 3 months are especially at risk of pneumococcal meningitis. Even in economically developed regions, invasive pneumococcal disease carries mortality rates of 10% to 20%, and the rate may exceed 50% in high-risk groups.

S pneumoniae is a gram-positive encapsulated bacteria of which about 90 different polysaccharide capsule serotypes have been identified. Most pneumococcal disease in infants is associated with the 11 most common serotypes, which cause at least 75% of invasive disease in all regions. Pneumococcal resistance to essential antibiotics is a serious and rapidly increasing problem worldwide.

Protective immunity against pneumococci is provided by type-specific anticapsular antibodies. However, capsular polysaccharide vaccines do not regularly elicit protective levels of antibodies in children aged younger than 2 years, or in immunocompromised individuals. One of the currently licensed vaccines contains purified capsular polysac-charide from each of the 23 capsular types of *S pneumoniae*, which together account for most cases (90%) of serious pneumococcal disease in Western industrialized countries. Relatively good antibody responses are elicited in adults. In some countries, vaccination is recommended for elderly people, particularly those living in institutions.

Experience with *Haemophilus influenzae* type B conjugate vaccines has shown that the immunogenicity of polysaccharide can be improved by chemical conjugation to a protein carrier, thereby eliciting a T-cell–dependent antibody response. Unlike polysaccharide vaccines, conjugate vaccines induce high antibody levels and elicit an immune response in infants and in immunodeficient persons. Moreover, these vaccines induce immunological memory. Therefore, they could reduce bacterial transmission in the community. Introduction of a 7-valent conjugate vaccine in the United States resulted in a dramatic decline in the rates of invasive disease. The vaccine also showed moderate protection against otitis caused by vaccine serotypes. However, the decrease in vaccine-type otitis media was partially offset by an increase in disease caused by nonvaccine types of *S pneumoniae* and by *H influenzae*, a phenomenon referred to as "replacement disease."

The development and introduction in developing countries of a conjugate *S pneumoniae* vaccine is now one of the highest-priority projects. Several conjugate vaccines that provide more optimal serotype coverage in developing countries than the currently licensed 7-valent vaccine are in clinical development. They may be available by 2008 to 2010 for vaccination programs in developing countries, although presumably at a high price.

MENINGOCOCCAL MENINGITIS

Bacterial meningitis remains a serious threat to global health, accounting for an estimated 170 000 deaths yearly worldwide. Even with antimicrobial therapy and the availability of sophisticated intensive care, case fatality rates remain at 5% to 10% in industrialized countries and are higher in the developing world. Between 10% and 20% of survivors develop permanent sequelae. Since the introduction of *H influenzae* type b

conjugate vaccines, *Neisseria meningitidis* has become the commonest cause of bacterial meningitis in the world. *N meningitidis* is spread by person-to-person contact through the airborne respiratory droplets of infected people. The disease affects mainly young children, but it is also common in older children and young adults. Serogroups A, B, C, Y, and W-135 account for 90% of all disease.

Group A meningococcus has historically been the main cause of epidemic meningococcal disease and still predominates in Africa during both endemic and epidemic periods. The highest burden of disease occurs in sub-Saharan Africa in an area extending from Senegal and Ethiopia, referred to as the "meningitis belt." Epidemics occur in irregular cycles, lasting for 2 to 3 dry seasons and dying out during the intervening rainy seasons. The size of these epidemics can be enormous: in 1996, around 200 000 cases were reported, with 20 000 deaths. In the last few years, the emergence of group W-135 as the cause of epidemics has added complexity to the epidemiological situation in the region.

Group B meningococcus accounts for approximately 50% of meningococcal meningitis cases in North America and Europe. In all countries, the incidence of group B disease is highest in infants. Group B epidemics have occurred in the United States, Cuba, Brazil, and Chile. Since 1991, New Zealand has experienced a large epidemic of group B meningococcal infection, with incidence rates up to 10 times the background incidence. Altogether, meningococcus serogroup B incidence may be estimated at between 20 000 and 80 000 cases per year, with 2000 to 8000 deaths.

Polysaccharide vaccines against *N meningitidis* groups A, C, Y, and W-135 are available worldwide, although in restricted quantities, and with a price for the tetravalent vaccine that does not allow widespread use in sub-Saharan Africa. The emergence of the W-135 serogroup in some countries of Africa has prompted the development of a cheaper trivalent polysaccharide

A/C/W-135 vaccine. However, polysaccharide vaccines are poor immunogens in young infants and fail to induce immunological memory. In 1999, meningococcal group C conjugate vaccine was successfully introduced into the routine British immunization program, opening the way for the development of conjugate vaccines against the other *N meningitidis* serogroups. Vaccine manufacturers are currently developing conjugate vaccine combinations incorporating groups A, C, Y, and W-135 polysaccharides.

These multivalent meningococcal polysaccharide–protein conjugate vaccines will be available in the United States and Europe within a few years. Nevertheless, it is unlikely that these new vaccines will be available at a price affordable to most of the countries in the African meningitis belt. Therefore, a public partnership between the World Health Organization (WHO) and the Program for Appropriate Technology in Health (a US-based nongovernmental organization), the Meningitis Vaccine Project, is currently developing a serogroup A conjugate vaccine tailored for Africa that will be available at a price of less than US $1 per dose.

Serogroup B capsular polysaccharide is a poor immunogen, probably because it is structurally identical to glycoproteins expressed by host tissues. Consequently, vaccine research directed against serogroup B meningococcus has focused largely on cell-surface protein antigens (outer membrane proteins). The 2 most-studied outer-membrane-protein vaccines are those produced in response to outbreaks in Norway and Cuba. Both have been used for epidemic control in their respective countries and were found to be 50% to 80% effective.

HIV/AIDS

More than 40 million adults and children are living with HIV/AIDS worldwide and close to 5 million people (including 800 000 children) become infected each year. HIV infections are now almost equally distributed between men and women, with an estimated 17.6 million women aged 15 to 49 years living with HIV/AIDS. HIV/AIDS is the leading cause of death in sub-Saharan Africa and the fourth biggest killer worldwide. Asia currently experiences the world's fastest-growing HIV/AIDS epidemic. Highly active antiretroviral therapy has reduced progression to AIDS, deaths, and HIV transmission from mother to child in North America and Western Europe. However, success with treatment has not been matched by progress toward prevention, and evidence of rising HIV infection rates is emerging, particularly in marginalized communities. A new determination to fight the epidemic emerged following the United Nations General Assembly Special Session on HIV/AIDS in July 2001, and a general effort is being made to make antiretroviral drugs available to the underprivileged populations. A new initiative (called "3 by 5") launched by WHO in 2003 aims at providing effective therapy to at least 3 million patients by 2005. However, despite these encouraging trends, a preventive vaccine is needed more than ever, particularly in developing countries.

Human immunodeficiency viruses belong to the Lentivirus group of the Retroviridae family. Two types have been described: HIV-1 and HIV-2, the former appearing more aggressive and spreading more rapidly. The development of a safe and effective HIV vaccine is hampered by the tremendous genetic variability of the virus and the paucity of knowledge on possible immune mechanisms of protection. The first clinical trial of an HIV vaccine was conducted in the United States in 1987. Since then, over 30 candidate vaccines have been tested in over 80 phase I/II clinical trials, involving over 10 000 healthy volunteers. Most of these trials have been conducted in the United States and Europe. A few trials also have been conducted in developing countries (Brazil, China, Cuba, Haiti, Kenya, Thailand, Trinidad, and Uganda). The effort to develop and evaluate HIV vaccines will be strengthened by the African AIDS Vaccine Programme, which was established following an initiative of WHO and the

Joint United Nations Programme on HIV/AIDS (UNAIDS), and by a new initiative involving, among others, the Bill and Melinda Gates Foundation, the International AIDS Vaccine Initiative, and the US National Institutes of Health.[4]

Only 2 efficacy trials have been completed so far, both using the same approach of a subunit gp120 envelope glycoprotein, one in the United States (with sites in Canada and Europe) and the other in Thailand. The 120 kDa glycoprotein (gp120) is the major antigenic determinant present on the surface of HIV particles. Definite results from both trials were reported in 2003, demonstrating that immunization did not result in a statistically significant reduction of HIV infection within the study populations. A third efficacy trial involves a live recombinant vector (canarypox-HIV) expressing the *gag*, *env*, and *pol* genes of HIV-1 and combined in a prime-boost vaccination regimen with a gp120 subunit vaccine; begun in Thailand in late 2003, it aims to include 16 000 volunteers. Other interesting approaches being tested in humans are based on DNA prime and recombinant poxvirus boosts. These vaccines are not intended to prevent HIV infection but to elicit a T-cell immune response that could prevent or delay the occurrence of the disease.

Recombinant adenoviruses represent another promising approach of the same type, especially when combined with a recombinant canarypox in a prime-boost vaccination regimen. Other candidate vaccines include other recombinant bacterial or viral vectors, some of which have shown some promise in controlling viral replication in preclinical studies in nonhuman primate models. Subunit HIV vaccines based on engineered recombinant envelope glycoproteins alone or combined with the non-structural Tat, Nef, and Rev proteins, DNA vaccines and peptides also are under development.

There is no doubt that the development of a safe, effective, and affordable HIV vaccine remains the scientific and public health challenge of this new century.

HUMAN PAPILLOMAVIRUS

Human papillomavirus (HPV) causes cervical cancer, the second biggest cause of female cancer mortality worldwide with 288 000 deaths yearly. Approximately 500 000 cases of cervical cancer are reported each year, with nearly 80% occurring in developing countries. In the absence of screening programs, cervical cancer is detected too late and leads to death in most cases. The highest incidences are found in some countries of Latin America (93.8 per 100 000 women in Haiti, the highest national incidence in the world), in Africa (61.4 per 100 000 women in Tanzania), and in Asia (30 per 100 000 in India). Epidemiological studies have reported that 75% of the 15- to 50-year-old population in the United States is infected with HPV, with 1% presenting clinical lesions. The prevalence of HPV infection among sexually active women may range from 18% to 25%, especially in some populations of sexually active teenagers.

HPV belongs to the Papovaviridae family. More than 30 types of HPV have been identified that can infect the genital mucosa. It has been established that over 95% of cervical cancer biopsies contain HPV DNA, with oncogenic HPV-16, -18, -33, and -45 comprising more than 80% of the cases. The association of cervical cancer with the presence of sexually transmitted HPV DNA has substantiated the basis for vaccine development. Viral recombinant proteins are being studied as antigenic components of vaccine candidates. Prophylactic vaccine candidates are based on the recombinant capsid proteins L1 and L2, which self-assemble into viruslike particles (VLPs) that can induce virusneutralizing antibodies, while therapeutic vaccine candidates, based on viral oncogenic proteins E6 and E7, are designed to induce cell-mediated immune responses able to eliminate infected cells.

The results of a controlled efficacy trial of HPV-16 VLPs became available recently and showed that the incidence of persistent HPV-16 infection and

HPV-16-related cervical intraepithelial neoplasia was reduced in vaccinated women, with a 100% efficacy rate over a 1.7-year follow-up period. These results suggest that immunizing HPV-16-negative women will eventually reduce the incidence of cervical cancer. Two prophylactic vaccine candidates are at the level of phase III efficacy evaluation: a bivalent HPV-16/18 VLP vaccine produced in insect cells using a recombinant baculovirus, and a tetravalent HPV-6/11/16/18 VLP vaccine produced in recombinant yeast.

CONCLUSION

The biotechnology revolution, culminating in the sequencing of the genome of a great many pathogens, together with increased knowledge of the immune responses to infections, has allowed the unprecedented rational development of new recombinant vaccines that will hopefully help control infectious diseases, including those that appear most complex, such as HIV/AIDS, tuberculosis, and malaria.[5] However, despite these new tools, the challenges remain formidable.[6] The development and registration of a new vaccine can take more than 10 years[7] and cost $200 million to $500 million.[8] The world vaccine market is estimated at approximately $6.5 billion,[9] a meager 2% of the global pharmaceutical market, making vaccine research and development considerably less attractive to private investors than drug development. Moreover, many of the diseases for which new vaccines are urgently needed mainly affect developing countries whose market characteristics fail to attract private capital investment.

It is nevertheless vital to continuously develop new vaccines and to improve existing ones.[10] In this context, a new paradigm needs to be developed to include and coordinate the actions of the WHO, international and national funding agencies, the pharmaceutical industry and manufacturers in emerging developing countries, nonprofit foundations, and nongovernmental humanitarian organizations. Working together, these organizations could harness existing potentials and accelerate the development and testing of new vaccines and the improvement and implementation of existing vaccines. The goal is to offer better safety, efficacy, and delivery methods with lower costs of production, leading to a more efficient distribution and better availability of vaccines, especially in developing countries.

About the Authors

Marie Paule Kieny is with the World Health Organization, Geneva, Switzerland. Jean-Louis Excler is with the International AIDS Vaccine Initiative, Delhi, India. At the time of this study, Marc Girard was with the Foundation Biomérieux, Annecy, France.

Correspondence: Requests for reprints should be sent to Marie Paule Kieny, PhD, Initiative for Vaccine Research, World Health Organization, Avenue Appia 20, CH1211-Genève 27, Switzerland (e-mail: kienym@who.int).

Acknowledgments

Dr Daniel Tarantola, previously director of the WHO Department of Immunization, Vaccines and Biologicals, has been an inspiration for this work. Nadia Fisher is acknowledged for expert secretarial assistance.

References

1. Biellik R, Madema S, Taole A, et al. First 5 years of measles elimination in southern Africa: 1996–2000. *Lancet.*2002;359:1564–1568.
2. *State of the World's Vaccine and Immunization.* Rev ed. Geneva, Switzerland: World Health Organization; 2003.
3. Widdus R. Public–private partnerships for health: their maintargets, their diversity, and their future directions. *Bull World Health Organ.*2001;79(8): 713–720.
4. Klausner RD, Fauci AS, Corey L, et al. The need for a global HIV vaccine enterprise. *Science.*2003;300: 2036–2039.
5. Ellis RW. Technologies for making new vaccines. In: Plotkin SA, Orenstein WA, eds. *Vaccines.* 4th ed. Philadelphia, Pa: Elsevier Saunders; 2004:1177–1197.
6. *Proceedings of the Fourth Global Vaccine Research Forum.* Geneva, Switzerland: World Health Organization; 2004.
7. Struck MM. Vaccine R&D success rates and development times. *Nat Biotechnol.*1996;14(5):591–593.
8. André FE. How the research-based industry approaches vaccine development and establishes priorities. *Dev Biol (Basel).*2002;110:25–29.
9. Greco M. The future of vaccines: an industrial perspective. *Vaccine.*2001; 20(suppl 1):S101–S103.
10. Bloom BR, Lambert P-H, eds. *The Vaccine Book.* San Diego, Calif: Academic Press; 2003.

Can We Capitalize on the Virtues of Vaccines? Insights from the Polio Eradication Initiative

| R. Bruce Aylward, MD, MPH and David L. Heymann, MD

ABSTRACT

Twenty-five years after the eradication of smallpox, the ongoing effort to eradicate poliomyelitis has grown into the largest international health initiative ever undertaken.

By 2004, however, the polio eradication effort was threatened by a challenge regularly faced by public health policymakers everywhere—misperception about the benefits and risks of vaccines. The propagation of false rumors about oral poliovirus vaccine safety led to the reinfection of 13 previously polio-free countries and the largest polio epidemic in Africa in recent years.

With deft management of such challenges by local, national, and international health authorities, poliomyelitis, a disease that threatened children everywhere just 2 generations ago, could soon be relegated to history like smallpox before it.

INTRODUCTION

Disease eradication "attacks inequities and provides the ultimate in social justice and equity," as by design the benefits should accrue to all peoples in perpetuity.[1(p112)] The only completed eradication initiative to date was based on the widespread application of a vaccine, and this demonstrates the rare potential of immunization as a public health tool.[2] Although endemic polio has now been eliminated from all but 6 countries in the world,[3] the ultimate success of this massive initiative is still threatened by the same challenge that faces public health policymakers everywhere—misperceptions held by government officials, health professionals, the media, and the general public about the benefits and risks of vaccines, both now and in the future.

We examine the progress that has been made toward the eradication of poliomyelitis and the prospects for its completion, including the eventual cessation of polio immunization, against a background of recent events, both local and international, that have influenced these prospects.

A GLOBAL EFFORT FOR A GLOBAL GOOD

In 1988, the World Health Assembly adopted the goal of polio eradication by the year 2000.[4] This World Health Assembly consensus was the result of a broad combination of influences ranging from the increasing evidence that human-to-human transmission of polioviruses could be interrupted to the ceaseless promotion of a global eradication target by many scientifically respected advocates.[5] Most important, in the Americas polio was rapidly being eliminated through a 4-pronged strategy consisting of high routine immunization coverage with oral poliovirus vaccine (OPV); national immunization days targeting every child younger than 5 years for supplementary OPV doses; surveillance for, and laboratory investigation of, all cases of acute flaccid paralysis among children younger than 15 years; and massive, house-to-house "mop-up" campaigns to interrupt the final chains of transmission.[6]

Despite the global consensus to eradicate polio, the number of countries implementing the strategies initially grew very slowly because of limited promotion of the goal internationally, a lack of resources, and other health priorities both within and outside immunization programs.[7] With the certification of polio eradication in the Americas in 1994[8] and the elimination of polio from China shortly thereafter, there was a rapid scale-up of the global effort, with striking examples of international cooperation. In April 1995, 18 countries of the Middle East, Caucasus, Central Asian Republics, and Russia launched Operation MECACAR, beginning a multiyear effort to immunize 85 million children against polio during synchronized national immunization days.[9] In 1996, then-President Nelson Mandela of South Africa and 45 other heads of state from throughout Africa launched the Kick Polio Out of Africa campaign.[10]

As the result of these and similar collaborative efforts throughout the world,[11] every country had introduced the key polio eradication strategies by 2000, including conflict-affected countries such as Afghanistan, the Democratic Republic of the Congo, and Somalia. Globally, an estimated 10 million health workers and volunteers immunized 600 million children in 100 countries during multiple rounds of national immunization days in that year.[12] By that time, a truly global surveillance and laboratory network had been established, with district-level weekly or monthly reporting from every country in which polio was endemic or recently endemic. More than 60 000 diagnostic specimens from more than 30 000 acute flaccid paralysis patients were being analyzed in the network every year to identify the remaining chains of polio transmission and target supplementary immunization activities.[13]

These national efforts were supported by a robust partnership that was spearheaded by the World Health Organization, Rotary International, the US Centers for Disease Control and Prevention, and the United Nations Children's Fund (UNICEF). The polio partnership grew to include national governments, foundations, international humanitarian organizations, national and international nongovernmental organizations, donor agencies, the private sector, and development banks. The most extraordinary partner was the international service organization Rotary, which in addition to countless hours donated by its 1.2 million volunteers in 140 countries, contributed over US$600 million to the global effort. By the end of 2003, more than US$3 billion in external financing and US$2.5 million in in-kind contributions had been expended to eradicate polio in the countries in which it was endemic.[14] The capacity to mobilize resources on this scale for a single disease control effort was very much attributable to the concept of polio eradication as a global public good.[15] That all children everywhere might benefit in perpetuity from this initiative proved a powerful investment incentive to a broad range of stakeholders from community leaders to national health policymakers to ministers of international development and even G8 leaders.[16]

By the end of 2003, this international eradication effort had eliminated polio from all but 6 countries in the world, demonstrating that with the proper application of the eradication strategies and international cooperation, poliovirus transmission could be rapidly interrupted anywhere (Figure 1). In the 6 remaining countries in which polio was endemic (Nigeria, India, Pakistan, Egypt, Afghanistan, and Niger), the disease was either

highly localized or had been interrupted in large geographic areas, setting the stage for global eradication. Despite this extraordinary progress and massive international investment, in 2003 a series of misunderstandings and misrepresentations about the safety of OPV in 1 state of 1 country rapidly escalated, leading to the suspension of polio campaigns in that area, a nationwide epidemic, and the reinfection of many previously polio-free countries. For the first time in history, more countries suffered importations of polio than were actually endemic for the disease, putting the entire eradication initiative at risk.

STOPPING POLIO TRANSMISSION

This most recent and perhaps most insidious threat to the interruption of wild poliovirus transmission globally began in mid-2003, in the key state of Kano in northern Nigeria,

when a small number of local opinion leaders began questioning the basis for the mass polio immunization campaigns. Some of these local leaders soon began voicing a wide range of theories about OPV itself, suggesting that it contained, among other things, HIV and antifertility agents.[17] Within weeks, the local media were full of reports of conspiracy theories, the most popular being that the polio campaign was in fact an effort to depopulate the north of the country using "contaminated" OPV. Using the Internet for its research, several members of the local press soon found material to further sustain these theories, such as long-debunked theories linking OPV to the origins of HIV.[18]

By the end of August 2003, political leaders in Kano and adjoining states had decided to suspend the polio campaigns until the rumors could be addressed. Unfortunately, within months hundreds of children

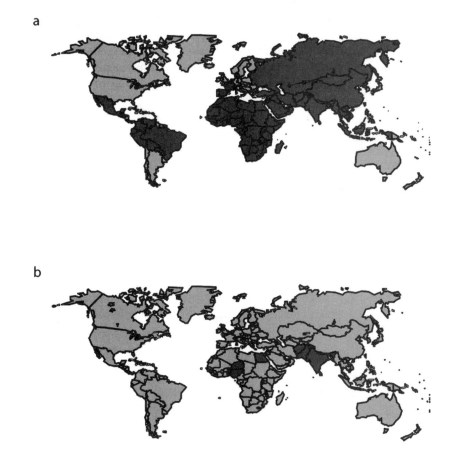

FIGURE 1— Distribution of endemic poliomyelitis (dark gray) (a) in 1988, the year the World Health Assembly voted to eradicate the disease and at which time polio was present in more than 125 countries, and (b) at the end of 2003, when endemic polio was limited to 6 countries.

had been paralyzed in Nigeria as epidemic polio returned to the country. The virus rapidly spread from Kano to other states within Nigeria that had long been polio-free (e.g., the megacity of Lagos) as well as to other, polio-free, countries of sub-Saharan Africa (Figure 2) and beyond, costing over US$100 million in emergency response activities.[19] One of Africa's most impressive achievements in health and international cooperation was at risk, as well as the global eradication effort.

Recognizing that a failure to implement the strategies in any remaining area in which polio was endemic would put the entire global eradication effort and investment at risk, on January 15, 2004, the leaders of the World Health Organization and UNICEF convened an emergency meeting of the health ministers of the 6 remaining polio-infected countries and 3 of the recently reinfected countries. The meeting also brought together political and health leaders from key states and provinces within those countries in which polio was endemic. After a day of deliberations, the ministers issued the Geneva Declaration on the Eradication of Poliomyelitis, stating that 2004 presented the best, and possibly last, chance to achieve this global public good.[20] The declaration introduced an aggressive plan to immunize a total of 250 million children during up to 6 door-to-door polio immunization campaigns in each country within the next 12 months. The Nigerian minister outlined an extensive program of joint work with Kano state authorities to resolve the remaining doubts about the safety of the polio vaccine and then allow the resumption of the polio immunization campaigns.

As of January 18, 2005, the "intensified" effort in Asia was on track. After a marked increase in polio immunization campaign quantity and quality, poliovirus transmission in India, Pakistan, and Afghanistan was highly focal, with 182 cases reported for 2004 compared with 336 in 2003. In all 3 countries, large-scale mop-up activities had been added to the national program to interrupt transmission as rapidly as possible. Although there continued to be widespread low-level poliovirus transmission in Egypt, the quality of eradication activities in that country had also improved markedly since early 2004. In contrast, sub-Saharan Africa was still experiencing epidemic polio; cases in Nigeria and Niger had soared to 788 (vs 395 in 2003), and since January 2003, a total of 260 children had been paralyzed in 13 previously polio-free countries by polioviruses that were genetically linked to viruses that had originated in northern Nigeria. However, the health ministers of 23 west and central African countries had initiated a series of massive, synchronized campaigns for late 2004 and 2005, targeting 80 million children, to get that eradication effort back on track for an end-of-2005 target.[21]

The success of this intensified polio eradication effort now depends on (1) direct oversight by all political, traditional, religious, and community leaders in each area in which the disease is endemic to ensure that every child is reached during each immunization campaign, and (2) action by the international community to close rapidly the US $275 million funding gap for intensified eradication activities worldwide during 2005–2006.

STOPPING POLIO IMMUNIZATION

Even before this new challenge to polio eradication appeared, 3 events had led some commentators to question whether the eventual cessation of polio immunization, an implicit goal of the eradication program, would ever be feasible, regardless of the success of the ongoing efforts to interrupt wild poliovirus transmission. First, through the application of new molecular tools, virologists demonstrated that a 1999–2000 polio outbreak in Hispaniola was not attributable to a wild poliovirus, but rather a circulating vaccine-derived poliovirus (cVDPV).[22] Second, a team of virologists succeeded in synthesizing a viable poliovirus de novo from the genetic code, which was by then available on the Internet.[23] Third, an individual with a primary immunodeficiency syndrome was found to have excreted a neurovirulent vaccine-derived poliovirus (iVDPV) for as long as 10 years.[24]

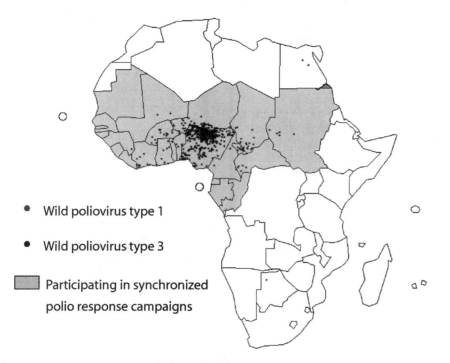

● Wild poliovirus type 1

● Wild poliovirus type 3

▨ Participating in synchronized polio response campaigns

FIGURE 2— Reported polio cases in Africa (January 1, 2003, to July 31, 2004) and countries participating in synchronized outbreak response campaigns in late 2004.

TABLE 1— Risk Estimates of Paralytic Disease Owing to Polioviruses After Interruption of Wild Poliovirus Transmission Globally[a]

Source of Risk	Specific Risks	Frequency[b]	Annual Burden (Cases of Paralysis)	Expected Evolution of Specific Risks
Vaccine-derived poliovirus	VAPP	2–4/million birth cohort	250–500	Stable
	cVDPV	4 episodes during 2000–2004	6[c]	Increase
	iVDPV	24 cases identified since 1961	< 1	Decrease
Wild-type poliovirus	Release from an IPV production site	1 event resulting in 1 infection (1990s)	< 1	Decrease
	Release from a laboratory stock	2 events during 2000–2003 (10 polio cases)	Unknown	Decrease
	Intentional release	None observed	Unknown	Unknown

Note. VAPP = vaccine-associated paralytic poliomyelitis; cVDPV = circulating vaccine-derived poliovirus; iVDPV = prolonged excretion of a vaccine-derived poliovirus by an individual with a primary immunodeficiency syndrome; IPV = inactivated poliovirus vaccine.
[a]Assuming continuation of oral poliovirus vaccine for routine immunization against polio.
[b]Based on World Health Organization unpublished data.
[c]Estimate based on incomplete information.

Although all these developments had for some time been deemed possible, these events began a new debate about the technical feasibility and wisdom of ever stopping immunization with OPV. This debate was further heightened by the events of, and subsequent to, September 11, 2001, most notably the use of biological agents for malicious purposes in the United States and the resumption of limited immunization with smallpox vaccine.[25] Some argued that given the challenges of ensuring the safe containment of laboratory stocks of wild polioviruses in a post–September 11 world, and establishing and maintaining a vaccine stockpile of sufficient size to respond to future outbreaks, it would be necessary to continue polio immunization indefinitely.[26] One commentator suggested that although the inactivated poliovirus vaccine (IPV) could provide population immunity while avoiding the risks of OPV, the much higher price of IPV made continued OPV a more appropriate strategy for developing countries.[27]

The potential "prisoners' dilemma" that was emerging, in which the continued use of OPV after eradication of wild-type polioviruses might lead to the emergence of new virulent vaccine-derived strains, required acceleration of the ongoing research program to define the magnitude of these risks and potential strategies for dealing with them (Table 1). More than 7000 Sabin-derived polioviruses were screened to search for cVDPVs, and collaborative studies were established with clinics that treated individuals with primary immunodeficiencies. Within 2 years, a substantial body of data demonstrated that cVDPVs and iVDPVs were in fact rare and posed decreasing risks with time after OPV cessation.[28] All 4 cVDPV outbreaks had been rapidly controlled with mass OPV campaigns. Of the 19 iVDPVs identified to date worldwide, only 2 of the original hosts are still known to be excreting virus, with no evidence of secondary transmission. In addition, by the end of 2003, 157 countries had initiated the necessary nationwide survey of facilities for stocks of wild and vaccine-derived polioviruses and potentially infectious materials, and 81 countries, including the United States, had completed inventories.[29]

In September 2003, a World Health Organization–convened meeting of international experts concluded that the continued use of OPV after eradication of wild-type polioviruses, in an environment of decreasing OPV coverage because of the cessation of polio campaigns, posed a medium- to long-term risk to the international goal of eliminating paralytic poliomyelitis caused by circulating polioviruses.[30] The group stated that OPV immunization should be stopped as soon as possible after interruption of wild poliovirus transmission, while high population immunity and surveillance sensitivity could reduce the risk of cVDPV emergence and facilitate the prompt detection and response to such events if they occurred. Recognizing that IPV will not substantially change the future risk of polio in many countries, particularly those with low routine immunization coverage, the World Health Organization is providing countries with the evidence needed to make their own risk analysis on the costs and benefits of IPV for routine childhood immunization after OPV cessation. In addition to providing guidance on IPV policy, the World Health Organization is giving particular attention to helping individual countries establish and maintain the surveillance and response capacity needed before, during, and after OPV immunization cessation.[31] This work includes the development of stockpiles of monovalent OPV, to allow type-specific responses to future polio outbreaks, and, potentially, Sabin-based IPV to limit a proliferation in the number of facilities undertaking large-scale amplification of wild poliovirus strains after the cessation of OPV immunization. The ultimate success of this strategy will depend on (1) negotiating international concurrence to stop OPV use in all countries over a very short time period (to avoid the risk of exposing other areas to vaccine-derived strains, particularly those that choose not to introduce IPV), and (2) establishing and maintaining an international stockpile of poliovaccines to manage the cVPDVs that might emerge during the cessation of OPV immunization.

CONCLUSIONS

Since its launch in 1988, the Global Polio Eradication Initiative has grown into the largest international health effort ever, generating broad international collaboration and community participation. In 2004, the initiative was intensified to interrupt polio transmission in the 6 remaining countries in which polio was endemic and, eventually stop the routine use of OPV. The greatest recent challenge to interrupting polio transmission has been the promotion of false rumors about OPV safety in 1 state of 1 country. Ironically, the greatest challenge to the cessation of OPV immunization in the future may be establishing international consensus on the real risks of that vaccine once wild poliovirus transmission has been interrupted. With

deft management of these challenges by local, national, and international health policymakers, poliomyelitis, a disease that threatened children everywhere just 2 generations ago, could soon be relegated to history like smallpox before it.

About the Authors

The authors are with the Polio Eradication Initiative, World Health Organization, Geneva, Switzerland.

Correspondence: Requests for reprints should be sent to R. Bruce Aylward, MD, Coordinator, Polio Eradication Initiative, World Health Organization, 20, Avenue Appia, CH-1211 Geneva 27, Switzerland (e-mail: aylwardb@who.int).

Acknowledgments

The authors thank Dr Daniel Tarantola for his extensive and valuable comments during the preparation and revision of this article.

Contributors

The authors originated and developed this article jointly. R.B. Aylward wrote the initial draft, incorporating the comments of D.L. Heymann, and finalized the article on receipt of the reviewer comments.

References

1. Foege WH. Conference synthesis and vision for the future. *Bull World Health Organ.* 1998;76(suppl 2):109–112.
2. Aylward B, Hennessey KA, Zagaria N, Olivé JM, Cochi S. When is a disease eradicable? 100 years of lessons learned. *Am J Public Health.* 2000;90:1515–1520.
3. Progress towards global eradication of poliomyelitis, 2003 and January–April 2004. *Wkly Epidemiol Rec.* 2004; 79:229–234.
4. *Global Eradication of Poliomyelitis by the Year 2000.* Geneva, Switzerland: World Health Organization; 1988. World Health Assembly resolution WHA41.28.
5. Dowdle WR, Cochi SL. Global eradication of poliovirus: history and rationale. In: Semler BL, Wimmer E, eds. *Molecular Biology of Picornaviruses.* Washington DC: ASM Press; 2002.
6. De Quadros CA, Hersh BS, Olivé JM, Andrus JK, da Silveira CM, Carrasco PA. Eradication of poliomyelitis: progress in the Americas. *Pediatr Infect Dis J.* 1991; 10:222–229.
7. Aylward RB, Tangermann R, Sutter R, Cochi SL. Polio eradication: capturing the full potential of a vaccine. In: Levine MM, Kaper JB, Rappuoli R, Liu MA, Good MF, eds. *New Generation Vaccines.* New York, NY: Marcel Dekker; 2003: 145–157.
8. *Expanded Programme on Immunization. Report of the First Meeting of the Global Commission for the Certification of the Eradication of Poliomyelitis.* Geneva, Switzerland: World Health Organization; 1995. WHO document WHO/EPI/GEN/95.6.
9. Expanded Programme on Immunization. Update: mass vaccination with oral poliovirus vaccine—Asia and Europe, 1996. *Wkly Epidemiol Rec.* 1996; 71:329–332.
10. Okwo-Bele JM, Lobanov A, Biellik RJ, et al. Overview of poliomyelitis in the African region and current regional plan of action. *J Infect Dis.* 1997:175(suppl 1): S10–S15.
11. Andrus JK, Thapa AB, Withana N, Fitzsimmons JW, Abeykoon P, Aylward B. A new paradigm for international disease control: lessons learned from polio eradication in Southeast Asia. *Am J Public Health.* 2001;91:146–150.
12. Expanded Programme on Immunization. Progress towards global poliomyelitis eradication, 2001. *Wkly Epidemiol Rec.* 2002;77;98–107.
13. Department of Vaccines and Biologicals. Expanding contributions of the global laboratory network for poliomyelitis eradication. *Wkly Epidemiol Rec.* 2002;77:133–137.
14. Aylward RB, Acharya A, England S, Agocs M, Linkins J. Global health goals: lessons from the worldwide effort to eradicate poliomyelitis. *Lancet.* 2004; 362:909–914.
15. Woodward D, Smith RD. Global public goods and health: concepts and issues. In: Smith RD, Beaglehole R, Woodward D, Drager N, eds. *Global Public Goods for Health.* Oxford, England: Oxford University Press, 2003: 3–29.
16. The White House Web page. G-8 Commitment to Help Stop Polio Forever. Available at: http://www.whitehouse.gov/news/releases/2004/06/20040610-44.html.

Accessed January 27, 2005.

17. Samba E, Nkrumah F, Leke R. Getting polio eradication back on track in Nigeria. *N Engl J Med.* 2004;350: 645–646.

18. Cohen J. AIDS origins: disputed AIDS theory dies its final death. *Science.* 2001;292:615.

19. World Health Organization. Polio outbreak threatens West and Central Africa. Press Release. June 2004.

20. *Geneva Declaration on the Eradication of Poliomyelitis.* Geneva, Switzerland: World Health Organization; 2004.

21. Aylward RB, Nshimirimana D, Rosenbauer O, Gasasira A, Heymann D, Konaré A. Polio Eradication—African Union (AU) Flagship Programme Back on Track? *MERA: Medical Education Resource in Africa.* 2004;13:5–6.

22. Kew O, Morris-Glasgow V, Landaverde M, et al. Outbreak of poliomyelitis in Hispaniola associated with circulating type 1 vaccine–derived poliovirus. *Science.* 2002;296:356–359.

23. Cello J, Paul AV, Wimmer E. Chemical synthesis of poliovirus cDNA: generation of infectious virus in the absence of natural template. *Science.* 2002;297:1016–1018.

24. Khetsuriani N, Prevots DR, Quick L, et al. Persistence of vaccine-derived polioviruses among immunodeficient persons with vaccine-associated paralytic poliomyelitis. *J Infect Dis.* 2003;188:1845.

25. Centers for Disease Control and Prevention. Recommendations for using smallpox vaccine in a pre-event vaccination program. Recommendations of the Advisory Committee on Immunization Practices (ACIP) and the Healthcare Infection Control Practices Advisory Committee (HICPAC). *MMWR Morb Mortal Wkly Rep.* 2003;52(RR-7):1–16.

26. Nathanson N, Fine P. Poliomyelitis eradication—a dangerous endgame. *Science.* 2002;296:269–270.

27. Henderson DA. Countering the posteradication threat of smallpox and polio. *Clin Infect Dis.* 2002;34:79–83.

28. Aylward RB, Cochi SL. Framework for evaluating the risks of paralytic poliomyelitis after global interruption of wild poliovirus transmission. *Bull World Health Organ.* 2004;82(1):40–46.

29. World Health Organization. Progress in certification of poliomyelitis eradication and in laboratory containment of wild poliovirus. *Wkly Epidemiol Rec.* 2003;44:410–414.

30. *Vaccines and Biologicals. Report of an Informal Consultation on the Identification and Management of Vaccine-Derived Polioviruses (VDPVs).* Geneva, Switzerland, World Health Organization; 2004.

31. Global Polio Eradication Initiative. *Strategic Plan, 2004–2008.* Geneva, Switzerland: World Health Organization; 2004.

Assembling a Global Vaccine Development Pipeline for Infectious Diseases in the Developing World

| Irina Serdobova, MBA, PhD and Marie-Paule Kieny, PhD

ABSTRACT

Commercial realities have drastically reduced private investment in the development of new public health tools, but increased awareness of this situation has resulted in the emergence of a variety of research-based, nonprofit organizations. We reviewed current vaccine developments and developed a framework for efficient research and development investments in this area.

We have identified several key "push" and "pull" forces within the vaccine research and product development environment and have examined their impacts on the process. These forces affect the global vaccine pipeline, which is composed of all individual vaccine initiatives and global partnerships (i.e., stakeholders), All of these research and development stakeholders must work together to establish and promote a global, sustainable research and development pipeline that delivers optimal vaccines and immunization technologies.

INTRODUCTION

Vaccines are the cornerstone of the fight against communicable diseases. This has been proven by the success of smallpox eradication, the drastic reduction in polio cases during the past 20 years, the progress toward tetanus elimination, and the reduction of measles mortality. Despite these achievements, infectious diseases are still responsible for nearly 30% of all deaths worldwide; more than 15 million people die every year, mostly in low-income and middle-income countries.[1]

Approximately 1.5 million of these deaths could have been prevented if the currently available vaccines were made universally available. Additionally, licensed vaccines to combat many deadly childhood diseases do not yet exist (Figure 1).[2]

Achievement of the United Nations (UN) Millennium Development Goals relies in part on the availability of new tools through research and product development, innovation, and breakthroughs. Goals (such as halving current child mortality figures by the year 2015 [Goal 4]; combating HIV/AIDS, malaria, and other diseases [Goal 6]; forging a global partnership for development; and partnerships ensuring access to medicines [Goal 8]) are highly pertinent to the vaccine community. In 2005 the World Health Assembly adopted an ambitious and comprehensive plan, the Global Immunization Vision and Strategy 2006–2015 (GIVS), for fighting vaccine-preventable diseases.[3] This strategy has 3 priority objectives: (1) immunize more people against more diseases, (2) introduce a range of newly available vaccines and technologies, and (3) provide a number of critical health interventions through immunization. Development of new and improved vaccines, and enhanced coverage for old and new vaccines alike, will contribute substantially to global efforts to reduce disease burden and, in so doing, will reduce poverty.

DRIVING FORCES FOR RESEARCH AND DEVELOPMENT

The research and product development process bridges the gap between scientific discovery and the delivery of tools for health intervention. Vaccines used today are the product of discovery and development during past decades. The aim of the research and product development process[4] is to design effective and consistent methods for the identification and production of potential vaccines, test them for safety and efficacy in preclinical studies, and establish their efficacy in humans. There is a clear responsibility throughout vaccine development to both adhere to and be guided by a structured framework that embodies registration requirements and normative guidelines. This framework collectively ensures the ethics, safety, and quality of the research, manufacturing, and clinical development during the research and product development process.

It often takes more than 10 years to deliver a final, licensed vaccine,[5] and requires not only excellence during research and product development but also managerial and funding commitment throughout the endeavor. The cost of developing a vaccine—from research and discovery to product registration—is estimated to be between US $200 million and US $500 million per vaccine.[6] This figure includes vaccines that are abandoned during the development process. In short, vaccine research and product development is lengthy, complex, and loaded with binary outcome risks.

Several driving forces have an impact on the research and product development process that develops vaccines for nonprofit or low-profit markets that can be grouped into 2 categories: "push" and "pull"—terms that are commonly used when business strategies are being developed. Abstractly, a product is developed either because of a clear demand—a "pull"—for the vaccine in the marketplace or because it becomes technically and operationally feasible—a "push." In practice, the actual delivery of the product to the population in need is dependent on the concerted action of both forces (Figure 2).

Within the context of vaccine development, push forces are principally composed of scientific and technological advances, management and coordination support, and availability of research and product development funding. Pull forces reflect governmental and public recognition and commitment to the fulfillment of health needs and the potential profitability of a future product within a specific free-market segment.

Balancing both forces is necessary for establishing a sustainable product pipeline that consistently yields new vaccines and contributes new public health tools. Additionally, the reality of these forces must be credibly articulated in language that resonates with all stakeholders (i.e., immunization partners). Investing resources and efforts that strengthen any of the push and pull forces can affect the product-oriented pipeline and the impact of unilateral (i.e., asymmetric) disturbances on any point of the process. This investment should be viewed holistically within the context of the entire development environment. In the commercial world, all push forces are united by company operations that target either existing or emerging markets. With publicly funded research, there is additional complexity because of numerous independent entities that have their own discrete mandates.

Technology Push

During the past few decades, scientific advances in fields such as biotechnology, immunology, bioinformatics, genomics, and proteomics and the development of DNA-based and peptide-based vaccine technologies have provided large numbers of poten-

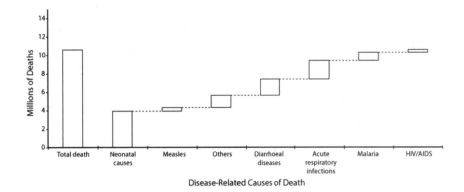

FIGURE 1— Causes of death in children aged younger than 5 years.

Note. "Neonatal causes" includes infectious diseases (neonatal tetanus, pneumonia, meningitis, sepsis/septicemia, diarrhea and other infections during the neonatal period) as well as noncommunicable diseases (birth asphyxia, congenital abnormalities, and preterm birth). "Others" represents mortality in 10% of children aged younger than 5 years and includes causes unrelated to AIDS, diarrhea, measles, malaria, acute respiratory disease, and neonatal causes and injuries.

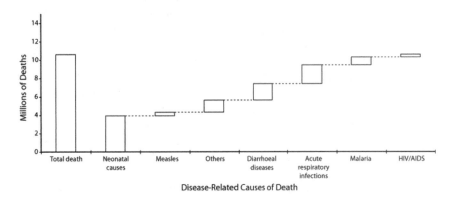

FIGURE 2— Driving forces for public health research and product development.

Note. The shape of the cones mimics a balloon pushed and pulled through the "eye" of the registration "needle." The arrows inside the cones represent the movement along the Push and Pull continuum. Black boxes represent potential vaccine candidates that will eventually yield 1 licensed product.

tial new molecules that can be selected for vaccine development. Preclinical vaccine-testing platforms and new approaches to the development of animal models of disease (such as transgenic animals, i.e., animals that have been genetically altered to exhibit disease symptoms) have moreover broadened the range of potential approaches for validating the potential vaccine. Finally, innovative drug delivery methods and improved understanding of pharmaceutical formulation and clinical testing allow for the potential enhancement of both existing and potential vaccines. Several publicly funded research funding entities— including the National Institutes of Health (NIH), the Medical Research Council, the US Agency for

International Development (USAID), the World Health Organization's (WHO) Initiative for Vaccine Research, the United Nations' Children's Fund (UNICEF)-United Nations' Development Programme (UNDP)-World Bank-WHO Special Programme for Research and Training in Tropical Diseases, the Program for Appropriate Technology in Health, and the International Vaccine Institute—are actively involved in these efforts.

It is appropriate to use technology as the departure point for promoting collaborative initiatives. Because science is a common language, technology exchanges between established and developing health initiatives, as well as between north and south and south and south countries, can be readily implemented. The ultimate goal of these networks is to focus collective research efforts on the challenges within disease-endemic countries. The effective engagement of all research communities can ensure that the issues most relevant to health are addressed with the most effective technological approaches available.

Research and Product Development Funds Push

Developing countries' public spending on research and product development is insufficient for supporting effective internal development of new or improved tools that combat the wide spectrum of infectious diseases in these countries. The low capacity that is the result of internally derived funds has recently been bolstered by a positive trend in contributions from industrialized countries to the developing world. This funding has come from bilateral development agencies, including USAID, the Canadian International Development Agency, the United Kingdom's Department for International Development, and the Swedish International Development Agency; multilateral organizations, including WHO, the UNDP, the World Bank, and the European Commission, and public and private foundations and grant support programs, including NIH, the Rockefeller Foundation, the Wellcome Trust, and the Bill and Melinda Gates Foundation. However, despite this increase in funding, research and product development funds for vaccine research are still insufficient.

Management Push

Effective vaccine research and product development relies on efficient management and access to long-term committed resources. Without effective and experienced management, successful vaccine development is virtually impossible, because the process is both complex and lengthy. During the past 2 decades, several international initiatives, public–private partnerships, and alliances have been created and are active in vaccine research and product development, including the UNICEF-UNDP-World Bank-WHO Special Programme for Research and Training in Tropical Diseases, the Program for Appropriate Technology in Health, and the International Vaccine Institute. Several entities that are focused on single diseases—including the Aeras Global TB Vaccine Foundation, the International AIDS Vaccine Initiative, and Program for Appropriate Technology in Health's Malaria Vaccine Initiative—have been created to manage product development processes.

In addition to these initiatives, many established programs and dedicated international and national institutions have provided ad hoc support, advocacy, and funds for managing vaccine research and product development projects.[7] Often, these new research and product development initiatives (e.g., the International AIDS Vaccine Initiative) have responsibility for all product-related push forces (technology, funds, and management) that are supported by fundraising and advocacy, although for the most part, their coordination with disease control programs and vaccine procurement mechanisms still needs to be effectively integrated.

Market and Procurement Funds Availability Pull

Today, all publicly funded vaccine research and product development require at least 1 industrial partner, or at a minimum 1 established manufacturing entity, because of capital expenditure barriers resulting from the need to produce vaccines in accordance with good manufacturing practices. For the industrial partner, factors that have an impact on the minimum level of pull forces necessary for attracting significant funding are the same whether the products are developed for the developing world or for an established market economy. These factors include developmental and commercialization costs and risks, which culminate in the risk-adjusted chance of generating acceptable stakeholder return from a finite budget.

Throughout the decisionmaking process about whether to favor one development program over another, opportunity costs prevail, i.e., the value of using resources in one way versus the value of pursuing other available alternatives. The commercial third party considers the minimum acceptable market pull forces in a public–private partnership to be where the opportunity cost is neutral. The public sector realizes it must consider the expected return of a specific investment in terms of public health gain rather than invest limited resources in competing priorities. For example, the Global Alliance for Vaccines and Immunization is currently developing and testing framework-based investment cases for future fund allocation. The combination of developmental risks and manufacturing risks, compounded by politically and economically driven uncertainties in the end-consumer marketplaces, collectively often result in unattractive investment propositions for commercial vaccine development organizations.[8]

To overcome the vacuum left by the lack of an innate market pull, it has been proposed that public funds be set aside to guarantee procurement of new vaccines at a fixed price during a predetermined time period.[9] If uncertainty in the commercialization risk is reduced well in advance, developmental risk becomes the main variable that the managerial decisionmakers must consider. Reducing the risk should facilitate the inclusion of vaccines in a commercial product portfolio. This approach has already been effective. For example, public sector increases in procurement commitments and funding has been successful in attracting commercial entities to invest in the development and production of the relatively low-cost hepatitis B and combination vaccines for developing markets. In the future, there may be investments in rotavirus and pneumococcal vaccines once they are introduced.

Control Priorities and Health Systems Capacity Pull

Governments are the key players in the formulation and implementation of national immunization policies.

Public sector entities, such as international organizations and disease control programs, should therefore provide countries with sufficient information about disease burden and the cost-effectiveness of new vaccines, which will allow governments to include evidence-based decisions about the introduction of new vaccines in their immunization programs. If governments present clearly articulated and consistent national program policy statements about the introduction of new vaccines, including recommendations from international partners, global demand for new products can be better ascertained and used as a pull factor to stimulate vaccine research and product development.

Additionally, major investment is necessary for strengthening health systems before the introduction of new products. Indeed, the health systems in many developing countries are struggling to sustain their existing vaccine programs. Today, many international agencies, alliances, nongovernmental organizations, and bilateral initiatives—including WHO, UNICEF, the World Bank, and the Global Alliance for Vaccines and Immunization—are helping national governments to strengthen their immunization and health systems. Future strengthening of health systems should overcome this capacity barrier and lead to the development of a more dependable pull force for vaccine research and product development efforts.

Advocacy Pull

Evidence-based advocacy can have a great impact on attracting the attention of researchers and funding bodies for vaccine development projects. Surveillance data, global and national burden of disease estimates, and demand projections can emphasize the true health value of particular research and product development investments. Through this process, investment in neglected diseases may potentially be rendered more attractive for commercial development and may have an increased likelihood of attracting public funds and management efforts. Advocacy support is therefore

important for the sustainability of research and product development programs and for the delivery of nonmonetary credits to all partners who contribute to the enterprise.

The existence of push and pull forces, and an appropriate balance between them, is necessary for establishing a sustainable product pipeline. The odds for research product attrition rates are dictated by empirically determined probabilities of success. Several potential, independently produced products should be pulled and pushed into the pipeline to beat these odds, which will result in at least 1 licensed product eventually being launched. The driving forces should not favor one potential vaccine or clinical trial. Rather, the forces should favor an entire product pipeline of numerous projects to promote fair competition and diversification of research approaches. The result will be successful, sustainable pipelines of research projects that will deliver tools for future efficient global immunization efforts (Figure 2).

The imbalance of forces, or the lack of 1 or some of them, impairs the formation of an efficient research and development pipeline. The malaria vaccine research and product development is a case in point, because, during the past 3 decades, effective push forces (substantial investment by academic institutions into upstream research, availability of the complete sequence of the *P. falciparum* genome, etc.) were insufficient for establishing a credible product pipeline. The recent creation of 2 initiatives dedicated to malaria vaccine research and development—the European Malaria Vaccine Initiative and the United States' Malaria Vaccine Initiative—has provided an additional element in the form of a management and funding push. The previously modest pull forces also have been reinforced. The Malaria Research and Development Alliance intends to increase the level of advocacy for malaria interventions, and USAID and the Malaria Vaccine Initiative have conducted a study in Africa that assessed the future market for a malaria vaccine. It is hoped that

a clearer definition of the demand (market pull) for such products will stimulate industry investment in this area and accelerate discussions within ministries of health about strategies for introducing this prevention tool (health priority pull).

Finally, the malaria vaccine research and product development community has recently completed a technology road mapping exercise, which the industry is using to define new pathways for innovation and increased efficiency. The goal of technology road mapping is to accelerate and improve the development of promising malaria vaccines by providing a cohesive framework for defining critical needs, focusing technology investments, producing a blueprint to align and guide activities within the global malaria community, catalyzing new investment, and directing donor funds to the highest-priority needs. In addition to these promising malaria vaccine efforts, several recent investments in dedicated research and development funding, technologies, and management—in the form of nonprofit enterprises[10–12]—also bring hope for a breakthrough in other vaccine research and development, including HIV and tuberculosis.

All these driving forces are instrumental in ensuring that enough potential vaccines are moved through the research and product development process and that 1 or more effective products will eventually be licensed and introduced into immunization programs. In this manner, the concept of a global vaccine research and product development portfolio pipeline emerges by combining all the individual efforts and initiatives for researching and developing vaccines that target infectious diseases.

A GLOBAL VACCINE RESEARCH AND DEVELOPMENT PIPELINE ALREADY EXISTS

The various vaccine research and product development stages include discovery, preclinical research, clinical and regulatory research, and postlicensing research. Because of this

TABLE 1— Global Vaccine Research Development Pipeline

Disease or *Pathogen*	Major Partners Promoting Vaccine Development Against Diseases of Developing World	Most Advanced Candidate Stage			Research for Introduction
		Discovery	Clinical	Postregistration	
HIV	ANRS, IAVI, MRC, NIH, private sector		X		X
Malaria	EMVI, EU, MVI, NIH, USAID, private sector		X		X
Tuberculosis	Aeras, EU, NIH, private sector		X		X
Influenza (broad spectrum)	EU, NIH, private sector	X			
Pneumococcus	EU, Johns Hopkins pneumoADIP, MRC, NIH, PATH, USAID, private sector			X	X
Cholera	IVI, NIH, private sector			X	X
Enterotoxigenic *Escherichia coli*	CVD, private sector		X		
Rotavirus	CDC, PATH rotaADIP, USAID			X	X
Shigellosis	CVD, IVI, NIH, WRAIR, private sector		X		
Typhoid	IVI, NIH, private sector			X	
Caliciviruses	CDC, CVD		X		
Dengue	PDVI, WRAIR, private sector		X		X
Japanese encephalitis	PATH, private sector			X	X
Hookworm	Public sector		X		
Leishmaniasis	IDRI, public sector		X		
Schistosomiasis	EU, NIH, USAID		X		
Buruli ulcer	GBUI		X		
Neisseria meningitides A,C,W135,Y	MVP, private sector			X	X
Streptococcus A	NHMRC, NIH, private sector		X		
Streptococcus B	NIH, private sector		X		
Trachoma	Private sector		X		
Herpes simplex virus 2	NIH, private sector		X		
Human papilloma virus	IARC, NIH, PATH, private sector			X	X
Measles (aerosol)	ARC,CDC, WHO, private sector		X		

Note. ADIP = accelerated development and introduction plan; Aeras = Aeras Global Tuberculosis Vaccine Foundation; ANRS = Agence Nationale de Recherches sur le Sida (France); ARC = Amercian Red Cross; CDC = Centers for Disease Control and Prevention (USA); CVD = Center for Vaccine Development (USA); EMVI = European Malaria Vaccine Initiative; ETEC = *Enterotoxigenic Escherichia coli;* EU = European Union (funded projects), Hib = *Haemophilus influenzae* type b; HIV = human immunodeficiency virus; HPV = human papillomavirus; HSV = herpes simplex virus; GBUI = Global Buruli Ulcer Initiative; IAVI = International AIDS Vaccine Initiative; IDRI = Infectious Disease Research Institute; IVI = International Vaccine Institute; MRC = Medical Research Council (England); MVI = Malaria Vaccine Initiative at PATH; MVP = Meningitis Vaccine Project; NHMRC = National Health and Medical Research Council; NIH = National Institutes of Health (USA); PATH = Program for Appropriate Technology in Health; PDVI = Paediatric Dengue Vaccine Initiative; USAID = United States Agency for International Development; WHO = World Health Organization; WRAIR = Walter Reed Army Institute of Research. Although this review focuses on international and national entities supporting global vaccine research initiatives, it is of note that the private sector and developing country institutions also greatly contribute to the global pipeline.

process, work on future access to vaccines should be undertaken early for all infectious diseases in developing countries. To increase both the efficiency and the probability of successful outcomes for individual vaccine-related initiatives, the work of all partners should be viewed as the component elements of a concerted global effort. The integrity of the individual entities will be respected, and an informally integrated and common global pipeline can emerge (Table 1).

Vaccine research and product development is a high-risk undertaking. From a statistical view, the global product pipeline requires many early-stage development projects to generate 1 successful product; the probability of a pre-clinical vaccine reaching the market has been estimated at 0.22, i.e., about 5 to 1 odds against success. As a result, to register a single vaccine, there needs to be 4 to 5 independent potential vaccines under development.[5] The uncertainty of research outcomes makes establishing and maintaining such a pipeline a necessity. To ensure the likelihood that a vaccine will actually emerge on the market, the pipeline must be composed of a research and product development portfolio of different potential vaccines in different stages of development for each of the targeted diseases and postregistration activities that will ensure future accelerated introduction and access of vaccines.

Certain gaps can be identified in the current global vaccine pipeline. For example, there is only 1 potential recombinant vaccine for leishmaniasis (supported by the Infectious Disease Research Institute) that has entered clinical trials in the United States and Latin America. In the case of malaria, many potential vaccines concentrate on the same parasite proteins, which potentially repeats similar trial results while neglecting novel target opportunities. For bacterial pneumonia, the current vaccines do not cover all of the disease serotypes required in developing countries, and new vaccines would need substantial investment to reach the market. For human papillomavirus and cervical cancer, the

issue of vaccine accessibility among adolescent girls in poor countries has not been adequately addressed, and vaccines have been licensed in 2006 without sufficient data for an effective introduction in developing countries.

The importance of carrying out research in a true partnership with developing countries should not be underemphasized. To ensure the global pipeline operates efficiently and delivers optimal vaccines to poor countries, all of the partners must coordinate their efforts to strengthen research, product development, regulatory evaluation, ethical evaluation, and post-marketing surveillance. Moreover, the participation of developing countries in setting research priorities and defining the most appropriate target product characteristics for new vaccines is essential for the future success of vaccine development and implementation.

Even when efficient vaccines are developed and introduced, research and product development cannot then cease. Implementation research, post-marketing surveillance, and additional clinical studies that enable optimal evaluation in the target population and of the impact of immunization are all necessary and vital components of successful vaccine introduction and deployment. Collectively, these postapproval activities ensure the maximization of a vaccine's life-saving impact. Similar to the life-cycle management approaches that are applied to commercial vaccines, innovation and research that is focused on providing both better vaccines and enhanced vaccine delivery systems and improving the manufacturing process to continually reduce vaccine unit cost to the end-user also should continue. In short, the existence of an "ever-green" (always updated) vaccine pipeline that constantly delivers new or improved products to the market is critical.

CONCLUSIONS

Despite positive trends, the current level of investment in building sustainable research and product development driving forces has not yet reached a sufficient level. The appar-

ently complex global pipeline does not cover all essential aspects of the vaccine development continuum. There are many gaps in this continuum that prevent successful delivery of some essential vaccines. Additionally, the participation of developing countries' research and disease-control entities during the process is often underweighted.

To meet the challenges of the United Nations' Millennium Development Goals, a new coordinated vaccine research and product development paradigm needs to be built through the active participation of all stakeholders. In addition to this convergence of efforts and increased coordination, developing countries should play a central role in identifying and communicating the specific vaccine products they need. WHO will be a critical player in ensuring that all occur.

About the Authors

Irina Serdobova is with Axensus, Ltd, consultants, Cheltenham, Gloucestershire. Marie-Paule Kieny is with the Initiative for Vaccine Research, World Health Organization, Geneva, Switzerland.

Correspondence: Requests for reprints should be sent to Marie-Paule Kieny, PhD, Initiative for Vaccine Research, World Health Organization, Ave Appia 20, CH1211-Geneva 27, Switzerland (e-mail: kienym@who.int).

Note. The views expressed in this article are those of the authors and do not necessarily represent the policy of the World Health Organization.

References

1. World Health Report 2004, World Health Organization, Geneva, Switzerland. Available at: http://www.who.int/whr/2004/en/. Accessed July 1, 2005.
2. World Health Report 2005, Annex Table 3, World Health Organization, Geneva, Switzerland. Available at: http://www.who.int/whr/2005/en/. Accessed July 1, 2005.
3. Global Immunization Vision and Strategy 2005, World Health Organization, Geneva, Switzerland. Available at: http://www.who.int/gb/ebwha/pdf_files/WHA58/A58_12

-en.pdf and http://www.who.int/ gb/ebwha/pdf_files/WHA58/A58_12 Add1-en.pdf. Accessed July 1, 2005.

4. Initiative on Public-Private Partnerships for Health (IPPPH). Available at: http://www.ippph.org/. Accessed July 1, 2005.

5. Struck MM. Vaccine research and product development success rates and development times. *Nat Biotechnol.* 1996;14:591–593.

6. Andre FE. How the research-based industry approaches vaccine development and establishes priorities. *Dev Biol (Basel).* 2002;110:25–29.

7. Davey S, ed. *The 10/90 Report on Health Research 2001–2002.* Arusha, Tanzania: Global Forum for Health Research; 2002.

8. *Lessons Learned: New Procurement Strategies for Vaccines. Final Report to the GAVI Board.* Mercer Management Consulting; 2002. Available at: http://www.vaccinealliance.org/resour ces/lessons_learned_draft_final.pdf. Accessed July 1, 2005.

9. Levine R, Kremer M, Albright A. Making markets for vaccines. Ideas to action. Available at: http://www.cgdev.org/doc/books/vac-

cine/MakingMarkets-complete.pdf. Accessed August 4, 2006.

10. International AIDS Vaccine Initiative. Available at: http://www.iavi.org/. Accessed July 1, 2005.

11. Klausner RD, Fauci AS, Corey L, et al. The need for a global HIV vaccine enterprise. *Science.* 2003;300:2036–2039.

12. Aeras Global TB Vaccine Foundation. Available at: http://www.aeras.org/. Accessed July 1, 2005.

The Global Alliance for Vaccines and Immunization: Is It a New Model for Effective Public–Private Cooperation in International Public Health?

| *William Muraskin, PhD*

ABSTRACT

The Global Alliance for Vaccines and Immunization (GAVI) has in many ways been remarkably successful in revitalizing the international coalition of institutions and organizations concerned with getting vaccines to the children of the poorest countries. Many have seen this high-profile venture in public–private cooperation as a model for other groups concerned with more effectively helping to solve health problems in the developing world. We examined major flaws in the GAVI and argue that in fact the alliance does not represent a new paradigm for international public health. However, the experience of the GAVI may suggest an alternative, and more effective, way to conceptualize future global initiatives.

INTRODUCTION

At the end of 1999, an alliance of international health agencies, private industry, bilateral donors, philanthropic foundations, and other parties concerned with the health of children in the poorest nations was formed to both finance and speed the delivery of new and improved vaccines to children in the developing world. The coalition was called the Global Alliance for Vaccines and Immunization (GAVI)—and it was backed up by a heavily endowed entity called the Vaccine Fund (for a more intensive treatment of this subject, see Muraskin[1]).

Despite its laudable efforts to pioneer a new and more effective model of international cooperation, the GAVI is handicapped by 2 fundamental flaws and thus runs a high risk of ultimate failure, with the danger of hurting other efforts as well (such as alliances like the Global Fund for AIDS, Malaria and Tuberculosis, which has considered the GAVI a model for dealing with developing countries' problems). First, the GAVI, as currently constituted, has failed to achieve a balance between "top-down" and "bottom-up" in its relations with countries, a fact that continues to plague and undermine the initiative. A second and closely related flaw is that the international public health community has still not been able to reach a genuine consensus on the exact role that immunization should play in protecting the health of children in developing countries.

Top-down globalism plays a necessary and powerful role in initially moving the public health community forward, but it cannot succeed in the long run without genuine bottom-up input and support. Unfortunately, global initiatives are handicapped in generating support, because conflict so frequently arises between the priorities of the founders of global initiatives and those of the countries the initiatives purport to assist. In the absence of genuine grassroots espousal, pressure is placed on global organizers to seduce participants and manipulate enthusiasm rather than actually develop it.

Although the creation and commencement of innovative programs simultaneously in many countries appears to make organization at the global level indispensable, such high-level initiation often lacks, and in fact undermines, local support. Can we solve this problem? The answer is yes, but the solution requires a radically different conceptualization of the proper role of individuals and groups working at the global level. It requires a greater degree of humility than now exists and a radically changed sense of what constitutes "service" to developing countries. Those aspiring to exert global "leadership" will need to see themselves more as facilitators than as movers and shakers. This change in perspective will require more effort than the lip service currently paid to the bottom-up approach; such a transformation will require finding a way to generate real bottom-up initiation.

Supporters of this new approach do not deny that global initiatives have a vital role to play. Getting truly bottom-up initiatives organized and running will be difficult, and top-down assistance will be required. However, the legitimate global role of top-down initiatives requires a markedly greater level of restraint and a genuine willingness to subordinate global initiatives to the priorities of the people they are intended to help than is currently apparent. We can see this need very clearly in the case of the GAVI.

The GAVI was the creation of deeply committed and morally energized people working at the top level of the international health community. Such dedicated individuals were especially important at the Bill and Melinda Gates Children's Vaccine Program; the Program for Appropriate Technology in Health (PATH), which housed it; the International Federation of

Pharmaceutical Manufacturers Association; the World Bank; the Gates Foundation; US Agency for International Development headquarters in Washington, DC; World Health Organization (WHO) headquarters in Geneva, Switzerland; UNICEF headquarters in New York, NY; and the Rocke-feller Foundation. People in these organizations were global players, with both the strengths and the weaknesses that accompany that position. Although they benefited from seeing the big picture, they were too often severely handicapped by their lack of familiarity with the details on the ground. Not only were in-country field workers from UN agencies, bilateral donors, nongovernmental organizations, and indigenous governments not part of the core group advocating the creation of the GAVI, these workers were to a remarkable extent not consulted by those who created the GAVI. Part of this lack of participation was structurally caused—that is, high-level globalists communicate primarily with their peers rather than with those working at other levels of the system. However, part of the problem was a conscious choice: people focused on the big picture do not want to be bogged down and nitpicked to death by localists who raise a barrage of "parochial" and country-specific objections. Global activists are by nature interested in hearing what can be done, not in hearing about the myriad obstacles to rapid and effective action.

A strong case can be made for employing a bird's-eye view of the world, and Tore Godal, the executive secretary of the GAVI, has made this case. Workers close to developing countries "see the differences and not the commonalities," he says, but without some "simple global principles," one is forced into bilateral negotiations, which consume time, severely slow down the process, and are so country-specific that it is hard to generate usable lessons (interview by the author, December 2000). As a result, a globalist approach is the only way to speed things up. In a world that is increasingly globalized, the legitimacy of this global perspective must be taken into account.

THE LOCAL VS THE GLOBAL

However, workers with long familiarity with conditions in the field are painfully aware of the problems facing any large-scale and ambitious new venture originating on the international level. They have had a great deal of experience with global interventions, not only in trying to actually implement them but also in dealing with the aftermath when donors have moved on to newer, hotter issues. In her classic study of Nepal, *Politics, Plans, and People: Foreign Aid and Health Development*,[2] Judith Justice of the University of California, San Francisco, has documented the constant changes in global priorities—the flavor-of-the-month—club types of interventions—that have been forced on developing countries over time. She has highlighted the disarray, wasted effort, skewed priorities, and disillusionment that have followed in their wake. Field workers are well aware of that sorry legacy of global activism and are anxious not to relive it. They are forced to know intimately—in a way that global leaders simply cannot, or will not, understand—the limitations of local government, infrastructure, finance, and human resources that plague the developing world and what they mean in practice.

In the case of the GAVI, one of its initial flaws was that its vision came from leaders who were inadequately informed regarding field workers' opinions about what could realistically be accomplished within a relatively short space of time—the imbalance of "top-down" and "bottom-up" referred to in the introduction.

Bjorn Melgaard, who was head of the WHO's Expanded Programme on Immunization, and subsequently of its entire combined vaccine division, has expressed his sympathy with the anxieties of in-country workers confronted with new global initiatives (interview by the author, December 2002):

> My major criticism . . . of the [Vaccine] Fund, the GAVI and the Global Fund [for AIDS, Malaria and Tuberculosis] . . .

[is that they] operate . . . as new donors on the block and require new formats for planning, implementation, monitoring, reporting, etc. [This] imposes a tremendous burden on countries. . . . New alliances demand their own new systems, and [such demands] undermine the implementation capacity of the Ministries of Health.

What one hears over and over again from those working in-country, whether with the WHO, UNICEF, the nongovernmental organizations, the bilateral donors, or others, is that at the provincial (and often the national) level only a handful of skilled people manage to "do everything." The pool is small, and global initiatives keep placing the burden of ever-shifting priorities onto the shoulders of the same small group of people. This limitation of human capacity makes it difficult to take on even generously funded programs. Godlee, in a 1994 critique of the WHO in BMJ,[3] highlighted the importance of the problem—and her words apply even better to the impact of global initiatives in general than to that of one organization:

> It may seem harsh to suggest that WHO's impact on countries may be not just minimal but negative. Such a suggestion is, however, widely acknowledged. The phrase is "donor robbery." By this, people mean that WHO—and other international agencies—rob countries of precious expertise. Skilled and effective professionals are in short supply in some areas and are therefore snapped up by the international organizations.[3]

Just as field-savvy expatriate agency workers in developing nations were not part of the global groups creating the GAVI, neither were governments in the developing world participants in the process. The GAVI was designed for the countries' good but not *by* the countries. It is vital to realize that the demand for this initiative did not emanate from the designated beneficiaries. Rather, the countries as a group have had to be wooed, "educated," and financially enticed to accept the GAVI's goals as their own.

A good example of such seduction can be found in Uganda. In an unpublished report to USAID on immunization written in 1999, right at the time that the GAVI was being formed, Justice states the following:

"Although the National Immunization Program had earlier been given the highest priority in Uganda, current priorities were stated to be malaria among the infectious diseases, followed by respiratory conditions and pneumonia, malnutrition and kwashiorkor, and diseases related to water and sanitation such as severe diarrhea. . . . Hepatitis B [which would be the first GAVI-supported vaccine] does not have a champion, no one who is passionate about it or interested enough to commit time and energy to its promotion and, therefore, it is most unlikely to be placed on the health agenda in the near future. . . ."[4]

Nevertheless, within an astonishingly short period of time after new money for hepatitis B vaccine became available, Uganda had applied for, and received, hepatitis B vaccine funds.

A GAVI BLIND SPOT

The full implications of this situation have been very difficult for the most committed GAVI supporters to assimilate fully. Many of these supporters insist that the mission of the GAVI is simply to carry out aims that the countries themselves have voted for on numerous occasions in the World Health Assembly and elsewhere. For example, the World Health Assembly, with the support of all of its member countries (99% of the countries in the world), voted for making hepatitis B a universal childhood vaccine. Developing countries have supported the concept of 80% diphtheria, pertussis, tetanus vaccine coverage in 80% of all country districts, with a specific date agreed on by everyone. Both targets and dates are core GAVI goals. Nevertheless, such broad statements of goals, or even narrowly set timetables, often have little connection to what developing countries' governments can muster the desire or political will to stand behind.

Many scientists who support the GAVI have explained the obvious reluctance of many countries to actually champion immunization goals as their own by arguing that if the leaders "really understood" the importance of those objectives, they would change their minds and support them—all they need is to be given "the facts." This may be true, but the need for such "education" is the key point—the countries remain pupils who need to be helped to see the light and change their actual—as opposed to rhetorical—priorities.

VACCINATION ABOVE ALL ELSE

This brings us to the second major flaw of the GAVI: the nonnegotiable status of immunization as the initiative's core goal. Most in-country workers and most developing countries' governments—even their ministries of health—would not place a series of new children's vaccines at the top of their priorities without a major financial enticement. For everyone familiar with conditions in the field, child immunization is only one of a backbreaking press of challenges, and the introduction of new and improved children's vaccines has by no means been the most urgent.

The GAVI champions immunization, and yet its core constituencies—field workers and developing countries' governments—have been unenthusiastic supporters of that goal. And when it comes to questioning the centrality of vaccination, they are joined by a third group, the European bilateral donors. Although bilateral donors have been among the nations most committed to the struggle for equity for all children of the developing world, they have entertained very strong doubts about whether vaccination is the best means of achieving that goal. That very same reservation alienated the bilateral donors from a previous vaccine alliance, the Children's Vaccine Initiative,[4] and made them its chief critic.

THE BILATERAL DONOR POSITION

The bilateral donor position was clearly presented by Jorn Heldrup of Dandida, the Danish foreign aid agency, who was present at the GAVI board meeting in November 2002. As he put it in an interview in November 2002:

There are good things to support about the GAVI. . . . The problem is [that] it . . . may undermine the health in developing countries. In Tanzania, for example, there are 10—only 10 people—in the whole country who can deal with the various international initiatives that are thrown at the country. They must deal with them all . . . [and the] GAVI is only one of them. They are pulled one way, then another. What should be important is the countries' own priorities and their looking at all the possibilities [available to them] and [then their] choosing priorities with the limited resources that they have. But that is not possible when these initiatives come down [from on high].

And so Dandida and the other European bilateral donors have pushed for a method that would avoid undermining local decisionmaking. The bedrock on which bilateral donors stand is the "systems approach" to health development, which emphasizes allowing countries to set their own priorities. From that perspective, the donors have been concerned with the entire health system and careful not to overemphasize one type of intervention (such immunization) at the expense of others. They have also strongly emphasized the vital importance of developing countries' governments setting their own priorities—not simply within the health sector, but also in the trade-offs between health, housing, education, industrial development, and so forth. The commitment of bilateral donors to this approach is at odds with the basic assumptions of the globalists who created the GAVI.

CAN BOTH APPROACHES WORK?

Many people of goodwill have tried to bridge the gap between those who support a systems approach and those who champion a vaccine-centric focus. Unfortunately, an inherent contradiction between the worldviews of the 2 groups cannot be reconciled, at least at this time.

The heart of the problem is that creators and core supporters of the GAVI have never believed that immunization is just one among many contending programs that should "freely compete" with one another for commitments from developing countries. The GAVI's assertion that vaccines are extremely cost-effective and could easily outdo other interventions in any competition for funds is an attractive rhetorical claim that nevertheless has not been tested. Although the creators of the GAVI have perfunctorily recognized the desirability of countries' setting their own priorities, the supporters of the systems approach have seen local decisionmaking as a paramount value. Saving lives through immunization, not having countries set their own priorities, has always been the GAVI's supreme goal.

For the small and dedicated cadre that enables the GAVI to function, and that constitutes its indispensable human infrastructure, the primacy of immunization is *nonnegotiable*. Immunization is the rock upon which the GAVI and its Vaccine Fund are built. Such is absolutely not the case for the individuals and groups that support the systems approach.

THE PROBLEM WITH INVERTED PYRAMIDS

Ultimately the GAVI is a partnership of organizations, countries, and individuals, almost all of whom have substantial reservations about its goals. Its core base of support is located in the Bill and Melinda Gates Children's Vaccine Program (the name of the project has been changed to the Children's Vaccine Program at PATH), the Vaccine Fund, the Gates Foundation, the key GAVI infrastructural units (the secretariat, working group, and task force on finance), and scattered individuals in the international agencies and developing countries. These people have been the driving force of the GAVI and the cadre that has energized it and made it a dynamic and pioneering initiative. Yet the majority of the GAVI's partners have remained only lukewarm adherents. Most countries that partner with the GAVI have been supporters primarily because of the substantial new money available for the initiative—starting with the $750 million from the Gates Foundation. Although bilateral donors have cooperated to varying degrees, as a group they have shown no desire to pledge themselves to pick up the long-term costs of the new vaccines, without which the short-term benefits of the GAVI's Vaccine Fund money are not sustainable. The field workers remain skeptics, and the WHO and UNICEF continue to be distracted with a host of other pressing priorities and remain keenly aware that their own institutional self-interests often differ significantly from that of the GAVI.

The bottom line is that the GAVI is a giant inverted pyramid that rests on the backs of a very small committed base. For its core supporters, the GAVI is a mission, a cause, and a grand experiment. For everyone else, however, it is merely one of numerous initiatives—many of them more urgent. As a consequence, it is dubious that the GAVI represents a model of private–public effective action and that it can serve as a useful guide for other high-level initiatives.

TO MAKE THE GAVI SUSTAINABLE

The GAVI on the surface looks healthy and strong. It continues to move ahead at a breakneck pace with continuous milestones reached and goals achieved. But under the surface, the GAVI suffers from fundamental flaws, some of which pose a potentially fatal threat both to the GAVI and to its long-term goals. What, if anything, can be done?

An indispensable part of any solution would involve openly and purposefully turning the existing inverted pyramid of the GAVI on its head so that the supporters of a systems approach to health development—who constitute a large majority of the international public health community—become core supporters of the GAVI. This cannot happen as long as the GAVI overly privileges immunization in fact as well as in name.

The quite laudable goal of introducing new and improved vaccines would not have to be totally abandoned, but it would have to be integrated with, and subordinated to, broader systems objectives. Where an irresolvable conflict arises, the timetable for vaccine introduction would have to be determined by its effect on the overall mission of strengthening the entire health system. The continued active engagement of vaccine-centric groups and individuals within the GAVI, despite their inability to dominate it, would guarantee that the importance of immunization was never lost from sight—a danger of the systems approach.

A reformulation of the goals of the GAVI to emphasize building strong foundations that will support lasting achievements can be the start of a painful but necessary way out of the dilemma. Donors (governments, philanthropies, and the general public that supports them both) must face up to the fact that short-term gains, no matter how much they lend themselves to public relations sound bites or fit neatly into donor funding cycles, do not achieve their stated humanitarian objectives. It is time to try another approach.

About the Authors

William Muraskin is with the Department of Urban Studies, Queens College, City University of New York, Flushing, NY.

Correspondence: Requests for

reprints should be sent to William Muraskin, PhD, Professor of Urban Studies, Department of Urban Studies, Queens College, City University of New York, Kissena Blvd, Flushing, NY 11367 (e-mail: muraskin@yahoo.com).

Acknowledgments

The author was supported by a 4-year grant (2000 HE 024) from the Rocke-feller Foundation to study the origins and development of the Bill and Melinda Gates Children's Vaccine Program and the Global Alliance for Vaccines and Immunization.

I thank the Rockefeller Foundation for support of this project.

References

1. Muraskin W. Revolution in International Public Health? The Origins and Development of the Bill and Melinda Gates Children's Vaccine Program (CVP) and the Global Alliance for Vaccines and Immunization (GAVI). Rochester, NY: University of Rochester. In press.
2. Justice J. Politics, *Plans, and People: Foreign Aid and Health Development.* Berkeley, Calif: University of California Press; 1986.
3. Godlee F. The World Health Organization: WHO at country level—a little impact, no strategy. *BMJ.* 1994;309:1636–1639.
4. Justice J. Study of Factors Influencing the Introduction of New and Underutilized Vaccines Into Uganda; 1999. Report to Children's Vaccine Initiative/ USAID.
5. Muraskin W. *The Politics of International Health: The Children's Vaccine Initiative and the Struggle to Develop Vaccines for the Developing World.* Albany, NY: State University of New York Press; 1998.

A Global Perspective on Vaccine Safety and Public Health: The Global Advisory Committee on Vaccine Safety

| Peter I. Folb, MD, FRCP, Ewa Bernatowska, MD, PhD, Robert Chen, MD, MA, John Clemens, MD, Alex N. O. Dodoo, PhD, MSc, MPSGH, MRPharmS, BPharm, Susan S. Ellenberg, PhD, C. Patrick Farrington, PhD, T. Jacob John, PhD, DCH, MBBS, MRCP, Paul-Henri Lambert, MD, Noni E. MacDonald, MD, MSc, BSc, Elizabeth Miller, FRCPath, MB, David Salisbury, CB, FRCP, FFPHM, Heinz-J. Schmitt, MD, Claire-Anne Siegrist, MD and Omala Wimalaratne, MD, MBBS

ABSTRACT

Established in 1999, the Global Advisory Committee on Vaccine Safety advises the World Health Organization (WHO) on vaccine-related safety issues and enables WHO to respond promptly, efficiently, and with scientific rigor to issues of vaccine safety with potential global importance. The committee also assesses the implications of vaccine safety for practice worldwide and for WHO policies. We describe the principles on which the committee was established, its modus operandi, and the scope of the work undertaken, both present and future. We highlight its recent recommendations on major issues, including the purported link between the measles–mumps–rubella vaccine and autism and the safety of the mumps, influenza, yellow fever, BCG, and smallpox vaccines as well as that of thiomersal-containing vaccines.

INTRODUCTION

The successful implementation of large-scale comprehensive national immunization programs and the consequent eradication or reduction of smallpox, polio, measles, pertussis, meningococcal meningitis, diphtheria, hepatitis B, congenital rubella syndrome, and tetanus were among the most notable public health achievements of the 20th century. Even in countries where resources for national health programs are severely limited, it has been possible to achieve significant progress.[1] There is good reason to expect that these advances will be sustained in the 21st century. It has been suggested that there are 4 elements of successful public health efforts: highly credible scientific evidence, passionate advocates, media campaigns, and law and regulation, usually at the national level[2] (to which might be added adequate resources and political will).

It is thus paradoxical that, as vaccines have become increasingly more effective, safe, and of good quality, public concerns about their safety have increased, especially in the developed world.[3] In recent years, the World Health Organization (WHO) has taken steps to meet these modern challenges to vaccination, including the establishment, in 1999, of the Global Advisory Committee on Vaccine Safety (GACVS). The GACVS provides advice to the WHO on all vaccine-related safety issues, enabling the organization to respond promptly, efficiently, and with scientific rigor to safety issues of potential global importance.[4] The committee also assesses the implications of vaccine safety issues for practice worldwide and for WHO policies. In doing so, the GACVS often draws on the advice, experience, and analysis of outside experts.

We report on the principles upon which the GACVS was established, the modus operandi of the committee, and the scope, rather than the details, of the work undertaken by the committee over the past 4 years. We also consider future challenges facing the committee.

THE GACVS: TERMS OF REFERENCE

Several specifications and guidelines led the establishment of the GACVS. First, the committee should be able to consider and make recommendations regarding all aspects of vaccine safety that might be of interest and importance to member states and to the WHO and that are of sufficient importance to affect WHO or national policies. The decisions of the committee should be free of vested interests, including the interests of the WHO itself or of other organizations involved in achieving the goals of universal immunization coverage and national programs for immunization.

Second, committee members should collectively bring the expertise necessary for evaluation and decision-making in the field of vaccine safety, including familiarity with the drug regulatory process, with special reference to the needs of the developing world. The committee should be free to make decisions and recommendations not necessarily in line with the special interests of the institutions at which the committee members work, in accordance with the high standards set by the WHO in terms of absence of conflicts of interest among members of the organization's various committees. Third, all decisions and recommendations of the committee should be based on the best available scientific evidence and expertise and should be authoritative, defensible, and explicable in terms of fact, scientific evidence, and process.

CAUSALITY ASSESSMENT OF ADVERSE POSTIMMUNIZATION EVENTS

One of the first responsibilities of GACVS was to determine a set of criteria according to which the causes of adverse postimmunization events could be judged. Building on the work of the United States surgeon general and his team from 1964, the committee decided that the following generally established criteria are most relevant in determining causality in assessments of vaccine-related events.[5,6]

- *Consistency*: The association of a purported adverse event with the administration of a vaccine should be consistent; that is, the findings should be replicable in different localities, by different investigators not unduly influencing one another, and by different methods of investigation, all leading to the same conclusion(s).
- *Strength of the association*: The association should be strong in terms of magnitude (in an epidemiological sense) and the dose–response relationship of the vaccine with the adverse effect.
- *Specificity*: The association should be distinctive; that is, the adverse event should be linked uniquely or specifically with the vaccine concerned rather than occurring frequently, spontaneously, or commonly in association with other external stimuli or conditions.
- *Temporal relation*: There should be a temporal relationship between the vaccine and the adverse event, in that receipt of the vaccine should precede the earliest manifestation of the event.
- *Biological plausibility*: The association should be coherent, that is, plausible and explicable according to known facts in the natural history and biology of the disease.

Not all of these criteria need be present for a causal relationship to be determined, and neither does each carry equal weight. In addition to these principles, there are a number of conditions and provisos that should be applied in evaluating causality in the field of vaccine safety. First, the requirement for biological plausibility should not unduly influence consideration of causality. Biological plausibility is a less robust criterion than the others. If an adverse event does not fit with known facts and the previous understanding of the adverse event or the vaccine under consideration, it does not necessarily follow that new or hitherto unexpected events are improbable.

Second, there must be consideration of whether the vaccine is serving as a trigger. A *trigger* in this context is an agent that causes an event to occur earlier that would have occurred some time later anyway. When acting as a trigger, the vaccine could hypothetically expose an underlying or preexisting condition or illness. Finally, with live attenuated vaccines, the adverse event may be attributable to the pathogenicity of the attenuated vaccine–related microorganism and not distinguishable (except in severity) from the disease for which the vaccine is administered. Identification of the vaccine strain of the microorganism or its genetic material in diseased tissue or the patient's body fluids in such a situation would add weight to causality.

An association between vaccine administration and an adverse event is most likely to be considered *strong and consistent* when the evidence is based on the following:

- Well-conducted human studies that demonstrate a clear association with a design testing a priori the hypothesis of such an association. Such studies will normally be randomized controlled clinical trials, case–control investigations, or cohort studies. Case reports, however numerous and complete, do not fulfill the requirements for testing hypotheses.
- Associations demonstrated in more than one human study and showing consistency between studies conducted by different investigators in different settings, with results that are consistent despite different research designs. An association between dose and adverse effect strengthens the causal association between the vaccine and the effect. This is not necessarily the case if there is a hypersensitivity effect.
- Similarity of the adverse event to the disease the live vaccine is intended to prevent, with a nonrandom temporal relationship between administration and the adverse incident.

There should ideally be a strict definition of the adverse event in clinical, pathological, and biochemical terms. The frequency of the adverse event should be substantially lower in the nonimmunized population than in the immunized population in which the event is described, and there should not be obvious alternative reasons for its occurrence that are unrelated to immunization.

SCOPE OF THE WORK CONSIDERED BY THE GACVS

The committee has reviewed the following safety issues: macrophagic myofasciitis and aluminum-containing vaccines, the health effects of thiomersal-containing vaccines, autoimmune diseases and vaccines, potential contamination of vaccines with transmissible spongiform encephalopathy, adverse events following mumps vaccination, mortality following routine infant immunizations, the safety of yellow fever vaccine, risks following immunization in HIV-infected children, the safety of BCG vaccine in immunocompromised individuals, the measles–mumps–rubella (MMR) vaccine and autism, the safety of MMR versus rubella vaccine in the postpartum period, multiple sclerosis and hepatitis B vaccination, acute lymphatic leukemia and hepatitis B vaccination, oculorespiratory syndrome following influenza vaccination, Bell's palsy following vaccination with an inactivated intranasal flu vaccine licensed in Switzerland, influenza vaccination of women during pregnancy, the safety of smallpox vaccines, the safety of polio vaccination in the context of eradication, and enhancement of electronic communications of vaccine safety issues and establishment of a Web site reference.

Outcomes of the deliberations of the committee on these and other issues are reported routinely in the *Weekly Epidemiological Record*, and relevant information can be found at http://www.who.int/vaccine_safety/en. What follows has been selected as illustrative of the work of the committee, in terms of both its proactive approach and its reactive response to reports and concerns brought to it.

NONSPECIFIC EFFECTS OF VACCINES

The GACVS has given considerable attention to the purported nonspecific adverse effects of the diphtheria–tetanus–pertussis (DTP) vaccine on infants aged 18 months or younger in low-income countries.[7–9] It has also been suggested by Kristensen et al. that BCG has an overall non-specific beneficial effect and that measles vaccine is associated with reduced mortality and morbidity that cannot be explained by prevention of measles alone.[7] The GACVS believes that this set of theories raises critical issues pertaining to the safety of vaccines and immunization practices and that there is a need for further systematic research in the area of vaccine safety. For the time being, the GACVS has found that the reported results and conclusions are not without potential bias and that the results have not been confirmed by others in different settings.

MMR AND AUTISM

There is ongoing debate as to whether autism has a genetic or environmental cause (including the possibility of a prenatal insult), or both. Autistic spectrum disorders represent a continuum of cognitive and neurobehavioral disorders, including autistic disorder or autism. Prevalence rates of autism vary considerably according to intensity of case ascertainment, ranging from 0.7 to 21.1 per 10 000 children (median: 5.2 per 10 000).

Concerns about a possible link between vaccination with MMR and autism were raised in the late 1990s, after the publication of a series of studies claiming an association

between both natural and vaccine strains of the measles virus and inflammatory bowel diseases and autism. The authors of more recent studies have also claimed findings supporting such an association. Since public concerns have remained high, in 2002 WHO, on the recommendation of the GACVS, commissioned a review of the risk of autism associated with MMR vaccination. The findings of the review, conducted by an independent researcher, were presented to the GACVS for its consideration. Eleven epidemiological studies were reviewed in detail, taking into consideration study design and limitations.[10–20] Three laboratory studies were also reviewed.[21–23] The conclusion of the review was that existing studies do not show evidence of an association between the risk of autism or autistic spectrum disorders and the MMR vaccine.

On the basis of the results of this review, the GACVS agreed and concluded that there is no evidence for a causal association between MMR vaccine and autism or autistic spectrum disorders. It is the opinion of the committee that additional epidemiological studies are unlikely to add to the existing data but that there is a need for a better understanding of the causes of autism. The committee also concluded that there is no evidence to support the preferred use of monovalent MMR vaccines over the combined vaccine. On the grounds that administration of the single vaccines at intervals carries a higher risk of incomplete immunization and longer periods during which children are unprotected from these diseases, the GACVS did not recommend a change in current MMR vaccination practices.

SAFETY OF MUMPS VACCINES

In 2003, the committee commissioned a comprehensive review of the literature on the safety of mumps vaccination, with special attention to vaccine-derived mumps meningitis. High rates of aseptic meningitis have been described for the Urabe, Leningrad–Zagreb, and Leningrad-3

vaccines relative to the Jeryl–Lynn vaccine. There is no known viral explanation for this difference based on virus genotype or phenotypic properties. Intensive surveillance of the safety of mumps vaccines during and after mass vaccination campaigns[24–28] may have contributed to distorted assessments of risk. Risk estimates have varied between studies, reflecting differences in study settings and circumstances and in degrees of surveillance. The available data are insufficient to distinguish between the safety profiles of the Urabe, Leningrad–Zagreb, and Leningrad-3 strains with respect to risk for aseptic meningitis. All reported cases of vaccine-derived mumps meningitis have been associated with recovery, without neurological sequelae.

Now that all mumps virus strains can be characterized by nucleotide sequencing and polymerase chain reaction, it should be possible to address scientifically a number of unresolved questions regarding mumps vaccine safety. These issues include defining the molecular determinants of virus attenuation; characterizing the genetic determinants of virulence; determining the safety of the vaccines in relation to either pure or mixed virus populations, along with their antigenicity; and determining at what stage mutations occur in the virus. The presence of sub-variant viruses in different vaccines could be studied. Such knowledge would support the development of more scientifically based mumps vaccines and contribute to a better understanding of the pathogenesis of adverse effects. Molecular assays would distinguish wild-type from vaccine strains of the mumps virus and thus assist quality control assessments of both existing and future vaccines. The committee has recommended establishment of an international reference laboratory for mumps vaccine virus isolates from vaccinated subjects.

SAFETY OF YELLOW FEVER VACCINE

The GACVS considered the cases of fatal viscerotropic disease following yellow fever vaccination reported in the United States, Brazil, and Australia.[29–31] The cases were attributable to a vaccine-type virus and not to a reversion of the vaccine strain to wild type. In contrast to the viscerotropic complications of yellow fever vaccination, recent neurotropic cases have not been fatal. The latter have been presumed to fall into one of 3 different clinical forms: Guillain–Barré syndrome (immune mediated), encephalopathy (owing to virus invasion), and acute demyelinating encephalomyelitis (caused either by direct virus invasion or by an immune-mediated response). Neurotropic complications of yellow fever vaccine are age related; individuals aged 65 years or older who are first-time vaccine recipients are at higher risk than younger individuals, but the young are not excluded from risk.

The GACVS noted the need for improved ability to predict who is at risk of the serious complications of yellow fever vaccine and what are the predisposing factors. An important and unresolved issue is the safety and efficacy of yellow fever vaccine among HIV-positive individuals. It remains to be determined whether HIV-positive status and the resultant immune deficiency affect seroconversion, risk of invasion of the nervous system, and risk of encephalopathy and at what stage of HIV disease yellow fever immunization should be regarded as contraindicated. Clarification is needed to determine whether there are differences in the incidence rates of minor and major adverse reactions to the vaccine among HIV-positive individuals.

INFLUENZA VACCINATION OF WOMEN DURING PREGNANCY

The committee has considered the safety of influenza vaccination of women during pregnancy. Manufacturers and national drug regulatory authorities tend to caution against routine use of influenza vaccine in pregnancy because there is a dearth of information regarding the vaccine's safety during the first trimester. The concern is that influenza during pregnancy carries a risk of morbidity signif-icantly higher than usual, along with a greater prospect of hospitalization and of a fatal outcome. The committee has concluded that the risks and benefits of influenza virus vaccination during all stages of pregnancy should be reconsidered, taking into account the high risk to the mother—and to the fetus—of the disease itself. Such advice would not apply to situations in which risk of influenza is low or to live attenuated influenza vaccines, which are not indicated in pregnancy.

BCG IMMUNIZATION IN HIV-POSITIVE INFANTS

The committee recently reviewed the available data on the benefits and risks of BCG immunization in the case of infants living in areas with high prevalence rates of tuberculosis, with and without concurrent high rates of HIV infection. Only limited population-based data are available on the effectiveness of BCG vaccine in preventing severe tuberculosis in HIV-positive infants, as well as on its safety. On the basis of the evidence available, the committee has advised that (1) no changes be made in the current recommendations for BCG immunization of infants in countries with high prevalence rates of tuberculosis; (2) that population-based studies be undertaken to determine the efficacy and safety of BCG and related vaccines in HIV-negative and HIV-positive children, respectively, in instances in which there are high endemic rates of tuberculosis; and (3) an international reference laboratory be established to systematically differentiate BCG strains and relate data to the antigenicity, efficacy, and safety of different strains.

SAFETY OF SMALLPOX VACCINATION

The committee has considered the safety of smallpox vaccination, including an updated account of the safety of vaccination practices in the United States since January 2003. Interim reports of the US experience have been published in *Morbidity and Mortality Weekly Report*.[32,33] Adverse effects consistently reported have included myopericarditis at frequencies that exceeded what might occur by coincidence. The committee has noted the importance for smallpox immunization programs to be supported by adverse event monitoring and recognizes that data are insufficient to define the incidence of adverse events among primary vaccinees as opposed to individuals revaccinated after a long interval.[34,35]

THIOMERSAL IN CHILDREN'S VACCINES

In the late 1990s, concerns were raised in the United States about the safety of thiomersal, a preservative used in some vaccines that has the ability to prevent bacterial contamination of multidose vials and contains ethyl mercury. These concerns were based on the realization that as the number of immunizations increased, the cumulative amount of mercury in the US infant immunization schedule could potentially exceed the most conservative recommended threshold for exposure to methyl mercury set by US government agencies. Methyl mercury has been reported to cause neurological abnormalities in newborns after fetal exposure resulting from mothers ingesting large doses over a long period of time.

In 1999, as a result of concern regarding this theoretical risk, 2 US immunization advisory bodies and the European Commission on Proprietary Medicinal Products recommended the expedited removal of thiomersal from vaccines. The change in the United States has placed pressure on other countries to follow this country's lead. However, removal of thiomersal may lead to changes in vaccine potency, stability, and reactogenicity, and this process must proceed with great caution. Furthermore, since thiomersal is an important component in terms of maintenance of sterility in certain multidose vaccine vial preparations, its removal might have serious repercussions for safe vaccine delivery.

Subsequent to the decision having been made in the United States, reassuring additional information about the safety of thiomersal-containing vaccines has become available. In particular, it has been shown that the pharmacokinetic profile of ethyl mercury is substantially different from that of methyl mercury, the former being rapidly excreted through the gut. In addition, several recently completed epidemiological studies have provided reassuring evidence with respect to the safety of thiomersal in the amounts contained in vaccines. The GACVS has reviewed the issue and found no scientific evidence of toxicity from thiomersal-containing vaccines. As a result, the WHO Strategic Advisory Group of Experts,[36] at its June 2002 meeting, strongly affirmed that vaccines containing thiomersal should continue to be available so that safe immunization practices can be maintained.

Thiomersal has been used for more than 60 years as an antimicrobial agent in vaccines and other pharmaceutical products to prevent unwanted growth of microorganisms. There is a specific need for preservatives in multidose presentations of inactivated vaccines such as DTP and hepatitis B. Repeated puncture of the rubber stopper to withdraw additional amounts of vaccine at different intervals poses risks of contamination and consequent transmission to children. Removal of thiomersal could potentially compromise the quality of childhood vaccines used in global programs. Live bacterial or viral vaccines (e.g., measles vaccines) do not contain preservatives because they would interfere with the active ingredients. In the case of certain vaccines, thiomersal is also used during the manufacturing process.

THE WAY FORWARD

Since there will probably continue to be challenges raised by allegations of adverse events linked to immunization, it is expected that the role of the GACVS will continue to expand, with special attention to the following:

• Standards involving consultations with the pharmaceutical industry, national governments, and drug

regulatory authorities need to be improved. Decisions will increasingly be made on the basis of the comprehensive vaccine safety database being developed by the committee, which will contain all of the relevant materials, published as well as unpublished, that the committee takes into account. The critiques of data made by the committee will be openly available for consideration and review by others. Decisions of the committee may be appealed or challenged. The committee aims at generating a growing sense of confidence that its decisions and recommendations are open-minded, thoroughly sound scientifically and medically, and in the interests of public health.

• The committee has a desire to work more with, and give support to, national drug regulatory authorities in promoting sound and informed regulatory practices, including ongoing review of vaccine safety issues after registration.

• In the future, the committee can be expected to provide more support for the initiatives of the WHO Department of Immunization, Vaccines, and Biologicals to facilitate the department's work with countries (especially developing countries) with vaccine manufacturing capabilities and high numbers of vaccine exports to other countries.

About the Authors

Peter I. Folb is with the Medical Research Council, Cape Town, South Africa. Ewa Bernatowska is with the Department of Immunology, Children's Memorial Health Institute, Warsaw, Poland. Robert Chen is with the Immunization Safety Branch, Centers for Disease Control and Prevention, Atlanta, Ga. John Clemens is with the International Vaccine Institute, Seoul, Korea. Alex N.O. Dodoo is with the Centre for Tropical Clinical Pharmacology and Therapeutics, University of Ghana Medical School, Accra. Susan Ellenberg is with the Office of Biostatistics and Epidemiology, Food and Drug Administration, Rockville, Maryland. Patrick Farrington is with the Department of Statistics, Open University, Milton Keynes, England. T. Jacob John is with the Kerala State Institute of Virology and Infectious Diseases, Vellore, India. Paul-Henri Lambert and Claire-Anne Siegrist are with the World Health Organization Collaborating Centre for Neonatal Vaccinology, Centre Médical Universitaire, Geneva, Switzerland. Noni E. MacDonald is with the Department of Paediatrics, Dalhousie University, Halifax, Nova Scotia, Canada. Elizabeth Miller is with the Immunisation Department, Health Protection Agency, London, England. David Salisbury is with the Communicable Disease and Immunisation Team, Department of Health, London. Heinz-J. Schmitt is with the Center for Preventive Pediatrics, Johannes Gutenberg-Universität, Mainz, Germany. Omala Wimalaratne is with the Department of Rabies and Vaccines, Medical Research Institute, Colombo, Sri Lanka.

Correspondence: Requests for reprints should be sent to Peter I. Folb, Medical Research Council, PO Box 19070, Tygerberg, 7505, Cape Town, South Africa (e-mail: pfolb@mrc.ac.za).

Acknowledgments

The committee wishes to acknowledge with appreciation the support received from the WHO secretariat, with special thanks to Drs Adwoa Bentsi-Enchill, Dina Pfeifer, and Philippe Duclos. Dr Daniel Tarantola, director of the WHO Department of Immunization, Vaccines, and Biologicals, and Dr Bjorn Melgaard, previous director, have been a great support to the work of the committee while respecting and advocating its independence from the other functions of WHO and its partners.

Note

The views expressed in this article are those of the Global Advisory Committee on Vaccine Safety and do not reflect the official positions of any of the agencies or institutions with which the authors are affiliated.

Contributors

All of the authors substantially contributed to the review of the issues presented in their capacity as members of the Global Advisory Committee on Vaccine Safety, and all actively participated in the drafting and editing of the article.

References

1. Biellik R, Madema S, Taole A, Kutsulukuta A, Allies E, Eggers R, et al. First 5 years of measles elimination in southern Africa: 1996–2000. *Lancet*.2002;359:1564–1568.
2. Isaacs SL, Schroeder SA. Where the public good prevailed: lessons from success stories in public health. *Am Prospect*. 2001;12:26.
3. *State of the World's Vaccines and Immunization*. Geneva, Switzerland: World Health Organization; 2002.
4. Vaccine Safety Advisory Committee. Vaccine safety. *Wkly Epidemiol Rec*.1999;74:337–340.
5. Causality assessment of adverse events following immunization. *Wkly Epidemiol Rec*.2001;76:85–92.
6. *Surgeon General's Advisory Committee Report on Smoking and Health*. Washington, DC: US Dept of Health and Welfare; 1964. PHS publication 1103.
7. Kristensen I, Aaby P, Jensen H. Routine vaccinations and child survival: follow up study in Guinea-Bissau, West Africa. *BMJ*.2000;321:1435–1438.
8. Fine P. Commentary: an unexpected finding that needs confirmation or rejection. *BMJ*.2000;321:1439.
9. Aaby P, Jensen H, Samb B, et al. Differences in female-male mortality after high-titre measles vaccine and association with subsequent vaccination with diphtheria-tetanus-pertussis and inactivated poliovirus: a re-analysis of the West African studies. *Lancet*. 2003;361:2183–2188.
10. Gillberg C, Steffenburg S, Schaumann H. Is autism more common now than 10 years ago? *Br J Psychiatry*. 1991;158:403–409.
11. Taylor B, Miller E, Farrington CP, et al. Autism and measles, mumps, and rubella vaccine: no epidemiological evidence for a causal association. *Lancet*. 1999;353:2026–2029.
12. Patja A, Davidkin I, Kurki T, Kallio MJ, Valle M, Peltola H. Serious adverse events after measles-mumps-rubella vaccination during a fourteen-year prospective follow-up. *Pediatr Infect Dis J*.2000;19:1127–1134.
13. Dales L, Hammer SJ, Smith NJ. Time trends in autism and in MMR immunization coverage in California. *JAMA*. 2001;285:1183–1185.
14. Peltola H, Patja A, Leinikki P, Valle M, Davidkin I, Paunio M. No evidence for measles, mumps, and rubella vaccine-associated inflammatory bowel disease or autism in a 14-year prospective study. *Lancet*. 1998;351:1327–1328.
15. Kaye JA, del Mar Melero-Montes M, Jick H. Mumps, measles, and rubella vaccine and the incidence of autism recorded by general practitioners: a time trend analysis. *BMJ*. 2001;322:460–463.
16. Madsen KM, Hviid A, Vestergaard M, et al. A population-based study of measles, mumps, and rubella vaccination and autism. *N Engl J Med*. 2002;347:1477–1482.
17. Farrington CP, Miller E, Taylor B. MMR and autism: further evidence against a causal association. *Vaccine*. 2001;19:3632–3635.
18. DeWilde S, Carey IM, Richards N, Hilton SR, Cook DG. Do children who become autistic consult more often after MMR vaccination? *Br J Gen Pract*. 2001;51:226–227.
19. Fombonne E, Chakrabarti S. No evidence for a new variant of measles-mumps-rubella-induced autism. *Pediatrics*. 2001;108:E58.
20. Taylor B, Miller E, Lingam R, Andrews N, Simmons A, Stowe J. Measles, mumps, and rubella vaccination and bowel problems or developmental regression in children with autism: population study. *BMJ*. 2002;324:393–396.
21. Kawashima H, Mori T, Kashiwagi Y, Takekuma K, Hoshika A, Wakefield A. Detection and sequencing of measles virus from peripheral mononuclear cells from patients with inflammatory bowel disease and autism. *Dig Dis Sci*. 2002;45:723–729.
22. Martin CM, Uhlmann V, Killalea A, Sheils O, O'Leary JJ. Detection of measles virus in children with ileo-colonic lymphoid nodular hyperplasia, enterocolitis and developmental disorder. *Mol Psychiatry*. 2002;7(suppl 2):S47–S48.
23. Singh VK, Lin SX, Newell E, Nelson C. Abnormal measles-mumps-rubella antibodies and CNS autoimmunity in children with autism. *J Biomed Sci*. 2002;9:359–364.
24. Da Cunha SS, Rodrigues LC, Barreto ML, Dourado I. Outbreak of aseptic meningitis and mumps after mass vaccination with MMR vaccine using the Leningrad-Zagreb mumps strain. *Vaccine*. 2002;20:1106–1112.
25. Dourado I, Cunha S, Teixeira MG, et al. Outbreak of aseptic meningitis associated with mass vaccination with a Urabe-containing measles-mumps-rubella vaccine: implications for immunization programs. *Am J Epidemiol*.2000;151:524–530.
26. Dos Santos BA, Ranieri TS, Bercini M, et al. An evaluation of the adverse reaction potential of three measles-mumps-rubella combination vaccines. *Rev Panam Salud Publica*.2002;12:240–246.
27. Fullerton KE, Reef SE. Ongoing debate over the safety of the different mumps vaccine strains impacts mumps disease control. *Int J Epidemiol*.2002;31:983–984.
28. Galazka AM, Robertson SE, Kraigher A. Mumps and mumps vaccine: a global review. *Bull World Health Organ*.1999;77:3–14.
29. Chan RC, Penney DJ, Little D, Carter IW, Roberts JA, Rawlinson WD. Hepatitis and death following vaccination with 17D-204 yellow fever vaccine. *Lancet*. 2001;358:121–122.
30. Martin M, Tsai TF, Cropp B, et al. Fever and multisystem organ failure associated with 17D-204 yellow fever vaccination: a report of four cases. *Lancet*. 2001;358:98–104.
31. Vasconcelos PFC, Luna EJ, Galler R, et al. Serious adverse events associated with yellow fever 17DD vaccine in Brazil: a report of two cases. *Lancet*.2001;358:91–97.
32. Cardiac and other adverse events following civilian smallpox vaccination—United States, 2003. *MMWR Morb Mortal Wkly Rep*.2003;52:639–642.
33. Adverse events following civilian smallpox vaccination—United States, 2003. *MMWR Morb Mortal Wkly Rep*.2003;52:819–820.
34. Global Advisory Committee on Vaccine Safety. *Wkly Epidemiol Rec*. 2003;78:282–284.
35. Global Advisory Committee on Vaccine Safety. *Wkly Epidemiol Rec*. 2004;79:16–20.
36. *Report of the Strategic Advisory Group of Experts (SAGE)*. Geneva, Switzerland: World Health Organization; 2003.

Overview of Health Disparities Section
Health Disparities: A Global Perspective

| *Dr. Garth Graham, Director, U.S. Office of Minority Health and Deputy Assistant Secretary for Minority Health*

Martin Luther King once said, "Injustice anywhere is a threat to justice everywhere." Viewed globally, there are massive disparities in health outcomes and healthcare access that affect the vulnerable and underserved populations of the world. The reasons for these differences are myriad, including natural and manmade disasters, economic insecurity, political instability, and lack of resources and infrastructure in the delivery of healthcare—to name a few. It is also true that, within any given country, health disparities are likely to exist—regardless of the extent to which a country is economically rich or poor, developed or undeveloped. In many cases these differences in health outcomes or access to health care fall along the fault line of socioeconomic status. Despite the fact that medical breakthroughs in the last century have significantly improved health outcomes for most populations—it is still also true that a health/healthcare gap exists between the "haves" and the "have-nots" of the world. Even though health disparities by race, ethnicity, class, or gender often correlate or overlap with social or economic status, other factors such as cultural beliefs and values, lifestyle behaviors, availability of healthcare, ability to communicate with healthcare providers, health literacy, participation in clinical research studies, or genetic risk factors also contribute to health/healthcare disparities between races, ethnicities, classes, or genders. It is fair to say, however, that the underserved, undervalued, or vulnerable individuals of any society are at far greater risk of experiencing poor health outcomes than are their more privileged counterparts.

The readings in this section offer a range of strategies and insights for reducing health disparities. Casas-Zamora and Ibrahim provide an overview of efforts to confront global health inequities, noting that, "there is a global movement for health equity that began in the last decade of the 20th century and continues to grow." These authors draw attention to the priority for developed countries to address health disparities at both a national and international level. Developed nations have recognized that health disparities exist for their own populations as well as abroad. For example, pivotal public inquiries in the United Kingdom (e.g., the 1980 Black Report[1] and the 1988 Acheson Report[2]), and in the United States (e.g. the 1987 Report of the Secretary's Task Force on Black and Minority Health[3] and the 2003 Institute of Medicine Report[4]) drew attention to the existence of racial/ethnic health disparities within each nation.

In the United States experience, the 1987 Secretary's Report[3] prompted the establishment of the Office of Minority Health (OMH) within the Federal Department of Health and Human Services. The mission of OMH is to "improve and protect the health of racial and ethnic minority populations through the development of health policies and programs that will eliminate health disparities." Today in the United States, governmental agencies at the local, State and Federal levels have programs and policies with this same mission.[5] As the dialogue on health disparities in the United States has continued, the conversation has included, to an increasing extent, the integration of quality improvement measures as a strategy to deal with health disparities. For example, in 1999, a congressional mandate formed the Agency for Healthcare Research and Quality. This agency produces a yearly National Healthcare Disparities Report (NHDR), which tracks numerous quality measures of minority health from multiple national databases. Improvements in data collection and health information technology hold potential for providing evidence-based research to identify and solve health inequities.

The populations of the United States and other developed nations have become increasingly diverse for a number of reasons including increased immigration patterns. The global community has, in effect, come to the doorstep of these countries. Because of this trend, cultural and linguistic competencies (i.e., the ability to understand and communicate with individuals in the idioms of their own language and culture) have become crucial elements in national efforts to eliminate health disparities.

Casas-Zamora and Ibrahim also discuss key efforts of developed nations and the international community to look beyond their borders and sponsor campaigns aimed at reducing health disparities worldwide. Apart from the interventions mentioned in their chapter, a wide array of non-profit and faith-based organizations have long been active, and continue to be major players in combating adverse health issues worldwide. The global

HIV/AIDS epidemic, emerging threats from viral and bacterial diseases, and the effects of poverty on health outcomes have attracted widespread public concern, especially through the efforts of media outlets and celebrity individuals who generate increased levels of public awareness of these problems. In the United States, for example, the non-profit *One Campaign* (www.one.org/about), and the government-sponsored *PEPFAR* initiative (www.pepfar.gov) mobilize large numbers of individuals and organizations to work for positive health outcomes in the world's poorest communities. The constellation of governmental, business, private sector, non-profit, faith-based, and individual efforts to reduce health disparities is a healthy (in every sense of the word) development that can only be improved by increased cooperation and interaction among these various entities.

Two readings provide specific examples of health disparities by social status and by race/ethnicity. MacNeil, Lobato, and Moore describe disparities in risk factors and treatment for tuberculosis between incarcerated and non-inmate populations in the United States. They note that tuberculosis case rates are substantially higher in prison populations than in the general population. This study highlights the practical value of identifying communities with elevated rates of a particular disease. Interventions not only protect the affected individuals but may also reduce risk of disease outbreak in the general population. Bramley, Hebert, Tuzzio, and Chasin compare health disparities between majority and indigenous populations in the United States (American Indians/Alaska Natives) and in New Zealand (Maoris). This study confirms that these minority populations have significantly poorer health status than do their majority counterparts across a range of health indicators. This study is useful for its discussion of appropriate measures that can detect health disparities, i.e. measures for health outcome, preventive care, modifiable risk factors, and treatment services. The authors also discuss the interventions that have been successful in each country.

Gravlee, Dressler, and Bernard provide an intriguing analysis of skin color and race as variables in health disparities research. Their research finds that "blood pressure is associated with culturally ascribed 'color' [in Puerto Rico]—but not with skin pigmentation." This study touches on the long-standing and controversial debate as to the meaning of "race" as a sociocultural construct or genetic/biological construct—and its usefulness or reliability as a variable in clinical studies of disease.

The answer to the question of what to do about global and country-wide health disparities depends on the specific situation, or the endpoint to be achieved, but must always include strategies based on wisdom, will, and wherewithal. *Wisdom* and knowledge are gained by using evidence-based research (such as is presented in the following readings) to identify the problems and determine what works to solve them. Further, individuals, institutions, and governments must intentionally develop a moral, political, and intellectual *will* to reduce health disparities and to work cooperatively with all sectors of society—most especially those that are targets for intervention—to find and implement solutions. Finally, societies must allocate financial and intellectual resources to provide the *wherewithal* to act on their collective wisdom and will.

It has always been a matter of justice for the "haves" to care about and attempt to facilitate the healthcare needs of the "have-nots." In today's global marketplace. with the reality of population fluidity within and between countries (migration from rural to urban settings, displacement due to war and calamity, increased immigration), it also makes practical sense. When health disparities go unchecked, everyone pays the price—in the spread of disease, the potential for social instability, and the loss of human intellectual and leadership capital.

References

1. Black D. *Inequities in Health.* London, United Kingdom: Penguin; 1980.
2. Acheson, D. *Independent Inquiry into Inequalities in Health.* London: The Stationery Office; 1998.
3. Heckler MM. *Report of the Secretary's Task Force on Black and Minority Health.* Washington, D.C.: U.S. Department of Health and Human Services; 1985.
4. Smedley BD, Stith AR, Nelson AC, eds. *Unequal treatment: confronting racial and ethnic disparities in health care.* Washington, D.C.: National Academies Press; 2003.
5. Graham GN. Quality of Care and Health Disparities: The Evolving Role of the Government. IN: Williams, RA (Ed.), *Eliminating Healthcare Disparities in America. Beyond the IOM Report.* Totowa, NJ: Humana Press; 2007.

An Unanswered Health Disparity: Tuberculosis Among Correctional Inmates, 1993 Through 2003

| Jessica R. MacNeil, MPH, Mark N. Lobato, MD and Marisa Moore, MD, MPH

ABSTRACT

Objectives: We sought to describe disparities and trends in tuberculosis (TB) risk factors and treatment outcomes between correctional inmate and noninmate populations.

Methods: We analyzed data reported to the national TB surveillance system from 1993 through 2003. We compared characteristics between inmate and non-inmate men aged 15–64 years.

Results: Of the 210976 total US TB cases, 3.8% (7820) were reported from correctional systems. Federal and state prison case rates were 29.4 and 24.2 cases per 100000 inmates, respectively, which were considerably higher than those in the noninmate population (6.7 per 100000 people). Inmates with TB were more likely to have at least 1 TB risk factor compared with noninmates (60.1% vs 42.0%, respectively) and to receive directly observed therapy (65.0% vs 41.0%, respectively); however, they were less likely to complete treatment (76.8% vs 89.4%, respectively). Among inmates, 58.9% completed treatment within 12 months compared with 73.2% of noninmates.

Conclusions: Tuberculosis case rates in prison systems remain higher than in the general population. Inmates with TB are less likely than noninmates to complete treatment.

INTRODUCTION

Tuberculosis (TB) is an important health problem in correctional systems in many parts of the United States.

Although the incident TB case rate for the general population has remained at fewer than 10 cases per 100 000 persons since 1993,[1] substantially higher case rates, some as high as 10 times that of the general population, have been reported in correctional populations.[2–4] The TB case rate reported from 1 urban jail was 72.1 cases per 100 000 inmates, representing 10% of the county's cases.[5] Furthermore, studies have found the prevalence of latent TB infection (LTBI) among inmates to be as high as 25%.[6–10] Other studies have shown a correlation between length of incarceration and positive tuberculin skin test responses, indicating transmission may have occurred in these facilities.[11,12]

A disproportionately high percentage of TB cases in the United States occur among persons incarcerated in correctional facilities. In 2003, 3.2% of all TB cases nationwide occurred among residents of correctional facilities.[1] In contrast, 0.7% of the total US population were confined in prisons and jails in 2003, a population that was increasing at an average annual rate of 3.7% from 1995 through 2003.[13] One notable reason for the high rates of TB in correctional institutions is the greater proportion of persons who are at high risk for TB but who can not access standard public health interventions. Transmission risks particular to correctional institutions include close living quarters, poor ventilation, and overcrowding.[5,14,15]

Owing to the occurrence of TB outbreaks and the documentation of high rates of TB in correctional systems, the Centers for Disease Control and Prevention (CDC), in 1993, began asking state health departments to report whether those newly diagnosed with TB were residents of correctional facilities. We analyzed data reported to the national TB surveillance system from 1993 through 2003 to define trends in correctional TB cases and describe characteristics of individuals with TB who are residents of correctional facilities.

METHODS

An inmate TB patient was defined as a person who was incarcerated in a correctional facility at the time TB was diagnosed. We analyzed data from TB cases reported to the national TB surveillance system from 1993 through 2003 among inmates of correctional systems (including federal and state prisons, local jails, and juvenile facilities, and other facilities such as immigration detention centers) in the 50 states and the District of Columbia. For comparative purposes, all calculations and comparisons for risk-factor characteristics, clinical presentation, drug resistance, and treatment outcomes were performed only for males aged 15 to 64 years, a group that comprised 85.5% of inmate cases.

Variables in the national TB case report are collected uniformly throughout the country with the exception of human immunodeficiency virus (HIV) status. California does not report individual HIV test results but does submit the results of TB and AIDS registry cross-matches. California TB patients with an AIDS match were classified as HIV-infected; all others were classified as having an unknown HIV status. All 2003 California cases are classified as unknown HIV status.

Completion-of-therapy calculations were done for persons who were alive at diagnosis, had an initial drug regimen of 1 or more anti-TB drugs, did not die during therapy, and did not have an initial *Mycobacterium tuberculosis* isolate resistant to rifampin. Timely completion of therapy was defined as completion of treatment within 12 months. The latest year for which information on treatment outcomes is available is 2001.

State and federal prison population case rates were calculated with data from the US Bureau of Justice Statistics.[13,16,17] Estimates of correctional populations are based on year-end counts of inmates for state and federal prisons in the 50 states, the District of Columbia, and the Federal Bureau of Prisons. Case rates were not calculated for jail inmates because accurate estimates for this population were not available, in part owing to the difficulty of removing recidivists from the population count.

RESULTS

From 1993 through 2003, US jurisdictions reported 210976 cases of TB to the national TB surveillance system. Information about residence at a correctional facility at the time of TB diagnosis was reported for 208468 (98.8%) patients, of whom 7820 (3.8%) were inmates. The percentage of TB cases in males aged 15 to 64 years reported as residing in a correctional facility was 9.2% for those born in the United States and 4.2% for those not born in the United States (odds ratio [OR] = 2.2; 95% confidence interval [CI] = 2.08, 2.33; $P < .001$).

Trends in Tuberculosis Cases and Rates

From 1993 through 2003, the percentage of TB cases among local jail inmates increased from 42.8% of all inmates with TB to 53.5% (2 for trend = 57.8; $P < .001$), whereas cases among federal inmates increased from 2.9% to 11.8% (Table 1). Case rates for the 11 years studied were 29.4 per 100 000 for federal prisons and 24.2 for state prisons. In contrast, federal prisons in 1993 and in 2003 had nearly level TB case rates. In state prisons, case rates decreased from 52.3 in 1993 to 6.6 in 2003, a decline of 87.4%.

Two states, California and Texas, accounted for 42.7% of the 7820 reported TB cases among inmates from 1993 through 2003, and another 4 states (Florida, Georgia, Illinois, and New York) accounted for an additional 28.6% of reported TB cases. These same 6 states accounted for 56.9% of the 200 648 reported TB cases among noninmates.

Demographic Characteristics

The characteristics of individuals with TB in correctional facilities differed from those with TB who did not reside in correctional facilities: inmates with TB were more likely to be male (89.4% vs 61.9%, respectively), US born (77.0% vs 58.3%, respectively), younger (median: 37 vs 45 years of age, respectively), and from racial and ethnic minority groups (81.7% vs 75.5%, respectively). Over time, an increasing proportion of TB cases were among foreign-born persons in both inmate and noninmate populations. The proportion of foreign-born inmates with TB had increased from 15.5% in 1993 to 40.3% by 2003; similarly, 30.6% of those with TB in the general population were foreign-born in 1993, and 53.6% were foreign-born in 2003.

TABLE 1— Tuberculosis Cases Among Inmate and Noninmate Populations, by Prison Facility Category and Year: United States, 1993–2003

Year			Cases, No. (%) [Rate][a,b]		
	Noninmate	Inmate[c]	Federal Prison	State Prison	Local Jail
1993	23 027 (96.0) [8.5]	953 (4.0)	28 (2.9) [31.3]	462 (48.5) [52.3]	407 (42.8)
1994	22 330 (95.2) [8.1]	1119 (4.8)	31 (2.8) [32.6]	470 (42.0) [48.9]	571 (51.1)
1995	21 545 (95.8) [7.8]	938 (4.2)	24 (2.6) [26.8]	332 (35.4) [33.5]	539 (57.5)
1996	20 319 (96.3) [7.3]	784 (3.7)	28 (3.6) [29.4]	295 (37.6) [28.4]	409 (52.2)
1997	18 951 (96.2) [6.7]	746 (3.8)	30 (4.0) [29.5]	220 (29.5) [20.5]	445 (59.7)
1998	17 601 (96.4) [6.2]	657 (3.6)	32 (4.9) [29.8]	188 (28.6) [16.8]	382 (57.9)
1999	16 873 (96.7) [5.9]	577 (3.3)	33 (5.7) [26.3]	163 (28.3) [14.4]	343 (59.3)
2000	15 707 (96.4) [5.4]	587 (3.6)	39 (6.6) [29.9]	172 (29.3) [14.6]	327 (55.6)
2001	15 384 (96.7) [5.3]	523 (3.3)	37 (7.1) [25.8]	141 (27.0) [11.6]	281 (53.5)
2002	14 556 (96.9) [4.9]	461 (3.1)	39 (8.5) [26.2]	124 (26.9) [10.3]	238 (51.6)
2003	14 355 (96.8) [4.8]	475 (3.2)	56 (11.8) [35.2]	81 (17.1) [6.6]	254 (53.5)
Total	200 648 (96.2) [6.7]	7820 (3.8)	377 (4.8) [29.4]	2648 (33.9) [24.2]	4196 (53.7)

[a]Rates are for cases per 100 000 persons per year from estimates of the US resident population.43
[b]Inmate denominators include all inmates held in public and private adult federal and state facilities.
[c]Inmates are residents of federal prisons, state prisons, local jails, juvenile facilities, and other facilities; hence, the national total exceeds the number of inmates in federal and state prisons and jails.

TABLE 2— Risk-Factor Characteristics of Inmate and Noninmate Populations (Males Aged 15–64 Years) With Tuberculosis, by Year: United States, 1994–2003

	Inmate			Noninmate		
	1994	2003	1994–2003	1994	2003	1994–2003
Excess alcohol use[a]						
Yes	214 (21.4)	140 (33.6)	1762 (29.2)	2113 (21.0)	1489 (23.1)	18 682 (23.7)
No	505 (50.6)	245 (58.8)	3249 (53.8)	5357 (53.1)	4727 (73.4)	51915 (65.8)
Unknown	279 (28.0)	32 (7.7)	1033 (17.1)	2616 (25.9)	226 (3.5)	8366 (10.6)
Injecting drug use[a]						
Yes	121 (12.1)	49 (11.8)	733 (12.1)	529 (5.3)	175 (2.7)	3197 (4.1)
No	570 (57.1)	327 (78.4)	4169 (69.0)	6806 (67.5)	6012 (93.3)	66 837 (84.6)
Unknown	307 (30.8)	41 (9.8)	1142 (18.9)	2751 (27.3)	255 (4.0)	8929 (11.3)
Noninjecting drug use[a]						
Yes	211 (21.1)	127 (30.5)	1523 (25.2)	825 (8.2)	671 (10.4)	7754 (9.8)
No	480 (48.1)	251 (60.2)	3349 (55.4)	6326 (62.7)	5498 (85.4)	61 681 (78.1)
Unknown	307 (30.8)	39 (9.4)	1172 (19.4)	2935 (29.1)	273 (4.2)	9528 (12.1)
Homelessness[a]						
Yes	126 (12.6)	65 (15.6)	906 (15.0)	1005 (10.0)	676 (10.5)	8359 (10.6)
No	726 (72.8)	326 (78.2)	4605 (76.2)	8165 (81.0)	5615 (87.2)	67 528 (85.5)
Unknown	146 (14.6)	26 (6.2)	533 (8.8)	916 (9.0)	151 (2.3)	3076 (3.9)
HIV status[b]						
Yes	321 (32.2)	47 (11.3)	1454 (24.1)	2455 (24.3)	720 (11.2)	13 635 (17.3)
No	182 (18.2)	229 (54.9)	2261 (37.4)	2114 (21.0)	3243 (50.3)	30 678 (38.9)
Unknown	495 (49.6)	141 (33.8)	2329 (38.5)	5517 (54.7)	2479 (38.5)	34 650 (43.9)

Note. The proportions of inmates and noninmates have 1994 as the baseline year owing to a substantially high proportion of missing data for 1993.
[a]Reported in the year prior to diagnosis.
[b]All 2003 California cases are classified as unknown HIV status.

Risk-Factor Characteristics

Excess alcohol use, injection drug use, non-injection drug use, and homelessness within 1 year prior to TB diagnosis in adult males aged 15 to 64 years were all more frequent in inmates with TB than in noninmates with TB (Table 2). Additionally, inmates were more likely than noninmates to report at least 1 TB risk factor including HIV-infection (60.1% vs 42.0%, respectively).

Inmates with TB were also more likely than noninmates with TB to be HIV infected. From 1993 through 2003, HIV infection was documented in 35.8% of inmates with TB in state prisons, in 20.7% of those in jail, and in 13.2% of those in federal prisons. Overall, of males with TB aged 15 to 64 years, 25.2% who were inmates were known to be HIV infected versus 18.0% of those who were noninmates. A positive finding, however, is that HIV prevalence is declining in this setting. Among those with TB in state prisons, the prevalence of HIV infection decreased from 43.1% in 1993 to 11.6% in 2003. In federal prisons, the prevalence of HIV infection decreased from 23.8% in 1993 to 9.3% in 2003. In local jails in 1993, 22.8% of inmates with TB also were infected with HIV, whereas in 2003, 12.4% of inmates with TB were HIV infected.

Clinical Presentation and Drug Resistance

A higher proportion of inmates (90.3%) than noninmates (84.4%) had pulmonary TB. Results of sputum smears for acid-fast bacilli and sputum cultures were reported more often for inmates than for noninmates. Inmates compared with noninmates were less likely to have extrapulmonary TB (OR = 0.60; 95% CI = 0.55, 0.66; $P <$ .001).

TABLE 3— Characteristics of Persons Reported to Have Anti–Tuberculosis (TB) Drug-Resistance, by Inmate and Noninmate Populations (Males Aged 15–64 Years): United States, 1993–2003

	Cases, No. (%)			
	Inmate		Noninmate	
	No Prior TB	Prior TB	No Prior TB	Prior TB
Isoniazid resistance[a]				
US born	301 (8.1)	26 (11.7)	2235 (5.8)	178 (8.2)
HIV infected	108 (9.5)	13 (18.6)	782 (8.4)	47 (9.5)
HIV noninfected	100 (7.6)	5 (6.0)	728 (4.8)	73 (8.2)
Foreign born	136 (11.0)	23 (34.2)	3319 (11.9)	308 (23.1)
Multidrug resistance[b]				
US born	75 (2.0)	14 (6.3)	589 (1.5)	80 (3.7)
HIV infected	46 (4.0)	6 (8.6)	330 (3.5)	33 (6.7)
HIV noninfected	15 (1.1)	2 (2.4)	107 (0.7)	19 (2.1)
Foreign born	16 (1.5)	7 (9.2)	457 (1.6)	135 (10.2)
Resistance to at least 1 first-line drug				
US born	453 (12.1)	37 (16.6)	3875 (10.0)	289 (13.3)
HIV infected	155 (13.6)	20 (28.6)	1294 (13.8)	89 (18.1)
HIV noninfected	145 (10.9)	8 (9.5)	1218 (8.0)	109 (12.2)
Foreign born	234 (18.9)	31 (40.8)	5114 (18.2)	407 (30.5)

Note. HIV = human immunodeficiency virus.
[a] Resistance to at least the drug(s) indicated, but also may have resistance to additional first-line drugs.
[b] Resistance to isoniazid and rifampin.

Table 3 presents the frequency of drug resistance of *M tuberculosis* isolates among inmate and noninmate patients. In general, drug-resistance levels were higher in those with a prior history of TB, those not born in the United States, those with HIV infection, and inmates. From 1993 through 2003, declines in drug resistance were greater for inmates than for noninmates: isoniazid resistance decreased (inmates, from 10.9% to 6.7%; noninmates, from 9.9% to 8.8%), as did levels of multidrug-resistant TB (inmates, from 3.3% to 0.6%; noninmates, from 3.4% to 1.1%), and resistance to any drug (inmates, from 15.2% to 11.5%; noninmates, from 14.9% to 13.6%).

Treatment Outcomes

In 1993, among patients for whom extended treatment was not warranted, treatment was completed within 12 months in 47.9% of inmates compared to 60.4% of noninmates. In 2001, rates of completion of therapy had improved to 63.6% and 80.1%, respectively. Rates of completion of therapy within 12 months were lower in persons with TB risk factors and lowest for those who had HIV infection at the time of TB diagnosis, in both inmates and noninmates, but lower among inmates (Table 4).

Inmates were more likely to receive directly observed therapy for at least part of their therapy than were noninmates (Table 4); however, inmates were less likely to complete therapy. Lower completion rates among inmates compared with noninmates reflect higher levels of "incomplete treatment" categories (moved, lost, other, or unknown). A higher percentage of federal inmates (27.9%) were classified as "treatment incom-

plete" owing to a reported treatment outcome of "moved out of jurisdiction" compared with other inmates (9.0%) and noninmates (4.4%). In addition, 11.0% of local jail inmates had a reported treatment outcome of "lost," compared with 7.1% of other inmates and 3.9% of noninmates.

DISCUSSION

The success of TB control in the United States is evident by the steady decline in cases among incarcerated populations along with declining rates in the communities from which inmates are drawn. Yet, our findings call attention to the epidemiology and health-related outcomes in correctional inmates that demonstrate marked disparities in TB rates, measures of risk including HIV infection, and TB treatment outcomes.

TABLE 4— Tuberculosis (TB) Treatment Outcomes for Inmate and Noninmate Populations (Males Aged 15–64 Years): United States, 1993–2001

	Cases, No. (%)	
	Inmate	Noninmate
Directly observed therapy		
Yes, total direct	3499 (65.0)	27 320 (41.0)
Yes, direct and self	1018 (18.9)	16 761 (25.1)
No, self-administered	654 (12.2)	21 200 (31.8)
Unknown	211 (3.9)	1374 (2.1)
Completion of therapy		
Completed therapy	4133 (76.8)	59 629 (89.4)
Moved	550 (10.2)	2917 (4.4)
Lost	514 (9.6)	2621 (3.9)
Refused	36 (0.7)	540 (0.8)
Other/Unknown	149 (2.8)	998 (1.5)
Completion of TB therapy within 12 months by risk factor (%)		
Injecting drug use[a]	57.9	62.9
Noninjecting drug use[a]	61.8	69.6
Excess alcohol use[a]	63.8	73.4
Homelessness[a]	59.1	67.7
HIV-infected at TB diagnosis	44.8	54.5

[a] Reported in the year prior to TB diagnosis.

Substantially greater case rates in correctional systems are indicative of this disparity, especially in the federal prison system. In 2003, the TB case rate for federal prisons was 6.9 times the case rate in the general US population (5.1 cases per 100 000 population).[1] Paradoxically, enhanced screening in federal prisons may have resulted in better case detection and thus an apparent rise in the number of TB cases.[18] The increasing proportion of inmates who are born in countries other than the United States also may be partly responsible for the increase in TB cases in federal prisons.[19] Although we did not calculate the case rate among jail inmates because of unreliable population estimates, local studies indicate that case rates in jail populations are also greater than in the general population. In San Francisco, for example, jail inmates had a case rate of 72.1 cases per 100 000 inmates compared with a rate of 26.2 cases per 100 000 persons in the local population.[5]

Inmates, in contrast to noninmates, are more likely to have multiple risk factors for infection with M tuberculosis and for progression to TB disease. Inmates are also more likely to have drug-resistant TB. Special efforts are needed to mitigate the personal and public health toll created by these risk factors.[20,21] The concentration of these factors in a congregate population has resulted in explosive outbreaks of TB, as demonstrated in a North Carolina outbreak involving 25 homeless patients, 72% of whom had a history of incarceration in the local county jail.[22] Tuberculosis outbreaks and ongoing transmission have occurred even after inmates were screened for TB[23–25] and also have been attributed to failure to complete treatment by inmates known to have LTBI.[26,27]

Despite elevated rates of HIV infection—the strongest risk factor for developing TB among adults who have LTBI[28]—the HIV status of more than one third of inmates with TB is unknown. In a study of 20 large city

and county jails, a review of inmate medical records found that only 48% of 376 inmates with LTBI had a known HIV status.[29] Although the CDC recommends routine HIV counseling and testing at intake to the correctional facility,[30] the majority of correctional systems currently do not offer universal HIV testing, a critical limitation for effective TB prevention and control and for the medical management of individual patients.[31] Moreover, in HIV-infected persons infected with M tuberculosis, the progression to TB disease is often rapid and can cause difficult-to-control outbreaks.[27]

Outbreaks of both multidrug-resistant and drug-susceptible TB related to HIV coinfection have been documented in correctional facilities.[3,4,27,32,33] These outbreaks are often attributed to the failure to detect TB disease early after entry into the facility or failure to complete treatment for LTBI resulting in TB transmission to other inmates, correctional facility employees,[3,34,35] and community members.[36]

Epidemiologic and operational studies have helped elucidate problem areas for TB prevention and control in correctional systems and the surrounding community.[5,7,10,14,25,34–37] One such study in Memphis, Tenn, showed that 43% of community residents with TB had been incarcerated in the same jail at some time before their diagnosis, and this jail had experienced a TB outbreak lasting several years.[14] A subsequent study revealed the strain in question was more prevalent in the surrounding community than it was prior to the jail outbreak.[35] In Maricopa County, Ariz, 24% of persons reported with TB during 1999 and 2000 had been incarcerated in the county jail prior to their TB diagnosis.[37] Additionally, it was discovered that the majority of persons (83%) who later had TB had not received any TB screening while in jail. These and other reports have highlighted the need for implementing infection control measures in correctional facilities.[24]

Our data confirmed that health disparities in treatment outcomes exist for inmates with TB. Inmates have lower treatment completion rates; even when individual risk groups are compared, the discrepancy in treatment completion for inmates persists (Table 4). Tuberculosis screening at entry to a correctional facility provides a unique opportunity for identifying individuals at risk for TB who might not otherwise have access to medical care and prevention services.[37] Correctional systems, especially jails, offer distinct logistical obstacles to screening and treatment; inmates are moved frequently or are released, making evaluation and completion of therapy difficult at best.[14] Inmates are more likely to have treatment outcomes classified as "incomplete" owing to their moving out of the jurisdiction or being lost to treatment supervision.[38] Failure to complete treatment for TB is a cause for concern for the health of those individuals who did not receive a full course of curative therapy and for the communities in which they live.

One limitation of our study is that the national surveillance data identified only case-patients diagnosed during incarceration. Those with TB who may have progressed to disease before or after incarceration are not separately defined in our analysis. Standard TB-control activities and investigations may not elicit information about incarceration, resulting in possible underreporting of cases that are epidemiologically linked with incarceration.[34,36] Failures to establish these connections hamper the effectiveness of public health interventions.[22,35,36] Another limitation of the study is the difficulty of tracking outcomes when inmates are transferred within or between correctional systems. For that reason, our data may underestimate completion rates for some prison inmates.

Poor access to TB services and socioeconomic status play a role in the elevated TB rates among correctional inmates.[39] However, inmates are more likely to receive treatment by directly observed therapy, a patient-management practice that generally improves the success of treatment completion. Our finding of unacceptably low rates for the therapy completion among inmates is disturbing because of the possibility that these individuals may be the cause of future TB outbreaks in a given community.[40] To better ascertain and improve treatment completion rates among inmates, health departments should enhance their capacity for tracking TB patients diagnosed or treated in correctional systems. To ensure that TB medical evaluations and therapy are completed for inmates, public health and corrections officials are obliged to develop policies that optimize discharge planning and case management for inmates released during TB evaluation or treatment.[38,40] These policies should be reevaluated periodically to determine whether such practices should be modified to improve outcomes.[2,41]

About the Authors

At the time of the study, Jessica R. MacNeil, Mark N. Lobato, and Marisa Moore were with the Division of Tuberculosis Elimination, National Center for HIV, STD, and TB Prevention, Centers for Disease Control and Prevention, Atlanta, Ga.

Correspondence: Requests for reprints should be sent to National Center for HIV, STD, and TB Prevention, Office of Communications, Centers for Disease Control and Prevention, 1600 Clifton Road, Mail Stop E-06, Atlanta, GA 30333.

Acknowledgments

We thank Robert Pratt for his careful scrutiny during data verification.

Human Participation Protection

No protocol approval was needed for this study. The national surveillance system has been classified by the CDC as a project not involving human subjects or research because the primary intent is a public health practice disease control activity, specifically routine disease surveillance. The data are used for disease control program or policy purposes.

Contributors

The authors all conceptualized the study. J. R. MacNeil conducted analyses. M. Moore supervised the analyses. M. N. Lobato assisted with the interpretation of the data analyses and coauthored the article. All authors conceptualized ideas, interpreted findings, and reviewed drafts of the article.

References

1. Centers for Disease Control and Prevention. *Reported Tuberculosis in the United States, 2003*. Atlanta, Ga: US Department of Health and Human Services, Centers for Disease Control and Prevention, September 2004.
2. Centers for Disease Control and Prevention. Prevention and control of tuberculosis in correctional facilities: recommendations of the Advisory Council for the Elimination of Tuberculosis. *MMWR Morb Mortal Wkly Rep.* 1996;45(No. RR-8):1–27.
3. Centers for Disease Control and Prevention. Probable transmission of multidrug-resistant tuberculosis in a correctional facility—California. *MMWR Morb Mortal Wkly Rep.* 1993;42:48–51.
4. Braun MM, Truman BI, Maguire B, et

al. Increasing incidence of tuberculosis in a prison inmate population: association with HIV infection. *JAMA.* 1989;261: 393–397.

5. White MC, Tulsky JP, Portillo CJ, Menendez E, Cruz E, Goldenson J. Tuberculosis prevalence in an urban jail:1994 and 1998. *Int J Tuberc Lung Dis.* 2001;5:400–404.

6. Spencer SS, Morton AR. Tuberculosis surveillance in a state prison system. *Am J Public Health.* 1989;79: 507–509.

7. Alcabes P, Vossenas P, Cohen R, Braslow C, Michaels D, Zoloth S. Compliance with isoniazid prophylaxis in jail. *Am Rev Respir Dis.* 1989;140:1194–1197.

8. Salive ME, Vlahov D, Brewer TF. Coinfection with tuberculosis and HIV-1 in male prison inmates. *Public Health Rep.* 1990;105:307–310.

9. Centers for Disease Control and Prevention. Tuberculosis prevention in drug-treatment centers and correctional facilities—selected US. sites, 1990–1991. *MMWR Morb Mortal Wkly Rep.* 1993;42:210–213.

10. Lobato MN, Leary LS, Simone PM. Treatment for latent TB in correctional facilities: a challenge for TB elimination. *Am J Prev Med.* 2003;24:249–253.

11. Stead WW. Undetected tuberculosis in prison: source of infection for community at large. *JAMA.* 1978;240:2544–2547.

12. Bellin EY, Fletcher DD, Safyer SM. Association of tuberculosis infection with increased time in or admission to the New York City jail system. *JAMA.* 1993; 269:2228–2231.

13. US Department of Justice. *Prison and Jail Inmates at Midyear 2003.* Bureau of Justice Statistics Bulletin. May 2004, NCJ 203947.

14. Jones TF, Craig AS, Valway SE, Woodley CL, Schaffner W. Transmission of tuberculosis in a jail. *Ann Intern Med.* 1999;131:557–563.

15. Koo DT, Baron RC, Rutherford GW. Transmission of Mycobacterium tuberculosis in a California state prison, 1991. *Am J Public Health.* 1997;87:279–282.

16. US Department of Justice. *Prison and Jail Inmates at Midyear 1996.* Bureau of Justice Statistics Bulletin. June 1997, NCJ 164619.

17. US Department of Justice. *Prison and Jail Inmates at Midyear 2001.* Bureau of Justice Statistics Bulletin. July 2002, NCJ 195189.

18. Saunders DL, Olive DM, Wallace SB, Lacy D, Leyba R, Kendig NE. Tuberculosis screening in the federal prison system: an opportunity to treat and prevent tuberculosis in foreign-born populations. *Public Health Rep.* 2001;116:210–218.

19. US Department of Justice. *Prison and Jail Inmates at Midyear 2004.* Bureau of Justice Statistics Bulletin. April 2005, NCJ 208801.

20. Selwyn PA, Hartel D, Lewis VA, et al. A prospective study of the risk of tuberculosis among intravenous drug users with human immunodeficiency virus infection. *N Engl J Med.* 1989;320:545–550.

21. Zolopa AR, Hahn JA, Gorter R, et al. HIV and tuberculosis infection in San Francisco's homeless adults. Prevalence and risk factors in a representative sample. *JAMA.* 1994;272:455–461.

22. McElroy PD, Southwick KL, Fortenberry ER, et al. Outbreak of tuberculosis among homeless persons coinfected with human immunodeficiency virus. *Clin Infect Dis.* 2003;36:1305–1312.

23. Bock NN, Reeves M, LaMarre M, DeVoe B. Tuberculosis case detection in a state prison system. *Public Health Rep.* 1988;113:359–364.

24. Chaves F, Dronda F, Cave MD, et al. A longitudinal study of transmission of tuberculosis in a large prison population. *Am J Respir Crit Care Med.* 1997; 155:719–725.

25. MacIntyre CR, Kendig N, Kummer L, Birago S, Graham NM, Plant AJ. Unrecognised transmission of tuberculosis in prisons. *Eur J Epidemiol.* 1999;15: 705–709.

26. Bergmire-Sweat D, Barnett BJ, Harris SL, Taylor JP, Mazurek GH, Reddy V. Tuberculosis outbreak in a Texas Prision, 1994. *Epidemiol Infect.* 1996;117:485–492.

27. Centers for Disease Control and Prevention. Drug-susceptible tuberculosis outbreak in a state correctional facility housing HIV-infected Inmates—South Carolina, 1999–2000. *MMWR Morb Mortal Wkly Rep.* 2000; 49:1041–1044.

28. Shafer RW, Edlin BR. Tuberculosis in patients infected with human immunodeficiency virus: perspective on the past decade. *Clin Infect Dis.* 1996;22:683–704.

29. Reichard AA, Lobato MN, Roberts CA, Bazerman LB, Hammett TM. Assessment of tuberculosis screening and management practices of large jail systems. *Public Health Rep.* 2003;118:500–507.

30. Centers for Disease Control and Prevention. Routine HIV Testing of Inmates in Correctional Facilities. Available at http://www.cdc.gov/hiv/partners/Interim/routinetest.htm. Accessed March 14, 2005.

31. Hammett TM, Maruschak LM. *1996–1997 update: HIV/AIDS, STDs, and TB in correctional facilities.* Issues and Practices in Criminal Justice, Washington DC: US Department of Justice, National Institute of Justice, 1999, NCJ 176344.

32. Valway SE, Richards SB, Kovacovich J, Greifinger RB, Crawford JT, Dooley SW. Outbreak of multi-drug-resistant tuberculosis in a New York State prison, 1991. *Am J Epidemiol.* 1994;140:113–122.

33. Centers for Disease Control and Prevention. Tuberculosis outbreaks in prison housing units for HIV-infected inmates—California, 1995–1996. *MMWR Morb Mortal Wkly Rep.* 1999;48:79–82.

34. Steenland K, Levine AJ, Sieber K, Schulte P, Aziz D. Incidence of tuberculosis infection among New York State prison employees. *Am J Public Health.* 1997;87: 2012–2014.

35. Jones TF, Woodley CL, Fountain FF, Schaffner W. Increased incidence of the outbreak strain of Mycobacterium tuberculosis in the surrounding community after an outbreak in a jail. *South Med J.* 2003;96:155–157.

36. Bur S, Golub JE, Armstrong JA, et al. Evaluation of an extensive tuberculosis contact investigation in an urban community and jail. *Int J Tuberc Lung Dis.* 2003; 7:S417–423.

37. MacNeil JR, McRill C, Steinhauser G, Weisbuch JB, Williams E, Wilson ML. Jails, a neglected opportunity for tuberculosis prevention. *Am J Prev Med.* 2005;28: 225–228.

38. Cummings KC, Mohle-Boetani J, Royce SE, Chin DP. Movement of tuberculosis patients and the failure to complete antituberculosis treatment. *Am J Respir Crit Care Med.* 1998;157:1249–1252.

39. Cantwell MF, McKenna MT, McCray E, Onorato IM. Tuberculosis and race/ethnicity in the United States: impact of socioeconomic status. *Am J Respir Crit Care Med.* 1998;157:1016–1020.

40. Tuberculosis outbreak in a homeless population—Portland, Maine,

2002–2003. *MMWR Morb Mortal Wkly Rep.* 2003;52:1184–1185.

41. Klopf LC. Tuberculosis control in the New York State Department of Correctional Services: a case management approach. *Am J Infect Control.*

1998;26: 534–537.

42. Lobato MN, Roberts CA, Bazerman LB, Hammett TM. Public health and correctional collaboration in tuberculosis control. *Am J Prev Med.* 2004;27:112–117.

43. US Census Bureau. Population Estimates. Available at: www.census.gov/popest/archives/php. Accessed March 15, 2005.

Confronting Health Inequity: The Global Dimension

| Juan Antonio Casas-Zamora, MD, MScSM and Said A. Ibrahim, MD, MPH

INTRODUCTION

Since the days of Hippocrates, health inequities and the role of social and environmental factors in the determination of marked differences in health status have been well recognized. For some time now, the driving force behind public health has been understanding and intervening in the underlying causes of health inequity. The publication of the Black Report[1] in the United Kingdom in 1980 brought a more focused approach to this discourse by identifying specific factors, such as social class, gender, and race/ethnicity, as the social and economic determinants of health inequities. With this evolution came a conceptual and operational distinction between health disparities/inequalities and health inequity/equity.[2]

These distinctions aside, the issue of health inequity has moved beyond the academic discourse into the arena of policy and action. In the United States, the 2002 Institute of Medicine report *Unequal Treatment: Confronting Health Care Disparities* marked a turning point.[3] It is, however, important to recognize that like the problem of health inequity itself, the struggle to confront it is neither unique to the United States nor simply a local matter. Many nations, both developed and developing, have adopted strategies to reduce health inequities.

EFFORTS IN THE DEVELOPED WORLD

Confronting health inequities is increasingly a priority for health policy-makers, both nationally and internationally. There are several recent examples of national governments in developed countries undertaking major initiatives to reduce health inequities. For instance, in the United Kingdom one of the first decisions of the incoming Labor government in 1997 was to commission the "Independent Inquiry into Inequalities in Health." Under the direction of Sir Donald Acheson, the commission's mandate was to establish the facts and suggest why, despite the increase in prosperity and substantial reductions in mortality evinced in the United Kingdom in the previous 2 decades, the gap in health status between those at the top and bottom of the social scale, as well as between various ethnic groups and between the sexes, had continued to widen.[4] On the basis of the commission's recommendations, the government formulated a comprehensive plan that recognizes the structural determinants of health, such as the social environment and the wider community, with the overarching goal of reducing avoidable health disparities.[5,6]

In 1998, the EURO Health for All policy (Health 21) was published.[7] This policy specifies that by 2020 the health gap between countries and between socioeconomic groups within countries should be reduced by at least one fourth in all member states. Since that time, other European countries have undertaken similar comprehensive reviews and action plans at regional, national, and local levels.[8,9] The following EURO Health for All policy recommendations are being implemented, at least partially, in member states of the European Union and various other neighboring countries, providing a useful model for similar action in other regions[10]:

1 Establish national health inequity targets by identifying and advocating relevant national and regional health targets and by tackling health determinants to reduce health inequalities.

2 Integrate health determinants into other policy areas at national, regional, and local levels, using cross-sectoral approaches.

3 Work at the local level by supporting community development approaches and the integration of local services, multi-disciplinary approaches, and partnerships.

4 Reduce barriers to ensure access to and use of effective health care and prevention services by socially disadvantaged and vulnerable groups.

5 Develop indicators and systems for monitoring health inequalities, including systems for collecting data on structural factors and determinants of health, such as social class, gender, and ethnicity.

6 Assess health impact by developing and applying procedures, methods, and tools by which policies, programs, and projects may be judged as to their potential effects on the health of a population and the distribution of those effects within the population.

7 Evaluate financial and human resources to ensure sufficiency and to increase knowledge on how to effectively tackle health inequities.

8 Create and support opportunities to disseminate models of good practice and evidence-based approaches to tackle health inequalities, including databases of successful interventions.

Other developed countries, such as Australia, New Zealand, and Canada, are also in the process of incorporating health equity and social determinants of health into regional or national public health policies.[11–13]

In the United States in 1998, the Clinton administration established the Initiative to Eliminate Racial and Ethnic Disparities in Health, which set a national goal of eliminating long-standing racial/ethnic disparities in health status by 2010 and, for the first time, set high national goals for all Americans, ending a practice of separate, lower goals for racial and ethnic minorities.[14] There are mounting public and private coalition efforts aimed at "closing the gap" in health and health care that have continued under the Bush administration.[15]

In contrast to the European approach to health inequities, it is racial and ethnic disparities that are of greater policy relevance in the United States. First, there are obvious historical reasons for the extensive overlap of socioeconomic and racial inequalities in the United States. Second, the predominant use of ethnic and racial group categories in most vital statistics, census, economic, and other population and health related data greatly facilitates monitoring disparities by race instead of by social class.[16] In fact, it has been well demonstrated in the United States that socioeconomic differences between races account for much of the racial differences in health, even though race per se—or rather, the results of societal discrimination based on race—may have an independent effect on health status and health care access/utilization.[17–19]

STRATEGIES IN THE DEVELOPING WORLD

The emergence of health equity as a public health issue is also occurring

in the developing world. Following the Alma-Ata Primary Health Care Summit in 1979, many national governments in Latin America, Asia, and Africa came together to formulate a strategy for achieving the goal of "Health for All."

The Alma-Ata summit advocated the achievement of greater health equity and the reduction of health disparities as national goals. Prior to the emergence of the HIV/AIDS epidemic in the 1990s, many developing countries achieved noteworthy improvements in national average life expectancy and mortality rates, even though health disparities between socioeconomic and ethnic groups within countries actually increased in most cases. For example, in Latin America and the Caribbean, the region that experienced the highest rate of improvement in health indicators in that period, health disparities were also the greatest. The ratio between the highest and lowest national infant mortality rates in the region of the Americas was 7:1 in 1964 and had risen to 14:1 by 1994. Similarly, within Brazil, even though the national infant mortality rate fell by 40% between 1977 and 1995, the ratio between the rural northeast and the rest of the country actually increased from 1.7:1 to 2.0:1.[20]

In response to these disparities, from 1996 to 2002 the Pan American Health Organization undertook an ambitious effort to promote health equity in its technical cooperation programs in the Americas by promoting research, benchmarking, strengthening information dissemination, establishing databases, and improving health information analysis for monitoring and reducing health disparities within and between countries in the region.[21,22] In fact, some Latin American countries—for example, Costa Rica, Chile, Peru, Bolivia, and Brazil—have incorporated equity goals into their national public health programs.

THE ROLE OF THE INTERNATIONAL COMMUNITY

The international community also has a role in the global campaign to

confront health inequalities. Some international organizations are already in the forefront of this campaign. For example, the Poverty and Health Network of the World Bank[23,24] has developed a methodology for the analysis of socioeconomic differences in health, nutrition, and population in developing countries that is based on the World Bank's demographic and health surveys. This methodology provides a much needed empirical approach for monitoring intracountry trends and intercountry comparisons of health disparities.[25,26]

In 1996, the Rockefeller Foundation and the Sweden International Development Cooperation Agency established a Global Health Equity Initiative, with a network of more than 100 researchers in more than 15 countries, for the purpose of raising global awareness and building capacity to address health inequities. The most visible product of this effort was the publication in 2001 of a groundbreaking report[27] that established a solid conceptual and operational framework, based on a global perspective and country-specific analysis, of health equity in which global and national determinants are closely interrelated (via the economic and social consequences of economic and financial globalization, political stability and governance, poverty and development, ethnic conflicts, migration, etc.). The report emphasized the need to strengthen the capacity of the health sector in all countries and provide it with tools for tackling health disparities, in partnership with all potential partners in government and civil society.

Various current global initiatives have emerged from the Global Health Equity Initiative and other aforementioned efforts. One is the Global Equity Gauge Alliance, also supported by the Rockefeller Foundation and the Sweden International Development Cooperation Agency, which was created to participate in and support an active approach to monitoring health inequalities and promoting equity within and between societies. The Alliance currently includes 11 member-teams, called Equity Gauges, located in 10 countries in the Americas, Africa, and Asia.[28] In sub-Saharan Africa, an initiative closely linked to the Global Equity Gauge Alliance is EQUINET, the Regional Network on Equity in Health in Southern Africa. EQUINET involves professionals, civil society members, policymakers, state officials, and academic, government, and civic institutions from Botswana, Malawi, Mozambique, South Africa, Tanzania, Zambia, Zimbabwe, and the South African Development Community who have come together as an equity catalyst to promote shared values of equity and social justice in health.[29]

The International Society for Health Equity, founded in 2000, has successfully held 3 international conferences with hundreds of participants from all continents; today it constitutes the most authoritative international professional association of health equity researchers, analysts, and advocates.[30] The most recent conference, held in Durban, South Africa, in June 2004, dealt with a myriad of emerging issues for effectively reducing health disparities in the developing and developed world. Some of these issues included insurance and finance, resource allocation, access to care, special population groups, analytical methods for time trends and life-course determinants, community action, social empowerment, gender and health, law and human rights, local governance and planning, and the impact of HIV/AIDS.[31]

The United Nations organizations, such as the World Health Organization (WHO), also have a leadership role to play in the global effort to confront health inequalities. Such action is consistent with the 1998 World Health Assembly resolution, which confirmed that a reduction in socioeconomic inequalities in health was a priority for all countries.[32] In 2000, a special issue of the *Bulletin of the World Health Organization*[33] was devoted to inequalities in health, and the WHO Global Health Survey, initiated in 2001, provides valuable health indicators that can be crossed with socioeconomic

data to provide the basis for the monitoring of health disparities.[34]

Since 2003, under the leadership of Director General Lee Jong-Wook, the issue of health equity has acquired a new place in the priorities of WHO.[35] An equity team has been established within the area of evidence and information for policy, with the objective of supporting innovation and strengthening knowledge sharing on a global level. An expressed goal is to develop new forms of collaboration between health experts and decision-makers to translate current evidence on the social and environmental determinants of health disparities into effective public policy.[36] In his speech to the 57th World Health Assembly in May of this year, the WHO director general announced his intention to set up and launch a new global commission formed by expert public health scientists and policymakers to gather evidence on the social and environmental causes of health inequities and ways to overcome them, with the purpose of providing guidance for all WHO programs.[37]

In summary, there is a global movement for health equity that began in the last decade of the 20th century and continues to grow. The role of information and knowledge sharing is key in linking this global effort to local actions and challenges; international and national health organizations in the developed and developing countries, be they in the public sector or in civil society, must join hands with local communities and governments if health inequities are to be effectively reduced.

The optimists among us believe that the road toward globalization can lead us to a future in which development becomes freedom[38] and in which all human beings can enjoy complete citizenship, wherever they may be; exercise the right to gainful employment; and fully share in the benefits of knowledge and information.[39] Such a world is one in which avoidable and unfair differences in the opportunity to lead a healthy life—differences between men and women; among Black, White, and brown;

among inhabitants of the North and South, East and West—would cease to exist. The road to this world is a long one, one that will take us far beyond the horizon. Although it begins on our very doorstep, it has global dimensions.

About the Authors

Juan Antonio Casas-Zamora is with the Liaison Office to the European Union, World Health Organization, Brussels, Belgium. Said A. Ibrahim is with the Center for Health Equity Research and Promotion, VA Pittsburgh Healthcare System, Pittsburgh, Pa.

Correspondence: Requests for reprints should be sent to Said A. Ibrahim, MD, MPH, Center for Health Equity Research and Promotion, VA Pittsburgh Healthcare System, University Drive C, 11-East (130 A-U) Pittsburgh, PA 15240 (e-mail: said.ibrahim2@med.va.gov).

References

1. Black D. *Inequities in Health.* London, United Kingdom: Penguin; 1980.
2. Macinko JA, Starfield B. Annotated bibliography on equity in health, 1980–2001. *International Journal for Equity in Health.* 2002;1(1):1–20.
3. *Unequal treatment: confronting racial and ethnic disparitites in health care. A report of the Institute of Medicine.* Washington, DC: National Academy Press; 2002.
4. Acheson D. Independent Inquiry into Inequalities in health report. London, United Kingdom: The Stationery Office; 1998. Available at: http://www.archive.official-documents.co.uk/document/doh/ih/ih.htm. Accessed September 27, 2004.
5. Exworthy M, Stuart M, Blane D, Marmot M. *Tackling Health Inequalities Since the Acheson Inquiry.* London, United Kingdom: The Policy Press; 2003.
6. Department of Health. Health inequalities. 2004. Available at: http://www.dh.gov.uk/policyandguidance/healthandsocialcaretopics/healthinequalities. Accessed September 27, 2004.
7. World Health Organization Regional Office for Europe. Health 21: an introduction to the health for all policy framework for the WHO European

Region. Available at: http://www.euro.who.int/document/EHFA5-E.pdf. 1998. Accessed September 27, 2004.

8. World Health Organization Regional Office for Europe. Update of the regional Health for All Policy framework. 2003. Available at: http://www.euro.who.int/document/rc53/edoc08.pdf. Accessed September 27, 2004.

9. Menke R, Streich W, Rossler G, Brand H. *Report on Socio-Economic Differences in Health Indicators in Europe: Health Inequalities in Europe and the Situation of Disadvantaged Groups.* Bilthoven, the Netherlands: National Institute for Public Health and the Environment (RIVM); 2003.

10. European Network of Health Promotion Agencies. The role of health promotion in tackling inequalities in health: policy recommendations. Available at: http://www.euro-healthnet.org/eurohealthnet/ressources/brochure.pdf (PDF file). Accessed September 27, 2004.

11. New South Wales Department of Health. Social determinants of health. Updated October 24, 2002. Available at: http://www.health.nsw.gov.au/public-health/chorep/soc/soc_intro.htm. Accessed September 27, 2004.

12. Ministry of Health. Social inequalities in health–New Zealand 1999. 2000. Available at: http://www.moh.govt.nz/moh.nsf/0/65b8566b2ac3a9684c2569660079de90?OpenDocument. Accessed September 27, 2004.

13. Health Canada. The social determinants of health: an overview of the implications for policy and the role of the health sector. 2003. Available at: http://www.hc-sc.gc.ca/hppb/phdd/pdf/overview_implications/01_overview_e.pdf. Accessed September 27, 2004.

14. Ibrahim SA, Thomas SB, Fine MJ. Achieving health equity: an incremental journey. *Am J Public Health.* 2003;93: 1619–1621.

15. Department of Health and Human Services, Office of Minority Health. Health disparities. Available at: http://www.omhrc.gov/OMH/Health%20Disparities/index.htm. Accessed September 27, 2004.

16. National Research Council, Panel on DHHS Collection of Race and Ethnic Data. Ver Ploeg M, Perrin E, eds. *Eliminating Health Disparities: Measurement and Data Needs.* Washington, DC: National Academies Press; 2004. Also available at: http://www.nap.edu/catalog/10979.html. Accessed September 27, 2004.

17. Krieger N, Sidney S. Racial discrimination and blood pressure: the CARDIA study of young black and white adults. *Am J Public Health.* 1996; 86:1370–1378.

18. Krieger N, Rowley DL, Herman AA, Avery B, Phillips MT. Racism, sexism, and social class: implications for studies of health, disease, and well-being. *Am J Prev Med.* 1993;9(suppl 6): 82–122.

19. House J, Williams DR. Understanding and reducing socioeconomic and racial/ethnic disparities in health. In: Hofrichter R, ed. *Health and Social Justice: Politics, Ideology, and Inequity in the Distribution of Disease.* San Francisco, Calif: Jossey-Bass; 2003.

20. Casas JA, Dachs NW, Bambas A. Health disparities in Latin America and the Caribbean: the role of social and economic determinants. In: *Equity and Health: Views From the Pan American Sanitary Bureau.* Washington, DC: Pan American Health Organization; 2001: 22–49.

21. Casa-Zamora JA, Gwatkin DR. The many dimensions of health equity. *Rev Pan Am Salúd Publica.* 2002;11(5–6). Available at: http://www.scielosp.org/scielo.php?script=sci_issuetoc&pid=1020-498920020005&lng=en&nrm=iso. Accessed September 27, 2004.

22. EQIDAD electronic mailing list. Available at: http://equidad.bvsalud.org.

23. Gwatkin DR. Reducing health inequalities in developing countries. In: Detels R, McEwen J, Beaglehole R, Tanaka H, eds. *Oxford Textbook of Public Health.* Vol 3. 4th ed. New York, NY: Oxford University Press; 2002: 1791–1810.

24. Wagstaff. A. Poverty and health sector inequalities. *Bull World Health Organ.* 2002;80:97–105.

25. Round I country reports on health, nutrition, population conditions among poor and better-off in 45 countries. 2000. Available at: http://www1.worldbank.org/prem/poverty/health/data/round1.htm. Accessed September 27, 2004.

26. Round II Country Reports on Health, Nutrition, Population Conditions among Poor and Better-Off in 56 Countries. 2004. Available at: http://www1.worldbank.org/prem/poverty/health/data/round2.htm. Accessed September 27, 2004.

27. Evans T, Whitehead M, Diderichsen F, Bhuiya A, Wirth M, eds. *Challenging Inequities in Health: From Ethics to Action.* New York, NY: Oxford University Press; 2001.

28. McCoy D, Bambas L, Acurio D, et al. Global equity gauge alliance: reflections on early experiences. *J Health Popul Nutr.* 2003;21:273–287.

29. EQUINET Africa. Available at: http://www.equinetafrica.org. Accessed September 27, 2004.

30. Toronto declaration on equity in health. *Pan Am J Public Health.* 2002; 12:465–467.

31. International Society for Equity in Health, Third International Conference. Conference program. 2004. Available at: http://www.iseqh.org/documents/Agenda-DETAILEDJune12004-Printer.doc. Accessed September 27, 2004.

32. World Health Organization. Health-for-all policy for the 21st century. Available at : http:www3.who.int/whosis/discussion_papers/pdf/paper43.pdf . Accessed September 27, 2004.

33. World Health Organization. *Bull World Health Organ.* 2000;78(1).

34. Sandana R, Tandon A, Murray CJL, et al. Describing population health in six domains: comparable results from 66 household surveys. March 2002. Available at: http://www3.who.int/whosis/discussion_papers/pdf/paper43.pdf. Accessed September 27, 2004.

35. Lee JW. Global health and WHO: shaping the future. *Lancet.* 2003;362:2083–2088.

36. Vega J, Irwin A. Tackling health inequalities: new approaches in public policy. *Bull World Health Organ.* 2004; 82:432–433.

37. World Health Organization. Fifty-Seventh World Health Assembly, Address by the Director-General. May 17, 2004. Available at: http://www.who.int/dg/lee/speeches/2004/wha57/en. Accessed September 27, 2004.

38. Sen AK. *Development as Freedom.* New York, NY: Knopf; 1999.

39. Hardt M, Negri A. *Empire.* Cambridge, Mass: Harvard University Press; 2001.

Disparities in Indigenous Health: A Cross-Country Comparison Between New Zealand and the United States

| Dale Bramley, MBChB, MPH, FAFPHM, Paul Hebert, PhD, Leah Tuzzio, MPH and Mark Chassin, MD, MPP, MPH

ABSTRACT

Objectives. We compared the health statuses of the indigenous populations of New Zealand and the United States with those of the numerically dominant populations of these countries.

Methods. Health indicators compared included health outcome measures, preventive care measures, modifiable risk factor prevalence, and treatment measures.

Results. In the case of nearly every health status indicator assessed, disparities (both absolute and relative) were more pronounced for Maoris than for American Indians/Alaska Natives. Both indigenous populations suffered from disparities across a range of health indicators. However, no disparities were observed for American Indians/Alaska Natives in regard to immunization coverage.

Conclusions. Ethnic health disparities appear to be more pronounced in New Zealand than in the United States. These disparities are not necessarily intractable. Although differences in national health sector responses exist, New Zealand may be well placed in the future to evaluate the effectiveness of new strategies to reduce these disparities given the extent and quality of Maori-specific health information available.

INTRODUCTION

The indigenous peoples of New Zealand and the United States have much in common. Both have had a history of colonization. In addition, they have become, in numerical terms, "minority" populations relative to the predominant European and White groups in each country. Maoris (who represent 10%–15% of New Zealand's population) and American Indians/Alaska Natives (who represent 1%–1.5% of the US population) also exhibit substantially poorer health outcomes than the majority populations over a range of health indicators.[1,2] Reducing health disparities has recently become a central focus of health care policies in both countries.

In New Zealand, the national health strategy aims to reduce inequalities in health status and to ensure accessible and appropriate services for Maoris, Pacific peoples, and those of low socioeconomic status.[3] In the United States, *Healthy People 2010* is the federal government's blueprint for building a healthier nation.[4] It is designed to achieve 2 major overarching goals: increasing Americans' quality of life and years of healthy life and ending racial/ethnic disparities in disease burden.

Our study's aims were to compare the health status of the indigenous populations of New Zealand and the United States with that of the majority (European/White) populations of these countries over a range of health-related indicators, including health outcomes (i.e., life expectancy, infant mortality, mortality risk ratios), preventive services (i.e., immunization, cervical cancer and breast cancer screening coverage), modifiable risk factors (i.e., smoking, obesity, diabetes), and treatment services (i.e., access to coronary artery bypass grafting, coronary angio-plasty, renal transplantation). We discuss gaps in the current availability of health indicator data.

The 2 countries differ in regard to the approaches they are taking to reduce the large disparities in the health status of indigenous populations. There are a number of reasons for these different approaches, including differences in historical understandings of the nature of health disparities, the way in which the health sector is organized, legislative and funding incentives associated with reducing disparities, and the availability of indigenous data to monitor disparities.

METHODS

We compared health indicators related to the Maori indigenous population of New Zealand and the American Indian/Alaska Native indigenous population of the United States with indicators for the numerically dominant population group in each country: those of European background (or non-Maori/non-Pacific people when European data were unavailable) in New Zealand and non-Hispanic Whites in the United States. It should be noted, however, that other minority groups in both countries experience poorer health outcomes than the majority group; examples are Pacific peoples in New Zealand and Hispanic, indigenous Hawaiian, and African American groups in the United States.

We selected health indicators on the basis of availability of data, impact on health status, meaningfulness, and susceptibility to influence by the health system.[5] We used the most recent, representative, and comparable data available. Although these data are not always directly comparable between the 2 countries, they do fairly assess the differences that exist within countries in terms of the racial/ethnic groups examined. (Details on the data sources used are available from the first author.)

Health Outcome Measures

New Zealand data on life expectancy at birth and infant mortality were obtained from the country's Ministry of Health.[6,7] US data for these measures were obtained from the National Center for Health Statistics and the Indian Health Service (IHS), an agency housed within the US Department of Health and Human Services.[8–10]

The mortality measures we used in our comparisons were those accounting for the leading causes of death in the 2 countries,[11,12] including lung, bowel, cervical, breast, and prostate cancers; ischemic heart disease; cerebrovascular disease; chronic obstructive pulmonary disease; suicide; diabetes; HIV; and homicide. Mortality data for New Zealand are compiled by the New Zealand Health Information Service,[11] and causes of death are defined according to *International Classification of Diseases* (*ICD*; 9th revision) codes. Mortality data for the United States are compiled by the National Center for Health Statistics,[13] which uses codes from the *ICD*, 10th revision, to identify causes of death. (Details on the *ICD* codes used in the present analyses are available from the first author.)

In the case of both countries, we used crude data to calculate 1999 mortality rates for the indigenous and majority populations by primary cause of death. In addition, we calculated age-adjusted mortality rates using direct standardization[14] and weights based on the 1999 New Zealand population. We also conducted analyses using US-based weights and Segi population-based weights,[11] and these analyses produced results similar to

those presented here. In our study, mortality risk ratios refer to the age-adjusted mortality rate in the indigenous population divided by the age-adjusted rate in the majority population.

Preventive Care Measures

Measles, mumps, rubella, tetanus, pertussis, diphtheria, polio, and hepatitis B immunization data were collected. New Zealand data were derived from the 1996 North Health Survey (the country's most recent immunization survey)[15]; US data were derived from the country's 2001 National Immunization Survey.[16]

Screening coverage data for New Zealand (for 2002 and 2003) were obtained from the Ministry of Health.[17] Breast screening data are presented for women aged 50 to 64 years who had undergone a mammography in the preceding 2 years as part of the country's national breast cancer screening program. Papanicolaou test data are presented for women aged 20 to 69 years who had undergone testing in the preceding 3 years as part of the national cervical cancer screening program.

Self-reported data on use of screening services in the United States were obtained from the 1998 National Health Interview Survey. Breast cancer screening data are presented for women 40 years or older who had undergone a mammography in the preceding 2 years. Cervical cancer screening data are reported for women 18 years or older who had undergone a Papanicolaou test in the preceding 3 years.[4]

Modifiable Risk Factors

Smoking prevalence data for New Zealand (among individuals 15 years or older) were derived from a 2001 tobacco use survey.[18] Smokers were defined as those who smoked either readymade or "roll-your-own" cigarettes.[18] US smoking data (among individuals 18 years or older) were obtained from the 2001 National Health Interview Survey.[19] Smokers were defined as those who had smoked 100 cigarettes in their lifetime

and who now smoked every day or some days.[20]

Obesity prevalence data for New Zealand (among those 15 years or older) were obtained from the 2002–2003 New Zealand Health Survey. Adult obesity levels were defined as measured body mass indexes (BMIs) of 30 or above among the majority population and 32 or above among Maoris. Overweight levels were defined as BMIs between 25 and 29 among the majority population and between 26 and 31 among Maoris.[21] In the United States, data for White men and women older than 20 years were obtained from the 1999–2000 National Health and Nutrition Examination Survey (NHANES).[22] Obesity was defined as a BMI of 30 or above; overweight was defined as a BMI between 25 and 29. The NHANES sampling design does not include American Indians/Alaska Natives living on reservations. Thus, obesity data for American Indians/Alaska Natives were derived from the Strong Heart Survey (data were available for adults aged 45–74 years).[23]

New Zealand diabetes prevalence data (among those 15 years or older) were obtained from the 1996–1997 New Zealand Health Survey. Prevalence rates were based on self-reported data.[24] US diabetes prevalence data (among those 20 years or older) were obtained from the Behavioral Risk Factor Surveillance System and from the IHS.[25,26]

Treatment Services

The rates we present here are relative rates according to racial/ethnic group membership. We did not calculate absolute values, because medical practice characteristics and access to procedures may vary between the 2 countries. In the United States, no national databases exist containing information on treatment procedures (making any comparison of such services difficult). However, the Medicare program maintains administrative data on all US residents older than 65 years. Therefore, these data were deemed to be the most consistent with

TABLE 1— Health Outcome Measures, by Gender and Ethnicity: United States and New Zealand

	New Zealand				United States			
	Maori/European Difference	Maori	European	Total	AIAN/White Difference	AIAN	White	Total
	Life expectancy[a]							
Male	8.9	68.0	76.9	76.2	7.4	67.4	74.8	79.5
Female	9.4	72.3	81.7	81.0	5.8	74.2	80.0	74.1
	Infant mortality[b]							
Total	3.6	7.7	4.1	5.4	3.3	9.3	6.0	7.2

Note. AIAN = American Indian/Alaska Native.

[a]Life expectancy at birth (years). European life expectancy refers to non-Maori population.

[b]Number of deaths in a calendar year among children younger than 1 year per 1000 live births in the same calendar year.

those available from New Zealand. We made no distinctions regarding whether the use of particular procedures is appropriate or degrees of overuse or underuse that may exist.

The New Zealand Ministry of Health supplied treatment service data regarding cardiac procedures.[27] Renal transplant data were derived from the Australia and New Zealand Dialysis and Transplant Registry.[28] US treatment procedure data were derived from published studies involving the Medicare database.[29,30]

RESULTS

Health Outcome Measures

Overall life expectancy was higher in New Zealand (Table 1). Maori males had a life expectancy 8.9 years less than that of non-Maori males, whereas Maori females had a life expectancy 9.4 years less than that of non-Maori females. In the United States, American Indian/Alaska Native males had a life expectancy 7.4 years less than that of White males, and American Indian/Alaska Native females had a life expectancy 5.8 years less than that of White females.

The infant mortality rate was lower in New Zealand (5.4 per 1000 live births) than in the United States (7.2 per 1000 live births). However, the Maori infant mortality rate was higher than the New Zealand European rate, and a similar pattern was seen in the United States in regard to American Indians/Alaska Natives and Whites.

New Zealand and US mortality rates are shown in Table 2. Mortality rates (among members of all racial/ethnic groups) from cerebrovascular disease were higher in New Zealand than in the United States, and mortality rates from most cancers were slightly higher. Mortality rates from ischemic heart disease and suicide were similar in the 2 countries. Mortality rates from diabetes, chronic obstructive pulmonary disease, HIV, and homicide were lower in New Zealand.

In New Zealand, age-adjusted mortality rates were generally higher for Maoris than for those of European backgrounds. With the exception of bowel cancer, risk ratios between Maoris and the majority population were greater than 1 for all causes of death reported. The same was not true for risk ratios between American Indians/Alaska Natives and Whites. American Indians/Alaska Natives exhibited lower age-adjusted death rates than Whites for most causes of death; exceptions were suicide, diabetes, HIV, and homicide.

The relationships just described are illustrated in Figure 1; the horizontal axis shows the American Indian/Alaska Native–White risk ratio, and the vertical axis shows the Maori/European risk ratio. The vertical and horizontal lines are drawn at a risk ratio of 1.0 (no racial/ethnic difference in mortality risk); the diagonal line is drawn where the US risk ratio equals that of New Zealand (i.e., no difference in racial/ethnic disparities

between the countries). It can be seen that most causes of death are above the diagonal line, indicating greater disparities in New Zealand than in the United States. It also can be seen that causes of death tend to be above the horizontal 1.0 risk-ratio line for New Zealand but to the left of the vertical 1.0 risk-ratio line for the United States.

Modifiable Risk Factors

Maoris exhibited the highest smoking prevalence; 48.6% of Maori adults were smokers, twice the smoking prevalence of the majority population (Table 3). Almost 33% of American Indians/Alaska Natives were smokers, a rate 36% higher than that among White Americans. The highest prevalence of obesity was found among Americans, with 44% and 57% of male and female American Indians/Alaska Natives, respectively, being obese. The diabetes prevalence was higher in the United States, with American Indians/Alaska Natives exhibiting the highest observed overall prevalence (15.3%). In both countries, the indigenous populations exhibited an almost 3-fold higher diabetes prevalence than the majority populations.

Preventive Services

In the United States, immunization coverage rates were marginally higher among White American children (Table 3). However, in the case of measles/mumps/rubella, the highest coverage rate observed was that among American Indians/Alaska

TABLE 2— Age-Adjusted Mortality Rates (per 100 000 Population) and Mortality Risk Ratios for Major Causes of Death, by Race/Ethnicity: New Zealand and United States, 1999

Cause of Death	New Zealand				United States			
	Maori	European	All Races	Maori/European Risk Ratio	AIAN	White	All Races	AIAN/White Risk Ratio
Malignant neoplasms	292.2	180.2	201.3	1.62	117.9	187.5	186.4	0.63
Malignant neoplasm of trachea, bronchus, and lung	95.6	31.6	37.8	3.03	33.0	54.1	52.3	0.61
Malignant neoplasm of breast	22.4	14.9	17.0	1.50	8.0	14.0	14.1	0.57
Malignant neoplasm of prostate	21.2	13.3	14.5	1.59	4.4	9.5	10.3	0.46
Malignant neoplasm of cervix	6.5	1.2	1.9	5.42	1.0	1.3	1.5	0.77
Malignant neoplasm of colon, rectum, and anus (bowel)	20	28.6	29.8	0.70	10.9	19.0	19.1	0.57
Ischemic heart disease	281.1	156.9	172.3	1.79	112.6	171.6	171.0	0.66
Cerebrovascular disease	85.2	69.5	74.2	1.23	35.4	51.7	53.1	0.68
Other chronic obstructive pulmonary disease	49.8	28.4	30.8	1.75	22.1	35.3	32.7	0.63
Suicide (intentional self-harm)	11.9	11.7	13.5	1.02	11.9	11.8	10.5	1.01
Diabetes	79.0	13.6	19.4	5.81	46.7	19.7	22.8	2.37
HIV	1.1	0.4	0.6	2.75	3.0	2.3	5.3	1.30
Homicide (assault)	3.8	0.7	1.3	5.43	10.6	2.9	6.2	3.66

Note. AIAN = American Indian/Alaska Native.

Natives. New Zealand children exhibited lower immunization rates than US children, and Maori children had the lowest rates. Self-reported breast and cervical cancer screening coverage rates were lower in New Zealand, and again Maoris exhibited the lowest levels. In New Zealand, the risk ratio for screening coverage (Maori population vs majority) was 0.67 in the case of both breast and cervical cancer. American Indians/Alaska Natives had lower screening coverage rates than Whites. Racial/ethnic differentials were greater in the United States than in New Zealand for breast cancer screening, but the converse was true for cervical cancer screening.

Treatment Services

In regard to access to coronary angioplasty, Maoris underwent approximately 50% fewer procedures than those of European backgrounds, while American Indians/Alaska Natives underwent 25% fewer procedures than White Americans (Table 3). Coronary artery bypass grafting rates were similar among Maoris and New Zealand Europeans, but American Indians/Alaska Natives underwent 20% fewer such procedures than White Americans. Among all people aged 15 to 59 years undergoing dialysis in New Zealand in 2001, 3.6% of Maoris went on to receive transplants, compared with 15.5% of the majority population. Among Americans 55 years or younger undergoing dialysis

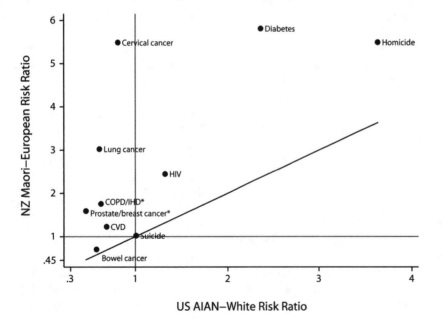

FIGURE 1— Comparison of mortality risk ratios for Maoris versus Europeans in New Zealand and American Indians/Alaska Natives versus Whites in the United States.
Note. NZ = New Zealand; COPD = chronic obstructive pulmonary disease; IHD = ischemic heart disease; CVD = cerebrovascular disease; AIAN = American Indian/Alaska Native.

TABLE 3— Data on Modifiable Risk Ratios (RRs), Preventive Services, and Treatment Services: United States and New Zealand

Outcome Measure	New Zealand			United States American Indian		
	RR	Maori	European	RR	Alaska Native	White
Modifiable risk factors						
Smoking, %	2.0	48.6	23.9	1.4	32.7	24.0
Obesity, %						
Obese						
Male	1.9	31.5	16.5	1.6	44.2	27.7
Female	1.4	26.7	19.1	1.9	57.4	30.6
Overweight						
Male	0.9	37.0	40.6	1.0	38.7	39.9
Female	1.2	32.5	26.3	1.1	29.3	26.6
Both overweight and obese						
Male	1.2	68.5	57.1	1.2	82.9	67.6
Female	1.3	59.2	45.4	1.5	86.7	57.2
Self-reported diabetes, %	2.7	8.3	3.1	2.6	15.3	5.9
Preventive service coverage, %						
Immunization[a]						
3 or more DTP	0.87	77.6	90.6	0.98	92.7	94.6
3 or more polio	0.62	49.7	79.7	0.97	87.5	90.1
3 or more hepatitis B	0.74	62.8	85.3	0.96	85.7	89.6
1 or more MMR	0.73	63.7	87.5	1.03	94.2	91.7
Cancer screening						
Breast	0.67	43.0	64.0	0.62	45.0	67.0
Cervical	0.67	46.0	68.0	0.91	72.0	79.0
Treatment services						
Angioplasty[b]	. . .	0.54	1.00	. . .	0.75	1.00
CABG[b]	. . .	1.01	1.00	. . .	0.79	1.00
Transplant[c]	. . .	3.6	15.5	. . .	12.1	22.7

Note. DTP = diphtheria/tetanus/pertussis vaccine; polio = poliovirus vaccine; MMR = measles/mumps/rubella vaccine; angioplasty = coronary angioplasty; CABG = coronary artery bypass grafting; transplant = renal transplantation.
[a]Risk ratios.
[b]Risk ratios. New Zealand: 2000–2001 non-risk-adjusted standardized discharge ratios by ethnicity for coronary angioplasty. The European rate is for non-Maori/non-Pacific peoples. United States: data based on number of persons receiving selected cardiac procedures per 100 Medicare beneficiaries with at least 1 ischemic heart disease hospitalization in 1998.
[c]New Zealand: transplant rate among those aged 15–59 years as a proportion of those undergoing dialysis. United States: percentage of individuals receiving transplants at 1 year of those Medicare end stage renal disease beneficiaries younger than 55 years following renal failure.

for end-stage renal failure in 1995, 12.1% of American Indians/Alaska Natives went on to receive transplants, compared with 22.7% of White Americans.

DISCUSSION

In the case of nearly every health indicator we examined, disparities (both absolute and relative) between indigenous and majority populations were more pronounced among Maoris in New Zealand than among American Indians/Alaska Natives in the United States. Relative to the majority populations, both indigenous groups were shown to experience large disparities in health status across most of the indicators assessed, even though, over the past 50 years, these groups have exhibited rapid gains.

For example, life expectancy among Maoris increased 27% between 1950 and 1997, from approximately 55 years to 70 years. Recent analyses show that most of this increase took place prior to the mid- 1980s. However, since that period, life expectancy among non-Maoris has continued to rise, while that among Maoris has been mostly static, thus producing a widening in disparities.[1]

In the United States, life expectancy for American Indians/Alaska Natives increased by 39% between 1940 and 1995, from 51 years to 71 years. Coinciding with this increase, however, has been a parallel increase in mortality rates associated with chronic diseases.[31]

To date, relatively few studies have involved comparisons across countries of the health status of indigenous peoples with that of numerically dominant populations.[32–38] Many of the studies available have originated from Australia, and few have included comparisons with New Zealand Maoris.[32,33,35,36] Furthermore, most have reviewed mortality trends only and have not provided wider overviews of health indicators.[32,33,36,37]

US Successes in Decreasing Disparities

Concerning our findings, of particular interest is the fact that, in the United States, disparities in rates of childhood immunization and cervical cancer screening coverage have largely been eliminated. In the case of immunization, Strine et al. recently noted some of the probable reasons for this success,[39] including comprehensive health services provided through the IHS, integrated primary care services provided in collaboration with tribes (e.g., public health nurse home visits, tracking of immunization status of children, and field clinics held at community centers, schools, and reservations), and free vaccines administered

through immunization programs. Community outreach programs also exist to reach remote areas.[39] New Zealand health policymakers could benefit from studying this approach. New Zealand's low immunization coverage levels, compounded by a lack of accurate coverage data,[40] have been a major public health concern for many years.

Smoking prevalence disparities are also less pronounced in the United States. Although smoking prevalence is high among American Indians/Alaska Natives (33% of the adult population), it is only 36% higher in relative terms than the prevalence among White Americans, whereas smoking prevalence among Maoris are twice the New Zealand European levels (49% of adult Maoris are current smokers). These findings may partially explain why ischemic heart disease and lung cancer mortality rates among American Indians/Alaska Natives are lower than the corresponding Maori rates.

The IHS is likely to have played a significant role in regard to factors that may have contributed to the health gains experienced by American Indians/Alaska Natives.[41] This agency is unique in the United States in delivering health care to a specific ethnic group. Such coordinated mechanisms of health care delivery, if provided adequate resources, could potentially lead to dedicated efforts to reduce health care disparities.

The IHS has an annual operating budget of $2.8 billion, contingent on an annual appropriation from Congress and thus susceptible to change. A work group commissioned by the IHS that compared IHS personal health benefits with federal employee health benefit plans estimated that expenditures on IHS services are 46% less than those on federal employee health benefit plans.[42] Despite this apparent underfunding of services, the IHS actively seeks to maximize tribes' involvement in meeting the health needs of the registered American Indian/Alaska Native population and to maximize the health care gains available.

New Zealand Successes in Decreasing Disparities

New Zealand has had particular success in reducing infant mortality rates. From 1950 to 1998, the overall New Zealand infant mortality rate declined from 28 per 1000 births to 6 per 1000. More striking has been the decline in the Maori rate over this same period, from 70 to 8 per 1000 births. Recent reductions in the Maori rate are largely due to the drop in deaths caused by sudden infant death syndrome.[43] Infant mortality rates were one of the few health status indicators in which Maoris exhibited "better" health outcomes than American Indians/Alaska Natives, although relative indigenous–majority disparities were greater for Maoris.

Recent data from the New Zealand Ministry of Health suggest that Maoris' access to coronary artery bypass grafting has increased. This pattern of improvement is encouraging given that previous studies reported large disparities in access to this procedure.[44] However, it should be noted that, in the present study, rates were not adjusted for severity, incidence, or appropriateness of treatment.

The New Zealand Health Services have only recently focused on reducing health care disparities experienced by Maoris. This study demonstrates that disparities are large and that there is considerable room for improvement. However, a number of coordinated strategies are now being put in place, including increasing the number of Maori health care providers and health care workers, increasing funding for regions in which there are high levels of deprivation and large numbers of minority residents, requiring health agencies to produce specific strategies for enhancing the health status of Maoris, and increasing Maoris' presence in terms of governance of the health sector.[3,45–47]

Data Availability and Methodological Considerations

According to the IHS, 2.6 million American Indians/Alaska Natives reside in the United States. Approximately 60% of these individuals are eligible for health services provided by the IHS.[48] Health information on the 40% of American Indians/Alaska Natives not covered by the IHS is largely unavailable. Furthermore, because American Indians/Alaska Natives represent such a small proportion of the overall American population, health surveys undertaken to gather population prevalence data frequently do not have the statistical power to elicit information related to this group. In New Zealand, such problems have largely been eliminated, in part because Maoris represent a significantly higher proportion of the population and in part because of efforts to increase the size of Maori populations sampled in national health surveys.[21]

It should also be noted that, according to the US Bureau of the Census, 4.1 million people identify themselves as American Indians/Alaska Natives in contrast to the figure of 2.6 million just mentioned.[49] The source of this higher figure is the 2000 census; in that year, for the first time, individuals could indicate membership in multiple racial/ethnic groups. Given these differences, there has not been agreement to date as to which population denominator values to use for the American Indian/Alaska Native population. Any change in such denominator values may affect all national health statistics involving American Indians/Alaska Natives (including those described here).

Collection of race/ethnicity-specific health information in the United States is also hampered by the lack of national health databases. Furthermore, many health care providers do not collect such data. New Zealand, by comparison, does not experience such difficulties owing to the establishment of national health data sets that include information on race/ethnicity. To measure progress toward reductions in health disparities, it is essential that quality indigenous health data exist, and the United States would benefit from improvements in the collection of these data.

In terms of methodological considerations associated with our study,

several limitations are inherent in any cross-country comparison of health outcome indicators. Data comparability can be problematic, especially in the case of types of treatment, because guidelines, thresholds for action, and medical practice cultures may vary between countries. However, these potential differences do not have an impact on the relative disparities observed among Maoris and American Indians/Alaska Natives in terms of access to the procedures assessed here.

Concerning comparability of mortality data, important issues to consider include differences in *ICD* coding practices, accuracy of race/ethnicity data within and between countries, and numerator or denominator undercounting among indigenous peoples. In both New Zealand and the United States, studies have shown that there is considerable under-reporting of indigenous deaths and other indigenous health indicators.[50–55] Researchers in New Zealand have recently undertaken work designed to better enumerate the magnitude of such problems.[50,51] However, we did not use these data; rather, we used 1999 mortality data, which were outside of the scope of the research just mentioned. Comparable data were also not available for American Indians/Alaska Natives.

Another potential limitation of our study is that some of the data relate to national population data sets and some were derived from population samples. In regard to the time periods and age groups for which results are presented, we have attempted to harmonize these data, but there were minor differences.

In the case of all of the data collected, the varying degrees to which the indigenous health information that exists for the 2 countries is complete and accurate are likely to have influenced the findings presented here. It is not possible to quantify the exact amount of the measurement bias that may exist. The data presented here, however, are the most reliable currently available.

Finally, we have not addressed other factors that may affect the relative size of disparities, particularly dif-

ferences in socioeconomic status. The importance of socioeconomic variables in influencing health outcomes cannot be underestimated, but it was not our aim to explore such differences. Furthermore, because of the lack of available data and differences between countries in variables such as cost of living, income levels, and definitions of poverty and educational achievement, such a comparison would be methodologically difficult.

Conclusions

In the case of nearly every health indicator examined here, disparities experienced by Maoris in New Zealand (both absolute and relative to the majority population) were more pronounced than those experienced by American Indians/Alaska Natives in the United States. This situation is not necessarily intractable, as evidenced by the success of the United States in eliminating disparities in immunization coverage among American Indians/Alaska Natives. Although national health sector responses differ, New Zealand may be well placed in the future to evaluate the effectiveness of policies to reduce disparities given the high levels of Maori-specific health information available and the new strategies being put in place.

About the Authors

At the time of this study, Dale Bramley, Paul Hebert, Leah Tuzzio, and Mark Chassin were with the Department of Health Policy, Mount Sinai Medical School, NY.

Correspondence: Requests for reprints should be sent to Dale Bramley, Waitemata District Health Board, DHB Board Office, Level 1, 15 Shea Terrace, Private Bag 93-503, Takapuna, Auckland Department of Health Policy, Auckland, New Zealand (e-mail: dale.bramley@waitematadhb.govt.nz).

Acknowledgments

Dale Bramley was on a Harkness Fellowship in health policy for the duration of the present research. Funding for this fellowship was made available by the Commonwealth Fund of New York.

We acknowledge the following people who provided advice on or reviews of the article: Rod Jackson (University of Auckland), Nicole Laurie (RAND, Washington, DC), Robin Osborn (Commonwealth Fund, New York), and Dr Anne Beal (Commonwealth Fund).

Note. The views presented here are those of the authors and not necessarily those of the Commonwealth Fund.

Contributors

D. Bramley originated the study; oversaw all aspects of design, analysis, and interpretation; and led the writing of the article. P. Hebert conducted the mortality analysis and assisted with study design and the writing of the article. L. Tuzzio and M. Chassin assisted with design, interpretation, and the writing of the article.

References

1. *Decades of Disparity: Ethnic Mortality Trends in New Zealand 1980–1999.* Wellington, New Zealand: Ministry of Health; 2003.

2. Zuckerman S, Haley J, Roubideaux Y, Lillie-Blanton M. Health service access, use and insurance coverage among American Indians/Alaska Natives and Whites: what role does the Indian Health Service play? *Am J Public Health.* 2004;94: 53–59.

3. King A. *The New Zealand Health Strategy.* Wellington, New Zealand: Ministry of Health; 2000.

4. *Healthy People 2010: Understanding and Improving Health.* Washington, DC: US Dept of Health and Human Services; 2000.

5. Institute of Medicine. *Envisioning the National Quality Report.* Washington, DC: National Academy Press; 2001.

6. Stefanogiannis N. *Provisional Life Expectancy Data, New Zealand, 2001.* Wellington, New Zealand: Ministry of Health; 2004.

7. *An Indication of New Zealanders' Health.* Wellington, New Zealand: Ministry of Health; 2002. Occasional report 1.

8. Keppel K, Pearcy J, Wagener D. *Trends in Racial and Ethnic-Specific Rates for Health Status Indicators: 1990–1998.* Atlanta, Ga: Centers for Disease Control and Prevention; 2002:1–16.

9. National Center for Health Statistics. United States life tables, 2000. *Natl Vital Stat Rep.* 2002;51(3).

10. Moore B. *Life Expectancy: Data Years 1996–1998.* Rockville, Md: Indian Health Service; 2001.

11. New Zealand Health Information Service. *Mortality and Demographic Data 1999.* Wellington, New Zealand: Ministry of Health; 2003.

12. *1999 United States Mortality File.* Atlanta, Ga: Centers for Disease Control and Prevention; 1999.

13. Hoyert D, Arias E, Smith B, Murphy S, Kochanek K. *Deaths: Final Data for 1999.* Hyattsville, Md: National Center for Health Statistics; 2001:1–113.

14. Fleiss J. *Statistical Methods for Rates and Proportions.* 2nd ed. New York, NY: John Wiley & Sons Inc; 1981.

15. *Immunisation Coverage in North Health: Comparative Results From North Health's 1996 Immunisation Coverage Survey.* Auckland, New Zealand: North Health; 1997.

16. Centers for Disease Control and Prevention. Estimated vaccination coverage with individual vaccines and selected vaccination series among children 19–35 months of age by poverty level and race/ethnicity, US National Immunization Survey 2001, 2002. Available at: http://www.cdc.gov/nip/coverage/NIS/01/TAB32-pov_race.htm. Accessed February 1, 2005.

17. Bloomfield A. *Screening Data Coverage for New Zealand.* Wellington, New Zealand: Ministry of Health; 2003.

18. *Tobacco Facts 2002.* Wellington, New Zealand: Ministry of Health; 2002.

19. Centers for Disease Control and Prevention. Cigarette smoking among adults, United States, 2001. *MMWR Morb Mortal Wkly Rep.* 2003;52:953–956.

20. Centers for Disease Control and Prevention. National Center for Health Statistics definitions used for tobacco use. Available at: http://www.cdc.gov/nchs/datawh/nchsdefs/cigarettesmoking.htm. Accessed February 1, 2005.

21. *A Snapshot of Health: Provisional Results of the 2002/03 New Zealand Health Survey.* Wellington, New Zealand: Ministry of Health; 2003.

22. *Health, United States, 2002, With Chartbook on Trends in the Health of Americans.* Hyattsville, Md: National Center for Health Statistics; 2002:Table 70.

23. Welty T, Rhoades D, Yeh F, et al. Changes in cardiovascular disease risk factors among American Indians: the Strong Heart Study. *Ann Epidemiol.* 2002;12: 97–106.

24. *Taking the Pulse: The 1996/1997 New Zealand Health Survey.* Wellington, New Zealand: Ministry of Health; 1999.

25. Centers for Disease Control and Prevention. Diabetes prevalence among American Indians and Alaska Natives and the overall population– United States, 1994–2002. *MMWR Morb Mortal Wkly Rep.* 2003; 52:702–704.

26. Centers for Disease Control and Prevention. Behavioral Risk Factor Surveillance System—diabetes prevalence grouped by race, 2002. Available at: http://apps.nccd.cdc.gov/brfss/race.asp?cat=DB&yr=2002&qkey=1364&state=US. Accessed February 1, 2005.

27. Lambie L. *Standardised Discharge Ratios for Coronary Procedures in New Zealand 2002.* Wellington, New Zealand: Ministry of Health; 2003.

28. Chadham S. ANZDATA 25th annual report. Available at: http://www.anzdata.org.au/anzdata/AnzdataReport/download.htm#25th%20Report. Accessed February 1, 2005.

29. Eggers P. Racial differences in access to kidney transplantation. *Health Care Financing Rev.* 1995;17(2): 89–103.

30. Eggers P, Greenberg L. Racial and ethnic differences in hospitalization rates among aged Medicare beneficiaries, 1998. *Health Care Financing Rev.* 2000; 21(4):91–105.

31. Centers for Disease Control and Prevention. Cancer mortality among American Indians and Alaska Natives—United States, 1994–1998. *MMWR Morb Mortal Wkly Rep.* 2003;52:704–707.

32. Paradies Y, Cunningham J. Placing aboriginal and Torres Strait Islander mortality in an international context. *Aust N Z J Public Health.* 2002;26:11–16.

33. Ring I, Firman D. Reducing indigenous mortality in Australia: lessons from other countries. *Med J Aust.* 1998;169:528–533.

34. Michael J, Michael M. Health status of the Australian aboriginal people and the Native Americans—a summary comparison. *Asia Pacific J Public Health.* 1994;7:132–136.

35. Kunitz S, Brady M. Health care policy for aboriginal Australians: the relevance of the American Indian experi-

ence. *Aust J Public Health.* 1995;19:549–558.

36. Hogg R. Indigenous mortality: placing Australian aboriginal mortality within a broader context. *Soc Sci Med.* 1992;35:335–346.

37. Trovato F. Aboriginal mortality in Canada, the United States and New Zealand. *J Biosoc Sci.* 2001;33:67–86.

38. Ring I, Brown N. Indigenous health: chronically inadequate responses to damning statistics. *Med J Aust.* 2002;177:629–631.\

39. Strine T, Mokdad A, Barker L, et al. Vaccination coverage of American Indian/Alaska Native children aged 19 to 35 months: findings from the National Immunization Survey, 1998–2000. *Am J Public Health.* 2003;93:2046–2049.

40. Turner N, Baker M, Carr J, Mansoor O. Improving immunisation coverage: what needs to be done? *N Z Public Health Rep.* 2000;7(3/4):11–13.

41. Katz R. Addressing the health care needs of American Indians and Alaska Natives. *Am J Public Health.* 2004;94:13–14.

42. Frias H. Should Indian health care be an entitlement? *IHS Provider.* 2003;60:60–64.

43. Statistics New Zealand. Infant mortality 1950–1998. Available at: http://www.stats.govt.nz/looking-past-20th-century/changes-in-society/infant-mortality.htm. Accessed February 1, 2005.

44. Tukuitonga C, Bindman A. Ethnic and gender differences in the use of coronary artery revascularisation procedures in New Zealand. *N Z Med J.* 2002;115:179–182.

45. *He Korowai Oranga.* Wellington, New Zealand: Ministry of Health; 2001.

46. *Reducing Inequalities in Health.* Wellington, New Zealand: Ministry of Health; 2002.

47. *Whakataka: Maori Health Action Plan 2002–2005.* Wellington, New Zealand: Ministry of Health; 2002.

48. *Indian Health Service Fact Sheet.* Rockville, Md: Indian Health Service; 2003.

49. US Bureau of the Census. The American Indian and Alaska Native population 2000. Available at: http://www.census.gov/prod/2002pubs/c2kbr01–15.pdf. Accessed February 1, 2005.

50. Blakely T, Robson B, Atkinson A, Sporle A, Kiro C. Unlocking the numerator-denominator bias I: adjustment ratios by ethnicity for 1991–1994 mortality data. The New Zealand Census Mortality Study. *N Z Med J.* 2002;115:39–43.

51. Blakely T, Kiro C, Woodward A. Unlocking the numerator-denominator bias II: adjustment to mortality rates by ethnicity and deprivation during 1991–94. The New Zealand Census Mortality Study. *N Z Med J.* 2002;115:43–48.

52. Stehr-Green P, Bettles J, Robertson L. Effect of racial/ethnic misclassification of American Indians and Alaskan Natives on Washington State death certificates, 1987–1997. *Am J Public Health.* 2002;92:443–444.

53. Frost F, Tollestrup K, Ross A, Sabotta E, Kimball E. Correctness of racial coding of American Indians and Alaska Natives on Washington State death certificates. *Am J Prev Med.* 1994;10:290–294.

54. Sugarman J, Holliday M, Ross A, Castorina J, Hui Y. Improving American Indian cancer data in the Washington State cancer registry using linkages with the Indian Health Service and tribal records. *Cancer.* 1996; 78(suppl 7):1564–1568.

55. Sugarman J, Lawson L. The effect of racial misclassification on estimates of end-stage renal disease among American Indians and Alaska Natives in the Pacific Northwest, 1988 through 1990. *Am J Kidney Dis.* 1993;21:383–386.

Skin Color, Social Classification, and Blood Pressure in Southeastern Puerto Rico

| Clarence C. Gravlee, PhD, William W. Dressler, PhD and H. Russell Bernard, PhD

ABSTRACT

Objectives. We tested competing hypotheses for the skin color–blood pressure relationship by analyzing the association between blood pressure and 2 skin color variables: skin pigmentation and social classification.

Methods. We measured skin pigmentation by reflectance spectrophotometry and social classification by linking respondents to ethnographic data on the cultural model of "color" in southeastern Puerto Rico. We used multiple regression analysis to test the associations between these variables and blood pressure in a community-based sample of Puerto Rican adults aged 25–55 years (n=100). Regression models included age, gender, body mass index (BMI), self-reported use of antihypertensive medication, and socioeconomic status (SES).

Results. Social classification, but not skin pigmentation, is associated with systolic and diastolic blood pressure through a statistical interaction with SES, independent of age, gender, BMI, self-reported use of antihypertensive medication, and skin reflectance.

Conclusion. Our findings suggest that sociocultural processes mediate the relationship between skin color and blood pressure. They also help to clarify the meaning and measurement of skin color and "race" as social variables in health research.

INTRODUCTION

Throughout the Americas, people of African ancestry have higher mean blood pressures and higher rates of hypertension than do others in the same societies. This pattern was first observed in the United States in 1932.[1] Over 70 years later, excess hypertension still contributes more to the diminished life expectancy of African Americans than does any other major cause of death, including cancer, diabetes, stroke, or HIV/AIDS.[2] Although the prevalence of hypertension and the magnitude of inequalities vary by country, a general pattern of elevated blood pressure holds elsewhere in the African Diaspora.[3-7]

There remains no consensus as to why this pattern exists, leading some to call it "the puzzle of hypertension in African-Americans."[8] One key piece of the puzzle is that, within populations of African ancestry, darker-skinned individuals tend to have higher mean blood pressures than do their lighter-skinned counterparts. Previous researchers have proposed 2 major explanations for this relationship. The first is that dark skin color, as a marker of African ancestry, is linked to a genetic predisposition for high blood pressure.[9,10] The second is that dark skin color, as a marker of subordinate social status, exposes dark-skinned individuals to racial discrimination, poverty, and other stressors related to blood pressure.[11-13] These competing hypotheses—1 genetic, 1 sociocultural—encapsulate the debate over race and health in general, making the skin color–blood pressure relationship a convenient microcosm of the broader problem.

Our purpose was to test competing explanations for the relationship between skin color and blood pressure more directly than has been done before. We address an important limitation of previous studies by recognizing that genetic and sociocultural hypotheses refer to distinct dimensions of skin color. The hypothesis that skin color is linked to a genetic predisposition for high blood pressure refers to the *phenotype of skin pigmentation*. The hypothesis that skin color is a marker of exposure to social stressors refers to the *cultural significance of skin color* as a criterion of social classification. These conceptually distinct variables require distinct measurement operations. However, previous studies have not aimed to isolate the cultural and biological dimensions of skin color or to test their associations with blood pressure.

Measuring the biological dimension of skin color is straightforward in principle. Reflectance spectrophotometry provides an objective measurement of skin pigmentation attributable to melanin, the implicit skin color variable in genetic hypotheses for the skin color–blood pressure relationship. The key measurement challenges involve the choice of instrument and use of proper technique.[14,15] Measuring the cultural dimension of skin color presents a different set of challenges. It first requires a test of the assumption that there is a shared cultural model that assigns meaning to skin color variation. It then requires a way to estimate how the color status of any given individual would be defined according to that model. In short, it requires treating the notion that race is a cultural construct as an empirical matter, not a mantra.

We use data from a preliminary study in Puerto Rico to test the hypothesis that blood pressure is associated with the cultural rather than biological significance of skin color. Two factors make Puerto Rico an appropriate setting. First, an earlier study reported an association between skin pigmentation and systolic blood pressure (SBP) among 4000 urban men, but it did not address the extent to which this association reflected genetic or sociocultural mechanisms.[16] Second, previous ethnography[17–19] indicates that the local cultural model of *color* (ko-lór) differs from the American model of *race* in important ways. In particular, *color* classification is shaped not only by skin color but also by other physical features and, possibly, by social status markers like wealth, family background, or residential area. One consequence is that, for a given level of skin pigmentation, there should be variability in social classification, making it possible to measure the cultural and biological dimensions of skin color as distinct variables.

METHODS

Research Setting and Sampling

The research was set in Guayama, Puerto Rico, a southeastern coastal town of approximately 44 000 residents.[20] Guayama was a center of the Puerto Rican sugar economy in the 19th century and now has a substantial manufacturing base, especially in the petroleum and pharmaceutical industries. This trajectory of economic development ensures adequate variation in 2 key independent variables in our study: skin color and socioeconomic status.

The sample was designed to maximize contrasts in these variables, rather than to estimate population parameters. On the basis of ethnographic data, we identified 4 residential areas that span the range of variation on socioeconomic status and skin color, and selected a probability sample for each area. This strategy has been used in previous studies of skin color and blood pressure, and is

appropriate when the goal is to maximize internal validity.[21]

The first sampled residential area consisted of the 5 *caseríos,* or public housing facilities in Guayama. The second was a lower–middle class *barrio,* the typical residents of which include secretaries, teacher's assistants, factory workers, and others in the service sector. The third was a large middle-class *urbanización,* or planned subdivision, the typical residents of which include teachers, bankers, or technical workers in area pharmaceutical plants. The fourth was the only gated *urbanización* in Guayama, favored by physicians, lawyers, and scientists and engineers from local petroleum and pharmaceutical plants. Further details about the 4 residential strata are given elsewhere.[22] Sampling from these residential types limits the generalizability of our findings, but it improves the efficiency of our attempt to detect sociocultural processes related to class and *color.*

Within each residential type, we drew a random sample of 25 households. One adult, aged 25–55 years, was selected randomly from each household, for a total sample size of 100. If the sampled household had no eligible members, refused to participate, or could not be reached after 3 attempts, another household was substituted at random. Response rates ranged from 80.6 to 89.3% across neighborhoods, with an overall rate of 85.5%.

Interviews were conducted in participants' homes by a European American researcher and a Puerto Rican research assistant, who self-identified as *negra,* or Black. The interview schedule was designed to be executed with handheld computers and software designed for mobile computer-assisted personal interviewing. The advantages of this technology for data quality are described elsewhere.[23] Data were collected in June and July 2001.

Skin Color Measures

Recent developments in culture theory and ethnographic methods allow us to estimate how *color* is defined according to the salient cultur-

al model in Puerto Rico. Specifically, cultural consensus analysis[24] formally tests the assumption that respondents share a coherent cultural model, and estimates the culturally appropriate responses to a set of questions. Gravlee[19] used cultural consensus analysis to describe the cultural model of *color* in southeastern Puerto Rico. He asked respondents to identify the *color* of 72 standardized facial portraits that vary systematically in gender, skin tone, hair texture, nose shape, and lip form; the portraits were originally developed to elicit folk racial categorizations in Brazil.[25] Cultural consensus analysis of respondents' categorizations in Puerto Rico provides evidence of a shared cultural model of *color,* which enables classification of the standardized portraits into 5 culturally salient categories.[19]

We matched survey respondents to the same standardized portraits in order to estimate the culturally appropriate classification of each respondent's *color.* Interviewers independently selected the portrait that most closely resembled each survey respondent. Initial interrater reliability was moderately strong (=.64, 95% confidence interval [CI] = .51, .76); disagreements were resolved through discussion. Because cultural consensus analysis estimates the culturally appropriate categorization of each portrait, matching survey respondents to portraits estimates the culturally appropriate categorization of each respondent's *color.* This estimate approximates how respondents are perceived by others in mundane social interaction.

Skin pigmentation was measured with a handheld narrow-band reflectometer (Derma-Spectrometer; Cortex Technology, Hadsund, Denmark) designed and validated for measuring human skin pigments.[15] The Derma-Spectrometer emits light at green (568 nm) and red (655 nm) wavelengths. It separates the reflected light attributable to melanin from that attributable to hemoglobin and summarizes this value as the melanin index (M). Analyses here use the mean melanin index from 3 measurements taken at the upper inner arm (an unexposed site), following Shriver and Parra.[15] This index estimates constitutive skin pigmentation, the implicit skin color variable in genetic explanations for the relationship between skin color and blood pressure.

Blood Pressure and Covariates

Blood pressure measurements were made with an automatic blood pressure monitor, Omron Model HEM-737AC (Omron Health-care, Inc., Vernon Hills, IL). This device has been validated for use in population-based studies[26] and has been recommended by the European Society of Hypertension.[27] Three blood pressure measurements were taken at standardized intervals in the beginning, middle, and end of the hour-long interview. Respondents were seated with their left arm supported at heart level. Prior to each blood pressure measurement, respondents had been seated for at least 10 minutes and had not ingested caffeine or tobacco for at least 30 minutes. We measured the circumference of the left arm to determine correct cuff size. Mean SBP and mean diastolic blood pressure (DBP) were computed from 3 measurements and treated as dependent variables.

Standard covariates were used to control for competing explanations: gender (0 = female, 1 = male), age (in years), socioeconomic status (SES), body mass index (BMI, weight in kg/height in m2), and current antihypertensive medication (0 = no, 1 =

yes). Weight (± 0.1 kg) was measured with a digital scale; height (± .1 cm) was measured with a portable stadiometer. Education was measured by self-reported years of schooling completed, and household income was measured by asking respondents which of 9 income ranges described total household income from all sources, before taxes, in the last 12 months. We tested multiple ways of modeling SES, including raw household income, household income adjusted for household size, education (years), highest degree attained, and factor loadings on the first principal component of education (years) and household income. We used the principal component score because it captures in a single measure 88% of the variance in education and income, and because other ways of modeling SES do not alter the substantive results.

Statistical Analysis

We conducted multiple regression analysis separately for SBP and DBP. We constructed cross-product interaction terms to test for interactions between *color*, SES, and gender. Predictors were mean-centered to reduce multicollinearity and to facilitate interpretation of interaction terms. We examined variance inflation factors for evidence of multi-collinearity and case diagnostics (Cook's statistic, studentized residuals, hat matrix values, dfbetas) for evidence of influential observations. Because we did not aim

to estimate population parameters, our analyses did not require sampling weights.

In all models, ascribed *color* was entered as 2 categorical variables using the Helmert coding scheme. The first variable tests for differences between the intermediate category *trigueño* (literally, "Wheat-colored") and *blanco* (White); the second tests for differences between *negro* (Black) and the mean of *trigueño* and *blanco*. This coding scheme reflects both the natural ordering of categories and the expectation from ethnography that the stigmatized category *negro* would differ from the mean of *trigueño* and *blanco*.[18]

RESULTS

Table 1 reports descriptive statistics for study variables in the total sample and within categories of ascribed color. Respondents classified as negro have slightly higher SBP, on average, but this bivariate association is not statistically significant. Women comprise 62% of the sample, attributable to random sampling within residential types and to the uneven gender distribution in public housing facilities.

Figure 1 depicts the relationship between ascribed *color* and skin pigmentation. As expected, median pigmentation is lightest for respondents assigned to the category *blanco* and darkest for those assigned to *negro*. Intermediate pigmentation is evident for *trigueño* and *indio* ("Indian"). For our

TABLE 1— Mean (±SD) or Frequency for Study Variables, by Cultural Consensus Classification of Color: June and July 2001

	Blanco (n = 46)-	Trigueño (n = 32)-	Negro (n = 22)-	Total (N = 100)-
Systolic blood pressure	125.2 (15.6)	124.1 (20.3)	127.8 (16.8)	125.4 (17.4)
Diastolic blood pressure	80.4 (9.8)	80.0 (11.1)	79.6 (11.7)	80.1 (10.6)
Age, y	40.4 (7.3)	37.8 (8.0)	38.9 (9.2)	39.2 (8.0)
Gender, % female	60.9	75.0	45.5	62.0
BMI	28.8 (5.3)	28.7 (6.5)	27.9 (7.1)	28.6 (6.1)
Education, y*	15.6 (2.6)	13.2 (4.6)	12.4 (2.5)	14.1 (3.6)
Household income (imputed), $*	51 097.8 (35 003.0)	31 265.6 (38 276.6)	20 386.4 (19 878.8)	37 995.0 (35 536.1)
Antihypertensive medication, %	13.0	12.5	0.0	10.0
Skin pigmentation, M*	32.8 (2.6)	40.8 (4.8)	45.9 (5.6)	38.2 (6.7)

Note. BMI = body mass index. Tests of significance by analysis of variance (ANOVA) for continuous variables and χ^2 for categorical variables; for household income, mean and standard deviation computed for midpoint of selected category.
* $P < .05$

purposes, the distributions of pigmentation by *color* are more important than are the central tendencies, i.e., the mean, median, or mode. In particular, overlapping interquartile ranges for respondents assigned to *trigueño, indio,* and *negro* confirm the expectation that individuals at a given level of skin pigmentation may vary in social classification. This finding makes it possible to evaluate the association of blood pressure with the cultural and biological dimensions of skin color. In subsequent analyses, the 2 respondents assigned to *indio* are collapsed into *trigueño.* This coding decision is based on the affinity between these categories in the local cultural model.[19]

Table 2 gives multiple regression coefficients for SBP and DBP. More complex models (data not shown) provide no evidence of statistical interaction between SES and skin pigmentation or between gender, SES, and *color.* Table 2 indicates that ascribed *color,* but not skin pigmentation, is associated with blood pressure. At specific levels of SES, being culturally defined as *negro,* or Black, is associated with SBP and DBP, independent of skin pigmentation and covariates.

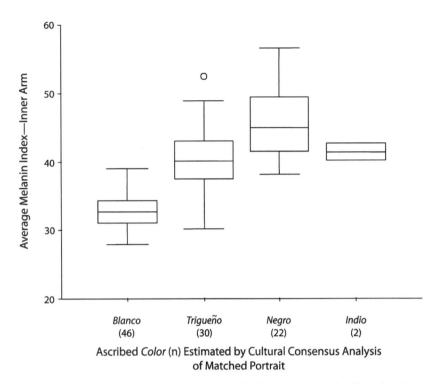

FIGURE 1— Melanin index at upper inner arm by ascribed *color*, as determined by cultural consensus estimate of matched standardized facial portrait.

TABLE 2— Regression of Systolic and Diastolic Blood Pressure on Pigmentation, Ascribed *Color*, and Covariates (N = 100): June and July 2001

	Systolic Blood Pressure[a]		Diastolic Blood Pressure[b]	
	B (95% CI)	P	B (95% CI)	P
Constant	123.99 (119.69, 128.29)	.000	79.95 (76.97, 82.93)	.000
Age, y	1.12 (0.77, 1.48)	.000	0.54 (0.29, 0.78)	.000
Gender (1 = male, 0 = female)	7.25 (1.21, 13.28)	.019	1.48 (−2.71, 5.66)	.485
Body mass index	0.02 (−0.44, 0.48)	.934	0.18 (−0.14, 0.50)	.264
Antihypertensive medication	13.20 (3.75, 22.64)	.007	7.05 (0.51, 13.60)	.035
Skin pigmentation, M	−0.60 (−1.28, 0.08)	.083	−0.26 (−0.74, 0.21)	.268
Socioeconomic status, SES	−0.68 (−4.45, 3.10)	.723	−1.43 (−4.05, 1.18)	.279
Ascribed *color*				
Trigueño versus *Blanco*	3.99 (−4.58, 12.57)	.357	0.61 (−5.33, 6.55)	.839
Negro versus Trigueño/Blanco	14.07 (3.94, 24.19)	.007	4.29 (−2.72, 11.31)	.227
SES x ascribed *color*				
SES x *Trigueño* versus *Blanco*	−5.48 (−12.12, 1.16)	.105	−1.31 (−5.91, 3.29)	.572
SES x *Negro* versus *Trigueño/Blanco*	14.91 (5.89, 23.94)	.001	7.31 (1.05, 13.56)	.023

Note. B = unstandardized regression coefficient; CI = confidence interval.
[a]Adjusted R2 = 0.403
[b]Adjusted R2 = 0.225

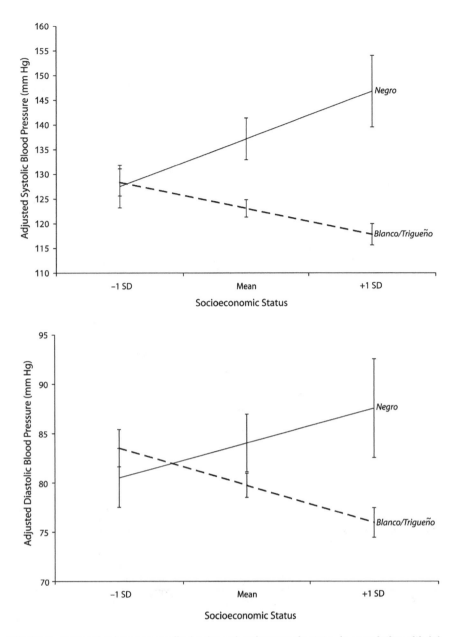

FIGURE 2— Interaction between ascribed *color* and socioeconomic status in association with (a) systolic and (b) diastolic blood pressure, independent of skin pigmentation and covariates.

Figure 2 illustrates this interaction. At low levels of SES, there is no detectable difference in blood pressure across categories of *color*. However, as SES increases, those who are estimated to be *negro* by cultural consensus analysis of matched facial portraits have higher mean blood pressures. Those who are estimated to be *trigueño* or *blanco* have lower mean blood pressures as SES increases. This interaction effect and the simple main effect of *color* explain an additional 7.9% of variance in SBP and 1.7% of variance in DBP, as compared with

reduced models omitting these variables (data not shown). There is borderline evidence ($P=.08$) for an association between SBP and skin pigmentation, independent of covariates; the direction of that association is the opposite of that predicted by the genetic hypothesis.

Regression diagnostics were found to be satisfactory. Variance inflation factors (maximum = 2.94) indicate that multicollinearity is not a significant problem. Case diagnostics identify 2 respondents with noteworthy values of Cook's statistic; excluding these

cases does not alter the substantive results.

DISCUSSION

We argue that genetic and sociocultural hypotheses for the relationship between skin color and blood pressure entail 2 distinct skin color variables: the phenotype of skin pigmentation and the cultural significance of skin color as a criterion of social classification. Our measurement strategy operationalizes this distinction, and results suggest that the cultural rather than biological dimension of skin color may be the key variable of interest.

Among respondents who are at or above mean SES, those who are culturally defined as *negro,* or Black, have higher SBP and DBP, on average, than do those classified as *blanco*, White, or *trigueño*, Intermediate. This relationship holds independent of age, gender, body mass, skin pigmentation, or reported use of antihypertensive medication. We found no evidence of darker skin pigmentation being associated with higher blood pressure in this sample.

The nature of the relationship between ascribed *color* and blood pressure is consistent with the ethnographic record in Puerto Rico. First, the interaction between *color* and SES corresponds to ethnographic evidence that status distinctions based on *color* are relatively insignificant in low-SES contexts, and that racism is most pernicious in the middle and upper classes.[28–31] Thus, respondents who are classified as *negro* in high-SES contexts may experience more frequent, frustrating social interactions as a result of institutional and interpersonal discrimination. Experimental and observational studies suggest that chronic exposure to such interactions may be linked to cardiovascular responses, including sustained high blood pressure.[32,33]

Second, the absence of statistically significant differences in blood pressure between the categories *trigueño* and *blanco* is consistent with ethnographic evidence. One notable feature of ethnic classification in Puerto Rico, as opposed to the mainland United

States, is the existence of intermediate categories, such as *trigueño*, that do not carry the stigma of "Blackness." Whereas people defined as *negro* are likely to encounter institutional and interpersonal constraints on social mobility, those defined as *trigueño* face relatively few such constraints as a consequence of *color*.[30,31] The finding that high-SES respondents estimated to be *negro* but not *trigueño* have the highest blood pressures is therefore consistent with the hypothesis that sociocultural processes mediate the link between skin color and blood pressure.

Despite speculation about possible genetic links between skin color and blood pressure,[9,10] it should not be surprising that skin pigmentation and blood pressure are not significantly associated in our sample. Recent studies show that skin pigmentation is associated with molecular estimates of continental ancestry, with correlations ranging from weak (Mexico, =.21) to moderately strong (Puerto Rico, =.63) across populations.[34] Yet the central question is whether continental ancestry is informative about alleles related to blood pressure. Available evidence suggests that it is not.[35,36] Skin pigmentation is informative about continental ancestry precisely because its distribution differs from most human genetic variation. Most genetic markers show relatively small differences between human populations,[37] but skin pigmentation shows marked regional variation in response to geographic differences in the intensity of ultraviolet radiation.[38] Our findings thus reinforce criticism that skin color should not be used uncritically as a marker of racial–genetic predisposition to disease; genetic hypotheses require genetic data.[34]

Our findings also relate to recent discussions about causal inference and the measurement of "race" as a cultural construct in social epidemiology. Kaufman and Cooper[39] suggest that standard comparisons of racially defined groups are ill suited to explaining racial differences in health. In particular, they point out that causal reasoning in epidemiology is based on a counterfactual framework that asks, "What would the outcome have been if the exposed individual were not exposed to the alleged cause?" When the alleged cause is race, they argue, this model breaks down, because there is no logical counterfactual state: "a Black person who is not Black cannot be considered the same person."[39(p115)]

Yet, as others have noted,[40,41] the constraint on this counterfactual state is empirical, not logical. To imagine a Black person who is not Black, it is necessary only to distinguish between 2 exposures: having dark skin and being culturally defined as "Black." It is difficult to operationalize this distinction in the mainland United States, because the prevailing cultural model of racial classification defines dark-skinned people with any detectable trace of African ancestry as "Black." However, as the Puerto Rican case shows, the relative salience of skin color as a basis of social classification is variable across societies, such that people with a given skin tone may be assigned to different folk ethnoracial categories in everyday social interaction.

A key innovation of our study is the attempt to estimate how survey respondents would be classified in everyday social interaction by linking survey measurement to ethnographic data on the salient cultural model of *color*.[19] This strategy treats the notion that race is a cultural construct as a mandate for research. Some well-meaning commentators argue that, because race is a cultural construct and not a biological reality, public health researchers should abandon it as a variable. For example, Fullilove asks, "Why continue to accept something that is not only without biological merit but also full of evil social import?"[42(p1297)] We suggest that this question contains the answer. Because racial classification in the United States—and other folk classification schemes in other societies—are full of evil social import, social scientists must devise strategies to operationalize racial classification as a sociocultural variable. Our approach to this problem complements other strategies to explain racial health inequalities, including what Krieger[40] identifies as the direct and indirect impacts of racism on health.

Perhaps because research on skin color and blood pressure often reflects the assumptions of a racialized world-view,[43] previous studies have not distinguished between skin pigmentation and the cultural significance of skin color as potentially independent predictors of blood pressure. However, once we recognize that distinction, existing evidence favors the cultural rather than biological significance of skin color. Seven previous studies of skin color and blood pressure[7,9,44–48] measured skin pigmentation with reflectance spectrophotometry; none reported an association between pigmentation and blood pressure in the entire sample after control for age, gender, and SES. One of these studies found an association only in low-SES respondents,[46] whereas another reported an association only in Egyptian women.[48] By contrast, 5 studies[16,49–52] that measured skin color by observer ratings reported a consistent association between skin color and blood pressure across the sample. Thus, studies that measure skin pigmentation precisely using reflectance spectrophotometry provide the weakest evidence for an association between skin color and blood pressure. Those that approximate social classification with observer ratings provide the strongest evidence of such an association.

This set of findings underscores the importance of our measurement approach. However, limitations of the research design moderate the strength of our results. First, by comparison to previous studies, our sample is small. It is noteworthy that, despite the small sample size, we observed a statistically significant relationship between ascribed color and blood pressure. Case diagnostics also indicate that this relationship does not depend on a small number of unusual cases. Still, it remains to be seen whether our findings can be replicated in other parts of Puerto Rico or elsewhere. A larger sample would also increase the statistical power to detect more complex interactions between SES, *color,* and other important factors, such as gender, perceived discrimination, or access to health care. Second, although our measure of ascribed *color* is linked to ethnographic data regarding the salient cultural model, it is unclear how well it estimates everyday social classification. This unresolved question is a critical area for future research. One important extension of this work would be to examine whether nonbiological markers of social status influence the ascription of *color* and, if so, how this effect alters the association with blood pressure. Third, we did not collect data on dietary intake or energy expenditure. There is evidence that both skin color and exposure to social stressors are associated with blood pressure, independent of such measures,[16,21] but attention to nutritional status and physical activity would enhance future research. Fourth, the biological significance of skin pigmentation may differ in Puerto Rico and the mainland United States, given different historical processes of admixture. This difference limits direct comparability between Puerto Rico and the mainland. However, the fact that skin color and blood pressure are related in societies with different histories of genetic admixture, but with common histories of slavery and racial discrimination, suggests that nongenetic factors may provide a more parsimonious explanation.

Given these limitations, our study is significant, more for the questions it raises than for the answers it provides. Skin pigmentation is central to debates about race and genetics, but most researchers fail to distinguish its significance as a biological parameter from its significance as a marker of social status and exposure to stressors.[34] Our measurement strategy provides one way to make this distinction explicit. Our finding that blood pressure is associated with culturally ascribed *color*—but not with skin pigmentation—does not exclude a genetic basis to population differences in blood pressure. Yet it does cast doubt on genetic explanations for the relationship

between skin color and blood pressure. This finding highlights the need for testable hypotheses and appropriate measurement operations in future research on the causes of poor health in the African Diaspora.

About the Authors

Clarence C. Gravlee is with the Department of Anthropology, Florida State University, Tallahassee. William W. Dressler is with the Department of Anthropology, University of Alabama, Tuscaloosa. H. Russell Bernard is with the Department of Anthropology, University of Florida, Gainesville.

Correspondence: Requests for reprints should be sent to Clarence C. Gravlee, PhD, Department of Anthropology, Florida State University, Tallahassee, FL 32306-7772 (e-mail: cgravlee@fsu.edu).

Acknowledgments

This work was funded by the National Science Foundation (BCS 0078793) and by the American Heart Association, Florida and Puerto Rico Affiliate (0010082B).

We thank Mark D. Shriver for providing the reflectometer; Alejandrina Ramos for assistance in data collection; Prof. Nydia Garcia, Dr. Jeffrey Quiñones, Doña Marta Almodóvar, and Lillian Torres Aguirre for their support of the project; and James Eberwine for comments on a previous draft.

Human Participant Protection

This study was conducted with approval from the institutional review board of the University of Florida.

Contributors

C. C. Gravlee originated the study, collected the data, completed all analyses, and led the writing. W. W. Dressler and H. R. Bernard critically reviewed the study design and assisted with the analyses and interpretation of data. All authors reviewed drafts of the article.

References

1. Adams JM. Some racial differences in blood pressure and morbidity in groups of white and colored workmen. *Am J Med Sci.* 1932;184:342–350.

2. Wong MD, Shapiro MF, Boscardin WJ, Ettner SL. Contribution of major diseases to disparities in mortality. *N Engl J Med.* 2002;347:1585–1592.

3. Cooper RS, Rotimi C, Ataman S, et al. The prevalence of hypertension in seven populations of West African origin. *Am J Public Health.* 1997;87:160–168.

4. Cooper RS, Rotimi CN. Hypertension in blacks. *Am J Hypertens.* 1997;7:804–812.

5. Halberstein RA. Blood pressure in the Caribbean. *Hum Biol.* 1999;71:659–684.

6. James SA, Aleida-Filho N, Kaufman JS. Hypertension in Brazil: a review of the epidemiologic evidence. *Ethn Dis.* 1991;1:91–98.

7. Frisancho AR, Farrow S, Friedenzohn I, et al. Role of genetic and environmental factors in the increased blood pressures of Bolivian blacks. *Am J Hum Biol.* 1999;11:489–498.

8. Cooper RS, Rotimi CN, Ward R. The puzzle of hypertension in African-Americans. *Sci Am.* 1999;280(2): 56–63.

9. Boyle E, Jr. Biological patterns in hypertension by race, sex, body weight, and skin color. *JAMA.* 1970; 213:1637–1643.

10. Gleiberman L, Lackland DT, Egan BM. Nativity and race: response. *Hypertension.* 1999;34(5):e7.

11. Tyroler HA, James SA. Blood pressure and skin color. *Am J Public Health.* 1978;68:1170–1172.

12. Dressler WW. Social class, skin color, and arterial blood pressure in two societies. *Ethn Dis.* 1991;1(1): 60–77.

13. Klonoff EA, Landrine H. Is skin color a marker for racial discrimination? Explaining the skin color–hypertension relationship. *J Behav Med.* 2000;23:329–338.

14. Takiwaki H. Measurement of skin color: practical application and theoretical considerations. *J Med Invest.* 1998;44(3–4):121–126.

15. Shriver MD, Parra EJ. Comparison of narrow-band reflectance spectroscopy and tristimulus colorimetry for measurements of skin and hair color in persons of different biological ancestry. *Am J Phys Anthropol.* 2000;112:17–27.

16. Costas R, Jr., Garcia-Palmieri MR, Sorlie P, Hertzmark E. Coronary heart disease risk factors in men with light

and dark skin in Puerto Rico. *Am J Public Health*. 1981;71:614–619.

17. Seda Bonilla E. *Requiem para una cultura: ensayos sobre la socialización del puertorriqueño en su cultura y en el ámbito del poder neocolonial*. Rio Piedras: Ediciones Bayoan; 1972.

18. Duany J. *The Puerto Rican nation on the move: identities on the Island and in the United States*. Chapel Hill, NC: University of North Carolina Press; 2002.

19. Gravlee CC. Ethnic classification in southeastern Puerto Rico: the cultural model of "color." *Soc Forces*. 2005;83:949–970.

20. United States Bureau of the Census. *Profiles of General Demographic Characteristics, Census 2000: Puerto Rico*. Washington, DC: US. Department of Commerce; May 2001.

21. Dressler WW, Balieiro MC, Dos Santos JE. Culture, skin color, and arterial blood pressure in Brazil. *Am J Hum Biol*. 1999;11:49–59.

22. Gravlee CC, Dressler WW. Skin pigmentation, self-perceived color, and arterial blood pressure in Puerto Rico. *Am J Hum Biol*. 2005;17:195–206.

23. Gravlee CC. Mobile computer-assisted personal interviewing (MCAPI) with handheld computers: the Entryware System v3.0. *Field Methods*. August 2002; 14:322–336.

24. Romney AK, Weller SC, Batchelder WH. Culture as consensus: a theory of culture and informant accuracy. *Am Anthropol*. 1986;88:313–339.

25. Harris M. Referential ambiguity in the calculus of Brazilian racial identity. *Southwest J Anthropol*. 1970; 26(1):1–14.

26. Anwar YA, Giacco S, McCabe EJ, Tendler BE, White WB. Evaluation of the efficacy of the Omron HEM-737 IntelliSense device for use on adults according to the recommendations of the Association for the Advancement of Medical Instrumentation. *Blood Press Monitoring*. 1998;3(4):261–265.

27. O'Brien E, Waeber B, Parati G, Staessen J, Myers MG. Blood pressure measuring devices: recommendations of the European Society of Hypertension. *BMJ*. 2001;322(7285):531–536.

28. Mintz SW. Cañamelar: the subculture of a rural sugar plantation proletariat. In: Steward JH, Manners RA, Wolf ER, Padilla Seda E, Mintz SW, Scheele RL, eds. *The People of Puerto Rico: a Study in Social Anthropology*. Urbana, Ill: University of Illinois Press; 1956:314–417.

29. Gordon MW. Cultural aspects of Puerto Rico's race problem. *Am Sociol Rev*. 1950;15:382–392.

30. Muñoz Vázquez M, Alegría Ortega IE. *Discrimen por razón de raza en los sistemas de seguridad y justicia en Puerto Rico*. San Juan, PR: Comisión de Derechos Civiles; 1999.

31. Hoetink H. "Race" and Color in the Caribbean. In: Mintz SW, Price S, eds. *Caribbean Contours*. Baltimore, MD: The Johns Hopkins University Press; 1985:55–84.

32. Harrell JP, Hall S, Taliaferro J. Physiological responses to racism and discrimination: an assessment of the evidence. *Am J Public Health*. 2003;93:243–248.

33. Wyatt SB, Williams DR, Calvin R, Henderson FC, Walker ER, Winters K. Racism and cardiovascular disease in African Americans. *Am J Med Sci*. 2003;325:315–331.

34. Parra EJ, Kittles RA, Shriver MD. Implications of correlations between skin color and genetic ancestry for biomedical research. *Nat Genet*. 2004;36(Suppl 11): S54–S60.

35. Daniel HI, Rotimi CN. Genetic epidemiology of hypertension: an update on the African diaspora. *Ethn Dis*. Summer 2003;13(2 Suppl 2):S53–S66.

36. Nesbitt S, Victor RG. Pathogenesis of hypertension in African Americans. *Congest Heart Fail*. 2004;10(1): 24–29.

37. Rosenberg NA, Pritchard JK, Weber JL, et al. Genetic structure of human populations. *Science*. 2002; 298:2381–2385.

38. Jablonski NG. The evolution of human skin and skin color. *Annual Review of Anthropology*. 2004;33:585–623.

39. Kaufman JS, Cooper RS. Seeking causal explanations in social epidemiology. *Am J Epidemiol*. 1999; 150(2):113–120.

40. Krieger N. Does racism harm health? Did child abuse exist before 1962? On explicit questions, critical science, and current controversies: an ecosocial perspective. *Am J Public Health*. 2003;93(2):194–199.

41. Muntaner C. Invited commentary: social mechanisms, race, and social epidemiology. *Am J Epidemiol*. 1999;150(2):121–126.

42. Fullilove MT. Comment: abandoning 'race' as a variable in public health research—an idea whose time has come. *Am J Public Health*. 1998;88:1297–1298.

43. Smedley A. *Race in North America: origin and evolution of a worldview*. 2nd ed. Boulder, CO: Westview Press; 1998.

44. Keil JE, Tyroler HA, Sandifer SH, Boyle E. Hypertension: effects of social class and racial admixture. *Am J Public Health*. 1977;67:634–639.

45. Keil JE, Sandifer SH, Loadholt CB, Boyle E. Skin color and education effects on blood pressure. *Am J Public Health*. 1981;71:532–534.

46. Klag MJ, Whelton PK, Coresh J, Grim C, Kuller LH. The association of skin color with blood pressure in US Blacks with low socioeconomic status. *JAMA*. 1991; 265:599–602.

47. Ernst FA, Jackson I, Robertson RM, Nevels H, Watts E. Skin tone, hostility, and blood pressure in young normotensive African Americans. *Ethn Dis*. 1997;7(1):34–40.

48. Mosley JD, Appel LJ, Ashour Z, Coresh J, Whelton PK, Ibrahim MM. Relationship between skin color and blood pressure in Egyptian Adults: results from the National Hypertension Project. *Hypertension*. 2000;36:296–302.

49. Harburg E, Gleibermann L, Roeper P, Schork MA, Schull WJ. Skin color, ethnicity, and blood pressure I: Detroit blacks. *Am J Public Health*. 1978;68:1177–1183.

50. Harburg E, Erfurt JC, Hauenstein LS, Chape C, Schull WJ, Schork MA. Socio-ecological stress, suppressed hostility, skin color, and black-white male blood pressure: Detroit. *Psychosom Med*. 1973;35:276–296.

51. Sichieri R, Oliveira MC, Pereira RA. High prevalence of hypertension among black and mulatto women in a Brazilian survey. *Ethn Dis*. 2001;11:412–418.

52. Gleiberman L, Harburg E, Frone MR, Russell M, Cooper ML. Skin colour, measures of socioeconomic status, and blood pressure among blacks in Erie County, NY. *Ann Hum Biol*. 1995;22(1):69–73.

Overview of Children, Adolescents, and Family Health Section

| Prof. A. Mushtaque R. Chowdhury, Dean, James P. Grant School of Public Health, BRAC University, Dhaka, Bangladesh;
Prof. Allan Rosenfield, Dean, Mailman School of Public Health, Columbia University, New York

This anthology includes papers published in the *American Journal of Public Health* in various years between 2001 and 2007. These can be grouped into several clusters. Three of them cover issues related to inequalities as variously defined and identified. For example, the paper by Burstrom et al. (2005) provides a historical analysis of the introduction of improved water and sanitation in the later 19th and early 20th century in the city of Stockholm, Sweden and how it had an equitable impact on some of the immediate outcome indicators. The paper by Rodwin et al. (2005) also covers four major urban settlements in the developed world—New York, London, Paris, and Tokyo—±and analyzes the link between income and infant mortality rates in these cities between 1988-1992 and 1993-1997. The third study in this cluster is by Pickett et al. (2005) which reported the contribution of poor socioeconomic status, represented by income, in increased births and violence amongst the adolescents in selected rich countries.

The above three papers originate from higher-income countries. Over the past decade or so, there have been a number of initiatives that systematically considered inequities in health, particularly in low-income countries. These represented inequities in terms of access and coverage of health services and their impact on health status. One such initiative is the Global Health Equity Initiative (GHEI), spearheaded by the Rockefeller Foundation and supported by several other agencies including the World Health Organization (WHO), Canadian

International Development Agency (CIDA), the World Bank, and the Swedish International Development Cooperation Agency (SIDA). It resulted in the publication of a major volume with 13 essays and a foreword by the then-serving Prime Minister of Bangladesh, Sheikh Hasina (Evans et al. 2001).

The issue of equity has been in discussion and discourse in health literature for centuries. It is central to and one of the major pillars of Primary Health Care (PHC), articulated in 1978 in Alma Ata, to which the world is reverting back after a couple of decades of uncertainties and indecision. Evans et al reported studies from different parts of the world which demonstrated convincingly the existence of huge inequities in health access and status. There were inequities not only in terms of income entitlement, but also in terms of gender, social status represented by education, ethnicity, geographical residence (rural, urban and slums) and so on. These inequities are pervasive and unfortunately drag on. Although our knowledge about the levels and causes of inequities in health are quite robust and extensive, our knowledge and experience on how to deal with these is scant at best.

As health and health inequities affect other outcomes such as income, education, environment, etc., and are also affected by these, the interventions to address health inequities may be found here, in addition to direct health measures. Evans and colleagues cite measures that have been found effective in reducing inequities in

health status of children. This study, which comes from Bangladesh, reports on a women-centered poverty alleviation program run by a local non-governmental organization (BRAC) with major emphasis on micro credit and children's education. The study demonstrates this approach having reduced inequities in under-5 mortality and in bringing the rates of children of poor women at par with those of the well-to-do sections in the community (Chowdhury and Bhuiya 2001). Such micro credit and poverty alleviation programs are now being implemented all over the world, and its impact on other aspects of human well-being such as women's empowerment, nutrition, education, fertility and so on is well documented (Chowdhury and Bhuiya 2004; Bhuiya and Chowdhury, 2002). For changing health status and improving health inequities, we need to think outside the box and look for solutions in other sectors. Health measures including curative and preventive care are essential to reduce mortality and morbidity, but interventions targeted to the social determinants of health may bring the desirable results faster and in a more sustained fashion (Chowdhury, 2007; CSDH 2007).

Two papers presented in this anthology deal with post-disaster health situations. While the paper by Desai and Perry (2004) tried to track the human rights violations against women in postwar Kosovo, the paper by Becker (2006) describes a program that provided psychosocial care to child and adult survivors of the Asian Tsunami in Southern India. The Kosovo study lamented the paucity of appropriate data to track "the scope and frequency of violent acts committed against women." Indeed this is true for most low income countries where availability of credible information on violence against women is a major limitation in undertaking any systematic monitoring and advocacy work. For many such countries the basic statistics which gives a child its basic human rights, the birth registration, is absent or faulty at best. In Bangladesh, for example, birth registration is available for less than ten percent of the population, and that too is often incomplete and faulty. In the absence of data, governmental and development agencies often depend on decennial censuses or periodic surveys. However, the censuses are too infrequent for use in development programs and the surveys are expensive.

An issue related to this is the question of research capacity. Since the publication of the report by the Commission on Health Research for Development in 1990 (COHRED 1990), there have been a number of international initiatives to promote research in low income countries. The issue of the "10/90" gap (implying that only ten percent of the resources are spent in researching health problems of 90 percent of the world's population) has caught the imagination of many agencies. With support from donor agencies, the Council on Health Research for Development (COHRED) and the Global Forum for Health Research (GFHR) are working to reduce the 10/90 gap. The Global Forum claims that there has been a sustained increase in the global spending on health research. Nobody, however, seems to know whether the gap has been reducing or not.

One issue at hand is the question of research capacity in low income countries. Research is not a part of the academic culture in most of these countries. Research is hardly taught in universities and the government decisions are hardly based on research findings. Indeed, most of the decisions and plans are made on an *ad hoc* basis without the benefit of any evidence base. Those who feel obliged to do

research often get frustrated as their research is seldom translated into policies. For a sustained improvement of health in low income countries, promotion and development of research culture and capacities are essential. Birn (2005) also addresses the importance of research in the case of Uruguay, when she examines the historical reasons behind the country's institutionalizing child health as a priority.

The two papers by Rosenfield & Figdor (2001) and Bassett (2001) have brought forth the issue of MTCT (mother-to-child transmission) of HIV and the place of the *mother* in it. "Maternal" was a low priority in MCH (maternal and child health) programs in the 1980s-1990s, which led to asking the question 'Where is the M in MCH?' (Rosenfield and Maine, 1985), as a result of which the Safe Motherhood program was born. The authors, for very valid reasons, similarly draw attention to the role of mothers in MTCT.

Over the past couple of decades, the world has made significant progress in many health related fields, child health being one. Over the past few years, Bangladesh, like some other low income countries, has been able to reduce its infant and under-5 mortality rates by more than half. Unfortunately, the maternal mortality rate has not been reduced to a similar extent. "Magic bullets" for child mortality like oral rehydration therapy (ORT), immunizations, and vitamin A have been successfully scaled up to reach most of the population. Reducing maternal mortality, however, requires a more system-wide approach which involves a responsive health system that can provide emergency obstetric care (EmOC). Many of the low income countries are trailing behind in this, and unless health systems are strengthened to respond to emergencies, the health of pregnant women will remain at stake.

The paper by Foege (2001) deserves attention in this respect as well. He critiques a manual on managing newborn health, published by APHA. He says that the technology and scientific know-how to save newborns are all known. The only issue is

what he calls *management*. Indeed, this remains true for most diseases that kill children and women prematurely. In its report, the Task Force on Child Health and Maternal Health of the UN Millennium Project echoed this by pointing out that the world has all the resources to prevent most maternal and child deaths—but the real challenge is how to make these available to the vast majority of the world's poor (Freedman et al, 2005). In other words, this is a question of scaling up of known and effective interventions. The Task Force report also strongly advocated for increased attention to strengthening the health system so that it is able to entertain the health needs of all: poor and rich, men and women, dominant and the minorities.

The last two papers are by Miller et al. (2006) and Roggero et al. (2007). The former, a study from Botswana where the world's highest percentage of AIDS orphaned children live, assessed the ability of households to adequately take care of the orphans. This brings to light once again the plight of a most neglected and unheard group of children whose parents fell victim to the AIDS epidemic. Botswana, even as one of the richest countries of the African continent, neither has the public sector nor the individual household-level support to provide adequate care to orphans. As the paper concludes, lessons from Botswana "provide valuable insights to policy-makers throughout sub-Saharan Africa." The latter paper presents a meta-analysis of the relationship between child labor and status of health as represented by different indicators such as mortality rate, nutritional level, and infectious morbidity.

In a way, these findings are neither surprising nor unexpected. The children who (have to) resort to labor hail from poorer households where their support is needed for the family's day-to-day survival. For many of these children, going to schools is a luxury which their households feel they can scarcely afford. The study also speculates on the longer-term health impacts of child labor. There are some policy implications associated with child labor as well: the practice is banned in most countries, yet it continues unabated in many low income settings. The reason is simple: poorer families perceive the need for their children's support to supplement the household income. Taking a partial view of this scenario is not helpful to remove the ill effects of child labor. One has to instead recognize the facts and come up with practical, workable solutions. As a small example of the real-life clash between child health and child labor, consider that in the rural setting of countries like Bangladesh, children can provide real assistance to their parents in agriculture, e.g., by taking food to the field or herding the cattle. The school hours clash with the work hours, setting up a simple conflict. One can resolve this by setting flexible school timings; the school may be in session during times (or seasons) when there is a reduced need for children's work. This approach has been tried successfully by some Bangladeshi NGOs, and highlights the need, again, for creative solutions to intractable problems (Ahmed et al. 1993).

Lastly, the papers presented in this anthology are a substantial, thought-provoking addition to the literature and to efforts for continuing education. They provide a variety of topics with experiences from different parts of the world. They remain essential for public health practitioners and people who wish to expand their knowledge in this area.

References
1. Evans, T.;Whitehead, M.;Diderichsen, F.;Bhuiya, A.; Wirth, M. *Challenging Inequities in Health: From Ethics to Action.* New York: Oxford University Press. 2001.
2. Chowdhury A.M.R. and Bhuiya A. Do poverty alleviation programmes reduce inequitities in health? In: D. Leon and G Walt (ed.s) *Poverty Inequality and Health.* Oxford, Oxford University Press, 2001 (pages 312-331).
3. Chowdhury A.M.R. and Bhuiya A. 2004. The wider impact of BRAC poverty alleviation programme in Bangladesh. *Journal of International Development* 16.
4. Bhuiya, A. and Chowdhury, A.M.R. 2002. Beneficial effects of a woman-focused development programme on child survival: evidence from rural Bangladesh. *Social Science and Medicine* 55.
4. Chowdhury A. Rethinking interventions for women's health. *Lancet,* Volume 370, Issue 9595, Pages 1292 – 1293.
5. Report of the Commission on Social Determinants of Health. Accessed at http://www.who.int/social_determinants/resources/mekn_report_10oct07.pdf
6. COHRED. 1990 Report of Commission on Health Research for Development. Accessed at: http://www.cohred.org/Assests/PDF/Papers/ComReports.pdf
7. Rosenfield A, Maine D. Maternal mortality - a neglected tragedy. Where is the M in MCH? *Lancet.* 1985 Jul 13;2(8446):83-5
8. Freedman LP, Waldman R, de Pinho H, Wirth M, Chowdury AMR, Rosenfield A. Transforming health systems to improve the lives of women and children. *Lancet.* March 12, 2005; 365: 997-1000.
9. Ahmed M, Chabbott C, Joshi A, Pande R and Prather CJ. 1993. Primary Education for All: Learning from the BRAC Experience. Washington DC: Academy for Educational Development.

Infant Mortality and Income in 4 World Cities: New York, London, Paris, and Tokyo

| Victor G. Rodwin, MPH, PhD and Leland G. Neuberg, PhD

ABSTRACT

Objectives. We investigated the association between average income or deprivation and infant mortality rate across neighborhoods of 4 world cities.

Methods. Using a maximum likelihood negative binomial regression model that controls for births, we analyzed data for 1988–1992 and 1993–1997.

Results. In Manhattan, for both periods, we found an association (.05% significance level) between income and infant mortality. In Tokyo, for both periods, and in Paris and London for period 1, we found none (5% significance level). For period 2, the association just missed statistical significance for Paris, whereas for London it was significant (5% level).

Conclusions. In stark contrast to Tokyo, Paris, and London, the association of income and infant mortality rate was strongly evident in Manhattan.

INTRODUCTION

The nationwide infant mortality rate in the United States is notoriously high in comparison with the national rates of other wealthy nations belonging to the Organization for Economic Cooperation and Development (OECD).[1,2] This problem is often attributed to bias in reporting differences among nations.[3,4] However, no one would argue that reporting bias constitutes a complete explanation. The higher US infant mortality rate may also be attributable to our more heterogeneous population and our lack of universal health care coverage (leading to inadequate access to services, including prenatal care for pregnant mothers). More generally, the higher US rate may result from socioeconomic conditions (e.g., the relatively high level of poverty and the extent of income inequality in the United States compared with other OECD nations).[5]

We departed from more conventional comparative analyses of national health statistics. We took as our units of analysis large administrative neighborhoods in New York, London, Paris, and Tokyo. These world cities have heterogeneous populations (albeit much less so in Tokyo) and increasing income disparities between rich and poor. Within each city, we investigated the relationship between infant mortality rate and an income-related variable across its neighborhoods.

METHODS

City Definition, Neighborhood Selection, and Period Choice

New York City (population, 8 million), greater London (population, 7.3 million), Paris and its surrounding first ring (population, 6.2 million), which includes the Seine-Saint Denis, Hauts-de-Seine, and Val-de-Marne départements, and central Tokyo (population, 8.1 million) are the largest cities among the higher income nations of the OECD. They also have the highest number of births in their respective nations. These world cities function as hubs in the global economy of transnational corporations, financial services, and information exchange.[6,7] One can define them, spatially, as enormous "city-regions."[8] In this article, however, as in previous ones growing out of the World Cities Project,[9,10] we study their "urban cores"[11]: Manhattan (1.5 million population), inner London (2.7 million population), Paris (2.1 million population), and inner Tokyo (2.1 million population). For simplicity, we refer to these units as Manhattan, London, Paris, and Tokyo in the remainder of the article.

These urban cores share a number of convergent characteristics. They are medical capitals with a disproportionate share of hospitals and specialist physicians. They are destinations for large immigrant communities from around the world (with the exception of Tokyo). The foreign-born population of Paris (1999), London (2001), and Manhattan (2000) is 22.7%, 33.7%, and 29.4%, respectively.[12] In Paris, of the foreign-born from outside the European Union, most are from northern Africa (40.3%), Asia (21.1%), and sub-Saharan Africa (16.9%). In London, those from outside the European Union are mostly from Africa (30.8%), the Caribbean (25.6%), and Bangladesh (17.3%). In Manhattan, recent immigrants are predominantly from Latin America (including the Caribbean [48%], Asia [27%], and Europe [18%]). However, despite these differences, in all 3 cities, recent immigrants have exacerbated social and spatial inequalities.[13–15]

To some extent, defining neighborhoods is arbitrary. We relied on 2 criteria: existing designations or administrative boundaries and data availability. We obtained data on live births, infant deaths, and an income-related measure that is as similar as possible across cities (our data set is posted at http://www.ilcusa.org/_lib/pdf/ajph.dataappendix.pdf). For Manhattan, we used the 10 subborough units for which the New York City Housing and Vacancy Survey provides mean household income estimates during periods between the decennial census. For London, we used the 14 boroughs of inner London; for Paris, the 20 *arrondissements*; and for Tokyo, 11 *ku*.

Infant mortality—deaths in the first year of life—is an important indicator of social well-being, which reflects multiple social determinants of health. The infant mortality rate is defined as the number of infant deaths for a period divided by the number of live births for that period. Neighborhoods with relatively small numbers of births have less stable neighborhood rates. Because some neighborhoods in the 4 cities we examined have a relatively small number of annual live births, to increase the stability of the rates for these neighborhoods, we chose (as we did in a previous study) to study 5-year rather than 1-year periods.[10] By studying 2 such periods (1988–1992 and 1993–1997), we can learn whether the relation between infant mortality rate and an income-related measure changes from 1 period to the next. Data for births and infant deaths are as comparable as one can find in making international comparisons of infant mortality rates.[2–4]

Research Questions

Figure 1 shows the infant mortality rate distributions in the 4 cities for both periods. Except for Tokyo, median neighborhood rates fell between the 2 periods. For both periods, the Manhattan distribution exhibits greater spread than those of the other cities and is also more skewed in the direction of high rates. However, the figure reveals nothing about the relationship of income and infant mortality rate in the cities. Do lower income neighborhoods of a city tend to have higher rates than neighborhoods in the rest of the city? If so, does the magnitude of the difference change from 1 period to the next?

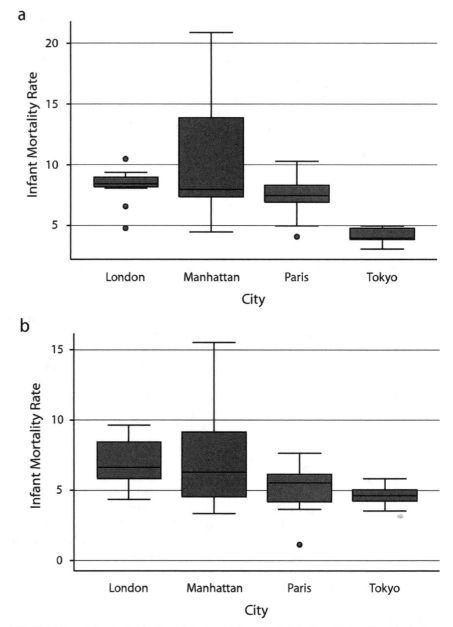

FIGURE 1— Box plots of neighborhood infant mortality rate distributions for London, Manhattan, Paris, and Tokyo for (a) 1988–1992 and (b) 1993–1997, showing differences in spread and symmetry in the distribution of neighborhood infant mortality rates for the 4 cities.

Note. The common vertical axis is the neighborhood infant mortality rate. The thick middle horizontal line across the full rectangle is at the median neighborhood rate on the vertical axis. The upper and lower horizontal lines of the full rectangle are at the 75th and 25th percentile rates, respectively. The remaining 2 horizontal lines, the whiskers, are at the largest and smallest rates of the distribution on the vertical axis, unless there are rates a substantial distance from the others. Such rates are outliers, and a box plot represents them as dots. For inner London, we included each of the 14 boroughs (Camden, City of London, Hackney, Hammersmith and Fulham, Haringey, Islington, Kensington and Chelsey, Lambeth, Lewisham, Newham, Southwark, Tower Hamlets, Wandsworth, and Westminster); for Manhattan, each of the 10 subborough units used by the Housing and Vacancy Survey (Greenwich Village/Financial District, Lower East Side, Chinatown, Stuyvesant Town/Turtle Bay, Upper West Side, Upper East Side, Morningside Heights/Hamilton Heights, Central Harlem, East Harlem, and Washington Heights/Inwood; for Paris, each of the well-known 20 arrondissements (1–20); and for inner Tokyo each of the 11 ku: Chiyoda, Chuo, Minato, Shinjuku, Bunkyo, Taito, Sumida, Koto, Shibuya, Toshima, and Arakawa.

Source. The birth and death data on which these rates were based are available from the authors. London: Office of National Statistics, birth registration and linked mortality files, number of live births (1990–1997), population < 1 year of age and number of infant deaths (1988–1997). Manhattan: Data were extracted from birth and death files, Division of Vital Statistics, Department of Health and Mental Hygiene. Paris: 1988–1992 number of live births and infant deaths are from "La santé de la mère et de l'Enfant à Paris," Département des Affaires Sanitaires et Sociales, Ville de Paris, July 2000. For the period 1993–1997, data were provided by Eric Jougla, Institut Nationale Scientifique d'Etudes et de Recherches Médicales (INSERM). Tokyo: 1988–1992 data are from Tokyo Eiseikyoku (1993), Annual Report on Health in Tokyo. Data on 1993–1997 are from Fiscal Year 2000 Report of the Bureau of Public Health, Tokyo Metropolitan Government, 2000.

American Journal of Public Health | January 2005, Vol 95, No. 1

TABLE 1— Results of Maximum-Likelihood Negative Binomial Regression That Controls for Births

City	1988–1992				1993–1997			
	IRR	SE	Stat	P Value	IRR	SE	Stat	P Value
London	.941	.046	−1.24	.107	.814	.082	−2.03	.021
Manhattan	.441	.101	−3.59	< .0005	.391	.082	−4.50	< .0005
Paris	.999	.058	−0.01	.496	.871	.074	−1.52	.065
Tokyo	.922	.098	−0.77	.221	1.002	.121	.01	.506

Note. IRR = incident rate ratio; SE = standard error; Z Stat = Z statistic. The model controls for births and regresses deaths on an indicator variable for the lower quartile of income (or the upper quartile of deprivation). With births fixed, IRR is the ratio of the infant mortality rate of those in the upper (lower) three quartiles of income (deprivation) to those in the lower (upper) quartile of income (deprivation). Estimations use a maximum-likelihood negative binomial regression. P values are for 1-sided tests and are asymptotic. The number of neighborhoods or observations for each period for London, Manhattan, Paris, and Tokyo, respectively, are 14, 10, 20, and 11.

If 1 neighborhood has 1000 births and 10 deaths and another has 10000 births and 100 deaths, they would both have infant mortality rates of 10 per 1000 and would be indistinguishable in a model that did not control for births. However, intuitively, variation in births is likely to influence variation in deaths or variation in infant mortality rate. Thus, we sought a model that controls for births.

Because deaths is a nonnegative count variable, a Poisson regression model was a possibility. However, to account for greater variation than in a true Poisson process, we used instead a maximum likelihood negative binomial regression model that constrains the predicted number of deaths to a nonnegative number. Number of deaths is the response, number of births is the exposure, and an income-related variable is the explanatory variable.

For income, a similar measure of pretax, average household income, by neighborhood, is available for Manhattan, Paris, and Tokyo, so we began with this variable for these 3 cities. Since household income data are not available in the United Kingdom, for London, following British custom, we began with "deprivation" indices in place of direct income measures. Income figures for Manhattan, Paris, and Tokyo are in dollars, francs, and yen, respectively. For London, we began with the Carstairs Deprivation Index (http://census.ac.uk/cdu/Datasets/1991Census_datasets/Area_Stats/Derived_data/Deprivation_scores/Carstairs_index.htm) for period 1 and the Department of the Environment, Transport and the Regions Deprivation Index (http://www.detr.gov.uk) for period 2.

Using income and 2 different deprivation indices as explanatory variables in the models would make London and the other 3 cities hard to compare. Therefore, we used income and the deprivation indices to define an indicator variable that we used as the explanatory variable in the models. For Manhattan, Paris, and Tokyo, we let income (I) = 0 for a neighborhood if it was in the lower income quartile of neighborhoods. These are the 2 lowest income neighborhoods in Manhattan, the 5 lowest in Paris, and the 3 lowest in Tokyo. For the other neighborhoods in these cities, we let I = 1. For London, we let I = 0 for each of the 4 neighborhoods in the highest deprivation index quartile. For the other neighborhoods of London, we let I = 1. If both deprivation indices in London included the 4 lowest income neighborhoods in their upper deprivation quartile, our combination of income and deprivation indicators selected the lower income quartile of neighborhoods for all 4 cities.

We reported not the estimate of the underlying coefficient of I but the exponential of the estimate (i.e., the estimated incident rate ratio). The incident rate ratio here is the ratio of the value of the infant mortality rate in the rest of the city to its value in the low-income (or high-deprivation) neighborhoods. Our null hypothesis in each city and period was that the true value of the incident rate ratio for I is 1, that is, that there was no difference in infant mortality rates between the low-income (or high-deprivation) neighborhoods and those of the rest of the city. Our alternative hypothesis was that the incident rate is less than 1, that is, the low-income (or high-deprivation) neighborhoods have higher infant mortality rates than those in the rest of the city.

RESULTS

Except for Tokyo in the second period (Table 1), all of the incident rate ratios were less than 1, as expected. That is, with births fixed, shifting a neighborhood out of the lower income (or higher deprivation) quartile lowered its number of deaths or infant mortality rate. More income for the neighborhood was associated with a lower infant mortality rate.

The findings were most dramatic for Manhattan, where we found strong support for the alternative hypothesis since the downward shift in infant mortality rate from low-income to high-income neighborhoods was significant at the .05% level in both periods. The first period estimate was that the rate in the high-income neighborhoods was 44% of the rate in the low-income neighborhoods; for the second period estimate, it was 39%.

In London, we estimated that the low-deprivation neighborhoods had a rate 94% of the rate in the high-deprivation neighborhoods in the first period and 82% in the second period. However, only the second period estimate was statistically significant at the 5% level.

In Paris, we found no difference in the low-and high-income neighborhood rates in the first period. We estimated that the high-income neighborhood rate was 87% of the low-income neighborhood rate in the second period, a figure that just missed statistical significance at the 5% level.

Finally, in Tokyo we found no significant difference (at the 5% level) between low-and high-income neighborhood rates in either period.

DISCUSSION

In summary, after controlling for births, we found that between the two 5-year periods, each city, except for Tokyo, experienced a widening of the infant mortality rate gap between its low-income (or high-deprivation) neighborhoods and the rest of the city. Despite this apparent "manhattanization" of London and Paris, Manhattan still stood out conspicuously in comparison with London, Paris, and Tokyo in 2 respects. First, after controlling for births, Manhattan was the only city with a statistically significant association (at the 5% level) between infant mortality rate and income (or deprivation) indicator in both periods. Second, the magnitude of the infant mortality rate gap was dramatically greater in Manhattan than in any of the other cities. In Manhattan, we estimated that the low-income neighborhoods had an infant mortality rate approximately 2.5 times that of the rest of the city. In the other 3 cities, in contrast, we estimated that the infant mortality rate of the low-income (or high-deprivation) neighborhoods was never greater than approximately 1.25 times that of the rest of the city in either period.

We found that the evidence of higher infant mortality rates in low-income neighborhoods, when births are fixed, was especially strong in Manhattan. Central and East Harlem were the Manhattan neighborhoods in the lower income quartile, and they were also the neighborhoods with the highest infant mortality rates. A causal reading of this finding suggests a clear policy strategy. To lower infant mortality rates in Central and East Harlem, New York City should promote economic development in these neighborhoods and thereby raise their average income levels.

The problem, of course, is that even after controlling for births, an association between income level and infant mortality rate does not establish that the former causes the latter. Even if our Manhattan model was perfectly specified, no conclusion that low income causes more infant deaths is warranted because our data were ecological. The infants who died in the low-income Manhattan neighborhoods could have been children of the higher income residents of those neighborhoods. Only if our data were at the individual level and experimental—not observational—would our findings support a causal argument. Nonetheless, our regression results and broader comparative analysis raise at least 3 important questions for debates about the direction of policy in Manhattan:

First, what characteristics of high-infant-mortality, low-income neighborhoods, other than insufficient income, contribute to raising infant mortality? Are such neighborhoods characterized by inadequate provision of family planning, prenatal care, and other health care services leading to low levels of maternal health?

The New York Department of Health and Mental Hygiene (DHMH) recently introduced several new initiatives all of which suggest an affirmative answer to this question. For example, after an internal study that reported an 80% rate of unintended pregnancies in neighborhoods with high infant mortality rates,[16] the DHMH established a citywide family planning initiative. In addition, the DHMH established an infant mortality case review committee to examine the causes of each infant death and now is attempting to coordinate citywide and regional perinatal forums to improve access to care for high-risk mothers and newborns. Perhaps most important of all, the DHMH established district public health offices in high-infant-mortality neighborhoods, including 1 for East and Central Harlem, whose responsibilities include leveraging resources and improving coordination of DHMH programs. For example in Central Harlem a strategic action committee designed a range of interventions that address health care as well as social factors related to mothers at risk.

Second, do high-infant-mortality, low-income neighborhoods reflect patterns of racial segregation and other forms of discrimination that might affect both the incomes and access to health care of minority women in Manhattan?

There is abundant evidence that race is an important determinant of infant mortality in the United States.[17,18] Ellen's evidence on this issue has the strength of analyzing individual rather than ecological data, but because the Internal Revenue Service does not disclose household income data at the individual level, the relative role of race and income level as sources of health outcomes cannot be explored.[19] Had we included percentage of African Americans in our Manhattan model, the incident rate ratio for our income indicator might well have been 1.

Third, why do inequalities among high-and low-infant-mortality Manhattan neighborhoods remain so flagrant in spite of the well-known decrease in the overall citywide rate?

Based on our findings, one might suspect that Manhattan provides inadequate levels of health care access to mothers in poorer neighborhoods. New York State's Prenatal Care Assistance Program (PCAP) became part of the Medicaid program after expansion in income eligibility thresholds in 1990. Nevertheless, Joyce's evaluation of the PCAP's impact on birth outcomes of Medicaid recipients in New York City suggests that expansion of prenatal care for women at risk is an inadequate strategy with which to achieve significant birth outcomes.[20] A broader range of services, including family planning, comprehensive health care coverage, and targeted outreach efforts would probably be more effective than the PCAP. In this sense, the absence of universal health insurance in the United States exacerbates the problem of access in comparison to what Joseph White has called the "international standard."[21] For example, Great Britain ensures health care coverage under its National Health Service; France and Japan ensure universal coverage under their national health insurance programs. Perhaps the extent to which a country lacks a commitment to universal coverage strengthens the connections between infant mortality and income.

Most research on the determinants of infant mortality highlights the importance of 3 types of variables in explaining variation in infant mortality rates across geographic units: material conditions (income and deprivation indicators, including race), income inequalities, and levels of available health services for mothers.[22–33] The research is less clear on the relative importance of these variables. Moreover, the range of relevant health services is wide. It includes health education, contraception services, pregnancy counseling and abortion services, prenatal care (particularly for high-risk mothers), routine primary health care, and neonatal medical care and follow-up of high-risk mothers after birth.

Because we have neither a measure of income inequality nor a measure of health service use for each of our neighborhoods, our analysis does not shed light on the relative importance of neighborhood average income, health service use, and income inequality on infant mortality. Just as the absence of race in our Manhattan model could account for the importance of income there, the absence of income inequality and health service use in our models could account for the significant effect of income in Manhattan in contrast to Paris and Tokyo.

We know that local governments in Paris, Tokyo, and London operate nationally funded programs to identify high-risk mothers and offer them special services.[34–36] In Paris, Tokyo, and

London (albeit less so), there are aggressive efforts, at the neighborhood level, to follow all mothers in the course of their pregnancies and after birth. Moreover, in Paris, there are even financial incentives from the central government—the *Protection Maternelle et Infantile*—for mothers to seek out these services.[37,38]

Unfortunately, comparable data across all 4 cities on the extent and effectiveness of these services and on the spatial distribution of primary health care and public health professionals, by neighborhood units, are difficult to obtain. Could differences in the distribution of services and personnel responsible for them explain the differences we found for the role of income or deprivation among these cities? Only models that include all 3 variables at once—income level, income inequality, and a measure of accessible services—can begin to answer this question. In the meantime, there is increasing recognition at the New York City DHMH, and within the new Strategic Health Authorities responsible for London, that reducing disparities among neighborhood infant mortality rates will require intense targeting of high-rate neighborhoods and disproportionate resources directed to them.

About the Authors

Victor G. Rodwin is with the World Cities Project, a joint venture of the Wagner School, New York University, and the International Longevity Center–USA, New York. Leland G. Neuberg is with the Department of Mathematics and Statistics, Boston University, Boston.

Correspondence: Requests for reprints should be sent to Victor G. Rodwin, MPH, PhD, Wagner School, New York University, The Puck Building, 295 Lafayette St, New York, NY 10012 (e-mail: victor.rodwin@nyu.edu).

Acknowledgments

This work was supported by an Investigator Award in Health Policy Research, from the Robert Wood Johnson Foundation, to Victor G.

Rodwin, and by the International Longevity Center–USA.

We thank Michael Gusmano and 3 anonymous reviewers for helpful suggestions, and Robert N. Butler, Françoise Forette, Sally Greengross, Dominique Jolly, Philip R. Lee, Roland Moreau, and Shigeo Morioka for helping us incubate the idea of this project from its most embryonic stage. We also thank Gabriel Montero who assisted with the preparation of our data set posted on the International Longevity Center Web site.

Finally, in each city, we are grateful for assistance from the following colleagues in obtaining and interpreting publicly available data on infant mortality and income: Melanie Besculides, Birgit Bogler, Tamara Dumanovsky, Fabienne Laraque, Kai-Lih Liu, all at the New York City Department of Health and Mental Hygiene (New York); Justine Fitzpatrick, London Health Observatory (London); Marie Claude Bonnefoi, Christine Grouas, Robert Poinsard (Paris Department of Health and Social Affairs), Eric Jougla (INSERM), Jeanne Fagnani (CNRS), and Diane Slama-Lequet (DRESS) (Paris); and Yukiko Kudo, Yoshiko Yamada (International Longevity Center–Japan), and Keiko Honda (International Longevity Center–USA) (Tokyo).

Contributors

V. R. Rodwin conceived the study and obtained the data. L. G. Neuberg performed the statistical modeling. Both authors worked closely together in writing and interpreting the findings.

Human Participant Protection

Local institutional review board approval was not sought, because this study was a secondary analysis of publicly available data that contained no individual identifying information.

References

1. *OECD Health Data, 2004.* Paris, France: Organization for Economic Cooperation and Development; 2004.
2. Sepkowitz S. International rankings of infant mortality and the United States'

vital statistics natality data collecting system: failure and success. *Int J Epidemiol.* 1995;24:583–588.

3. Howell E, Blondel B. International infant mortality rates: bias from reporting differences. *Am J Public Health.* 1994;84:850–852.

4. Liu K, Moon M, Sulvetta M, Chawla J. International infant mortality rankings: a look behind the numbers. *Health Care Financ Rev.* 1992;13:105–118.

5. Hogue CJ, Hargraves MA. Class, race and infant mortality in the United States. *Am J Public Health.* 1993;83:9–12.

6. Hall P. *The World Cities.* 3rd ed. London, UK: Weidenfeld and Nicholson; 1984.

7. Sassen S. *The Global City: New York, London, Tokyo.* 2nd ed. Princeton, NJ: Princeton University Press; 2001.

8. Scott A. *Global City-Regions: Trends, Theory, Policy.* New York, NY: Oxford University Press; 2001.

9. Rodwin VG, Gusmano MK. The World Cities Project: rationale and design for comparison of megacity health systems. *J Urban Health.* 2002;79:445–463.

10. Neuberg L, Rodwin V. Neighborhood matters—infant mortality rates in four cities: London, Manhattan, Paris, and Tokyo. *Indicators.* 2002–3;2:15–38.

11. Savitch HV. *Post-Industrial Cities: Politics and Planning in New York, Paris and London.* Princeton, NJ: Princeton University Press; 1988.

12. World Cities Project Fact Sheet. International Longevity Center-US. Available at: www.ilcusa.org/_lib/pdf/wcp_fact.pdf. Accessed September 28, 2004.

13. Sassen S. Economic restructuring as class and spatial polarization. In: Sassen S, ed. *The Global City: New York, London, Tokyo.* 2nd ed. Princeton, NJ: Princeton University Press; 2001:251–325.

14. Preteceille E. *La ségregation sociale dans les grandes villes.* Paris, France: Documentation Française, Problèmes Politiques et Sociaux No. 684; 1992.

15. Hamnett C. Social polarization in glob-al cities: theory and evidence. *Urban Stud.* 1994;3:401–424.

16. Besculides M, Laraque F. Unintended pregnancies among the urban poor. *J Urban Health.* 2004;81: 340–348.

17. Racial and ethnic disparities in infant mortality rates: 60 largest US cities, 1995–1998. *MMWR Morb Mortal Wkly Rep.* 2002;51:329–332.

18. Hogue CJ, Hargraves MJ. Class, race and infant mortality in the United States. *Am J Public Health.* 1993;83:9–12.

19. Ellen I. Is segregation bad for your health? The case of low birth weight. In: *Brookings-Wharton Papers on Urban Affairs.* Washington, DC: Brookings Institution Press; 2000.

20. Joyce T. Impact of augmented prenatal care on birth outcomes of Medicaid recipients in New York City. *J Health Econ.* 1999;18:31–67.

21. White J. *Competing Solutions: American Health Care Proposals and International Experience.* Washington, DC: Brookings Institute; 1995.

22. Séguin L, Xu Q, Potvin L, Zunzunegui MV, Frohlich KL. Effects of low income on infant health. *Can Med Assoc J.* 2003;168:1533–1538.

23. DiLiberti J. The relationship between social stratification and all-cause mortality among children in the United States: 1968–1992. *Pediatrics.* 2000;105:e2.

24. Bird ST, Bauman KE. State-level infant, neonatal, and postneonatal mortality: the contribution of selected structural socioeconomic variables. *Int J Health Serv.* 1998;28:13–27.

25. Pearce N, Davey Smith, G. Is social capital the key to inequalities in health? *Am J Public Health.* 2003;1: 122–129.

26. Davey Smith G. Income inequality and mortality: why are they related—income inequality goes hand in hand with underinverstment in human resources. *BMJ.* 1996;312:987–988.

27. Ben-Shlomo Y, White IR, Marmot M. Does the variation in the socioeconomic characteristics of an area affect mortality? *BMJ.*

1996;312:1013–1014.

28. Kawachi I, Kennedy BP, Wilkinson RG, eds. *The Society and Population Health Reader, Vol. I: Income Inequality and Health.* New York, NY: The New Press; 1999.

29. Mellor JM, Milyo J. Reexamining the evidence of an ecological association between income inequality and health. *J Health Polit Policy Law.* 2002;3:487–522.

30. House JS. Relating social inequalities in health and income. *J Health Polit Policy Law.* 2001;26: 523–532.

31. Kawachi I, Blakely T. When econo-mists and epidemiologists disagree. . . . *J Health Polit Policy Law.* 2001;26:534–541.

32. Daniels N, Kennedy B, Kawachi I. Justice is good for our health. *Boston Rev.* 2000;25:4–21.

33. Sohler N, Arno P, Chang C, Fang J, Schecter C. Income inequality and infant mortality in New York City. *J Urban Health.* 2003;80:650–657.

34. Child Health in 1990: The United States compared to Canada, England and Wales, France, the Netherlands and Norway. Proceedings of a confer-ence: Washington, DC; March 18–19, 1990. *Pediatrics.* 1990;86 (suppl, part 2):1025–1127. Theme issue.

35. Leppert PC. An analysis of the rea-sons for Japan's low infant mortality rate. *J Nurse Midwifery.* 1993;38: 353–357.

36. Richardson G. *A Welcome for Every Child: How France Protects Maternal and Child Healt. A New Frame of Reference for the United States.* Arlington, Va: National Center for Education in Maternal and Child Health; 1994.

37. Bergman B. *Saving Our Children from Poverty: What the United States Can Learn from France.* New York, NY: Russell Sage; 1996.

38. Rodwin VG. The health care system under French national health insur-ance: lessons for health reform in the United States. *Am J Public Health.* 2003; 93:31–37.

Psychosocial Care for Adult and Child Survivors of the 2004 Tsunami Disaster in India

| Susan M. Becker, PhD, MPH

ABSTRACT

The tsunami disaster in South Asia affected the mental health of thousands of survivors, but psychological aspects of rehabilitation are frequently overlooked in public health initiatives. From January to March 2005, teams from the National Institute of Mental Health and Neurosciences in Bangalore, India, traveled to south India and implemented a "train the trainer" community-based mental health program of psychosocial care to facilitate the recovery of child and adult survivors. Psychosocial care has applications to natural and man-made disasters in developing countries.

INTRODUCTION

The tsunami disaster in South Asia affected the emotional health of thousands of child and adult survivors, but mental health aspects of relief and rehabilitation frequently have been neglected in disaster initiatives.[1,2]

The National Institute of Mental Health and Neurosciences, located in Bangalore, India, has been at the forefront of providing mental health care in disasters and has developed and implemented a model of psychosocial care that provides a broad range of community-based interventions to promote psychological rehabilitation of survivors and community cohesion. Teams of psychiatrists, psychologists, and psychiatric social workers from the National Institute of Mental Health and Neurosciences traveled to the most devastated areas in the states of Tamil Nadu and Kerala and the Andaman Islands in January 2005 to provide training in mental health interventions for child and adult survivors. We describe the experience of professional teams who traveled to the cities of Nagappattinam and Cuddalore in Tamil Nadu, where most of the Indian fatalities occurred.

METHODS

A "train the trainer" model was used; a 3-day experiential training program in psychosocial care was provided for nongovernmental organization workers, teachers, and local health care providers who subsequently trained 1050 community-level workers at the disaster areas to offer basic mental health care to adult and child disaster survivors. The training format, along with structured therapeutic activities and instructive manuals, had been developed by the National Institute of Mental Health and Neurosciences teams in the aftermath of the Gujarat earthquake in 2001 and the Gujarat riots in 2002.[3] second tsunami wave. Trainees also were taught to identify individuals with severe reactions, such as despair, guilt, recurrent flashbacks, and feelings of loss which required referral to professionals.

In the training program, the following essentials of psychosocial care for adults were taught:

- Feelings must be normalized and ventilated to help survivors understand the disaster and the changes they experienced in body and mind.
- Somatic and psychological symptoms could be decreased by listening, encouraging relaxation, promoting externalization of interests, and engaging in recreational activities in a group setting.
- Culturally appropriate proverbs, metaphors incorporated into storytelling, and cultural rituals may be used to facilitate a reinterpretation of the meaning of the disaster with attention to restoration of coping mechanisms.
- Community cohesion would be strengthened by facilitating group activities and support groups.

RESULTS

As described in the previous section, emotional support was incorporated into relief and rehabilitation efforts. Group sessions were held in the affected communities on a daily (and later a twice-weekly) basis, often in temporary housing camps where disaster survivors resided. Local community workers trained in psychosocial care were able to relate to survivors in terms of their language and cultural traditions and maintain continuity of care. This cascading model was used in the tsunami area to train 1050 volunteers in the field during the first 3 months after the disaster.

Many child victims and survivors experienced the violence of the tsunami disaster; lost parents, siblings, and friends; and required mental health intervention. The initial response was to reunite children with their families, but many children lost their parents and were placed into temporary refugee camps. To restore normalcy to their lives, routines of daily living were put into place, and structured routines were initiated to promote a sense of security and predictability for the children. Playgroups were established by trained community workers within the camp settings, which minimized the stigmatization that is inherent in individualized psychotherapy in this culture. For more severe cases, the option of referral to a psychiatric facility was available.

In areas that were less affected, primary schools were reopened, and teachers trained by the National Institute of Mental Health and Neurosciences teams administered psychological support in the form of play therapy to their students. By conducting group sessions with children in a natural school setting, officials attempted to normalize the children's experience and provide needed group support to traumatized children who verbalized anxieties about loss of their school, their teacher, their school records, and their future educational opportunities.

DISCUSSION

Developing countries with large, impoverished populations experience the most severe consequences of disasters. The "train the trainer" model of psychosocial care has implications for natural and man-made disasters in resource-poor settings where mental health professionals are in short supply. Studies that test the effectiveness of psychosocial care in emergencies are needed but are limited by the ethical dilemma of withholding interventions to control groups and the logistics of performing research in disaster situations.

About the Author

The author is with the National Institute of Mental Health and Neurosciences, Bangalore, India.

Correspondence: Requests for reprints should be sent to Susan M. Becker, PhD, MPH, Assistant Professor, Department of International Health, School of Nursing and Health Studies, Georgetown University, 3700 Reservoir Rd, Washington, DC 20057 (e-mail: susanbecker@hotmail.com).

Acknowledgments

Susan M. Becker was funded by The Fulbright Foundation at the time of her participation in this project.

Sincere thanks to K. Sekar and R. Parthasarathy, from the Department of Psychiatric Social Work at the National Institute of Mental Health and Neurosciences, who provided psychosocial care to the survivors.

Human Participant Protection

Institutional review board approval was provided through the Ethics Committee at the National Institute of Mental Health and Neurosciences.

References

1. VanRooyen M, Leaning J. After the Tsunami—facing the public health challenges. *N Engl J Med.* 2005;352:435–438.
2. Norris FH, Friedman MJ, Watson P. 60 000 disaster victims speak, part II: summary and implications of the disaster mental health research. *Psychiatry.* 2002;65:240–260.
3. Sekar K, Dave SA. *Psychosocial Care in Disaster Management: My Work Book.* Bangalore, India: National Institute of Mental Health and Neurosciences and Care India; 2004.

Orphan Care in Botswana's Working Households: Growing Responsibilities in the Absence of Adequate Support

| Candace M. Miller, ScD, MHS, Sofia Gruskin, JD, MIA, S.V. Subramanian, PhD, Divya Rajaraman, MPH and S. Jody Heymann, MD, PhD

ABSTRACT

Objectives. Botswana has one of the world's highest HIV-prevalence rates and the world's highest percentages of orphaned children among its population. We assessed the ability of income-earning households in Botswana to adequately care for orphans.

Methods. We used data from the Botswana Family Health Needs Study (2002), a sample of 1033 working adults with caregiving responsibilities who used public services, to assess whether households with orphan-care responsibilities encountered financial and other difficulties. Thirty-seven percent of respondents provided orphan care, usually to extended family members. We applied logistic regression models to determine the factors associated with experiencing problems related to orphan caregiving.

Results. Nearly half of working households with orphan-care responsibilities reported experiencing financial and other difficulties because of orphan care. Issues of concern included caring for multiple orphans, caring for sick adults and orphans simultaneously, receiving no assistance, and low income.

Conclusions. The orphan crisis is impoverishing even working households, where caregivers lack sufficient resources to provide basic needs. Neither the public sector nor communities provide adequate safety nets. International assistance is critical to build capacity within the social welfare infrastructure and to fund community-level activities that support households. Lessons from Botswana's orphan crisis
can provide valuable insights to policymakers throughout sub-Saharan Africa.

INTRODUCTION

The AIDS pandemic is creating a generation of orphaned children who have lost 1 or both parents to the deadly disease. By 2004, an estimated 15 million children between the ages of 0 and 17 years had been orphaned by HIV/AIDS,[1] and the rate of orphaning is increasing. Worldwide, the number of orphans increased by 23% between 2001 and 2003, although it would have declined in the absence of HIV.[1]

Almost 80% of children orphaned by HIV/AIDS, or 12.3 million infants and youth, are living in sub-Saharan Africa.[1] Nearly 1 in 5 children in Zimbabwe and Lesotho, and 15% of children in Zambia, Swaziland, and Mozambique, require fostering and care.[1] In Botswana, the nation with the highest rate of orphanhood (20%), an estimated 120000 children aged 0 to 17 years had lost their mother, father, or both parents to AIDS by the end of 2003.[2] In addition, an estimated 200 000 children in Botswana will be orphaned by 2010.[3]

Twenty-five million people in sub-Saharan Africa are infected with HIV, and the orphan population is likely to expand as parents with HIV/AIDS continue to die. Botswana has the second-highest rate of HIV in the world.[4] In 2003, 37% of adults aged 15 to 49 were HIV-positive,[5] placing Botswana in danger of losing one third of its adult population by 2010.[6] Although antiretroviral treatment is

becoming more accessible in countries such as Botswana, Zambia, and South Africa, still only a portion of the people requiring treatment receives it.[7] Even with declines in the rate of orphaning because of uptake in access to antiretroviral treatment, the orphan population in sub-Saharan Africa is expected to increase to 18 million children younger than 18 years by 2010.[1]

Historically, the fostering of children by extended family members, including aunts, uncles, grandparents, and other relatives, is common throughout sub-Saharan Africa.[8] Extended family members have fostered children for a variety of reasons including the deaths of mothers in childbirth, for youth to gain access to education, and so that the children could be used for domestic labor.[8] The tradition of fostering by extended family continues today and is a vital coping mechanism in nations with high HIV prevalence and growing orphan populations. Throughout sub-Saharan Africa, an estimated 90% of orphaned children in households live with extended family members,[9] and the working or income-earning households are considered to be in the best financial position to meet the costs of care, including providing basic needs such as food and shelter.

The advantages of extended-family fostering are that it is culturally acceptable and assumed to be sustainable throughout a child's development, partially because communities will band together to support these households.[8,10,11] In most cases, children can find stability, love, and emotional support in relatives' homes.

By contrast, institutional care in orphanages or residential facilities is recommended only in desperate situations, such as when there is abuse, child-headed households without support, or homelessness.[9,12] Institutional care generally lacks the capacity to meet emotional needs,[9,13] costs more per child than family care, and is potentially unsustainable in the long term because of a reliance upon charitable giving.[9,12]

Consequently, fostering by extended-family households is the preferred choice guiding policy,[1,14–18] even when it is unclear whether households are able to provide adequate care. In truth, the African tradition of strong extended-family networks sustaining households in times of need may no longer be viable.[9,19] In some nations, urbanization has diminished the strength of extended-family networks and kinship obligations have become less compelling.[20] Moreover, reports of breakdown in family ties have emerged when adults have expressed reluctance to care for orphans, fearing that additional children will be a drain on household finances.[21] Subsequently, there are growing gaps for children to slip through in what were previously thought to be impermeable traditional extended-family networks.[22]

Furthermore, community members are commonly believed to provide the resources that sustain AIDS- and orphan-affected households.[13,23] In reality, communities are often providing little or no support to individual households.[10] In Botswana, rapid development has eroded the custom of reciprocity among community members.[20] Families in Lesotho and Malawi reported that the burden of care lay with extended family households despite care policies stressing the role of communities.[24] Community-based and nongovernmental organizations are also credited with supporting orphan households. However, one study from Uganda revealed that only 5% of orphans were reached by the combined efforts of nongovernmental organizations, government, and other donors, and community-based organizations reached only 0.4% of orphans.[10]

In 2004, 20% of sub-Saharan African households with children were caring for orphans,[23,25] even though 2001 data shows that nearly 50% of households in the region were living on less than US $1 per day.[26] Ample evidence confirms that households living in extreme poverty, such as those headed by nonworking and elderly grandparents, lack the resources to adequately care for orphans[10] and that orphan care provided by destitute families can be disastrous for all concerned.[17,27,28] Therefore, given that large-scale institutional care is impractical, impoverished households provide inadequate care, and communities and organizations lend minimal assistance, it would appear that economically productive, working households represent the greatest hope for providing adequate orphan care. Still, the feasibility of working households providing care and economically surviving over time is unclear. Nonetheless, there is a paucity of scientific research describing the impact of fostering on households.

Several existing studies examining orphan households have used snowball sampling and small sample sizes, which frequently capture the poorest of households.[29,30] Analyses of national household surveys have provided insight into aspects of orphan care, yet these data sources may underrepresent working households where 1 or more adults are in the workplace during daytime hours when surveys are administered.[23] In addition, much of the existing literature is based on data from the early- to mid-1990s, which may not be relevant given the rapid rate of HIV transmission and orphaning.[30,31] In this study, working households are defined as those in which at least 1 adult had both working and caregiving responsibilities in the previous year.

Human and social development throughout sub-Saharan Africa is contingent upon the ability of working households to survive economically while caring for orphans. The purpose of this study is to assess whether, in light of current realities and policies, working households can adequately care for orphans without becoming impoverished. We examined whether working households encountered problems and whether they received assistance with orphan care.

METHODS

The Botswana Family Health Needs Study was conducted in 2002. A questionnaire was administered to adults waiting for services at government outpatient health centers in Gaborone, a major city; Molepolole, an urban village; and Lobatse, a small town. The number of surveys administered at each site was based on population estimates from the 2001 census.[32] The sample was designed to reflect Botswana's population distribution, where 40% live in cities, 44% live in urban villages, and 16% live in small towns. Adults who were aged at least 18 years, worked in the past year, and had caregiving responsibilities were included in the study.

Respondents were recruited at general, maternal and child health, and pediatric outpatient clinics in government hospitals. Many of the participants were seeking routine services for themselves or dependents, rather than treatment for an illness. Respondents were asked to list all household members, the vital status of each child's parents, where each child's surviving parents lived, and the reason for each child living away from the home, if applicable. Data were collected on income, housing characteristics, and problems caring for orphans and adults. Respondents were also asked if they received any financial or material support from other household members, relatives, community volunteers, or the government to assist with orphan care.

The overall response rate for the Botswana Family Health Needs Study was 96% resulting in 1033 surveys. Children aged 0 to 17 years who had reportedly survived their mother or their father, or both parents, were categorized as orphans. Orphan households were those where working adults provided care for at least 1 child whose parent had died. Of the 1033 working households surveyed,

379 or 37% were providing orphan care and these comprised the final sample for this study.

Household problems because of orphan caregiving were modeled with 2 outcomes. The first outcome was reported financial difficulties because of orphan care. The second outcome was a combined measure of 3 reported difficulties because of orphan care: financial difficulties, household shortages in basic needs, or trouble meeting household and community responsibilities, such as housework or other caregiving. This outcome serves as a combined measure of orphan-related financial, resource, and time restraints that might negatively affect the health and well-being of other household family members or the respondent.

The relation between reporting difficulties because of orphan care and key household characteristics was estimated in logistic regression models. The models were built stepwise and covariates were added if parameter estimates were significant at $P < .05$ in bivariate models. Differences in the -2 log likelihood statistic between models were calculated and the resulting 2 statistics were used to determine the best model. The functional form of each model was checked graphically and was found to have met the assumption of linearity in the log odds. Data were analyzed using SAS Statistical Software, Version 8.02 (SAS Institute Inc, Cary, NC).

RESULTS

Working, Orphan Household Characteristics

Eighty percent of respondents in the Botswana Family Health Needs Study were female, which is not surprising given that women may be more likely than men to accompany their dependents when seeking health services. Forty percent of respondents were living with a spouse or partner, whereas 60% were single, separated, divorced, or widowed. The mean age of respondents was 35 years.

Of the 379 working households providing orphan care, 50% had electricity and 78% had running water,

and 64% of household heads had completed secondary school or higher. Mean monthly household income was 1981 pula (US $396).

The mean household size was 5.84 persons and households ranged from caring for 1 to 9 orphans, with 54% caring for 1, 29% caring for 2, and 17% caring for 3 or more orphans. Extended family members provided the vast majority of orphan care. Fifty-nine percent of households reported caring for nieces and nephews, 28% cared for another relative, 6% cared for siblings, 5% cared for grandchildren, and 7% cared for a friend, neighbor, or had some other relationship to the orphan.

In many households, caregivers had additional responsibilities beyond providing orphan care and working. Forty-one percent also cared for sick adults and 45% cared for someone who had died in the past 5 years.

Caregiving Assistance

Only 2% of households reported receiving assistance from friends or neighbors and less than 1% reported receiving any type of support from community volunteers. Orphan households typically received support from other household members (43%), from relatives (39%), or from the government (34%). However, 15% of households received no assistance.

Problems Because of Caregiving

Forty-seven percent of working households reported financial difficulties because of orphan care and 48% reported financial problems; trouble providing food, shelter, or transportation; or difficulties meeting household and community responsibilities.

Logistic regression models illustrate the relation between household problems and the caregiving burden, income, and assistance (Table 1). Working households receiving no outside help were more than 3 times as likely to report financial difficulties as households receiving assistance. Households with high caregiving burdens, such as those caring for 3 or more orphans, were more than twice as likely to report financial difficulties

as households that cared for a single orphan. The burden of caring for someone who met the clinical diagnosis for AIDS also showed a strong association with household difficulties, making these households nearly twice as likely to have problems. As expected, higher income reduced the likelihood of reported difficulties.

Figure 1a displays the fitted probability of having financial difficulties in households caring for 2 orphans and an adult with AIDS, at each level of income, depending on whether assistance was received. These households are bearing overwhelming care-giving responsibilities, and the lower-income households are nearly guaranteed to have problems in the absence of outside assistance. In working households with average monthly incomes of 1500 to 2000 pula, the probability of having financial difficulties drops from about 97% to 54% with orphan assistance. The fitted probability of having financial difficulties in households that care for 2 orphans and no adults is about 75% in households with average incomes, but drops to about 14% when assistance is provided (Figure 1b).

Figure 2a displays the fitted probability that a household that receives orphan assistance will experience problems at low, middle, and high levels of income depending on the number of orphans cared for in the home. Low-income households (monthly income < 1000 pula) are 62% more likely to face problems when they care for more than 1 orphan, whereas middle- (1001 to 2000 pula) and high- (> 2000 pula) income families are able to care for 2 and 4 orphans, respectively, before being more than 50% likely to have problems. The probability of experiencing problems in working households that do not receive orphan assistance is illustrated in Figure 2b. Low- and middle-income households will assuredly experience problems without orphan assistance when caring for even a single orphan.

DISCUSSION

Our analysis demonstrates that even Botswana's working households

TABLE 1— Logistic Regression Analyses of the Fitted Relationship Between Reporting Financial and Other Problems From Orphan Care, Household Characteristics, and Receiving Assistance (n = 376): Botswana, 2002

	Model 1: Financial Difficulties, OR (95% CI)	Model 2: Any Problems Because of Caring for Orphans,[a] OR (95% CI)
Income		
0–1000 pula	1.00	1.00
1001–2000 pula	0.71 (0.42, 1.22)	0.73** (0.42, 1.25)
2001–13 500 pula	0.31** (0.18, 0.55)	0.31 (0.17, 0.54)
Number of orphans cared for		
1	1.00	1.00
2	1.20 (0.72, 1.97)	1.19 (0.72, 1.97)
≥3	2.02* (1.10, 3.68)	2.09* (1.14, 3.82)
Caring for adults and orphan assistance		
Caring for adult who meets the World Health Organization clinical definition for AIDS	1.95* (1.14, 3.34)	1.98* (1.15, 3.41)
No orphan assistance provided	3.34** (1.75, 6.36)	3.54** (1.84, 6.83)
	Model diagnostics	
–2 log likelihood	476.71	475.23
–2 log likelihood from null model	519.71	520.57
C index	0.68	0.69

Note. OR = odds ratio; CI = confidence interval.

[a]Combined measure of 3 reported difficulties because of orphan care: financial difficulties, household shortages in basic needs, or trouble meeting household and community responsibilities, such as housework or other caregiving.

*$P < .05$; **$P < .001$.

are struggling with orphan caregiving responsibilities and that low- and middle-income households lack the resources to provide basic needs. However, households receiving financial or material assistance have a greatly reduced probability of experiencing difficulties because of orphan care. Thus, extended-family caregiving may be sustainable with the support of an adequate public-sector safety net.

Regrettably, though, Botswana's public sector lacks system capacity to fulfill existing duties as well as to respond to new AIDS- and orphan-related demands because of severely limited resources and inadequately developed infrastructure.[33] The limited capacity of Botswana's Social Welfare Division diminishes the effectiveness of the National Orphan Care Programme.

Although an estimated 120 000 children are orphaned in Botswana, the Social Welfare Division had registered only 47 725 by March 2005 (Program Coordinator, Orphans and Vulnerable Children, Social Welfare Division, oral communication, March 2005). This large discrepancy is important because registration is a precursor to the receipt of public-sector material and financial support. Additional problems are surfacing as well. In 2005, only 42 social workers were responsible for care of more than 100 000 orphans in the 15 districts of Botswana (Program Coordinator, Orphans and Vulnerable Children, Social Welfare Division, oral communication, February 2005). According to department officials, capacity is far exceeded, retention is low, frustration

is high, and the number of orphans is growing.

In the fiscal year 2003/2004, the government of Botswana spent an estimated US $50 million on activities related to the HIV/AIDS epidemic,[34] but orphan care accounted for a mere 2% of the budget. Orphan care must compete with other priorities, including the scaling up of antiretroviral treatment distribution. Subsequently, the portion of resources allotted to orphan care is not commensurate with the costs of meeting the needs of orphans and caregiving households. Botswana's District and Village Multisectoral AIDS Committees have proposed community-level interventions, including income-generating projects, support centers, and activities aimed at improving orphan registration. However, there is a desperate lack of funding for these activities despite the fact that they are frequently touted as the "orphan response."

Our study captured a broad sector of households that use public services, thus including working households that might not be proportionally represented in home-based surveys administered during working hours. Though this study is building upon previous qualitative research, a limitation of this clinic-based sample is that findings can only be generalized to others in a position to use public services, rather than the entire population.

Additionally, the cross-sectional study design did not allow us to measure changes that occurred in caregiving households over time. Furthermore, we did not collect expenditure data or other information that would permit us to describe the actual mechanisms that result in household problems. This is a limitation in our study as well as in the national household surveys, which provide much of the data used in other research on orphan households. For example, do households become impoverished because caregiving duties reduce employment options or simply because orphan-related expenses exceed resources? Future studies should collect income and expenditure data, along with other theory-driven explanatory variables that help explain the mechanisms by which orphan care affects households. Longitudinal studies are essential if policymakers are to understand how orphan caregiving affects households through different stages of fostering.

These data were collected in 2002. At that time, many households lacked the capacity to provide basic needs. Since then, the social and economic crisis caused by HIV/AIDS has worsened as more households have lost family members to AIDS and have begun caring for orphans. If current trends continue, the number of orphans requiring care will surpass the material ability of households with limited resources to absorb children, regardless of their willingness.[10,15]

Furthermore, when households

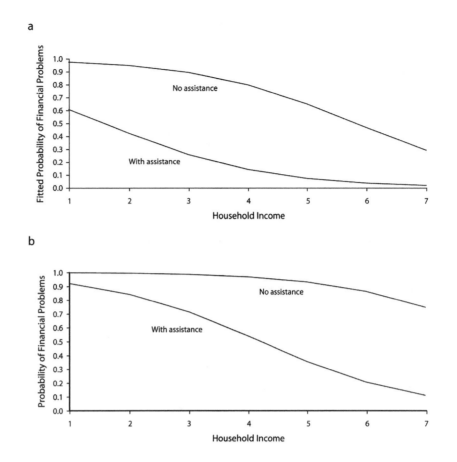

FIGURE 1— Fitted probability that a household will have financial difficulties because of orphan care based on income level and receiving orphan assistance in households not caring (a) and caring (b) for adults.

lose food security[30] and sink into debt,[10] children may lose access to health services and schools,[23,35,36] enter the labor force,[23] trade sex for money, and suffer from malnutrition and psychological distress.[37] The long-term negative consequences of these impacts is immeasurable. Child welfare deteriorates in households where orphanhood is compounded by poverty.[11,38] The high percentage of financially destabilized households identified in this study can potentially tip Botswana's economic and social stability with implications for years to come.

The findings from the Botswana Family Health Needs Study have implications for households in all high HIV-prevalence countries, particularly those where the number of orphans has overwhelmed traditional support networks. Botswana has a history of good governance and investments in health and social welfare,[7] and yet the public

sector is unable to provide an adequate safety net. Furthermore, Botswana has 2 to 4 times the per capita gross domestic product of other nations with high orphan rates in sub-Saharan Africa (US $9200 in Botswana vs US $3200 in Lesotho, US $5200 in Swaziland, US $900 in Zambia, and US $1900 in Zimbabwe, in 2004).[26] The prospects for southern Africa are of tremendous concern when, even in Botswana, working households are unable to provide adequate care and the public sector is unable to offer sufficient support.

Results from this study demonstrate that an immediate allocation of funds from the international community is necessary to improve public sector safety nets so that households can adequately care for orphans. Action is crucial to prevent growing orphan-based disparities in health and education, the financial collapse of house-a

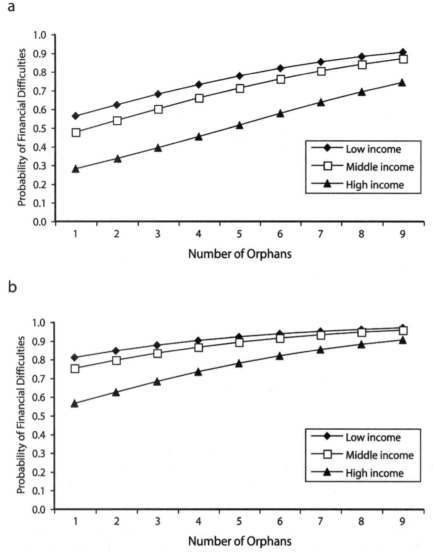

FIGURE 2— Fitted probability that a household will have financial difficulties because of orphan care based on the number of orphans cared for in low-, middle-, and high-income households with assistance (a) and without assistance (b).

holds, the unraveling of communities, and, within several generations, the descent of national economies, and the emergence of failed states.

The world community recognizes that the orphan crisis has the potential to cause vast reversals in human and economic development in sub-Saharan Africa, where already one third of children do not finish primary school, 40% of adults are illiterate, and 1 in 6 children dies before reaching age 5.[39] In 2001, the United Nations General Assembly Special Session Declaration of Commitment on HIV/AIDS set specific targets for all participating nations,

including, " . . . implement national policies and strategies to build and strengthen governmental, family and community capacities to provide a supportive environment for orphans . . . affected by HIV/AIDS."[40] In June 2005, at the summit in Gleneagles, Scotland, Group of Eight nations acknowledged the crisis and declared their commitment to support all children orphaned and left vulnerable by AIDS.[41] The Group of Eight leaders pledged to increase official development assistance for Africa by US$25 billion per year by 2010,[41] with a portion of these resources directed at improving

the situation of orphans by increasing home support and cash transfers. Although these resources would be divided among governance, economic, and human development goals, if truly delivered, they would have great potential for improving public services that can support orphan households.

Furthermore, at the United Nations World Summit in New York City in September 2005, the world community agreed to "[e]nsure that the resources needed for prevention, treatment, care and support . . . in particular [for] orphan children . . . are universally provided . . . "[42] Although previous international assistance has included some contributions and technical support, the international community's response to the orphan crisis has been sorely limited, with efforts largely entailing unheeded calls for action.[35] The degree to which these and other funding requests—such as The Africa Commission's call for US$2 billion per year to meet orphans' material and psychosocial needs[43]—are heeded will have an enormous impact on the health and development of a generation of children and the households that care for them.

The weight of orphan responsibilities is destabilizing working households in sub-Saharan Africa, and in Botswana in particular, where one third of the population may die within 8 to 12 years. Even in Botswana, where there is a strong policy framework, gaps in the social welfare infrastructure leave orphan households lacking basic needs and nearly impoverished. Social welfare infrastructures require immediate capacity building, management training, additional staff, and increased budgets to provide the safety net that stabilizes households.

Caregivers, community-based organizations, the public sector, and international partners must collaborate in implementing long-term solutions. A combination of funding and technical assistance is required to strengthen public-sector infrastructure and ultimately support orphan households. In addition, community-level responses must be supported, funded, evaluated, and replicated when successful.

Supporting orphan households is critical to the future of sub-Saharan Africa and urgent action is essential. Both national and international responses must be proportional to the gravity of the situation. With a long-standing commitment to policies promoting human development and economic growth, Botswana is poised to be a leader in developing and sustaining a viable orphan response, but desperately needs technical and financial resources to overcome substantial obstacles.

About the Authors

At the time of this study, Candace M. Miller and S. Jody Heymann were at the Department of Society, Human Development, and Health at the Harvard School of Public Health, Boston, Mass. S.V. Subramanian is with the Department of Society, Human Development and Health, at the Harvard School of Public Health. Sofia Gruskin is with the Department of Population and International Health at the Harvard School of Public Health. At the time of this study, Divya Rajaraman was with the Botswana–Harvard Partnership, Gaborone, Botswana.

Correspondence: Requests for reprints should be sent to Candace M. Miller, Center for International Health and Development, School of Public Health, Boston University, 111 East Concord Street, Boston, MA 02115 (email: candace_miller@post.harvard.edu).

Acknowledgments

S.V. Subramanian is supported by the National Institutes of Health Career Development Award (1 K25 HL081275).

Our warm thanks to members of the research and administration teams at the Botswana–Harvard School of Public Health AIDS Initiative Partnership in Botswana and the Project on Global Working Families at the Harvard School of Public Health who facilitated and contributed to this study. We are particularly grateful to our diligent and conscientious data collection team; to the Mashi study teams in Lobatse, Mochudi and Molepolole; to Ria Madison for administrative support; to Karen Bogan for assistance with data management and programming; and to the staff of the clinics where we conducted interviews.

We are most indebted to those who took the time to participate in the study.

Human Participant Protection

The Human Subjects Committee at the Harvard School of Public Health deemed the Botswana Family Health Needs Study exempt because of its confidential and anonymous nature.

Contributors

C. M. Miller conceptualized the research questions, conducted the data analysis, interpreted results, and wrote and revised the article. D. Rajaraman helped to draft the survey instrument and managed the data collection. S. Gruskin helped to conceptualize ideas and interpret findings, and reviewed drafts. S. V. Subramanian contributed to data analysis. S. J. Heymann developed the survey instrument, oversaw the fielding of the survey, helped to conceptualize ideas and interpret results, and reveiwed drafts.

References

1. The Joint United Nations Programme on HIV/AIDS, United Nations Children's Fund, US Agency for International Development. *Children on the Brink 2004: A Joint Report of New Orphan Estimates and a Framework for Action.* New York, NY: United Nations Children's Fund; 2004.

2. The Joint United Nations Programme on HIV/AIDS, World Health Organization, United Nations Children's Fund. *Epidemiological Fact Sheets on HIV/AIDS and Sexually Transmitted Infections: 2004 Update Botswana.* Geneva, Switzerland: World Health Organization; 2004.

3. MacFarlan M, Sgheri S. *The Macroeconomic Impact of HIV/AIDS in Botswana.* Working paper 01/80. Washington, DC: International Monetary Fund; 2001.

4. The Joint United Nations Programme on HIV/AIDS, World Health Organization, United Nations Children's Fund. *Epidemiological Fact Sheets on HIV/AIDS and Sexually Transmitted Infections: 2002 Update Botswana.* Geneva, Switzerland: World Health Organization; 2002.

5. *Botswana 2003 Second Generation HIV/AIDS Surveillance.* Gaborone, Botswana: The National AIDS Coordinating Agency; 2003.

6. *Botswana Human Development Report 2000.* Gaborone, Botswana: United Nations Development Programme; 2000.

7. The Joint United Nations Programme on HIV/AIDS. *AIDS Epidemic Update December 2004.* Available at: http://www.unaids.org/wad2004/EPI_1204_pdf_en/EpiUpdate04_en.pdf. Accessed May 31, 2005.

8. Madhavan S. Fosterage patterns in the age of AIDS: continuity and change. *Soc Sci Med.*2004;58: 1443–1454.

9. *Africa's Orphaned Generations.* New York, NY: United Nations Children's Fund; 2003.

10. Deininger K, Garcia M, Subbarao K. AIDS-induced orphanhood as a systemic shock: magnitude, impact, and program interventions in Africa. *World Dev.*2003; 31:1201–1220.

11. Foster G, Williamson J. A review of current literature on the impact of HIV/AIDS on children in sub-Saharan Africa. *AIDS.*2000;14(suppl 3):S275–S284.

12. Subbarao K, Mattimore A, Plangemann K. *Social Protection of Africa's Orphans and Other Vulnerable Children.* Washington, DC: The World Bank, Human Development Sector, Africa Region; 2001.

13. United Nations Children's Fund, The Joint United Nations Programme on HIV/AIDS. *Children Orphaned by AIDS: Frontline Responses From Eastern and Southern Africa.* New York, NY: United Nations Children's Fund; 1999.

14. Bhargava A, Bigombe B. Public policies and the orphans of AIDS in Africa. *BMJ.*2003;326: 1387–1389.

15. Hunter SS. Orphans as a window on the AIDS epidemic in Sub-Saharan Africa: initial results and implications of a study in Uganda. *Soc Sci Med.*1990;31: 681–690.

16. Muchiru S. *The Rapid Assessment of the Situation of Orphans in Botswana.* Gaborone, Botswana: Oakwood Management and Development Consultants, AIDS/STD Unit, Ministry of Health; 1998.

17. Smart R. *Policies for Orphans and Vulnerable Children: A Framework for*

Moving Ahead. Washington, DC: US Agency for International Development, Futures Group International, Policy Project; 2003.

18. Social Welfare Division. *Short Term Plan of Action on Care of Orphans in Botswana 1999–2001.* Gaborone, Botswana: Ministry of Local Government; 1999.

19. Kamali A, Seeley JA, Nunn AJ, Kengeya-Kayondo JF, Ruberantwari A, Mulder DW. The orphan problem: experience of a sub-Saharan Africa rural population in the AIDS epidemic. *AIDS Care.*1996;8:509–515.

20. Milligan A, Williams G. *Botswana: Towards National Prosperity: Common Country Assessment 2001.* Gaborone, Botswana: United Nations System in Botswana; 2001.

21. Botswana Ministry of Health, AIDS/STD Unit. *The Rapid Assessment on the Situation of Orphans in Botswana.* Gaborone, Botswana: Republic of Botswana; 1998.

22. Nyamukapa C, Gregson S. Extended family's and women's roles in safeguarding orphans' education in AIDS-afflicted rural Zimbabwe. *Soc Sci Med.*2005;60: 2155–2167.

23. Monasch R, Boerma J. Orphanhood and childcare patterns in sub-Saharan Africa: an analysis of national surveys from 40 countries. *AIDS.*2004;18(suppl 2): S55–S65.

24. Ansell N, Young L. Enabling households to support successful migration of AIDS orphans in southern Africa. *AIDS Care.*2004;16:3–10.

25. AIDS Education and Research Trust Web site. Available at: http://www.avert.org/aidsmoney.htm. Accessed March 12, 2005.

26. World Bank. *World Development Indicators.* Available at: http://www.worldbank.org/data/wdi2

005/pdfs/Table2_5.pdf. Accessed May 31, 2005.

27. Lewis S. UN Secretary-General's Special Envoy on HIV/AIDS in Africa. Paper presented at: XIIIth International Conference on AIDS and STIs in Africa; September 21–26, 2003; Nairobi, Kenya.

28. *Children in a World of AIDS.* Westport, CT: Save the Children; 2001.

29. *Situation Analysis on Orphans and Vulnerable Children.* Gaborone, Botswana: United Nations Children's Fund, Social Welfare Division; 2003.

30. Cross C. Sinking deeper down; HIV/AIDS as an economic shock to rural households. *Soc Transition.*2001;32:133–147.

31. Bicego G, Rutstein S, Johnson K. Dimensions of the emerging orphan crisis in sub-Saharan Africa. *Soc Sci Med.*2003;56:1235–1247.

32. Central Statistics Office. *Population and Housing Census: Population of Towns, Villages and Associated Localities in August 2001.* Gaborone, Botswana: Government of Botswana; 2001.

33. Simms C, Rowson M, Peattie S. *The Bitterest Pill of All. The Collapse of Africa's Health Systems.* London, England: Save the Children; 2001.

34. National AIDS Coordinating Committee. *Status of the 2002 National Response to the UNGASS Declaration of Commitment on HIV/AIDS.* Gaborone, Botswana: Republic of Botswana, United Nations Children's Fund, Joint United Nations Programme on HIV/AIDS, Africa Comprehensive HIV/AIDS Partnership; 2003.

35. Miller CM. *The Orphan Epidemic in Botswana.* Boston, Mass: Society Human Development and Health, Harvard University; 2005.

36. Case A, Paxson C, Ableidinger J. Orphans in Africa: parental death, poverty, and school enrollment. *Demography.*2004;41:483–508.

37. Atwine B, Cantor-Graaea E, Bajunirwe F. Psychological distress among AIDS orphans in rural Uganda. *Soc Sci Med.*2005;61:555–564.

38. Urassa MB, Ng'weshemi JT, Isingo R, Schapink D, Kumogola Y. Orphanhood, child fostering and the AIDS epidemic in rural Tanzania. *Health Transit Rev.*1997;7(suppl):141–153.

39. *Human Development Report 2005.* New York, NY: United Nations Development Programme; 2005. Available at http://hdr.undp.org/reports/global/2004/pdf/hdr04_HDI.pdf. Accessed September 12, 2005.

40. *United Nations General Assembly Special Session on HIV/AIDS. June 25–27, 2001.* Available at: http://www.unaids.org/whatsnew/others/un_special/index.html. Accessed October 4, 2005.

41. *Gleneagles Summit Documents: Signed Version of Gleneagles Communique on Africa, Climate Change, Energy and Sustainable Development: July 2005.* Available at: http://www.fco.gov.uk/Files/kfile/Post G8_Gleneagles_Communique,0.pdf. Accessed October 4, 2005.

42. *United Nations World Summit. High-level Plenary Meeting of the General Assembly 14–16 September 2005. Draft Outcome Document.* Available at: http://www.un.org/ga/president/59/draft_outcome.htm. Accessed October 4, 2005.

43. *Our Common Interest: Report of the Commission for Africa.* London, England: Commission for Africa; 2005.

Uruguay on the World Stage: How Child Health Became an International Priority

| *Anne-Emanuelle Birn, ScD, MA*

ABSTRACT

The evolution of international health has typically been assessed from the standpoint of central institutions (international health organizations, foundations, and development agencies) or of one-way diffusion and influence from developed to developing countries.

To deepen understanding of how the international health agenda is shaped, I examined the little-known case of Uruguay and its pioneering role in advancing and institutionalizing child health as an international priority between 1890 and 1950.

The emergence of Uruguay as a node of international health may be explained through the country's early gauging of its public health progress, its borrowing and adaptation of methods developed overseas, and its broadcasting of its own innovations and shortcomings.

INTRODUCTION

The history of international health has typically been examined from the perspective of metropolitan institutions such as the World Health Organization, the International Red Cross, and the Rockefeller Foundation.[1–5] While some works trace the interactions of these agencies with far-flung actors, the motives, ideas, and operations of international health are invariably portrayed as centrally determined, then diffused around the world. To broaden this account of the development of the international health agenda, I examine the little-known case of Uruguay and its pioneering role in advancing child health as an international priority between 1890 and 1940.

Uruguay became involved in international health at least in part to search for solutions to its intractable infant mortality problem, and it ended up offering local approaches—including a children's code of rights—that had global appeal. As the home of the International American Institute for the Protection of Childhood (Instituto Internacional Americano de Protección a la Infancia, or IIPI), the first permanent organization of its kind, founded in 1927, Montevideo became a node of international health which—though lacking the political cachet of Washington, DC, or Geneva, Switzerland—helped shape a worldwide children's health agenda.

The transformation of Uruguay's domestic debates into an influential institute can be observed through the international networks of Uruguayan doctors and child health advocates, the opportunities and interests that gave rise to the IIPI, and its repercussions, including Uruguay's Children's Code. My analysis, unlike a conventional history, highlights the emergence of a significant initiative from a peripheral location through the interplay of local political and social conditions with widely shared health priorities.

THE URUGUAYAN WAY

Despite its small size and its distance from the centers of power, Uruguay became engaged with international health developments beginning in the late 19th century. Founded in 1830 following a longstanding conflict between Spain/Argentina and Portugal/Brazil over possession of its territory, Uruguay enjoyed relative stability and a cattle-based economy after its civil wars subsided in 1851. Its high levels of urbanization and school attendance, tiny indigenous population, secular government, uniform and accessible geography, and mild, Mediterranean-like climate differentiated Uruguay from most of its neighbors. The country was peopled largely by Spanish and Italian immigrants, with a small elite of French ancestry and a few descendants of African slaves. Uruguay's approximately 1 million residents (one third of whom lived in the capital, according to the 1908 census)[6] shared a self-effacing longing for Europe while developing their own brand of state protectionism.

Uruguay differed from most Latin American countries in that the Catholic Church and the landed elites were relatively weak forces as the modern state began to take shape in the late 19th century. Moreover, the country's sparse institutional infrastructure in the social arena left room for state growth.[7,8] The rapid expansion of public education for both sexes that started in the 1870s—making Uruguay the region's leader in literacy, with 54% literacy in 1900[9]—presaged the welfare state, which emerged in full force under the reformist Colorado Party administrations of President José Batlle y Ordóñez (1903–1907 and 1911–1915). Enabled by relative prosperity and the sidelining of the opposition Blanco Party, Batlle's first administration opened a wide-ranging dialogue on issues such as universal suffrage, maternal benefits, and working conditions. Concretely, it established retirement and other benefits for the civil service.[10]

A severe economic crisis in 1913 accelerated the implementation of various Batllista policies—including an 8-hour workday and exemption from taxes on essential goods—that seemed to prefigure Keynesian approaches to mitigating the social and economic inequalities provoked by capitalism. Indeed, Batlle conceived of a protective state that offered compensation for injustices suffered by various segments of the population. His ambitious agenda of centralization and redistribution included old-age pensions, worker protections, state monopoly of finance and other sectors, and public assistance for women, children, and the poor.[11,12] That progress in enacting reforms was slow—in part because the reforms yielded contradictory results, such as lower wages[13–15]—did not cause the country to be viewed as a failed experiment. Instead this stepwise approach elicited attention: a variety of voices engaged in decades of lively debate, domestically and internationally, over the effectiveness of the Batllista state and of its particular features, such as those improving child health and welfare.

Uruguay's place in the globalizing health system was at once peculiar and typical. Like Central and Eastern European countries at the time, Uruguay shared many of the modern state-building and cultural values of Western Europe but had a still largely rural economy. Like other Latin American countries, Uruguay was not tied to a single international mandate, instead interacting with a changing panorama of public health examples.

Mid–19th-century European concerns with preventing the spread of epidemic diseases—and the economic consequences of the resulting trade interruptions—were echoed in a series of meetings held in Montevideo and Rio de Janeiro starting in 1873 aimed at standardizing quarantine measures and maritime sanitation. The meat- and hide-exporting economies of Argentina and Uruguay were particu-

larly intent on guarding against yellow fever from Brazil, since most ships entering the Río de la Plata after leaving Brazil stopped in both Buenos Aires and Montevideo. The 1887 sanitary convention signed by Brazil, Argentina, and Uruguay—the first of its kind to be ratified in the Americas—detailed quarantine periods for ships bearing cholera, yellow fever, and plague and was in effect for 5 years before it broke apart. A 1904 successor convention included reciprocal notification. These treaties presaged pan-American efforts to prevent infectious outbreaks originating from immigrant and commercial vessels.[16]

GAUGING INFANT MORTALITY

In the late 19th century, Uruguay began to consider social policy an important underpinning of public health. Initially it was French legislation—maternity leave, welfare provisions, mandatory breastfeeding for abandoned infants, milk hygiene, and other puericultural (from Adolphe Pinard's notion of the scientific cultivaiton of childhood and the improvement of child health and welfare through better conditions of childrearing) measures—that was most influential. In the 1930s many Uruguayan social policy-makers and doctors admired the Soviet health system. By the 1950s, Uruguayan public health was increasingly influenced by the technical and biomedical approach of the United States. Uruguay was never "passively derivative"[17] of these models, instead selecting features from abroad and melding them with the ideas, reality, and politics at home.

A particular mark of Uruguay's early participation in international health discussions was the founding of the Civil Registry in 1879, mandating the regular collection of birth and death records. Most of the nations that developed comprehensive vital statistics systems before 1900 were major powers concerned with population health as a sign of economic vitality. Rapidly industrializing England, France, and Germany, for example, monitored the survival of children as an indicator of

workforce and military readiness and imperial strength.[18,19] Though it had little industry and no pretense to empire-building, Uruguay had plenty of livestock to count: its first statistical annual, published for the 1873 World Exhibition in Vienna, was sponsored by the Uruguayan Agricultural Association.[20]

The European connections of the Uruguayan elites also propelled data collection. The country's statistical annuals were self-consciously modeled after Parisian volumes,[21] second half of the 19th century: more than 40 medical periodicals were founded, numerous hospitals and clinics were organized, and the country's first friendly society (providing mutual aid for unemployment and medical care) was established in 1854. The University of the Republic's Faculty of Medicine was founded in 1875, and by the time its state-of-the-art research facility was built in 1911, there were several dozen graduates per year.[22,23]

Statistical annuals compiling cause-specific mortality data were first published in 1885,[24] with infant deaths added in 1893. This allowed health experts to follow the country's uneven but sure decline in infant mortality from 104 deaths per 1000 live births in 1893 to 72 per 1000 in 1905. Over the next 35 years infant mortality stagnated, fluctuating between 85 and 113 deaths and averaging 95 deaths per 1000 live births. Only after 1940 did infant mortality resume its decline. Although other countries reported higher levels of infant mortality than Uruguay at particular points in time, virtually every other setting experienced continuous—if sometimes bumpy—declines[25–27] (Figure 1).

Uruguay was thus unusual on several counts: in establishing a functioning civil registry early on, in achieving lower infant mortality rates than several European countries, and in experiencing a prolonged stagnation in infant mortality rates. The country's early successes and its subsequent setbacks with infant mortality impelled health experts to identify the underpinnings of local circumstances and to search for international approaches that might prove helpful.

URUGUAYAN PUBLIC HEALTH ABROAD AND AT HOME

In 1895, approximately a decade after Uruguay's civil registry achieved regular coverage, public health powers were consolidated under the National Council of Hygiene. Uruguay now had information, centralized authority, and a cadre of medical and public health experts keen to participate in international health developments. This group of experts documented Uruguayan health and mortality domestically and comparatively; advised policymakers; ran health and welfare institutions; saw patients in clinical settings; and participated in international congresses, publications, and other scientific activities.[28,29]

An early member of this group was Joaquin de Salterain (1856–1926), whose career illustrates the back-and-forth between international and Uruguayan developments in health. Of French and Spanish parentage, de Salterain was among the first graduates of Uruguay's Faculty of Medicine in 1884 and won a government scholarship to go to Paris for specialized training in ophthalmology. Rather than narrowing his focus, his fellowship widened it, and on his return to Uruguay he became involved in a range of health activities. De Salterain was a constituting member of the National Council of Hygiene, and in the mid-1890s he began to publish detailed analyses of Montevideo's mortality statistics.[30,31] De Salterain headed Montevideo's Department of Public Health and was a program director in the Pereira Rossell Children's Hospital (founded in 1905) and the Dámaso Larrañaga children's asylum (established in 1818). His work helped set the stage for Uruguay's role abroad, but he was perhaps most effective at using his international interchanges to leverage increased attention and resources at home.

From the 1890s on, Uruguayans participated in virtually every international congress related to public health and social welfare. They published their own presentations in either Uruguayan or international journals and typically issued analytic summaries of the confer-

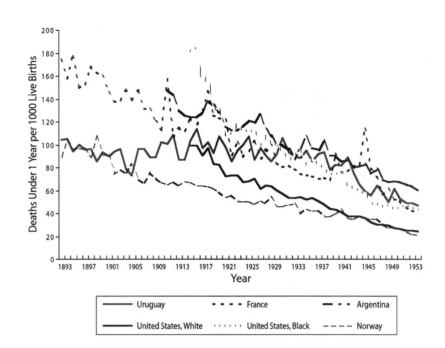

FIGURE 1– International comparisons of infant mortality rate, 1893–1953.

ence discussions in Uruguay's *Boletín del Consejo Nacional de Higiene (Bulletin of the National Council of Hygiene).* Medical elites from throughout the Americas received advanced training in Europe during this period, making contacts, attending congresses, joining scientific networks, and pressing their own governments to expand activities. But few countries, particularly small countries, achieved as consistent an international presence as did Uruguay. Most countries sent 1 representative to the 1900 Paris conference at which the *International Classification of Diseases* was first revised; Uruguay sent 2.[32] Similarly, the 7-person delegation Uruguay sent to Washington, DC, for the 15th International Congress on Hygiene and Demography in 1912 was larger than that of all but a handful of countries.[33] That this attendance was at state expense—at a time when the National Council of Hygiene relied on a largely volunteer labor force—implies that politicians and bureaucrats believed Uruguay's health learning would take place internationally.

Uruguay's reorganization and expansion of social welfare fit with this notion of selectively adapting foreign developments. In 1907 Uruguay was among the first countries outside Europe and its colonies to found a milk

station (*gota de leche*) based on the French model (*goutte de lait*) to distribute pasteurized milk and provide medical attention to needy mothers and their infants.[34] By 1927, 33 milk stations had been established throughout the country, arguably covering the largest proportion of mothers and infants in the world. This number was exceeded only in France.

The 1910 nationalization of Uruguay's charity institutions into the Asistencia Pública Nacional was likewise self-consciously patterned on France's Assistance Publique, then expanded into one of the most far-reaching social assistance programs in the world.[35] Uruguay also maintained Anglo-America–style private aid agencies (typically run by women), some of which received government grants to deliver services.[36–38] The full legalization of divorce (including divorce unilaterally initiated by women) in 1913[39]— giving the country one of the world's most liberal divorce laws—was further evidence of Uruguay's "borrow and change" social policy approach.

THINKING COMPARATIVELY, CONTRIBUTING INTERNATIONALLY

Uruguayans were clearly adept at participating in international health

FIGURE 2— Stamp commemorating the 100 years since Dr. Luis Morquio became the Chair of Pediatrics at the Faculty of Medicine at Uruguay's University of the Republic. Bottom right corner includes the statue of Morquio with a child that stands along one of Montevideo's main boulevards. The stamp was designed by Daniel Pereyra. *(Courtesy Administración Nacional de Correos, Uruguay.)*

networks and adapting foreign innovations to serve local needs. Equally striking is how Uruguay's self-publicized problems catapulted the country to regional and international attention.

In the late 19th century European countries began to conduct mortality comparisons, a practice Uruguay fully adopted. De Salterain observed in 1896 that Uruguay's mortality rate was dropping steadily and that Montevideo's rate was lower than those of Paris, London, St Petersburg, and Buenos Aires. De Salterain boasted, "What other explanation could there be for such pleasing results than the progress of our public welfare institutions, health administration, and hygiene education?"[40]

Other colleagues followed suit, especially after the infant mortality rate emerged as an international indicator around 1900.[41] In 1913, Julio Bauzá, the doctor heading Montevideo's milk stations, went so far as to argue that little attention needed to be paid to infant mortality because Uruguay's

rates were so much lower than those of Chile, France, Russia, and Germany. He affirmed, "The truth is we are in an enviable position for a myriad of European and American countries."[42]

These early comparative analyses were aimed mostly at domestic audiences, but local experts soon recognized that Uruguay's well-documented mortality patterns had relevance far beyond the country's borders. Luis Morquio (1867–1935), the founding father of Uruguayan pediatrics and a leading authority on both medical and social aspects of child health, was the most prominent translator of the local experience to the international scene. In 1895, upon returning to Montevideo from training in Paris, he became medical director of the external services of the Orphanage and Foundling Home. There he oversaw an extraordinarily low—for the time—mortality rate of 7% of children, which he attributed to careful attention to infant feeding, including weekly visits to his clinic by wet-nurses and their charges.[43,44]

Morquio was presenting his analyses of Uruguay's experience to Latin American medical congresses by 1904 and to European audiences soon after. If Morquio agreed that Uruguay's infant mortality rates—rates favored, he believed, by environmental cleanliness, low population density, and high levels of breastfeeding[45]—deserved some international appreciation, he did not dwell on success, arguing that half of the infant deaths were avoidable[46] (Figure 2).

Morquio's moderation proved perceptive. As of 1915 Uruguay's infant mortality record, although still better than most European levels, was stationary, if not worsening. This was particularly troubling given that the national birth rate was steadily declining.[47] Morquio—who by this time had served as the medical director of the largest children's asylum, chief of the pediatric clinic in the main public hospital, and a professor of clinical pediatrics—believed that some of the international measures adopted by Uruguayan health authorities had unintended consequences. He worried that milk stations discouraged

breast-feeding by offering free or subsidized milk, and that this milk was often contaminated.[48]

Thereafter, numerous doctors chimed in on sometimes acerbic debates over the role of public health institutions, social and economic conditions, illegitimacy, abandonment, sanitation, climate, and cultural factors in Uruguay's stagnating infant mortality.[49] Such discussions were not unique to Uruguay, but they were unusual in the international attention they generated. Uruguayan authors were extremely prolific on this question, publishing more than 1000 journal articles related to child and infant health between 1900 and 1940 (estimate based on a bibliographic database compiled by A.-E.B.).

Morquio himself was a major contributor to Uruguay's international renown, writing an average of 9 articles per year between 1900 and 1935. Almost half of his output appeared in foreign publications, including *Archives de Médecine des Enfants* (France), *La Nipiología* (Italy), *Journal of Nervous and Mental Diseases* (United States), and the *Archivos Latino Americanos de Pediatría*, which he cofounded.[50] Most of his articles focused on specific childhood medical problems, giving him credibility in the worlds of medicine and research as well as public health. Morquio became widely known for his 1917 book on gastrointestinal problems of infants, which was published in several languages and bridged his various interests. Numerous pieces he published in Uruguay were reissued by international journals. In 1928, for example, a talk he gave in Montevideo on infant mortality was reprinted in the *Boletín de la Oficina Sanitaria Panamericana*,[51] which introduced it by emphasizing its "universal relevance."

Almost as soon as they began to be compiled, Uruguay's infant mortality statistics were viewed simultaneously in national and international terms. Scrutinized through comparative lenses, Uruguay initially deemed itself a success story. Conversely, as the problem of infant mortality stagnation unfolded domestically, the repercussions went far beyond the national realm.

URUGUAY'S HEALTH INTERNATIONALISM

By the 1920s the international health landscape consisted of a handful of permanent agencies, based principally in Europe and North America, with limited but growing prestige. In December 1902 the Union of the American Republics (precursor to the Organization of American States) sponsored the International Sanitary Convention in Washington, DC, at which the International Sanitary Bureau was founded. The International Sanitary Bureau, renamed the Pan American Sanitary Bureau (PASB) in 1923, was the world's first international health agency.[52]

Operating out of the US Public Health Service under the directorship of the US surgeon general until the mid-1940s, the PASB worked on treaties and commercial concerns related to epidemic diseases, with quadrennial congresses creating an important venue for public health exchange among the region's professionals. In 1907 the PASB established an International Sanitary Office in Montevideo for the collection of health statistics from South American countries, but the precariously funded office disappeared within a decade. The PASB's sixth conference in Montevideo in 1920, at which US Surgeon General Hugh Cumming became director, marked a renewal of activity. The PASB's widely distributed *Boletín de la Oficina Sanitaria Panamericana* was founded in 1922, the Pan American Sanitary Code was passed in 1924, and cooperative activities with member countries were also initiated in the 1920s.[53,54]

Another key agency involved in international health was the New York–based Rockefeller Foundation, founded in 1913. The foundation's International Health Board launched a series of campaigns against hookworm, yellow fever, and malaria in Latin America and throughout the world, as well as establishing schools of public health in Europe, the Americas, and beyond.[55,56] Interestingly, Uruguay was virtually the only country in the region untouched by the Rockefeller

FIGURE 3— Paulina Luisi, Uruguay's first female doctor, with her Faculty of Medicine classmates in September 1901. (Photo courtesy of the Department of History of Medicine, Faculty of Medicine, University of the Republic, Montevideo, Uruguay.)

Foundation (perhaps because it no longer experienced any of the foundation's showcase diseases), leaving the country all the more inclined to pursue public health approaches broadly.

In Europe it took more than half a century to transcend imperialist jealousies in order to establish a uniform system of disease notification and maritime sanitation. The culmination of 11 international sanitary conferences held since 1851, the Office International d'Hygiène Publique was founded in Paris in 1907 to hold periodic conferences, regulate quarantine agreements, and conduct studies on epidemic diseases. It also served as the international repository for health statistics before this responsibility was assumed by the World Health Organization in 1948.

The devastation of World War I lent new urgency to international health organizations. In 1921 the Geneva-based League of Nations founded an epidemic commission to control outbreaks of typhus, cholera, smallpox, and other diseases in Eastern and Southern Europe. The head of the epidemic commission, the Polish hygienist Ludwik Rajchman, ably transformed it into the League of Nations Health Organization (LNHO) in 1923. The LNHO helped war-torn nations reorganize their health bureaucracies and pursued an ambitious program of surveillance, research,

standardization, professionalization, and technical aid. Under Rajchman (who later helped found UNICEF), the LNHO expressed a special concern for the health and welfare of children, working closely with the war relief agency Save the Children (founded in Britain in 1919, with an international counterpart established in Geneva in 1920).[1,57]

Uruguay became involved with the LNHO in the early 1920s, most notably through Paulina Luisi, the country's first woman doctor and its leading liberal feminist.[58–60] Active in regional feminist, scientific, and child welfare circles, Luisi soon leapt to prominence on the international scene. She was the only Latin American woman delegate to the first League of Nations Assembly, participating in various treaty, disarmament, and labor conferences. In 1924 she became an expert delegate on the League of Nations advisory commission on white slavery, and for 10 years she was one of only 2 Latin American delegates on the Committee for the Protection of Childhood (the other being an IIPI representative). Luisi forcefully advocated increased Latin American perspectives in the League of Nations' work for children, including surveys of needs and policies as well as greater representation in governing bodies[61–64] (Figure 3).

THE BIRTH OF THE IIPI

Another key dimension of international organizing in this period consisted of periodic congresses, mostly held in Europe, devoted to questions of hygiene, demography, statistics, and child welfare.[41] Two international associations for childhood protection were conceived in Brussels in 1907 and 1913, but their institutionalization was aborted and their activities were absorbed by League of Nations committees in the 1920s.

In the Americas, meanwhile, Pan American Child Congresses were launched in Buenos Aires in 1916, serving as a vibrant forum for Latin American reformers, feminists, physicians, lawyers, and social workers devoted to improving the health and welfare of poor and working-class women and children. The 8 hemispheric meetings held before World War II influenced the passage of dozens of laws delineating rights in such areas as adoption, infant health, state assistance, and child labor.[65] Although the first Pan American Child Congress was organized by "maternalist feminists" who viewed the lot of children as inextricably linked to the rights of women as mothers,[60,66] control over the Latin American child welfare movement was soon seized by male professionals, as evidenced by the preponderance of male presenters at the successful second congress, held in Montevideo in 1919. Even presider Paulina Luisi was upstaged by Luis Morquio's high profile.[67]

It was at this congress that Morquio called for an international institute for childhood protection to be based in Montevideo, a proposal enthusiastically sanctioned by the Uruguayan government through a 1924 decree and approved by the fourth Pan American Child Congress, held in Santiago later that year.[68] But the founding of the IIPI awaited an outside impetus, which—apparently thanks to Luisi—came in the guise of LNHO sponsorship of a conference held in June 1927 in Montevideo.

This conference, the South American Conference on Infant Mortality, was the first League of Nations conference of any kind to be held in Latin America. Attended by both Rajchman and the LNHO's president, Danish bacteriologist Thorvald Madsen, the conference was a prestigious forum for Morquio and other experts in infant health and welfare.[69] Through the IIPI, the LNHO backed a set of infant mortality surveys in Argentina, Brazil, Chile, and Uruguay similar to surveys it had sponsored in Europe.[70,71] The results, presented at the Sixth Pan American Child Congress in Lima in 1930, demonstrated the need for improvements in vital statistics, centralization of services, and a range of public health, social assistance, economic, and educational measures to reduce infant mortality.[72–74]

The IIPI itself was launched by 10 participating countries (Argentina, Bolivia, Brazil, Chile, Cuba, Ecuador, Peru, the United States, Uruguay, and Venezuela; by 1949 the founders were joined by all other countries in the region), each with 1 official delegate. After 1936 the IIPI requested 2 representatives from each country—one technical and based in the home country, the other resident in Montevideo (a diplomat, for example). In the early years, most IIPI operating funds were provided by the Uruguayan government, with intermittent support from other member countries.

The IIPI's charge was to collect and disseminate research, policy, and practical information pertaining to the care and protection of infants, children, and mothers. It sought to "[Latin] Americanize" the study of childhood so that the region was understood as distinct from and not just derivative or reflective of Europe.[75] At the same time, the IIPI ensured that the region's problems, research, and policies entered into international discussions. The IIPI's widely circulated *Boletín del Instituto Internacional Americano de Protección a la Infancia*, its library, its health education materials, and the child congresses it sponsored rapidly established its strong reputation and generated a large network of collaborators throughout Latin America and the world.[76]

In its first decade, the IIPI was governed by a group of distinguished physicians. Gregorio Aráoz Alfaro of Argentina served as president for the first 25 years of IIPI's existence, with Uruguayan Víctor Escardó y Anaya as secretary. Morquio was the IIPI's first director; after his death in 1935 his compatriot Roberto Berro held the position until 1956. In addition to editing the *Boletín* and working with the international advisory board, the director oversaw a small permanent staff who ran the Institute's library and archive; collected laws, statistics, and reports on child protection from member countries and beyond; and sent information to correspondents around the world.[76,77]

The IIPI navigated complicated waters between independence and patronage. It was a consulting agency to both the League of Nations and the Panamerican Union until World War II, and in 1949 it was integrated into the Organization of American States. (The IIPI is now known as the Instituto Internacional del Niño, or International Institute of the Child.) The LNHO had hoped that its role in the IIPI would give it a foothold in various South American research and educational instititions,[69] but tight resources in Geneva meant that the LNHO could do little more than encourage activities at the IIPI. (A lingering question is why the LNHO rather than the PASB provided the organizing spark for the IIPI, and whether the PASB's territoriality—based as it was in US isolationist politics and a Monroe Doctrinism applied to health—helped derail the LNHO's ambitious plans in Latin America.)

The IIPI propelled Uruguay to international attention. In 1930 Morquio was named to the presidency of Save the Children in Geneva, providing a worldwide platform for the policies and practices he and other Uruguayans had developed. The Pan American Child Congresses continued to meet until 1942, offering a key venue for exchange of ideas and learning during a period of fertile social policy activity throughout the region.[65]

Perhaps most visibly, the IIPI's *Boletín*, founded shortly after the 1927 conference, brought considerable acclaim to Uruguay. Unique in its scope, the IIPI's *Boletín*—published quarterly in English, French, and Spanish—covered topics ranging from the organization of children's social services to summer camps, school health, sports, education, health campaigns, marginalized children, and the causes of infant or child mortality. It was one of the most international journals of its day: of the 1000 authors published in the journal's first 2 decades, approximately one fifth were from Europe and North America and four fifths from throughout Latin America. Slightly more than one third of the authors were Uruguayan. A small number of Uruguayan pieces profiled child welfare systems in other countries, but for the most part Uruguayans used the IIPI's *Boletín* to highlight domestic problems and achievements in infant, child, and maternal welfare.

URUGUAY'S CHILDREN'S CODE

As the Uruguayan public health community grappled with the continued stagnation of its infant mortality rates, it became clear that increasingly specialized medical approaches were insufficiently integrated with social provisions for child health. This realization offered a chance for IIPI influences to be expressed through local developments, but in 1933 Uruguay's liberal era came to a sudden end with the dictatorship–cum–conservative-populist government of Gabriel Terra. Rather than impede integrated child welfare policy, however, Terra's efforts to rationalize and centralize power reinforced the country's widely supported protectionism[78,79]: the IIPI served as a social policy umbrella under which new initiatives were researched and debated.

In 1933 Morquio, Bauzá and other colleagues were invited by the just-founded Ministry of Child Protection—the first of its kind in the world—to form a legislative advisory commission to organize the various programs and agencies involved in infant and child welfare in Uruguay. Under the leadership of Roberto Berro, a disciple of de Salterain and Morquio and an advocate of "childhood social medicine,"[80] the commission did not limit itself to the administrative process of merging overlapping agencies. Instead, it called on the country to adopt a children's code spelling out children's rights to health, welfare, education, legal protections, and decent living conditions and creating specific institutions to run and oversee child and maternal aid programs.

Following a lively debate in Uruguay's national Assembly, the unanimous recognition by foreign delegates to the Seventh Pan American Conference in 1933 that such a code would put Uruguay "in the vanguard," and expressions of broad professional and popular support, the Uruguayan parliament approved the Children's Code in 1934. With passage of the code, the Uruguayan government explicitly recognized the importance of integrating medical approaches to the improvement of child health with social approaches, including better housing, sanitation, road-paving, schools, and family allowances[81] (Figure 4).

To enable its interdisciplinary work and avoid turf battles with other ministries, the Ministry of Child Protection was refashioned into the Consejo del Niño (Children's Council) under the Ministry of Public Education. Although the Consejo was headed by a series of doctors, it was purposely separated from the new Ministry of Public Health (established in 1934) to emphasize its social, rather than medical, approach to child well-being. The Consejo organized its services by age group (prenatal, infant, child, and adolescent divisions) and jurisdiction (education, law, social services, and school health divisions), establishing offices throughout the country and absorbing a series of kindergartens, orphanages, asylums, homes, camps, and reform institutions. With this purview, the Consejo reached virtually every Uruguayan child, at minimum through school health exams and, for poor and work-ing-class children, through extensive coordinated services.[82,83]

The relationship between the IIPI and the Consejo was very close, with ongoing exchange of staff and ideas. Berro, for example, directed the Consejo before becoming head of the IIPI; Bauzá was an IIPI representative before becoming a division head and then director of the Consejo. Descriptions and assessments of Consejo projects were frequently published in the IIPI's *Boletín*, probably bringing Consejo activities to greater international attention than the children's services of any other country.[84,85]

Although several other countries had previously enacted children's codes—and Save the Children founder Eglantyne Jebb's Declaration of the Rights of the Child had been adopted by the League of Nations in 1924—these efforts were more symbolic than substantive. It was Uruguay—with its well-developed welfare state, close links to the IIPI, anxiety about infant mortality, and international profile—that offered an implementable model of children's rights in a particular national setting. Through the IIPI, the PASB, the LNHO, and other networks, Uruguay's experience became widely

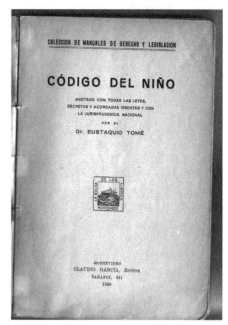

FIGURE 4— Annotated version of Uruguay's Children's Code.

known and discussed, particularly as its infant mortality rates finally began to improve in the late 1930s. Countries with active social medicine movements, such as late-1930s Chile under the leadership of Minister of Health Salvador Allende,[86] built upon and strengthened Uruguay's efforts. The IIPI and PASB jointly issued the Pan American Children's Code in 1948, and in 1989 the United Nations General Assembly adopted the Convention on the Rights of the Child, both of which drew extensively on the Uruguayan code.

Uruguay's Children's Code was the effort of decades of activism on the part of several generations of Uruguayan public health and social welfare advocates whose domestic work enjoyed international recognition. It was the interaction between Uruguay's international leadership and the protectionist Batllista state that, despite its flaws and slow pace, provided a laboratory of legislation and practice in the area of children's well-being.

CONCLUSIONS

As this examination of the founding and activities of the IIPI demonstrates, the institutional panorama of international health included more than the "usual suspects" among metropolitan organizations. With existing agencies in place in the United States and Europe, Uruguay did not seem a propitious locale for a new international health office. But the country used its strengths—a stable welfare state, well-placed professionals, leadership in child health—and its weaknesses—small size, remoteness, persistent infant mortality problems—to secure a place on the world stage. A key additional ingredient for establishing the IIPI in Uruguay was the legitimacy provided by the country's ties to another international agency—the League of Nations. In obtaining the League's support, the cosmopolitan physicians who anchored Uruguay's international engagement in public health benefited from the essential legwork of the "maternalist feminists" who had launched the Pan American Child

Congresses.

It might be suggested that Uruguay was able to carve out a niche in international health that was of little moment to the larger community. But given the LNHO's early interest in the IIPI, the extensive worldwide concern with maternal and child health that was manifested during this period,[19] and the international attention that was later paid to children's health through such organizations as UNICEF,[87] this thesis holds little water. Still, in 1927 children did not top the list of concerns of the PASB, which would have been the IIPI's logical patron. With several PASB conferences in the 1920s (including the 1920 Montevideo meeting), there was ample opportunity for sponsorship. But the PASB spent its first decades focused on the interruption of commerce caused by epidemic diseases, even as the delegates to its conferences requested attention to other health priorities.[88] Making faraway Montevideo into "the Geneva of South America" does not seem to have irked PASB Director Cumming: the PASB was officially supportive of the IIPI,[89] though Cumming failed to mention the IIPI in several key overviews of health cooperation that he published.[90]

Once the IIPI was established, maternal and child health took on a higher profile at the PASB, particularly in its *Boletín de la Oficina Sanitaria Panamericana*. Child well-being finally reached the PASB's agenda at its ninth conference, held in Buenos Aires (together with the Latin American Eugenics and Homiculture Congress) ("Homiculture" is a Cuban-coined term expanding Pinard's concept of puericulture to include cultivation of the child from prebirth to adulthood.) in 1934, shortly after the passage of Uruguay's Children's Code. The PASB supported the position articulated by the IIPI's Berro, which fostered "positive" eugenics as embracing a "broad, non-coercive public health and social welfare approach directed toward the child" in contrast to the United States's focus on heredity and sterilization.[91] Given the IIPI's activities and its very existence—bolstered by the advocacy

of several member countries—the PASB could no longer overlook maternal and child health.

The IIPI's modus operandi differed significantly from that of other international health agencies. Rather than evolving into a regional outpost of the LNHO or the PASB, it maintained cordial relations free of "parental" constraints. Owing to the combination of fortunate timing, Uruguayan government support, and the regional backing of child health Pan-Americanists, the IIPI remained unencumbered by imperial or industrial interests. It drew its agenda from the concerns of health experts, feminists, and child advocates grounded in local problems in settings where child health policies were intertwined with burgeoning protectionism. The "Uruguay round" of international health suggests that the field is shaped by more than center–periphery logic.

About the Author

Correspondence: Requests for reprints should be sent to Anne-Emanuelle Birn, ScD, MA, Department of Public Health Sciences, University of Toronto, 1st Floor, McMurrich Bldg, 12 Queen's Park Crescent W, Toronto, ON M5S 1A8, Canada (email: ae.birn@utoronto.ca).

Acknowledgments

Partial funding for the writing of this paper was provided by the Global Health Trust's Joint Learning Initiative on Human Resources for Health and Development and the Canada Research Chairs program. The initial research was funded by the National Institute on Aging (grant 16813-01) and the National Institutes of Health, National Institute on Child Health and Human Development (grant 37962-02).

I am grateful to Gregory Kim for carrying out the analysis of the *Boletín* of the IIPI. My thanks to Sandra Burgues, Fernando Mañé Garzón, Raquel Pollero, Wanda Cabella, and Nikolai Krementsov for their helpful comments and suggestions, as well as to the "Public Health Then and Now" editors and the anonymous reviewers.

References

1. Weindling P. *International Health Organisations and Movements, 1918–1939.* Cambridge, United Kingdom: Cambridge University Press; 1995.

2. Packard R. "No other logical choice": global malaria eradication and the politics of international health in the post-war era. *Parassitologia.* 1998;40:217–230.

3. Siddiqi J. World Health and World Politics: The World Health Organization and the UN System. Columbia: University of South Carolina Press; 1995.

4. Hutchinson JF. Champions of Charity: War and the Rise of the Red Cross. Boulder, Colo: Westview Press; 1996.

5. Farley J. To Cast Out Disease: A History of the International Health Division of Rockefeller Foundation (1913–1951). New York, NY: Oxford University Press; 2004.

6. Anuario Estadístico del Uruguay. *Censo General de la República en 1908.* Montevideo, Uruguay: Imprenta Juan Dornaleche; 1911.

7. Panizza F. Late institutionalisation and eary modernisation: the emergence of Uruguay's liberal democratic political order. *J Latin Am Stud.* 1997;29:667–691.

8. López-Alves F. *State Formation and Democracy in Latin America, 1810–1900.* Durham, NC: Duke University Press; 2000.

9. Engerman SL, Haber S, Sokoloff KL. Inequality, institutions, and differential paths of growth among New World economies. In: Menard C, ed. *Institutions, Contracts, and Organizations.* Cheltenham, United Kingdom: Edward Elgar Publishing; 2000.

10. Nahum B. La Epoca Batllista, 1905–1929. In: *Historia Uruguaya.* Montevideo, Uruguay: Ediciones de la Banda Oriental; 1994:140.

11. Vanger MI. *The Model Country: José Batlle y Ordeñez of Uruguay, 1907–1915.* Lebanon, NH: University Press of New England; 1980.

12. Pelúas D. José Batlle y Ordóñez : el hombre. Montevideo, Uruguay: Editorial Fin de Siglo; 2001.

13. Barrán JP, Nahum B. Crisis y radicalización 1913–1916. In: *Batlle, los Estancieros y el Imperio Británico.* Montevideo, Uruguay: Ediciones de la Banda Oriental; 1985:257.

14. Bértola L. Ensayos de historia económica: Uruguay y la región en la economía mundial, 1870–1990. Montevideo, Uruguay: Ediciones Trilce; 2000.

15. Filgueira F. *A Century of Social Welfare in Uruguay: Growth to the Limit of the Batllista Social State.* Notre Dame, Ind: Kellogg Institute for International Studies; 1995. Democracy and Social Policy Series, Working Paper No. 5.

16. Moll A. The Pan American Sanitary Bureau: its origin, development and achievements: a review of inter-American cooperation in public health, medicine, and allied fields. *Boletín de la Oficina Sanitaria Panamericana.* 1940; 19:1219–1234.

17. Peard JG. Race, Place, and Medicine: The Idea of the Tropics in Nineteenth-Century Brazilian Medicine. Durham, NC: Duke University Press; 1999.

18. Koven S, Michel S. Mothers of a New World: Maternalist Politics and the Origins of Welfare States. New York, NY: Routledge; 1993.

19. Fildes V, Marks L, Marland H. Women and Children First: International Maternal and Infant Welfare, 1870–1945. London, United Kingdom: Routledge; 1992.

20. Vaillant A. *La República Oriental del Uruguay en la Esposición de Viena.* Montevideo, Uruguay: Imprenta a vapor de La Tribuna; 1873.

21. Rial J. *Población y Desarrollo de un Pequeño País: Uruguay, 1830–1930.* Montevideo, Uruguay: Centro de Informaciones y Estudios del Uruguay; 1983.

22. Mañé Garzón F, Burgues Roca S. *Publicaciones Médicas Uruguayas de los Siglos XVIII y XIX.* Montevideo, Uruguay: Universidad de la República, Facultad de Medicina, Oficina del Libro AEM; 1996.

23. Buño W. Nómina de egresados de la Facultad de Medicine de Montevideo entre 1881 y 1965. *Apartado de Sesiones de la Sociedad Uruguaya de Historia de la Medicina.* 1992;IX (1987–88).

24. Dirección de Estadística General. Anuario Estadístico de la República Oriental del Uruguay. Año 1884. Libro I del Anuario y XV de las Publicaciones de esta Dirección. Montevideo, Uruguay: Tipografía Oriental; 1885.

25. Ramiro FariñasD, Sanz Gimeno A. Cambios estructurales en la mortalidad infantil y juvenil española. *Boletín de la Asociación de Demografía Histórica.* 1999;17:49–87.

26. Wolleswinkel–van den Bosch JH, Poppel FW, Looman CW, Mackenbach JP. Determinants of infant and early childhood mortality levels and their decline in the Netherlands in the late nineteenth century. *Int J Epidemiol.* 2000;29:1031–1040.

27. Corsini CA, Viazzo PP. The Decline of Infant and Child Mortality: The European Experience 1750–1990. Cambridge, Mass: Kluwer Law International; 1997.

28. *Catálogo de la Exposición Internacional de Higiene. Enero–Abril de 1907.* Montevideo, Uruguay: Talleres Gráficos A. Barreiro y Ramos; 1907:39.

29. El Uruguay en el V Congreso Médico Latino-Americano (VI Pan-Americano) y Exposición Internacional de Higiene anexa. Lima, Noviembre de 1915. *Boletín del Consejo Nacional de Higiene.* 1913;8:515–524.

30. Soiza Larrosa A. La mortalidad de la ciudad de Montevideo durante el año 1893, por el Dr. Joaquín de Salterain, miembro del Consejo de Higiene Pública. Del retrospecto de El Siglo. *Sesiones de la Sociedad Uruguaya de Historia de la Medicina.* 1987;5:188–191.

31. de Salterain J. Boletín demográfico de la ciudad de Montevideo. *Revista Médica del Uruguay.* 1899;2:41–43.

32. Bertillon J. Nomenclature des Maladies (Statistiques de Morbidité–Statistiques des Causes de décès). Commission Internationale Chargée de Reviser les Nomenclatures Nosologiques. Paris, France: Imprimerie Typographique de l'Ecole d'Alembert; 1900.

33. *Transactions of the Fifteenth International Congress of Hygiene and Demography.* Washington, DC: Government Printing Office; 1912.

34. Rollet C. Le modèle de la goutte de lait dans le monde: diffusion et variantes. In: *Les Biberons du Docteur Dufour.* Fécamp, France: Musées Municipaux de Fécamp; 1997:111–117.

35. Becerro de Bengoa M. Los problemas de la asistencia pública. *Segundo Congreso Médico Nacional.* Montevideo, Uruguay: Imprenta El Siglo Ilustrado; 1921.

36. Ehrick C. Affectionate mothers and the colossal machine: feminism, social assistance and the state in Uruguay, 1910–1932. *The Americas.* 2001;58:121–139.

37. Asistencia Pública Nacional. Acta 312 (asunto: Sociedad Bonne Garde solici-

ta una subvención). *Boletín de la Asistencia Pública Nacional.* 1918;8:19–21.

38. *El Año de los Niños.* Montevideo: Asociación Uruguaya de Protección a la Infancia; 1925.

39. Cabella W. La evolución del divorcio en Uruguay (1950–1995). *Notas de Población.* 1998;XXVI.

40. de Salterain J. La mortalidad en la ciudad de Montevideo durante el año de 1895. *Año III del Retrospectivo de "El Siglo."* Montevideo, Uruguay: Museo Histórico Nacional, Casa de Lavalleja, Archivo y Biblioteca Pablo Blanco Acevedo; 1896.

41. Rollet C. La santé et la protection de l'enfant vues à travers les congrès internationaux (1880–1920). *Annales de Démographie Historique.* 2001:97–116.

42. Bauzá J. Mortalidad infantil en la República del Uruguay en el decenio 1901–1910. *Revista Médica del Uruguay.* 1913;16:45–81.

43. Morquio L. Cuatro años del servicio externo del Asilo de Expósitos y Huérfanos. *Revista Médica del Uruguay.* 1900;3.

44. Escardó y Anaya V. Biografía del Profesor Luis Morquio. *Archivos de Pediatría del Uruguay.* 1935;6:250–276.

45. Morquio L. La mortalidad infantil de Montevideo. In: *Tercer Congreso Médico Latinoamericano, Montevideo 1907.* Montevideo, Uruguay: Imprenta El Siglo Ilustrado; 1907:547–585.

46. Morquio L. Causas de la Mortalidad de la Primera Infancia y Medios de Reducirla. Informe Presentado al 2do Congreso Médico Latino-Americano Celebrado en Buenos Aires en Abril de 1904. Montevideo, Uruguay: Imprenta El Siglo Ilustrado; 1904.

47. Primer Congreso Médico Nacional: Sección de Pediatría, presidida por el Dr. Luis Morquio. *Revista Médica del Uruguay.* 1916;19:666–678.

48. Morquio L. Protección a la primera infancia. *Primer Congreso Médico Nacional.* Montevideo, Uruguay: Imprenta El Siglo Ilustrado; 1916.

49. Birn A-E, Pollero R, Cabella W. No se debe llorar sobre leche derramada: el pensamiento epidemiológico y la mortalidad infantil en Uruguay, 1900–1940. *Estudios Interdisciplinarios de América Latina.* 2003;14:35–65.

50. Escardó y Anaya V. *Bibliografía del Profesor Morquio.* Montevideo, Uruguay: Instituto de Pediatría y Puericultura "Profesor Luis Morquio"; 1938.

51. Morquio L. La mortalidad infantil en Uruguay. *Boletín de la Oficina Sanitaria Panamericana.* 1928;7: 1466–1475.

52. Transactions of the First General International Sanitary Convention of the American Republics, Held at the New Willard Hotel, Washington, D.C., December 2, 3, and 4, 1902, Under the Auspices of the Governing Board of the International Union of the American Republics. Washington, DC: Government Printing Office; 1902.

53. Bustamante M. Los primeros cincuenta años de la Oficina Sanitaria Panamericana. *Boletín de la Oficina Sanitaria Panamericana.* 1952;33: 471–531.

54. Moll A. The Pan American Sanitary Bureau: its origin, development and achievements: a review of inter-American cooperation in public health, medicine, and allied fields (continued). *Boletín de la Oficina Sanitaria Panamericana.* 1941;20:375–380.

55. Cueto M. Missionaries of Science: The Rockefeller Foundation and Latin America. Bloomington: Indiana University Press; 1994.

56. Fosdick R. *The Story of the Rockefeller Foundation.* New York, NY: Harper & Row; 1952.

57. Balinska M. *Une Vie pour L'humanitaire: Ludwik Rajchman (1881–1965).* Paris, France: Editions la Découverte; 1995.

58. Ehrick C. Madrinas and missionaries: Uruguay and the Pan-American women's movement. *Gender Hist.* 1998; 10:406–424.

59. Sapriza G. *Memorias de Rebeldía: Siete Historias de Vida.* Montevideo, Uruguay: Punto Sur Editores; 1998.

60. Lavrin A. Women, Feminism, and Social Change in Argentina, Chile, and Uruguay. Lincoln: University of Nebraska Press; 1995.

61. Scarzanella E. Proteger a las madres y los niños: el internacionalismo humanitario de la Sociedad de las Naciones y las delegadas sudamericanas. In: Potthast B, Scarzanella E, eds. *Mujeres y Naciones en América Latina: Problemas de Inclusión y Exclusión.* Madrid, Spain: Iberoamericana Editorial Vervuert; 2001.

62. Luisi P. Otra voz clamando en el desierto (Proxenetismo y reglamentación). Montevideo, Uruguay: CISA; 1948:1.

63. Rooke PT, Schnell RL. "Uncramping child life": international children's organisations, 1914–1939. In: Weindling P, ed. *International Health Organisations and Movements, 1918–1939.* Cambridge, United Kingdom: Cambridge University Press; 1995:176–202.

64. Miller C. The Social Section and Advisory Committee on Social Questions of the League of Nations. In: Weindling P, ed. *International Health Organisations and Movements, 1918–1939.* Cambridge, United Kingdom: Cambridge University Press; 1995:154–175.

65. Guy D. The Pan American Child Congresses, 1916 to 1942: Pan Americanism, child reform, and the welfare state in Latin America. *J Family Hist.* 1998;23:272–291.

66. Miller F. *Latin American Women and the Search for Social Justice.* Lebanon, NH: University Press of New England; 1991.

67. Guy DJ. The politics of Pan-American cooperation: maternalist feminism and the child rights movement, 1913–1960. *Gender Hist.* 1998;10: 449–469.

68. *Antecedentes Publicados por la Comisión Honoraria.* Montevideo, Uruguay: Instituto Internacional Americano de Protección a la Infancia; 1925:21.

69. Madsen T. Report by the president of the Health Committee on his technical mission to Certain South American Countries. Geneva, Switzerland: League of Nations Archives, Assemblée 8, 1927, Decs 39–133; September 16, 1927.

70. Scarzanella E. "Los pibes" en el Palacio de Ginebra: las investigaciones de la Sociedad de las Naciones sobre la infancia latinoamericana (1925–1939). *Estudios Interdisciplinarios de América Latina y el Caribe.* 2003;14.

71. Madsen T. Report on the work of the Conference of Health Experts on Infant Welfare held at Montevideo from June 7th to 11th, 1927. Geneva, Switzerland: League of Nations Archives, Assemblée 8, 1927, Decs 39–133; September 16, 1927.

72. Debré R, Olsen EW. Société des Nations, Organisation d'Hygiène. Les enquêtes entreprises en Amérique du Sud sur la mortalité infantile. *Boletín del Instituto Internacional Americano de Protección a la Infancia.* 1931;4: 581–605.

73. Morquio L. Société des Nations, Organisation d'Hygiène. Conférence d'experts hygiénistes en matière de protection de la première enfance. *Boletín del Instituto Internacional Americano de Protección a la Infancia.* 1931;4:535–580.

74. Aráoz Alfaro G. Société des Nations, Organisation d'hygiène. Experts hygiénistes en matière de protection de la 1ère enfance. *Boletín del Instituto Internacional Americano de Protección a la Infancia.* 1931;4:373–425.

75. Fournié E. Séptima Conferencia Internacional Americana, Capítulo V: problemas sociales. *Boletín del Instituto Internacional Americano de Protección a la Infancia.* 1934;7:229–249.

76. Escardó y Anaya V. Veniticinco anos del Consejo Directivo y de la Dirección General. *Boletín del Instituto Internacional Americano de Protección a la Infancia.* 1952;26:91–105.

77. Morquio L. Instituto Internacional Americano de Protección a la Infancia: noticia presentada al VI congreso panamericano del niño. *Boletín del Instituto Internacional Americano de Protección a la Infancia.* 1930;4:215–229.

78. Caetano G. Prólogo. In: *El Uruguay de los Años Treinta: Enfoques y Problemas.* Montevideo, Uruguay: Ediciones de la Banda Oriental; 1994:7–15.

79. Caetano G, Jacob R. *El Nacimiento del Terrismo, 1930–1933.* Montevideo, Uruguay: Ediciones de la Banda Oriental; 1989.

80. Berro R. La medicina social de la infancia. Boletín del Instituto Internacional Americano de Protección a la Infancia. 1936;9:594–609.

81. Tomé E. Código del Niño. Anotado con todas las leyes, decretos y acordadas vigentes y con la jurisprudencia nacional. In: *Colección de Manuales de Derecho y Legislación.* Montevideo, Uruguay: Claudio García Editor; 1938.

82. *Consejo del Niño. Consejo del Niño, Su Organización y Funcionamiento 1934–1936.* Montevideo, Uruguay: Imprenta de Monteverde & Cia; 1937?:81.

83. Guía Informativa de las Funciones que Desarrolla el Consejo del Niño. Montevideo, Uruguay: Consejo del Niño; 1950.

84. Quesada Pacheco R. Informe sobre la Obra de Protección a la Infancia realizada por el Consejo del Niño del Uruguay. *Boletín del Instituto Internacional Americano de Protección a la Infancia.* 1937;11:261–283.

85. Bauzá JA. Acción futura del Consejo del Niño. Boletín del Instituto Internacional Americano de Protección a la Infancia. 1943;17:291–300.

86. Illanes MA. *En el Nombre del Pueblo, del Estado y de la Ciencia . . . : Historia Social de la Salud Pública, Chile 1880–1973.* Santiago, Chile: Colectivo de Atención Primaria; 1993.

87. Gillespie J. International organizations and the problem of child health, 1945–1960. *Dynamis.* 2003;23: 115–142.

88. Birn A-E. No more surprising than a broken pitcher? Maternal and child health in the early years of the Pan American Sanitary Bureau. *Can Bull Med Hist.* 2002;19:17–46.

89. Moll A. Las obras sanitarias de protección a la infancia en las Américas. *Boletín de la Organización Sanitaria Panamericana.* 1935;14:1040–1055.

90. Cumming HS. Development of international cooperation among the health authorities of the American republics. *Am J Public Health.* 1938;28: 1193–1196.

91. Stepan N. *The Hour of Eugenics: Race, Gender, and Nation in Latin America.* Ithaca, NY: Cornell University Press; 1991.

Adolescent Birth Rates, Total Homicides, and Income Inequality In Rich Countries

| Kate E. Pickett, PhD, Jessica Mookherjee, MSc and Richard G. Wilkinson, MMedSci

ABSTRACT

Income inequality has been associated with both homicides and births to adolescents in the United States and with homicides internationally. We found that adolescent birth rates and general homicide rates were closely correlated with each other internationally ($r = 0.95$) and within the United States ($r = 0.74$) and with inequality internationally and within the United States. These results, coupled with no association with absolute income, suggested that violence and births to adolescents may reflect gender-differentiated responses to low social status and could be reduced by reducing income inequality.

INTRODUCTION

Violence and births to adolescents seem to stand out as gender-differentiated markers of the corrosive effects of poverty among young people.[1–3] Although adolescent births and levels of violence are strongly associated with poverty *within* developed countries, national rates of both violence and adolescent births are nevertheless higher in several wealthy countries compared with poor countries. In other words, homicides and adolescent pregnancies appear to be associated with relative rather than absolute poverty. Indeed, the degree of income distribution within a society has been linked to homicide rates within and outside the United States (see, for example, Hsieh and Pugh,[4] Wilkinson et al.,[5] Daly et al.,[6] and Fajnzylber et al.[7]), but only within the United States

for adolescent births.[8,9] We decided to investigate how much these 2 social problems were related to each other and, if they have common roots, whether these roots might lie in relative or in absolute deprivation.

METHODS

International Comparisons

Countries were included if they were among the 50 countries with the highest gross national income per capita by purchasing power parity in 2002, had populations of more than 3 million, and had data on income inequality. The eligible countries were Australia, Austria, Belgium, Canada, Denmark, Finland, France, Germany, Greece, Ireland, Israel, Italy, Japan, The Netherlands, New Zealand, Norway, Portugal, Singapore, Slovenia, Spain, Sweden, Switzerland, the United Kingdom, and the United States.

Data on income inequality came from the United Nations Development Program Human Development Indicators; dates for each country vary slightly from country to country but are within the period 1992–1998.[10] Income inequality was measured as the ratio of the total annual income received by the richest 20% of the population to the total average annual income received by the poorest 20% of the population. Gross national income per capita by purchasing power parity was measured in US dollars and obtained from the World Bank World Development Indicators database.[11] Data on births per 1000 women aged 15 to 19 years for 1998 came from UNICEF.[12] Adolescent

birth rates were unavailable for Israel, Singapore, and Slovenia, and these countries were excluded from our study. Data on homicides came from the United Nations' *Survey on Crime Trends and the Operations of Criminal Justice Systems*.[13] Homicide data were period averages of available rates per 100000 persons for 1990–2000.

US Comparisons

Data on income inequality for the 50 United States and the District of Columbia were obtained from the US Census Bureau.[14] Income inequality was measured as the Gini coefficient based on family income for 1999. Per capita income in 1999 was obtained from the US Census Bureau *Census 2000 Summary File 3*.[15] Data on births to adolescents in 2000 came from the US National Vital Statistics System.[16] Data are presented as births per 1000 females aged 15 to 19 years. Homicide rates per 100 000 persons came from the Federal Bureau of Investigation's annual report on crime statistics for the United States for 1999.[17] Data were unavailable for Wyoming and the District of Columbia. From a national report on juvenile offenders and victims, we also extracted juvenile homicide arrest rates per 100 000 juveniles (aged 10–17 years) for 46 states in 1997.[18]

Statistical Methods

We first estimated simple correlations between homicide rates and adolescent birth rates both within the United States and internationally. We then measured the independent effects of income inequality and per capita (absolute) income on homicide rates and adolescent birth rates internationally and within the United States. Within the United States only, this analysis was repeated for juvenile homicide rates. We also examined the effect of income inequality on each outcome while controlling for the other outcome.

RESULTS

Figure 1 shows a plot of adolescent birth rates and homicide rates in the United States. The Pearson correlation coefficient between adolescent birth rates and homicide rates was 0.95 ($P < .001$) internationally and 0.74 ($P < .001$) across the United States. The independent effects of income inequality and per capita income on adolescent births and homicides are shown in Table 1. The partial correlation coefficients for income inequality and both outcomes in both settings were statistically significant ($P < .01$) and ranged from 0.51 to 0.73. Figure 2 shows a plot of income inequality and adolescent birth rates for 21 developed countries.

The effect of per capita income differed in the 2 comparisons. Internationally, higher per capita income was associated with *higher* rates of adolescent births and homicides ($P < .001$), whereas in the United States, higher per capita income was associated with lower adolescent birth rates ($P < .001$) and was not significantly related to homicide rates. The Pearson correlation coefficient for juvenile homicides and income inequality was 0.31 ($P = .035$), and for juvenile homicides and per capita income it was effectively zero (0.001; $P = .994$) (data not

shown). The international associations between each outcome and income inequality were removed by controlling for the other. In the United States, an attenuated correlation remained between income inequality and adolescent births.

DISCUSSION

Our findings suggested that the links between deprivation and both violence and adolescent births reflect the destructive psychosocial and behavioral effects of inequality. As Luker[19] put it, it is "the discouraged among the disadvantaged" who become adolescent mothers. Gilligan[20] and others pointed out how often violence among young men is triggered by humiliation and disrespect.

Successful programs for preventing adolescent pregnancy and violence have often focused on personal development, attempting to undo the psychosocial costs of low social status.[1,21] But these patterns demand a common explanation. Our study suggests that levels of relative deprivation may be an underlying cause. Interestingly, the decline in US homicide and adolescent birth rates since the 1990s was accompanied by declining unemployment and improved relative income among the poorest individuals.[17,22]

About the Authors

Kate E. Pickett is with the Department of Health Sciences, University of York, York, England. Jessica Mookherjee is with the Department of Anthropology,

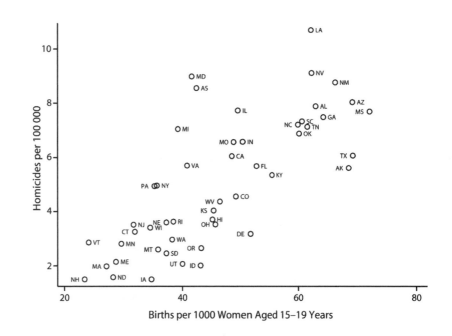

FIGURE 1— Homicide rates and rates of adolescent births in 49 states (indicated by postal codes): United States, Federal Bureau of Investigation, 1999, and US National Vital Statistics System, 2000.

TABLE 1— Independent Effects of Absolute Income and Income Inequality on Homicide Rates and Births to Adolescents Among Rich Countries and Within the United States

Per capita income	Among Rich Countries				Within the United States			
	Adolescent Births		Homicides		Adolescent Births		Homicides	
	r	P	r	P	r	P	r	P
Per capita income	0.73	<.001	0.71	<.01	0.72	<.001	0.51	<.001
Per capita income	0.75	<.001	0.78	<.001	-0.55	<.001	-0.17	.245

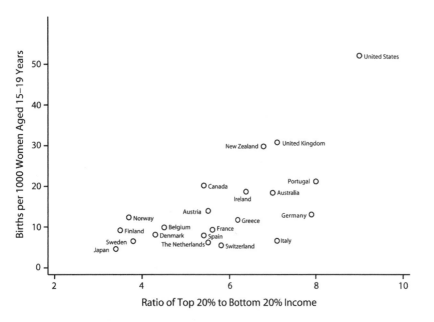

FIGURE 2— Income inequality and rates of adolescent births among 21 of the richest developed countries: United Nations, 1990–2000, and UNICEF, 1998.

University College London, London, England. Richard G. Wilkinson is with the Division of Epidemiology and Public Health, University of Nottingham Medical School, Nottingham, England.

Correspondence: Requests for reprints should be sent to Kate E. Pickett, PhD, Department of Health Sciences, University of York, Seebohm Rowntree Building—Room A/TB/220, Heslington, York YO10 5DD UK (e-mail: kp6@york.ac.uk).

Contributors

All authors contributed to the origination and design of the study and to the writing and revising of the brief. K. E. Pickett conducted the statistical analysis.

References

1. Health Development Agency. *Teenage Pregnancy and Parenthood: A Review of Reviews.* London, England: Health Development Agency, National Health Service; 2003. Evidence Briefing.

2. The Alan Guttmacher Institute. *Teen Sex and Pregnancy: Facts in Brief.* New York, NY: The Alan Guttmacher Institute; 1999.

3. Wilson M, Daly M. Competitiveness, risk-taking and violence: the young male syndrome. *Ethol Sociobiol.*1985;6:59–73.

4. Hsieh C-C, Pugh MD. Poverty, income inequality, and violent crime: a meta-analysis of recent aggregate data studies. *Crim Justice Rev.*1993;18:182–202.

5. Wilkinson RG, Kawachi I, Kennedy BP. Mortality, the social environment, crime and violence. *Sociol Health Illn.*1998;20:578–597.

6. Daly M, Wilson M, Vasdev S. Income inequality and homicide rates in Canada and the United States. *Can J Criminol.*2001;43:219–236.

7. Fajnzylber P, Lederman D, Loayza N. Inequality and violent crime. *J Law Econ.*2002;45:1–40.

8. Gold R, Kawachi I, Kennedy BP, Lynch JW, Connell FA. Ecological analysis of teen birth rates: association with community income and income inequality. *Matern Child Health J.*2001;5:161–167.

9. Gold R, Kennedy B, Connell F, Kawachi I. Teen births, income inequality, and social capital: developing an understanding of the causal pathway. *Health Place.*2002; 8(2):77–83.

10. United Nations Development Program. *Human Development Report.* New York, NY: Oxford University Press; 2003.

11. World Development Indicators [database online]. Washington, DC: World Bank; 2004. Available at: http://www.worldbank.org/data/wdi2 004. Accessed December, 2004.

12. *A League Table of Teenage Births in Rich Nations: Innocenti Report Card.* Florence, Italy: UNICEF Innocenti Research Centre; 2001. Report No. 3.

13. United Nations Crime and Justice Information Network. *Survey on Crime Trends and the Operations of Criminal Justice Systems (Fifth, Sixth, Seventh).* New York, NY: United Nations; 2000.

14. Table S4: Gini ratios by state: 1969, 1979, 1989, 1999. Washington, DC: Income Statistics Branch/Housing and Household Economic Statistics Division, US Census Bureau; 2004. Available at: http://www.census.gov/hhes/income/ histinc/state/state4.html. Accessed April 13, 2005.

15. *Census 2000 Summary File 3.* Washington, DC: US Census Bureau; 2003.

16. Ventura SJ, Mathews TJ, Hamilton BE. Teenage births in the United States: state trends, 1991–2000, an update. *Natl Vital Stat Rep.* May 30, 2002;50(9): 1–4.

17. *Crime in the United States.* Washington, DC: Federal Bureau of Investigation; 1990–2000.

18. Office of Juvenile Justice and Delinquency Prevention. *Juvenile Offenders and Victims: 1999 National Report.* Pittsburgh, Pa: National Center for Juvenile Justice; 1999.

19. Luker K. *Dubious Conception: The Politics of Teen-age Pregnancy.* Cambridge, Mass: Harvard University Press; 1996.

20. Gilligan J. *Violence: Our Deadly Epidemic and Its Causes.* New York, NY: GP Putnam; 1996.

21. Center for the Study and Prevention of Violence. *Blueprints Model Program Descriptions, FS-BP02.* Boulder: University of Colorado; 2004. Available at: http://www.colorado.edu/cspv/blue-prints/model/overview.html. Accessed April 13, 2005.

22. The Alan Guttmacher Institute. *The Guttmacher Report on Public Policy.* New York, NY: The Alan Guttmacher Institute; 1998.

Managing Newborn Health in the Global Community

| William Foege, MD, MPH

ABSTRACT

The largest health disparities in the world are found in maternal and neonatal mortality figures between the industrialized countries and the poorest sections of the poorest countries. Young lives would be saved if the skills and knowledge that have been accumulated by health workers aroundthe world could be readily applied. The problems reside with lack of management resources rather than lack of scientific knowledge. The Healthy Newborn: A Reference Manual for Program Managersis a graduate course in management aimed at providing health to newborns and healthy newborns to communities.

INTRODUCTION

The responsibility of caring for a newborn child is awesome, even for those who do such work professionally. Often everything goes as it should. When it does not, however, a lifetime can be determined by actions that take only minutes.

In precisely the places with the fewest resources, we find the largest problems. The transition from intrauterine to extrauterine existence is a period of drama and comparatively high risk. But more than that, it is a period of the largest health disparities in the world, namely those found in maternal and neonatal mortality figures between the industrialized countries and the poorest sections of the poorest countries.

Why such disparities? There is no unalterable reason. The differences come down to whether or not the skills and knowledge that have been accumulated by workers around the world, especially in recent decades, are actually applied. In the final analysis, the problem is usually one of management rather than of science. How can systems be developed, and how can health workers receive the training and support, to make those skills and knowledge available for the care of each child?

Occasionally, a publication turns out to be so useful that with its appearance a tradition is born. *Control of Communicable Diseases in Man*, a publication of the American Public Health Association, is an example. It filled a pressing need in the early years of the 20th century, and after 84 years and 17 editions it continues to assemble pertinent knowledge of communicable diseases and to update that knowledge periodically, providing public health officers with concise guidelines for diverse situations. I predict that *The Healthy Newborn: A Reference Manual for Program Managers* will have a similar destiny, proving so useful in salvaging young lives that frequent editions will update the information it contains.

A VALUABLE TOOL

Because newborn morbidity and mortality are a management problem, this manual is quite intentionally a management document. It focuses immediately on the needs of managers, who can make a difference for an entire geographic area. It provides a road map for district medical officers and program managers, outlining, in 4 sections, logical steps to improve newborn health.

Part 1 reviews what has been learned about why children die before birth or in the neonatal period. The section makes clear what can go wrong and the urgency that is required to avoid delays in care. The section also reinforces how much is known, emphasizing that the problem is not one of knowledge but of action and that much of the needed action can be accomplished at low cost. Part 1 ends with a useful summary table of the relationships between maternal conditions and perinatal outcomes.

Part 2 provides the tools to fill in the framework developed in Part 3. It includes the usual tools of epidemiology but also offers a simple mnemonic to introduce assessment principles for the health worker. Reminiscent of the UNICEF mnemonic "GOBI" ("growth monitoring, oral rehydration, breastfeeding, and immunization") to keep health workers thinking about priorities, the authors introduce "BABIES" ("birthweight, age at death, and boxes for intervention and evaluation system") as the basis for a health management information system to determine what goes wrong in local settings and what improvements are possible. The BABIES mnemonic provides readers with the useful concept of thinking in 2 dimensions— time of death and weight at birth—to summarize what can go wrong and what can be done to intervene.

Part 3 introduces a management model that a program manager can apply to a specific problem: define the problem, assess performance, design appropriate interventions, and monitor and evaluate the results. Step by step, this section takes the manager through every challenge to be faced, from collecting the right information in the right way to making the right decisions with that information. What is surprising is the completeness of the manual. Program managers can use their energy to apply the information contained in the manual to their districts and to get the pertinent information from their jurisdictions, rather than being forced to seek more information from the literature.

What is noteworthy about the approach is the involvement of the community in every step of the process. This is not a mysterious medical system doing something to the community. It is the community understanding the problem and therefore helping to solve the problem. The result will be stronger newborns in a stronger community. After studying part 3, a program manager who start-

ed with the most rudimentary understanding of the problems of newborn mortality can be in a position to comprehend and change the risks for an entire district and to fully engage the community.

Part 4 gets to the reason for all of the preliminaries. It packages the possible interventions, summarizes the delays that lead to adverse outcomes, and provides very specific intervention instructions for every period from pregnancy through birth to emergency newborn care. And finally, for those who want even more detail, it includes an impressive list of references for additional information and a CD-ROM with additional resources.

The manual is not restricted to theory. The reader can be inspired by examples such as the case of Gadchiroli district in Maharastra State, India, where neonatal mortality was documented at 60 per 1000 live-born children. A management package was introduced that included training of mothers, training of traditional birth

attendants, resuscitation skills, and detection and management of neonatal problems. The program reduced neonatal mortality by more than 60% within 3 years. The cost of the package was $5.30 per child, and the cost per life saved was calculated to be less than the cost of a measles vaccination program.

A SHORT COURSE IN MANAGEMENT

Reviewing the manual took me back to an experience I had 3 decades ago. Having been given the responsibility of running a large public health program, I felt the need to enroll in a management course. It was one of the most useful educational experiences of my life. I realized, however, that although medical school had also been a course in management, that fact had been carefully and cleverly camouflaged by a focus on the science. As medical students, we were given the feeling that we could always go into administration if our clinical skills were inadequate. Management was degraded. Never mentioned was the fact that the entire purpose of medical school was management.

Patients are seen because they are not in an ideal health position. By taking a careful history, performing a physical examination, and ordering appropriate laboratory and radiologic tests, the physician attempts to understand the gap between where the patient is and where he or she should be. (This is in fact a surveillance system or health management information system.) A plan is then developed to move the patient to the selected goal—with monitoring and evaluation carried out via temperature and blood pressure readings, laboratory tests, and so forth—and midcourse corrections are made if progress is less than ideal. Classic management techniques are employed, but somehow they are never called management.

This manual is transparent. The difference between whether a body of knowledge improves health or does not improve health comes down to management. *The Healthy Newborn* is a

Cover of *The Healthy Newborn: A Reference Manual for Program Managers.* Joy E. Lawn, Brian J. McCarthy, and Susan Rae Ross. (CARE–CDC Health Initiative, Atlanta, Ga, 2001.)

graduate course in management aimed at providing health to newborns and healthy newborns to communities. It is a wonderful and practical addition to our global-health tool chest that will be useful to everyone—to the minister of health attempting to develop appropriate health programs for an entire country, to district medical officers focusing on a particular region, to those who train local traditional birth attendants, and to those attempting to educate an entire community. The authors deserve our gratitude.

About the Author

William Foege is with the Department of International Health, Rollins School of Public Health, Emory University, Atlanta, Ga.

Correspondence: William Foege, MD, MPH, Rollins School of Public Health, Emory University, 1518 Clifton Rd, Atlanta, GA 30322 (e-mail: wfoege@sph.emory.edu).

The production and publication of *The Healthy Newborn: A Reference Manual for Program Managers* was made possible through the CARE–CDC Health Initiative, an initiative funded by the R. W. Woodruff Foundation through CARE, the CDC Foundation, and the World Health Organization Collaborating Center in Reproductive Health in Atlanta. Information about availability, distribution, cost, and contact persons can be found at www.cdc.gov/nccdphp/drh.

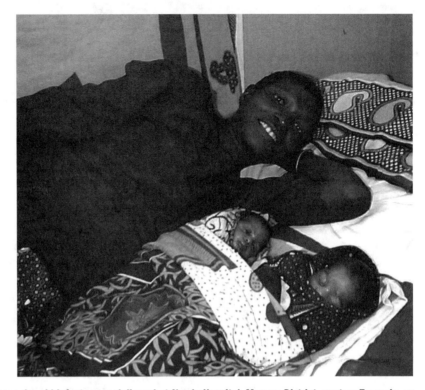

These day-old infants were delivered at Ngudu Hospital, Mwanza District, western Tanzania, on February 1, 2001. (Photo: Michelle Kouletio.)

The Health Impact of Child Labor in Developing Countries: Evidence From Cross-Country Data

| Paola Roggero, MD, MSc, Viviana Mangiaterra, MD, PhD, Flavia Bustreo, MD and Furio Rosati, PhD

ABSTRACT

Objectives. Research on child labor and its effect on health has been limited. We sought to determine the impact of child labor on children's health by correlating existing health indicators with the prevalence of child labor in selected developing countries.

Methods. We analyzed the relationship between child labor (defined as the percentage of children aged 10 to 14 years who were workers) and selected health indicators in 83 countries using multiple regression to determine the nature and strength of the relation. The regression included control variables such as the percentage of the population below the poverty line and the adult mortality rate.

Results. Child labor was significantly and positively related to adolescent mortality, to a population's nutrition level, and to the presence of infectious disease.

Conclusions. Longitudinal studies are required to understand the short- and long-term health effects of child labor on the individual child.

INTRODUCTION

Child labor is an important global issue associated with poverty, inadequate educational opportunities, gender inequality, and a range of health risks.[1] Child labor is defined by the relevant international conventions (UNICEF's Convention on the Rights of the Child,[2] International Labor Organization [ILO] Convention 138,[3] and especially, 182[4]) not by the activities performed by the child, but by the consequences of such activities (exceptions are the so-called unconditional worst forms of child labor such as prostitution and bondage, as noted in ILO Convention 182). For instance, work affecting a child's health and schooling should, according to these conventions, be eliminated.[5] Identifying the health effects of child labor is essential because it enables policymakers to decide which types of child labor to target for eradication.

The ILO estimates that there are approximately 250 million child laborers worldwide, with at least 120 million of them working under circumstances that have denied them a childhood and in conditions that jeopardize their health and even their lives. Most working children are ages 11 to 14 years old, but as many as 60 million are between the ages of 5 and 11.[6] Although the exact numbers are not known, available statistics indicate that approximately 96% of child workers reside in developing countries in Africa, Asia, and Latin America; there are also pockets of child labor in many industrialized countries.[5,7,8] In spite of a reported decline in child labor during the period 1995 to 2000,[9] child labor remains a major concern.

Most child laborers begin working at a very young age, are malnourished, and work long hours in hazardous occupations; frequently they do not attend school. They receive very low wages or are unpaid, and their income or help is usually essential for family survival. They are mainly employed in the informal sector, with agriculture accounting for more children workers than any other sector. It is estimated that, in developing countries, at least 90% of economically active children in rural areas are employed in agriculture.[10] Recent ILO statistics from 20 developing countries categorized the proportion of economically active children aged 5 to 14 years as employed in agriculture, animal husbandry, and related work at 74% (73.3% of boys and 78.8% of girls).[11]

Short term, the most obvious economic impact of child labor at the family level is an increase in household income. Long term, the underaccumulation of human capital caused by low school attendance and poor health is a serious negative consequence of child labor, representing a missed opportunity to enhance the productivity and future earnings capacity of the next generation.[12] Child laborers grow up to be low-wage–earning adults; as a result, their offspring will also be compelled to work to supplement the family's income. In this way, poverty and child labor is passed from generation to generation.[13,14]

Although child labor is recognized as a global health problem, research on its health impact on children has been limited and sometimes inconsistent. In 1998, Graitcer and Lerer published the first comprehensive review of the effect of child labor on children's health by extrapolating data from the Global Burden of Disease Study.[15] The occupational mortality rate among children matched the adult occupational mortality rate, such that the occupational mortality rate indicates mortality associated with child labor. In another study, in 2000, Graitcer and Lerer did not find any differences in the health status of working and nonworking Egyptian children in the short run (the children were not followed to adulthood).[16] A 2003 report on children's work in Morocco,[17] Yemen,[18] and Guatemala,[19] and a review developed under the aegis of Understanding Children's Work Project[20] provide an overview of the nature and extent of child labor, its determinants, and its consequences for the health and education of children in these countries. Several case–control and cohort studies have reported on the association of child labor, impaired growth, and malnutrition.[21–26]

The health effects of child labor on children and the correlation between current health and future health status are difficult to investigate and are compounded by short-term versus long-term health consequences. The situation is further complicated because work can contribute to an improvement in a poor child's nutritional status (a positive health effect).[14] Finally, the anthropometric measurements that traditionally have been used to evaluate children's health status are of limited value for those who are age 10 years and older.

We provide evidence, garnered from a cross section of countries, on the relation between child labor and children's health. To our knowledge, this study represents the first use of cross-country data to examine the issue. The benefit of cross-country data is that they allow us to synthesize indicators, creating a set of indicators unavailable in micro- or individual-country data. The drawback to using different data sources is that the statistics may not be comparable. To avoid problems of comparability, we limited ourselves to data that were standardized by the institutions that collected or compiled them. We analyzed the health effects of child labor on children by correlating existing health indicators and the prevalence of child labor in a large group of developing countries (Algeria, Angola, Bangladesh, Belize, Benin, Bolivia, Botswana, Brazil, Burkina Faso, Burundi, Cambodia, Cameroon, Chad, Chile, China, Congo, Colombia, Cote d'Ivoire,

Costa Rica, Democratic Republic of Congo, Dominican Republic, Egypt, Ecuador, El Salvador, Eritrea, Gabon, Gambia, Ghana, Guatemala, Guinea, Guinea Bissau, Haiti, Honduras, India, Indonesia, Iran, Iraq, Jamaica, Jordan, Kenya, Laos, Liberia, Libya, Lesotho, Madagascar, Malaysia, Malawi, Mali, Mexico, Mongolia, Mozambique, Morocco, Myanmar, Namibia, Nepal, Nicaragua, Niger, Nigeria, Oman, Pakistan, Panama, Papua New Guinea, Paraguay, Peru, Philippines, Rwanda, Senegal, Sierra Leone, Solomon's Islands, Sri Lanka, Sudan, Swaziland, Syrian Arab Republic, Uganda, Uruguay, Tanzania, Venezuela, Vietnam, Thailand, Togo, Yemen, Zambia, Zimbabwe).

METHODS

Data and Indicator Sources

We derived our estimates on the prevalence of child labor among children aged 10 to 14 years from only 1 data set: the World Bank's *World Development Indicators*.[27] This source limits its estimates of working children to the "economically active population," which means that children who are in non economic activities or are employed in hidden forms of work such as domestic service, prostitution, and armed conflict are not included.

Health indicators, such as health status, and health determinant indicators, which give information about the health of a community or population relative to some criteria or in comparison with other communities or populations, were obtained from the *World Development Indicators*, the Global Burden of Disease Study,[28] and the life tables for 191 countries (our study included only the 83 developing countries).[29]

The following rates and percentages were obtained from the World Bank database: male and female adult mortality rates, fertility rates, the prevalence of undernourishment (percentage of population), the prevalence of HIV/AIDS among adults (percentage of population), and national poverty levels (percentage of population below the national poverty line, as

determined using the World Bank's country poverty assessments).

The World Bank's data set came from multitopic welfare surveys, such as the Living Standard Measurement Study (LSMS), which measure and analyze poverty. Dozens of countries have implemented multitopic surveys, and many of them have conducted the same survey repeatedly, allowing for relevant comparisons across time. Multitopic surveys can also be used to measure the effect of public policies and programs on poverty. The LSMS—one of the best known and most useful of these surveys—has a questionnaire designed to study multiple aspects of household welfare and behavior; it also incorporates extensive quality-control features. The main objective of LSMS surveys is to collect household data that can be used to assess household welfare, understand household behavior, and evaluate the effect of various government policies on the quality living conditions of the population. Accordingly, LSMS surveys collect information on employment, household income and expenditures; asset ownership, such as housing or land; health; education; fertility; nutrition; migration; and access to services and social programs. To minimize errors and delays in data processing, LSMS surveys are implemented with distinct procedures that resolve most inconsistencies in the raw data before the data reach the central statistical office.

Data on HIV/AIDS infections, non-HIV infections, and malaria among children aged 5 to 14 years, associated with 4 major risk factors (malnutrition, poor water and lack of sanitation and hygiene, unsafe sex, and dangerous occupation), came from the Global Burden of Disease Study. These indicators are expressed as disability-adjusted life years calculated as the sum of years of life lost because of disability and years of life lived with disability. Mortality rates among children, both boys and girls, aged 10 to 14 years were obtained from these life tables.

The data, all from the year 2000, were collected from 83 countries in 6 geographic regions, as defined by the Global Burden of Disease Study (sub-

Saharan Africa, Latin America and the Caribbean, Asia and Pacific Islands, China, India, and North Africa/Middle East).

Data Analysis

The data on child labor (expressed as a percentage of children aged 10 to14 years who were workers) and health indicators were analyzed by multiple regression to ascertain the effect of child labor on the various health indicators. All data were aggregated at the national level. The strength of the association between the percentage of children who were workers and HIV/AIDS infections, non-HIV infections, and malaria as expressed by disability-adjusted life years were also correlated using SPSS version 10 for Windows (SPSS Inc, Chicago, Ill).

The following were designated as dependent variables: the mortality rate among boys aged 10 to 14 years, the mortality rate among girls aged 10 to 14 years, and the percentage of the population aged 10 to 14 years undernourished.

Mortality rate among children aged 10 to 14 years is an important health indicator, commonly related to accidents. We chose mortality rate among children as a dependent variable because we could test independent variables against it to determine which independent variables most influence mortality in this age range. For each of the first 2 dependent variables, 2 separate regression models were developed, 1 using only the adult mortality rate for women and the other using only the adult male mortality rate. This avoided possible colinearity between these 2 independent variables, a problem that could have occurred had we used a combined version of the adult mortality rate. We

chose prevalence of malnutrition in the population as a dependent variable because it reflects the health environment of households and we wished to determine which variables were significantly related to it.

The independent (or predictor) variables used to predict the dependent variables were the following, in various combinations: adult mortality rate for men, adult mortality rate for women, percentage of the population below the poverty line, percentage of adults infected with HIV/AIDS, percentage of the population undernourished, percentage of children aged 10 to14 years who were workers (child labor prevalence).

RESULTS

Figures 1 and 2 show the associations between the predictor variables and the dependent variables; Table 1 presents the multiple regression results. Figures 1 and 2 show that child labor appeared to be negatively correlated with the health status of the population, supporting the hypothesis that child labor affects child health.

This association could be caused by other factors affecting the population's health status that were also correlated with the percentage of children engaged in paid labor. Therefore, we included control variables such as the percentage of the population below the poverty line and the adult mortality rate in the regression. The results of the regression confirmed that several variables played a determining role in the mortality rates of children aged 10 to 14 years and that 2 of these variables also affected the level of undernourishment. The prevalence of child labor was a significant predictor of undernourishment in a population and of the mortality rate for children aged 10 to 14 years (boys and girls), confirming that child labor affects children's health.

We also looked at the association between childhood morbidity, as measured by disability-adjusted life years, and the prevalence of child labor in the 6 regions we studied (Figure 3). In each of the regions with

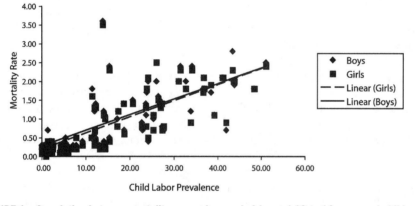

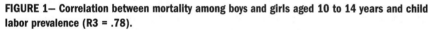

FIGURE 1— Correlation between mortality among boys and girls aged 10 to 14 years and child labor prevalence (R3 = .78).

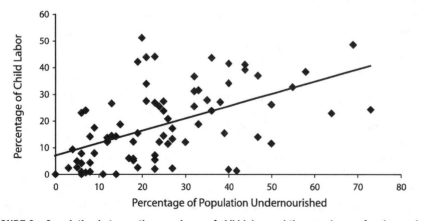

FIGURE 2— Correlation between the prevalence of child labor and the prevalence of undernourishment in the population (R3 = .47).

TABLE 1— Multiple Regression Results (Unstandardized Coefficients) for Mortality, Undernourishment, and Labor: Children Aged 10–14 Years, 2000

	Boys	Girls	Undernourished Population
Child labor prevalence	0.016*	0.016*	0.003*
Percentage of population below national poverty lines	0.012*	0.015*	0.003*
Adult mortality rate			
Men	0.023*	0.023*	
Women	0.017*	0.019*	
Percentage of population undernourished	−0.004	−0.006	
Percentage of HIV/AIDS among adults	NA	NA	0.01*

Note. NA = not applicable.
*P ” .05.

a high prevalence of child labor, there was a high correlation between child labor and childhood morbidity associated with HIV/AIDS, non-HIV infectious diseases, and malaria.

DISCUSSION

Child labor remains one of the most provocative and controversial challenges facing the world at the beginning of the 21st century. Furthermore, child labor's close links to poverty, lack of education, poor health, and gender inequalities highlight the need for broad-based social and economic progress.

By extrapolating data from the Global Burden of Disease Study, Graitcer and Lerer estimated mortality, morbidity, and disability associated with child labor.[15] Despite the limits of the Global Burden of Disease Study— for example, the health statistics were constrained by the age stratification used, and the injury data were not provided by occupation—Graitcer and Lerer were able to estimate work-related injury and mortality. They concluded that in all regions the occupational mortality rate among children matched the adult occupational mortality rate, indicating that children may be working in conditions that are as hazardous as, or even more hazardous than, those of adults. Burn injury estimates from the Global Burden of Disease

Study show that work-related burns constituted more than one third of all burn injuries sustained among children aged 5 to 14 years. It is worth noting that this statistic did not take into account burns sustained during housework, the most common of which occur while cooking over an open fire.

Graitcer and Lerer did not find any health problems in working Egyptian children,[16] but they argued that a child's exposure to poor working conditions and health hazards may result in health consequences much later in life. In reports on child labor

in Morocco,[17] Yemen,[18] and Guatemala,[19] the researchers of the Understanding Children's Work project found few or no ill health effects resulting from work and suggested that this might be because the healthiest children are selected for work or because health consequences may not become apparent until a later stage in a child's life. They also showed that it is not work per se that is damaging to a child's health, but rather certain kinds of work.

Studies with an ecological design have proven valuable in descriptive

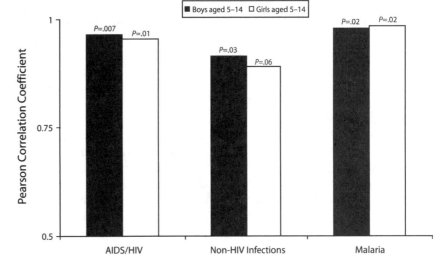

FIGURE 3— Correlation between child labor, HIV/AIDS, non-HIV infections, and malaria among children and adolescents (aged 5–14 years).

and etiological epidemiology, as well as in economics, social planning, and policy evaluation.[30] Our study is the first to analyze the health effects of child labor with cross-sectional data, showing that some health indicators are affected by child labor.

In Table 1, the independent variables account for approximately 77% of the mortality rates for children, both boys and girls, aged 10 to 14 years. This significance ($P < .001$) suggests that the model is both valid and statistically significant. Child labor, poverty, and adult mortality rates explain, at a significant level, the variance in adolescent mortality among boys and girls aged 10 to 14 years. The percentage of the population that is undernourished does not explain adolescent mortality rates for either boys or girls. For each 1 of the first 2 dependent variables (adolescent mortality rates for boys and girls aged 10 to14 years), we developed 2 regression models, one taking into account only the adult mortality rate for women and the other the combined adult mortality rate for men and women. We did this to avoid any colinearity between these 2 independent variables.

The percentage of the population living below the poverty line was designated an independent variable because of its relevance to policy decisions on education, health, decentralization of resource management, and preventive measures. As predictor variables, child labor and poverty both were significantly correlated with malnutrition (as measured by the percentage of population that was undernourished), whereas the percentage of HIV/AIDS among adults was not significantly related to malnutrition.

Mortality rates for different age groups are important indicators of health status in a country. In the absence of incidence and prevalence rates for disease (morbidity data), they serve to identify vulnerable populations. They are also among the indicators most frequently used to compare levels of socioeconomic development across countries. The finding that child labor prevalence is significantly correlated with adolescent mortality, a population's

nutrition level, and the presence of infectious disease among children suggests that countries with high child labor prevalence have low health status.

Work can limit a child's opportunities to obtain an education, especially for girls, whose educational attainment is a recognized determinant of child survival and health.[31] Work can expose children to physical and social environments conducive to high-risk sexual behavior. Because child labor is significantly correlated with infectious diseases among children, including HIV/AIDS, interventions that reduce child labor rates could have a direct health benefit.

We have identified a set of health indicators affected by child labor, and our data support the hypothesis that child labor affects children's health, particularly as measured by adolescent mortality rates. Given the nature of the available data, it is difficult to carry out a proper causality analysis. The methodological weakness of an ecological study is that estimates of effect at the ecological level cannot be extrapolated to individuals. The ecological design did not permit us to obtain direct estimates of the effect of child labor in exposed versus unexposed populations. Therefore, we could not be certain, for instance, that the children experiencing greater morbidity and mortality in a given population were actually child laborers. Other drawbacks to the ecological method are that the method relies on existing data sources, which are often flawed and may involve confounding variables for which control may be difficult.[32] Problems with the ecological approach, however, are minimized when measurement, analysis, and interpretation are all at the group level and the data sources are reliable. The ecological design lends itself to the study of structural or sociological effects on human behavior and concomitant disease or injury. The principal characteristic of the ecological design—namely, that it examines differences between groups—makes it well suited to evaluating social and health policies, such as those related to injury prevention.[33]

Although our findings indicate that child labor may be affecting the health of children, more data are needed to develop a better understanding of the short- and long-term health problems associated with child labor. Most important, longitudinal studies are required to understand the short- and long-term health effects of child labor on the individual child.

About the Authors

At the time of the study, Paola Roggero was a consultant for the University of Bocconi at the World Bank, Human Development Network, Washington, DC. Viviana Mangiaterra and Flavia Bustreo are with the World Bank, Human Development Network, Washington, DC. Furio Rosati is with the Understanding Children's Work Project, Rome, Italy.

Correspondence: Requests for reprints should be sent to Paola Roggero, Viale Gran Sasso 11, 20131, Milan, Italy (e-mail: roggero@unimi.it).

Acknowledgments

This work was supported by the Understanding Children's Work (Inter-Agency Research Cooperation Project), University of Rome, Italy.

Contributors

P. Roggero originated the study and supervised all aspects of its implementation. V. Mangiaterra assisted with the study and supervised research input. F. Bustreo contributed ideas and reviewed drafts of the article. F. Rosati synthesized analyses and interpreted findings. All authors reviewed the drafts of the article.

References

1. Parker D. Health effect on child labor. *Lancet.* 1997;350:1395–1396.
2. UNICEF guide to the convention on the rights of the Child. Available at: http://www.unicef.org/crc/crc.htm. Accessed December 28, 2006.
3. International Labour Organization. ILO Convention 138: Minimum age Convention, 1973. Available at: http://www.ilo.org/public/english/standards/ipec/publ/law/ilc/c1381973.Accessed December 28, 2006.
4. International Labour Organization.

ILO Convention 182: Worst forms of Child labor, 1999. Available at: http://www.ilo.org/public/english/standards/relm/ilc/ilc87/com-chic.htm. Accessed December 28, 2006.

5. US National Research Council. Committee on the Health and Safety Implications of Child Labor. *Protecting Youth at Work: Health, Safety, and Development of Working Children and Adolescents in the United States.* Washington, DC: National Academy Press; 1998.

6. UNICEF. *The State of the World's Children 1997.* Oxford, UK: Oxford University Press, 1997.

7. Parker D. Child labor: the impact of economic exploitation on the health and welfare of children. *Minn Med.* 1997;80:10–13, 52–55.

8. *Eliminating the Worst Forms of Child Labour. A Practical Guide to ILO Convention No. 182.* Handbook for Parliamentarians no. 3. Geneva, Switzerland: International Labor Organization and Inter-Parliamentary Union; 2002.

9. International Labor Organization. *Child Labor: Targeting the Intolerable.* Conference Report VI (1). Geneva, Switzerland: 1998.

10. Forastieri V. *Children at Work: Health and Safety Risks.* Geneva, Switzerland: International Labor Organization; 1997.

11. Kebebew Ashagrie. *Statistics on Working Children and Hazardous Child Labour in Brief.* Rev ed. Geneva, Switzerland: International Labor Organization; 1998.

12. Heady C. The effect of child labor on learning achievement. *World Dev.* 2003;31:385–398.

13. Galli R. *The Economic Impact of Child Labour.* Geneva, Switzerland: International Labor Organization; 2001.

14. Harper C, Marcus R, Moore K. Enduring poverty and the conditions of childhood: life course and inter-generational poverty transmissions.

World Dev 2003; 31:535–554.

15. Graitcer PL, Lerer LB. *Child Labor and health: quantifying the global health impacts of child labors.* Washington, DC: World Bank; 1998.

16. Graitcer PL, Lerer LB. *The Impact of Child Labor on Health: Report of a Field Investigation in Egypt.* Washington DC: World Bank; 2000.

17. Understanding children's work in Morocco. Report prepared for the Understanding Children's Work Project, a joint research initiative of the International Labor Organization, UNICEF, and the World Bank. 2003. Available at: http://www.ucw-project.org/pdf/publications/report_morocco_draft.pdf. Accessed December 28, 2006.

18. Understanding children's work in Yemen. Report prepared for the Understanding Children's Work Project, a joint research initiative of the International Labor Organization, UNICEF, and the World Bank. 2003. Available at: http://www.ucw-project.org/pdf/publications/report_yemen_draft.pdf. Accessed December 28, 2006.

19. Understanding children's work in Guatemala. Report prepared for the Understanding Children's Work Project, a joint research initiative of the International Labor Organization, UNICEF, and the World Bank. 2003. Available at: http://www.oit.org.pe/ipec/documentos/gua-national_report.pdf. Accessed January 5, 2006.

20. Susser M. The logic of the ecological: II. The logic of the design. *Am J Public Health.* 1994;84:830–835.

21. O'Donnell O, Rosati CF, Van Doorslaer E. *Child Labour and Health: Evidence and Research Issues.* Florence, Italy: Innocenti Research Centre; 2002.

22. Shah PM. The health care of working children. *Child Abuse Negl.* 1984;8:541–544.

23. Singh M, Kaura VD, Khan SA.

Working Children in Bombay—A Study. New Delhi, India: National Institute of Public Cooperation and Child Development; 1980.

24. Gross R, Landfried B, Herman S. Height and weight as a reflection of the nutritional situation of school-aged children working and living in the street of Jakarta. *Soc Sci Med.* 1996;43:453–458.

25. Ambadekar NN, Wahab SN, Zodpey SP, et al. Effect of child labor on growth of children. *Public Health.* 1999;113:303–306.

26. Hawamdeh H, Spencer N. Effect of work related variables on growth among working boys in Jordan. *J Epidemiol Community Health.* 2003;57:154–158.

27. World Bank. *World Development Indicators.* Washington, DC: World Bank; 2003.

28. Murray CJL, Lopez AD, eds. *The Global Burden of Disease: A Comprehensive Assessment of Mortality and Disability From Diseases, Injuries and Risks Factors in 1990 and Projected to 2020.* Cambridge, Mass: Harvard School of Public Health; 1996.

29. *The World Health Report: Reducing Risks, Promoting Healthy Life.* Geneva, Switzerland: World Health Organization; 2002.

30. Lopez AD, Salomon J, Ahmad O, Murray CJL. *Life Tables for 191 Countries: Data, Methods and Results.* Global Program on Evidence discussion no. 9. Geneva, Switzerland: World Health Organization; 2000.

31. Raju T. Child labor, adult illiteracy and employment rates in India. *Indian J Pediatr.* 1989;56:193–200.

32. Walter SD. The ecologic method in the study of environmental health. I. Overview of the method. *Environ Health Perspect* 1991;94:61–5.

33. Rothman KJ. Methodologic frontiers in environmental epidemiology. *Environ Health Perspect Suppl.* 1993;101(suppl 4):19–21.

Equitable Child Health Interventions: The Impact of Improved Water and Sanitation on Inequalities in Child Mortality in Stockholm, 1878 to 1925

| Bo Burström, MD, PhD, Gloria Macassa, MD, Lisa Öberg, PhD, Eva Bernhardt, PhD and Lars Smedman, MD, PhD

ABSTRACT

Today, many of the 10 million childhood deaths each year are caused by diseases of poverty—diarrhea and pneumonia, for example, which were previously major causes of childhood death in many European countries. Specific analyses of the historical decline of child mortality may shed light on the potential equity impact of interventions to reduce child mortality.

In our study of the impact of improved water and sanitation in Stockholm from 1878 to 1925, we examined the decline in overall and diarrhea mortality among children, both in general and by socioeconomic group. We report a decline in overall mortality and of diarrhea mortality and a leveling out of socioeconomic differences in child mortality due to diarrheal diseases, but not of overall mortality. The contribution of general and targeted policies is discussed.

INTRODUCTION

In a recent series of papers on child survival in the Lancet,[1–4] neonatal causes, diarrhea, and pneumonia were quoted as major causes of the 10 million childhood deaths that occur each year.[1] In spite of evidence that interventions reduce mortality, the coverage of such interventions is still too low,[2] and the delivery of services is not sufficient.[3] In addition, poor children are disadvantaged in terms of exposure to and resistance to disease, coverage levels for preventive interventions, and use of health care when they are sick.[4] A major issue for many governments is how to reduce mortality and ensure that interventions to reduce mortality also reach poor children.

Diseases such as diarrhea and pneumonia are diseases of poverty,[1] and they were major causes of childhood death in many European countries a century ago. Specific analyses of the historical decline of child mortality in these countries may shed light on the potential overall and equity impact of certain interventions to reduce child mortality, such as improvement of water and sanitation. The historical time period and cause-specific patterns of child mortality may also be informative. Previous studies of infant mortality in Stockholm from 1878 to 1925[5] showed a transition over time in the age structure and cause-specific composition of mortality analogous to the country typology described[1]; diarrhea and pneumonia initially were the main causes, and as they declined, neonatal causes subsequently increased in relative importance. Infant (< 1 year) mortality rates exceeded 200 per 1000 in Stockholm until 1900 and declined to 50 per 1000 by 1925. Most of the decline, which occurred in the postnatal (1–11 month) period, was driven by a decline in diarrhea mortality. Other important causes of death included congenital conditions; tuberculosis; meningitis; undernutrition; and other diseases associated with poverty, crowding, and adverse living conditions, which were a reality for the majority of the rapidly growing urban population in Stockholm.[5]

There were probably many causes of the decline in diarrhea mortality;

improvements in the provision of water and sanitation, changes in hygienic perception and behavior, and general socioeconomic improvements, including improved nutritional status, are all thought to have been contributing factors.[6] Obviously, the mortality decline occurred in the absence of other specific interventions such as immunization and effective curative interventions.

Against this background, we analyze the impact of improvements of water and sanitation in Stockholm from 1878 to 1925 on overall mortality and diarrhea mortality, both in general and by socioeconomic group.

DECLINE IN CHILD AND INFANT MORTALITY IN STOCKHOLM

Background

The historical decline of infant and child mortality in European countries previously has been studied extensively.[7,8] Other Swedish studies have addressed the issue, as well as the importance of health reform to the decline.[9–13] However, few studies have investigated the mortality decline in Stockholm.[14,15] In a recent study of health reforms in Swedish towns from 1875 to 1910, Edvinsson and Rogers studied the correlation between investments in the health care sector, sanitation, and water and changes in infant mortality.[16] They found a correlation between infant mortality and investments in health care (the creation of epidemic wards in hospitals), but not investments in water and sanitation.[16]

The McKeown thesis[17] states that improved nutrition and a general rise in the standard of living were the main explanations of the historical decline of child mortality in Europe. While this thesis was once generally accepted, it has now been questioned. Szreter argued that although an improved standard of living was important, organized public health and sanitary reform, including specific interventions such as improved water and sanitation, were crucial for the improvement of health.[18,19] Nathanson,[20] building on Szreter's work, further proposed that the implementation of health and sanitary reforms depends on the type of governance and is facilitated in highly centralized states.

Water Supply

Before 1860, the population of Stockholm got its water from wells and from surface water. Piped water was introduced to improve hygiene, reduce the risk of epidemics, enhance industrial access to water, and provide water for fire fighting. The first part of the water works opened in 1861. A total of 120 water posts providing water free of charge were installed across the city, and water pipes were extended to all inhabited parts of the city. Piped water became available indoors and in courtyards, streets, and squares.[21] An investigation of the housing conditions of the working classes in 1896 showed that almost half of all apartments inhabited by workers in the area studied had piped water in the apartment building, and more than one third had a tap in the courtyard; 14% of the apartments had no access to piped water on the premises.[22]

Disposal of Excreta

Following the last cholera epidemic in Stockholm in 1853, which left 3000 dead, public opinion for improved sanitation resulted in the establishment of a new sanitation office, which was charged with managing excreta disposal efficiently and cleaning streets and yards belonging to the city. A new sanitation ordinance was established in 1874.[12] Sanitation routines were reviewed to increase the effectiveness and efficiency in the work. In the first

half of the 19th century, excreta had been emptied into cesspools in the city. The last cesspool was closed in 1894. Increasingly, excreta was transported away from the city to central latrine terminals, from which some of it was sold as manure to farmers. Further legislation in 1892 regulated latrine vessels and their cleaning. New and uniform latrine vessels were introduced that could more easily be transported and cleaned. The collection and transport of the vessels was also made more efficient. Through changes made in the 30 years leading up to the early 1890s, excreta disposal in Stockholm was developed from an almost medieval system to a hygienic standard acceptable for the 20th century.[23]

In 1880, there were about 30 000 outdoor privies and the same number of indoor privies. The number of indoor privies increased to nearly 100 000 by the turn of the century. The number of collected vessels increased from about 120 000 in 1870 to a peak of almost 700 000 vessels in the period 1900 to 1910. Over the same period, the population of Stockholm nearly tripled, from 135 000 in 1870 to 340 000 in 1910. Sharing communal privies became less common. At the end of the 19th century, 3 of every 4 families had a privy at their private disposal, and only 3% shared facilities with more than 1 other family.[22] From 1910 onward, the number of water closets increased, while the number of outdoor and indoor privies successively decreased.[23]

Sewerage System

In the 1850s, wastewater was discharged into open ditches, some covered with planks or stones. The sewerage system was not developed in coordination with the piped water system, but some 10 to 20 years later. By the end of the 19th century, the central parts of the city had sewerage, still mainly for wastewater only. In 1895, there were only 40 premises in the city with water closets. By 1904, this number had increased to 1506, and in 1909 the city decided to grant permission to connect water closets to the

municipal sewerage system. In 1909, a second sewerage plan was launched, and a first wastewater treatment plant was constructed.[23]

Other Improvements

Economic development improved from the end of the 1890s onward, with recessions in 1906/07 and during World War I. The 1880s had been "the dark, desperate, impossible decade,"[24(p38)] with widespread malnutrition among the working class. In the 1890s, people had better opportunities for improved nutrition—not only because there was more money for food, but also because women could stay home to cook. At the turn of the century, prices increased, and a recession followed in 1906/07. In spite of temporary economic setbacks (particularly during World War I), living conditions improved, and class inequalities were reduced, primarily owing to improvements in the economic position of the working class.[24]

From the 1890s, the principles for governing the city changed from being purely economic to including concern for the health of the population.[25] A "sanitary police" department was instituted as part of the new emphasis on improvements in environmental hygiene. This authority was charged with inspecting food and milk and checking adherence to a local ordinance mandating the cleanliness and tidiness of outdoor premises. The department made 50 000 to 100 000 inspection visits a year. A voluntary organization modeled on the Sanitary Institute of Great Britain (the Public Health Association) was formed in 1881, bringing together physicians, lawyers, scientists, and engineers with representatives of charitable organizations. It became an influential body that pressed local policy-makers to make improvements conducive to health. In the early 20th century, local organizations inspired by philanthropic baby care in other European countries were also formed. They emphasized the promotion of breast-feeding and the distribution of controlled milk to infants and children when breastfeeding was not possible.[26]

DATA AND METHODS

We obtained information concerning the provision of piped water from historical records of the Stockholm city water works. The child mortality analysis is based on individual entries from computerized records originally collected for civil registration purposes in Stockholm for the years 1878 to 1925 (the Roteman Archives). These records include the child's sex and date of birth; the date of the child's entering the parish and moving out of the parish or death; and the child's age when these events occurred. Individuals are identified by their name and date of birth. Members of the same household are kept together through a special file number given to the household in the original register.

From this information, we used individual data on date of birth, date of moving into and out of the parish, the occupational title of the head of the household, and the date of death. These data were linked to computerized death certificates with information on the cause of death, through the date of birth and another identity number. The death certificates were filled out by physicians and include the name, date of birth, date of death, and primary and secondary cause of death. The data cover the period from 1878 to 1925, a very dynamic time in the history of Stockholm. Information for all residents of Södermalm (an island in central Stockholm) during this period has been computerized. The data set includes all children aged birth to 9 years who resided for some period of time in Södermalm—in all, 88 157 children before 1900 and 102 814 children from 1901 to 1925 (a total of 724 253 person-years of follow-up and 16 574 deaths among the children aged birth to 9 years). The population of Södermalm, which was predominantly working class, increased from about 50 000 in the 1870s to 120 000 in the 1920s. In a contemporary investigation, the 2 parishes of Maria and Katarina on Södermalm had higher rates of infant and child mortality than most other parishes in Stockholm.[14]

This study focuses on deaths due to diarrhea. Since 94% of the children who died from diarrhea were aged younger than 2 years, we restricted the study to this age group. The study included children aged younger than 2 years residing for some period of time in Maria and Katarina parishes during the study period (1878–1925). The outcome measure was death among children, measured as the incidence rate of death. Age- and cause-specific mortality rates were calculated for each year of study, and data were pooled into periods of years (1878–1883, 1884–1889, 1890–1895, 1896–1900, 1901–1908, 1909–1917, 1918–1925). Children could enter the follow-up by living in the parish from the start or by being born in or moving into the parish during the follow-up period. Each child was followed for a maximum of 365 days per year or until the day of death or moving out of the parish.

Classification of Cause of Death

From 1860 onward, deaths of residents in Stockholm were certified by doctors. As indicated on the death certificate, the death of 1 child may have more than one cause and may thus be counted under more than 1 cause of death. However, the overall death rates were not affected by this classification— a child's death was counted only once. Death due to diarrhea was defined as a death caused by cholera, colitis, diarrhea, gastritis, gastroenteritis, enteritis, intestinal inflammation, or typhoid fever. By this classification, diarrhea was 1 of the main causes of death. Out of the total 16 574 deaths, 3799 (22.9%) were due to diarrhea. Among children younger than 2 years, the proportion of deaths due to diarrhea was 30.2% (3569 out of a total 11 816).

Classification by Socioeconomic Group

The occupational title of the head of household from the original data (translated into a Historical International Classification of Occupations [HISCO] code for the particular title)[27] was used for a subsequent classification into socioeconomic group, based on the Erikson Goldthorpe system of classifica-

tion.[28] The 11 Erikson Goldthorpe categories were subsequently merged into 5 socioeconomic groups: group 1—higher and intermediate nonmanual group (5.9% of the sample); group 2—lower nonmanual group (9.1%); group 3—skilled manual workers (23.3%); group 4—unskilled manual workers (33.2%); group 5—persons lacking a HISCO code or not working (28.5%). This last group largely consisted of households headed by women who had no profession (68%); 49% of children in these households were born out of wedlock. The same coding of socioeconomic group was applied for the entire study period.

Analysis

The overall mortality rates and diarrhea mortality rates, calculated by year, are presented as incidence rates per 1000 person- years. Subsequently, overall mortality rates and diarrhea mortality rates were calculated by socioeconomic group and time period, with the individual years aggregated into 7 time periods. Finally, Cox regression analysis was used to obtain the hazard of death (referred to as relative risk of death) by socioeconomic group in relation to the hazard of death of children in socioeconomic group 1. Analyses were done with SAS software, version 8.1 (SAS Institute Inc, Cary, NC).

RESULTS

The overall mortality rate declined from an average of 130 per 1000 in the period 1878 to 1882 to 31 per 1000 in 1918 to 1925, while the diarrhea mortality rate declined from 59 per 1000 to 2 per 1000 over the same time (Figure 1). Figure 2 shows the cumulative expansion of new water pipes and the daily average water consumption per capita in relation to the annual diarrhea mortality rate from 1878 to 1925. By 1900, more than half of all new pipes were in place, and nearly all of the 7000 water pipe connections installed from 1875 to 1920 were completed by 1915. Average daily water consumption increased from about 40 L per person in the beginning of the period to about 80 L per person by 1900; it declined to about 60 L per person in 1920. The decline in water consumption after the turn of the century was partly due to the introduction of water meters that determined cost at the point of consumption and to thrift campaigns during World War I.[29]

The decline of diarrhea mortality rates and the relative risk of mortality by socioeconomic group and time period are shown in Figures 3 and 4 and in Table 1. In the first period, 1878 to 1882, the diarrhea mortality rate for children in socioeconomic group 4 was about 50% higher than the rate for children in group 1. The diarrhea mortality rate among children in group 5 (whose parents either were not working or lacked an HISCO code) was more than twice that of children in group 1. Although the absolute mortality rates declined and the rate differences varied over time, this pattern continued until the 2 last periods (1909–1917 and 1918–1925), when there was no longer an evident stepwise socioeconomic pattern in diarrhea mortality. In the period 1909 to 1918, the diarrhea mortality rates of children in socioeconomic groups 2, 3, and 4 were similar to the rate for children in group 1. The rate was still higher in group 5 than in group 1 in the period 1909 to 1918, but from 1918 to 1925, there were no significant socioeconomic differences in diarrhea mortality.

The socioeconomic differences in overall mortality rates and relative risk of mortality over time, shown in Figure 4 and Table 1, are similar to the pattern of diarrhea mortality in the earlier time periods. However, unlike the pattern in diarrhea mortality, the stepwise socioeconomic gradient in overall mortality rates by socioeconomic group remained throughout the study period, and the differences were statistically significant from 1918 to 1925.

DISCUSSION

There was a remarkable decline in overall child mortality, and particularly diarrhea mortality, in Stockholm from 1878 to 1925. The decline in diarrhea

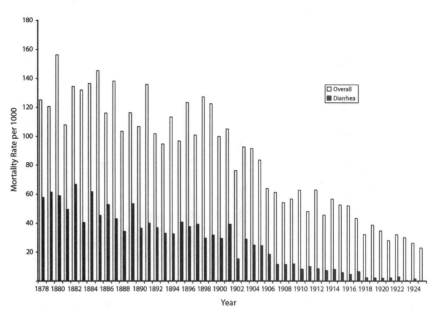

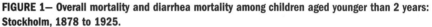

FIGURE 1— Overall mortality and diarrhea mortality among children aged younger than 2 years: Stockholm, 1878 to 1925.

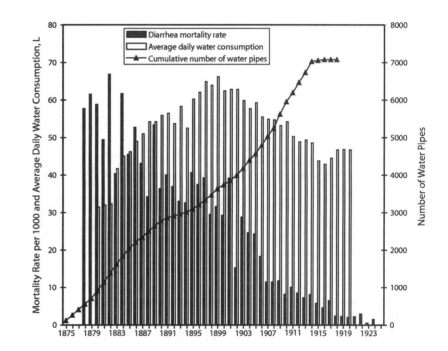

FIGURE 2— Diarrhea mortality rate in relation to daily average water consumption per person and cumulative number of new water pipe connections, Stockholm, 1878 to 1925.

mortality was initially more rapid in the highest socioeconomic group than in the lower socioeconomic groups, causing increased social differentials. However, there was soon considerable improvement among children in the other socioeconomic groups, not least in the periods 1890 to 1895 and 1909 to 1917. In the last period, there was no significant difference by socioe-

conomic group in the risk of dying from diarrhea. Diarrhea mortality was virtually eliminated by 1925, after having been one of the major causes of infant and childhood death before the turn of the century. The fact that death from diarrhea mainly affected infants suggests that breastfeeding was not generally practiced during the first months of life. The average age of

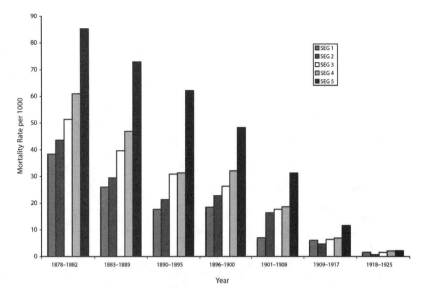

FIGURE 3— Diarrhea mortality rates among children aged younger than 2 years, by socioeconomic group (SEG), Stockholm, 1878 to 1925.

Note. Groups are numbered in order of descending socioeconomic status.

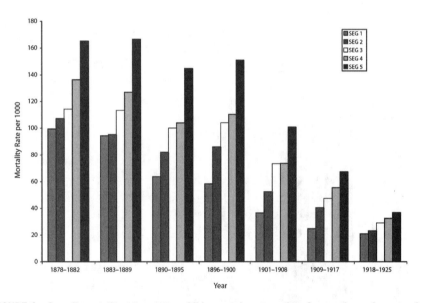

FIGURE 4— Overall mortality rates among children aged younger than 2 years, by socioeconomic group (SEG), Stockholm, 1878 to 1925.

Note. Groups are numbered in order of descending socioeconomic status.

death from diarrhea was 6 months before 1900 and 5.4 months after 1900. Children born out of wedlock died slightly younger than those born within wedlock. Unfortunately, data on the prevalence of breast-feeding in Stockholm are very scarce, but a survey of the whole of Sweden in the 1870s stated that there was "partial breast-feeding" in Stockholm,[30] and the intensive campaigns by doctors against bottle feeding support that statement.[29]

It may be difficult to disentangle the precise role of the different factors that brought about the decline in diarrhea mortality around the turn of the century or what caused the equalization of mortality risks. However, the decline of diarrhea mortality in Stockholm illustrates some features of the relationship between improvements in water and sanitation and the decline of diarrhea. Large interventions involving expansion of access to water and concurrent improvements in

sanitation, such as described in Stockholm, have been found to have greater impact than more limited interventions. Few studies have analyzed the impact of water and sanitation on diarrhea mortality, although the impact on severe diarrhea and mortality is hypothesized to precede the impact on morbidity.[31] In Stockholm, the decline of diarrhea mortality was quite rapid, but we have no records of the diarrhea morbidity rates. However, some studies suggest that sanitation is more important than water.[31,32]

Another factor likely to have had great importance to the decline of diarrhea mortality in Stockholm was the strong local political commitment to improvements in the sanitary environment, public education, and the enforcement of sanitary laws and regulations. Technical improvements in water and sanitation may not be sufficient unless accompanied by changes in health behavior. In Stockholm, several beneficial developments took place simultaneously that seem to have acted synergistically in reducing diarrhea mortality. The enforcement of the local sanitary ordinance appears to have been extensive and forceful, and the universal application of interventions regarding improved water supply and improved sanitary environment seems to have benefited the lower social classes as much as, or more than, the higher social classes.

Regarding recent debates on the health effects of different sanitation interventions in non-industrialized countries,[33,34] it is evident that in Stockholm most of the diarrhea mortality decline occurred before the expansion of water closets. Hence, water closets do not appear to be indispensable in reducing diarrhea mortality.

From the early 1890s, young children became a target for city health policies. A socioeconomic gradient prevailed throughout the study period for overall mortality rates, while it diminished in the last 2 time periods for diarrhea mortality rates. This fact suggests that improvements in water and sanitation and related interventions conducive to the decline of diarrhea

TABLE 1— Relative Risk of Diarrhea Mortality and Overall Mortality Among Children Younger than 2 Years, by Socioeconomic Group: Stockholm, 1878 to 1925

Socioeconomic Group[a]	1878–1882, RR (95% CI)	1883–1889, RR (95% CI)	1890–1895, RR (95% CI)	1896–1900, RR (95% CI)	1901–1908, RR (95% CI)	1909–1917, RR (95% CI)	1918–1925, RR (95% CI
Diarrhea mortality							
1	1.0	1.0	1.0	1.0	1.0	1.0	1.0
2	1.1 (0.7, 1.8)	1.1 (0.7, 1.8)	1.2 (0.6, 2.3)	1.2 (0.6, 2.4)	2.3 (1.1, 4.9)	0.8 (0.4, 1.6)	0.4 (0.1, 2.7)
3	1.3 (0.9, 2.0)	1.5 (1.0, 2.3)	1.7 (1.0, 3.0)	1.4 (0.8, 2.5)	2.5 (1.3, 5.0)	1.1 (0.6, 2.0)	1.0 (0.2, 4.2)
4	1.6 (1.1, 2.3)	1.8 (1.2, 2.7)	1.8 (1.0, 3.0)	1.7 (1.0, 3.0)	2.7 (1.4, 5.2)	1.1 (0.6, 2.1)	1.3 (0.4, 4.9)
5	2.2 (1.5, 3.2)	2.8 (1.9, 4.1)	3.5 (2.1, 5.8)	2.6 (1.5, 4.5)	4.4 (2.2, 8.5)	1.9 (1.0, 3.4)	1.3 (0.4, 4.5)
Overall mortality							
1	1.0	1.0	1.0	1.0	1.0	1.0	1.0
2	1.1 (0.8, 1.4)	1.0 (0.8, 1.3)	1.3 (0.9, 1.8)	1.5 (1.0, 2.1)	1.4 (1.0, 2.0)	1.7 (1.2, 2.3)	1.1 (0.8, 1.6)
3	1.1 (0.9, 1.5)	1.2 (1.0, 1.5)	1.6 (1.2, 2.1)	1.8 (1.3, 2.4)	2.0 (1.5, 2.7)	1.9 (1.4, 2.6)	1.4 (1.0, 2.0)
4	1.4 (1.1, 1.7)	1.3 (1.1, 1.6)	1.6 (1.2, 2.1)	1.9 (1.4, 2.6)	2.0 (1.5, 2.7)	2.3 (1.7, 3.0)	1.6 (1.1, 2.2)
5	1.6 (1.3, 2.1)	1.7 (1.4, 2.1)	2.2 (1.7, 2.9)	5 (1.8, 3.4)	2.7 (2.0, 3.6)	2.6 (2.0, 3.5)	1.7 (1.2, 2.3)

Note: RR=relative risk; CI=confidence interval.
[a]Numbered in order of descending socioeconomic status.

mortality that were implemented concurrently resulted in an equalization of the mortality risk from diarrhea but not in the risk of death from other causes. These interventions included higher standards of cleanliness of public areas, improved handling of excreta, intensified health inspection, milk inspection, better food handling, improved child feeding practices, and health education to improve hygienic practices. Furthermore, most of these improvements and interventions were implemented universally and not in a targeted way. Some specific reforms, however, were designed to support single mothers of illegitimate children and to foster families.[29]

Conversely, the equalization of mortality risks suggests that the lower socioeconomic groups benefited to a greater extent from the universal interventions than did the higher socioeconomic groups. Higher socioeconomic groups, however, are likely to have gained access to piped water earlier than lower socioeconomic groups, since water pipe connections had to be paid for by the proprietor. As others have shown previously, the decline of mortality is often accompanied by an increase in relative mortality differentials.[35,36] However, over time, these

differentials diminished in Stockholm. Our findings regarding diarrhea mortality are similar to those of Troesken,[37] who studied the impact of improved water and sanitation on survival rates in African American households in certain US cities in the first half of the 20th century. Where interventions to improve water and sanitation were implemented in mixed household neighborhoods, African Americans benefited disproportionately from such improvements; as a result, racial mortality differentials diminished considerably.[37]

What knowledge can be gained from analyses of the diarrhea mortality decline in Stockholm that can be of use for countries with high levels of diarrhea mortality today? First, the explanation of the McKeown thesis for the decline of mortality[17] can be questioned regarding diarrhea. It seems evident that economic development per se does not bring about a reduction in diarrhea mortality. Economic improvement may contribute to mortality decline, but it needs to be translated into specific interventions that affect risk factors or causes of mortality. In that regard, our findings are more in line with those of Szreter, highlighting the importance of specific

public health interventions (e.g., improved water and sanitation) rather than just economic improvement.[18,19]

Furthermore, our results support the hypotheses of Nathanson,[20] who stated that public health policies play a critical role in disease prevention and that the implementation of such policies is facilitated in strong, centralized states. Sweden was a precise example of a strong, centralized state that made the implementation possible. The enforcement and everyday implementation of practical public health policies, such as the removal of fecal matter and garbage, may be one key to reducing exposure to infectious agents from the fecally contaminated environment. The implementation of such policies needs to be guided by appropriate local research. Again, one reason for the decline in diarrhea mortality in Stockholm was probably the wide coverage of both water and sanitation interventions for all segments of the population. Therefore, in countries with high mortality, public health interventions need to be well organized and extensive if they are to have a substantial impact.

Second, in spite of the powerful interventions and action that took place, the decline of diarrhea mortality in Stockholm took quite some time. This demonstrates the need for patience when evaluating large-scale intervention projects in poor countries today. It may also be difficult to link the effect of 1 specific action to reduced morbidity and mortality rates, since these are the product of many different causes.

Third, interventions to reduce inequalities in child mortality ideally should help lower socioeconomic groups more than, or at least as much as, higher socioeconomic groups. This may be obvious, but it seldom happens in poor countries today. Since higher social classes have lower mortality, improvements in the average level of health in a country depend on wide coverage of interventions that have an impact among the lower social classes—for instance, wide coverage of improved water and sanitation and removal of environmental contamination. In our example from Stockholm at the turn of the 20th century, a general approach combined to some extent with targeted interventions for high-risk groups succeeded in benefiting lower socioeconomic groups as much as, or more than, higher socioeconomic groups, albeit with a time lag. In addition, as the example in our study suggests, improved access to piped water may be more effective if implemented in a comprehensive setting as part of a broader package of improved sanitation and handling of excreta, increased awareness of personal hygiene and food handling, and general socioeconomic development. We believe that further analysis of socioeconomic patterns in specific aspects of the historical decline of child mortality may contribute to knowledge on interventions and policies to improve equity in child survival.

About the Authors

Bo Burström and Gloria Macassa are with the the Centre of Health Equity Studies, Stockholm University/Karolinska Institutet, and the Department of Public Health Sciences, Division of Social Medicine, Karolinska Institutet, Stockholm, Sweden. Lisa Öberg is with the Centre of Health Equity Studies, Stockholm University/Karolinska Institutet and the Department of History, Södertörn University College, Huddinge, Sweden. Eva Bernhardt is with the Centre of Health Equity Studies, Stockholm University/Karolinska Institutet and the Department of Sociology, Stockholm University. Lars Smedman is with the Centre of Health Equity Studies, Stockholm University/Karolinska Institutet and the Department of Woman and Child Health, Karolinska Institutet.

Correspondence: Requests for reprints should be sent to Bo Burström, MD, PhD, Department of Public Health Sciences, Division of Social Medicine, Karolinska Institutet, SE-171 76 Stockholm, Sweden (e-mail: bo.burstrom@phs.ki.se).

Acknowledgments

This study was partly financed by the Swedish Council for Working Life and Social Research (grant 2001-2448).

Contributors

B. Burström and G. Macassa developed the study and performed the quantitative analyses. B. Burström wrote the article. L. Öberg provided the qualitative analyses and background information. E. Bernhardt and L. Smedman provided further interpretation of the results of the study. All authors assisted in revising the article and contributed to formulating the study objectives.

References

1. Black RE, Morris SS, Bryce J. Where and why are 10 million children dying every year? *Lancet.* 2003;361: 2226-2234.
2. Jones G, Steketee RW, Black RE, Bhutta ZA, Morris SS, Bellagio Child Survival Study Group. How many child deaths can we prevent this year? *Lancet.* 2003;362:65-71.
3. Bryce J, el Arifeen S, Pariyo G, Lanata CF, Gwatkin D, Haicht JP, Multi-Country Evaluation of IMCI Study Group. Reducing child mortality: can public health deliver? *Lancet.* 2003; 362:159-164.
4. Victora CG, Wagstaff A, Armstrong Schellenberg J, Gwatkin D, Claeson M, Habicht JP. Applying an equity lens to child health and mortality: more of the same is not enough. *Lancet.* 2003;362: 233-241.
5. Burström B, Bernhardt E. The changing cause of death pattern among infants, Stockholm 1878-1925. *Scand Popul Stud.* 2002;13:53-64.
6. van Poppel F, van der Heijden C. The effects of water supply on infant and child mortality: a review of historical evidence. *Health Transit Rev.* 1997;7:113-148.
7. Woods RI, Watterson PA, Woodward JH. The causes of rapid infant mortality decline in England and Wales, 1861-1921, Part I. *Popul Stud (Camb).* 1988;42:343-366.
8. Schofield R, Reher D, Bideau A, eds. *The Decline of Mortality in Europe.* Oxford, England: Clarendon Press; 1991.
9. Castensson R, Lövgren M, Sundin J. Urban water supply and improvement of health conditions. In: Brändström A, Tedebrand LG, eds. *Society, Health and Population During the Demographic Transition.* Umeå, Sweden: Umeå University; 1988:273-298.
10. Edvinsson S. *The Unhealthy Town: Social Inequalities Regarding Mortality in 19th Century Sundsvall* [thesis; in Swedish with English summary]. Umeå: Umeå University, Dept of History; 1992.
11. Sundin J. Culture, class and infant mortality during the Swedish mortality transition, 1750-1850. *Soc Sci Hist.* 1995;19:117-145.
12. Nelson MC, Rogers J. Cleaning up the cities: application of the first comprehensive public health law in Sweden. *Scand J Hist.* 1994;19:17-40.
13. Nilsson H. *Mot bättre hälsa. Dödlighet och hälsoarbete i Linköping 1860-94 [Towards Better Health. Mortality and Health Work in Linköping 1860-94*; thesis, with English summary]. Linköping, Sweden: Institutionen för Tema; 1994.
14. Linroth K. *Dödsorsakerna och dödligheten i Stockholm 1871-90 [Causes of Death and Mortality in Stockholm 1871-90].* Stockholm, Sweden: Beckmans; 1892
15. Nelson MC, Rogers J. Stockholm and Gothenburg and the urban mortality puzzle. In: Lundh C, ed. *Demography, Economy and Welfare.* Lund, Sweden: Lund University Press; 1995: 292-309.
16. Edvinsson S, Rogers J. Hälsa och hälsoreformer i svenska städer kring

sekelskiftet 1900 [Health reforms in Swedish towns 1875–1910; in Swedish, with English summary]. *Historisk Tidskrift.* 2001;4:541–564.

17. McKeown T. *The Modern Rise of Population.* London, England: Edward Arnold; 1976.

18. Szreter S. The importance of social intervention in Britain's mortality decline c. 1850–1914: a re-interpretation of the role of public health. *Soc Hist Med.* 1988;1:1–37.

19. Szreter S. Rethinking McKeown: the relationship between public health and social change. *Am J Public Health.* 2002;92:722–724.

20. Nathanson C. Disease prevention as social change: toward a theory of public health. *Popul Dev Rev.* 1996;22: 609–637.

21. Cronström A. *Vattenförsörjning och avlopp [Water and Sewerage].* Stockholm, Sweden: Stockholms stad; 1986.

22. Beredningsutskottets utlåtanden och memorial för år 1897. Bihang Nr 40. *Af stadsfullmäktige beslutad undersökning af arbetarnes bostadsförhållanden I Stockholm [City council survey of the housing conditions of workers in Stockholm].* Stockholm, Sweden: Stockholm City Council; 1897.

23. Dufwa A, Pehrson M. *Avfallshantering och återvinning [Waste Disposal and Recycling].* Stockholm, Sweden: Stockholms stad; 1989.

24. Hirdman Y. Magfrågan. *Mat som mål och medel 1870–1920 [The Issue of the Stomach. Food as a Means and as an End 1870–1920].* Kristianstad, Sweden: Rabén & Sjögren; 1983.

25. Sheiban H. *Den ekonomiska staden: stadsplanering i Stockholm under senare hälften av 1800-talet [The Economic City. City Planning in Stockholm During the Latter Half of the 19th Century].* Lund, Sweden: Arkiv; 2002.

26. Weiner G. *De räddade barnen: om fattiga barn, mödrar och fäder och deras möte med Filantropin i Hagalund 1900–1940 [The Saved Children: Poor Children, Mothers, Fathers and Their Encounter With Philanthropy in Hagalund 1900–1940].* Stockholm, Sweden: Hjelms förlag; 1995.

27. van Leeuwen MHD, Maas I, Miles A. *Historical International Classification of Occupations (HISCO).* Leuven, Belgium: Leuven University Press; 2002.

28. Erikson R, Goldthorpe J. *The Constant Flux: A Study of Class Mobility in Industrial Societies.* Oxford: Clarendon Press; 1992:29–64.

29. Öberg L. The city of Stockholm vs children's untimely death. Medico-political child health promotion in Stockholm 1878 to 1925, with special reference to the reduction of digestional diseases. Paper presented at: Social Science History Conference; March 2004; Berlin, Germany.

30. Brändström A, Edvinsson S. From the past to the present: dramatic improvements in public health. In: Lindberg G, Rosen M, eds. *National Atlas of Sweden. Public Health and Health care.* Uppsala, Sweden: National Land Survey and National Board of Health and Welfare; 2000:22–43.

31. Esrey SA, Feachem RG, Hughes JM. Interventions for the control of diarrhoeal diseases among young children: improving water supply and excreta disposal facilities. *Bull World Health Organ.* 1985;63:757–772.

32. Esrey SA, Habicht JP. Epidemiologic evidence for health benefits from improved water and sanitation in developing countries. *Epidemiol Rev.* 1986;8: 117–127.

33. Esrey SA. Water, waste and wellbeing: a multicountry study. *Am J Epidemiol.* 1996;143:608–623.

34. Cairncross S, Kolsky PJ. Re: "Water, waste and wellbeing: a multicountry study" [letter]. *Am J Epidemiol.* 1997; 146:359–360.

35. Antonovsky A, Bernstein J. Social class and infant mortality. *Soc Sci Med.* 1977;11:453–470.

36. Woods R, Williams N. Must the gap widen before it can be narrowed? Long-term trends in social class mortality differentials. *Continuity and Change.* 1995; 10:105–137.

37. Troesken W. *Water, Race and Disease.* Cambridge, Mass: MIT Press; 2004.

Tracking Gender-Based Human Rights Violations in Postwar Kosovo

| Sapna Desai, MS and Melissa J. Perry, ScD, MHS

ABSTRACT

Four years have passed since the institution of the cease-fire in Yugoslavia, and questions remain as to how Kosovar women are faring in the country's postwar reconstruction. Reports, albeit fragmented, suggest that violence against women began to increase in 1998 and 1999. This trend continued through 2001, even while rates of other major crimes decreased.

Despite considerable local efforts to address the conditions of women, there remains a lack of systematic data documenting the scope and frequency of violent acts committed against women. A centralized surveillance system focused on tracking human rights abuses needs to be established to address this critical need for empirically based reports and to ultimately guide reform efforts.

INTRODUCTION

In 1999, the North American Treaty Organization's bombing campaign in the Federal Republic of Yugoslavia brought Kosovo, a previously little known province, to world center stage. Amid reports of more than 800 000 refugees and more than 12 000 fatalities caused by the conflict, the international community learned of the plight of Kosovar women in particular.[1] While the bombing has stopped and the province is now working toward self-governance, questions have emerged in regard to how Kosovar women have recovered since the cease-fire 4 years ago and how they are faring in postwar reconstruction.

In the postconflict environment of continued interethnic tension and unstable economic conditions, women have emerged as particularly vulnerable to violence and other human rights violations. According to both women's rights organizations and an assessment conducted by the United Nations Development Fund for Women (UNIFEM), violence against women has increased since the end of the conflict. Furthermore, local police reports confirm that violence against women is on the rise and is at least as common as violence stemming from interethnic and political tensions.[2] Yet, international and local human rights data do not typically capture this trend.[3] Although political violence is methodically monitored, only anecdotal data are available to describe gender-based human rights violations. Despite considerable local efforts to address the issue, there remains a critical lack of systematic data documenting the scope and frequency of violent acts committed against women.

These systematic data are vital; from institution-building activities to training of health professionals, their absence may result in violence against women not being addressed in strategies and programming. Eliminating violence against women is critical to the growth of any society, whether it is rebuilding after conflict or at the height of development. However, in the absence of proper resource allocation or commitment, political declarations offer little potential for change.

The United Nations Interim Mission in Kosovo, more commonly known as UNMIK, functions as the main governing body in the region, with a joint interim administrative structure designed to incorporate local Kosovars into the transitional government.[4] In 2000, UNMIK established a policy advisory body, the Office of Gender Affairs (OGA), to address the needs of women. The OGA has declared violence against women as a key priority of its work.[5] As UNMIK builds efforts in this area, establishing sustainable, methodical data systems to track prevalence rates of gender-based violence emerges as a major challenge. It is in this context, as the postwar situation in Kosovo demonstrates, that public health and human rights professionals can develop concrete methods to monitor gender-based human rights violations and, ultimately, ensure that reform efforts are evidence based. Moreover, violence against women is a global phenomenon; the Kosovar experience can guide reconstruction efforts around the world.

VIOLENCE AGAINST WOMEN

The United Nations Declaration on the Elimination of Violence Against Women defines violence against women as "any act of gender-based violence that results in, or is likely to result in, physical, sexual or psychological harm or suffering to women."[6] A manifestation of gender inequality, gender-based violence encompasses a broad spectrum of acts, ranging from intimate partner abuse to trafficking of women with the intention of forced prostitution, directed at women solely because of their gender.[7] Violence against women is a pervasive public health problem, yet it is among the least recognized human rights violations. Largely as a result of lobbying efforts on the part of women's advocacy groups, eliminating gender-based violence has steadily emerged as a critical item on research, policy, and intervention agendas.

There are data, albeit piecemeal, suggesting that violence against women in Kosovo needs further attention. In UNIFEM's 2000 assessment of violence against the country's women, *No Safe Place*, the first study of its kind conducted by an international organization in the region, researchers surveyed women representative of the demographic diversity in Kosovo, and results were adjusted for the population at risk.[8] The study revealed that almost 1 in 4 women (23%) reported experiencing domestic violence. Notably, 44% of women reported their first exposure to violence as occurring in 1998 or 1999, suggesting a temporal connection to the escalating conflict in Kosovo in 1998. In attempting to provide an understanding of the situation, UNIFEM consultant Rachel Wareham pointed out that in postwar periods, when societal structures are weakened and traditional systems altered—and women move into roles previously unoccupied—societies are likely to witness an increase in violence against women.[8]

In addition to domestic violence, Kosovar women may be experiencing increased levels of sexual assault: UNMIK police reports indicate that while serious crimes such as murder, abduction, and arson decreased during 2000 and 2001, sexual assault was the only major violation to exhibit an increase, from 115 to 133 reported cases.[3] Fear of stigmatization, compounded by a lack of support services, has been reported[8] as a major obstacle to disclosure; accordingly, these estimates probably underrepresent actual prevalence rates of sexual assault.

There is also considerable anecdotal evidence that trafficking in women for the purposes of forced prostitution is on the rise in Kosovo. Societal factors such as poverty, increased vulnerability of women, and

gender discrimination—coupled with a huge influx of international aid workers—have contributed to creating a sustainable market for traffickers.[3] Reports of women forced or tricked into traveling to the region indicate that the area is primarily a destination point for women forced into prostitution, although there are also a few scattered reports of women being abducted out of the province.[9] Organizations addressing this issue report that a lack of systematic data collection, difficulty in investigation and enforcement, and limited social services available to victims of trafficking represent major obstacles to developing coordinated efforts.

ADDRESSING GENDER-BASED VIOLENCE

Although many urban women enjoy equality in education and professional life, the majority of Kosovar society is structured on a patriarchal, traditional system.[10] The extended family is the primary form of social support, and most women would not be inclined to threaten its cohesiveness by reporting violence. Male relatives are the primary protectors against violence; if this support does not exist, there is little expectation of intervention.[8] Moreover, male violence against women is generally unchallenged in Kosovar society, and victims who choose disclosure may be met with isolation or blame. Faced with a lack of economic opportunities outside of urban centers, female survivors of domestic violence may resist disclosure because, in many cases, they have little hope for an independent life apart from the family structure.

While a number of local and international organizations are working strenuously toward realizing women's equal societal status as well as safety, most women's organizations report that current efforts are far from adequate and that political will is considerably lacking. International observers have primarily acknowledged incidents that can be classified as war crimes. International recognition of gender-based violence in Kosovo has largely

concerned incidents occurring during the conflict. Prominent local activists have outwardly voiced concerns that the OGA does not effectively incorporate the concerns of local women and may serve as more of an obstacle than a source of support.[11] Despite the lack of strong women's voices within current political structures, local and international women's activist groups and organizations are steadily gathering force to establish both a firm voice and a firm agenda in addressing gender-based violence.

In the postconflict climate, however, women's groups report feeling overwhelmed, and some do not feel qualified to provide specific services such as domestic violence counseling. The influx of foreign assistance has been critical in providing resources, but, according to some nongovernmental organizations (NGOs), it has resulted in underestimation or hindrance of local efforts. There is an impressive contingent of organizations working in the field of gender and women's rights, yet most appear to be involved in welfare rather than education or prevention.[8]

The legal system does contain fragmented codes that could be used to prosecute violence committed against women in the home, although marital rape is excluded. A uniform protocol for addressing domestic violence cases does not exist, but ongoing efforts on the part of local and international organizations to train police and attorneys represent a promising development. Despite the increasing number of reports of sexual violence outside the home, there is little evidence of coordinated efforts on the part of existing institutions and organizations to address or monitor prevalence rates.

Significant levels of resources have been allocated in the area of trafficking of women. In particular, the International Organization of Migration, along with the OGA and the Organization for Security and Cooperation in Europe, has instituted training and investigation programs. However, there is a considerable need for increased interagency coordination and response.[9]

THE NEED FOR SURVEILLANCE SYSTEMS

While the organizations just described undoubtedly are playing a critical role in addressing violence against women, the potential gains of their work will remain undocumented without adequate data. Currently, no tracking system exists to monitor progress in reducing gender-based human rights violations. Data sources are fragmented, and there is no formal mechanism available to coordinate data collection, analysis, or report distribution. Numerous local organizations have reported experiencing frustration with foreign NGOs and visitors who have repeatedly solicited preexisting public health and human service data with little attempt to follow up on or distribute the information collected.

Organizations that do collect data typically report raw numbers unadjusted for the population at risk, increasing the perception that the data merely represent anecdotes with little proof to support them. Furthermore, data derived from police records, human rights organizations, and other civic groups have not been consolidated in a central database that can be shared and utilized by agencies in making priority assessments.

The Council for the Defense of Human Rights and Freedoms (CDHRF), a Kosovo NGO, and the Harvard School of Public Health are collaborating in an effort to establish a centralized system for collecting data on gender-based human rights violations. In a concentrated effort over the past year, CDHRF has been collecting anonymous incidence data on human rights abuses against women occurring during 2 target time periods: July 1999 through June 2001 and July 2001 through June 2003. As a result of the organization's long-term presence in human rights work, existing CDHRF networks have been included in data collection efforts. These networks include hundreds of medical, human service, and legal professionals, all of whom were working in Kosovo well before the ethnic strife in the province gained international attention.

In addition, CDHRF has established contact with the UNMIK administration and the many foreign NGOs that are relatively new to the province. In essence, any group or agency working toward women's rights and protection of women from violence is being asked to contribute to the data collection effort. Data on assorted human rights violations, including physical and sexual violence committed against any woman residing in the province, are being collected without personal identifiers via a standard 2-page data collection form used by all participating agencies. The 2 study periods (1999–2000 and 2001–2003) were targeted to allow retrospective and prospective comparisons, and population-at-risk estimates will be used for each period to compute incidence rates.

To the best of our knowledge, this is the first effort to establish a coordinated surveillance system designed to track gender-based human rights violations at the population level in Kosovo. We anticipate that this pilot effort will inevitably produce incomplete data, but its results will probably prove invaluable in terms of improving the system and planning a longer term effort. Critical to the longevity of this effort will be rapid distribution of the information collected, both to reinforce agencies' participation and to provide much needed (albeit incomplete) data to inform programmatic decisionmaking.

STRUCTURES AND ACTORS FOR EFFECTIVE MONITORING

Because the surveillance project just described originated from a research effort, it is all the more important that an infrastructure be established to maintain its continuity and longevity. To date, participation by existing agencies in recording and reporting the data has been solid, and at the moment it appears that these collaborations can be maintained over time. The critical elements that must be established are as follows: (1) linking the data-coordinating system to the efforts of the government authority to address gender-based violence and (2) identifying sustainable funding sources.

Given that the OGA has declared violence against women a priority area, and given that international human rights standards oblige governments to eliminate gender-based violence, there is a clear role for the Kosovo governmental authority in formally establishing and securing funding for the surveillance system. While establishing the data coordinating center outside the structure of the UNMIK may be preferable in terms of maintaining and further building collaborations at the community level, there will be a strong continued need for coordination and funding support from a central authority as well.

To ensure that future resources will be available to maintain the data collection system, the OGA might identify potential funding sources from varied donors such as multilateral and bilateral agencies and international NGOs and foundations. To determine where and how the data coordinating system will be permanently established, UNMIK also could distribute a "request for proposals" to all participating agencies. In this scenario, it would be important for both UNMIK and nongovernment professionals to be involved in reviewing the solicited proposals and making final decisions.

An additional responsibility of the OGA could be to ensure that the agency ultimately charged with coordinating the data center is responsible for maintaining the highest level of data security at all times, issuing regular reports to the other contributing data collection agencies, and making data available to outside agencies for programmatic purposes as needed. In regard to guaranteeing integration and maintenance of the centralized data-coordinating system over time, the involvement of the government authority will prove critical in further establishing these specific responsibilities, in accord with the authority's stated political commitment and obligation.

The strong presence in Kosovo of organizations working toward women's rights clearly demonstrates the potential to fill the obvious gaps in monitoring gender-based violations. Just as the international community systematically monitors cases of interethnic and political violence, current government structures must prioritize issues involving women and, accordingly, track and address violations of women's human rights. The development and administration of surveillance mechanisms has global ramifications as well. Reconstruction efforts throughout the world face similar challenges in developing interventions for violence against women and, in the absence of preestablished systems, probably lack the resources to initiate a data collection process.

Over time, the experience and monitoring mechanisms developed in Kosovo can serve as a basic model that can be adapted internationally. Professionals in the fields of human rights and public health can therefore productively work together to develop appropriate data collection systems in an effort to ensure that elimination of gender-based violence is accorded the global priority it deserves.

About the Authors

At the time of writing, Sapna Desai was with the Department of Population and International Health, Harvard School of Public Health, Boston, Mass. Melissa J. Perry is with the Department of Environmental Health, Harvard School of Public Health.

Correspondence: Requests for reprints should be sent to Melissa J. Perry, ScD, MHS, Department of Environmental Health, Harvard School of Public Health, 665 Huntington Ave, Boston, MA 02115 (e-mail: mperry@hsph.harvard.edu).

References

1. Speigel PB, Salama P. War and mortality in Kosovo, 1998–99: an epidemiological testimony. *Lancet.* 2000;355:2204–2206.
2. United Nations Interim Mission in Kosovo. Police crime statistics: 2000/2001. Available at: http://www.unmikonline.org/civpol/statistics.htm. Accessed April 25, 2002.
3. *Getting It Right? A Gender Approach to UNMIK Administration in Kosovo.* Stockholm, Sweden: Kvinna till Kvinna Press; 2001.
4. United Nations Interim Mission in Kosovo. Joint interim administrative structure fact sheet. Available at: http://www.unmikonline.org/1styear/jias.htm. Accessed April 25, 2002.
5. United Nations Interim Mission in Kosovo. UNMIK at two, people's rights: challenges still. Available at: http://www.unmikonline.org/2ndyear/unmikat2p4.htm. Accessed May 2, 2003.
6. *United Nations Declaration on the Elimination of Violence Against Women.* New York, NY: United Nations; 1993. UN document A/48/49.
7. Watts C, Zimmerman C. Violence against women: global scope and magnitude. *Lancet.* 2002;359:1232.
8. Wareham R. *No Safe Place: An Assessment on Violence Against Women in Kosovo.* Prishtine, Kosovo: United Nations Development Fund for Women; 2000.
9. Organization for Security and Cooperation in Europe Mission in Kosovo. Combating trafficking in Kosovo. Available at: http://www.osce.org/kosovo/documents. Accessed March 19, 2002.
10. International Helsinki Federation for Human Rights. Women 2000—investigation into the status of women's rights: Federal Republic of Yugoslavia (Kosovo and Serbia). Available at: http://www.ihf-hr.org/reports/women/yugoslavia.pdf. Accessed April 13, 2002.
11. Association for the Education of Women. Letter to United Nations office from Igo Rogovo on behalf of the Rural Women's Network. Available at: http://www.motratqiriazi.org/network.htm. Accessed February 25, 2002.

Where is the M in MTCT? The Broader Issues in Mother-to-Child Transmission of HIV

| Allan Rosenfield, MD and Emily Figdor, MPH

In 1985, a report subtitled "Where is the M in MCH?"[1] pointed out that most, if not all, maternal and child health (MCH) programs, both domestic and international, focused on health issues concerning infants and young children. Women were considered, if at all, only in relation to improving infant neonatal outcomes. This focus was partly justified in the developing world, where infant mortality rates of 100 per 1000 or higher meant that millions of infants and young children were dying each year. With maternal mortality ratios as high as 500 to 1000 per 100000 live births, however, each year an estimated 600 000 women were dying from pregnancy-related complications. The vast majority of these deaths were preventable. In addition, several million more women were suffering serious complications, most notably vesical vaginal fistula and rectal vaginal fistula, which result in permanent urinary or rectal incontinence, essentially making outcasts of the women who survive.

At the end of the 19th century, maternal mortality ratios in North America and Europe were similar to those today in most developing countries. Antibiotics, safe blood transfusions, and ready access to both emergency surgical care and safe, legal abortion services have dramatically reduced these ratios (to 8 to 12 deaths per 100000 live births). But with great worldwide inequities in income distribution and access to health and social services, rates of maternal mortality and morbidity in developing countries remain extraordinarily high, even though the solution requires no new technologies, no new drugs, and no new vaccines. Access to

emergency care is the single most important component in lowering maternal mortality. In Africa, Asia, and Latin America, access to such services is either very limited or entirely absent.

HIV: MTCT

A similar dynamic underlies efforts to decrease mother-to-child transmission (MTCT) of HIV. At the July 2000 international AIDS conference in Durban, South Africa, much of the discussion focused on preventing maternal–infant transmission of HIV. In 1999, an estimated 500000 neonates were infected with HIV during the prenatal, intrapartum, or breastfeeding periods.[2] Further estimates suggest that as many as 50% of all deaths among children younger than 5 years in such countries as South Africa and Zimbabwe are from AIDS; in Botswana, that figure reaches 64%.

With 50% of all AIDS cases in Africa and Asia occurring among women, MTCT will continue at an astounding pace. The overall rate of perinatal transmission is approximately 25%; among breastfeeding women, the rate is as high as 45%.[2] Effective treatment to substantially decrease transmission is available in the West—but not in sub-Saharan Africa and Asia.

A long course of treatment during pregnancy can reduce MTCT to minimal levels.[3] Research in Africa and Asia has demonstrated that shorter, much less expensive courses of therapy also decrease transmission rates, although not to the same extent as the longer ones.[4,5] However, as Berer states, "Short course AZT treatment is an intervention that uses women's bodies to deliver pre-

ventive treatment to infants. Although the anti-HIV benefit to infants is clear, there is no benefit to the women."[6]

Impact on Women

There is a paucity of research examining the health impact of short-course therapy on women. Many clinicians have assumed that single-dose nevirapine and the slightly longer short-course therapies do not increase viral resistance to these drugs. However, one report suggests that viral resistance may be induced following a single dose of nevirapine.[7] Clearly, further research is needed to determine the effects of anti-retroviral interventions on women's health. Although resistance may not be crucial if the woman does not receive treatment in the future, treatment for women may well become available. Efforts by South Africa to negotiate drug pricing and possible initiatives by both the pharmaceutical industry and Western nations could result in more widespread drug availability, which would be beneficial in reducing MTCT but could have a negative impact on HIV-positive women.

If indeed funds become available to make short-term therapy available to decrease the chances of MTCT, should we not be giving serious consideration to finding ways to offer women treatment simply because they are infected with HIV, not just because they are pregnant? In other words, should we not value saving women's lives as an equal priority to decreasing transmission to infants?

Breastfeeding

Another issue of tremendous complexity relates to breastfeeding.[8] The available data indicate that breastfeeding increases the risk of MTCT above and beyond the in utero and intrapartum risks of transmission. We do not know whether short-course therapy to reduce MTCT is effective when women breast-feed, nor do we have data to assess which is greater: the increased risk of a breastfed infant's being infected with HIV and subsequently dying from AIDS or the increased risk of childhood death from diarrheal disease and malnutrition because of unclean water and inadequate amounts of formula milk. Data on the comparative risks are vitally needed at both the country and regional levels. The very successful 1974–1984 Nestlé boycott revolved specifically around the issue of the high rates of infant mortality from bottle-feeding in cultures where sterilizing water is difficult and funds to purchase sufficient quantities of formula milk are inadequate. This advocacy campaign resulted in a United Nations Children's Fund/World Health Organization (UNICEF/WHO) code on the marketing of formula milk in developing countries. If it is recommended that women in poor communities forgo breastfeeding, then programs must be implemented to make certain that bottle-feeding does not increase infants' risk of death.

Orphans

One final issue—perhaps one of the most complex from a moral and ethical standpoint— is that decreasing maternal–infant transmission of HIV without treating the mother or father adds to the already high numbers of orphaned children. Many of these orphans become street people, because AIDS has ravaged their traditional extended families.[9] Do we expand treatment to decrease MTCT without treating women, only to increase the number of orphans? It is difficult to believe that this question even needs to be asked.

Conclusions

The following imperatives need to be considered in relation to MTCT:
* treatment of women, but not just to decrease MTCT;
* treatment of infants who are HIV positive;
* access to clean water and adequate

amounts of formula milk; and
* significant investment in the infrastructure needed to fulfill these goals.

What a sad commentary on the priorities of both the donor community (the United Nations system, the World Bank, the International Monetary Fund, and bilateral agencies) and local governments that none of these issues is currently a priority initiative in most developing nations. Consider what a reallocation of the vast amount of funding invested in the military alone could do for programs to improve health and well-being. The Clinton Administration's suggestion that $1 billion in loans be made available through the Import–Export Bank for the purchase of drugs and for infrastructure development was inappropriate and ill conceived at a time when poor nations are struggling to abolish their high debt. If such funds are to be made available, they should be outright grants, not loans that will only further increase the burden of debt in poor countries.

Why have we been unable to establish a health care system that can deliver emergency obstetric services to reduce high rates of maternal mortality and preventive testing and treatment services for HIV/AIDS? The differentials between the haves and the have-nots within and among countries are unconscionable. Why have both international and local governments not given higher priority to the impact of poverty and the lack of resources for vital services? Where is the outrage that we still have to ask these questions? These are the multiple tragedies that societies, their political structures, and the international community must recognize and prioritize—and then implement strategies to bring about real change. As a first step, government agencies, bilateral donors, nongovernmental organizations, and others working to decrease MTCT of HIV should join with their counterparts advocating for women's health and rights to reach a consensus that does not ignore the M in MTCT.

About the Authors

Allan Rosenfield is with the Mailman School of Public Health, Columbia University, New York, NY. Emily Figdor is with the National Family Planning and Reproductive Health Association, Washington, DC.

Requests for reprints should be sent to Allan Rosenfield, MD, Mailman School of Public Health, 600 W 168th St, New York, NY 10032.

References

1. Rosenfield A, Maine D. Maternal mortality—a neglected tragedy: where is the M in MCH? *Lancet.* 1985;2(8446):83–85.
2. Piot P, Coll-Seck A. Preventing mother-to-child transmission of HIV in Africa. *Bull World Health Organ.* 1999;77:869–870.
3. Conner EM, Sperling RS, Gelber R, et al. Reduction of maternal–infant transmission of human immunodeficiency virus type I with zidovudine treatment. *N Engl J Med.* 1994;331: 1173–1180.
4. Shaffer N, Chuachoowong R, Mock PA, et al. Short-course zidovudine for perinatal HIV-1 transmission in Bangkok, Thailand: a randomised controlled trial. *Lancet.* 1999;353: 773–780. 5. Guay L, Musoke P, Fleming T, et al. Intrapartum and neonatal single-dose nevirapine compared with zidovudine for prevention of mother-to-child transmission of HIV-1 in Kampala, Uganda: HIVNET 012 randomised trial. *Lancet.* 1999; 354:795–802.
6. Berer M. Reducing perinatal HIV transmission in developing countries through antenatal and delivery care, and breastfeeding: supporting infant survival by supporting women's survival. *Bull World Health Organ.* 1999;77: 871–877.
7. Becker-Pergola G, Guay L, Mmiro F, et al. Selection of the K103N nevirapine resistance mutation in Ugandan women receiving NVP prophylaxis to prevent HIV-1 vertical transmission. Paper presented at: 7th Conference on Retroviruses and Opportunistic Infections; January 30–February 2, 2000; San Francisco, Calif. Abstract available at: http://64.58.70.224/2000/ abstracts/658.htm. Accessed October 30, 2000.
8. Kuhn L, Stein Z. Infant survival, HIV infection, and feeding alternatives in less-developed countries. *Am J Public Health.* 1997;87: 926–931.
9. Drew RS, Makufa C, Foster G. Strategies for providing care and support to children orphaned by AIDS. *AIDS Care.* 1998;10(suppl 1):S9–S15.

Keeping the M in MTCT: Women, Mothers, and HIV Prevention

| Mary T. Bassett, MD, MPH

When the results of ACTG 076, a clinical trial supported by the National Institutes of Health, were published in 1994, it was already clear that the AIDS toll in sub-Saharan Africa and Asia would be immense. This landmark study showed that a single antiretroviral drug taken for a short time (i.e., not a lifetime) could reduce mother-to-child transmission (MTCT) of HIV by a stunning 67%.[1] Although the regimen was not practical for use in developing countries, its success pointed to a whole new avenue of prevention: antiretroviral drugs taken by pregnant HIV-infected women to prevent transmission to the infant.

We now have data on the effectiveness of several short-course oral regimens using zidovudine, zidovudine plus lamivudine, and nevirapine. [2–6] All but nevirapine require multiple dosing regimens, usually for several weeks, but they all work, some perhaps as effectively as the original complex 076 regimen.[7] Breastfeeding, widespread in Africa, attenuates the reduction of HIV transmission achieved by intrapartum antiretroviral regimens. However, the short-course zidovudine and nevirapine regimens have been shown to have long-term benefits to the breastfed infant.[8,9]

Today in North America and Europe, MTCT of HIV has declined greatly as a public health problem, and there are data to suggest that adoption of the 076 findings in standard pregnancy care has contributed to this decline.[10] In the poor countries of the developing world, however, not a single country is able to offer antiretroviral drugs routinely for the prevention of MTCT outside of the private sector. Not Thailand, where the first short-course zidovudine regimen of proven efficacy was introduced in early 1998.[11] Not Uganda, where the nevirapine regimen was proved to be about 50% efficacious in 1999.[4]

At the end of 1999, there were 15.7 million HIV-infected women and 1.3 million HIV-infected children worldwide.[12] Nearly all HIV-infected children younger than 10 years acquired HIV from their mothers and live in developing countries. To date, the nevirapine regimen tested in Uganda is the simplest and cheapest. It amounts to giving 1 dose of nevirapine to the HIV-positive mother while she is in labor and 1 dose to the infant within 3 days of birth. What accounts for this failure to translate such a simple regimen into saving lives?

Rosenfield and Figdor[13] tackle some of these concerns in this issue of the *Journal.* They do well to remind us that if we take care of mothers, mothers can take care of their infants. The question is not the safety of these regimens to the mother or infant; all available data show that the regimens are safe.[14] At issue is how we prioritize public health interventions and how we view, in the context of child survival, the benefits and obligations of women who are mothers.

COST: THE MAIN BARRIER

It is not universally agreed that saving an infant born to an HIV-infected mother is a sensible use of public funds in poor countries. The infant will be born into extremely difficult circumstances; death is predicted at least for its mother and probably for its father. Should we invest public dollars in preventing infant deaths—an investment that will translate into a rising tide of orphans? In hard-hit countries, such as Zimbabwe, it is predicted that by 2005, 1 in 3 children younger than 15 years will be orphaned. The social cost of so many young people's being raised without parental or adult guidance will surely be very high.

It would be misleading, however, to suggest that policy debates have delayed implementing MTCT reduction, except possibly in South Africa. In sub-Saharan Africa, apart from South Africa and Botswana, the first and still insurmountable obstacle is that of cost. Africa will not see the declines in HIV infection among children that are seen in North America and Europe, unless funds are provided to governments to support these efforts. And this support must come from the rich countries— as debt forgiveness by the International Monetary Fund and World Bank, reduced pricing by pharmaceutical companies, generic drug production, and grants.

MODELS FOR HIV TESTING

Despite the lack of national programs, experience in implementing reductions in MTCT in sub-Saharan Africa is growing. The combined efforts of United Nations agencies (Joint United Nations Programme on HIV/AIDS [UNAIDS], United Nations Children's Fund [UNICEF], and the World Health Organization [WHO]) have supported 11 pilot projects in different African countries, and more recently, the Call for Action initiative launched 18 projects in 6 African countries. In addition, antiretroviral drugs are being offered as part of the "best practice in obstetric care" in research initiatives that examine other interventions to reduce MTCT. These special projects suggest that delivering effective drugs to HIV infected mothers for the reduction of MTCT will not be as simple as doling out pills. Indeed, the challenges of intrapartum management of syphilis—a condition treatable with a single penicillin injection—might have warned us of the difficulty of translating an effective program into care.[15]

Many pregnant African women do not choose to have an HIV test when offered one. As a consequence, most HIV-infected women are not identified and are not offered drugs, even in the adequately supported pilot setting. For example, in our site in a working-class area outside of Harare, we estimate that only 15% of HIV-infected women in the target population presently benefit from drugs to reduce MTCT.[16] The main obstacle is low rates of participation in counseling and testing. We use the standard approach of individual pretest and posttest counseling. This "package" was developed for adults who wished to learn their status at a time when there was little or nothing in the way of therapy. One of our key aims was to prepare people for bad news by offering positive advice on healthy living and prevention.

Transferred to the care setting, where pregnant women are accustomed to following health workers' advice, voluntary counseling and testing makes new and unusual demands on the woman who has come for prenatal care. She must talk to a stranger about her thoughts and feelings. She is advised to try to raise these issues with her husband, with whom she probably rarely discusses such matters. Furthermore, she is told that the decision is hers to make. The responsibility (and presumably the blame) is hers. Is this fair?

Another approach is to make a positive recommendation, offer universal screening, and allow women to decline if they choose. But preliminary experience suggests that using an "opt out" approach (with universal HIV counseling and testing), instead of the standard "opt in" approach, to increase women's willingness to be tested may not result in greater access to antiretroviral drugs.[17] More women may have HIV tests, but they may not return for the results. In settings with high prevalences of HIV, where stigma and denial continue to characterize the response to HIV infection, we must conclude that women have very good reasons for not wishing to know their HIV status. In the tragic calculus of possibly saving her unborn child from HIV infection vs the social cost of knowing her own HIV-positive status, the cost of known HIV status is higher.

Why would this be so? Because a woman who learns her positive HIV status before her husband learns his own status very likely will be blamed for "bringing the infection home." And having a husband is crucial to the survival of the mother and her children. What sort of benefit is it to know that one is HIV positive, to face certain death, to be isolated and possibly cast out? For reduction of MTCT to occur, this social context must change. A program that increases the perception that women are to blame for HIV infection—a notion already entrenched in the public's awareness of prostitution—will not gain women's widespread support. It does no good to blame women or suggest that they are not good mothers. That men are "bringing HIV home" has been well established.

PCTC AND BLAME

Because it takes two to transmit HIV and two to make a child, women's health advocates and others have suggested we replace the "M" in MTCT with a "P" for "parent." Use of the term "PTCT" emphasizes the joint responsibility of both parents in the transmission of HIV to an infant. The father infects the mother and the mother then infects the child in a cascade of parent-to-child transmission.

In reminding us all that it is the infection of women as partners and wives that creates the problem of mother-to-child transmission, PTCT is a useful term. But that is its only utility. The father may not be the man who infected his wife, although he usually is. It might have been a previous partner. Should we use "adult-to-child transmission" (ATCT)? But this term, like PTCT, lacks biological specificity. It is true but vague, and greater vagueness will not help our prevention efforts.

One of the challenges of building the social context into our prevention strategies is to retain the biological specificity of what we know about HIV. Yes, AIDS is a disease of poverty, and it is a disease of inequality between the sexes. But it is also an infectious disease caused by a virus. For the infant, it is maternal infection that matters, and it is mother-to-child transmission that we seek to interrupt. Mother-to-child transmission is an accurate phrase, and as a paradigm it has yielded the highly effective antiretroviral approaches. There are millions of women in the world today who are HIV positive. We cannot prevent their HIV infection. Women are more than mothers, but many women see motherhood as a benefit, not only an obligation. For many HIV-infected women, a better chance to have an uninfected child is the only good news there is.

TAKING CARE OF WOMEN

This brings us to the last point raised by Rosenfield and Figdor: What about the treatment of women? If we care about child survival, what should be done about maternal survival? Certainly the death of a young mother carries high social costs. A recent review by Foster and Williamson[18] suggests that the loss of a father is just as costly, because he is often the breadwinner. Here we should ask, "What about the treatment of parents?" If we look carefully at how MTCT is being vanquished in the wealthy nations, we see that success increasingly is due not to specific

MTCT regimens but to the treatment of adult HIV infection. [19] Intensive antiretroviral therapy for the mother's infection also reduces HIV transmission to her infant.

If we take care of women, we will take care of mothers. If we take care of mothers, we will take care of infants. If we fail to begin to think about the therapeutic use of antiretroviral drugs in Africa, we risk (as DeCock and others[20] wrote in the Journal in 1993) caring about AIDS in Africa but not about Africans with AIDS.

About the Author

The author is with the Department of Community Medicine, University of Zimbabwe Medical School, Harare, Zimbabwe. Requests for reprints should be sent to Mary T. Bassett, MD, MPH, PO Box A-178, Avondale, Harare, Zimbabwe (e-mail: mbassett@healthnet.zw).

References

1. Connor EM, Sperling RS, Gelber R, et al. Reduction of maternal-infant transmission of human immunodeficiency virus type 1 with zidovudine treatment. *N Engl J Med.* 1994;331: 1173–1180.
2. Shaffer N, Chuachoowong R, Mock PA, et al. Short-course zidovudine for perinatal HIV-1 transmission in Bangkok, Thailand: a randomised controlled trial. *Lancet.* 1999;353: 773–780.
3. Dabis F, Msellati P, Meda N, et al. Six-month efficacy, tolerance and acceptability of a short regimen of oral zidovudine to reduce vertical transmission of HIV in breastfed children in Côte d'Ivoire and Burkina Faso: a double-blind placebo-controlled multicentre trial. *Lancet.* 1999;353:786–792.
4. Guay LA, Musoke P, Fleming T, et al. Intrapartum and neonatal single-dose nevirapine compared with zidovudine for prevention of mother-to-child transmission of HIV-1 in Kampala, Uganda. HIVNET 012 randomised trial. *Lancet.* 1999;354:795–802.
5. Gray G, for the PETRA Trial Management Committee. The PETRA study: early and late efficacy of three short ZDV/3TC combination regimens to prevent mother-to-child transmission of HIV-1. Paper presented at: 13th International AIDS Conference; July 9–14, 2000; Durban, South Africa. Abstract LbOr5.
6. Moodley D, on behalf of the SAINT investigators team. The SAINT trial: nevirapine (NVP) versus zidovudine (ZDV) + lamivudine (3TC) in prevention of peripartum HIV transmission. Paper presented at: 13th International AIDS Conference; July 9–14, 2000; Durban, South Africa. Abstract LbOr2.
7. Lallemant M, Jourdain G, Le Coeur S, et al. A trial of shortened zidovudine regimens to prevent mother-to-child transmission of the human immunodeficiency virus type 1. Perinatal HIV Prevention Trial (Thailand) Investigators. *N Engl J Med.* 2000;343:982–991.
8. Wiktor SZ, Leroy V, Ekpini ER, et al. Twentyfour- month efficacy of short-course maternal zidovudine for the prevention of mother-to-child HIV-1 transmission in a breast feeding population: a pooled analysis of two randomized clinical trials in West Africa. Paper presented at: 13th International AIDS Conference; July 9– 14, 2000; Durban, South Africa. Abstract TuOrB354.
9. Owor M, Deseyve M, Duefield C, et al. The one year safety and efficacy data of the HIVNET 012 trials. Paper presented at: 13th International AIDS Conference; July 9–14, 2000; Durban, South Africa. Abstract LbOr1.
10. Lindegren ML, Byers RH Jr, Thomas P, et al. Trends in perinatal transmission of HIV/AIDS in the United States. *JAMA.* 1999;286:531–538.
11. Joint statement by the Centers for Disease Control and Prevention, the Joint United Nations Programme on HIV/AIDS (UNAIDS), the National Institutes of Health (NIH), and the Agence Nationale de Recherche sur le SIDA (ANRS) [press release]. Atlanta, Ga: Centers for Disease Control and Prevention; February 18, 1998.
12. *Joint United Nations Programme on AIDS (UNAIDS) Report on the Global HIV/AIDS Epidemic.* Geneva, Switzerland: UNAIDS; June 2000. Report UNAIDS/00,13E.
13. Rosenfield A, Figdor E. Where is the M in MTCT? The broader issues in mother-to-child transmission of HIV. *Am J Public Health.* 2001; 91:703–704.
14. *WHO Technical Consultation of Behalf of the UNFPA/UNICEF/WHO/ UNAIDS InterAgency Task Force on MTCT: Conclusions and Recommendations.* Geneva, Switzerland: World Health Organization; October 11–13, 2000.
15. Fonck K, Claeys P, Bashir F, Bwayo J, Fransen L, Temmerman M. Syphilis control during pregnancy: effectiveness and sustainability of a decentralized program. *Am J Public Health.* 2001; 91:705–707.
16. Moyo S, Mhazo M, Mateta P, et al. Acceptability of short course AZT prevention regimen by HIV infected pregnant women: should VCT in the antenatal setting be modified? Paper presented at: 13th International AIDS Conference; July 9–14, 2000; Durban, South Africa. Abstract TuPpB1158.
17. Sibailly TS, Ekpini ER, Kamelan-Taneh A. Zidovudine for the prevention of mother-to-child transmission of HIV in Abidjan, Côte d'Ivoire. Paper presented at: 13th International AIDS Conference; July 9–14, 2000; Durban, South Africa. Abstract WeOrC549.
18. Foster G, Williamson J. A review of the current literature on the impact of the HIV/AIDS literature on children in sub-Saharan Africa. *AIDS.* 2000;14(suppl 3):S275–S284.
19. Cooper ER, Charurat M, Burns DN, Blattner W, Hoff R. Trends in antiretroviral therapy and mother-infant transmission of HIV. The Women and Infants Transmission Study Group. *J Acquir Immune Defic Syndr.* 2000;24:45–47.
20. DeCock KM, Lucas SB, Lucas S, Agness J, Kadio A, Gayle HD. Clinical research, prophylaxis therapy and care for HIV disease in Africa. *Am J Public Health.* 1993;83:1385–1389.

Overview of Infectious Diseases Section

| Beth Kirkpatrick, MD, Associate Professor of Medicine, Unit of Infectious Diseases, University of Vermont College of Medicine

The global burden of infectious diseases is a vast and complicated subject area, as evidenced by this review of manuscripts dated 2001-2006. Of the top ten causes of death in low-income countries, five are due to infectious diseases (lower respiratory infections, HIV/AIDS, diarrheal diseases, malaria and tuberculosis)[1], many of which disproportionately affect young children. This collection of articles makes no attempt to summarize the breadth of global infectious diseases. Instead, it offers the reader a sample of public health coordination efforts, new models, and behavioral science approaches to infectious diseases, most of which are broadly applicable to other infectious diseases or epidemics.

The first chapter by Andrus and colleagues summarizes the massive coordination and operational effort required in the global Polio eradication campaign[2]. Andrus and colleagues describe the campaign's aims for complete interruption of wild polio transmission, but also for routine polio immunizations, national immunization days, and house-to-house "mop-up" campaigns. They describe in detail the paradigm required to sustain this effort, including maintenance of intense international collaborations (which include governments and 14 additional non-governmental partners), surveillance strategies, a global laboratory network, and rigorous performance indicators. This paradigm will serve as a well-tested model for future disease eradication efforts as well as control of infectious disease transmission across international borders. The description of scale and complexity of this international coordi-

nation will also serve to increase our appreciation for the difficulty of the Polio eradication efforts.

Two chapters in this series address lessons learned from the SARS epidemic of 2003. SARS has not (thus far in 2008) reemerged. However, the lessons of the response to this newly described infectious agent, including the rapidity of the international effort and the economic, social, and public health impact, are well worth remembering for the next unanticipated public health crisis. The chapter by Tang and Wong was researched during the 2003 SARS outbreak in Hong Kong and focuses specifically on SARS infection[3]. Their work studied predictors of preventative health behaviors and the effect of community preventative health education. Perceived susceptibility to SARS infection, self-efficacy, and age were the best predictors of those persons who practiced preventative health behaviors.

Des Jarlais, et al. address the issue of stigmatization of newly emerging infectious diseases and evaluate perceptions of SARS as well as Acquired Immunodeficiency Syndrome (AIDS)[4]. Drawing from phone interviews performed in 2002 in New York City, the authors demonstrate the associations between individuals with less personal resources (income, social support, education) and support of stigmatizing actions and opinions, such as requiring infected persons to wear identification tags. In addition, the authors make evident the contribution of depression to these behaviors. This information will prove useful in predicting responses and attitudes toward future emerging

infectious diseases and in targeting educational programs.

The chapter by Tolley and Severy focuses on the importance of behavioral research in clinical trials investigating the use of vaginal microbiocides for the prevention of HIV transmission.[5] The authors argue strongly for integrating behavioral and social science (BSS) practices into early-stage clinical trials for products of public health importance (such as vaginal microbicides). Their discussion challenges the linear model of clinical research, which implies that BSS data are too subjective and should only be addressed once a product has demonstrated efficacy, presumably after a phase III field trial. The authors note that an integrated approach to issues such as cultural acceptability and an individual's perception of risk are critical to the success of a new product. Rather than being a burden on the clinical trial system, BSS information may be critical to the collection of accurate data and final acceptance of the new product.

Two chapters discuss point-of-use water treatment systems. Dunston et al. describe the lessons learned in a rapid scale-up of a point-of-care water disinfectant system in Madagascar in response to an ongoing cholera epidemic[6]. The authors emphasize the importance of social marketing and community mobilization in the success of the introduction of this water treatment system. The complementary chapter by Mintz and colleagues outlines broadly the issues surrounding access to point-of-care water treatment systems, including water treatment options, as well as the importance of safe water storage, behavioral changes, and low-cost technologies[7].

References

1. http://www.who.int/mediacentre/factsheets/fs310/en/index.html

2. J Andrus JK, Thapa AB, Withana N, Fitzsimmons JW, Abeykoon P, Aylward B. A new paradigm for international disease control: lessons learned from polio eradication in Southeast Asia. *Am J Public Health.* 2001 Jan;91(1):146-50.

3. Tang CS, Wong CY. An outbreak of the severe acute respiratory syndrome: predictors of health behaviors and effect of community prevention measures in Hong Kong, China. *Am J Public Health.* 2003 Nov;93(11):1887-8.

4. Des Jarlais DC, Galea S, Tracy M, Tross S, Vlahov D. Stigmatization of newly emerging infectious diseases: AIDS and SARS. *Am J Public Health.* 2006 Mar;96(3):561-7

5. Tolley EE, Severy LJ. Integrating behavioral and social science research into microbicide clinical trials: challenges and opportunities. *Am J Public Health.* 2006 Jan;96(1):79-83.

6. Dunston C, McAfee D, Kaiser R, Rakotoarison D, Rambeloson L, Hoang AT, Quick RE. Collaboration, cholera, and cyclones: a project to improve point-of-use water quality in Madagascar. *Am J Public Health.* 2001 Oct;91(10):1574-6.

7. Mintz E, Bartram J, Lochery P, Wegelin M. Not just a drop in the bucket: expanding access to point-of-use water treatment systems. *Am J Public Health.* 2001 Oct;91(10):1565-70.

A New Paradigm for International Disease Control: Lessons Learned From Polio Eradication in Southeast Asia

| Jon Kim Andrus, MD, Arun B. Thapa, MD, MS, Nalini Withana, MD, John W. Fitzsimmons, MURP, Palitha Abeykoon, MD, MPH, and Bruce Aylward, MD, MPH

ABSTRACT

Objectives. This study evaluated the impact of international coordination on polio eradication in Southeast Asia.

Methods. Active surveillance systems for acute flaccid paralysis were assessed. Analyses focused on surveillance proficiency and polio incidence.

Results. Ten countries coordinated activities. Importations occurred and were rapidly contained in China and Myanmar. Countries that have been free of indigenous polio transmission for at least 3 years include Sri Lanka, Indonesia, Myanmar, and Thailand. In the remaining endemic countries—India, Nepal, and Bangladesh—poliovirus transmission has been substantially reduced; however, these countries still harbor the world's largest polio reservoir.

Conclusions. Unprecedented international coordination in Southeast Asia resulted in dramatic progress in polio eradication and serves as a paradigm for control of other infectious diseases such as malaria and tuberculosis. (*Am J Public Health.* 2001;91:146–150)

Complete interruption of wild poliovirus transmission is the goal of the global polio eradication initiative.[1] High-quality surveillance of acute flaccid paralysis and wild poliovirus ultimately demonstrates whether the target has been achieved.[2] Such surveillance directs the allocation of resources to areas with ongoing virus transmission requiring more concentrated efforts, such as areas with heavy migration and large numbers of border crossings.[3]

Other strategies for polio eradication are (1) routine immunization with at least 3 doses of oral polio vaccine, (2) national immunization days on which every child younger than 5 years receives 2 extra doses of oral polio vaccine, and (3) extensive house-to-house immunization "mop-up" campaigns in the final stages.[2]

A major challenge to the success of polio eradication is reintroduction of wild poliovirus from the remaining endemic countries into polio-free countries and countries that are rapidly becoming polio free. Repeated importations of polio from Southeast Asia to industrialized countries demonstrate the critical importance of Southeast Asia to global disease control.[4–9] International borders impose other operational impediments, but genomic sequencing data demonstrate shared reservoirs of wild poliovirus transmission that cross borders.

In this report, we focus on (1) international coordination in the area of polio eradication, (2) progress toward polio eradication in the 10 member states of the World Health Organization (WHO) Southeast Asia Region (total population: 1.2 billion), and (3) lessons learned for effective control of infectious disease transmission across international borders.

METHODS

To evaluate lessons learned in international disease control through the polio eradication initiative, we undertook a review of the working papers, reports, and recommendations of the international technical oversight body for polio eradication in the WHO Southeast Asia Region, the Technical Consultative Group, and its partner coordinating body, the Interagency Coordinating Committee. The Interagency Coordinating Committee meets to assess how funds are being used and to review resource requirements for the plan of action. The Technical Consultative Group and the Interagency Coordinating Committee coordinate activities between governments and assist partner agencies.

To evaluate progress toward polio eradication, we analyzed data from the Southeast Asia Region acute flaccid paralysis surveillance system. For the purposes of eradication, WHO recommends that every case of acute flaccid paralysis be reported and immediately investigated (i.e., within 48 hours of paralysis onset) and that 2 stool samples from each case subject be collected for analysis in a WHO accredited laboratory.[10] The results of clinical follow-up and virus isolation studies are used to classify acute flaccid paralysis cases as polio or nonpolio. Wild-virus-confirmed polio is defined as a case of polio associated with the isolation of wild poliovirus. With the exception of Sri Lanka (in 1993) and India (in 2000), all countries have reported both clinically confirmed and wild-virus-confirmed cases as polio.[10]

Surveillance sensitivity is demonstrated via the monitoring of standardized proficiency indicators: nonpolio acute flaccid paralysis reporting rate (target rate: more than 1 per 100000 residents younger than 15 years) and stool collection (target rate: more than

TABLE 1—Number of Reported Acute Flaccid Paralysis (AFP) Cases, Nonpolio AFP Rates, Confirmed Polio Cases, and Poliovirus Strains Detected, by Country: Southeast Asia Region, 1997 and 1999

Country	No. of Reported AFP Cases		Nonpolio AFP Rate		AFP Cases With Adequate Specimens,[a] %		No. of Confirmed Cases[b] (No. of Wild Virus Cases)		Wild Virus Detected[c]
	1997	1999	1997	1999	1997	1999	1997	1999	
Bangladesh	244	761	0.14	0.71	34	49	173 (5)	384 (28)	P1/P3
Bhutan	0	0	0.00	0.00	0	0	0 (0)	0 (0)	…
India	3047	9578	0.22	1.83	34	72	2275 (702)	2794 (1126)	P1/P2/P3
Indonesia	801	671	0.78	0.94	53	83	293 (0)	55 (0)	…
Maldives	1	0	0.84	0.00	100	0	0 (0)	0 (0)	…
Myanmar	172	181	0.75	0.81	58	66	55 (0)	41 (4)	P1
Nepal	36	234	0.26	1.99	39	76	12 (1)	39 (2)	P1
North Korea	3	14	0.01	0.00	0	36	0 (0)	0 (0)	…
Sri Lanka	115	105	2.12	1.86	45	88	0 (0)	0 (0)	…
Thailand	131	337	0.50	1.90	65	85	19 (1)	21 (0)	…
Total	4550	11881	0.32	1.57	39	71	2827 (709)	3334 (1160)	…

Note. The nonpolio AFP rate is the rate per 100000 children younger than 15 years. It does not include AFP cases pending classification, which would inflate the estimate.
[a]Two specimens collected within 14 days of paralysis onset.
[b]Reported confirmed polio cases based on clinical and virologic findings.
[c]Reported wild poliovirus types isolated in 1999.

80% of acute flaccid paralysis cases with 2 adequate stools collected fewer than 15 days after paralysis onset).

A unique case identification number is assigned to each case to link the epidemiologic and laboratory data. Data are reported on a weekly basis to the national immunization section and then to the WHO Southeast Asia Regional Office. Case investigation data and laboratory results are entered into a software program, Information for Action, developed for polio eradication by WHO and the Centers for Disease Control and Prevention (CDC). Epi Info 6.14 (CDC, Atlanta, Ga) was used in analyzing data.

RESULTS

International Coordination of Polio Eradication Strategies

Since 1994, the Technical Consultative Group has met at least yearly to review progress, provide recommendations, and, when appropriate, revise strategies. In 1999, the group met twice to provide guidance on doubling polio immunization activities in India and Bangladesh to meet the eradication target by 2000. Given several issues—accurate epidemiologic profile of transmission, low vaccination coverage, large annual birth cohorts, and a high prevalence of densely populated communities with poor sanitary

conditions—India decided, with guidance from the Technical Consultative Group, to make dramatic adjustments in its eradication strategies. [11–13] In the winter of 1999–2000, India decided to conduct 4 rounds of national immunization days followed by 2 rounds of subnational immunization days statewide in 8 selected high-risk states in the northern part of the country. Bangladesh, another major polio reservoir and a country sharing a border with India, also needed to make major adjustments in its strategies consistent with India's.

In 1994, a core group of partners emerged to support polio eradication in Southeast Asia, including WHO, the United Nations Children's Fund (UNICEF), Rotary International, and the CDC. By 2000, 14 partners had been successfully recruited to assist governments in funding polio eradication activities. Many of these partners work in multiple countries of Southeast Asia, also providing assistance with international coordination of efforts.

In 1994, Thailand was the first Southeast Asian country to conduct national immunization days; by 1997, all 8 polio endemic or recently endemic countries of the region had conducted national immunization days. Because countries of Southeast Asia form an epidemiologic block with simi-

lar high-transmission months for poliovirus, the Technical Consultative Group recommended that these countries synchronize their national immunization days. In December 1997 and January 1998, Bangladesh, Bhutan, China, India, Myanmar, Nepal, Pakistan, and Thailand synchronized national immunization days, vaccinating nearly 248 million children, 38% of the world's population of children younger than 5 years (Table 1).

Since 1997, weekly surveillance data have been sent electronically from districts to the national level and the WHO regional office, providing a mechanism for health officials at all levels to receive a weekly overview of the polio situation for the region. Nepal sends its stool specimens to Bangkok's laboratory for culture; Myanmar sends stool specimens for intratypic differentiation to Bangkok. WHO publishes a weekly polio bulletin that serves to link and strengthen coordination of activities among all countries.

The Southeast Asia Regional Office coordinates and manages the polio network of 17 laboratories by providing technical assistance and essential reagents, transferring technologies such as genetic sequencing, and convening yearly meetings to address operational constraints. The office also coordinates the accreditation of laboratories using 6 standardized performance indicators. By November 1999, of the 17 network laboratories conducting poliovirus isolation from stool specimens collected in acute flaccid paralysis cases, 14 were fully accredited by WHO. One (Jakarta) is being reviewed for accreditation, and 2 (Dhaka and Pyongyang) are being strengthened for review.

The response of WHO's global polio laboratory network to the finding of wild poliovirus type 1 in 1999 in China in a paralyzed boy aged 16 months was critical for determining the origin and coordinating responses in neighboring countries. China had last isolated indigenous wild poliovirus in 1994, and the identification of a wild poliovirus case in 1999 threatened to seriously compromise the polio-free status of China and WHO's Western Pacific Region. WHO coordinated the molecular epidemiologic investigation between the National Poliovirus Laboratory in Beijing, the CDC in the United States, and the Enterovirus Research Center in Mumbai. The evaluation showed that the virus strain found in China was closely related to poliovirus strains circulating in northern and central India during 1998 and 1999, suggesting an imported virus from that country.[14]

To further strengthen international coordination, the Southeast Asia Regional Office convened a meeting of health officials from Bangladesh, India, and Nepal in February 1999 to discuss mechanisms for immediate reporting of acute flaccid paralysis cases and control activities across borders. Countries recommended that the group be expanded to include other neighboring countries of Southeast Asia. It was recognized that WHO region designations could impose bureaucratic constraints in regard to promoting effective coordination between neighboring countries of different regions, Pakistan (Eastern Mediterranean Region) and India (Southeast Asia Region) being important examples.

To that end, WHO and UNICEF, with assistance from the South Asian Association for Regional Cooperation,

convened a meeting of high-level representatives from Afghanistan, Bangladesh, India, Iran, Myanmar, Nepal, and Pakistan in March 2000 to reach consensus on synchronizing polio immunization activities and streamlining communication strategies to expedite immediate reporting of acute flaccid paralysis cases across borders.

North Korea and South Korea are also in different WHO regions, but it is unlikely that transmission exists in either. However, to be certified polio free, North Korea will need to rapidly improve its surveillance performance, and this presents a challenge for partnership coordination between 2 countries with longstanding political tensions.

The Southeast Asia Regional Office estimates that since 1994, contributions from external partner agencies have totaled approximately $350 million. These contributions have been used to establish and coordinate surveillance activities and national immunization days across the region. It is also estimated that government in-kind contributions have been at least double the contributions from external sources, helping to cover costs of personnel, transport, and logistics.

Impact of Coordination on Polio Surveillance and Epidemiology

By 1999, all Southeast Asia Region countries had implemented active acute flaccid paralysis surveillance. Since 1997, 108 trained national surveillance medical officers in India have been strategically posted nationwide to assist health authorities in implementing active surveillance. In that country, 10 069 reporting units have been established to report acute flaccid paralysis cases weekly. Similarly, in 1999 Nepal deployed 8 surveillance medical officers, and Bangladesh deployed 16 officers (the latter was increased to 32 in 2000).

The nonpolio acute flaccid paralysis rate in Southeast Asia increased from 0.32 per 100 000 residents younger than 15 years in 1997 to 1.57 in 1999 (Table 1). In 1997, only Sri Lanka had a nonpolio acute flaccid paralysis rate above 1 per 100000. By 1999, India, Nepal, Sri Lanka, and

Thailand had rates above 1 per 100 000, and India, Myanmar, and Bangladesh had rates above 0.7 per 100000. In 1999, North Korea reported 14 acute flaccid paralysis cases, all pending classification.

The percentage of acute flaccid paralysis patients with 2 adequate stools (2 stools collected within 2 weeks of paralysis onset) in Southeast Asia increased from 39% in 1997 to 71% in 1999 (Table 1). In 1999, 2 adequate stools were collected for more than 80% of the acute flaccid paralysis cases reported in Indonesia, Sri Lanka, and Thailand; more than 70% of the cases reported in India and Nepal; and more than 60% of the cases reported in Myanmar.

Because the investment in surveillance occurred in 1997, the peak reported number of polio cases occurred in 1998 (see Figure 1 for a distribution of cases in the region). Southeast Asia accounted for 75% (4775) of all polio cases reported globally in 1998 and 52% (3334) in 1999. In addition, the region accounted for 85% (1942) of the wild-virus-confirmed polio cases reported globally in 1998 and 63% (1160) in 1999. Of all wild-virus-confirmed cases reported globally, India alone accounted for 85% in 1998 and 43% in 1999.

Even with improved surveillance, indigenous wild poliovirus was last isolated in Sri Lanka in 1993, in Indonesia in 1995, in Myanmar in 1996, and in Thailand in 1997 (Table 1). Bhutan and Maldives have been polio free for more than 10 years. Limited data are available from North Korea. In 2000, India, Bangladesh, and Nepal remained polio endemic.

Of the 1160 wild-virus-confirmed cases reported in Southeast Asia in 1999, 97% occurred in India (385 wild type 1, 11 wild type 2, 718 wild type 3, and 12 both type 1 and type 3), 2.3% occurred in Bangladesh (26 wild type 1 and 2 wild type 3), and the remainder occurred in Myanmar (4 wild type 1 due to importations) and Nepal (2 wild type 1). Bangladesh reported 28 virus-confirmed cases in 1999 (vs 8 in 1998), a number consistent with improved quality of surveillance (Tables 1 and 2). Nepal reported 2 wild-virus-confirmed cases in 1999 (vs 0 in 1998). Neither country reported virus-confirmed polio cases in January and February 2000.

The 4 wild type 1 poliovirus cases isolated in Myanmar were from the southern area bordering Bangladesh and were characterized, via genetic sequencing, as similar to those isolated in Bangladesh in 1999. The 2 wild type 1 poliovirus cases isolated in Nepal were from districts bordering Bihar and Uttar Pradesh.

India reported 1126 wild-virus-confirmed cases in 1999, as compared with 1942 in 1998, representing a 42% reduction in cases. Of the wild-virus-confirmed cases reported in India in 1999, 88% occurred in the northern states of Bihar (123), Delhi (730), Uttar Pradesh (773), and West Bengal (121). Delhi was the only state in India that reported an increase in wild-virus confirmed cases from 1998 (47 cases) to 1999 (73 cases). In 1999, the 11 wild-virus-confirmed cases due to type 2 occurred in Uttar Pradesh (10) and West Bengal (1).

Of the 47 wild-virus-confirmed polio cases reported in India in January and February 2000, 19 occurred in Bihar, 20 occurred in Uttar Pradesh, 3 occurred in West Bengal, and 1 each occurred in Gujarat, Karnataka, Madhya Pradesh, Maharashtra, and Manipur; no cases were reported in Delhi. The 42 wild-virus confirmed cases reported from Bihar, Uttar Pradesh, and West Bengal during January and February 2000 represented a 7% increase from the 39 cases occurring during the same period in 1999. Excluding Bihar, Delhi, Uttar Pradesh, and West Bengal, the 5 wild-virus-confirmed cases reported from India in January and February 2000 represented a 74% reduction from the 19 cases occurring during the same period in 1999.

Discussion

Effective international coordination of polio eradication activities requires well functioning technical oversight and partner coordination groups, such as the Technical Consultative Group and the Interagency Coordinating Committee, to ensure that strategies stay on track and sufficient resources are available to do the job. Cross-border meetings between neighboring countries have proven essential for interrupting transmission of wild poliovirus in reservoirs that extend beyond national boundaries. These meetings have aided collaboration between countries toward synchronizing massive supplementary disease control campaigns, such as national immunization days, and have improved disease surveillance and reporting through less formal but more rapid channels of communication.

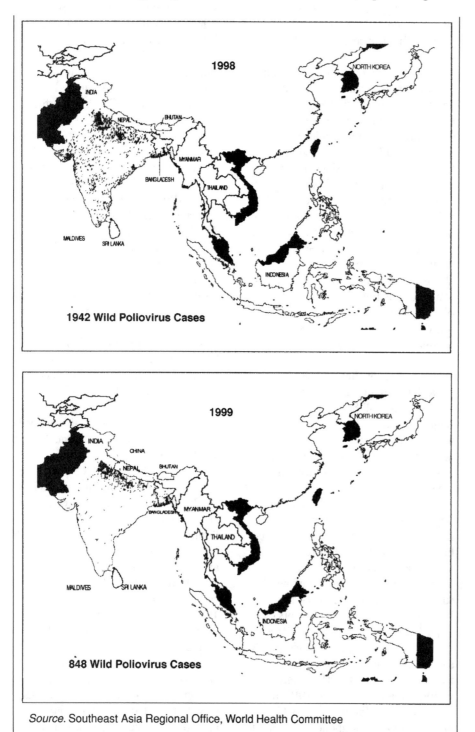

Source. Southeast Asia Regional Office, World Health Committee

FIGURE 1—Distribution of wild poliovirus cases: Southeast Asia Region (SEAR), 1998 and 1999

TABLE 2—Wild Poliovirus Isolation: Southeast Asia Region, 1997–1999

Poliovirus Type	1997	1998	1999
Type 1	634	1741	429
Type 2	3	83	11
Type 3	78	192	732
Total	715	2016	1172

Note. Data include mixtures.

Data from the Southeast Asia Regionwide active acute flaccid paralysis surveillance system now provide an accurate description of the current status of wild poliovirus transmission, allowing resources to be properly targeted. The global burden of polio in Southeast Asia member states decreased from more than 75% in 1998 to 52% in 1999. Indonesia, Thailand, and Myanmar appear to be joining the polio-free countries of Bhutan, Maldives, and Sri Lanka. From 1998 to 1999, reported cases of polio increased in Bangladesh, a change consistent with improvements in surveillance. Although polio has been markedly reduced in India, in northern India transmission of wild poliovirus has remained intense and most likely was a source of importations of virus into China in 1999, which had not isolated indigenous poliovirus cases since 1994.[14,15]

The persistent circulation of wild poliovirus type 2 in parts of Bihar, Uttar Pradesh, and West Bengal in India suggests that pockets of susceptible children are not being vaccinated via either routine services or national immunizationdays.[13]

Lessons learned from polio eradication may serve as a paradigm for the international control of other infectious diseases such as malaria and tuberculosis. Essential elements of this paradigm include effective leadership; appropriate use of, and new ways of working within, United Nations agencies such as WHO to streamline methods of work and communication between countries; a standardized surveillance strategy between countries; active surveillance supported by a team of qualified surveillance medical officers; an accredited laboratory network supported by state-of-the-art technologies such as genetic sequencing for tracking origins of infectious agents; performance indicators for monitoring progress and quality of activities; a technical oversight group that reviews and modifies control strategies; a partner coordinating body that ensures sufficient resources; powerful civic society partners (e.g., Rotary International) that can effectively lobby national governments from within the country; and rapid dissemination of information to those who need it most.

Effective cross-border coordination of polio eradication activities requires a high level of commitment. Efforts such as the mobilization of 2.4 million volunteers and the involvement of 500 district immunization officers, 108 surveillance medical officers, a national polio surveillance unit, and other Ministry of Health and Family Welfare staff in India are enhanced when such approaches are duplicated and synchronized in highly endemic neighboring countries. In such situations, chains of transmission of wild poliovirus in migrant populations are less likely to be missed.

About the Authors

Jon Kim Andrus, Arun B. Thapa, Nalini Withana, John W. Fitzsimmons, and Palitha Abeykoon are with the World Health Organization Southeast Asia Regional Office, New Delhi, India. Bruce Aylward is with the World Health Organization Polio Eradication Initiative, Geneva, Switzerland. Requests for reprints should be sent to Jon Kim Andrus, MD, SEARO/WHO, World Health House, Indraprastha Estate, Mahatma Gandhi Rd, New Delhi, 110002, India (e-mail: andrusj@whosea.org).

Contributors

J. K. Andrus directed WHO's Southeast Asia Region polio eradication initiative and is the primary investigator and author of the paper. A.B. Thapa, J.W. Fitzsimmons, N. Withana, P. Abeykoon assisted with the analysis of the data. B. Aylward coordinates the global polio eradication initiative and contributed to the discussion section of the paper.

References

1. World Health Assembly. *Global Eradication of Poliomyelitis by the Year 2000.* Geneva, Switzerland: World Health Organization; 1988. WHA resolution WHA41.28.
2. Hull HF, Ward NA, Hull BP, de Quadros C. Paralytic poliomyelitis: seasoned strategies, disappearing disease. *Lancet.* 1994;343: 1331–1337.
3. Aylward B, Andrus J, Bilous J, Smith J, Sanders R. Poliomyelitis immunisation programmes [letter]. *Lancet.* 1997;349:574–575.
4. Bijkerk H. Surveillance and control of poliomyelitis in the Netherlands. *Rev Infect Dis.* 1984;6 (suppl 2): S451–S456.
5. Kim-Farley RJ, Bart KJ, Schonberger LB, et al. Poliomyelitis in the USA: virtual elimination of disease caused by wild virus. *Lancet.* 1984;2: 1315–1317.
6. de Quadros CA, Andrus JK, Olive JM, de Macedo CG, Henderson DA. Polio eradication from the Western Hemisphere. *Annu Rev Public Health.* 1992;13:239–252.
7. Oostvogel PM, van Wijngaarden JK, van der Avoort HG, et al. Poliomyelitis outbreak in an unvaccinated community in the Netherlands, 1992–93. *Lancet.* 1994;344:665–670.
8. Centers for Disease Control and Prevention. Isolation of wild poliovirus type 3 among members of a religious community objecting to vaccination—Alberta, Canada, 1993. *MMWR Morb Mortal Wkly Rep.* 1993;42: 337–339.
9. *Progress Toward the Global Interruption of Wild Poliovirus Type 2 Transmission.* Atlanta, Ga: Centers for Disease Control and Prevention; 1999.
10. *Field Guide for Supplementary Activities Aimed at Achieving Polio Eradication.* Geneva, Switzerland: World Health Organization Expanded Programme on Immunization; 1995.
11. Banerjee K, Andrus JK, Hlady G. Conquering polio in India [letter].

Lancet. 1997;349:1630.

12. Andrus JK, Banerjee K, Hull BP, Smith JC, Mochny I. Polio eradication in the World Health Organization South-East Asia Region by the year 2000: midway assessment of progress and future challenges. *J Infect Dis.* 1997;175(suppl 1):S89–S96.

13. Banerjee K, Hlady G, Andrus JK, Sarkar S, Fitzsimmons J, Abeykoon P. Poliomyelitis surveillance: the model used in India for polio eradication. *Bull World Health Organ.* 2000;78: 321–329.

14. Centers for Disease Control and Prevention. Importation of wild poliovirus into Qinghai Province—China, 1999. *JAMA.* 2000;283:1414–1415.

15. Wang K, Zhang L, Otten MW, et al. Status of the eradication of indigenous wild poliomyelitis in the People's Republic of China. *J Infect Dis.* 1997;175(suppl 1):S105–S112.

An Outbreak of the Severe Acute Respiratory Syndrome: Predictors of Health Behaviors and Effect of Community Prevention Measures in Hong Kong, China

| Catherine S. K. Tang, PhD and Chi-yan Wong, MSSc

INTRODUCTION

The current global outbreak of the severe acute respiratory syndrome (SARS) poses an international public health threat.[1] Hong Kong, China, remains one of the most severely affected areas. We aimed to identify psychosocial factors associated with SARS preventive health behaviors and to assess whether preventive health behaviors increased after launching SARS community prevention activities.

METHODS

We telephone interviewed 1002 adult Chinese in wave 1 (March 17–18, 2003), which represented the early stage of the SARS outbreak in Hong Kong. A separate sample of 1329 adult Chinese were also telephone interviewed in wave 2 (March 29–April 1, 2003), which represented a period of vigorous community-wide SARS prevention activities by local health authorities. Response rates of the participants, calculated as percentages of completes to completes plus refusals, were 53% and 65% for waves 1 and 2, respectively. These two samples were comparable in various demographic information. The overall age distribution was 20% for 18 to 29 years, 50% for 30 to 49 years, 15% for 50 to 59 years, and 15% for 60 years or older.

We used key concepts of psychosocial models of health behaviors[2–4] to design our survey, which included the following measures.

Practice of Preventive Health Behaviors

Local health authorities have recommended the following preventive health behaviors to prevent the contracting and spreading of SARS: maintaining good personal hygiene, developing a healthy lifestyle, ensuring good ventilation, and wearing face masks. We asked participants in wave 1 to indicate how often in the past week they had practiced at least 1 of the above preventive health behaviors. In wave 2, we specifically asked participants how often they wore face masks to prevent contracting SARS during the last week. Participants responded with (1) never, (2) only a few times, (3) sometimes, or (4) almost all the time. We classified the first 3 responses as inconsistent preventive health behaviors (coded as 0) and "almost all the time" as consistent preventive health behaviors (coded as 1).

Perceived Knowledge About SARS, Susceptibility to SARS, and Self-Efficacy in Performing the Suggested Preventive Health Behaviors

These 3 psychosocial factors were each measured by 1 item. Participants indicated their perceptions on 4-point scales, with high scores representing high levels of these factors.

Attitudes Toward SARS Prevention Measures

Participants in wave 2 were assessed on their attitudes toward SARS community prevention measures by 5 items (on 4-point scales): (1) whether enough information was provided, (2) whether health guidelines were clear, (3) whether they believed that the suggested preventive health behaviors were effective, (4) whether they were satisfied with the government, and (5) whether they had confidence in the government's ability to control the spread of SARS. High scores corresponded to very favorable attitudes. The value for this scale was .73.

Demographics

All participants were asked about their age, education, income, and employment status.

RESULTS

We used SPSS 10.0 (SPSS Inc, Chicago, Ill) statistical software to conduct data analyses. The rates of preventive health behaviors for waves 1 and 2 are presented in Table 1. Results of a logistic regression analysis indicated that higher rates of preventive health behaviors in wave 1 (before exposure to SARS community prevention measures) were significantly related to greater perceived susceptibility to contracting SARS (odds ratio [OR] = 1.468; 95% confidence interval [CI] = 1.089, 1.979), greater self-efficacy in performing the preventive health behaviors (OR = 2.304; 95% CI = 1.672, 3.175), and older age (OR = 1.125; 95% CI = 1.063, 1.190).

The practice of SARS-specific preventive health behaviors (wearing of face masks) in wave 2 was expressed as a function of preventive health behaviors before exposure to SARS community prevention measures and attitudes toward these measures. The probability of preexposure preventive

TABLE 1— Rates of Preventive Health Behaviors

	Wave 1: No. Practicing Preventive Health Behaviors/Total (%)	Wave 2: No. Wearing Face Mask/Total (%)
Sex		
Male	136/449 (30.3)	281/533 (52.7)
Female	190/549 (34.6)	531/794 (66.9)
Age, y		
19–29	52/225 (23.1)	142/269 (52.8)
30–49	177/513 (34.5)	383/620 (61.8)
50–59	42/137 (30.7)	133/195 (68.2)
> 60	49/109 (45.0)	154/243 (63.4)
Education		
Primary school	48/145 (33.1)	169/280 (60.4)
High school	188/610 (30.8)	434/717 (60.5)
Community college/university	88/235 (37.4)	198/311 (63.7)
Employment		
Full-time/part-time	177/552 (32.1)	426/701 (60.8)
Homemakers	63/180 (35.0)	190/277 (68.6)
Students	26/95 (27.4)	47/103 (45.6)
Retired	39/89 (43.8)	105/164 (64.0)
Unemployed	19/70 (27.1)	35/68 (51.5)
Personal monthly income, $		
< 1000	16/69 (23.2)	42/91 (46.2)
1000–2500	96/281 (34.2)	229/377 (60.7)
2501–5000	37/108 (34.3)	75/127 (59.1)
> 5000	8/22 (36.4)	28/41 (68.3)
Overall	327/1002 (32.6)	812/1329 (61.2)

health behaviors was calculated from estimated coefficients of various psychosocial and demographic factors as derived from wave 1. Results of the logistic regression analysis indicated that higher rates of preventive health behaviors in wave 2 were associated with more favorable attitudes toward prevention measures (OR = 1.493; 95% CI = 1.097, 2.033) and higher probability of preexposure preventive health behaviors (OR = 2.662; 95%

CI = 2.154, 3.289; Table 2). The marginal effect of favorable attitudes toward prevention measures was estimated to be a 9.2% increase in preventive health behaviors in wave 2 with 1-unit change in these attitudes (measured on 4-point scale). In waves 1 and 2, 32.7% and 61.2%, respectively, of the participants reported consistent practice of preventive health behaviors (OR = 3.245; 95% CI = 2.735, 3.852; power = 1.00).

DISCUSSION

Our results were supportive of the contribution of perceived susceptibility,[2] selfefficacy,[4] and age[5–7] in predicting the practice of preventive health behaviors. Favorable attitudes toward SARS prevention measures also were associated with higher rates of SARS-specific preventive health behaviors. Furthermore, we supported that community-level prevention meas-

TABLE 2— Logistic Regression Results on Preventive Health Behaviors

	Coefficient	SE	OR	95% CI	P
Wave 1: Before exposure to prevention measures					
Constant	-5.463	. . .	. . .	. . .	. . .
Knowledge	0.165	0.128	1.179	0.918, 1.514	.197
Perceived susceptibility	0.384	0.152	1.468	1.089, 1.979	.012
Self-efficacy	0.835	0.164	2.304	1.672, 3.175	.000
Sex (male)	0.200	0.152	1.221	0.906, 1.646	.189
Age	0.117	0.029	1.125	1.063, 1.190	.000
Education	0.118	0.081	1.125	0.960, 1.319	.147
Wave 2: After exposure to prevention measures					
Constant	-0.671	. . .	. . .	. . .	. . .
Estimated preexposure preventive health behaviors	0.979	0.108	2.662	2.154, 3.289	.000
Attitudes toward prevention measures	0.401	0.157	1.493	1.097, 2.033	.011

Note. OR = odds ratio; CI = confidence interval. Wave 1: number of observations = 1002; log likelihood = 1094.19; χ^2 = 55.41 (*P* = .000). Wave 2: number of observations = 1329; log likelihood = 1501.84; χ^2 = 96.41 (*P* = .000).

ures against SARS were related to significant increases (28.5%) in individuals' practice of the recommended preventive health behaviors. We suggest that SARS community prevention activities should focus on the perception of personal vulnerability as well as the promotion of self-efficacy and favorable attitudes toward prevention measures. Finally, it should be noted that increases in the suggested preventive health behaviors might have been influenced by other extraneous factors in addition to being exposed to SARS community prevention measures.

About the Authors
Catherine S. K. Tang and Chi-yan Wong are with the Chinese University of Hong Kong, Shatin, NT, Hong Kong, China.

Correspondence: Requests for reprints should be sent to Catherine S.K. Tang, PhD, Department of Psychology, The Chinese University of Hong Kong, Shatin, NT, Hong Kong, China (e-mail: ctang@cuhk.edu.hk).

Contributors
Both authors contributed to the conception and design of the study, data analysis, and interpretation of findings. C. S. K. Tang took the lead in writing the brief.

References
1. World Health Organization. Update 27: One month into the global SARS outbreak: status of the outbreak and lessons for the immediate future. Available at: http://www.who.int/csr/sars/archive/2003_04_11/en. Accessed April 11, 2003.
2. Rosenstock IM, Strecher VJ, Becker MH. Social learning theory and the health belief model. *Health Educ Q.*1988;15:175–183.
3. Ajzen I, Fishbein M. *Understanding Attitudes and* Predicting Social Behavior. Englewood Cliffs, NJ: Prentice-Hall; 1980.
4. Bandura A. *Self-Efficacy: The Exercise of Control.* New York, NY: WH Freeman Co; 1997.
5. Berrigan D, Dodd K, Troiano RP, Krebs-Smith SM, Barbash RB. Patterns of health behaviors in US adults. *Prev Med.*2003;36:615–623.
6. Pappas G. Elucidating the relationships between race, socioeconomic status, and health. *Am J Public Health.*1994;84:892–893.
7. Shi L. Socio-demographic characteristics and individual health behaviors. *South Med J.*1998;91:933–941.

Stigmatization of Newly Emerging Infectious Diseases: AIDS and SARS

| Don C. Des Jarlais, PhD, Sandro Galea, MD, Melissa Tracy, BA, Susan Tross, PhD and David Vlahov, PhD

ABSTRACT

Objectives. We assessed relationships between sociodemographic characteristics and mental health status and knowledge of, being worried about, and stigmatization of 2 emerging infectious diseases: AIDS and SARS.

Methods. We conducted a random-digit-dialed survey of 928 residents of the New York City metropolitan area as part of a study of the effects of the September 11, 2001, terrorist attacks. Questions added for this study concerned respondents' knowledge of, worry about, and support of stigmatizing actions to control AIDS and SARS.

Results. In general, respondents with greater personal resources (income, education, social support) and better mental health status had more knowledge, were less worried, and were less likely to stigmatize. This pattern held for both AIDS and SARS.

Conclusions. Personal resources and mental health factors are likely to influence the public's ability to learn about, rationally appraise the threat of, and minimize stigmatization of emerging infectious diseases such as AIDS and SARS.

INTRODUCTION

Both the fear of people who are different and the fear of disease can lead to social stigmatization.[1] Occasionally these fears co-occur, resulting in severe stigmatization of strangers with diseases. Such stigmatization can increase the adverse consequences of a disease in multiple ways.

First, stigmatization can substantially increase the suffering of persons with the disease. Second, persons with or at risk for the disease may avoid seeking health care, making it much harder for public health authorities to control the disease. Third, professionals and volunteers working in the field may also become stigmatized, leading to higher rates of stress and burnout.[2] Finally, stigmatization may generate considerable economic losses if people avoid groups or geographic areas associated with the disease.

Many diseases have been stigmatized throughout history. For example, persons with the plague were stigmatized during the Middle Ages, and sexually transmitted diseases have been stigmatized throughout the last several centuries.[3,4] Acquired immunodeficiency syndrome (AIDS) has been one of the most feared and stigmatized diseases of the last 20 years. There is abundant evidence that the stigmatization of AIDS has been detrimental to the health of those with AIDS and has played a role in limiting public health and medical efforts to control the disease.[5,6] For example, early stigmatization of AIDS as a disease of homosexual men contributed to low levels of funding for AIDS research in the1980s.[3,4,7]

Over the last several years, severe acute respiratory syndrome (SARS) has emerged as a new feared disease associated with strangers (Asians, particularly Chinese) and has generated considerable stigmatization.[8,9] Reduced travel to SARS-affected areas clearly led to large economic losses for those areas,[10,11] but there has been relatively little systematic research on fear of SARS or stigmatization of persons with or at risk for the disease.[12] In one study of medical access patterns in Taiwan, Chang and colleagues found that "fear of SARS" led to substantial reductions in seeking medical care: a 23.9% reduction for ambulatory care, a 35.2% reduction for inpatient care, and a 16.7% reduction for dental care.[13] Presumably, people avoided seeking medical care out of fear of becoming infected with SARS in these medical settings. Studying the stigmatization of SARS may provide us with insight into the stigma associated with emerging infectious diseases and the potential consequences of such stigmatization.

A potentially useful model for considering stigmatization of SARS and other newly emerging infectious diseases may be found in the work of Pryor et al.[14] They suggest a 2-factor theory of HIV- related stigma: (1) an immediate affective reaction, based on multiple negative qualities associated with the disease (e.g., death, promiscuity, drug use, homosexuality), possibly followed by (2) a cognitive rule-based system that ameliorates stigmatization "if perceivers have enough time, motivation, and cognitive resources."[14(p1189)] Within this formulation, availability of additional information about the disease should lead to a reduction in stigmatization. This prediction is consistent with the activities of many public health authorities who hope to reduce stigmatization through increased public education on diseases such as AIDS.

We compared stigmatizing attitudes toward AIDS and SARS in a representative sample of persons living in the New York City (NYC) metropolitan area and examined factors associated with these attitudes.

METHODS

Participants

We obtained data from a cohort of persons who were living in the NYC metropolitan area on September 11, 2001. Briefly, the cohort was recruited through a random-digit-dialed telephone survey between March 25 and June 25, 2002, for the purpose of understanding the consequences of the September 11 terrorist attacks in the NYC area. The sampling frame consisted of all adults (aged 18 years and older) in the NYC metropolitan area. (Additional details are provided elsewhere.[15]) Interviews were conducted in English, Spanish, Mandarin, and Cantonese by trained interviewers using translated and back-translated questionnaires and a computer-assisted telephone interview system. In each eligible household, the adult whose birthday was closest to the interview date was chosen to participate. Up to 10 attempts were made to conduct the interview. The response rates among those eligible for survey participation were 56% in the metropolitan area and 60% in New York City itself.

Contact information for follow-up interviews was obtained from respondents and their key family members. Follow-up was conducted between September 25, 2002, and January 31, 2003, and between September 24, 2003, and February 29, 2004. We completed follow-up interviews with 1832 (67%) of the 2748 baseline respondents during the second follow-up, at which time we asked the questions reported on here. Each participant received a nominal $10 incentive to participate in each survey wave, and each interview was approximately 35 minutes long.

Survey Instrument

Demographic data for this analysis came from the baseline interview, during which we collected information on respondents' age, race/ethnicity, gender, and education. Data about self-assessed knowledge of and attitudes toward SARS and AIDS were collected from a randomly selected subset of participants in the second cohort follow-up. These questions were modified from previous work (J. Ahern, J. Stuber, and S. Galea, unpublished data, 2005).

We first asked if the respondent had heard about SARS; those who said yes were asked if they had heard "a great deal," "some," or "not much" about the disease. We then asked respondents who had heard about SARS how much they agreed or disagreed with each of the following statements as a method for controlling the disease: "requiring Americans with SARS to wear identification tags," "the government announcing it will execute people who knowingly spread SARS," "quarantining or separating all people with SARS from others in the United States," "avoiding areas in the United States that are heavily populated by Chinese," "forcing all Chinese people to be medically checked for SARS," and "not allowing Chinese people to enter the United States." An additional statement concerned whether people who developed the disease could be blamed: "People with SARS got what they deserved." Response options were "agree strongly," "agree somewhat," "disagree somewhat," or "disagree strongly." We asked equivalent questions about AIDS, substituting "HIV or AIDS" for "SARS" and "gay men" for "Chinese."

We also constructed a summary stigmatization scale for each disease by summing the responses to the 6 questions about stigmatizing methods of controlling the disease. The Cronbach was 0.80 for the AIDS stigmatization scale and 0.72 for the SARS stigmatization scale. We also asked respondents how worried they were about contracting SARS or AIDS— "not at all worried," "somewhat worried," or "very worried."

We were interested in whether worry and stigmatization were associated with psychological conditions such as depression. To assess depression, we used an adapted version of the major depressive disorder scale from the non-patient version of the structured clinical interview for the *Diagnostic and Statistical Manual of Mental Disorders, Revised Third Edition* (*DSM III-R*),[16] which has been used in other population studies.[17,18] We followed *DSM-IV* guidelines, considering that respondents met the criteria for depression if they had experienced 5 or more symptoms for at least 2 weeks. We also asked when was the last time the respondent experienced these symptoms. The Cronbach for the 8 symptoms used in this scale was 0.79.[19] We asked about depressive symptoms in the previous 12 months and in the 1 month before the interview.

Analyses

We used means to summarize responses to each of the questions about AIDS and SARS attitudes and then assessed the correlations between responses. We used 2 tests, t tests, and Pearson correlations to assess relationships between various factors and knowledge of and attitudes toward AIDS and SARS. The analyses were weighted to correct potential selection bias related to the number of household telephones, the number of persons in the household, and oversampling, as well as to make the sample demographically similar to the NYC metropolitan area population according to 2000 US Census estimates. We used SUDAAN software (release 8.0; Research Triangle Institute, Research Triangle Park, NC) to estimate standard errors and to adjust analyses for weighting.

RESULTS

The sample was weighted to approximate the 2000 US Census data for the NYC metropolitan area: 45% male, 55% female; 54% White, 19% African American, 5% Asian, 20% Hispanic, 3% other; 11% aged 18 through 24 years, 26% aged 25 through 34 years, 21% aged 35 through 44 years, 18% aged 45 through 54 years, 12% aged 55 through 64 years, and 12% aged 65 years or older.

TABLE 1— Mean Responses to Survey Questions About AIDS and SARS: New York City Metropolitan Area, 2003 (n = 928)

	Mean Response, AIDS	Mean Response, SARS	r
How much have you heard about AIDS (SARS)?[a]	3.78	3.78	0.327
Should Americans with AIDS (SARS) be required to wear identification tags?[b]	1.77	1.77	0.674
Should people who knowingly spread AIDS (SARS) be executed?[b]	1.92	1.92	0.710
Should people in the United States with AIDS (SARS) be quarantined?[b]	1.62	1.62	0.287
Should people avoid areas in the United States heavily populated by gay men (Chinese)?[b]	1.68	1.68	0.339
Should all gay men (Chinese) be forcibly checked for AIDS (SARS)?[b]	2.24	2.24	0.508
Should gay men (Chinese) not be allowed to enter the United States?[b]	1.43	1.43	0.138
Did people with AIDS (SARS) get what they deserve?[b]	1.23	1.23	0.492
How worried are you about getting AIDS (SARS)?[c]	1.34	1.34	0.288

Note. Parenthetical wording pertains only to questions regarding SARS. All Ps < .0001.
[a]Coded from 2 (not much) to 4 (a great deal).
[b]Coded from 1 (disagree strongly) to 4 (agree strongly).
[c]Coded from 1 (not at all) to 3 (very).

Table 1 shows the means for the responses to the questions on AIDS and SARS and the correlations between the AIDS and SARS responses. The means were quite similar for both sets of responses. There was only 1 question with a 1-point difference in the means: there was substantially more agreement on quarantining people with SARS than on quarantining people with AIDS ($t=-38.8$; $P<.0001$). Thus, given the modes of transmission and length of incubation period for the 2 diseases, quarantine would be an acceptable public health measure for controlling SARS, but not AIDS, in New York City. There was a 0.5-point difference between mean responses to the question "How much have you heard about [AIDS/SARS]?" Respondents reported having heard more about AIDS than about SARS ($t=25.2$; $P<.0001$). There was relatively little agreement with the "blaming" question ("People with [AIDS or SARS] got what they deserved") for either AIDS or SARS (means of 1.23 and 1.11, respectively, on a scale of 1 [disagree strongly] to 4 [agree strongly]).

The correlations between responses to the AIDS questions and responses to the SARS questions were statistically significant for all questions and ranged from a low of 0.14, for allowing gay men or Chinese into the country, to a high of 0.71, for executing persons who knowingly spread AIDS or SARS. The correlation for the question on being worried about getting AIDS/SARS was significant but modest at 0.29.

Responses to the questions concerning relatively extreme forms of stigmatization (requiring persons with the disease to wear identification tags, executing persons who knowingly spread the disease, forcing all gay men to be checked for AIDS or Chinese for SARS) were highly correlated, with correlation coefficients between 0.51 and 0.71. The correlation for the question on blaming persons with the disease ("They got what they deserved") was also relatively high (0.49).

There were few significant associations between sociodemographic variables (age, gender, and race/ethnicity) and knowledge of and attitudes toward AIDS and SARS. Younger respondents (younger than 45 years) and Whites were less likely than others to express stigmatizing attitudes toward AIDS. Younger respondents were more likely than older respondents to report being "somewhat" or "very" worried about getting AIDS, and women were more likely than men to report that they were "somewhat" or "very" worried about getting SARS. Whites were less likely than those of other races to be concerned about getting AIDS and SARS (data available from the first author).

As shown in Table 2, educational level was related to almost all of the responses on the AIDS and SARS questions. There were multiple significant relationships between higher educational levels and decreased agreement with the stigmatizing methods of controlling the diseases. The relationships were generally negative, with more educated respondents expressing less agreement with the stigmatizing methods of disease control. The question on the use of quarantine was a notable exception to this general pattern.

Table 3 shows, for each disease, correlations between knowledge ("heard about"), the summary stigmatization scale, blaming, and being worried about getting the disease. There were consistent patterns among knowledge, stigmatization, blaming, and worry for both diseases. Greater knowledge was modestly associated with less stigmatization and less blaming. Within the group of respondents

TABLE 2— Survey Respondents' Knowledge and Attitudes About AIDS and SARS, by Educational Attainment: New York City Metropolitan Area, 2003 (n = 928)

Question	AIDS							SARS						
	Not much, %	Some/a great deal, %	Agree, %	Disagree, % / Not at all, %	Somewhat, %	Very, %	P	Not much, %	Some/a great deal, %	Agree, %	Disagree, % / Not at all, %	Somewhat, %	Very, %	P
How much have you heard about AIDS (SARS)?							.215							.224
<High school	6.0	94.0						22.0	78.0					
High school or equivalent	6.4	93.6						18.1	82.0					
Some college	1.6	98.4						13.2	86.8					
College degree	4.7	95.3						11.3	88.7					
Graduate work	0.7	99.4						7.4	92.6					
Should Americans with AIDS (SARS) be required to wear identification tags?							.0003							.010
<High school			47.6	52.4						38.2	61.8			
High school or equivalent			33.5	66.5						37.6	62.4			
Some college			21.2	78.8						28.8	71.2			
College degree			21.6	78.4						25.4	74.6			
Graduate work			10.4	89.6						12.4	87.6			
Should people who knowingly spread AIDS (SARS) be executed?							.005							.315
<High school			45.0	55.0						28.6	71.4			
High school or equivalent			36.4	63.7						20.8	79.2			
Some college			29.0	71.0						25.5	74.5			
College degree			24.8	75.3						20.2	79.8			
Graduate work			15.0	85.0						12.7	87.3			
Should people in the United States with AIDS (SARS) be quarantined?							.0002							.091
<High school			34.8	65.3						55.4	44.6			
High school or equivalent			25.6	74.4						73.3	26.7			
Some college			19.4	80.6						76.0	24.0			
College degree			11.8	88.2						73.6	26.4			
Graduate work			6.1	93.9						60.9	39.1			
Should people avoid areas in the United States heavily populated by gay men (Chinese)?							.001							.009
<High school			30.9	69.1						16.0	84.0			
High school or equivalent			25.4	74.6						22.1	77.9			
Some college			23.3	76.7						20.8	79.2			
College degree			12.4	87.6						19.8	80.2			
Graduate work			7.2	92.8						5.5	94.5			

TABLE 2– CONTINUED

	AIDS								SARS							
Question	Not much, %	Some/a great deal, %	Agree, %	Disagree, %	Not at all, %	Somewhat, %	Very, %	P	Not much, %	Some/a great deal, %	Agree, %	Disagree, %	Not at all, %	Somewhat, %	Very, %	P
Should all gay men (Chinese) be forcibly checked for AIDS (SARS)?																
<High school			77.9	22.1				<.0001			48.6	51.4				<.0001
High school or equivalent			53.4	46.7							48.7	51.3				
Some college			43.1	56.9							38.9	61.2				
College degree			34.9	65.1							26.2	73.8				
Graduate work			17.4	82.6							11.0	89.0				
Should gay men (Chinese) not be allowed to enter the United States?																
<High school			9.7	90.3				.012			28.1	72.0				.002
High school or equivalent			14.8	85.2							20.8	79.3				
Some college			13.4	86.6							25.8	74.2				
College degree			5.4	94.6							12.2	87.8				
Graduate work			3.2	96.8							6.2	93.8				
Did people with AIDS (SARS) get what they deserve?																
<High school			6.5	93.5				.121			3.5	96.5				…
High school or equivalent			7.0	93.0							2.7	97.3				
Some college			5.3	94.7							0.8	99.2				
College degree			1.7	98.3							0.0	100.0				
Graduate work			6.9	93.1							0.0	100.0				
How worried are you about getting AIDS (SARS)?																
<High school					59.2	22.0	18.9	<.0001					53.3	33.4	13.3	.098
High school or equivalent					64.6	25.0	10.4						53.6	42.9	3.6	
Some college					66.7	31.9	1.4						48.9	43.9	7.2	
College degree					71.1	26.9	2.0						56.6	38.6	4.9	
Graduate work					86.2	12.8	1.0						70.9	27.4	1.7	

Note. Parenthetical wording pertains only to questions regarding SARS.

TABLE 3— Correlations Between Survey Respondents' Knowledge and Attitudes About AIDS and SARS, Overall and by Degree of Worry About Getting the Disease: New York City Metropolitan Area, 2003 (n = 928)

	AIDS (n = 917)						SARS (n = 863)					
	How Much Heard About the Disease[a]		Stigmatization Scale[b]		People With the Disease Got What They Deserve[c]		How Much Heard About the Disease[a]		Stigmatization Scale[b]		People With the Disease Got What They Deserve[c]	
	r	P	r	P	r	P	r	P	r	P	r	P
Stigmatization scale[b]	−0.177	<.0001	...	...	...	...	−0.160	−<.0001	...	...	...	...
People with the disease got what they deserve[c]	−0.117	.0004	0.349	<.0001	...	...	−0.216	<.0001	0.208	<.0001	...	...
How worried about getting the disease[d]	−0.035	.290	0.170	<.0001	0.028	.402	0.027	.423	0.213	<.0001	0.039	.249

Not at all worried about getting the disease

	AIDS (n = 669)						SARS (n = 498)					
Stigmatization scale[b]	−0.203	<.0001	...	...	...	...	−0.134	.003	...	...	...	...
People with the disease got what they deserve[c]	−0.141	.0003	0.375	<.0001	...	...	−0.191	<.0001	0.208	<.0001	...	...

Somewhat worried about getting the disease

	AIDS (n = 199)						SARS (n = 318)					
Stigmatization scale[b]	−0.209	.003	...	...	...	...	−0.276	<.0001	...	...	...	...
People with the disease got what they deserve[c]	−0.096	.182	0.311	<.0001	...	...	−0.274	<.0001	0.216	.0001	...	...

Very worried about getting the disease

	AIDS (n = 45)						SARS (n = 45)					
Stigmatization scale[b]	0.258	.091	...	...	...	...	−0.155	.311	...	...	...	...
People with the disease got what they deserve[c]	−0.150	.332	0.197	.205	...	...	−0.086	.575	0.103	.502	...	...

Note. Ns do not fully add up because of missing data.
[a]Coded 2 (not much) to 4 (a great deal).
[b]Coded 6 (less stigmatization) to 24 (more stigmatization).
[c]Coded 1 (disagree strongly) to 4 (agree strongly).
[d]Coded 1 (not at all worried) to 3 (very worried).

TABLE 4— Associations Between Depression and Worry About Getting AIDS or SARS: New York City Metropolitan Area, 2003

| How Worried | Worried About Getting AIDS | | | | Worried About Getting SARS | | | |
| | Symptoms of Depression in Past Year | | Symptoms of Depression in Past Month | | Symptoms of Depression in Past Year | | Symptoms of Depression in Past Month | |
	No. (%)	P	No. (%)	P	No. (%)	P	No. (%)	P
Not at all	75 (8.6)	.0003	37 (4.5)	.039	54 (8.0)	.015	26 (3.8)	.054
Somewhat	52 (19.4)		22 (10.0)		58 (15.3)		27 (7.8)	
Very	13 (30.8)		6 (13.7)		12 (22.9)		5 (15.7)	

Note. "No." reflects the actual count of respondents in each cell; "%" is the percentage of people reporting different levels of depression symptoms within the categories of worry about the disease. This percentage is based on the weighting procedures described in Methods.

who were "very worried" about getting either disease, however, having heard more about the disease was associated with greater stigmatization ($r = 0.26$ for AIDS, $r = 0.16$ for SARS; both $Ps > .05$).

Table 4 shows associations between concern about getting AIDS or SARS and having experienced symptoms of depression in the year before the interview. All of the associations were of positive-response form, with higher rates of depression within each category of increasing worry. In a cross-sectional study we cannot ascertain the direction of cause and effect.

DISCUSSION

We found a number of similarities between attitudes toward AIDS and attitudes toward SARS. Some sociodemographic characteristics, especially lower educational levels, were associated with endorsement of a variety of stigmatizing methods for the control of each disease. Increasing levels of worry about getting each disease were associated with depression.

Similarities and Differences Between AIDS and SARS

There are several strong similarities between AIDS and SARS from a psychological perspective, suggesting that they may serve as a model for stigmatizing attitudes toward serious emerging infectious diseases in general. Both AIDS and SARS are relatively

new, both are fatal for a high percentage of persons who develop the disease, and both are associated with "stranger" groups (gay men and injection drug users for AIDS, Asians in general and Chinese in particular for SARS). However, there are very important differences in the epidemiology of the 2 diseases, and New York City's experiences with AIDS and SARS have been radically different.

HIV/AIDS has truly been a public health catastrophe for the city, with a cumulative total of 122062 cases of AIDS[20] and an estimated 3105 new HIV infections per year in the city at the time of data collection (September 2003).[21] In contrast, there were only 9 cases of SARS reported in the metropolitan area, there was no known local transmission of SARS, and by the time of data collection the World Health Organization had officially declared that SARS had been contained globally.[22] The modes of transmission (and thus, the ability of an individual to avoid infection) are also quite different for the 2 diseases—primarily sexual and blood-to-blood contact for AIDS, and primarily droplet transmission for SARS.

This study showed great consistency in attitudes toward both diseases, suggesting that the psychological similarities between the 2 diseases may be more important in shaping attitudes toward them than the epidemiological differences. For example, the means of responses on the "worried" question

were almost identical for the 2 diseases (approximately 1.5 on a 3-point scale from "not at all worried" to "very worried"). The associations between educational level and attitudes toward the diseases were nearly identical as well. Also, for each disease there were relatively high correlations between the severe stigmatization questions and blaming people with the disease. This suggests that the responses to these questions may be relatively independent of the specific characteristics of AIDS and SARS, including the objective likelihood of contracting the diseases.

Zajonc has described the "primacy of affect" in psychological processes,[23] and our findings do strongly suggest that the negative emotions aroused by the 2 diseases generate similar patterns of stigmatization and override the differences in their epidemiology.

Stigmatization of Emerging Infectious Diseases

People with diseases appear to have been stigmatized throughout history. This stigmatization and the resulting social shunning may have served to reduce transmission of infectious diseases in the past, and quarantine and avoidance of people and places associated with a disease may still be useful in controlling some diseases. With emerging infectious diseases in the context of economic globalization, however, stigmatization and the fear of stigmatization may also actively increase the spread of the diseases. Individuals with or at risk for stigmatized diseases may avoid seeking health care in order to avoid being stigmatized. Governments may attempt to suppress information about emerging infectious diseases in their jurisdictions because of the potentially severe economic consequences associated with stigmatization of an infectious disease. Thus, in the current era, control of emerging infectious diseases will require that we increase our ability to ameliorate the stigmatization associated with such diseases.

Reducing Stigmatization of AIDS and SARS

Public health authorities have used a variety of methods to attempt to reduce stigmatization associated with HIV/AIDS.[24] These methods have included (1) basic public education about HIV/AIDS, such as national mailing of an informational pamphlet from the US surgeon general; (2) mass media (print, radio, and television) campaigns; (3) publicized symbolic acts by public leaders indicating that there is no need to fear people and places associated with the disease, such as pictures of the US president with AIDS patients; (4) creating or invoking laws or policies prohibiting stigmatization and discrimination, such as invoking the Americans with Disabilities Act to protect the rights of people with HIV/AIDS; and (5) drawing attention to sympathetic people with AIDS, such as Ryan White.

These efforts have been partially successful. National probability sample telephone surveys conducted throughout the 1990s[5] showed that overt expressions of stigmatization declined over time. However, inaccurate beliefs, such as a belief in transmission via casual contact, and punitive beliefs (that people with HIV/AIDS deserved the disease) increased. In 1999, one third of the sample expressed negative reactions to and discomfort with people with HIV.

There have been some attempts to reduce fear and stigmatization of SARS, such as public education campaigns.[25,26] There has also been a con-

certed attempt by health officials worldwide to keep the public informed of new developments regarding SARS, including the occurrence of infections through laboratory accidents.[27,28] Determining whether these efforts have been effective will require additional research.

Our data indicate some potential effectiveness of providing accurate information to the public as a strategy to reduce stigmatization. For both AIDS and SARS, the more subjects had heard about the disease, the less likely they were to express stigmatizing attitudes. However, some limitations of this strategy were also indicated. For the subgroup who were "very worried" about contracting the diseases, having heard more about the diseases was not associated with less stigmatization. Additionally, being depressed was associated with being worried about the diseases, suggesting that there may be important nonrational linkages between a person's general emotional status and his or her reaction to emerging diseases.

Interestingly, there also appears to be a carryover in time of worry about these types of diseases. Our data were collected after SARS was officially declared contained by the World Health Organization, but many of our respondents were still worried about contracting the disease. Indeed, the level of worry about contracting SARS was equal to the level of worry about contracting AIDS.

Limitations

There seems to be little doubt that both AIDS and SARS could evoke stigmatizing behaviors, which we were not able to directly assess. Actual enactment of stigmatizing behaviors may depend upon a variety of situational factors in addition to the possession of stigmatizing attitudes. Whether the patterns of stigmatizing behaviors would be similar for the 2 diseases remains to be addressed.

Our study was an exploratory effort added to an existing telephone survey. The time that we could add to the existing interview was limited, and some variables had to be measured

with single questions. We did not have prior work from which to formulate hypotheses and, thus, did not attempt multivariate analyses for testing hypotheses. Most of the correlation coefficients we observed were in the range of 0.3 to 0.7. Although these were highly significant, given our sample size, these coefficients correspond to between 10% and 50% of variance explained in the dependent variable. We expect that in future research, it will be possible to develop formal multivariate models that will explain higher percentages of variance in the dependent variables.

Conclusions

The data reported here concern AIDS and SARS, 2 "naturally occurring" infectious diseases. Whether the same stigmatization processes would occur in the context of a bioterrorist attack using infectious agents is an important issue for further investigation.

Additional new infectious diseases are likely to emerge in the coming years, some of which will arise in foreign countries and spread through international air travel. Some will also have high fatality rates. Many different strategies will be needed to control these new diseases, from improved laboratory facilities to better communication networks among health authorities in different countries. Better methods for ameliorating the fear and stigmatization associated with these diseases are also needed, and we suggest that this be considered an urgent matter for additional research.

About the Authors

Don C. Des Jarlais and Susan Tross are with Beth Israel Medical Center, New York, NY. Sandro Galea, Melissa Tracy, and David Vlahov are with the New York Academy of Medicine, New York, NY.

Correspondence: Requests for reprints should be sent to Don C. Des Jarlais, PhD, Beth Israel Medical Center, 160 Water St, 24th floor, New York, NY 10038 (e-mail: dcdesjarla@aol.com).

Acknowledgments

This work was supported in part by the National Institutes of Health (grants DA017642, MH066391, and DA003574).

Human Participants Protection

The institutional review board of the New York Academy of Medicine reviewed and approved this study.

Contributors

D.C. Des Jarlais and S. Galea planned the study, analyzed the data, and wrote the article. M. Tracy analyzed the data and contributed to the writing of this article. S. Tross and D. Vlahov contributed to the writing of this article.

References

1. Goffman E. *Stigma: Notes on the Management of a Spoiled Identity.* New York, NY: Simon & Schuster; 1963.
2. Snyder M, Omoto AM, Crain AL. Punished for their good deeds: stigmatization of AIDS volunteers. *Am Behav Sci.* 1999;42:1193–1211.
3. Brandt AM. *No Magic Bullet: A Social History of Venereal Disease in the United States Since 1880.* Expanded ed. New York, NY: Oxford University Press; 1987.
4. Brandt AM, Rozin P. *Morality and Health.* New York, NY: Routledge; 1997.
5. Herek G, Capitanio J, Widaman K. HIV-related stigma and knowledge in the United States: prevalence and trends 1991–1999. *Am J Public Health.* 2002;92: 371–377.
6. Parker R, Aggleton P. HIV and AIDS-related stigma and discrimination: a conceptual framework and implications for action. *Soc Sci Med.* 2003;57:13–24.
7. Shilts R. *And the Band Played On: Politics, People, and the AIDS Epidemic.* New York, NY: St Martins Press; 1987.
8. Arnold W. In travel to Singapore, suspicion is a form of defense. *New York Times.* April 21, 2003: A31.
9. Chang I. Fear of SARS, fear of strangers. *New York Times.* March 21, 2003: A1.
10. Bradsher K. Outbreak of disease brings big drop-off in China's economy. *New York Times.* April 28, 2003:A1, A14.
11. Bradsher K. Economies sickened by a virus, and fear. *New York Times.* April 21, 2003:A1, A8.
12. Person B, Sy F, Holton K, Govert B, Liang A, National Center for Infectious Disease/SARS Community Outreach Team. Fear and stigma: the epidemic within the SARS outbreak. *Emerg Infect Dis.* 2004;1: 358–363.
13. Chang H-J, Huang N, Lee C-H, Hsu Y-J, Hsieh C-J, Chou Y-J. The impact of the SARS epidemic on the utilization of medical services: SARS and the fear of SARS. *Am J Public Health.* 2004;94:562–564.
14. Pryor JB, Reeder GD, Landau S. A social-psychological analysis of HIV-related stigma: a two-factor theory. *Am Behav Sci.* 1999;42:1212–1228.
15. Galea S, Vlahov D, Tracy M, Hoover DR, Resnick H, Kilpatrick D. Hispanic ethnicity and post-traumatic stress disorder after a disaster: evidence from a general populations survey after September 11. *Ann Epidemiol.* 2004;14:520–531.
16. Spitzer RL, Williams JB, Gibbon M. *Structured Clinical Interview for DSM-III-R–Non-Patient Version.* New York, NY: Biometrics Research Department, New York State Psychiatric Institute; 1987.
17. Boscarino JA, Galea S, Adams R, Ahern J, Resnick H, Vlahov D. Mental health service and medication use in New York City after the September 11, 2001, terrorist attack. *Psychiatr Serv.* 2004;55:274–283.
18. Galea S, Ahern J, Resnick H, et al. Psychological sequelae of the September 11 terrorist attacks in New York City. *N Engl J Med.* 2002;346:982–987.
19. Boscarino JA, Galea S, Ahern J, Resnick H, Vlahov D. Utilization of mental health services following the September 11th terrorist attacks in Manhattan, New York City. *Int J Emerg Ment Health.* 2002;4(3): 143–155.
20. Centers for Disease Control and Prevention. *HIV/AIDS Surveillance Report.* 2001;13(1). Available at: http://www.cdc.gov/hiv/stats/hasr130 1.htm. Accessed December 10, 2005.
21. New York City Department of Health and Mental Hygiene. HIV Epidemiology Program 3rd Quarter Report. July 2004. Available at: http://www.nyc.gov/html/doh/html/di res/epi_reports.shtml. Accessed December 10, 2005.
22. World Health Organization. China's latest SARS outbreak has been contained, but biosafety concerns remain–Update 7. May 18, 2004. Available at: http://www.who.int/csr/don/2004_0 5_18a/en. Accessed December 10, 2005.
23. Zajonc RB. On the primacy of affect. *Am Psychol.* 1984;39:124–129.
24. Cumulative number of reported probable cases of severe acute respiratory syndrome (SARS). Available at: http://www.who.int/csr/sars/country/en. Accessed December 10, 2005.
25. Singapore begins SARS TV channel. *New York Times.* May 24, 2003:A1.
26. Kahn J. Quarantine set in Beijing areas to fight SARS. *New York Times.* April 25, 2003:A1, A20.
27. Normile D. Infectious diseases. Mounting lab accidents raise SARS fears. *Science.* 2004;304(5671):659–661.
28. Walgate R. SARS escaped Beijing lab twice: laboratory safety at the Chinese Institute of Virology under close scrutiny. Available at: http://www.the-scientist.com/news/20040426/05. Accessed April 26, 2004.

Integrating Behavioral and Social Science Research Into Microbicide Clinical Trials: Challenges and Opportunities

| Elizabeth E. Tolley, PhD and Lawrence J. Severy, PhD

ABSTRACT

It has been argued that rigid thinking about the types and progression of research needed to evaluate health promotion interventions has stymied the process by which research is translated to action. This argument is particularly salient in the field of HIV/AIDS prevention.

We examined microbicide research and identified challenges that obstruct the integration of clinical trial and behavioral and social science research, thereby reinforcing linear programs of research. We found that behavioral and social science research can both support microbicide clinical trial performance and anticipate the information most needed for a rapid and successful introduction of future microbicide products.

INTRODUCTION

In the August 2003 issue of the Journal, Glascow et al. argued for a more integrated approach to the development of behavioral interventions rather than the linear process of efficacy to effectiveness and the postmarketing research favored by the pharmaceutical industry.[1] We concur and have extended their argument to the field of microbicide development by considering both the challenges and the opportunities of a more integrated program of research.

As researchers enter their third decade of searching for an effective means of preventing HIV transmission, topical microbicides—gels, films, or other substances that can be self-applied vaginally or rectally—have

shown great potential. While no topical microbicide has yet been proven effective, these products are appealing for several reasons. First, they are one of the few technologies that can be initiated by women—the fastest growing population of HIV-infected individuals in many parts of the world[2]—and many believe microbicide use will require less active involvement from a male partner than male or female condoms do.[3] Second, topical microbicides may reach the market more quickly than other HIV prevention methods that are in development.[4] Third, microbicide products could potentially have additional properties that are desirable to users, such as being a contraceptive or non-contraceptive and having lubricating characteristics.[3] Finally, because microbicides are designed as a temporary rather than a systemic barrier to HIV, some potential users may consider microbicides to be a more flexible prevention option than a vaccine would be. One of the many challenges for microbicide researchers has been determining whether candidate products effectively prevent transmission of HIV. This seemingly straightforward requirement is, in fact, rather complex. Some researchers believe the biological ability of a first-generation microbicide product to prevent transmission when used perfectly (i.e., its efficacy) may be quite low when compared with condoms. However, others argue that even with lower efficacy rates, the product's effectiveness—its ability to prevent HIV transmission during everyday circumstances—may be higher than condoms. Such a paradox could happen if a less efficacious microbicide product were

used more consistently and by more people than condoms.[5,6] It is clear that effectiveness will ultimately be influenced by women's (or men's) willingness and ability to use microbicides consistently and correctly with high-risk partners. In turn, the choice to initiate and to sustain use (i.e., its acceptability) will undoubtedly be influenced by a range of other factors, including how risky a particular sexual partner is perceived to be or how sexually disruptive or enhancing the product is.[7] Behavioral and social science (BSS) research that addresses these issues could therefore play a crucial role in determining overall effectiveness.

Some BSS research has been undertaken since the earliest Phase I microbicide clinical trials began. Data collection has included structured questions for assessing microbicide and/or condom use, vaginal cleaning practices, and overall appreciation of the gel or other specific product attributes. Some Phase I trials have incorporated focus group discussions with women who have completed the trial to better understand their experiences with both gel use and participation in a research study.[8–10] However, plans for using BSS methods during the Phase II/III trials to examine longer-term acceptability and use patterns have been limited. Whereas some have called for a better incorporation of social science into biomedical research processes,[8,11,12] there have been numerous barriers to integrating BSS research and clinical trials research. We examined various perspectives and challenges that have obstructed this integration.

CHALLENGE 1: AN EFFICACIOUS PRODUCT WILL BE USED IF IT IS AVAILABLE

This perspective stems in part from a belief that "risk factors associated with HIV transmission are well defined, and education and behavioral modification programs proven effective."[13(p459)] However, we can look at condom use to see that this is a myth. Male condoms, when used consistently and correctly, offer upward of 95% protection from both pregnancy and HIV.[14] However, despite high efficacy, worldwide condom use is low, even within populations most at risk for HIV.[15,16]

Social science literature on the determinants of condom use provides important clues into the kinds of mediators that will influence the uptake and the effectiveness of an eventual microbicide product. For example, cultural context shapes an individual's or a couple's perceptions of HIV risk, which can lead married women or those in stable relationships to ignore their partner's behavior as an important source of HIV risk.[15–21] Service delivery policies and provider attitudes may determine whether an unmarried sexually active adolescent will have access to HIV-related information and services, such as condom provision. Additional mediators mitigate the effect of HIV risk perception on condom uptake. For example, as condom use has become associated with illicit sexual behavior, even those with knowledge about and a desire to use condoms may be unable to do so. Thus, even sex workers with a known risk for HIV have been unwilling or unable to use condoms with their husbands or romantic partners.[22,23] Also, the immediate circumstances of a sexual encounter will often determine whether or not an available condom is used.[22,24]

CHALLENGE 2: CLINICAL TRIALS DIFFER FROM SERVICE DELIVERY INTERVENTIONS

Stein et al. have shown that trial participants will receive the intervention generally under more rigorous and demanding circumstances than they would in a normal service delivery setting.[25] For example, trial participants will likely receive more information about the study product and how to use it than would family planning clients or pharmacy customers if a microbicide became widely available. They also will have greater access to tests for HIV, sexually transmitted diseases (STD), and other conditions than would those outside a trial. Sexual partners will be more involved in discussions about trial participation than they would be about everyday use of a microbicide product. Because of this, some might argue that little can be learned about use behavior within a randomized controlled trial.

However, not all clinical trials diverge significantly from the context of individuals' everyday health services. Trial managers can design the trial to reflect standard care in terms of the types and the amount of information provided to participants (Robinson J, FIBS, oral communication, April 2004). In such situations, lessons drawn from BSS research may be directly transferable to posttrial settings. Even within the most carefully planned and highly controlled trial settings, a BSS research component that focuses on the clinical trial context could provide valuable information for trial implementation and future product introduction. BSS questions can examine how well participants understand written or oral instructions on product use and how the delivery of such instructions and ongoing access to providers can contribute to correct use. For example, misunderstandings associated with the timing of gel application or the quantity of gel necessary could then be rectified to improve adherence. Insight into the relative importance of counseling versus experience via trial-and-error will provide important clues about the kinds of information or counseling that can support more consistent use outside of a trial setting.

One clear difference between a clinical trial and the everyday provision of microbicides is how providers discuss, and users comprehend, messages about product efficacy. Early microbicide acceptability research suggests that use is positively influenced by beliefs about product effectiveness. For example, our unpublished BSS research suggests that some women who have multiple partners may *selectively* use the study gel, i.e., they will use condoms only with clients, and they will use gel only with steady partners. Strategically targeted BSS research that examines the association between participants' perceptions of efficacy and product use will alert trial administrators to any false understanding about efficacy and, thus, enable them to address problems with adherence.

CHALLENGE 3: TRIAL PARTICIPANTS DIFFER FROM EVENTUAL USERS

Supporters of this argument believe that integration is inappropriate, because individuals involved in clinical trial research are generally not like those to whom the product will eventually be marketed. For example, individuals may be from lower-risk populations (if Phase I), higher-risk populations (if Phase II/III), or be more likely to use healthcare services than the population for whom microbicides might eventually be destined. Therefore, because generalization is not possible, the resources used to conduct BSS research are wasted.

Clearly, people have numerous reasons for participating or not participating in research.[26] With microbicide research, motivating factors are likely to include perception of personal risk for HIV/ AIDS, desire to contribute to society, financial gain, concerns about the experimental nature of the research, concerns about potential side effects, and fear of being associated with a stigmatized disease. Clinical trial administrators rely on randomization to distribute the confounding influence of individual characteristics across study arms. However, from a BSS perspective, examining individual motivations and concerns, couple dynamics, and broader sociocultural factors has direct application to clinical trial recruitment, retention, and adherence and to the acceptability and the introduction of an eventual microbicide product.

Consider an example from West Africa, where one of the authors recently traveled to assist sites with preparing for a Phase III microbicide trial. The trial intends to recruit women who have sexual relations with multiple partners and who are at risk for HIV. The experiences of local researchers suggest that the population of high-risk women is quite heterogeneous. They include self-identified sex workers—many of whom originated from neighboring countries—and numerous categories of local women who engage in clandestine high-risk sexual behaviors but do not consider themselves to be sex workers. Past research at those sites suggests that formal sex workers will be easy to recruit,[26] because they acknowledge their personal risk for HIV. Many have previously participated in HIV prevention trials, and many already use a vaginal gel to reduce the pain and discomfort of high-frequency sexual behavior and to prevent condom breakage. Because many of these women have experience with the dual use of condoms and gel, we can assume that adherence to both gel and condom use during the trial—and acceptance of an eventual gel product—will be good. However, past research also shows that these women are highly mobile and, therefore, difficult to retain during trials.[27] In contrast, local women who engage in clandestine or informal sex work might be more difficult to identify and recruit, but once they are, they should be easier to retain.

Evidence of low levels of condom use among these groups suggests that they might benefit greatly from the development of an effective microbicide product. During the trip, a peer educator from the informal sex worker community identified numerous factors that could inhibit the willingness of these local women to participate in a microbicide trial. These factors included concerns about being associated with sex work, low perceived risk for HIV, fear of side effects, and negative attitudes toward a vaginal gel. BSS research could help clarify potential participants' perceived benefits and concerns about the trial and develop messages and processes aimed at identifying and recruiting participants. Therefore, finding ways to include local women who have multiple sexual partners in the microbicide trial would not only benefit the trial but also inform strategies for reaching an important group of potential users postmarketing.

CHALLENGE 4: EFFICACY MUST BE PROVEN BEFORE RESEARCH IS CONDUCTED

This challenge is about timing. Those who support a linear program of research may agree that additional research is needed to determine the most effective means for making the drug available, but they believe it should be conducted only after efficacy has been proven.[28]

However, experience in the field of family planning suggests that BSS research is often conducted only after a less-successful-than-expected introduction of the drug rather than as a way of guiding introduction. For example, the IUD was introduced in India without the benefit of empirical research to determine issues about introduction, and Norplant went through a stage of introductory trials that were fashioned on the clinical trials preceding them.[29] As Simmons noted, a focus on the technology rather than the broader service delivery system and sociocultural context contributed to the failure of both these programs. Similarly, Potter said, "Historical events may result in contraceptive practices and service delivery systems that are far from optimal."[30(p732)] Clinical trials are likely to construct administrative systems (e.g., types of information provided to clients, the number and types of required follow-up visits, and resupply regimens) that are often retained long after trials have ended, without fully understanding the influence of those systems on the acceptability and use of the product or method. Because there is an urgency to slow the HIV epidemic, the pressure to move from efficacy to wide-scale introduction will be great. Strategies for microbicide introduction should be based on an understanding of the psychosocial, cultural, and service delivery factors that will affect demand for and use of the products.[7,31]

CHALLENGE 5: BSS DATA ARE SOFT, SUBJECTIVE, AND CONSEQUENTLY UNRELIABLE

This perspective stems in part from the idea that human behavior is messy and difficult to measure. Indeed, behavior is driven by the subjective cognitions and emotions of individuals who are in turn influenced by the social systems and cultures they inhabit. However, whereas the content of BSS research necessarily encompasses the subjective, its methods need not be wholly subjective. It is also relevant to note that social scientists do not always do a good job explaining, and sometimes adhering to, the rigorous standards that are possible with BSS research. We provide examples of behavioral measures and methods that respond to the needs of microbicide clinical trials in the following paragraphs.

At a minimum, microbicide effectiveness trials must be able to accurately assess delivery of the intervention (i.e., gel use) and disease exposure in order to attribute any differences between study arms in HIV or STD rates to the effect of the study product rather than to other reasons. Typically, clinical trial researchers attempt to obtain this information by requesting participants to report verbally or in diaries the number of sexual encounters in which they used the gel product alone, the gel and condoms together, condoms only, or neither. Such questions may require complex mental calculations, especially for participants who engage in high-frequency sexual relations or who have multiple partners. The use of cognitive testing or "think aloud" processes during the questionnaire design phase can both rationalize the sequencing and clarify the wording of questions so that they correspond more closely to the way participants derive their responses. For a woman engaged in sex work, mental calculations for determining the number of sexual acts engaged in during the last month for which they were protected by both gel and condoms might include (1) the number of clients during the last day of work, (2) whether that number was typical or not of the last week of work, (3) an estimation of a typical week times 4 weeks, (4) subtracting any period during the last month that she was sick or traveled, (5) whether there were any clients with whom she did not use a condom, and (6) whether there were any times she did not use the gel with a client. Unless prompted, she might not include the number of times she had sexual relations with a husband or romatic partners and whether condoms and/ or gel were used.

Rather than obtain use behavior on a per-act basis, it might be sufficient for trial purposes to group participants into more general categories of use and exposure. Usually, this approach entails asking participants to identify their behavior as always, sometimes, or never using condoms, gels, or both during sexual relations. Compared with this single-variable approach, psychometric scales could provide a more refined estimate of product compliance. A scale is composed of multiple items that, when combined, measure a single concept or variable.[32-34] The redundancy of items increases the precision of an estimate in much the same way that the redundancy of participants does in survey research (DeVillis R, PhD, oral communication, May 2004). At present, we know of no standardized adherence scales that could be integrated into microbicide trials; however, the development of such a scale would be a great contribution to the field.

One disadvantage to using highly structured questions for assessing acceptability and use behavior is that such questions may lack relevance for participants. In contrast, semistructured interviewing techniques have the advantage of increasing salience, because participants are encouraged to describe a set of behaviors in context and discuss in-depth only those topics

that are of personal concern.[35,36] The process of recounting a behavioral event may both jog a participant's memory (about whether she used a condom or gel with a particular partner or why she did not) and alert an interviewer to inconsistencies that can be further explored and resolved. When supplemented with more structured data, such qualitative information could be used to refine categories for gel adherence or HIV exposure. However, when using qualitative approaches, it is essential to identify and document the analytic steps taken to ensure that findings accurately represent the attitudes and the behaviors of participants rather than the researcher.[36-38]

CHALLENGE 6: BSS RESEARCH BURDENS CLINICAL TRIAL PARTICIPANTS AND STAFF

There is no doubt that clinical trial research places tremendous demands on all who are involved. Participants are required to rearrange their lives in multiple ways and then undergo procedures that are, at times, unpleasant or even risky. Trial managers must develop and maintain integrated systems for tracking participants, products, and data that adhere to the highest ethical and quality standards. Thus, it is little wonder that some may perceive the addition of BSS as overly burdensome. Although such concerns are not unwarranted, we suggest that well-integrated and carefully targeted BSS research will not only assist the clinical trial team in implementing the trial but also help with the translation of research findings to practical application.

When evaluating the usefulness of a BSS component, the clinical trial team should consider how confident they are in their ability to identify and recruit appropriate participants, whether they anticipate ethical concerns arising from community groups or participants themselves, what kinds of adherence and use data are required, and how aspects of the clinical trial or the broader social context might influence adherence and use.

Once areas for collaboration have been identified, a multidisciplinary team should determine the appropriate timing of, and approach to, BSS data collection and analysis. To date, many BSS assessments appended to microbicide clinical trials have recruited individuals who were no longer participating in the clinical trial.[9,10] Nonparticipants also may be recruited for BSS assessments during other phases of the clinical trial. For example, information collected from nonrecruited individuals during the screening phase can provide insight into the characteristics of potential acceptors. Both the nonrecruited and those who discontinue early may provide important information about barriers to microbicide use.

Nevertheless, some BSS questions are best assessed when the individual is actually using the product, i.e., during the clinical trial itself. We believe it is possible to add such questions without negatively affecting the trial. First, the BSS should consider clinical trial demands on participants' time when designing its protocol. For example, it is possible to schedule BSS interviews so that they do not coincide with particularly intensive phases of the clinical trial. During an upcoming microbicide clinical trial, limited baseline BSS data will be collected at enrollment; BSS follow-up will not occur until trial participants have concluded their third month of trial participation, before which time they are required to make monthly rather than quarterly visits to undergo a number of physical examinations. Once BSS follow-up begins, data collectors will work with trial participants to identify convenient dates, times, and locations for future follow-up interviews.

Second, coordination between the clinical trial and BSS assessment will ensure that there is no duplication of key questions associated with use behavior. For example, if the clinical trial measures variables associated with a BSS outcome (i.e., number of sexual acts protected by microbicide use), the BSS assessment will limit its assessment to measuring covariates of microbicide use (i.e., scaled measures of HIV risk perception, attitudes toward product attributes, and trial adherence motivation) or to qualitatively investigating participants' experiences with microbicides during the trial.

Finally, the choice of data collection method may influence participant burden. In general, structured questions, including the use of psychometric scales, tend to be less time-consuming. However, trial participants may welcome opportunities to talk about their experiences in a less structured format rather than in a formal format used by qualitative researchers. Participants in an HIV vaccine efficacy trial who took part in a qualitative study of their experiences with risk reduction counseling associated feelings about trial participation with counselor qualities. The kind of personal rapport and conversational quality adopted by trained qualitative interviewers was found to create overall positive experiences with trial participation.[39] Nevertheless, such techniques do demand special expertise in data collection and analysis.

CONCLUSIONS

There are many challenges to expanding the role of BSS research within the clinical trial context, but there are highly warranted grounds for doing so. As the size and the pace of the epidemic increase in some regions of the world, the character and the context of those at risk for HIV continue to change. The success of risk reduction products or strategies, including microbicides, will depend in part on our ability to incorporate them into public health programs that reach these different groups and empower them to use products effectively. We are not suggesting that every clinical trial of a health promotion product or strategy be accompanied by a BSS research component. However, we hope that researchers will conduct their own cost–benefit analyses and weigh the burden that might ensue against the additional information derived from expanding clinical trial research to incorporate unanswered questions associated with the contexts and determinants of intervention acceptability or use.

About the Authors

Both authors are with Family Health International, Durham, NC.

Correspondence: Requests for reprints should be sent to Elizabeth E. Tolley, Family Health International, 2224 East NC 54, Durham, NC 27713 (email: btolley@fhi.org).

Acknowledgments

We were supported by the US Agency for International Development. We thank Janet Robinson for her insightful comments and suggestions about the impact of integration on regulatory submissions to the Food and Drug Agency. We also thank Theresa Hatzell and Vera Grigorieva for their thoughtful reviews of earlier drafts. Finally, we appreciate the careful review and comments of the anonymous reviewers and Mary Northridge.

Contributors

Both authors originated the article and determined its content. E. E. Tolley had primary responsibility for writing the article.

References

1. Glasgow RE, Lightenstein E, Marcus AC. Why don't we see more translation of health promotion research to practice? Rethinking the efficacy-to-effectiveness transition. *Am J Public Health.* 2003;93: 1261–1267.
2. NAIDS. Women, Girls, HIV and AIDS—World AIDS Campaign 2004. Available at: http://www.unaids.org/wac_2004/index_en.htm. Accessed October 6, 2005.
3. Boonstra H. Campaign to accelerate microbicide development for STD prevention gets under way. *Guttmacher Rep Public Pol.* 2000;Feb:3–5.
4. Kresge K. Agreeing to disagree: the future of microbicides. *HIV/AIDS Treatment Insider.* 2003;4:1–6.
5. Speiler J. *Behavior Issues in Dual Protection.* Washington, DC: Population Association of America; 1997.
6. Stone A. Clinical Trials of Microbicides. *Microbicide Q.* 2003;1:13–18.
7. Elias C, Coggins C. Acceptability research on female-controlled barrier methods to prevent heterosexual transmission of HIV: Where have we been? Where are we going? *J Women's Health Gender-Based Med.* 2001;10:163–173.
8. Bentley ME, Fullem AM, Tolley EE, et al. Acceptability of a microbicide among women and their partners in a 4-country Phase I trial. *Am J Public Health.* 2004;94:1159–1164.
9. Bentley ME, Morrow KM, Fullem A, et al. Acceptability of a novel vaginal microbicide during a safety trial among low-risk women. *Fam Plann Perspect.* 2000;32:184–188.
10. Morrow K, Rosen R, Richter L, et al. The acceptability of an investigational vaginal microbicide, PRO 2000 Gel, among women in a phase I clinical trial. *J Women's Health.* 2003;12: 655–666.
11. Auerbach JD, Coates TJ. HIV prevention research: accomplishments and challenges for the third decade of AIDS. *Am J Public Health.* 2000;90: 1029–1032.
12. Bachrach CA, Abeles RP. Social science and health research: growth at the National Institutes of Health. *Am J Public Health.* 2004;94:22–28.
13. Folkers GK, Fauci AS. The AIDS research model: implications for other infectious diseases of global health importance. *JAMA.* 2001;286:458–461.
14. Warner DL, Hatcher RA. Male condoms. In: Hatcher RA, Trussell J, Stewart F, et al., eds. *Contraceptive Technology.* 17th ed. New York, NY: Ardent Media Inc; 1998:325–355.
15. Steiner MJ, Cates WJr, Warner L. The real problem with male condoms is nonuse. *Sex Transm Dis.* 1999;26: 459–462.
16. Gardner R, Blackburn RD, Upadhyay UD. *Closing the Condom Gap.* Baltimore, Md: Johns Hopkins University School of Public Health, Population Information Program; 1999.
17. Misovich SJ, Fisher JD, Fisher WA. Close relationships and elevated HIV risk behavior: evidence and possible underlying psychological processes. *Rev General Psychol.* 1997;1:72–107.
18. Castaneda D. The close relationship context and HIV/AIDS risk reduction among Mexican Americans. *Sex Roles.* 2000;42:551–579.
19. Worth D. Sexual decision-making and

AIDS: why condom promotion among vulnerable women is likely to fail. *Stud Fam Plann.* 1989;20:297–307.

20. de Zoysa I, Sweat MD, Denison JA. Faithful but fearful: reducing HIV transmission in stable relationships. *AIDS.* 1996;10(suppl A):S197–S203.

21. Heise LL, Elias C. Transforming AIDS prevention to meet women's needs: a focus on developing countries. *Soc Sci Med.* 1995;40:931–943.

22. Varga C. The condom conundrum: barriers to condom use among commercial sex workers in Durban, South Africa. *Afr J Reprod Health.* 1997;1:74–88.

23. Ortiz-Torres B, Williams SP, Ehrhardt A. Urban women's gender scripts: implications for HIV prevention. *Culture, Health Sexual.* 2003;5:1–17.

24. Beckman LJ, Harvey M. Factors affecting the consistent use of barrier methods of contraception. *Obstet Gynecol.* 1996;88:65S–71S.

25. Stein ZA, Myer L, Susser M. The design of prophylactic trials for HIV: the case of microbicides. *Epidemiology.* 2002;14:80–83.

26. Pedhazur EJ, Schmelkin LP. Artifacts and pitfalls in research. In: Pedhazur ED, Schmelkin LP, eds. *Measurement,*

Design, and analysis: An Integrated Approach. Hillsdale, NJ: Lawrence Erlbaum Associates; 1991:234–241.

27. Alary M, Mukenge-Tshibaka L, Bernier F, et al. Decline in the prevalence of HIV and sexually transmitted diseases among female sex workers in Cotonou, Benin, 1993–1999. *AIDS.* 2002;16:463–470.

28. Folkers GK, Fauci AS. AIDS Agenda Still Daunting. Available at: http://www.nap.edu/issues/19.4/folkers.html. Accessed August 26, 2003.

29. Simmons R, Hall P, Diaz J, Diaz M, Fajans P, Satia J. The strategic approach to contraceptive introduction. *Stud Fam Plann.* 1997;28:79–94.

30. Potter JE. The persistence of outmoded contraceptive regimes: the cases of Mexico and Brazil. *Popul Dev Rev.* 1999;25:703–739.

31. Rao Gupta G, Weiss E. Women's lives and sex: implications for AIDS prevention. *Cult Med Psychiatry.* 1993;17:399–412.

32. Bernard HR; *Social Research Methods Qualitative and Quantitative Approaches.* Thousand Oaks, Calif: Sage; 2000.

33. Mahoney CA, Thombs DL, Howe CZ.

The art and science of scale development in health education research. *Health Educ Res.* 1995;10:1–10.

34. DeVellis R. *Scale Development Theory and Applications.* Newbury Park, Calif: Sage; 1991.

35. Fitzpatrick R, Davey C, Buxton MJ, Jones DR. Evaluating patient-based outcome measures for use in clinical trials. *Health Technol Assess.* 1998;2:1–73.

36. Silverman D. The quality of qualitative health research: the open-ended interview and its alternatives. *Soc Sci Health.* 1998;4:104–118.

37. Ulin PR, Robinson ET, Tolley EE; *Qualitative Methods in Public Health: A Field Guide for Applied Research.* Indianapolis, Ind: Jossey-Bass; 2005.

38. Lincoln Y, Guba E. Establishing trustworthiness. In: Lincoln Y, Guba E, eds. *Naturalistic Inquiry.* Beverly Hills, Calif: Sage; 1985:397–444.

39. Guest G, McLellan E, Matia D, et al. HIV vaccine efficacy trial participation: men-who-have-sex-with-men's experiences of risk reduction counseling and perceptions of risk behavior change. AIDS Care. 2005;17:46–57.

Collaboration, Cholera, and Cyclones: A Project to Improve Point-of-Use Water Quality in Madagascar

| Chris Dunston, MPH, David McAfee, Reinhard Kaiser, MD, MPH, Desire Rakotoarison, MD, Lalah Rambeloson, Anh Thu Hoang, MPH and Robert E. Quick, MD, MPH

ABSTRACT

In November 1999, CARE Madagascar, Population Services International (PSI), and the Centers for Disease Control and Prevention (CDC) selected 30 poor communities in urban Antananarivo as the target population for launch of the Safe Water System. The system consists of behavior change techniques along with point-of-use treatment and safe storage of water. The project was launched in March 2000, ahead of schedule, because a cholera epidemic struck Madagascar in January.

Because of the enormous demand created by the cholera epidemic and by 3 cyclones that followed in the next 3 months, the project grew to national scale in less than a year. The combination of community mobilization and social marketing resulted in increased demand for and use of the Safe Water System.

INTRODUCTION

Poor water quality and sanitation infrastructure are major contributing factors to high rates of diarrhea and vulnerability to cholera in Madagascar. In March 1999, cholera was detected in the country for the first time in decades and, spreading rapidly, by January 2000 reached the capital, Antananarivo. In November 1999, some of the poorest communities in urban Antananarivo, where Community Assistance for Relief Everywhere (CARE) had been working, were chosen as the target population for piloting the Safe Water System[1] in Madagascar.

The implementation approach combined community mobilization by CARE Madagascar, social marketing by Population Services International (PSI), and program evaluation by the US Centers for Disease Control and Prevention (CDC). CARE's Program Mahavita had a well-established community mobilization process in 30 impoverished neighborhoods in Antananarivo. PSI had a national sales and distribution network for its other products, such as condoms. CDC drew on CARE's human and logistical resources to conduct evaluations.

In December 1999, CARE contracted PSI to socially market the Safe Water System in the areas where Mahavita was already operating. This involved local production of a 0.5% sodium hypochlorite solution packaged in a 500-mL bottle, an amount sufficient to treat approximately 2000 L of water. PSI contracted a local company to produce 20-L narrow-mouthed plastic jerry cans. The partners designed a brand name (Sûr'Eau, French for "safe water"), a logo, a label, packaging, usage instructions, and information, education, and communication materials.

In response to a major cholera epidemic that struck Antananarivo in January 2000, CARE and PSI launched the program in March 2000, 4 months ahead of schedule.

MARKETING THE SAFE WATER SYSTEM

PSI sold bottles of Sûr'Eau to wholesalers and retailers in the communities participating in the program and provided the product to CARE-trained community-based sales agents identified by neighborhood organizations. PSI designed radio and television spots and distributed brochures and posters.

PSI set an affordable consumer price for Sûr'Eau of US $0.30. At this price, the cost of treating 20 L of water was US $0.003. The price was US $0.18 for wholesalers and US $0.23 for retailers. PSI's cost recovery, excluding promotion and indirect costs, was approximately 46%.

Although the project originally was to be limited to the 30 Mahavita neighborhoods, the widening cholera epidemic resulted in demand for Sûr'Eau outside the project zone. In response, PSI and CARE broadened the intervention to cover all of Antanan-arivo. Within the first month of the project, private-sector suppliers were distributing Sûr'Eau in cholera-affected regions outside Antananarivo.

Between February 17 and April 3, 2000, three cyclones struck the east coast of Madagascar. The cyclones caused substantial wind, flood, and landslide damage, affecting 300 000 people and killing more than 200. CARE distributed more than 70 000 bottles of Sûr'Eau to affected populations. In recognition of the utility of Sûr'Eau in chol-era and cyclone emergencies, the US Agency for International Development provided funding to PSI to distribute the solution nationwide and to CARE to mobilize 4 additional project sites.

PSI monitored 4 indicators: production capacity, sales, number of retail outlets, and number of wholesalers. CARE evaluated the program's impact in Mahavita neighborhoods through baseline and follow-up surveys of a random sample of 375 households in 15 neighborhoods, stratifying them by the stage of the community mobilization process they had completed.

DISCUSSION AND EVALUATION

The Sûr'Eau Project has been characterized by rapid growth and high demand. Between March and December 2000, sales ranged from 8 000 to 80 000 bottles per month (Figure 1), with peaks during the rainy (cholera) season. PSI increased its monthly production capacity from 76 800 bottles in March 2000 to 250 000 in December 2000. Between March 2000 and January 2001, PSI's network of wholesalers increased from 78 to 725, and the number of retail outlets increased from 690 to 11 783. The remarkable success of the project was largely due to Sûr'Eau's usefulness and the project's easy deployment in response to emergencies.

The utilization rate of Sûr'Eau in Mahavita households was 11.2% after 6 months. Utilization in neighborhoods in the last stage of the community mobilization process was 19.7%, compared with 8.4% in those at an earlier stage (P = .01). Median free chlorine residuals in stored water were found to be 0.23 mg/L in households using Sûr' Eau, compared with 0.1 mg/L in households not using the product (P = .005).

The success of the project may have obscured several important questions. First, Sûr'Eau's sales curve was bimodal, with peaks occurring during cholera season. This finding suggests that Sûr'-Eau was perceived as a cholera prevention product rather than a general water treatment method. The challenge for PSI and CARE is to change consumer perceptions so that Sûr'Eau is used on a regular basis.

Second, because of the limited opportunity to do formative research, additional information was not obtained that might have helped with segmenting the audience, positioning the product, targeting desired behaviors, creating targeted messages, and defining appropriate communication channels.[2,3] Such research could help create increased demand.

Finally, the fact that PSI has not achieved full cost recovery raises questions about the sustainability of this project. Because the objective was to provide the highest-risk populations with affordable products, full cost recovery was not possible.[4] In fact, even though Sûr'Eau is sold at a very low price, economic barriers to its purchase still exist. For wide distribution of this product, therefore, partial subsidies and ongoing donor support will be necessary.

The combination of community mobilization and social marketing offers distinct advantages over social marketing alone.[5] Social marketing aims to increase access to and demand for products through low price, wide commercial distribution, and information, education, and communication materials; community mobilization creates demand for health interventions from a grassroots level through participatory approaches. Simultaneously increasing access and demand through a variety of techniques should increase adoption rates.

As the Sûr'Eau Project continues to evolve, opportunities for improving access and developing a replicable implementation model will arise. Already PSI is bringing private-sector partners into the project to take over production of Sûr'Eau so that PSI can focus on social marketing—creating demand during the non-cholera season; improving access in rural regions through the use of mobile information, education, and communication and sales teams; and reducing economic barriers through such innovations as refillable bottles, unit dose packaging, and coupons. Simultaneously, CARE is working to improve the partnership model by recruiting other nongovernmental organizations to increase demand for Sûr'Eau in high-risk populations through community mobilization and education methods. CARE is field-testing community mobilization methods in regions where the agency is converting disaster relief projects into development projects.

The combined approach of increasing access through social marketing and generating grassroots demand through community mobilization offers a promising and flexible model for development.

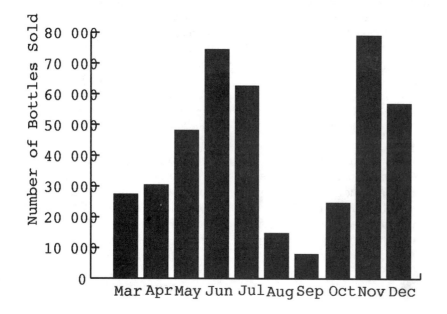

FIGURE 1— Number of bottles of Sûr'Eau water disinfectant sold in Madagascar from March through December 2000, by month.

HIGHLIGHTS

- Because of a cholera epidemic, a planned safe-water project in Madagascar was launched 4 months ahead of schedule.
- The cholera epidemic and the occurrence of 3 cyclones increased demand for water treatment and storage products, and the project was funded for national expansion.
- CARE's community mobilization process significantly increased communities' adoption of point-of-use water treatment and storage practices.

About the Authors

Chris Dunston, Desire Rakotoarison, and Anh Thu Hoang are with CARE Madagascar, Antananarivo. David McAfee and Lalah Rambeloson are with Population Services International Madagascar, Antananarivo. Reinhard Kaiser is with the National Center for Environmental Health and Robert E. Quick is with the National Center for Infectious Diseases, Centers for Disease Control and Prevention, Atlanta, Ga.

Correspondence: Requests for reprints should be sent to Robert E. Quick, MD, MPH, Foodborne and Diarrheal Diseases Branch, Mail Stop A38, Centers for Disease Control and Prevention, Atlanta, GA 30333 (e-mail: rxq1@cdc.gov).

Acknowledgments

C. Dunston, D. McAfee, and R. Quick designed the project, analyzed the data, and wrote the manuscript. R. Kaiser designed the evaluation, analyzed the data, and reviewed the manuscript. D. Rakotoarison and L. Rambeloson assisted with project design and reviewed the manuscript. A. T. Hoang contributed to the writing of the report.

Resources for this research were provided by the R. W. Woodruff Foundation to CARE and the CDC Foundation, as part of the CARE–CDC Health Initiative.

We would like to thank Patricia Riley, Dr Luke Nkinsi, Reema Jossy, and Lori Buhi of the CARE–CDC Health Initiative for their support, and Caran Wilbanks for her editorial assistance. We are grateful to the Assistant Développement Communitaires of CARE Madagascar for their work in implementing and evaluating this project in Antananarivo. We would also like to recognize the Sûr'Eau Project staff of PSI Madagascar for their diligent efforts to make their products available to the population.

Note. Use of trade names is for identification only and does not constitute endorsement by the Centers for Disease Control and Prevention or by the Department of Health and Human Services.

Top. Sûr'Eau production and bottling facility, Antananaviro, Madagascar.

Bottom. Five-hundred-mL bottle and label used to package Sûr'Eau, a water purification solution promoted by CARE Madagascar and Population Services International. *(Photo: Robert E. Quick.)*

References

1. *Safe Water Systems for the Developing World: A Handbook for Implementing Household-Based Water Treatment and Safe Storage Projects.* Atlanta, Ga: Centers for Disease Control and Prevention; 2000. Also available at: http://www.cdc.gov/safewater. Accessed July 3, 2001.

2. McDermott RJ. Social marketing: a tool for health education. *Am J Health Behav.* 2000;24:6–10.

3. Stanton B, Black R, Engle P, Pelto G. Theory-driven behavioral intervention research for the control of diarrheal diseases. *Soc Sci Med.*1992;35:1405–1420.

4. Smith WA. Social marketing: an evolving definition. *Am J Health Behav.* 2000;24:11–17.

5. Bryant CA, Forthofer MS, Brown KR, Landis DC, McDermott RJ. Community-based prevention marketing: the next steps in disseminating behavior change. *Am J Health Behav.* 2000;24:61–68.

Not Just a Drop in the Bucket: Expanding Access to Point-of-Use Water Treatment Systems

| *Eric Mintz, MD, MPH, Jamie Bartram, PhD, Peter Lochery, MSc(Eng) and Martin Wegelin, MSc*

ABSTRACT

Since 1990, the number of people without access to safe water sources has remained constant at approximately 1.1 billion, of whom approximately 2.2 million die of waterborne disease each year. In developing countries, population growth and migrations strain existing water and sanitary infrastructure and complicate planning and construction of new infrastructure.

Providing safe water for all is a long-term goal; however, relying only on time- and resource-intensive centralized solutions such as piped, treated water will leave hundreds of millions of people without safe water far into the future. Self-sustaining, decentralized approaches to making drinking water safe, including point-of-use chemical and solar disinfection, safe water storage, and behavioral change, have been widely field-tested. These options target the most affected, enhance health, contribute to development and productivity, and merit far greater priority for rapid implementation.

INTRODUCTION

We continue to allocate more money to conflict than to services, prestige projects take precedence over more mundane services, and populations without water and sanitation have neither the contacts nor the power to exert any influence. . . . [That] we have been unable or unwilling to ensure the access of one-quarter of the world's population to a safe supply of water and one-half of the world's population to adequate excreta disposal is among the most glaring examples of a failure to apply basic scientific principles to protect human health.

Paul Taylor[1]

Water is essential to life. We drink it, raise crops and livestock with it, clean our bodies and environment with it, and play in it. When it is contaminated with human or animal wastes, however, water carries illness and death. Approximately 1.1 billion persons, or one sixth of the world's population, lack access to safe water sources, and many more lack access to safe water.[2]

Important diseases that can be transmitted by the waterborne route include cholera, typhoid fever, amoebic and bacillary dysentery, and other diarrheal diseases; these diseases, which cause an estimated 2 187 000 deaths worldwide each year (A. Pruess, MPH; World Health Organization; written communication; May 10, 2001), account for most water-associated morbidity and mortality. Other contributors include (1) the water-washed diseases (e.g., scabies, trachoma), caused by poor personal hygiene and preventable through improved access to safe water; (2) the water-based diseases, caused by parasites found in intermediate organisms living in water (e.g., dracunculiasis, schistosomiasis); and (3) the water-related diseases, caused by insect vectors that breed in water (e.g., dengue, malaria).[3] The direct health burden is supplemented by the annual expenditure of over 10 million person-years of time and effort by persons carrying water from distant and often polluted sources.[4] In addition, indigent populations often pay exorbitant prices for limited quantities of poor-quality water, at costs that can represent 20% of a family budget,[5] while services to wealthier urban dwellers are heavily subsidized and of relatively high quality.[6] The claim has been made that no single type of intervention has greater overall impact on national development and public health than does the provision of safe drinking water and the proper disposal of human excreta.[4]

In 1980, the United Nations General Assembly proclaimed the period 1981 to 1990 as the International Drinking Water Supply and Sanitation Decade, with the primary goal of full access to water supplies and sanitation for all.[6] During the course of that decade, access to safe water was provided to an additional 1347 million people and access to sanitation facilities was provided to an estimated 748 million, at an estimated cost of US $133.9 billion.[6] Despite these major accomplishments, by the decade's end more than 1.1 billion people still lacked access to safe water and 2.4 billion were without adequate sanitation.[2] Reasons cited for the decade's failure to achieve more include population growth (estimated at 750 million), funding limitations, inadequate operation and maintenance, inadequate cost recovery, insufficient trained personnel,[7] and continuation of a "business as usual approach," drawing on traditional policies, resources, and technologies.[6] In particular, little progress was made in providing services to rapidly expanding, low-income, marginalized urban populations and to rural areas.[6,7] The most recent assessment of water supply and sanitation coverage shows that although more people than ever have access to water supply and sanitation services, the absolute numbers of unserved people remained constant throughout the period 1990 to 2000, when 1.1 billion were without access to improved water sources and 2.4 billion lacked access to basic sanitation.[2]

Water treatment plants and other large-scale projects remain an important and necessary objective of many development agencies; they were major advances in the sanitary revolution in industrialized countries at the end of the 19th century.[8] A century later, providing safe piped water to dispersed populations in rural areas of developing countries can be prohibitively expensive for governments, donors, and private utilities, calling into question the sustainability of this approach and whether anticipated health gains will be achieved, even from large investments. Meanwhile, in urban areas, rapid population growth and migrations motivated by cultural, economic, political, and environmental factors strain existing water and sanitary infrastructures and create enormous problems in planning and constructing new infrastructure. Residents of many of the world's largest cities enjoy only intermittent access to piped water, often of dubious quality and only from public taps at substantial distances from their homes. Others depend on water vendors for small volumes of costly water of unsure quality. Where providers cannot guarantee water quality at the point of supply, or where it cannot be guaranteed at the point of use, because of contamination during collection, transport, and storage, consumers face significant health risks.

Given the failure to reduce the numbers of people without access to basic water supply and sanitation during the 1990s, and the financial implications of even the apparently modest international development target of

halving the proportion of people not served with improved drinking water by 2015 (A. Pruess, MPH, written communication, May 10, 2001), it is evident that "business as usual" cannot provide a satisfactory response. Approaches that rely solely on time- and resource-intensive centralized solutions will leave hundreds of millions of people without access to safe water far into the foreseeable future; a radical reorientation toward interventions to support these populations is urgently required. This commentary reviews 2 low-cost decentralized technologies used to improve drinking water quality in developing countries and considers the role these technologies may play in future efforts to provide safe drinking water for all.

POINT-OF-USE CHEMICAL DISINFECTION

Where water sources are contaminated, drinking water must be treated to prevent waterborne disease. In the absence of functioning centralized water treatment systems, this responsibility falls to consumers by default. Treatment by boiling inactivates viral, parasitic, and bacterial pathogens, but it is economically and environmentally unsustainable.[9,10] Boiling provides no residual protection; after cooling, water can easily be recontaminated,[11] and it is associated with the risk of scalding, especially among infants. Safe and inexpensive chemical disinfectants that are suitable for household use in developing countries offer a practical alternative to boiling. Various point-of-use chemical agents for water treatment have been reviewed.[12] Overall, sodium hypochlorite, the active ingredient in commercial laundry bleach solutions, appears to be the safest, most effective, and least expensive chemical disinfectant for point-of-use treatment. As described in this issue, a dilute solution of sodium hypochlorite can be produced on-site through electrolysis of salt water[13] or can be commercially manufactured by a private company.[14]

In the past 5 years, several published field trials of hypochlorite for point-of-use water treatment have

established that it is acceptable for and effective at improving water quality in a number of settings, and that its use can reduce diarrheal illness by up to 85%.[15–19] It has been used to improve the safety of oral rehydration solutions and street-vended beverages,[20,21] and, as described in this issue, as an emergency response measure for persons displaced by natural disasters and threatened by epidemic cholera.[13, 22, 23] Among the limitations of hypochlorite-based disinfectants are their relative ineffectiveness against parasites and viruses and the reduced efficiency and disagreeable taste or odor that may result when they are used to treat water with excessive amounts of organic material.[12, 14] In their favor are the protective residual effect against bacterial contamination and the fact that they can be easily and reliably quantified in treated water by simple and inexpensive colorimetric assays.

POINT-OF-USE SOLAR DISINFECTION

The earth is bathed in electromagnetic radiation emitted from the sun, and solar radiation can be harnessed for point-of-use water disinfection.[24] Inactivation of pathogens in water may be achieved through the effects of ultraviolet radiation with or without the synergistic effects of increased temperature, or through increased temperature alone ("solar pasteurization" or "solar distillation"). The bactericidal effects of solar radiation obtained in different types of containers, at different exposure times and under different meteorologic conditions, have been documented.[25–27] Much of what has been learned has been incorporated into SODIS, a solar water disinfection project initiated by the Department of Water and Sanitation in Developing Countries (SANDEC). Clear plastic soda bottles or bags made of polyethylene terephthalate (PET) are used because they transmit ultraviolet A and are widely available, inexpensive, and chemically stable.[28] Thermal inactivation is significant only at water temperatures above 45°C.[28,29] Because heat increases the bactericidal effects of ultraviolet radiation, the bottom half of the bottle may be painted black or the clear bottles may be laid on a black surface to increase thermal effects. A paraffin-filled tube can be used to indicate temperatures at which sufficient disinfection is achieved. Turbidity markedly decreases the penetration of ultraviolet radiation; hence, it is advisable to treat water with turbidity greater than 30 nephelometric turbidity units by filtration, flocculation, or sedimentation before solar disinfection. Water can be aerated by vigorous shaking before exposure to solar radiation to take advantage of the increased bactericidal effects that occur in the presence of oxygen.[30]

> "Approaches that rely solely on time- and resource-intensive centralized solutions will leave hundreds of millions of people without access to safe water far into the foreseeable future."

Field trials of solar disinfection in Kenya demonstrated that it was an acceptable and effective means of improving water quality and significantly reduced the incidence of diarrhea and severe diarrhea in children.[31,32] Other health impact studies are under way. The limitations of solar disinfection are the need for sufficient solar radiation and relatively clear water and the difficulty in treating large volumes. Its advantages are simplicity, extremely low cost, and the fact that it leaves the taste of water unchanged.

SAFE WATER STORAGE

Water from potable sources, as well as water that has been made potable by boiling, chemical treatment, or solar disinfection, remains susceptible to the introduction of contaminants during collection, transport, and storage. The risk of diarrhea due to the contamination of drinking water during household storage, first noted in the 1960s,[33] has since been repeatedly observed.[34–38] It has been argued that people are less likely to suffer illness from organisms in their stored drinking water when the person introducing the organisms is a member of their household rather than a stranger.[39] While this may be true, infants and young children, who suffer the highest rates of diarrheal mortality, are vulnerable to infection from even small doses of waterborne pathogens that may be familiar to, and unlikely to cause illness in, other household members. Furthermore, studies have identified drinking water contaminated during collection, transport, and storage as a significant route of transmission during epidemics of cholera and dysentery.[40–42] Simply replacing unsafe water storage vessels with safer ones led to lower rates of cholera transmission in households in Calcutta[43] and less diarrhea in children in a refugee camp in Malawi.[38]

The principles of safe water storage, the characteristics of safe water storage vessels, and early intervention studies evaluating these vessels have been reviewed.[12] Safe water storage vessels with tight-fitting lids and narrow mouths, which allow users to remove water by pouring or through spigots but not by dipping, have been incorporated into both chemical and solar water treatment programs.[28, 44] The articles in this issue by Makutsa et al.[14] and Ogutu et al.[45] highlight the challenges of creating water storage vessels that meet traditional cultural standards and still fulfill the role of adequately protecting treated water from recontamination.

BEHAVIORAL CHANGE

To achieve significant reductions in the incidence or severity of diarrheal diseases, public health programs must change behavior.[46] Point-of-use water treatment adds to the time and expense required of consumers. Adopting a new vessel for water storage also adds expense and may have other disadvantages, such as the inability to maintain stored water at cooler temperatures.[19,45] The process by which new water treatment and storage behaviors are promoted is as critical as the disinfection and storage "hardware." Several innovative approaches have been applied to

change behavior in the context of programs to promote point-of-use disinfection and safe water storage. These include social marketing, motivational interviewing,[47] and, as described in this issue by Dunston et al.[13] and Makutsa et al.,[14] community mobilization.[44]

Improvements in the quality of drinking water provide far more benefit when coupled with improvements in hygiene and sanitation.[48, 49] Introducing treated drinking water into households in storage vessels with spigots or spouts enables families to reduce their exposure to waterborne pathogens and, in conjunction with hand washing and soap promotion, provides a platform for reducing the risk of water-washed diseases.[50] Safe storage of water in covered or closed containers may significantly reduce contamination by host organisms for the parasitic causes of water-based diseases and by mosquito vectors of water-related diseases such as dengue. Finally, safe water and, if available, hypochlorite disinfectant can be used for washing fruits, vegetables, and other foods consumed raw, thereby potentially reducing the incidence of food-borne infections.

THE ROLE OF LOW-COST, APPROPRIATE TECHNOLOGIES

In the past decade, low-cost decentralized approaches to making drinking water safer have been field-tested and have begun to be implemented in self-sustaining "real world" programs.[17, 44] A systems approach, incorporating elements of water treatment, safe water storage, and health education into a single program, will probably have greater, longer-lasting positive impacts on public health. Even greater impact may be attainable by increasing water availability and improving sanitation, according to the needs and resources of the communities served. Novel methods for safe disposal of human wastes, such as dehydrating toilets with urine separation, are already being evaluated in some areas.[51] The limiting factor for sustaining these interventions may be the economic capacity of the target population.

FIGURE 1. Promotional materials for branded, locally produced sodium hypochlorite solution manufactured and marketed in Bolivia (CLARO), Madagascar (Sûr'Eau), Zambia (Clorin), and Ecuador (Agua Pura). Social marketing of such safe water products is used to promote behavior change.

Safe water storage vessels with tightfitting lids and narrow mouths have been incorporated into both chemical and solar water treatment programs.

The problems of unsafe water and poor sanitation demand a multitude of varied and complementary solutions. In most areas, available options for point-of-use water treatment are limited and ineffective at preventing disease (filtration, sedimentation) or inconvenient and prohibitively expensive (boiling). Point-of-use programs in several countries have demonstrated that the market for safe water will readily absorb more effective treatment options if these are reasonably priced and properly promoted.[44]

We are witnessing unprecedented experimentation with new forms of privatization worldwide and increased attention to accountability and performance. People are increasingly perceived as consumers, rather than recipients, of development. Recognition of this trend favors an emphasis on con-

sumer choice and a more pluralistic approach toward water safety, with an increasing number of options of varying costs, convenience, and effectiveness more widely available.[1] Field trials, such as the ones reported in this issue from Kenya[14,45] and Madagascar,[13,22,23] can help define the optimal use of each of these options.

Cellular phones and satellite dishes revolutionized the telecommunications industry in developing countries, bypassing the expenditures and delays associated with traditional wire-based systems and allowing consumers rapid access to phone and television service. Similarly new scientific research and the current global economic and political climate offer dramatic opportunities to introduce new decentralized approaches for improving water quality. Capitalizing on these opportunities requires unique partnerships between the private and public sectors that can be brokered by the donor community. Multinational consumer products firms that produce, market, and distribute soap, bleach, and vessels suitable for safe water storage are well positioned to participate in this new sanitary revolution. But many barriers still need to be overcome and much work remains

to be done before safe water is made as widely available as tobacco, alcohol, or carbonated soft drinks.

CONCLUSIONS

Far too many people live without access to safe drinking water, and this is a primary determinant of continuing poverty. Progressive expansion of improved water supplies is important but often fails to address the immediate needs of the most disadvantaged. Options such as point-of-use water treatment target the most affected directly, enhance health benefit, and thereby contribute to development and productivity. Existing sector institutions are structured for traditional approaches and have a poor track record for promoting alternative technologies. Point-of-use water treatment merits far greater priority for achieving a meaningful rate of implementation.

About the Authors

Eric Mintz is with the Foodborne and Diarrheal Diseases Branch, National Center for Infectious Diseases, Centers for Disease Control and Prevention, Atlanta, Ga. Jamie Bartram is with Water, Sanitation, and

FIGURE 2: *Left.* A Chinese woman in Ningxia Province appreciating the good taste of SODIS-treated water. *Right.* A child from the Rachuonyo District, Nyanza Province, western Kenya, drawing water from the spigot of a clay pot that has been locally modified for safe water storage. *(Photo: Valerie Garrett.)*

Health, World Health Organization, Geneva, Switzerland. Peter Lochery is with Water, Sanitation, and Environmental Health, CARE, Atlanta, Ga. Martin Wegelin is with the Department of Water and Sanitation in Developing Countries, Swiss Federal Institute for Environmental Science and Technology, Duebendorf, Switzerland.

Correspondence: Requests for reprints should be sent to Eric D. Mintz, MD, MPH, Mailstop A-38, Centers for Disease Control and Prevention, Atlanta, GA 30333

Note. The views expressed in this commentary do not necessarily represent the decisions or the stated policy of the World Health Organization.

References

1. Taylor P. Regional perspectives on water safety: Africa. In: Craun GF, Robinson DE, Hauchman FS, eds. *Microbial Pathogens and Disinfection By-Products in Drinking Water: Health Effects and Management of Risks.* Washington, DC: International Life Sciences Institute Press; 2001.

2. World Health Organization, United Nations Children's Fund (UNICEF), Water Supply and Sanitation Council. *Global Water Supply and Sanitation Assessment 2000 Report.* New York, NY: UNICEF; 2000.

3. Bradley DJ, Emurwon P. Predicting the epidemiological effect of changing water sources. *East Afr Med J.*1968;45: 284–291.

4. Water and Sanitation. Fact Sheet Number 112. Geneva, Switzerland: World Health Organization; November 1996. Available at http://www.who.inl/inf-fs/en/factiiz.html.

5. *Urban Example–Prospective for the Future. Water Supply and Sanitation to Urban Marginal Areas of Tegucigalpa, Honduras.* New York, NY: UNICEF; 1989.

6. World Health Organization, UNICEF. *Water Supply and Sanitation Sector Monitoring Report 1990.* New York, NY: UNICEF; 1992.

7. *The International Drinking Water Supply and Sanitation Decade. End of Decade Review (as at [sic] December 1990).* Geneva, Switzerland: World Health Organization; 1992.

8. Melosi M. *The Sanitary City: Urban Infrastructure in America From Colonial Times to the Present.* Baltimore, Md: Johns Hopkins University Press; 2000.

9. Gilman RH, Skillicorn P. Boiling of drinking water: can a fuel-scarce community afford it? *Bull World Health Organ.* 1985;63:157–163.

10. deKonig HW, Smith KR, Last JM. Biomass fuel consumption and health. *Bull World Health Organ.* 1985;63: 11–26.

11. Luby S, Syed A, Atiullah N, Faizan K, Fisher-Hoch S. The limited effectiveness of home drinking water purification efforts in Karachi, Pakistan. *Int J Infect Dis.* 2000;4:3–7.

12. Mintz ED, Reiff FM, Tauxe RV. Safe water treatment and storage in the home: a practical new strategy to prevent waterborne disease. *JAMA.* 1995; 273:948–953.

13. Dunston C, McAfee D, Kaiser R, et al. Collaboration, cholera, and cyclones: a project to improve point-of-use water quality in Madagascar. *Am J Public Health.* 2001;91:1574–1576.

14. Makutsa P, Nzaku K, Ogutu P, et al. Challenges in implementing a point-of-use water quality intervention in rural Kenya. *Am J Public Health.* 2001; 91:1571–1573.

15. Quick RE, Venczel LV, Gonzales O, et al. Narrow-mouthed water storage vessels and in situ chlorination in a Bolivian community: a simple method to improve drinking water quality. *Am J Trop Med Hyg.*1996;54:511–516.

16. Semenza J, Roberts L, Henderson A, Bogan J, Rubin CH. Water distribution system and diarrheal disease transmission: a case study in Uzbekistan. Am J Trop Med Hyg. 1998;59:941–946.

17. Quick RE, Mintz ED, Sobel J, Mead P, Reiff F, Tauxe RV. A new strategy for waterborne disease prevention. In: Pickford J, et al., eds. Proceedings of the 23rd WEDC Conference, Durban, South Africa, 1997. Loughborough, England: Loughborough University; 1998.

18. Quick RE, Venczel LV, Mintz ED, et al. Diarrhea prevention in Bolivia through point-of-use disinfection and safe storage: a promising new strategy. *Epidemiol Infect.* 1999;122:83–90.

19. Luby S, Agboatwalla M, Raza A, et al. A low-cost intervention for cleaner drinking water in Karachi, Pakistan. *Int J Infect Dis.* In press.

20. Daniels N, Simons S, Rodrigues A, et al. First do no harm: making oral rehydration solution safer in a cholera epidemic. *Am J Trop Med Hyg.* 1999; 60:1051–1055.

21. Sobel J, Mahon B, Mendoza C, et al. A simple system for water purification and storage, handwashing, and beverage storage reduces fecal contamination of street-vended beverages in Guatemala. *Am J Trop Med Hyg.* 1998; 59:380–387.

22. Mong Y, Kaiser R, Ibrahim D, Rasoatiana, Razafimbololona L, Quick RE. Impact of the safe water system on water quality in cyclone-affected communities in Madagascar. *Am J Public Health.* 2001;91:1577–1579.

23. Reller M, Mong JM, Rabenjoelina, Hoekstra RM, Quick RE. Cholera prevention with traditional and novel water treatment methods: a report of an outbreak investigation in Fort-Dauphin, Madagascar. *Am J Public Health.*2001; 91:1608–1610.

24. Rolla TC. Sun and water: an overview of solar water treatment devices. *J Environ Health.* 1998; 60:30–32.

25. Acra A, Raffoul Z, Karahagopian L. *Solar Disinfection of Drinking Water and Oral Rehydration Solution.* Beirut, Leb-anon: Illustrated Publications SAL (for UNICEF); 1984.

26. Joyce TM, McGuigan KG, Elmore-Meegan M, Conroy RM. Inactivation of fecal bacteria in drinking water by solar heating. *Appl Environ Microbiol.*1996; 62:399–402.

27. Wegelin M, Canonica S, Meschner K, Fleischmann T, Pesaro F, Metzler A. Solar water disinfection: scope of the process and analysis of radiation experiments. *J Water Supply Res Technol AQUA.* 1994;43:154–169.

28. Wegelin M. Solar water disinfection (SODIS): a simple water treatment process. *J Water Supply Res Technol AQUA.* 2001;50:125–134.

29. McGuigan KG, Joyce TM, Conroy RM, Gillespie JB, Elmore-Meegan M. Solar disinfection of drinking water contained in transparent plastic bottles: characterizing the bacterial inactivation process. *J Appl Microbiol.*1998; 84: 1138–1148.

30. Reed R. Solar inactivation of faecal bacteria in water: the critical role of oxygen. *Lett Appl Microbiol.* 1997; 24: 276–280.

31. Conroy RM, Elmore-Meegan M, Joyce T, McGuigan K, Branes J. Solar disinfection of drinking water and diarrhoea in Maasai children: a controlled field trial. *Lancet.* 1996;348:1695–1697.

32. Conroy RM, Meegan ME, Joyce T, McGuigan K, Barnes J. Solar disinfection of water reduces diarrhoeal disease: an update. *Arch Dis Child.* 1999;81:337–338.

33. van Zilj WJ. Studies on diarrhoeal diseases in seven countries by the WHO Diarrhoeal Diseases Study Team. *Bull World Health Organ.* 1966; 35: 249–261.

34. Deb BC, Sircar BK, Sengupta PG, et al. Intra-familial transmission of *Vibrio cholerae* biotype El Tor in Calcutta slums. *Indian J Med Res.*1982;76:814–819.

35. Gunn RA, Kimball AM, Mathew PP, Dutta SR, Rifatt AHM. Cholera in Bahrain: epidemiological characteristics of an outbreak. *Bull World Health Organ.* 1981;59:61–66.

36. Echeverria P, Taylor DN, Seriwatnana J, et al. Potential sources of enterotoxigenic *Escherichia coli* in homes of children with diarrhoea in Thailand. *Bull World Health Organ.*1987; 65: 207–215.

37. Khairy AEM, Sebaie OE, Gawad AA, El Attar L. The sanitary condition of rural drinking water in a Nile Delta village, I: parasitological assessment of "zir" stored and direct tap water. *J Hyg Camb.*1982;88:57–61.

38. Roberts L, Chartier Y, Chartier O, Malenga G, Toole M, Rodka H. Keeping clean water clean in a Malawi refugee camp: a randomized intervention trial. *Bull World Health Organ.* 2001;79: 280–287.

39. VanDerslice J, Briscoe J. All coliforms are not created equal: a comparison of the effects of water source and in-house water contamination on infantile diarrheal disease. *Water Resources Res.*1993;29:1983–1995.

40. Swerdlow DL, Mintz ED, Rodriguez M, et al. Waterborne transmission of epidemic cholera in Trujillo, Peru: lessons for a continent at risk. *Lancet.* 1992;340:28–32.

41. Swerdlow DL, Malenga G, Begokyian G, et al. Epidemic cholera among refugees in Malawi, Africa: treatment and transmission. *Epidemiol Infect.*1997;118:207–214.

42. Tuttle J, Ries AA, Chimba R, Perera C, Griffin PM. Epidemic antimicrobial-resistant *Shigella dysenteriae* type 1 in Zambia: the hazards of stored water and street vended foods. *J Infect Dis.*1995;171:371–375.

43. Deb BC, Sircar BK, Sengupta PG, et al. Studies on interventions to prevent eltor cholera transmission in urban slums. *Bull World Health Organ.*1986; 64:127–131.

44. Safe Water Systems for the Developing World: A Handbook for Implementing Household-Based Water Treatment and Safe Storage Projects. Atlanta, Ga: Centers for Disease Control and Prevention; 2001. Available at: http://www.cdc.gov/safewater. Accessed July 14, 2001.

45. Ogutu P, Garrett V, Barasa P, Ombeki S, Mwaki A, Quick RE. Seeking safe storage: a comparison of drinking water quality in clay and plastic vessels. *Am J Public Health.* 2001;91: 1610–1611.

46. Stanton B, Black R, Engle P, Pelto G. Theory-driven behavioral intervention research for the control of diarrheal diseases. *Soc Sci Med.* 1992;35:1405–1420.

47. Thevos AK, Quick RE, Yanduli V. Application of motivational interviewing to the adoption of water disinfection practices in Zambia. *Health Promot Int.* 2000;15:207–214.

48. Esrey S, Feachem RG, Hughes JM. Interventions for the control of diarrhoeal diseases among young children: improving water supplies and excreta disposal facilities. *Bull World Health Organ.*1985;63:757–772.

49. VanDerslice J, Briscoe J. Environmental interventions in developing countries: interactions and their implications. *Am J Epidemiol.*1995;141:135–144.

50. Pinfold JV. Faecal contamination of water and fingertip-rinses as a method for evaluating the effect of low-cost water supply and sanitation activities on faeco-oral disease transmission, II: a hygiene intervention study in rural north-east Thailand. *Epidemiol Infect.*1990; 105:377–389.

51. Esrey S, Gough J, Rapaport D, et al. Ecological Sanitation. Stockholm, Sweden: Swedish International Development Cooperation Agency (SIDA); 1998.

An Annotated Bibliography of Global Health

| Omar A. Khan, MD MHS

The growing interest in global health, especially in the U.S., has meant a proliferation of reference material as well as popular texts on the topic. It is perhaps impossible, and likely not very useful, to present a full review of every book or periodical pertaining to global health. For example, it is likely that work in global health will require an understanding of epidemiology, health communication, and other broad public health disciplines. However, a review of each publication in those component sub-disciplines is far beyond the scope of this piece. We highlight here those publications and periodicals that are, in our subjective view and experience, authoritative or unique in their presentation of global health topics, and most relevant to the reader of this book.

Books

Title: *Global Health*
Subtitle: An Introductory Textbook
Authors/Editors: Ann Lindstrand, Steffan Bergstrom, Hans Rosling, Birgitta Rubenson, Bo Stenson, Thorkild Tylleskar
Publisher: Studentlitteratur
Notes: *A fine introduction to the field. One of the co-authors is the inimitable Prof. Hans Rosling, well-known for his work with Gapminder.org, on presentations depicting global inequalities and the multiple, complicated relationships in global health indicators. Not well marketed in the United States and consequently under-utilized.*

Title: *International Public Health*
Subtitle: Diseases, Programs, Systems, and Policies
Authors/Editors: Michael H. Merson,

Robert E. Black, Anne J. Mills
Publisher: Jones & Bartlett
Notes: *A fairly comprehensive overview of the major sub-topics within global health. The Editors are well-known in their fields; the section authors less so. Some (e.g. the section on Measures of Health) partner a senior author with a less experienced one; this approach has variable success. Overall, it will probably suit most readers to find more specific material in their area of interest, but for those wanting a general text on a challenging topic to summarize, this is as good a source as any.*

Title: *Disease Control Priorities in Developing Countries*
Authors/Editors: Dean Jamison, Joel Breman, Anthony Measham, George Alleyne, Mariam Claeson, David Evans, Prabhat Jha, Anne Mills, Philip Musgrove
Publisher: Oxford/World Bank
Notes: *Outstanding analysis of the title topic. A detailed look at the cross-cutting themes identified at the outset, with scholarly analysis of the issues and interventions. It's a shame that it will probably stay on the shelf due to its heft; it deserves to be read and absorbed since it reflects a great deal of interdisciplinary work in global health. Its companion volume is Global Burden of Disease and Risk Factors, edited by Alan Lopez, Colin Mathers, Majid Ezzati, Dean Jamison, Christopher Murray. The companion volume essentially updates the Global Burden of Disease volume by Murray and Lopez from some years ago.*

Title: *Hope in Hell*
Subtitle: Inside the world of Doctors Without Borders

Authors/Editors: Dan Bortolotti
Publisher: Firefly
Notes: *A gripping narrative account of the work of Medicins Sans Frontieres (Doctors without Borders). From background to real-life situations, Bortolotti provides an unflinching account of the harsh reality of the work of MSF and the harsher reality of the conditions which compel them to do so.*

Title: *Infections & Inequalities*
Subtitle: The Modern Plagues
Authors/Editors: Paul Farmer
Publisher: University of California Press
Notes: *Perhaps the definitive book by Paul Farmer, of the many by him (and one about him- Mountains Beyond Mountains). Eloquently addressed the fundamental issues of global health from the author's perspective of working in Haiti and elsewhere. Argues that the real reasons for global health problems are neither solely biological or technological but societal factors in poorer societies- a precursor to the formal idea of the 'social determinants of health'.*

Title: *Who Gave Pinta to the Santa Maria?*
Subtitle: Torrid Diseases in a Temperate World
Authors/Editors: Richard Desowitz
Publisher: Norton
Notes: *A fine and somewhat irreverent look at the history of infectious diseases in 'the new world'. You might learn more history of public health than you bargained for and enjoy it in the process.*

Title: *Social Determinants of Health*
Authors/Editors: Sir Michael Marmot

& Richard Wilkinson
Publisher: Oxford
Notes: Sir Michael Marmot, if he did not actually invent the Social Determinants of Health, certainly has done more than anyone to make them understandable, and to articulate the relationship of these determinants to health outcomes. This is a very manageably sized book and is virtually indispensable for anyone who seeks to understand the reasons of poor health around the globe.

Title: *Control of Communicable Diseases Manual*
Editor: David L. Heymann
Publisher: APHA Press/WHO
Notes: The oldest handbook of public health extant. It covers virtually every tropical disease known to man, and focuses on epidemiology, prevention, and control. Updated periodically (usually 4 years or so), and edited by one of the world's authorities on communicable disease (Dr. David Heymann of the WHO), it is authoritative and indispensable for the global health practitioner. The obvious disclosure here is that its publisher—APHA Press—also publishes the book you are now holding.

Title: *Oxford Handbook of Tropical Medicine*
Authors/Editors: Michael Eddleston, Robert Davidson, Robert Wilkinson, Stephen Pierini
Publisher: Oxford
Notes: A pocket-size clinical manual of tropical medicine. Rather than the exhaustive approach of the CCDM [see above] this focuses on several tropical disease of particular clinical importance such as diarrheal illnesses and malaria. More useful for the tropical medicine physician than for the public health practitioner, but this and the CCDM make for probably the only pair of books you would need on the proverbial tropical island (one which presumably has plenty of disease).

Title: *Global Change and Health*
Authors/Editors: Kelley Lee and Jeff Collin
Publisher: Open University Press/McGraw Hill
Notes: One of the most interesting books in this series by Open University Press.

Small and digestible, it presents overviews of global, environmental, and other changes, and their relationship to health. Quite suitable for introductory courses on the material.

Title: *Short Textbook of Public Health Medicine for the Tropics*
Authors/Editors: Adetokunbo O. Lucas and Herbert M. Gilles
Publisher: Arnold
Notes: Truly what it claims to be on the cover. A concise overview of the main disciplines relevant to tropical medicine, and of the thematic areas essential for the tropical medicine practitioner. Somewhat clinically oriented but many sections are very appropriate for introductory global health curricula.

Title: *Manson's Tropical Diseases*
Authors/Editors: Gordon C. Cook and Alimuddin I. Zumla.
Publisher: Saunders/Elsevier
Notes: The most venerable textbook in its field (now in its 21st edition), it has managed to stay current by simply being the most authoritative and comprehensive (2000 pages) resource in its field. The chapters are generally well-written and are stand-alone treatises on the diseases they cover. The book has a distinctly British flavor, but that has not kept it from the shelves of discerning tropical medicine experts in the U.S.

Title: *Hunter's Tropical Medicine and Emerging Infectious Diseases.*
Authors/Editors: G. Thomas Strickland
Publisher: Saunders
Notes: The American counterpart to Manson's, Hunter's is no less comprehensive in scope. Prof. Strickland of the University of Maryland has edited this 8th edition of a classic U.S. text on tropical medicine. Eleven sections cover all manner of tropical infections. Among the most useful are the section on Tropical Disease in a Temperate Climate; Laboratory Diagnosis; and, a somewhat surprising but welcome section, Poisonous & Toxic Plants & Animals.

Title: *A Practical Guide to Global Health Service*
Authors/Editors: Edward O'Neil Jr.

Publisher: American Medical Association Press
Notes: Also the author of Awakening Hippocrates: A Primer on Health, Poverty, And Global Service. Profiles roughly 300 organizations that place health volunteers abroad. The information herein may get dated quite quickly but it is a useful starting point nonetheless. There is little information on the quality or potential biases of the organizations.

Title: *Critical Issues in Global Health*
Editors: C. Everett Koop, Clarence E. Pearson, and M. Roy Schwarz
Publisher: Jossey-Bass
Notes: The editors have assembled contributions by prestigious leaders in the area of global public health who share their insights into what they see as the most pressing issues in global health. An excellent overview with the expected weaknesses of too much generalization and prescriptiveness. A useful text for an introductory course, or for a bedside reader with essays on global health by some of the world's leading thinkers such as Gro Harlem Brundtland and C. Everett Koop.

Journals
The following have as their mandate, to varying degrees, peer-reviewed scientific material pertaining to global health and/or tropical medicine. There is a wide variety of journals (as with the books) which cover material relevant to global health but not exclusively in its service, e.g., on general public health, or epidemiology, or behavioral health. URLs are provided, as is a notation on which were freely accessible (at the time of this writing).

Title: *Globalization & Health*
URL: http://www.globalizationand-health.com/
Notes: Open Access

Title: *Tropical Medicine and International Health*
URL: http://www.blackwellpublishing.com/journal.asp?ref=1360-2276&site=1

Title: *BMC International Health & Human Rights*
URL: http://www.biomedcentral.com/bmcinthealthhumrights/
Notes: Open Access

Title: *Global Public Health*
URL: http://www.tandf.co.uk/journals/titles/17441692.asp
Notes: Quarterly publication in 2007. Published in association with the Global Health Council.

Title: *Journal of Global Health Governance*
URL: http://diplomacy.shu.edu/academics/global_health/journal/
Notes: Open Access

Title: *Bulletin of the World Health Organization/The International Journal of Public Health*
URL: http://www.who.int/bulletin/en/
Notes: Open Access through the World Health Organization

Title: *American Journal of Tropical Medicine and Hygiene*
URL: http://www.ajtmh.org/

Title: Transactions of the Royal Society of Tropical Medicine and Hygiene
URL: http://intl.elsevierhealth.com/journals/trst/

Title: *Tropical Doctor*
URL: http://www.rsmpress.co.uk/td.htm

Title: *Acta Tropica*
URL: www.elsevier.com/wps/find/journaldescription.cws_home/506043/description#description

Title: *Annals of Tropical Medicine & Parasitology*
URL: http://www.maney.co.uk/search?fwaction=show&fwid=142

Title: *Emerging Infectious Diseases*
URL: http://www.cdc.gov/eid
Notes: Open Access through the US Centers for Disease Control & Prevention

Title: *Journal of Travel Medicine*
URL: http://www.istm.org